Europe or

to Self-De

MW01201401

Europe on the Path to Self-Destruction

Nationalism and the Struggle for Hegemony, 1815–1945

JACK L. SCHWARTZWALD

McFarland & Company, Inc., Publishers
Jefferson, North Carolina

LIBRARY OF CONGRESS CATALOGUING-IN-PUBLICATION DATA

Names: Schwartzwald, Jack L., 1958– author.
Title: Europe on the path to self-destruction : nationalism
and the struggle for hegemony, 1815-1945 / Jack L. Schwartzwald.
Description: Jefferson : McFarland & Company, Inc., Publishers, 2022. |
Includes bibliographical references and index.
Identifiers: LCCN 2022023574 | ISBN 9781476683409 (paperback : acid free paper) ∞
ISBN 9781476646855 (ebook)
Subjects: LCSH: Europe—History—1815-1871. | Europe—
History—1871-1918. | Europe—History—1918-1945. | World War,
1914-1918—Europe. | World War, 1939-1945—Europe. |
Nationalism—Europe—History. | Hegemony—Europe—
History. | Europe—Economic conditions. | Europe—Politics
and government. | BISAC: HISTORY / Europe / General
Classification: LCC D359.7 .S35 2022 | DDC 940.2/8—dc23/eng/20220525
LC record available at https://lccn.loc.gov/2022023574

BRITISH LIBRARY CATALOGUING DATA ARE AVAILABLE

ISBN (print) 978-1-4766-8340-9
ISBN (ebook) 978-1-4766-4685-5

On the cover: *top left to right*: Winston Churchill circa 1900,
Library of Congress; Kaiser Wilhelm II of Germany, Library
of Congress; Henry Morton Stanley, circa 1872 (National Portrait
Gallery, Smithsonian Institution); *bottom left to right*: "Tankdrome"
was a muster zone for tank squadrons on the Western Front, circa 1917
(© Everett Collection/Shutterstock); German troops in Russia, 1941
(National Archives); *background* Vintage map of Europe at the end
of 19th century - Picture from Meyers Lexicon books collection (written
in German language, published in 1908 in Germany (Nicku/Shutterstock)

Printed in the United States of America

*McFarland & Company, Inc., Publishers
Box 611, Jefferson, North Carolina 28640
www.mcfarlandpub.com*

In loving memory of my mother,
Frances "Frankie" Schwartzwald

Table of Contents

Preface

Between the years 1815 and 1945, the continent of Europe attained an unprecedented predominance in the world only to see it go up in smoke in two great global conflicts. The cause of Europe's rise—and of its fall—may be found in the immense societal changes that occurred in the intervening years. In 1815, Europe remained largely agricultural and dependent upon horsepower. By 1945, the power of the atom had been unleashed. Two industrial revolutions occurred in the interim—the first founded upon coal, iron and steam, the second upon oil, steel, electricity and internal combustion.

At the same time, the population of Europe increased from 188 million in 1800 to 400 million in 1900.[1] By 1913—the eve of the cataclysm—it would reach 498 million, or 28 percent of all the world's inhabitants.[2] Numbers alone, however, do not tell a complete story, for the character of the populace also underwent a dramatic change. The rise of manufacturing created whole new population centers and filled them with two new classes: one of relative wealth—the "bourgeoisie" (composed of the professional class and the leaders of commerce and industry), the other of poverty and toil—the urban working class or "proletariat."

The eminent European leaders who gathered at the Congress of Vienna in 1815—the "year one" of this transformative period—could not foretell the future. But they had a keen appreciation of the immediate past. The continent had only just emerged from twenty-five years of French Revolutionary and Napoleonic warfare—upheavals that added their own elements of social and economic dislocation. To them, it seemed that the font of all Europe's problems had been the French Revolution of 1789 with its novel ideas of liberty, egality and fraternity—and most especially of the "nation at arms." The obvious solution, now that it had been overthrown (or at least seemingly so) with Napoleon's defeat at Waterloo, was to put things back the way they had been before it all started, which is precisely what the assembled diplomatists attempted to do. In some ways this was analogous to applying a fresh coat of paint to a house fallen to ruin—and, indeed, it did not work in the end as evidenced by the fact that its architect, Klemens von Metternich of Austria, had to be spirited out of Vienna in a laundry cart amid new revolutionary violence in 1848.[3]

The revolutions of 1848 ended in failure with the apparent restoration of order across the continent. But the appearance was deceiving, for momentous changes were in train. In the same revolutionary year—1848—Karl Marx published his *Communist Manifesto* with its siren's-song promise of an inevitable proletarian utopia (and its unvarying culmination in a dystopian "bondage of the individual to the community"[4] wherever it has been tried). This was followed in 1862 and 1871, respectively, by Charles Darwin's publication of *The Origin of Species* and *The Descent of Man*, providing the first evidence-based alternative to the story of creation in the book of *Genesis*, but even more influential in the misapplication of its catch phrases, "struggle for existence" and "survival of the fittest," to the ongoing affairs of humankind.

In this same interim (1848–1871), nationalism came of age in its modern image, exemplified most vividly by the emergence of a unified Germany and a unified Italy. In the romantic view of the time, nationhood was seen to represent an expression of popular sovereignty among people sharing a common language, culture, history and economic interest (as opposed to the old idea of mere shared allegiance to a common ruling prince). "And the idea, once proclaimed," says the early 20th-century historian Alison Phillips, "spread with astonishing rapidity; till in all Europe there was not a race with a grievance, real or fancied, against the established order but based its resistance on the natural right of a 'nation' to be mistress of its own destinies."[5] To those familiar with Jean-Jacques Rousseau's *Social Contract*, the nation might even be understood to possess an innate "general will" making cooperation and brotherhood among the body politic the most natural of conditions (a rosy conception that ought to have been belied by the long lines at the Paris guillotine in 1793 and 1794, where the theory was first tried out).

In fact, the unification of Germany and Italy were not brought about "by speeches and majority decisions," as the romantics of 1848 presumed they might be. Rather, they were the product of "blood and iron"—i.e., power politics (*Realpolitik* in the parlance of the times)—carried to fruition by the likes of Otto von Bismarck. The scant role that romantic idealism played in this process may be discerned by the fate of the French provinces of Alsace and Lorraine—taken from France by Germany, in violation of the desires of their inhabitants, as part and parcel of German unification at the end of the Franco-Prussian War (1870–1871).

The present text is organized into three sections. The first—entitled *Evolution: The Nations Take Form*—catalogs the political and military events of the years between 1815 and 1871, including chapters on the restoration and final overthrow of the old order (1815–1848) and on the emergence of the modern nation-state as the agency tasked with managing the roiling undercurrents of societal change (1848–1870). Section II—entitled *Natural Selection: The Nations Take Sides*—begins with a survey of the momentous domestic developments that occurred within each of the major nation-states between 1870 and 1914 (Chapters 4, 5 and 6) as prelude to an examination of the era's international affairs (Chapter 7). Europe's brave new order is fraught with tension and rivalry during this period, driving the great nations to project their power beyond the confines of Europe in a global scramble for colonies, raw materials and markets. Closer to home, security considerations lead on the one hand, to an armaments race encompassing weaponry of previously unthinkable destructive capacity, and on the other, to a squaring-off of the European states into two rival alliance systems. The consequence of these processes is a swelling tide of "international anarchy," guaranteeing at one and the same time that the rival powers will be incapable of amicable relations and that a single false move must draw them all into a general war. Section III—entitled *Survival of the Fittest: The Nations Collide* (1914–1945)—covers the cataclysmic world wars which result (Chapters 9, 12 and 13), and the troubled interim between them wherein democracy falters and totalitarianism comes to encompass much of the globe (Chapters 10 and 11).

For the reader who is inclined towards happier tidings, the text includes more cheerful themes—for it is filled, too, with statesmen who attempt to steer a safe course through society's dilemmas and with liberal attempts to expand suffrage and constitutional freedoms. Each section concludes, moreover, with a chapter on societal achievements (Chapters 3, 8 and 14)—and there were many of them (indeed, from a technological standpoint, more than in all preceding periods of history taken together). There are also some thrilling examples of heroism in the forging of new frontiers, as in aviation and in the race to the North and South Poles.

The current volume does not presume to provide answers to the uncertainties of our own age, but in line with George Santayana's adage, that "those who cannot remember the past are condemned to repeat it," it is hoped that it might provide some historical perspective for readers currently contemplating them. Care has been taken to present the subject matter concisely enough to appeal to the general reader and comprehensively enough to appeal to the undergraduate student. The tone, it is hoped, will appeal to both. While it may be read independently without reference to other historical periods, it represents a direct continuation of the story of Western civilization begun in three preceding volumes—*The Ancient Near East, Greece and Rome*; *The Collapse and Recovery of Europe, AD 476–1648*; and *The Rise of the Nation-State in Europe: Absolutism, Enlightenment and Revolution, 1603–1815*.

The library collections at Brown University and the University of Rhode Island were an invaluable resource in building a bibliography for this book. While globalization continues to steer curricula toward "World History" courses in the academy, the scope of the current work, like its predecessors, is limited to European history except where outside events exercised a significant influence.

I have enjoyed much support in the writing of this volume, most especially from my wife, Cheryl, without whose unwavering encouragement the task would have proved impossible. Our two tuxedo cats, Cody and Crosby, veteran research companions from the three preceding volumes, agreed to stay on for this one provided that they had first dibs on the club chair in the home library. Sincere thanks are likewise owed to my sister, Ann, a career educator, who served in the dual capacity of proofreader and friend. Sadly, my mother, Frances "Frankie" Schwartzwald, likewise a career educator, who instilled a love of history in me from an early age, passed away during the writing of this volume, which is dedicated to her.

Finally, warmest thanks are extended to my loving niece, Liza Schwartzwald, who graciously donated her time as a proofreader.

Evolution:
The Nations Take Form

1

Reaction and Revolution, 1815–1848

The Congress of Vienna

At the end of the Napoleonic Wars, an exhausted Europe was presented with an exalted idea. It had taken a "Grand Alliance" of the major powers—England, Austria, Russia and Prussia—to bring Napoleon to heel. Now that he was safely closeted away on the distant island of St. Helena, mightn't a "Concert of Europe" emerge under the aegis of these same four powers to arbitrate the affairs of nations, guarding the independence of all member states while averting the possibility of renewed warfare? For good measure, the notion was touted that such a "concert" should rest upon the foundation of a "Holy Alliance"—a league of monarchs, each sworn to treat his fellows as brothers and to base his policymaking on the tenets of Christianity.

This last concept was the high-minded idea of Tsar Alexander I of Russia, a man of mystical leanings and impossible ideals, who had not conceived a project this big since agreeing on the raft at Tilsit to divide Europe with Napoleon (1807). (As the reader is likely aware, that misguided scheme ended with Moscow burnt and a French army of 450,000 buried beneath the Russian snow.) It is generally held that when he proposed his design in 1815, Alexander had but a decade left to live. The circumstantial evidence to that effect is compelling, given that his coffin was interred in 1825. What remains in question is whether he was in it. When Russia's communist regime opened the tomb well-nigh a century later, his remains were not to be found, and the speculation still persists that he survived into the 1860s as a reclusive monk living in accordance with the Christian precepts that he had formerly urged upon a continent.[1]

When the tsar first submitted his idea, he and his fellow European leaders were assembled at the Congress of Vienna amidst lavish entertainments and unceasing espionage. It is reported that the very maids were spies, hired to sift through the wastebaskets of the principals for state secrets. As a countermeasure, the British representative, Viscount Castlereagh, hired his own maids and burned any notes intended for the trash. The worst the spies seem to have gathered on him was that when he was alone, he sometimes danced about his quarters using a chair for a partner. (Before ridiculing him on this account, posterity should bear in mind that with so many balls to attend, a bit of preparation was only prudent.)[2]

The rulers of Prussia and Austria signed on to the Holy Alliance even before it was announced. Their sincerity in doing so, however, is open to question. Klemens Wenzel von Metternich, the Austrian foreign minister, called the project, to which his nation

Tsar Alexander I of Russia, equestrian portrait by Franz Krüger, Hermitage Museum, St. Petersburg, Russia (Wikimedia Commons).

was now a signatory, "a loud sounding nothing."[3] The cynical worldview encompassed by these words had been forged by a remote, traumatic episode. Twenty-one years earlier, Metternich's family had been driven into exile as French Revolutionary forces invaded the Rhineland (1794). The experience left an indelible imprint on young Klemens, then twenty-one, who, ever after, regarded the ideas of radicalism and nationalism with equal revulsion.[4] Arriving in Vienna as refugees, the Metternichs had hoped for resolute action on the part of the Hapsburg emperor to restore their properties, but as this was not feasible, the family was indemnified with lands in southern Germany.[5]

Born of noble blood, young Metternich contracted an advantageous marriage to the granddaughter of Wenzel Anton von Kaunitz, the celebrated 18th-century Austrian chancellor. A matrimonial pedigree of such distinction opened the door to a career in the Austrian diplomatic service and Metternich quickly rose through the ranks—becoming ambassador to Paris in the aftermath of the battle of Austerlitz (1805), and foreign minister following the Austrian defeat at Wagram (1809).[6] In this last capacity, he played an instrumental role in arranging the dynastic marriage between Napoleon and the Austrian princess Marie Louise (1810).

But the image of French troops storming into the Rhineland with the radical fervor of a nation at arms never ceased to torment Metternich. At a crucial juncture in 1813, he betrayed Napoleon—at least in the view of certain French historians—dallying a promise of neutrality before the French emperor until the Austrian army had had time to mobilize; then issuing an impossible 48-hour ultimatum before defecting to the anti–French coalition.[7] (Metternich's apologists have a contrary view of these events, reminding us that as a megalomaniac Napoleon could neither control his insatiable thirst for power nor appreciate the subtle, but important, concessions Metternich had been willing to offer in the name of peace.)

Once Napoleon was defeated, Metternich sought to fulfill his own agenda at the Congress of Vienna. In the Austrian diplomat's view, Europe must be put back into its natural equilibrium where the old order reigned. All remaining vestiges of the French Revolution—that "hydra with jaws open to swallow up the social order"[8]—must be expunged. Tsar Alexander might imagine that the exalted spirit of his Holy Alliance would lead naturally to liberal, constitutional rule throughout Europe,[9] but after the excesses of the Revolution, Metternich was of no mind to see sovereignty shared with the masses. Nor would he countenance the continent's growing nationalist fervor, heralded by the cries of intellectuals for a unified Germany and Italy.

Guided by Metternich, the Congress of Vienna remade the map of Europe—not to satisfy prevailing aspirations for national expression and popular sovereignty, but to restore the old order and render it immune to a repetition of the turmoil so recently extinguished. In working out the details, Metternich adroitly remained a step ahead of his fellow negotiators. Tsar Alexander had hoped to annex Poland in its entirety, replete with the partitions that had formerly belonged to Prussia and Austria. Vassal Poland would thus have become a Russian appendage, extending the tsar's influence deep into central Europe. Prussia was willing to acquiesce in the tsar's usurpation of her Polish lands provided she received all of Saxony in return—a prize that would have increased her own influence in Germany.

Were these neighborly aspirations to be fulfilled, Austria stood to be the loser.[10] A robust Russian presence in central Europe would infringe upon Austria's prerogatives there. Similarly, the absorption of Saxony by Prussia might render that kingdom

"Congress of Vienna by Jean-Baptiste Isabey" Identities of attendees: seated at far left is Prince Karl August von Hardenberg (Prussia); seated in the center with his left arm draped over the back of the chair is Robert Stewart, Viscount Castlereagh (10); standing in the foreground between them with one arm across his torso and the other seeming to direct attention to Castlereagh is Prince Metternich (6); seated far right, Charles Maurice de Talleyrand (France) and Count Gustav Ernst von Stackelberg (Russia); the others from left to right, retaining the numbers assigned to them are: 1. Arthur Wellesley, Duke of Wellington (UK); 2. Joaquim Lobo da Silveira (Portugal); 3. António de Saldanha da Gama (Portugal); 4. Count Löwenhielm (Sweden); 5. Louis Joseph Alexis de Noailles (France); 7. André Marie Dupin (France); 8. Count Nesselrode (Russia); 9. Pedro de Sousa Holstein, Duke of Palmela (Portugal); 11. Emmerich Joseph, Duke of Dalberg (France); 12. Ignaz Heinrich von Wessenberg (Confederation of the Rhine); 13. Andreas Razumovsky (Russia); 14. Charles Stewart, 3rd Marquess of Londonderry (UK); 15. Pedro Gómez Labrador, Marquis of Labrador; 16. Richard Le Poer Trench, 2nd Earl of Clancarty (UK); 17. Nikolaus von Wacken (Recorder); 18. Friedrich von Gentz (Congress Secretary); 19. Baron Friedrich von Humboldt (Prussia); 20. William Schaw Cathcart, 1st Earl Cathcart (UK). Identities courtesy of Jan Losenicky (Wikimedia Commons).

a rallying point for a strong, centralized Germany, which could only occur at Austrian expense, since Austria's influence there depended upon the German principalities remaining weak, divided and malleable.[11] By deft diplomacy—and, where that didn't work, by double dealing—Metternich forced Tsar Alexander to relinquish much of the Polish territory he coveted. In so doing, he demonstrated many of the qualities that had already gained him the epithet, "prince of diplomatists."[12] The tsar invoked a different epithet—calling Metternich a "liar" and suggesting that they settle their differences with pistols or swords.[13] He had no choice but to concede, however, for Britain and France had joined Austria in opposition to his designs. To console himself, Alexander fashioned the Polish territory he did obtain into an "independent" kingdom upon which he later conferred one of those liberal constitutions he had been touting. (Alas,

Europe After the Congress of Vienna by J.F. Horrabin, from H.G. Wells' *Outline of History* **(Wikimedia Commons).**

his magnanimity stopped short of allowing the Poles to exercise the freedoms granted therein.[14])

Prussia was outmaneuvered in the same fell swoop. Having had a portion of her Polish territory inconveniently restored to her by Metternich's labors, she could no longer lay claim to all of Saxony, and had to settle for a lesser territorial adjustment.[15] Her acquisitions left her less vulnerable to the whims of Russia, and more capable of defending herself against France than she had formerly been. But they denied her the leverage she coveted in Germany, and the bitterness thus engendered would simmer until Bismarck made Austria pay for Metternich's deviousness at Sadowa a half century later.[16] In the meantime, Germany remained an Austrian bailiwick.

So, too, did northern Italy, where Austria had acquired Venetia (Venice and its environs) and Lombardy as compensation for the loss of the former Austrian Netherlands. The trade, in Metternich's view, was a double victory. By relinquishing her Netherlands possessions, Austria removed herself from direct territorial contact with France, which meant that the defense of the Rhine against a resurgence of French aggression would be the immediate responsibility of others.[17] The acquisition of Venetia and

Lombardy, meanwhile, cemented Austrian predominance in northern Italy. While the independent Kingdom of Piedmont-Sardinia had attained a degree of prestige in this sphere through the repatriation of Savoy and the annexation of Genoa and Nice, this was but part and parcel of Metternich's same policy. For the augmented principality, while too weak to threaten Austria, was now strong enough to serve as a hurdle to French aggression in Italy. Thus, Austria had increased her own authority in Germany and Italy, while keeping the influence of Prussia, Russia and France strictly confined. With his grand design achieved on every front, Metternich might well confer upon himself his own epithet— the "Coachman of Europe."[18]

Among the quintessential priorities of the Congress of Vienna was the establishment of a defensive cordon around France. Although the first Treaty of Paris (May 1814) had restored the Bourbons to power within the boundaries existing in 1792, the French

Klemens von Metternich, 1815 portrait by Thomas Lawrence, Kunsthistorisches Museum, Vienna (Wikimedia Commons).

nation was universally distrusted as the wellspring of radical and nationalist ideas. The escape of Napoleon from Elba, and the fervor that transiently swept him back to power prior to his final overthrow at Waterloo (June 1815), served only to confirm the general suspicion. Consequently, the second Treaty of Paris (November 1815), while again restoring the Bourbons, imposed a sterner settlement. Keenly recollecting the humiliation of her defeats in the Napoleonic Wars, Prussia demanded that France pay reparations, and that she suffer occupation by a foreign army until the account was settled.[19] She also received territory along the Rhine, so that augmented Prussia, like augmented Piedmont-Sardinia might serve as a bulwark against French aggression.[20] To complete the cordon around France, Belgium (the former Austrian Netherlands) was incorporated into Holland, replete with a line of fortresses paid for out of the French reparations, in hopes of forging a serviceable barrier to the north.[21] Hence, on every frontier, a "watchdog" was in place to guard against French aggression.[22]

The fate of Belgium provides a fitting example of the determining "principle" behind the territorial decisions taken at Vienna. Far from attending to the aspirations of peoples, consultation was made only to expedience and the division of spoils. The Belgians were Catholic, the Dutch Protestant, and the former could never be content as subjects of the latter. The trend may be followed across the continent. France chafed at the reinstatement of the anti-egalitarian Bourbons. Polish patriots desired true independence, not the false veneer offered by the tsar. Denmark had cooperated too willingly with Napoleon. In consequence, she suffered the loss of Norway,[23] which was given, against the will of its people, to Sweden in compensation for the loss of Finland (to Russia) and Pomerania (to Prussia). While the "principle" of "legitimacy" was invoked in the restoration of the French Bourbons, Gustavus IV, the legitimate king of Sweden, was not restored to his throne, for the Congress had been too well served by the current ruler—Napoleon's turncoat former marshal, Jean-Baptiste Bernadotte.[24] St. Mark's Cathedral in Venice received back her famed bronze horses (stolen from the Byzantine hippodrome during the Fourth Crusade and then carted to Paris after the Napoleonic conquest), prompting Sir Samuel Romilly to ask the House of Commons whether it was honorable "to give [the Venetians] back their statues, but not to restore to them those far more valuable possessions, their territory and their republic."[25] Justice and expedience converged in Switzerland alone, which enjoyed the return of the three cantons seized by France in the recent wars with her neutrality henceforth guaranteed by the Congress.

Of the four great powers directing these affairs, Britain alone did not seek territorial compensation in Europe. Led by her Foreign Secretary, Viscount Robert Stewart Castlereagh, the island nation contented herself with additions to her colonial empire—Heligoland, Malta, Ceylon, and the Cape Colony being among the prizes that guaranteed her continued domination of the high seas where she hoped to put an end to the slave trade.[26] Britain desired above all else a balance of power on the continent in order to maintain the peace. Thus far, Metternich's schemes conformed to this desire. The parties were to diverge, however, on a question of no less import.

The Concert of Europe: Repression at Home and The Question of Foreign Intervention

In the popular view, Tsar Alexander's "Holy Alliance" became indelibly linked with the cloud of reaction that now settled over Europe. It is an ironic verdict, as the *Cambridge Modern History* notes, given that the tsar's mind was as yet enthralled with the liberal ideas he had learned in his youth. Although, he would later become a convinced reactionary, at the Congress of Vienna he still believed that Christian morals would promote liberality rather than restrain it.[27]

The true instrument of reaction to emerge from the Congress of Vienna was not the "Holy Alliance," which had no tangible effect on European politics, but the "Quadruple Alliance," signed by Britain, Austria, Russia and Prussia on November 20, 1815. The putative purpose of the latter agreement, which included a pledge of mutual military support, was to guard against the resumption of revolutionary activity in France. Article 6, however, enunciated a broader purpose, binding the sovereigns of the contracting powers to meet at "fixed intervals" to examine the taking of "such measures as … shall be judged most salutary for the peace and prosperity of the nations and for the maintenance of the peace of Europe."[28]

This single article, says Alison Phillips, "was the formal constitution of that Concert of Europe by which it was hoped the peace of the world might be preserved. But it was a departure from the Holy Alliance; for it substituted for the brotherhood of all sovereigns a dictatorship of the Great Powers whose ambassadors were to form, at Paris, an international court for the settlement of all questions arising out of the treaties concluded at Vienna and Paris…."[29] In the deft hands of Metternich, Article 6 would provide the means for "the conversion of [the Quadruple Alliance] into an engine of universal repression."[30]

Perhaps the earliest definite clue that the alliance would exceed its stated objective came at the Congress of Aix-la-Chapelle (1818), when, for all intents and purposes France was admitted to an alliance against itself.[31] The Quadruple Alliance, thereby, became a Quintuple Alliance, now including the venerable state of France and possessing as its mission the prevention of revolutionary activity … in France. With France onboard, one would think that the entire apparatus had become superfluous, but such was not the case.

Restored to his throne on the authority of the Allied army of occupation, King Louis XVIII of France had shown himself to be a sensible ruler. The judicious employment of his nominal "absolutism" was calculated to avoid any undue provocation of the French populace, for he well understood that the previous twenty-five years of French history could not be erased by absolutist decrees. The émigrés (French aristocrats who had fled the revolution) returning in his train might argue to the contrary, as they persistently did in the Chamber of Deputies. They might even force an unfortunate decision or two on the king—as when they compelled him to acquiesce in the imprudent execution of Marshal Ney (famed as the "bravest of the brave" for his service to Napoleon). But in Louis' view, the French throne was "the softest of chairs," and having been chased from it once (i.e., on Napoleon's return from Elba), he was determined not "to resume his travels."[32] Privately, he lampooned the Chamber of Deputies as the *Chambre Introuvable* or "Chamber of the Unobtainable," in reference to its desire to turn back the clock. Upon his restoration, he had promulgated a ruling "Charter" of some liberality, and he now stood by it. Although the document maintained that the king was ruler by divine right and reserved to him the prerogative of proposing new legislation, it gave royal affirmation to the immutable societal changes wrought by the Revolution—declaring equality before the law, protection against arbitrary arrest, freedom of worship and (with some reservations) freedom of the press. Land appropriated and sold during the Revolution would remain with its current owners with full protection of the law. Aristocratic titles, including those created during the Napoleonic period, would remain valid, but would carry no special privilege, including no exemption from taxation.[33] Despite a restricted franchise—not quite 100,000 of France's 29 million citizens were entitled to vote[34]—new elections in November 1816 cast out the reactionary *Chambre Introuvable*, an assembly "more royalist than the king,"[35] and replaced it with a body of moderate royalists with whom the king and his ministers could work.

Louis' attitude brought peace and stability—so much so, that the representatives of the Quadruple Alliance came to recognize that the greater provocation to revolutionary activity in France was not the forced restoration of the Bourbon monarchy, but the continuing presence of their own foreign army of occupation. Consequently, at Aix-la-Chapelle (1818), they decided to lower the war indemnity that had been imposed on France after Waterloo, and to withdraw the coalition army of occupation two years ahead of schedule. It naturally followed that France should be admitted to the very coalition of which it had formerly been the object—for to leave her in isolation would be to tempt her to intrigues of her own to find suitable allies in opposition to, and at the expense of, the alliance.[36]

While Louis XVIII was not Europe's only restored "absolutist" monarch, he alone seems to have understood the value of moderation. Spain's Ferdinand VII was particularly obtuse in this regard, as was Piedmont-Sardinia's Victor Emmanuel I, who "returned from his many years' exile in Sardinia, like a royal Rip Van Winkle, with the costume and ideas of a vanished generation, [and] cancelled with a stroke of the pen every act of government since 1787."[37] Moderation likewise received short shrift in Germany, where it might have been indulged at scant risk. The German people, by and large, had slight interest in politics. As industry had not taken hold to any great extent, there was no politically minded urban middle class. The bulk of the population was composed of peasants who were too busy tilling their fields for political theorizing. The only legislative organ representing the whole of Germany was the Diet of the "German Confederation," whose delegates were appointed by the rulers of their respective principalities. In all, there were thirty-eight such principalities, with Austria and Prussia heading the list. Of these, all but three—Bavaria, Baden and Württemberg—were ruled in absolutist fashion without constitutional charters. The Diet, consequently, was composed largely of reactionaries.

Organized at the Congress of Vienna as a league for the protection of greater Germany, the Confederation was instead enlisted by Metternich as a centralized tool for the suppression of liberal and nationalist ideas.[38] Given the make-up of the German population, such ideas had only a limited following—chiefly among university students. Filled with the romantic optimism of youth, these putative scholars formed patriotic fraternities, or "*Burschenschaften*," and staged rallies in favor of German unification and the removal of Austria from German affairs. A favorite icon of the movement was Friedrich Ludwig Jahn, a veteran of the wars against Napoleon, who established an open-air gymnasium, the *Turnplatz*, and used the practice of gymnastics as a means of building moral, as well as physical, strength. He bade his disciples "to regard themselves as members of a gild for the emancipation of their fatherland."[39] On October 18, 1817—the fourth anniversary of the victory over Napoleon at "the Battle of the Nations" at Leipzig (1813) and three hundred years to the month since Martin Luther issued his famous ninety-five theses—the *Burschenschaften* held a rally at Wartburg Castle, where the fugitive Luther had once taken refuge.[40] Following a series of reverential speeches, the students closed the ceremony with an irreverent parody of Luther's burning of the papal bull—building a bonfire, into which they cast a few reactionary symbols and anti-nationalist books. Included among the latter was a treatise by the dramatist August von Kotzebue, a much-hated foe of German constitutional strivings, who (unbeknownst to anyone) happened also to be a tsarist spy.[41]

Of little consequence in itself, the Wartburg festival was received within the halls of the Prussian government as the harbinger of revolution—a sentiment that was not assuaged when Karl Sand, a deranged theological student who had been present at Wartburg, thrust a knife into Kotzebue's heart at the latter's home in Mannheim in March 1819.[42] Metternich, who had kept abreast of the nationalist hubbub in Germany with an elaborate system of spies and secret police, wanted only a pretext to take action, and the murder of Kotzebue (which, incidentally, was followed by the spectacle of mourners dipping their handkerchiefs in Sand's blood at his execution as though he had been a saint[43]) seemed suited to the purpose. Seizing on this incident to proclaim the dangers of liberal and nationalist thought, Metternich drafted the infamous Carlsbad Decrees of 1819. Hastily approved at a congress of eight of Germany's thirty-seven principalities—the only ones on whom Metternich was sure he could rely—the decrees were submitted to the Diet at Frankfort for an emergency vote. The assembled delegates were given opportunity neither for debate nor to consult their respective princes (1819). "Thus," says Hazen, "the decrees, rushed by illegal ... methods through the Diet, became the law of Germany, binding upon every state."[44] The confirming ballot, on September 20, was said to have been unanimous. In fact, dissenting votes were simply excluded from the official count.[45]

The decrees disbanded the student societies, ousted liberals from the university faculties and clamped down on freedom of the press. Henceforth, imperial inspectors appeared in lecture halls, lending a censuring ear to all that was said.[46] Convicted of no crime, Jahn the gymnast was nonetheless incarcerated. Ernst Moritz Arndt, whose patriotic verse had spurred the youth of Germany to resist Napoleon, lost his faculty seat, and a reprint of Johann Gottlieb Fichte's equally patriotic *Address to the German Nation* was banned.[47] Believing that he had dealt German liberalism a fatal blow, Metternich wrote a letter to his wife, in which he modestly compared his own far-ranging brilliance to the narrow-mindedness of his contemporaries, declaring, "I cannot help saying to myself twenty times a day: 'Good God, how right I am, and how wrong they are!'"[48]

In England, however, Lord Castlereagh viewed the Carlsbad Decrees as an unwarranted encroachment on the sovereignty of the lesser German states, telling the tsar's ambassador, "that it was not in the interest of Governments to contract an alliance against the peoples."[49] Upon this issue the Concert of Europe would ultimately split asunder.

Robert Stewart, Viscount Castlereagh, 1817 portrait by Thomas Lawrence, Waterloo Chamber, Windsor Castle (Wikimedia Commons).

To be clear, Castlereagh's objection was not to the use of repression, for his own nation's legislation in these years was scarcely less repressive than were the Carlsbad Decrees. In contrast to the situation in Germany, England's industrial revolution was already well underway, leading not only to the rise of factories, but also to the rise of whole new urban centers. Overcrowded with downtrodden workers, the new cities were without parliamentary representation, for there had been no redistribution of seats to correspond to the population shifts. In a bid to keep disproportionate political clout in their own hands, the rural gentry clung to a patchwork of "rotten boroughs"— areas that were now almost bereft of population, but which still controlled the same number of parliamentary seats as they had in the bygone pre-industrial age.[50]

Compounding the political issue was the economic downturn

that followed Napoleon's defeat. "The sudden close of a long war," says the *Cambridge Modern History*, "dislocated commerce and industry.... A sudden cessation of demand caused great distress.... Half-a-million of men ... suddenly found themselves without employment.... The misery of the poor was extreme...." In response to this crisis, the British government "showed itself momentarily more ready to devise repressive than remedial measures."[51] In March 1817, a band of unemployed weavers from Manchester marched on London, many carrying blankets so that they could sleep along the route.[52] Mistaking these "Blanketeers" for Jacobins, the government suspended the right of habeas corpus, arrested their leaders and put them to flight.[53]

Two years later, a more notorious incident occurred in Manchester itself. There, in August 1819, eighty thousand protestors attended a rally for parliamentary reform at St. Peter's Field in violation of a local ruling. The gathering was peaceful, but when the event's main speaker—a certain radical named Henry Hunt—mounted the podium, the police stepped in to arrest him. Naturally enough, this gave rise to a chorus of angry boos from those in attendance,[54] which was answered—perhaps somewhat less naturally—by a charge of saber-wielding cavalrymen, who galloped into the unarmed crowd, hacking off heads and limbs. In all, eleven people were killed, and another 500 wounded or trampled.[55] Far from expressing remorse for the incident—which came to be called the "Peterloo Massacre"—the government passed a series of repressive measures known as the "Six Acts," which forbade further large gatherings, restricted freedom of the press[56] and facilitated the issuance of warrants to search for weapons in the homes of suspected troublemakers. When, three months later, the vigilant authorities thwarted the so-called "Cato Street Conspiracy"—a plot to assassinate the entire British cabinet—it appeared that the government had uncovered "exhibit one" in vindication of the Six Acts. In fact, the Cato Street affair (for which five plotters went to the gallows) was the work of an agent provocateur who had duped the other conspirators into the scheme, provided them with arms, and then betrayed them to the police in an elaborate scam to discredit radicalism.[57]

The suppression of radicalism, then, whether by means fair or foul, was not the divisive issue. What Castlereagh objected to was Metternich's desire to see the Carlsbad verdict endorsed by the European Powers and expanded to Europe generally—effectively granting authority to the Quadruple Alliance *to intervene collectively within the boundaries of sovereign independent nations* for the purpose of stamping out revolution, whether the targeted state or states desired such intervention or not.[58] Taken to its logical conclusion, the British government believed that such a policy "might ... in time present the spectacle of Cossacks encamped in Hyde Park to overawe the House of Commons."[59]

Although there was no open rupture in 1819, the issue would not long enjoy repose, for scarcely was Metternich's Carlsbad triumph complete before revolution broke out unexpectedly in Spain, where the restored regime was among the most reactionary in Europe (January 1, 1820). As his first act on returning from exile in 1814, Spain's Bourbon king, Ferdinand VII, revoked the liberal constitution of 1812, which had been promulgated in his absence by the guerrilla forces opposed to Napoleon and which he had sworn to uphold. Urged on by his coterie of reactionary ministers, Ferdinand resurrected the Inquisition, brought back the Jesuits, subjected liberals to a relentless persecution and annulled all legislation passed under the Constitution of 1812, bidding his people to resume their old ways "as if these things had never been done."[60] In 1819,

"The Massacre of Peterloo," caricature drawing by George Cruikshank (Wikimedia Commons).

the government laid plans to export the king's absolutism to Spain's American colonies, which had been in rebellion since the Napoleonic period. An expeditionary force of 20,000 men was fitted out at Cadiz. Hitherto, however, the king and his ministers had neglected the army and navy, which were both in an advanced state of decline, and rather than embark on a doomed mission, the soldiers of Cadiz mutinied in support of the Constitution of 1812. The revolution quickly spread, enveloping even Madrid, where the king, a virtual prisoner in his own riotous capital, conceded defeat, saying on March 20, 1820, "Let us advance frankly, myself leading the way, along the constitutional path."[61]

By this date, Tsar Alexander's enthusiasm for liberality had long been on the wane. In the estimation of one contemporary, the tsar "would gladly have everyone free, provided that everyone was prepared to do freely exactly what he wished."[62] As early as the Congress of Aix-la-Chapelle, Alexander had demanded an earnest from the French Foreign Minister, Armand Emmanuel Richelieu, that France would further restrict her suffrage in return for the early withdrawal of troops from French soil. Louis XVIII refused initially to honor this pledge, leaving an embarrassed Richelieu no choice but to resign. However, the election to the Chamber of Deputies of the notorious regicide, Abbé Grégoire, later that year forced Louis to amend the election laws after all.[63] This was followed, in February 1820, by the shocking assassination, outside the Paris Opera House, of the Duke of Berry—the sole member of the Bourbon line in France to have demonstrated the ability to father children. The knife-wielding assassin—an unrepentant Bonapartist named Louvel—hoped thus to seal the doom of the Bourbon dynasty, but the duke's wife, then two months pregnant, subsequently gave birth to a male heir.

The sole effects of the assassination, then, were to force Louis XVIII to abandon his moderate policy under pressure from the ultra-royalists in the legislative chambers, and to convince Tsar Alexander that revolution must be quashed wherever it reared its head. Toward this end, the tsar suggested the immediate mobilization of 15,000 Russian soldiers to invade Spain in concert with the other powers.[64]

If anything could dissuade Metternich from his design to use the Quadruple Alliance as a tool for stamping out revolution, it was the prospect of a Russian army crossing Germany and France to get to Spain. But even as he downplayed the need for intervention in Spain, the scourge of revolution spread to Naples—a circumstance that Metternich could not ignore. At the Congress of Vienna, Austria had received Lombardy and Venetia as direct possessions, ruled jointly by an Austrian viceroy. So apprehensive was Vienna about the prospect of revolutionary activity in these rich provinces, that to "make assurance doubly sure, a police was created whose special function was to watch the police."[65] In Lombardo-Venetian schools, children were taught that their provinces were intended by nature to be part of Austria rather than Italy, and it was thought prudent to revise Dante lest thoughts of nationalism be instilled in the mind of the student of medieval literature.[66] Precaution, too, was taken against the infiltration of liberal or nationalist ideas from outside. On being restored to the throne of Naples in 1815, the Neapolitan Bourbon ruler, Ferdinand I, was compelled by Metternich to sign a secret agreement, pledging that he would allow nothing in the way of liberal reform in his own kingdom that had not been conferred first by Austria upon the subjects of Lombardy and Venetia.[67]

While Ferdinand VII of Spain may have been the stupidest of the Bourbons, he had strong competition in the person of his uncle, the king of Naples, whose arbitrary rule and obtuse adherence to the clandestine Austrian pledge provoked the rise of a secret society of Italian nationalists known as the "Carbonari" or "charcoal burners." Inspired by the success of the revolution in Spain, a cadre of Neapolitan army officers touched off a rebellion on July 2, 1820. Joined by the Carbonari, the rebels gained control of the capital on July 13, and to keep his throne, Ferdinand I swore fealty to the Spanish Constitution of 1812, with the vow, "Omnipotent God, who ... lookest into the heart and into the future, if I lie, or if I should one day be faithless to my oath, do Thou, at this instant annihilate me."[68]

The eruption of revolutionary activity so close to the Austrian holdings of Lombardy and Venetia demanded a response. By the terms of Austria's secret treaty with Naples, which Ferdinand I had now breached (albeit under duress), Metternich had the prerogative to intervene unilaterally to quell the uprising, and could have done so without risking a breach with Britain.[69] He preferred, however, to pursue a course that Britain opposed, whereby Austria would intervene not on the basis of her treaty with Naples, but under the imprimatur of the Quadruple (now Quintuple) Alliance—thus establishing as fact his own conception of the alliance as an instrument of reaction possessing a "right of intervention" in revolutionary states.[70] He hoped moreover, to embark on this course without convoking a congress of the powers at which the tsar might press for Russian intervention in Spain in accordance with the same principle. Finding no support in the absence of such a congress, however, he agreed that one should be convened at Troppau in Silesia on October 20, 1820.[71]

Opposed in principle from the outset, England did not send a plenipotentiary to Troppau, although Lord Stewart, the British ambassador to Vienna, attended as an observer. France pursued a like course. The tsar, in contrast, proved most accommodating, for he was now a thoroughgoing reactionary, having been converted from his former liberal idealism by the spread of revolution and the assassination of the Duke of Berry. "To-day," he told Metternich in a private interview at the outset of the congress, "I deplore all that I said and did between the years 1815 and 1818.... You have correctly judged the condition of things. Tell me what you want and what you want of me, and I will do it."[72] With Prussia likewise supporting the Austrian position—and with Britain and France lacking an official say in the absence of plenipotentiaries—the congress promulgated the "Troppau Protocol," maintaining that "States which have undergone a change of government due to revolution, the result of which threaten other states, *ipso facto* cease to be members of the European Alliance, and remain excluded from it until their situation gives guarantees for legal order and stability. If owing to such alterations, immediate danger threatens other states the powers bind themselves, by peaceful means, or if need be, by arms, to bring back the guilty state into the bosom of the Great Alliance."[73]

This was precisely the principle that Castlereagh opposed. Brushing aside Metternich's contention that the powers would apply their "right of intervention" only when the internal affairs of a revolutionary state represented an external threat, the British Foreign Secretary asked "would the great Powers of Europe be prepared to admit the principle that their territories were to be thrown open to each other's approach upon cases of assumed necessity or expediency, of which, not the party receiving aid, but the party administering it, was to be the judge?" He answered that Britain would certainly *not consent* to such a principle. Nor would it "charge itself, as a member of the Alliance with the moral responsibility of administering a general European police...."[74]

Metternich hoped yet to beguile or cajole the British into agreement—first by creating the false impression that the Troppau Protocol might be amended at a follow-up congress to be held at Laibach in January 1821 (thereby convincing the British to send a representative), and then by insinuating that Britain's ongoing recalcitrance constituted a violation of her treaty obligations under the Quadruple Alliance. There ensued at the Congress of Laibach a most disconcerting exchange wherein the Russian foreign minister began reading a statement confirming the principles of the Troppau Protocol, and the British representative, Lord Stewart, interrupted to say that if the statement were read to completion, it would be followed by a formal British denunciation.[75]

The Congress of Laibach was attended by Ferdinand I of Naples who had promised on departing his kingdom to champion the cause of constitutionalism and to seek "to obtain the sanction of the powers for the newly acquired liberties" of his people.[76] Once arrived, however, he reneged on this pledge and requested that the powers intervene to suppress the revolution, which (Britain excepted) they agreed to do. The Congress thus ended with an affirmation of the Troppau Protocol by Austria, Russia and Prussia, and the dispatch of an Austrian army to Naples. In his report to the British government, a disillusioned Lord Stewart could say only that the three eastern powers had achieved "a triple understanding which bound the parties to carry forward their own views in spite of any difference of opinion between them and the two great constitutional governments [i.e., Britain and France]."[77]

France, as it turns out, was rather less "different" in its opinion than Lord Stewart might have supposed. Following the assassination of the Duke of Berry, a further restriction of the French electoral laws had delivered the French Chamber of Deputies once more to the ultra-royalists who were keen on sending an army into Spain for the dual purpose of restoring the absolutism of the kindred Bourbon ruler, Ferdinand VII, and of restoring France to the status of a major power.[78] Given that the tsar was now speaking of the dispatch of 100,000 troops for the suppression of revolution beyond the Pyrenees,[79] the alternative of a French intervention in Spain was not at all unappealing to Metternich. The result was yet another congress—convened at Verona on October 20, 1822—at which the French behaved as if their intervention had already been decided upon. Greatly vexed by the usurpation of his own Spanish design, the tsar announced indignantly that the size of his own hypothetical Spanish expeditionary force now stood at 150,000 hypothetical men.[80] During the course of ten days' deliberation, however, Metternich—that ever-facile "prince of diplomatists"—won the tsar over, with the result that Austria, Prussia and Russia jointly agreed that France should, indeed, intervene.

Britain's Lord Castlereagh had been slated to attend the Congress of Verona in person. Alas, he was not to make it. By the summer of 1822, the strain of his duties had driven him to a paranoid despondency, and in August of that year, he committed suicide by cutting his own throat with a penknife after others had taken the precaution of confiscating his razor.[81] George Canning succeeded to his position and sent the Duke of Wellington to Verona with instructions to oppose the French intervention. Now that the issue was decided, Wellington was instructed to participate no further in the discussions, thereby creating a formal rift in the Quadruple Alliance.[82]

There is a measure of irony in what ensued, for the French army of invasion that crossed into Spain on April 7 under the command of the Duc D'Angoulême (elder brother of the assassinated Duke of Berry) proceeded to take Madrid within seven weeks relying on a plan of operations privately recommended by Wellington.[83] On the promise of a general amnesty, the rebel government capitulated at Cadiz and liberated King Ferdinand on September 30. The following day, the king reneged on the promised amnesty. A reactionary organization calling itself the "Society of the Exterminating Angel" now carried out a bloodbath against the helpless rebels, despite remonstrations from the French government.[84] D'Angoulême, who was appalled by this barbarity, declined to accept the honors conferred upon him by Ferdinand before returning to France.[85]

The restored Spanish government desired now to regain authority over its rebellious colonies and requested that a congress of the powers convene in Paris to discuss the matter.[86] Britain, however, had been carrying on a vigorous commerce with these colonies and was overtly hostile to the establishment of a congress aimed at restoring them to Spanish rule. Warned by Metternich that persistence in this attitude would jeopardize Britain's influence in the alliance, Canning asked, "What is the influence we have had in the counsels of the Alliance, and which Prince Metternich exhorts us to be so careful not to throw away? We protested at Laibach, we remonstrated at Verona. Our protest was treated as waste-paper; our remonstrances mingled with the air."[87]

Fearing that the restoration of Spanish rule would deprive Britain of the commerce she now enjoyed, Canning toyed with the idea of formally recognizing the rebellious colonies as independent states.[88] Before he could act, however, another interested party beat him to the punch. In an address before the United States Congress on December 2, 1823, American President James Monroe promulgated the famous "Monroe Doctrine," saying that any effort by the European powers "to extend their system to any portion of this hemisphere," would be regarded "as the manifestation of an unfriendly disposition towards the United States."[89] Thus, says Alison Phillips, did "the great Republic of the West" respond "to the claim of the European powers to regulate the affairs of all the world" with its own principle of "America for the Americans." In combination with Britain's mastery of the seas, the American posture dealt the Concert of Europe a decisive defeat, prompting Canning's famous comment in declaring Britain's recognition of the South American states (1825), "We have called a new world into existence to redress the balance of the old."[90]

The Decembrist Revolt

Liberalism, quashed in Naples and Spain, now raised its head in the most unexpected of places. In 1825, Russia's Tsar Alexander I died (or faked his death) without a direct heir, leaving the throne to be contested by his two brothers: Constantine, the moderate governor of Poland, and Nicholas, a hopeless reactionary. Having been exposed to Western liberalism during the occupation of France, a clique of army officers declared for Constantine, hoping that his accession would bring desired reforms. Called the "Decembrists" (after the month of their rising), they convinced the St. Petersburg garrison to march to the seat of government chanting: "Constantine and Constitution." That the simpleton soldiers thought "Constitution" was Constantine's wife[91] portended ill enough, but worse was to come. Having never been to France, the populace at large could not perceive the merits of the Decembrist program and would not lend their support. When this became clear, several of the rebel leaders developed cold feet, and failed to carry out their assigned roles. But the greatest blow of all to the rebel cause was the status of their candidate. Constantine was actually ineligible for the throne. He had privately relinquished his claim in 1817 in order to marry Joanna Grudzinska, a Polish woman with no aristocratic ties.[92] A secret dossier containing Constantine's letter of renunciation and Tsar Alexander's manifesto confirming it was unsealed and read in a closed session of the Council of State on news of the tsar's decease.[93]

Unaware of this, the insurgents halted their march in the Great Square outside the St. Petersburg senate building. Nicholas, the lawful successor, rode up opposite them with a body of loyal troops. Eschewing the use of force, he directed a member of his coterie to attempt negotiation. But the mutineers shot the legate dead, and the scene was replayed when Nicholas sent forth a second conciliatory official. Finally, a few shots were aimed (badly) at Nicholas himself, whereat the eschewing of force ceased, and the tsar's artillery let loose a volley at point blank range. The mutineers scattered in all directions—some fleeing in a chaotic stampede across the frozen River Neva, only to be drowned when artillery fire smashed the ice.[94]

As these events unfolded, a second Decembrist outbreak occurred in southern Russia. Led by a certain Colonel Pavel Pestel, who espoused the lofty purpose of liberating the serfs and abrogating feudal privilege, this affair ended no less disastrously. After summary trials (in which the defendants were not allowed to testify and in which embellished confessions obtained by torture were entered into evidence[95]), Pestel and four other Decembrist ringleaders were condemned to the gallows, while the rank-and-file were sent to Siberia to die in snowy oblivion. Tsar Nicholas followed up the brutal suppression with a rigorous press censorship, tight restrictions on travel abroad (lest dangerous ideas filter home)[96] and, most notoriously, the establishment of a secret government police force—the hated "Third Section"—through which, he enforced

Decembrist Revolt, **by Vasily Timm, Hermitage Museum, St. Petersburg (Wikimedia Commons).**

his infamous "Nicholas System"—a merciless campaign against liberalism that would encompass three decades.[97]

The Revolutions of 1830

Disturbing as the sporadic outbursts of the 1820s might have been, Prince Metternich could at least be satisfied that each uprising had been isolated and had been dealt with in its turn. The same cannot be said of the revolutionary storm of 1830. The trouble of that year began in France. Louis XVIII had gone to his grave in 1824, and as with the Russian succession a year later, there was no direct heir to the throne. Thus, the crown fell to the king's brother—the recalcitrant Comte d'Artois, who took the throne as Charles X. In his youth, Charles had attempted to halt the French Revolution single-handedly by reserving the tennis court where the National Assembly had taken its famed Tennis Court Oath, thinking thus to prevent the assembly from convening ever again (1789). Although his tennis match failed to save the *Ancien Regime*, the scheming Bourbon learned nothing from the experience—or indeed, from the thirty-five-year interval between that day and his accession to the throne.

Lacking his brother's insight into the significance of the French Revolution, Charles was convinced that the calendar could be reset to 1789 by a firm enough hand.[98] He chose Reims as the site of his coronation, revivifying the old medieval ceremony wherein his body was anointed with holy oil, thus stressing the bond between Church and Crown and evoking memories of divine right rule. For this, he was lampooned in verse as "Charles the Simple" (a nickname conferred 900 years earlier on a hapless king of Carolingian France).[99] By 1827, his policies had taxed the patience of France to its limit. The new king curried favor with the Church, put clerics in charge of the schools and allowed the hated Jesuits (whose Order was still proscribed) to teach in the state seminaries.[100] He arbitrarily reduced interest payments on government bonds, and used the proceeds to compensate *émigrés* who had lost property during the Revolution. When his actions provoked an outcry, Charles merely surrounded himself with more obstinate ministers—the most notorious being Count Jules August Polignac, who became the king's chief minister in 1829. Finding Polignac insufferable, the Chamber of Deputies clamored for his dismissal. Charles instead closed its session and ordered new elections. When these gave the opposition an even greater majority, the king dissolved the Chamber altogether and opted to rule by decree, smugly declaring to his hesitant advisors: "I am an older man, gentlemen, than any of you ... and I recollect what happened in 1789, when the first retrograde step my unfortunate brother made ... was the signal for his destruction.... He yielded, and he was lost!"[101]

His initial decrees suspended freedom of the press and denied suffrage to the upstart bourgeoisie (July 26, 1830). Satisfied that he was in complete control, he withdrew to his hunting chateau at Rambouillet. Hardly was he gone, however, before the first barricades went up in Paris (July 27). To his own detriment, Charles had finally proved his point. The calendar *could* be turned back to 1789. Alas, it could be turned back no further, and Charles would have done well to remember that 1789 had not been a good year—at least not for the monarchy. Attempting to battle the revolutionaries in the Paris streets, his soldiers were pelted with furniture and other debris cast from upper story windows. Turning his field telescope toward the city on July 29, Charles was aghast to see the revolutionary tricolor fluttering over the city in place of the royalist *fleur de lis*.[102] He abdicated the same day. It was the first thoughtful act of his reign.

The era of Bourbon rule was at an end. But there was no unanimity as to what should succeed it. Bonapartists called for the abrogation of the humiliating treaties of 1815. Radicals lobbied for the resurrection of the Republic and dusted off the ancient Marquis de Lafayette to serve as their figurehead. But it was the moneyed bourgeois class who came up with the winning formula. Led by the propagandist, Adolphe Thiers, they pressed for the establishment of a constitutional monarchy wherein the king's ministers would answer to the legislature rather than to the crown. Under such a system, the bourgeoisie would be protected from arbitrary royal decrees. Moreover, by limiting suffrage to themselves—which is precisely what they intended to do when they gained power—they could protect themselves from the radicalism of the republicans. If all went well, the bourgeoisie would install themselves as a new ruling elite.

A suitable candidate for the watered-down throne was duly identified in Charles X's cousin, Louis Philippe, Duke of Orléans (son of Philippe Egalité, the aristocratic charlatan who had helped vote off the head of Louis XVI before meeting his own demise on the guillotine during the French Revolution). Louis Philippe had distinguished himself in the revolutionary wars by fighting under the tricolor at Jemappes, but he was implicated afterwards in a plot to overthrow the Republic and had fled (1793). In the France of 1830, this was not held against him, for it was known that his opinions were decidedly more liberal than those of Charles X.

If hardline republicans were nonetheless lukewarm about him, their leader, Lafayette was determined to see him rule. It had occurred to the old soldier that, given

Revolution of 1830, *Battle for l'Hôtel de Ville,* **1833, by Jean-Victor Schnetz, Palais Petit Collection (Wikimedia Commons).**

Europe's prevailing political climate, the establishment of a French republic might provoke an invasion by the great powers. This much Lafayette might have borne with sage equanimity. What he could not bear was the thought of being president of France when it happened—which was precisely the position he would be placed in if a republic was declared.[103] Thus, when Louis Philippe arrived at the Hotel de Ville to meet with him amidst mixed reviews from those manning the barricades, Lafayette escorted him to the Hotel balcony, embraced him, embraced the tricolor, and declared, "Here is the prince we need. This is the best of Republics!!!"[104] Although the logic of this utterance would not have withstood scrutiny, the crowd of onlookers cheered the spectacle enthusiastically enough to lower the curtain on the "July Revolution"—handing power to the House of Orléans and the bourgeoisie.

In Austria, Metternich viewed the episode as a threat to the system he had so laboriously constructed in the aftermath of the Napoleonic Wars. Unwilling to abide the revolutionary overthrow of the legitimate French regime, he sought support for combined intervention against France's new "king of the barricades."[105] Hardly had the thought occurred to him, however, before the embers of revolution spread beyond France's borders. In August, students rioted against Dutch rule in Belgium after watching an opera celebrating the 1820 Neapolitan revolt.[106] Dutch forces with artillery in tow attempted to occupy Brussels in September, only to be turned back by workers fighting from behind barricades. By October, Belgium had declared her independence. Austria and Russia demanded immediate intervention lest the Belgian success awaken the slumbering ogre of nationalism and revolution elsewhere on the continent. But Britain was staunchly opposed to the meddling of the eastern European powers in areas beyond their established spheres of influence. Nor, as it turns out, would she abide the petition of French nationalist agitators for Belgium's re-annexation to France as a step toward regaining their nation's "natural frontiers." Thus, when the Belgians offered their throne to Louis Philippe's son, a crisis seemed imminent. Luckily, the French king could sense the direction of international winds and knew they would be hostile to a renewed French presence in Belgium. He even summoned the old diplomat, Talleyrand, out of retirement to reassure the British of French neutrality in the Belgian revolt.[107] (This was the first of many instances where Louis Philippe would compromise French pride to avoid armed conflict with Britain.) On the other hand, the French king announced that France would not consent to armed intervention by the Eastern powers to quash the Belgian revolt, and that should an attempt be made toward that end, it would provoke French intervention "to hold the balance even" until the issue could be settled by negotiation.[108] The crisis was resolved on December 20, when all the European powers, save Holland,[109] joined hands in confirming Belgian independence. The Belgian Assembly promptly adopted the most liberal constitution in Europe, and conferred the crown upon Leopold of Saxe-Coburg, a German prince.

It would be a mistake to attribute this happy outcome wholly to the fortitude of England and France, for other factors had supervened. During the French and Belgian uprisings, Russia's Tsar Nicholas had fully intended to stem the tide of revolution by force of arms. His preparations, however, had to be abandoned owing to a crisis in Poland. In pursuing his aims, Nicholas proposed to mobilize and employ Polish troops. On hearing rumors to this effect, the Polish army (whose patriotic officer corps held liberal sympathies and considered France a benefactor) staged an insurrection rather than comply (November 29, 1830).[110] At Grochow, on February 25, 1831, they fought a costly draw with the tsar's forces that nonetheless handed them the strategic advantage. At Iganie in early April they won an outright victory over a Russian corps.

Alas, the auguries foretold a fatal outcome. Austria and Prussia—both of whom still possessed territory belonging to the former Poland—did not consider the reestablishment of Polish independence to be in their interests. Moreover, despite expressions of sympathy, England would not involve herself, and the new French regime did not feel secure enough to act without England.[111] (Indeed, France ultimately provided intelligence *against* Poland, hoping thus to diminish Nicholas' hostility toward the July Revolution.[112])

More significant than this, nationalism in Poland was largely confined to the landed aristocracy. Her ill-used peasantry did not rally to the cause. Lacking allies—or even broad-based support—the Polish army was badly mauled by the resurgent Russians at Ostrolenka in May 1831. A cholera epidemic that claimed the life of the German-born Russian commander, Hans Karl von Diebitsch, merely delayed the inevitable.[113] In September, Russian troops successfully stormed the defenses of Warsaw. The fall of the

Battle of Stoczek, **Polish Uprising, 1831, Jan Rosen, Polish Army Museum (Wikimedia Commons).**

Polish capital effectively ended the rebellion. In the aftermath, many Poles fled into exile. Others, less fortunate, were apprehended and deported to Siberia. Tsar Alexander's liberal Polish Constitution was revoked, Polish universities and libraries were closed, and the state was subjected to a military despotism.

While the Polish rebellion achieved nothing of lasting value for the Poles, it at least prevented Russian troops from intervening in France or Belgium. The fervor for revolution, indeed, had now spread beyond the boundaries of those states, making inroads into Germany and Italy. While Metternich's secret police and authoritarian decrees did much to limit the scope of these outbreaks, they did achieve some transient successes. In Parma and Modena, the reactionary rulers were chased into exile; in the Papal States, Pope Gregory XVI was deprived, for a time, of his temporal powers; and several German states were compelled to grant liberal constitutions. Alas, these gains were uniformly of short duration. The ebbing of the revolutionary tide in France, Belgium and Poland afforded Metternich the opportunity to take decisive action. In Italy, Austrian arms quashed the insurrections and restored the toppled regimes, while in Germany the Federal Diet adopted six articles effectively divesting the individual German states of the power to pursue liberal reform (1832).[114]

Liberal Reform in England, 1823–1848

In stark contrast to Metternich's policy, the British government sought in the years after the "Peterloo Massacre" to avert revolutionary violence by making liberal concessions. The trend began with a revision of the penal code in 1823, whereby the death penalty ceased to be applicable for a plethora of minor offenses such as pickpocketing or the theft of a fish. (Happily, the carrying out of such sentences had been in abeyance for some years prior to this revision.)[115] The reform had been the initiative of Sir Robert Peel, who likewise created a professional police force—nicknamed "Bobbies" or "Peelers" in his honor—to maintain the public safety.[116]

There followed, in 1827, the succession to the premiership of George Canning who attempted to reform the Corn Laws. Passed in 1815, these laws imposed tariffs on imported grain in order to protect the landed aristocracy against lower-priced foreign competition (with the expense being borne by the consumer). Canning's effort to reform them, however, was ruined in the House of Lords by the Duke of Wellington, the champion of landed interests, and this was followed in August by Canning's untimely death after just four months in office.[117] Repeal of the prejudicial grain imposts was thus delayed for another two decades.

The following year (1828), a critical election result in Ireland brought the issue of religious discrimination to the fore. Despite assurances made in the Act of Union of 1800 (whereby Great Britain and Ireland were forged into a "United Kingdom"), Catholics were still denied the right to hold parliamentary seats. In 1828, however, a talented Catholic orator named Daniel O'Connell challenged this injustice and was elected to the House of Commons for County Clare, Ireland, in violation of the ban. The government, in turn, had to decide whether to let him take his seat. King George IV (1820–30) favored a hard line, but this was certain to provoke violent protests. Indeed, there was fear of a new Irish civil war. Consequently, the government, now headed by Wellington, grudgingly declared Parliament open to Catholics and allowed O'Connell to sit. Of necessity, the "Test Act" of 1673 (which required disavowal of transubstantiation as a prerequisite to the assumption of government office) was revoked. While this concession was more than might have been expected in other nations, it was also less than it seemed; for, quite underhandedly, the government curtailed Catholic suffrage as part and parcel of the arrangement.[118]

The coming of the Revolutions of 1830 brought new disturbances to the English domestic scene. The "rotten borough" problem, which had led to the Peterloo Massacre, had only grown more acute in the intervening decade. While bustling manufacturing centers like Manchester were not yet represented in Parliament, Old Sarum, a town that had ceased to exist, still commanded two seats. Dunwich, too, was represented, even though it was now under water.[119] The outbreak of revolution on the continent was accompanied by rioting in the unrepresented urban centers of

Daniel O'Connell (1775–1847). Lithograph by Johann Stadler, 1843 (Wikimedia Commons).

England. The instigators, as it turns out, were not primarily the urban workers, upset with abysmal working conditions and long hours, but their bourgeois employers who wanted to replace the Tory government's protectionist trade policy with a laissez faire program that would better maximize their profits.[120] To achieve this aim they needed a say in government, which was impossible when their own urban centers were denied parliamentary representation.

On June 26, 1830, King George IV died. By quaint tradition, the British hold new elections upon the death of a reigning prince, and in the elections thus mandated, the reactionary Tories lost fifty seats, leaving them with a majority far less secure than they had formerly enjoyed. Moreover, by November, when the new Parliament opened its session, the success of the July Revolution in France had exercised a most prolific influence—demonstrating to the working class that a revolution could actually succeed, and to the bourgeoisie that they might gain political clout thereby (as the French bourgeoisie had) without necessarily risking a descent into Jacobinism, which had formerly been regarded as the inevitable outcome of all revolutions.[121]

Inside Parliament, however, the Whig opposition did not want revolution any more than did the Tories. To avert the looming crisis, they proposed the remedy of political reform. When asked in the House of Lords whether he intended to introduce a reform bill, however, the Duke of Wellington (now prime minister) answered to the effect that the British Parliament was the most excellent legislature mankind had ever encountered and that it enjoyed "the full and entire confidence of the country." Hence, he had no plan to sponsor any reform measures, and "should always feel it his duty to resist such measures when proposed by others."[122]

"Few speeches," says the *Cambridge Modern History*, "have ever had a greater effect than this one, though the effect was exactly the reverse of the speaker's intention. A storm of popular indignation ... swept the Tory Ministry from office, and placed the Whigs in power" for only the second time in forty-six years.[123] Despite unremitting protests from the ousted Tories, the prominent Whig figure, Lord John Russell, promptly laid before Parliament a major reform bill (introduced March 1, 1831), declaring, "A stranger who was told that this country is ... more civilized and more enlightened than any country was before it ... would be very much astonished if he were taken to a ruined mound and told that that mound sent two representatives to Parliament," while "large and opulent towns, full of enterprise and industry ... sent no representatives to Parliament." In reply, Sir Robert Inglis noted that if the boroughs now deemed to be unjustly represented had never existed, men like the elder and younger Pitt, Edmund Burke and Lord Canning would never have had the chance to serve their country. This was an excellent point, but it was ably countered by Thomas Babington (Lord Macaulay) who noted in turn, "we must judge of the form of government by its general tendency, not by happy accidents."[124]

After interminable speechmaking, the bill passed the Commons by a single vote amidst equal outbursts of cheers and howls. Before any action could be taken, however, the victory was overturned on the question of an amendment, and Parliament was dissolved (April 1831). To the amazement of both parties the ensuing elections revealed massive popular support for the Whigs, with polling places being surrounded by pro-reform mobs. The Whigs were returned with an even stronger majority and the bill was reintroduced. This time, it passed the Commons but was overruled by the House of Lords, many of whose members owned (and thus owed their generations-long influence to) boroughs that stood to be disenfranchised (October 1831).[125] The country was now in ferment. Mobs set fire to Bristol and were fired upon by government troops. Nottingham castle was reduced to ashes. In London, Wellington himself was accosted by rioters, and needed a military escort to get safely away.[126] Brought to the floor for a third time, the bill passed the Commons by 116 votes. In light of the ongoing demonstrations, King William IV (reigned, 1830–1837) reluctantly informed the upper house that if it attempted to overrule the bill again, he would be constrained to create enough new peerages to ensure its passage. The very thought brought the Lords to heel. They approved the bill in June 1832.[127]

By the terms of this famous "Reform Bill of 1832," suffrage was extended to the bourgeois merchant class, and many rotten boroughs were liquidated. But the result was far from democratic. The working class—which had done the lion's share of the rioting and demonstrating—remained without any political voice. This outcome was entirely intentional. Although there were a few radicals in Parliament who followed the "utilitarian" philosophy of Jeremy Bentham (1748–1832), the leading Whigs were not among them. Bentham had argued that "existing institutions should be valued, not for their antiquity, but ... for their utility in promoting 'the greatest happiness of the greatest number.'"[128] Furthermore, because humankind was ruled by self-interest, universal suffrage would be the best guarantee of "utilitarian" government—handing power to the majority ("greatest number"), which would naturally rule in its own self-interest ("greatest happiness"). Prior to the Reform Bill's passage, Lord Macaulay spent two years tearing this theory to shreds. "Whereas Bentham would have distributed votes to every man," says the *Cambridge Modern History*, "Macaulay would give it to every shopkeeper." In Macaulay's view, universal suffrage was a positive danger, for far from seeking "the greatest happiness of the greatest number," as Bentham had imagined, "large city populations were liable to become mobs and rabbles, selfish in prejudices, ungovernable in passions, and entirely at the mercy of unscrupulous demagogues." To extend the vote to everyone would thus be an invitation to revolution and anarchy. Limiting it to the commercial classes, in contrast, would serve the cause of orderly government—adding "the increasing influence of wealth and commerce" to "the decaying power of land and rank," as a bulwark in support of societal tranquility.[129]

This is an example of some very good thinking on Macaulay's part, but it does not address the issue of what was to occur when—inevitably—it dawned upon the working class that they had been left without representation. Macaulay and his fellow Whigs viewed the great Reform Bill they had authored as a long-term solution to the nation's woes. Indeed, Lord Russell had gone so far as to pronounce the reform "final" (for which he was afterwards lampooned by the radicals as "Finality Jack").[130] As the *Cambridge Modern History* notes, however, "The change the Whigs had accomplished was indeed greater than they had imagined.... It was not only that [they] had introduced a change; they had introduced the principle of change ... and proved that organic change might actually increase the efficiency, popularity, and stability of the Government."[131] Disappointed in thinking that they had produced a reform that would survive through the ages, the Whigs had nonetheless done a positive good, for their example gave the working class an alternative to revolution in pressing for change.

The working class promptly seized the mantle, embarking upon the so-called "Chartist Movement," which canvassed peaceably for further extension of the suffrage in a campaign lasting until 1848. Their goal was the implementation of a "Charter" comprised of "Six Points," with universal manhood suffrage, voting by secret ballot and uniformity in the size of voting districts heading the list. Alas, the program proved a fantastic failure. Parliament turned away the movement's petitions in 1839 and 1842 and then again in 1848, when a mass protest threatened to become violent. Charged with maintaining the peace on this last occasion, the elderly Duke of Wellington and his army of soldiers and constables found little to do, for a rainstorm sufficed to disperse the crowd. To complete the comedy, the Chartist leader, Feargus O'Connor, brought the group's petition (signed he claimed by five million souls) before Parliament, where a careful review revealed less than 40 percent of this number of signatures—many of which (for example, more than one purporting to be Wellington's) had been forged.[132]

We may note, however, that the post–Reform Bill era was not entirely bereft of reform. The newly enfranchised middle class improved the roads in the interest of commerce, granted parliamentary funds for the establishment of schools and instituted a penny-post whereby a penny stamp sufficed to get a letter delivered. Spurred on by the abolitionist clergyman William Wilberforce, Parliament, in 1833, passed legislation of pressing moral necessity—declaring an end to slavery on British colonial soil (with £20,000,000 being paid in compensation to the angry plantation owners).[133] A few acts of Parliament even benefited the workers. Already, the Tories had repealed the Combination Laws forbidding trade unions (1824), but a matter of far greater urgency was the plight of child laborers—impressed as early as age five and forced to work up to twelve hours a day in unsafe factories where the slightest transgression might result in a beating.[134] Following the Reform Bill of 1832, middle class sensibilities[135] prevailed upon parliament to lessen this injustice—however modestly—by passing the Factory Act (1833), which limited child labor to nine hours per day and made it illegal to employ children less than nine years old. There followed the Mines Act (1842), which forbade the employment of women or of children under the age of ten in the mines, and the Ten Hours Act (1847), limiting the length of the workday for adults. The mere thought of the conditions prevailing *after* these reforms appalls the modern mind—never mind those that prevailed before. But as bad as factory life might have been, the life of the indigent was even worse. A reformed "Poor Law"—passed in 1834 to address the increasing burden of the public dole as ever more people became dependent upon it—removed able-bodied individuals from the welfare rolls and forced them into workhouses. Here they labored under conditions made purposefully inhumane—husbands, for example, were forced to lodge separately from their wives—on the justification that their pauperism was a product of their own laziness rather than of the difficulties of the times.[136]

A Chartist Meeting, 1840, unknown artist (Wikimedia Commons).

The July Monarchy and the Revolutions of 1848

In reaction to the revolutionary climate of 1830, France and England had extended a role in government to the bourgeois class. In contrast, Austria, Russia and Prussia persisted in a policy of autocracy. Neither course proved satisfactory. By the 1840s, a new wave of discontent loomed on the horizon, and its eventual eruption would prove fatal to Metternich's system.

Predictably, the initial center of turmoil was France. By 1848, the new French king, Louis Philippe, could boast of peace and prosperity, but he could not boast of popular support. While the "July Monarchy" catered well enough to the needs of the bourgeoisie, which had brought it to power, its program was in all other respects repressive.[137] In the years prior to his enthronement, Louis Philippe had gained a reputation as a man of the people. He was often seen walking the streets of Paris unattended, sometimes stopping to drink a toast with members of the working class. His children attended the public schools. Once crowned, he proclaimed that he was "king by the grace of God *and* the will of the nation"—the theory being that sovereignty was imbued jointly in the king and in the people, and not in either of them alone.[138] Despite his inclinations, however, the experience of the Terror during the great Revolution had taught him to value order above all else. To allay the twin specters of "legitimist" reaction in favor of a Bourbon restoration and radical revolution in favor of democracy, he appointed the like-minded Casimir Périer as prime minister. Prior to his untimely death in 1832, Périer established a veritable "dictatorship of Liberal tendency," in support of which the king and government did not hesitate to employ force.[139]

When, for example, the silk workers of Lyons rose to protest their trifling wages (1831), government troops were called in to disperse them. No effort was made to address their grievances. Indeed, they were dealt a wage *decrease* in 1834 that provoked them to rebel anew. This time they gained a short-lived ascendancy over the city, before a bombardment by government artillery brought them to heel. The republicans who had backed the new regime in 1830 had expected greater liberalism and were now utterly disaffected. On hearing of the Lyons bombardment, they staged an insurrection in Paris. Here, too, the army delivered the government's answer, chasing the insurgents from their barricades at gunpoint. On the following morning the soldiery began dismantling the abandoned barricades in order to reopen the streets. Although they were not at this time threatening anyone, they were fired upon from a window on the rue Transnonain, and a popular officer was shot dead before their eyes. Identifying the building from which the fatal shot had come, the soldiers banged on the door until they were let in, and then went on a rampage, murdering several uninvolved persons, one of them a young woman who was bayoneted in the neck. (The soldier, says the contemporary historian and utopian socialist Louis Blanc, then discharged his weapon, resulting in the severance of her head.)[140]

Solemnized in an inflammatory drawing by the political satirist, Honoré Daumier (revered as the "Michelangelo of caricature"[141] for his skill at drawing Louis Philippe's head in the shape of a pear), the "Massacre in the rue Transnonain" became a metaphor for the king's tyranny.[142] Although he had had nothing to do with the incident directly, the government failed to set the record straight, opting instead to issue strong statements against the revolutionaries. This, of course, only kindled the flame. There ensued several attempts on the king's life—so many, in fact, that Louis Philippe asked

Massacre in the Rue Transnonain, April 15, 1934, painting by Honoré Daumier (Wikimedia Commons).

Louis Philippe in 1830 (left) looking serene, with curly hair and bushy sideburns giving his head the shape of a pear, and in 1833 (right) fatter and looking more worried; caricatures by Honoré Daumier (Wikimedia Commons).

whether some sort of monarchical hunting season had been proclaimed.[143] Inside the Chamber of Deputies, it was now traditional to greet the "Target King" with congratulations on another near miss.[144] The worst attack came in July 1835, when a dabbler in military engineering rigged twenty-four muskets to fire simultaneously on a royal procession. With the notable exception of its intended prey, the volley killed nearly everyone.[145] In response, the government cracked down—passing the repressive "September Laws," which provided for rigid press censorship and the unhindered arrest and detainment of troublemakers.

The muzzling of the opposition allowed the government to pretend for a time that discontent did not exist. But such was not the case. Discord smoldered beneath the surface over a variety of issues. Even the continuing respite from foreign war proved objectionable. Louis Philippe's prudent policy of neutrality in the Belgian and Polish rebellions of 1830 had averted a general European war, but had provoked riots in Paris.[146] As a sop to the growing nostalgia for the old days of conquest, the king dispatched his son, the Prince of Joinville, to St. Helena to collect Napoleon's coffin for reburial in France (1840). Simultaneously, however, he overruled his bellicose Prime Minister, Adolphe Thiers, and kowtowed to England rather than risk war over a brewing crisis in Turkey.

The evidence shows the king's foreign policy to have been subtle and wise.[147] The opposition castigated it as timid and hesitating. Under the stewardship of Louis Philippe's loyal foreign minister, Count Molé, a colonial venture in Algiers was brought to fruition, but the undertaking—dating to the reign of Charles X—had been precipitated by a heated diplomatic exchange in which the ruler of Algeria had batted the French consul with a flyswatter.[148] Final victory in such a matter did little to assuage French patriotism. Nor did the government's other major military endeavor, which involved the dispatch of a naval squadron to the Mexican port of Vera Cruz to seek redress for a variety of misdemeanors—the most infamous of which was the pillaging of a French-owned pastry store by Mexican revolutionaries. Although the foray nearly resulted in the capture of the notorious General Antonio López de Santa Anna,[149] it caused the French to be lampooned in Britain's *Annual Register* as bullies, "whose alacrity to hostilities seems too often to bear something of an inverse proportion to the means of the adversary."[150] As one might imagine, the "Pastry War" (as it was dubbed in the international press) did little to lift the prestige of the Orléans regime.

The government could have borne the opposition to its feeble hand in foreign policy, had it not been for an economic downturn in the mid–1840s. While the bourgeoisie flourished under the new monarchial regime, the pace of industrialization lagged behind the growth in population. Not enough jobs were produced, and poor harvests in 1846–47 compounded the economic misery. Hoping to compel the government to address the burdens of the working class, the republican Alexandre Auguste Ledru-Rollin initiated a campaign to broaden the suffrage. The realization of this goal seemed most unlikely, however, since Adolphe Thiers' "Movement Party," which supported democratic reform, had long been eclipsed in the Chamber of Deputies by François Guizot's "Resistance Party," which opposed it tooth and nail. The hated Guizot headed the king's ministry from 1840 until 1848, tampering with elections and buying off enough crooked deputies to maintain the status quo.[151] (His bribes, says Carlton Hayes, "converted the Chamber of Deputies into an employment bureau for dishonest politicians."[152]) As a standing testament to hypocrisy, Guizot declared that the government did not wish to deny the vote to anyone. Those who wanted it had only to make their desire known by becoming rich enough to meet the property qualification.[153] Out of 30 million Frenchmen, 100,000 could vote when Charles X was King. By enfranchising the upper bourgeoisie at the outset of his reign, Louis Philippe broadened the electorate to 170,000. Between 1830 and 1848, only 30,000 additional citizens were able to demonstrate to men like Guizot that they, too, wanted to vote.[154]

Thwarted in the Chamber of Deputies by the creatures of Guizot, those who favored extension of the suffrage took their ideas to a new forum. Because of a ban on public assemblies, they began holding public "banquets" where the topic of discussion just happened to be electoral reform. The most important of these banquets was scheduled to take place in Paris on February 22, 1848. The government forbade it. The people of Paris, many of whom were out of work owing to the continent-wide recession, responded with angry demonstrations. To the government's chagrin, several units of the Paris National Guard—whose middle-class rank-and-file stood to benefit from electoral reform[155]—sided with the protesters. But it was a squadron of loyal soldiers who sounded the regime's death-knell. Outside the government foreign office, they fired into an unruly crowd, leaving scores of unarmed civilians maimed or dead. At this, the city gave way to riot. Louis Philippe abdicated and fled the capital by carriage, leaving the succession to his nine-year-old grandson, the Count of Paris. The boy's mother proceeded in haste to the Chamber of Deputies to offer herself as regent, but before she could speak a mob stormed the Chamber demanding a provisional "republican" government. Such applause greeted this suggestion that the confused young Count added his own hurrah.[156] The crowd of hoodlums, meanwhile, continued to press into the Chamber—some rudely pointing their muskets at the duchess, who did well to slip out a side door with her son's scalp intact.[157]

In the initial rioting, the bourgeoisie and workers were comrades-in-arms, but it was widely recognized after the abdication of the king that this situation would not

Scene from the Revolution of 1848: Lamartine rejects the red flag in front of the Town Hall of Paris, February 1848, by Henri Félix Philippoteaux, Petit Palais, Paris (Wikimedia Commons).

endure. The Russian ambassador in Berlin wrote to his government that the collaboration between the bourgeoisie and the workers which had toppled Louis Philippe would now come apart since the former merely desired political reform while the latter wanted a redistribution of wealth.[158] His observation proved prophetic. Proletarian fervor was in the air—Karl Marx's *Communist Manifesto* had been published in Germany just weeks earlier—and radical activists now began to demand a government guarantee of jobs and significant reform of working conditions. In order to buy time, the government approved a National Workshop Program proposed by the renowned socialist Louis Blanc. Blanc's actual intention was to allow skilled tradesmen to establish and run their own factories, assisted at the outset by government subsidies. The profits, in this scheme would accrue not to the capitalist class, but to the involved workers and artisans, thus "to make him that works enjoy the fruits of his work."[159] Blanc, however, was given no control over the program, and had it not been for the Herculean efforts of Emile Thomas, a twenty-six-year-old engineer who served in the capacity of chief organizer, the project would have come to nothing at all. As it was, it did not amount to much. Owing to the hostility of Thomas' superior—the anti-socialist Minister of Public Works, Alexandre Marie—the program could find work for scarcely ten percent of those enrolled.[160] Moreover, it did not promote the establishment of durable manufacturing jobs, but simply assigned participants—skilled and unskilled alike—to work on temporary public works projects, including the digging of ditches. It was, in effect, a façade for the public dole (a concept Blanc deplored as the antithesis of his own vision even as the government attached his name to the project). As unemployed laborers streamed into the workshops by the tens of thousands, their idleness, coupled with the radical rhetoric of their leadership, caused the increasingly nervous propertied classes to regard them as the harbingers of social revolution.

It was a mistaken impression, but it was enough to produce a repetition of the events of 1830, whereby the workers, who had done all the work of the revolution, were to be denied the fruits of their labor. The country at large had no intention of catering to the social platform of the Parisian radicals. Thus, while the latter increased their demands, their candidates were soundly defeated in an election based on universal male suffrage (April 1848). Even the workers cast the bulk of their votes for moderate candidates.[161] Unwilling to accept defeat, the radicals organized a mass uprising in May, only to be subdued by the bourgeois-controlled National Guard. But when the government sought to finish the matter by abandoning the costly National Workshop Program, the vaunted volcano finally erupted. Driven more by hunger and privation than by notions of class warfare,[162] the workers fell in line behind the radicals and erected barricades (June 1848).

Having anticipated this response, the government deputed General Eugene Cavaignac, a veteran of the Algerian War, to restore the public peace. Cavaignac's soldiers promptly shattered the barricades with artillery fire, killing more than 1000 demonstrators (perhaps as many as 10,000)—many of whom were chased down and murdered after the fight was over.[163] Hailed as a hero in moneyed circles, Cavaignac was vilified by his victims as the "butcher of the barricades."

The violence of the so-called "June Days" created a nationwide desire for order. A new republican constitution was drawn up in November, providing for a one-house legislature and a single-term, four-year presidency. The latter office was imbued with extensive powers, civil and military, despite the prophetic oratory of the prominent Assembly

"**Remembrance of the Civil War,**" or *The Barricade, Rue de la Mortellerie*, June 1848, by Jean-Louis-Ernest Meissonier, Louvre (**Wikimedia Commons**).

member, Jules Grévy, who asked, "Are you quite sure that in that series of men who are to succeed each other every four years to the presidential throne, there will be only devoted republicans…. Are you sure there will never be anyone sufficiently ambitious to try to perpetuate his power?"[164]

In the presidential elections that followed (December 1848), the radical republican

Alexandre Auguste Ledru-Rollin garnered some 400,000 votes. Backed by moneyed interests, the decidedly more conservative Cavaignac easily outdid him, obtaining 1,500,000. But neither man won. Victory fell instead to a third candidate who received a landslide 5,500,000 of the ballots cast. The successful candidate spoke French with a German accent, having spent most of his life outside the country. He was not the favored candidate of those who had brought about the revolution, but they could do nothing to halt his popularity. His name was Louis Napoleon Bonaparte. He was the nephew of the great emperor—and he remains to this day one of the enigmas of modern European history.

Sixteen years earlier, in July 1832, a coffin interred at Vienna's Church of the Capuchins seemed to set seal to Bonapartist aspirations, for inside lay the corpse of Napoleon II, the hapless, neglected son of the great Bonaparte. His demise put an end to the direct line and delivered the succession to an imperial nephew—i.e., the aforementioned Louis Napoleon.[165] The early antics of this pretender made him a most unlikely candidate for success. In 1831, he and his elder brother, Napoleon Louis, participated in a doomed revolt against papal rule in Romagna, Italy. Napoleon Louis succumbed to measles as a result of this misadventure,[166] while a fellow freedom fighter named Orsini—whose surname will resurface later in our story—likewise lost his life. Following this escapade, the prince involved himself in two ill-conceived efforts to overthrow the government of Louis Philippe. In 1836, at age twenty-eight, he convinced the soldiers of the Strasbourg garrison to rise on his behalf. Sadly, he did not convince the garrison's commander, who promptly brought the enterprise to a halt. Still, the incident caused Louis Philippe untold anxiety, since news of it was relayed by semaphore telegraph—a medium requiring visual signals—and the weather turned bad before the nervous residents of the royal palace could be apprised of the outcome.[167]

Apprehended, the prince was sent into exile, spending time in America and then in Britain, where he published a Bonapartist political manifesto entitled *Napoleonic Ideas* (1839). The book gained Louis Napoleon sufficient notoriety to inspire a second, even less well-conceived, attempt at coup d'état.[168] Embarking from England, he landed on the French coast near Boulogne with a party of fifty-six followers—most of them drunk, since they had imbibed alcohol to fend off seasickness during the rough Channel crossing. His intent, says Charles Downer Hazen, was "to enact another 'return from Elba,' an event whose fascination for adventurers was lively, but an achievement difficult to repeat."[169] From start to finish, the enterprise was a disaster. Chased from the Boulogne garrison, the pretender and some of his associates returned to the coast and piled into a rowboat, but the little craft had not yet cleared the harbor when it came under fire and capsized. The prince had to grasp hold of a nearby buoy until his pursuers could rescue him.[170] At his trial, he argued that Louis Philippe was a usurper, since he had not been the legitimate claimant in 1830, and since his accession had never been approved by plebiscite, the method used by the great Bonaparte when he became emperor.[171] It was a reasonably good argument, but Louis Napoleon was sentenced to life imprisonment in the fortress of Ham, nonetheless. He served six years before escaping, dressed as a workman, in hopes of visiting his dying father in Florence (1846).

Undaunted by his failures, the prince seemed to regard his eventual triumph as preordained. Following his escape from the fortress of Ham, he told a confidante, "Though fortune has twice betrayed me, yet my destiny will none the less surely be fulfilled. I wait."[172] Two years later, the revolution brought him back to France. The effect, however, was less than stunning. Hardly did he arrive before official hostility convinced him to sail back to England, where, in one of history's ironies, he enlisted as a constable under Wellington—the conqueror of his famous uncle—in the tense days of April 1848 when the Chartist Movement threatened to become violent.[173] In June of the same year, he won a seat in the Chamber of Deputies in absentia, but the government threatened to arrest him if he returned, so he remained in exile. His ostracism proved a godsend, for he was absent from Paris during the brutal "June Days."

On being re-elected to the Assembly in September, he returned to take his seat. His first speech rebutted a motion (aimed against himself) that would have made "pretenders" ineligible for the four-year presidency established under the new constitution. So unimpressive were his remarks, delivered in a grating German accent, that the deputy who introduced the motion immediately withdrew it again, saying that he no longer considered it necessary.[174] (Years later, Louis Napoleon's German accent was to prove the source of another amusing anecdote, when, as emperor, he complimented Bismarck's immaculate French, telling him: "I have never heard a German speak French as you do," to which the German Chancellor replied: "Will you allow me to return the compliment, sire? ... I have never heard a Frenchman speak French as you do."[175])

But appearances are sometimes deceiving. One observer who met Louis Napoleon at this time said of him:

> Though I had not the slightest ground for expecting to see a fine man, I did not expect to see so utterly an insignificant one, and badly dressed in the bargain. On the evening in question, he wore ... a pair of yellowish trousers, the like of which I have never seen on the legs of any one off the stage.... When I entered the apartment on the evening in question, Louis Napoleon was leaning ... against the mantelpiece, smoking the scarcely ever absent cigarette, and pulling at the heavy brown moustache, the ends of which in those days were not waxed into points as they were later on. There was not the remotest likeness to any portrait of the Bonaparte family I had ever seen.... When.... I looked into his face, I felt almost tempted to put him down as an opium eater. Ten minutes afterwards I felt convinced that, to use a metaphor, he was the drug, and that everyone with whom he came in contact was bound to yield to its influence.[176]

Indeed, by the time of the presidential election he seemed to represent everything to everybody. His very name harkened to the former glory of France, a veritable magnet for French nationalists.

Louis Napoleon Bonaparte, President of the Second French Republic, 1848, lithograph by Eduard Kaiser (1820–1895) (Wikimedia Commons).

Additionally, he could put himself forth as an untarnished man of order, whereas Cavaignac, his chief rival in this sphere, had blood on his hands from the repressions of June. Even the workers could take heart, for Louis Napoleon had written a social-ist treatise entitled *On the Extinction of Pauperism* in which he had proposed a working wage of six francs per day—a significant increase over what the defunct national work-shop program had paid out.[177] On the heels of his victory, the nation elected a conser-vative Assembly that believed it could control the new president, since he had only just returned to France and had no influential supporters.[178]

The Other *Revolutions of 1848*

The turmoil begun in France proved every bit as infectious in 1848 as it had in 1830, engulfing Germany, Italy and most especially the Hapsburg Empire in a hydra of revo-lutionary activity. "Events," says Charles Downer Hazen, "were to succeed each other of a most sensational character, and the reaction of these events upon each other, of nation upon nation, of parts of nations upon other parts, was to be the most distinguishing as well as the most confusing characteristic of the time."[179]

As the reader will discern in the coming pages, the operative word in this supremely accurate quotation of Hazen's is "confusing." Confusing because there are multiple rev-olutions occurring at once, and in order to maintain some semblance of chronology we must skip back and forth between them. Confusing, too, because there is as yet no uni-fied Germany, and in the territory which we think of today as "German" there are two separate revolutions—one based in Frankfurt, which seeks to create a unified and lib-eral "Greater Germany" out of the patchwork of independent principalities that com-posed the German Confederation; the other in the streets of Berlin (capital of Prussia), which seeks to wring a liberal constitution from the Prussian King (Frederick William IV). In Italy, too, there are two revolutions to be considered. One in the north, spear-headed by King Charles Albert of Piedmont (who hopes at the very least to liberate Lom-bardy and Venetia from Italy), the other in Rome under the republican Mazzini. But it is in the Hapsburg Empire that confusion reigns in its most pristine form—for here we have simultaneous revolutions in four different places: In Vienna, the capital, where the radicals want a liberal constitution; in Bohemia, where liberalism and nationalism are at loggerheads; in Hungary, where the Magyars, though a minority, desire supremacy and independence; and in Italy, where Lombardy and Venetia want to throw off the Haps-burg yoke. With this as our framework, we will follow events as best we can.

In February 1848, a nationalist uprising in the Grand Duchy of Baden set Germany ablaze. In Berlin the following month, an attempt by saber-wielding cavalry to disperse a crowd of liberal agitators threw the entire city into open rebellion. Trapped in the whirlwind, Frederick William IV, the romantic Prussian king who dreamt of European unity under a medieval-style Holy Roman Empire even as his people clamored for lib-eral reform and national expression,[180] submissively paid his respects from the palace balcony to a funeral procession for those killed in the altercation. To mollify the rioters, he raised the German tricolor over the palace, lifted the ban on smoking in the Tiergar-ten—for this had been one of the mob's demands—and, on March 22, promised to draft a liberal constitution.[181] By May, with the fever of revolution consuming much of the German Confederation, a Federal Parliament of intellectuals convened in the free city of Frankfurt, presuming to speak for all Germany on the topic of unification, despite the fact that it possessed no army to back up its pronouncements.[182] All the states of Germany were invited to elect representatives to the new parliament by universal suffrage.

But if rebellious nationalism exercised a unifying influence in Germany, where a single "Germanic people" was artificially *divided* under a confederacy of rival sovereigns, it had a distinctly opposite effect in the Hapsburg Empire, where a confederacy of rival peoples—Germanic, Czech, Magyar, Italian, Polish, Serbo-Croatian, Slavic (*inter alia*)—was artificially *united* under a single sovereign.[183] Amid the swell of revolution, the rampart erected by Metternich against liberalism and nationalism in central Europe gave way like a house of cards.[184] On March 13, rioting in Vienna forced Metternich's resignation and flight to England after three and a half decades at Europe's helm. According to the account of Willis Mason West, the "Coachman of Europe" fled Vienna, as a stowaway in a laundry cart.[185]

"The effect produced by the news of Metternich's fall," says Alison Phillips, "was stupendous…. [His] name had become associated indissolubly with a system; and just as in 1789 the fall of the Bastille had been hailed as the symbol of the opening of a new era, so that of Metternich was welcomed in 1848 as marking the collapse of the combination of the reactionary Powers against liberty."[186] In the ensuing days, Hungarian nationalists inspired by the patriot-orator Louis Kossuth formed an autonomous government at Pressburg in Hungary while Czech nationalists declared Bohemian autonomy at Prague. In neither case was the Hapsburg Emperor deposed from his sovereign position,

Representatives of the Frankfurt Parliament convene in Frankfurt's St. Paul's Church, 1848, by Gerhard Delius (Wikimedia Commons).

but in all other respects Czechs and Hungarians alike intended to be masters of their own destiny. Hungary, indeed, went so far as to organize its own army and to appoint its own ambassadors to foreign courts.[187] Meanwhile, in riotous Vienna, the faint-hearted Emperor Ferdinand I (ruled, 1835–1848) agreed first to the establishment of a two-house Austrian Parliament and then to the convocation of a Constituent Assembly elected by universal suffrage to draft a constitution for the empire. Having failed to appease the mob by these concessions, he temporarily abandoned the capital for Innsbruck.[188]

As it turns out, the Austrian government's inability to deal with the escalating crisis was not due to the fall of Metternich, whose former talents at statesmanship had now withered to nothingness apart from a "capacity for more or less impressive phrase making."[189] Rather, it was due to the absence of the Austrian army—the bulk of which had been sent to northern Italy, where rebellion had been in the air for months.[190] Already, Milan had played host to the so-called "smoking riots" wherein local Milanese citizens boycotting an Austrian tax on tobacco, threw stones at Austrian soldiers who continued to smoke. When news of Metternich's flight arrived (March 18), this rebellion became generalized, spawning a bloody five-day street battle that forced the Austrians to evacuate the Lombard capital.[191]

Amid these events, Venetia, too, threw off the Austrian yoke, declaring an independent "Republic of St. Mark" in the Piazza San Marco (Saint Mark's Square) on March 22. Consequently, though the army was desperately needed in Vienna, Austria had either to dispatch more troops across the Alps or suffer the irreparable loss of her position in Italy.[192] Indeed, Italian hostility to Austria was not limited to Lombardy and Venetia where Austria ruled directly. While the remainder of the peninsula was sufficiently fractured in a political sense to evoke Metternich's famed assertion that Italy was nothing more than a "geographical expression,"[193] Italians of all stripes were, by 1848, seemingly agreed on at least one point—namely, that the time had come for an Italian "Risorgimento" or "resurrection" that required as its first step the expulsion of Austria from Italian affairs. Pressed to explain how this might come about, Charles Albert, King of Piedmont-Sardinia confidently replied that "Italy will do it alone."[194] On March 23, 1848, this same prince seized the mantle of Italian emancipation and declared war on the Austrian Empire. Crossing the Ticino into Milanese territory, he engaged the unready Austrians at Goito, gaining a victory that transiently extended his dominion across northern Italy (May 1848).[195]

Just as these various revolutions achieved their greatest momentum, however, the tide began to turn. In Bohemia, Czechs and Germans alike had clamored for liberalization at the outset of the revolution, but emerging nationalist sentiment now drove a wedge between them. The Czech rebels favored either an autonomous Czech Bohemia or a pan–Slav program aimed at bettering the status of all Slavs within the Hapsburg Empire. Bohemia's Germans, however, favored a vastly different course—namely, the incorporation of Bohemia into a unified "greater Germany" (something that had already been proposed by the Frankfurt Parliament). By June 1848, these competing ambitions had sown chaos among the Bohemian rebels.

In Vienna, too, the revolution lost impetus, as the new Austrian Parliament—composed of delegates of myriad nationalities—proved a House of Babel.[196] Ironically, the lone issue—liberal rather than national—upon which they all agreed proved their undoing. In fulfillment of the dream of Joseph I, the "enlightened despot" of the previous century, the Parliament abolished the last vestige of serfdom—dispensing with the hated "*robota*," which obliged the peasantry to provide free labor to the Austrian gentry at certain times of the year. Passed in September 1848, the abolition law—or Emancipation Act—was meant to appease the many peasants who had assisted in the revolution. Far from increasing the peasants' revolutionary zeal, however, the bill filled them with such contentment that they ceased to concern themselves with revolutionary matters. Thus, by their very magnanimity, the revolutionaries forfeited a critical support base.[197]

And now the military sands began to shift as well. On June 13, battle erupted in the streets of Prague between Czech and German revolutionaries. Barricades were thrown up near the residence of the city's Austrian military commandant, Prince Alfred von Windischgrätz. Beholding the proceedings from one of the windows, the prince's wife was struck dead by a musket ball. For Bohemia, this was the end. Windishgrätz unleashed his artillery on the agitators, delivering Prague back into the Hapsburg fold with a merciless bombardment. A month later, in Italy, the octogenarian Austrian General Joseph Radetsky defeated Charles Albert's Italians at Custozza to restore Hapsburg hegemony in Lombardy and Venetia (July 1848).

Meanwhile, in Hungary, as in Bohemia, nationalist rivalry had begun to play havoc with the revolutionary cause. Hitherto, the powerful Magyars had dominated the rebellion. But the Magyars did not constitute the majority of Hungarians, and the Slavs of the province—chief among them the Croats, led by the indomitable Count Joseph Jellačič—had no wish to cast off the rule of Vienna if Magyar mastery was to be established in its stead. Seeking to capitalize on this sentiment, Austria enlisted the Croats to combat the Magyar insurgency. In so doing, however, the government overstepped itself; for the task of battling the Magyars proved beyond the capability of the Croats, and when Austria tried to reinforce them, Vienna fell prey to riot. Believing that the fate of Hungary's revolution was intertwined with its own, the Viennese mob hanged the minister of war from a lamppost[198] and obstructed the soldiers' route of egress from the city.[199] So grave was the situation that Emperor Ferdinand perfunctorily granted the demands of the rioters and fled yet again—this time to Olmütz in Moravia (September 1848).

The mob's victory, however, proved ephemeral; for the situation was soon retrieved by Field Marshal Windischgrätz—now returned from Bohemia—who restored order in Vienna no less brutally than he had done in Prague (October 1848). It was the signal for reaction. Emperor Ferdinand, who had been no better than a broken reed throughout the crisis—fleeing hither and yon, while caving in, in turn, to Bohemian, Hungarian and Viennese demands—now abdicated at the insistence of his own supporters (December 2, 1848). Replacing him was his eighteen-year-old nephew, Franz Josef, who convened a new cabinet headed by Prince Felix Schwarzenberg, a stalwart reactionary intent on restoring power to the crown.

Schwarzenberg's opening move as prime minister was subtle—inviting the revolutionary Austrian Parliament to continue its deliberations on a constitution, but directing it to change its venue from the raucous capital to Kremsier, closer to Olmütz, where the imperial court had been sitting since Ferdinand's flight in September.[200] In the meantime, Prince Windischgrätz initiated operations against Hungary in cooperation with Count Jellačič. By January 1849, the advancing imperial forces had occupied Budapest. Hitherto, however, Prince Windischgrätz's troops had faced nothing more formidable than rioters and parliamentarians. In Hungary, they were up against the Magyar-dominated Hungarian army. Beginning in March 1849, the Magyars reeled off a string of victories, retaking Budapest and throwing the Austrians into retreat.[201]

The turnabout prompted the revolutionary flame to burst forth once more in Italy and Germany. In early April, the Frankfurt Parliament invited Frederick William IV of Prussia to assume the title of "emperor" of greater Germany—a decided challenge to Austria's traditional hegemony there. But the situation in Italy was more volatile still. On November 15, 1848, assassins slit the throat of the pope's advisor, Pellegrino Rossi, outside the Roman Parliament. The murder kicked off a nationalist uprising. On November 24, Pope Pius IX fled to Naples in the garb of a common priest, and on February 9, a Roman Republic was proclaimed.[202] The architect of the revolt was the radical republican Giuseppe Mazzini, who had been agitating for Italian liberty since the 1830s when he formed a secret society of revolutionaries whose members were all under forty years old. Known aptly enough as "Young Italy," the proselytes of the movement longed to throw off the Austrian yoke and to fashion Italy into a single republic, thus to assume the important standing in European affairs that destiny—and history—demanded for her. By 1834, when it staged its first uprising, the movement boasted a membership of 60,000—most famous among them the patriot-adventurer Giuseppe Garibaldi. The effort of that year failed disastrously, and in its aftermath, Mazzini fled to London, Garibaldi to South America. The year of 1848 brought both agitators back to the peninsula, and the defeat of Charles Albert ushered them to the forefront of Italian affairs. On March 5, 1849, a month after the flight of the pope, Mazzini entered Rome in triumph. Emboldened by these events, the Duchy of Tuscany ousted its grand duke and declared a republic, while Piedmont's Charles Albert renewed the war in northern Italy.

The "revitalized" rebellion proved a chimera in all quarters. At Novara on March 23, Charles Albert was defeated so decisively that he abdicated on the battlefield in favor of his son, Victor Emmanuel (March 23, 1849)—the campaign having lasted scarcely two weeks. The road to Rome was now seemingly open to Austrian arms. Unwilling to suffer the southward extension of Hapsburg influence in Italy, the French Assembly intervened, voting in April to send a French military expedition to Rome to restore the temporal authority of the pope. Though popular with French Catholics, this policy carried with it the great disadvantage of having to subdue some rather determined Roman freedom fighters.[203] After an initial setback and a bloody siege, the French finally gained control of the city on July 3, 1849. Mazzini and Garibaldi fled—the latter's ailing wife dying in his arms as he made a narrow escape.[204]

The restored pope, Pius IX, had once been a liberal. Indeed, on first assuming office in 1846, he had freed Rome's political prisoners, established a papal advisory council (thereby limiting his own prerogatives) and put an end to censorship of the press.[205] At the outset of the war between Austria and Piedmont in 1848, he had dispatched troops to the support of Charles Albert. But as head of the Catholic Church, he soon lamented the decision to make war on his fellow Catholics in Austria for the benefit of an Italian rival. By the so-called "Allocution" of April 1848, he summoned his troops to cease and desist before battle had been joined, sacrificing his reputation as a liberal, and provoking the citizens of Rome to riot.[206]

His subsequent forced exile at the hands of Mazzini's republicans transformed him into so thoroughgoing a reactionary that on restoring him to his post, France found that it could exert no influence over him. A stern missive from Louis Napoleon—who, as the reader may recall, had championed Roman liberty in his youth—proved entirely unavailing as Pius abolished all of Mazzini's liberal reforms.[207] On the whole, Austria had greater cause for satisfaction with Pius' policy than did his French deliverers.

(Indeed, the only Frenchman to obtain political capital from the Roman expedition may have been Louis Napoleon, who gained the plaudits of French Catholics by virtue of the intervention.)

By now, the revolutions in Vienna and Germany had also come apart. At Kremsier, the revolutionary Austrian Parliament finally completed its draft constitution on March 1, 1849. Before it could publish this document, however, Prince Schwarzenberg, on March 4, substituted one of his own, authored by his fellow cabinet member, Count Franz Stadion, a statesman of liberal reputation from Galicia. Brimming with liberal trappings that stole the fire of the Viennese revolutionaries—including the establishment of a bicameral legislature—the document preserved to the monarchy important prerogatives that would have been abolished under the Kremsier Constitution.[208] With its services no longer required the Kremsier Parliament was dissolved.

Soon thereafter, Prussia's Frederick William IV—unwilling to risk war with Austria for what he termed a "crown of mud" proffered by intellectuals and radicals—declined the Frankfurt Parliament's offer of the German imperial throne (April 28, 1849). The rebuff ended the German revolution at a blow. The Frankfurt Parliament collapsed; street riots aimed at keeping the insurrection alive in Breslau, Saxony and Baden were put down with cruel repression; and when it was over, a number of revolutionaries were executed in Baden despite a promise of amnesty.

With Vienna and Germany quiescent, Piedmont, Lombardy and Venetia defeated, and Rome besieged, Austria had but to overcome the Magyars to emerge from the tumultuous year of revolution with her power and prestige reconstituted. The task, however, proved beyond her. In March and April 1849, the Magyar armies gained victory upon victory. Powerless to stem the tide, Austria resorted to a drastic expedient, appealing for military assistance from a foreign power—Russia. In response, the Hungarian government made an error as romantic in intent as it was fatal in effect. It declared the accession of Franz Josef illegitimate in Hungary—for the emperor had not undergone the traditional Hungarian coronation with the crown of St. Stephen, and, furthermore, had reneged upon the liberties granted to Hungary by his inept predecessor, Ferdinand (who had been so crowned, and was thus, in Hungarian eyes, still the legitimate king). As the Austrian court would not yield before this compelling logic, Hungary declared its independence on April 14, 1849. In so doing, it unwittingly played into Austria's hands.[209]

Apprehensive that revolutionary success anywhere in Europe would rekindle nationalist sentiment among his own Polish subjects, Tsar Nicholas I, the "gendarme of Europe," would not brook the establishment of a free Hungary adjacent to his own dominions. Consequently, on receiving Franz Josef's plea to assist in the suppression of the Magyars, Nicholas was only too ready to oblige.[210] Russian troops advanced into Hungary in two columns—one moving toward central Hungary, the other along her eastern frontier—perhaps as many as 200,000 men in all. General Artur Gorgei, in command of a mere 30,000 Hungarian rebels, deftly attacked these columns in flank to slow their progress as he withdrew southwards in hopes of linking with other Hungarian forces, which were then assembling to fend off a simultaneous Austrian offensive. Unfortunately, the latter troops were utterly defeated at the town of Temesvar while Gorgei was still some thirty miles distant. Without hope of reinforcement, Gorgei surrendered to the Russians in August 1849.[211] Realizing that Hungary's cause was lost, Louis Kossuth—the oracle of the Hungarian revolution—fled to Turkey. Later, he would bedazzle audiences on the American and British lecture circuit with brilliant speeches delivered in impeccable English in support of Hungarian nationalism.[212] Most of his colleagues were not so fortunate—among them thirteen captured Hungarian officers who died on the gallows. (The valiant Gorgei was spared at the insistence of the tsar.)

Hence, by late summer 1849, the revolutions begun in the previous year had all been extinguished—many of them consumed to ashes in a rivalry between the very nationalist and liberal forces by which they had been spawned. In the end, embattled nationalism succeeded neither in uniting Italy or Germany nor in fracturing the Austrian Empire. Liberalism might have abolished feudal privilege within the Hapsburg domains, but it had left autocracy intact. In Prussia, Frederick William IV followed through on his promise of a constitution, nominally establishing election by universal suffrage; but the result, as we shall see, was wholly undemocratic.[213]

With the German revolution at an end, the question arose as to what was to be done with the German Confederation. To fill the void created by the collapse of the Frankfurt Parliament, Prussia and Austria put forward rival plans for its reorganization, the former providing for Prussian hegemony, the latter for continued domination by Austria. Tensions became acute, but in the end, Prussia backed down, for if it came to war, Frederick William feared that Russia would support Austria against him. In 1850, the Prussian king signed the Convention of Olmütz (November 1850), whereby he abandoned his own proposal so ignominiously that the agreement came to be known as the "Humiliation of Olmütz." Nevertheless, Prussia had the satisfaction of seeing Austria's plan founder, too, under international pressure. Ultimately, the antiquated Germanic Confederation of 1815 was simply restored, leaving the final struggle for German hegemony to be fought another day.[214]

2

Nationalism Triumphant, 1848–1870

The Establishment of the Second French Empire

Thus, despite their rapid and overwhelming success at the outset, each of the democratic revolutions of 1848 had ended in reaction. In France, the workers uprisings of the "June Days" of 1848 engendered so great a fear of social revolution that the majority of Frenchmen voted for "monarchist" rather than "republican" candidates in the first election under their new constitution. The Assembly thus elected celebrated its triumph by restricting suffrage and freedom of the press. Radical republican and socialist journals—published cheaply so as to be affordable to the working class—were effectively shut down by the imposition of a 50,000-franc licensing fee that was beyond the means of most editors. Similarly, control of the schools was taken away from secular educators (most of whom were pro-republican) and delivered into the hands of the clergy.[1] When, despite this, a number of radicals were elected to the Assembly in the 1850 by-elections, the conservative majority revised the constitution, over the objection of the new president, in order to deprive some three million Frenchmen of the right to vote.[2]

To this point in his term, Louis Napoleon had been the willing champion of property rights and law and order—desires that were shared by the majority of Assembly delegates (though as monarchists and republicans many of them held him in contempt). In order to form a more perfect union, the president now suggested that the constitution, so recently altered against his wishes, be revised yet again to include an amendment that would permit him to seek a second term in office—a modest proposal that was bolstered by a series of countryside tours in which he was popularly received.[3] Out of a concern for order, more than sixty percent of the Assembly voted in favor. But to pass an amendment required a seventy-five percent majority.[4] Consequently, the measure failed. Despite this apparent setback, Louis Napoleon boasted in private that he was "preparing the ruin of the Assembly," and that once it was "hanging over the precipice, I shall cut the rope."[5] In early November 1851, amid rising tensions, he asked the Assembly to reinstate universal suffrage. An expert schemer who played his cards close to his chest, he seems initially to have conceived this idea as a means of winning over the leftist deputies of the Assembly to his re-election amendment.[6] When, however, he perceived that it would cost him more votes on the right than he could possibly gain on the left, he was prepared to turn the Assembly's reactionary tendencies to his own advantage.[7] Employing his constitutional powers of appointment during the preceding month, he had packed key positions in his cabinet and in the police force with his own supporters. On the night of December

1, 1851, he sprang the trap. Thiers, Cavaignac and other leading opponents were placed under arrest. The next morning, the remaining deputies of the Assembly found themselves barred from their usual meeting hall, and when they convened at an alternative location, government troops barged in and arrested them. Placards posted throughout Paris proclaimed the president's noble intention of restoring to the people the sovereignty of which the Assembly had divested them. Lest the people be summoned to resist by the sounding of the church bells (a traditional revolutionary ploy) or by journalistic propaganda, the president had stationed police at the city's churches and printing offices.[8] The date was December 2, 1851—the anniversary of the battle of Austerlitz—and to secure popular support for his smartly timed coup, Louis Napoleon announced the restoration of universal male suffrage.

The people of the countryside (by and large) applauded their president's gallant effort to restore their votes, and the majority of Parisians might have done likewise had they not been dodging bullets. By December 3, the traditional barricades had gone up—albeit with considerably less enthusiasm than usual—and the army, just as traditionally, had commenced fire upon them. This was not so bad, but disaster ensued on the following day when a column of soldiers marching down the Boulevard Poissoniere went utterly berserk after being fired upon from an overhead window. Without attempting to identify the culprit, the troops leveled their rifles and shot everyone in sight, massacring over one hundred unsuspecting onlookers and innocent passersby, including a number of children.[9]

In those areas where die-hard republicans attempted to resist, they found that the working class was not interested in assisting them. The politician Jean Baudin martyred himself atop a barricade in a heroic but futile gesture to call them to arms. The resistance was handily put down—the perpetrators being denounced as a new *jacquerie* intent on wanton destruction[10]—while nationwide tens of thousands were placed under arrest on the ironic charge of conspiring against the state (their true crime being hostility to the coup d'état). Louis Napoleon would not have had it thus, for he was not without compassion,[11] but his co-conspirators—chief among them, his half-brother, Charles Morny, whom he had made Minister of the Interior—were anxious to prove, by these arrests, that they had acted in the interest of the "public safety."[12]

The repression and bloodletting tarnished Louis Napoleon's reputation. Victor Hugo, the famed poet and novelist (and the president's former friend), fled into exile, whence he penned scathing indictments, including one entitled *Napoleon the Little*.[13] But as Cobban notes, if there isn't a little repression attendant upon an escapade like this, people tend to wonder whether it had really been necessary in the first place.[14] Three weeks after the coup, the nation's re-enfranchised voters overwhelmingly approved a new constitution granting Louis Napoleon dictatorial powers styled upon the Consulate of Napoleon I. Budgetary control remained in the hands of the legislative chamber, but the new charter gave the Prince-President a ten-year term in office, and made him responsible only "to the French people, to whom he has always the right to make an appeal."[15] Thus he could resort to plebiscite at any time to demonstrate support for his policies. Nor was he long in doing so. Following another tour of the countryside in which he "spoke honeyed words to peasants, to artists, to capitalists, to rich and poor, to reactionaries and revolutionaries, to agnostics and those religiously inclined,"[16] he placed an imperial constitution before the people. On December 2, 1852, to the tune of eight million votes in favor versus just 250,000 opposed, the last vestiges of the tottering

Second Republic were swept aside by plebiscite to make way for a newly proclaimed Second French Empire. Louis Napoleon Bonaparte, the bungling adventurer and conspirator, had become Napoleon III, Emperor of the French.

Here, then, was the final overthrow of the French Revolution of 1848. Whereas the revolutionary tide had been beaten back in Austria, Hungary, Italy and Prussia by force of arms, says Alison Phillips, Louis Napoleon "had charmed the monster's ear with soothing phrases, had slipped a bit between its teeth and blinkers over its eyes, and harnessed it in triumph to the car of Empire."[17]

But if the specter of revolution had been exorcised from Europe, an end had been made, too, to the era of international stability that was the one definite fruit of the system of Metternich. As we have noted, the liberal cause in the revolutions of 1848, had foundered in part upon the rock of nationalist rivalry—a kinetic force that had by no means exhausted its energy. In the ensuing decades, the national unification movements in Italy and Germany were to render a profound change in the map of Europe. In France, the ascent of a new Bonaparte bade fair to rekindle that proud sense of French nationalism that had been studiously neglected by the restored Bourbons and Louis Philippe. Here was sufficient fodder for a new clash of titans, but the first blow to international quietude came from further afield in an oft-ignored quarter where an unanswered question had lingered since the dawn of the century.

The Eastern Question I: Turmoil in the Ottoman Empire, 1806–1841

The so-called "Eastern Question" was, in fact, a euphemism for the impending collapse of the Ottoman Empire—an event that was imminently expected in the courts of Europe. So precipitous was the Ottoman decline in the preceding half-century that the major European powers took to calling her the "Sick Man of Europe"—an epithet first coined by Nicholas I of Russia.[18] But if the European powers could agree on a nickname for the collapsing Sultanate, they could agree on little else. Russia anticipated the Turkish demise with bated breath, for she had long centered her hopes for a warm water port on the balmy Mediterranean, and hoped to achieve this aspiration at Turkish expense— either by dispatching her Black Sea Fleet to seize the Straits leading to the Mediterranean, or by marching her army southwards through the Balkans, a collection of Turkish principalities stretching from what is now Romania in the north to Greece in the south. In either case, the tsar might use his role as putative "protector" of the Sultan's Orthodox Christian population as a pretext. The first of these options, however, was anathema to Britain, which required access to the Straits for her own trade with India, while the latter, opposed by Britain on general principles, was doubly opposed by Austria— first, because Russian encroachment into the Balkans would give the tsar control of both banks of the Danube (thereby jeopardizing Austria's Black Sea commerce), and second, because liberation of the Balkan Slavic population might easily ignite nationalist aspirations among the millions of disgruntled Slavs living under Austrian rule.[19]

Even without Russian encroachment, however, the Balkan situation was palpably unstable. Since the dawn of the 19th century, the region's oppressed Christian population had been agitating openly for greater autonomy from the hated Turks. The Ottomans, as was their wont, answered this outcry with violent repression, for it considered these Christians to be "*rayahs*," or "herds of cattle," whose proper station was subservience.[20] Christians who failed to pay the *jizyah*, or tax on non–Muslims, "would be buried up to their necks in the ground, stripped naked and tied to trees, or roasted over slow fires."[21]

Despite the excellent track record of this policy in preceding centuries, this time it provoked a major insurrection in Serbia, led by the pig-dealer, Karageorge (i.e., "Black George"). Aided first by the Austrians, in whose army he had once served, and then by the Russians, Karageorge gained control of Belgrade (1806) and obtained a promise of Serbian autonomy (1812). Within the year, however, all was undone by Napoleon's invasion of Russia, which robbed the Serbs of Russian support, allowing the Turks to reassert their authority and to chase Karageorge into exile.

So matters stood until Palm Sunday, 1815, when a second pig-dealer, Milos Obrenovic, instigated a new uprising and drove the Turks back out. Karageorge returned, thinking to resume his leadership and expand the revolt into neighboring Greece, but Obrenovic, viewing him as a rival, had him murdered in his sleep by an axe-wielding assassin—an act which drove Karageorge's adherents to fury, but which greatly pleased the Sultan, who, on receiving the victim's head as a gift, allowed Serbia to resume her autonomy under Turkish suzerainty with Obrenovic serving as *Vozhd* or leader (1817).[22]

Four years later, an insurrection broke out in Greece, where the *Hetairia Philike*—a secret society dedicated to Greek independence—had enlisted 80,000 adherents. Urged on by Germanós, Bishop of Patras, the Greeks of the Morea (Greece's southern peninsula, classically known as the Peloponnesus) butchered the local Turks, and went in search of others, singing, "The Turk shall live no longer, neither in Morea nor in the whole earth" (1821).[23] Romantic Philhellenes from all over Europe—England's Lord Byron among them—rallied to the banner of these latter-day Athenians, only to find themselves in a death struggle among combatants who were deaf to the cry of mercy.

At Constantinople, reports of Greek atrocities (including the wanton murder of 2,000 Muslims after the storming of Tripolitza[24]) provoked anti–Christian riots. On Easter Sunday, 1821, Sultan Mahmoud II had Gregorias, the Patriarch of Constantinople, hanged from the gate leading to his palace. The corpse was entrusted to a party of Jews who refused to feed it to the dogs as the Sultan bade them, and instead threw it into the Bosphorus—inadequately weighted down, however, so that it floated in the water like a buoy until it was fished out again by a Russian commercial vessel and taken to Odessa where it was accorded a proper burial.[25] Mahmoud then dispatched a Turkish fleet to the isle of Chios, where his marines slaughtered 23,000 innocents out of a total population of 90,000, and sold 43,000 survivors into slavery.[26] Final victory proved elusive, however, until Mahmoud enlisted the support of his powerful Egyptian viceroy, Mehemet Ali (1825). Schooled in French tactics and weaponry, and led by Mehemet Ali's capable son, Ibrahim Pasha, the Egyptian troops proceeded to win seemingly decisive victories at Missolonghi (where the unfortunate Byron had succumbed to fever two years earlier) and on the Athenian Acropolis (1826–27).

To this point, the European powers had done nothing to intervene, for in this era they viewed all revolution—even against the Turk—with a jaundiced eye. "Three or four hundred thousand individuals hanged, butchered, impaled down there, hardly count," said Metternich in reference to the Greek plight.[27] But amid savage reprisals doled out by the Turks, Britain, France and Russia ultimately composed their differences on the

Eastern Question, and sent a joint naval squadron into the Mediterranean to support the rebels. On October 20, 1827, their combined armada stumbled upon the Turko-Egyptian fleet at Navarino Bay. The encounter might have come off without incident, for the European fleet did not have authority to open hostilities. But the unknowing Turks solved this dilemma by firing first, whereupon the Allies sent the entire Muslim fleet of sixty ships to the bottom at a cost of but one ship of their own.

In the battle's aftermath, the French landed a force of marines in the Morea to oust the Turks, while Russia, taking a broader view, attempted to force the Sultan into concessions in Moldavia and Wallachia (i.e., the "Danubian Principalities" which would be fused, one day, to form Romania—not that Moldavia or Wallachia had anything to do with Greece). When Sultan Mahmoud refused Russia's demands, Tsar Nicholas declared war, and sent his legions to the very gates of Constantinople (1829).

Throughout the 1820s, Mahmoud had been laboring feverishly to reform his corrupt government and decrepit army along European lines. In 1826, the Janissaries (formerly the elite corps of the Ottoman Army, but now dissolute and more concerned with being well-fed than with military discipline) had overturned their soup cauldrons at Constantinople—a traditional sign of rebellion[28]—rather than comply with the introduction of Western uniform and drill. Mahmoud had them gunned down in the streets and continued with his reforms. But he had not gotten far enough, and he was now out of time. Possessing no other choice, he appended his signature to the Treaty of Adrianople (1829), whereby he capitulated not only on the Danube, where the Principalities came under Russian protection, but also in Greece, where independence was formally proclaimed on February 3, 1830, and in Serbia, where Milos Obrenovic was elevated to the status of hereditary prince (1830).

Nor was this the end of Sultan Mahmoud's travails, for his Egyptian viceroy, Mehemet Ali, now demanded control of Syria as just reward for the help he had rendered against the Greeks. Naturally enough, Mahmoud refused, and no less naturally, Mehemet Ali dispatched his son, Ibrahim Pasha, into Asia Minor at the head of an Egyptian army. The Turkish forces proved no match for this sturdy force, which came within a hair's breadth of seizing the entire empire for Mehemet Ali after a victory at Konya in which the Sultan's Grand Vizier was taken prisoner (December 1832). Russia, however, would not countenance a strong man on the Ottoman throne when a perfectly good weak one was already in place.[29] Consequently, she intervened on the Sultan's behalf. The result was the Treaty of Unkiar-Skelessi (1833)—nominally a treaty of mutual defense pledging each nation to come to the other's aid in case of outside attack, but in effect reducing the Ottoman Empire to the status of a Russian protectorate. A secret clause of this agreement defined the obligation of the Ottoman Empire to Russia as excluding all foreign warships from the Straits leading to the Black Sea.

From the standpoint of Britain, which viewed the spread of Egyptian influence into Syria as a potential threat to her overland communications to India, the Treaty of Unkiar-Skelessi, giving Russia predominance in Constantinople, seemed very little improvement. France, to be sure, held an opposing view of the Egyptian advance, for Mehemet Ali was her ally and client. But she at least agreed with England that Russia had obtained entirely too much influence at the Ottoman court. Indeed, there was widespread (if unfounded) concern that the secret clause in the treaty regarding the Straits actually granted Russian warships free access while excluding the warships of all other nations.[30]

For the time being, then, Britain and France were united in opposition to Russia's newfound influence, and so they remained until 1839, when Sultan Mahmoud decided to seek revenge against Mehemet Ali by invading Syria. The assault was an unmitigated disaster. The Sultan's troops were immediately defeated at Nezib, whereupon the Ottoman fleet sailed to Alexandria and defected to Mehemet Ali. Russia might now have intervened in accordance with the Treaty of Unkiar-Skelessi, but Tsar Nicholas I thought it better to allow the situation to cause a rupture between Britain and France.[31] The result, after much diplomatic wrangling, was the bombardment of Beirut by a joint British-Russian-Austrian naval squadron commanded by Charles Napier, and the speedy retreat of Mehemet Ali's forces from Syria, despite much French sabre rattling on their client's behalf (September 1840). The subsequent appearance of this squadron off Alexandria convinced Mehemet Ali to return the Ottoman fleet to the Sultan and to surrender all claim to Syria in return for being named hereditary viceroy of Egypt—the agreement being guaranteed by the signatures of Britain, Russia, Austria and Prussia (February 1841). Utterly isolated, France could only join the other European powers in signing a joint agreement respecting the Sultan's closure of the Straits leading to the Black Sea to *all* foreign ships of war (thereby allaying any lingering doubts about the secret clause of the Treaty of Unkiar-Skelessi giving exclusive access to Russian warships).

The Eastern Question II: The Crimean War— A Badly Run Thing

For the remainder of the 1840s, the Eastern Question remained relatively quiescent. To be sure, when the inhabitants of Moldavia and Wallachia began agitating for the right to form an independent Romania in 1848, Russia sent troops into the region on the well-chosen pretext of "helping" the Turks maintain stability, but nothing of consequence came of it. Five years later, however, the Sultan granted the privilege of protecting the Holy Places of Palestine to France and the situation changed entirely. Tsar Nicholas I protested that he was the logical protector of these sites, given that the majority of Middle Eastern Christians were Greek Orthodox like himself, while France was overwhelmingly Catholic. The tsar's protest soon escalated into a demand that he be recognized as protector of all the Sultan's Orthodox Christian subjects—a status that would allow him to intercede in Turkish affairs at whim. Alarmed by his highhandedness, England and France dispatched a joint fleet to the Dardanelles. Nicholas promptly tested their resolve by invading Moldavia and Wallachia for a second time.[32] But the Allies were not bluffing, and when the Russians went on to decimate a Turkish naval squadron in its moorings at Sinope on the Black Sea coast, the Anglo-French fleet sailed through the Dardanelles into the Black Sea to force a showdown (January 1854).

Britain's steadfastness in this matter, as always, was rooted in strategic interest. Russian encroachment upon Turkey imperiled her commerce in the East. From the French standpoint, the potential gains were less palpable. In inaugurating his empire, Napoleon III had protested his desire for peace, saying that his conquests would be limited to the cultivation of fallow fields, the building of roads, harbors, canals and railroads. But in truth, his ascent to power was bound up inextricably with the nation's sense of lost glory dating to the fall of the great Napoleon. Thus, in bearing him to power, the Bonaparte name bore him also (and inexorably) towards war.[33] Then, too, there was personal animus. As ruler of Russia, Nicholas disdained the rise of the new Napoleon, addressing him merely as "my dear *friend*" when it was traditional to refer to a fellow monarch as "my dear *brother*."[34] The new French emperor did not forget this slight. Nor, as Carlton Hayes notes, was it lost on him that the "defeat of Russia would avenge the first Napoleon's Russian campaign and would redound to the eternal prestige of the Bonaparte family and of the French nation."[35]

In March 1855, war was declared. It was the first armed conflict between the major powers since Waterloo, four decades earlier—and the prospect was by no means universally welcomed. In England, the Conservative MP Benjamin Disraeli asked whether it was really necessary to go to war to prevent the Russian tsar from defending Christians in Turkey.[36] More alarming than statements made in Parliament, however, was the state of the army, which was officered by aristocrats who had gained their commissions by purchasing them—a system designed to keep the armed forces firmly in the grasp of the ruling class. Unfortunately, while it is true that no one outside the aristocracy made his way to the top under the purchase system (thereby greatly enhancing the cause of snobbery), neither did anyone with a talent for military affairs. At the outset of the war, the sole British officers with substantial field service were those serving in India, but only men of lesser standing had allowed themselves to be transferred to so ungodly a province, and such men were not encouraged to join their social betters in truly important matters such as war with Russia.[37] The Commander-in-Chief, a pleasant enough fellow named Lord Raglan, hadn't experienced combat since losing an arm at Waterloo—an experience that left such a vivid impression on him that in the present campaign he habitually alluded to his Russian enemies as "the French."[38] The real problem, however, was the rest of the British officer corps, consisting chiefly of petty-minded aristocrats, more concerned with internecine rivalry than with the great task at hand. According to one high-ranking authority, it was dangerous to charge such men with the responsibilities of a subaltern (an assessment that was soon borne out by events).[39]

The lack of readiness was immediately apparent. Supply and communications were handled in slipshod fashion (only twenty-one wagons were brought to service an army of 30,000[40]), and then disease—a cholera epidemic—exacted a frightful toll on the British and French armies prior to any actual fighting. Soldiers leaving Varna for Balchik Bay on the Black Sea coast were seen off at the former, and received at the latter, by a perverse audience of dead cholera victims bobbing head-up in the water where their corpses had been deposited.[41] Presently, enough live soldiers arrived so that the French and British High Commands could engage in some healthy bickering over strategy. It was agreed that the object of the campaign should be the capture of Sebastopol. Located at the southern tip of the Crimean Peninsula (which juts downward from the north coast of the Black Sea), Sebastopol was the chief port of call for the Russian Black Sea fleet. Without it, the Russian Navy would have no base from which to threaten Constantinople. Not only would the Allies win the war,[42] they would eliminate "a standing menace to the Turkish empire."[43]

So far, so good, but when the Allies finally came face-to-face with the enemy at the River Alma, a few miles shy of their goal, no unanimity on tactics could be reached. As a result, no tactics were employed. The infantry simply made a seemingly hopeless head-on thrust against their Russian counterparts, who were heavily dug in, high up on the opposite bank.[44] Although the thirsty infantrymen paused to drink as they crossed the river,[45] they miraculously waded to the far bank under fire and started their assault. Unable to view their progress, Lord Raglan proceeded across the river, and followed a trail that brought him uphill to an excellent observation point—flawed only in that it placed him, practically alone, *behind* the center of the enemy line.[46] The Russians assumed he could not have been so great an oaf as to sit there atop his horse without a formidable body of troops behind him, so they made no move against him. In short order, Raglan ordered up some field guns and commenced fire on the exposed Russian line. Pressed in front by the Allied infantry, and behind by Raglan's newly arrived guns, the Russians broke and ran. Had Raglan ordered a pursuit, or had the French (who had borne much less of the fighting) been willing to carry one out, the war might have ended then and there. As it was the Russians got safely away to Sebastopol.[47]

Following in their wake, the Allies bypassed the port's northern fortifications, and swung around to invest the citadel from the south. This flanking maneuver, heralded as brilliant back in the home country, took the Russians completely by surprise—not the least because the easily accessible northern fortifications were in disrepair and virtually abandoned, while the southern walls were intact and could be utilized for a stout defense.[48] It may be noted in justification of the Allied decision that if the northern half of the city had been taken, the southern half might have held out independently since an inlet of the Black Sea narrowed the approach to it.[49] Nevertheless, the time lost in altering the direction of approach allowed Russia's master engineer, Franz Eduard Todleben, to solidify the southern defenses.[50]

With the battle lines thus drawn, the British chose Balaclava as their base of operations. But their dispositions were soon upset by a Russian surprise attack that drove

Fragment of Franz Roubaud's panorama of the *Defense of Sebastopol* (Wikimedia Commons).

them from the southernmost ridge abutting Tennyson's celebrated "Valley of Death." Although a thin line of infantry and an outmanned heavy cavalry brigade quickly checked their advance, the Muscovites sought to carry off the guns of the captured ridge. Unwilling to let them get away with these trophies, Lord Raglan ordered his light cavalry to retake the ridge. Alas, his orders were imprecise, and his subordinates made a muddle of them, such that James Brudenell, Seventh Earl of Cardigan, led his men forward not against the ridge, but into the valley—now commanded by Russian artillery on both flanks and at the far end. Lord Raglan sat dumbfounded as he watched this misguided attack develop from a precipice overlooking the battlefield. In less than twenty minutes, over five hundred of the seven hundred cavalrymen initially engaged had become casualties.[51]

One of the enduring marvels of this brief encounter was the conduct of Lord Cardigan, who, as leader of the attack, was the first to reach (and gallop past) the Russian guns at the far end of the valley. Stationed to the rear of the guns was the main body of Russian cavalry. Advancing boldly, Cardigan was but twenty yards distant from this imposing force when he suddenly perceived that something was amiss. A quick glance over his shoulder—the first he had had occasion to take since starting forward—solved the mystery, revealing to Cardigan that he was entirely alone. No one else had made it that far. Approached by a troupe of Cossacks, he wheeled around and rode back into the mêlée in the valley. His men, who had been searching frantically for him, but could not see him through the whirl of smoke and shells, failed to notice as he calmly cantered past them en route to the British lines. When the two hundred-odd survivors finally emerged from the field of slaughter, Cardigan was back at base to greet them. Outraged, they asked him where he had been, and he had to call witnesses to the fact that he had even ridden as far as the guns.[52]

British Cavalry charging Russian forces at Balaclava, painting by Richard Caton Woodville (Wikimedia Commons).

Back in the valley, says the *Annual Register*, "The Cossacks, or some savages armed and accoutered like them, who had fled in crowds before a few British sabers, now faced about ... and, as our wounded lay writhing on the ground, pierced them through and through with their spears." Amidst this bloody business, some British survivors shammed dead or found hiding places. Later, when darkness descended, they crept to safety.[53] Such was the episode immortalized by Tennyson in his famed poem, *The Charge of the Light Brigade.*

To this point in the war, the British High Command had displayed an absolutely inspired capacity for throwing inferior numbers against overwhelming odds. That the Russians often retreated in disorder when this was done cannot be attributed to the viability of such tactics, but rather to the fact that the involved British units had to fight with the zeal of Tasmanian devils if they were to have any hope of survival. Confronted time and again by crazed handfuls of attackers, the Russians could only conclude that they were dealing with madmen who had no discernible regard for their own lives. While the British press gloried in the cavalry's Samurai death charges and the gallant stands of the infantry's "thin red line," the French were behaving in a decidedly more reserved manner. In councils of the High Command, they consistently voted against those actions—attacks, sorties and the like—that might be interpreted in the wrong way by the enemy. At the Alma, they had advanced practically unopposed onto the Russian flank. But instead of exploiting their coup with a spirited attack that could only have ended in an enemy rout, they came to a dead stop.[54] In the subsequent advance, it was the French who insisted on bypassing the northern fortifications of Sebastopol; and once arrived at the southern approaches, it was they who insisted upon a siege, rather than storming the city with reckless abandon as the British very much preferred to do. (Indeed, the initial plan had called for a direct assault.)[55]

The apparent reticence of her allies left the British no choice but to comply with the notion of a siege—the dilatory pace of which provided the Russians with the opportunity to attempt a counterstroke. At dawn on November 5, 1854, British pickets heard "a low rumbling noise" which they took to be a convoy of wagons. In fact, it was the tramp of infantry and the creak of field artillery. The first Russians to emerge from the mist were unarmed, pretending to surrender. The foremost British pickets went forward to apprehend them, only to be ambushed and taken prisoner themselves by armed troops coming up behind. A massive Russian surprise attack was underway, and owing to the capture of the British sentries, there was to be no advance alarm.[56]

The Battle of Inkerman was a seesaw, hand-to-hand affair fought largely with the bayonet. Ground was taken, lost and retaken by soldiers who had to traverse mounds of dead to get at one another. Vastly outnumbered at the point of attack, the British were nearly swept from the field. The French, however, proved their mettle in this struggle, providing timely succor to the beleaguered British. After a propitious start, the Russians were driven back to their fortifications with staggering losses—the battle ending toward midday.[57]

Britain's brave fighting men were again acclaimed as heroes at home. Sadly, the advantage of their victory was quite overmatched by the brutal Crimean winter of 1854–1855. Loss of the heights at the "Valley of Death" had severed the main British supply road, and rain soon transformed all lesser trails into bogs. In four piteously cold months, nine thousand British troops perished from starvation and exposure because the provisions in Balaclava harbor could not be brought up to them.[58]

The scandal engendered by this fiasco led to the fall of Lord Aberdeen's government. Lord Palmerston replaced him as Britain's prime minister in February 1855. Spring, however, saw the arrival of fresh British recruits, and in June, these went halves with the French in the most miserable repulse of the war. An assault was planned with no preliminary bombardment. The men moved into position in full view of the enemy on a brilliantly clear night, and the French jumped off prematurely after mistaking a stray shot for the signal to attack. Raglan had no choice but to send his men forward in support. They were greeted by repeated blasts of grapeshot.[59] The carnage was so abysmal that Raglan fell into despair. He died soon afterwards.[60]

The contest now became one of attrition, pitting the brilliant siege works of the French engineering corps against Franz Todleben's equally masterful Russian defenses. But for a shift in the diplomatic landscape, the war might have dragged on indefinitely. Disturbed by Russian encroachment in the Balkans (which posed a threat to her own free navigation of the Danube), Austria had threatened to enter the war on the Allied side in August 1854. To Tsar Nicholas this seemed a very poor expression of gratitude for the service he had rendered to Austria during the Hungarian revolution, and though he managed to secure Austria's continued neutrality by abandoning Moldavia and Wallachia, the bitterness thus engendered was enough to end the long period of friendship between the two nations. Thereafter, the blows fell in rapid succession. In January 1855, the kingdom of Piedmont-Sardinia—desiring Anglo-French support for its vision of Italian unity—declared war on Russia. Then, in September 1855, after softening up Sebastopol's defenses with twenty days of continuous bombardment at an expenditure of 1.5 million projectiles,[61] the Allies made a last-ditch effort to capture the fortress by storm. The attempt was everywhere thrown back except at the key point— known as Malakhov Hill—which was captured by determined French forces under General Patrice de MacMahon. "The fighting," says *Encyclopædia Britannica*, "was of

The attack on Malakhov Hill, painting by Yvon Adolphe, Collections du château de Versailles (Wikimedia Commons).

the most desperate kind. Every casemate, every traverse, was taken and retaken time after time, but the French maintained the prize...." The day's carnage claimed 23,000 lives (10,000 Allied, 13,000 Russian), with nineteen generals among the dead.[62]

The loss of Malakhov Hill rendered Todleben's entire fortress network indefensible, thus forcing a Russian withdrawal.[63] By this time, the reactionary Tsar Nicholas I had died after a reign of thirty years. His successor, Alexander II, was both more liberal and less bellicose. The war had cost Russia an estimated 250,000 lives and untold treasure.[64] The Allies were now adept at delivering supplies and reinforcements by sea, while Russian forces had to cross the cruel desert steppes.[65] Hence, when Austria again threatened intervention in the wake of the fall of Sebastopol, the new tsar agreed to send delegates to a peace congress (February 1856).

The Triumph of Nationalism in Italy

The ensuing Congress of Paris fulfilled the so-called "Four Points," encompassing the Allied war aims as elucidated during the conflict. In conformance with this outline, freedom of navigation was guaranteed on the Danube. Having already withdrawn its forces from Moldavia and Wallachia (i.e., the Danubian principalities), Russia was now obliged to cede a portion of Bessarabia so that its territory no longer abutted the riverbank. The revocation of Russia's claim to a protectorate over the Sultan's Orthodox Christian subjects was ensured by the admission of Turkey to the European Concert, with the Sultan pledging in return (emptily as it turns out) to maintain a generous attitude towards those subjects. Finally—and for Russia this was the bitterest pill to swallow—the Black Sea was entirely neutralized with its coast and waves declared off limits to the naval forces of any nation (including those of Russia and Turkey by whom the coastline was possessed).

Although the prosecution of the war had been far from masterful, and though it had cost the French nation 75,000 lives and 2 billion francs,[66] the peace brought new prestige to Napoleon III since the talks were held in Paris. Moreover, Eugénie de Montijo, the Spanish countess he had married in 1853, secured his dynasty by bearing him a son while the congress was ongoing. Yet it was Piedmont that took home the most currency from the peace conference. Her prime minister, Count Camillo Benso di Cavour, deftly parlayed Piedmont's participation in the war into a seat at the peace table—from which he championed the cause of Italian liberation and exposed before the world the cruelty of Austria's repressive hegemony in the peninsula.

A member of the Piedmontese nobility, Cavour had long been an ardent admirer of the British system of government, which he studied firsthand from the gallery of the House of Commons during a period of travel abroad and espoused to the Italian public as editor of the newspaper *Il Risorgimento* (*The Regeneration*). Charles Albert's grant of a constitution during the Revolution of 1848—subsequently upheld by his successor, Victor Emmanuel II, despite Austria's hostility[67]—was a life-changing event for Cavour. Elected to the first Piedmontese Parliament in 1848, he worked tirelessly to make the kingdom of Piedmont-Sardinia a model constitutional monarchy. By 1852, he rose to the position of prime minister, a post he would hold for most of the period until his untimely death in 1861. Had he wished, he could have ruled as a dictator, but he was committed in mind and spirit to constitutional rule. Though driven to distraction by the opposition he encountered in his dealings with the legislative chamber, he maintained that the process made him a better leader—forcing him to formulate his policies more clearly and to remain vigilant regarding public opinion. "Believe me," he was quoted as saying on one occasion, "the worst of Chambers is still preferable to the most brilliant of antechambers."[68] And on another: "I always feel strongest when Parliament is sitting."[69]

At home, the prime minister was a champion of liberal bourgeois policies, including free trade, the promotion of shipping, the building of railroads and the draining of marshes for agricultural use. (Prior to his entry into politics, he had founded the Piedmontese Agricultural Society, spurring agricultural modernization in the kingdom by employing chemical fertilizers and new irrigation techniques on his private estates.[70]) In foreign affairs, however, Cavour was a devotee of *Realpolitik*[71]—which is to say, of "power politics." In the

Camillo Benso di Cavour, circa 1860, drawn by A. Masutti, engraved by L. Calamatta (Wikimedia Commons).

entire peninsula, Piedmont alone was free from foreign domination. In Rome and the Papal States, foreign troops (French and Austrian) maintained the temporal authority of Pope Pius IX—that erstwhile champion of liberality who was now a confirmed reactionary and an enemy of Italian nationalism. The most pernicious influence, however, was exercised by Austria, which ruled Lombardy-Venetia directly, Tuscany, Modena and Parma indirectly (through Hapsburg princelings) and served as a prop for the inept Bourbon regime in Naples and Sicily. It was said that the hand of Austria was "felt even where her arms are absent,"[72] and from one end of the peninsula to the other, nationalist sentiment was cruelly suppressed.

Cavour was determined to oust Austria from the affairs of Italy, toward which end he overhauled the Piedmontese army. But the ruinous defeats of 1848–1849 proved that Piedmont could not match Austria in arms. To defeat the nemesis, an alliance with a major power would be necessary—and as a means of courting one, Cavour entered the Crimean War on the side of Britain and France, a seemingly reckless decision for which he was roundly criticized, since he could not publicize his true motive.[73]

The gambit paid off, for in the war's aftermath he found a benefactor for his designs in the person of Napoleon III. The French emperor was no stranger to the notion of Italian liberation. As a young man, he had fought for it. Now, however, his focus was economic not political. Free Italian principalities would offer a marvelous venue for commercial investment.[74] Deeming him too half-hearted in his support, a band of Italian fanatics led by a certain Felice Orsini—son of the Orsini who had died fighting alongside Louis Napoleon in the 1831 Romagna revolt—lobbed a bomb at the imperial coach outside the Paris Opera House killing scores of innocents. Had the detonation hit its mark, the cause of Italian liberation might have suffered. As it was, it exercised a most salutary influence. Anxious to avert further attempts on his life, Napoleon set to work in earnest on a Franco-Piedmontese alliance, to position himself as the champion of Italian nationalism. The pact was completed—ostensibly in secret—at Plombières in July 1858. By its terms, France agreed to come to the support of Piedmont in the event of a defensive war against Austria with the goal of ousting Austria from Italian affairs. Lombardy and Venetia would be annexed to Piedmont, creating a northern Italian kingdom, stretching from the "Alps to the Adriatic." In return, Piedmont would cede Nice and Savoy—Italy's lone French-speaking possessions—to France. Catching wind of the Plombières negotiations, Austria embarked on a military build-up along the Piedmont-Lombardy border—Piedmont doing likewise on its side of the frontier.

War appeared imminent. Prussia—the nominal ally of Austria—promised not to intervene against Piedmont provided that Piedmont did not instigate the hostilities. Britain and Russia—neither of which had forgiven Austria for her neutrality in the Crimean War—sought to avert a clash by offering mediation. Cavour reluctantly agreed to attend a congress for the purpose, but Austria unwisely refused, issuing an ultimatum demanding Piedmont's immediate demobilization. When Cavour answered that "his government had agreed to the congress proposed by the powers and that it had nothing more to say,"[75] Austria attacked, whereupon France fulfilled her Plombières' obligation by marching to Piedmont's assistance (April 1859).

A Franco-Piedmontese alliance harmonized perfectly with the foreign policy goals of Napoleon III, who wished first and foremost to solidify his regime by restoring to France something of the international prestige she had lost in 1815. A born schemer, he proposed to accomplish this aim by an imposture—posing as the champion of national self-determination for the oppressed peoples of Europe; by involving himself in the seemingly high-minded purpose of "giving freedom to the oppressed nations," he might also find opportunity for "restoring her natural frontiers to a liberty-giving France."[76] Stated in less lofty terms, says one historian, "Napoleon was known to contemplate the break-up of the settlement of 1815, in order that he might win something for himself in the scramble."[77]

Napoleon got off to an early, if abortive, start on his program during the Crimean War—alarming his English ally by suggesting that he might call the Poles to insurrection against their Russian overlords.[78] Likewise, at the ensuing Congress of Paris, he campaigned unsuccessfully for the union of Moldavia and Wallachia into an independent Romania.[79] But in light of his own—and, more to the point, his great uncle's—former exploits across the Alps, the liberation of Italy held a special allure.

At the outset of the war, he assumed nominal command of the army and, assisted by his capable generals, managed a series of untidy victories. At Magenta in early June, he was on the point of ordering his disorganized legions to fall back only to be informed by his staff that the battle was won.[80] Three weeks later, at Solferino (June 24, 1859), he managed a second ghastly triumph, which he observed from a nearby bell tower, smoking one cigarette after another and lamenting the fate of his men with the anguished phrase, "The poor people, the poor people, what a horrible thing war is."[81]

Enthusiasm did not come easy to Napoleon III, and the carnage at Solferino—where the Franco-Piedmontese forces lost 17,000 men as against 22,000 Austrians[82]—used up the last ounce of zeal he could muster for Cavour's Italian project. Unfortunately, he was now in over his head, for the Italian nationalist movement had already taken on a life of its own. After the Austrian defeat at Solferino, the states of central Italy—included among them the papal province of Romagna—rebelled against their respective governments and announced that they desired union with Piedmont. Napoleon could not support this challenge to the temporal powers of the pope without incurring the wrath of French Catholics. (Indeed, one French bishop was already denouncing him as a "modern Judas Iscariot."[83]) To complicate matters, Prussia, taken aback by France's unexpected and rapid success, was now threatening to intervene in the conflict.

Hoping to extricate himself from the evolving mayhem, the French emperor arranged an armistice with his Austrian counterpart at Villafranca (July 1859), believing he might buy off Cavour (who was not a party to the agreement) with the cession of Lombardy, while maintaining the stability of central Italy. Appalled, Cavour called upon Victor Emmanuel to continue fighting without the French, and when the prudent king refused, he resigned the premiership.[84]

The situation was retrieved, from the standpoint of Italian nationalism, by the rebels of the central Italian states—Tuscany, Parma, Modena and papal Romagna—who refused the Franco-Austrian summons to restore their former rulers, resolving instead to offer sovereignty to Victor Emmanuel. No one now dared make a move. Austria, defeated, had not the will to invade the rebellious states. Nor could Napoleon III (as a putative champion of national self-determination) have done so. Britain, too, declared against a forced restoration. Victor Emmanuel, on the other hand could not accept the offer of central Italian sovereignty without risking a breach with France, whose support was essential for consolidating the gains already made.[85]

Amid this diplomatic puzzle the erstwhile prime minister, Cavour, conceived a solution that would achieve Piedmont's aims while deflecting the diplomatic onus onto the shoulders of France. By treating separately with Austria in violation of the Plombières pact, Napoleon III had sacrificed his claim upon Nice and Savoy—prizes that might have gone far to deflect domestic attention from the Pandora's box he had opened in Italy. Taking a page from the Napoleonic playbook, Cavour secretly suggested to the French emperor that Nice, Savoy and the central Italian states should all hold plebiscites to decide their respective destinies for themselves in accordance with the principle of self-determination.[86] Properly managed, the plebiscites would almost certainly produce a desirable result. The plan fitted as nicely with Napoleon's enduring fondness for a good conspiracy as it did with Cavour's affinity for statesmanship. The agreement was signed at Turin, the plebiscites were held, and in conformance with the results, Piedmont received central Italy while France got Nice and Savoy.[87]

It soon became evident which of the leaders had thought matters through and which had not; for in aggrandizing itself, France had forfeited the goodwill of Britain, which approved the decision in central Italy but saw only French opportunism in the fate of Nice and Savoy. As Cavour put it to the French ambassador, "Now you are our accomplices."[88]

The war of 1859 delivered to King Victor Emmanuel II a formidable realm. But it lacked the prize jewel of Italy—namely Rome, where the pope enjoyed the combined backing of Austria and France. Against so formidable a coalition, it seemed that Cavour's Italian unification movement must stall. But the old Italian adventurer, Giuseppe Garibaldi, had fewer qualms about Piedmont's powerful neighbors than did Cavour or Victor Emmanuel. Setting sail from Genoa with a thousand followers, known as the "Red Shirts" after their chosen attire, he invaded the island of Sicily, already in rebellion against its Bourbon ruler, Francis II (May 1860). Facing a Bourbon garrison of 24,000 seasoned soldiers, Garibaldi nonetheless captured the road to Palermo, the island's capital, which subsequently fell in a hand-to-hand fight.[89] He then crossed over to the mainland to seize Naples, where the populace received him with wild enthusiasm (September 1860). Cavour feared that his progress would encourage him to attack Rome, thereby provoking foreign intervention. To forestall this, he mobilized Piedmont's army, marched it southwards through papal territory (sweeping aside a papal army en route), and invaded the kingdom of Naples. So popular was Garibaldi that he might have resisted and declared a republic with himself at its head, but his patriotism outweighed any desire for power or fame. He toured the city of Naples in an open carriage alongside Victor Emmanuel, while the cheering crowds overwhelmingly voted in favor of annexation to Piedmont.[90] Thus, after two years of conquest, the population of Victor Emmanuel's dominion had swelled from 5 million to over 22 million.[91] On March 14, 1861, the "Kingdom of Italy" was proclaimed. Only Austrian Venetia and papal Rome remained outside its confines. (The latter was, nonetheless, proclaimed capital of the Italian kingdom for symbolic purposes.)

The Vicissitudes of Empire in France

On the morrow of his victory at Solferino, Napoleon III seemed to be riding the crest of success. Hitherto, his military adventures had ended in victory—raising the prestige of France and making the emperor the arbiter of Europe. "For a time," says Schapiro, "...no treaty could be entered into, no territorial changes could be made, and no diplomatic policy inaugurated without his being consulted."[92]

At home he had restored order and prosperity. His belief in Saint-Simonian socialism—that the richer elements of society ought to see to the welfare of the poorer[93]—meshed well with his belief in industrial progress. Under the empire a great program of public works and public credit allowed for the drainage of marshes, the building of canals and the expansion of railroads. Not only did such projects bolster the nation's prosperity by modernizing its infrastructure; they also created an abundance of meaningful jobs, thereby fulfilling the essence of the workers' demand of 1848—that familiar slogan "the right to work." As part and parcel of the rebuilding program, Paris was modernized on a model created by the emperor himself[94] and carried through by the brilliant architect Baron Georges-Eugène Haussmann. Affordable tenements were built to house the working poor (though the number of units was insufficient, and many lacked running water[95]), and narrow winding streets were replaced by wide straight boulevards (which, it was hoped, would not be so inviting to the barricade builders at the next revolution).

Apart, then, from the scarcely veiled tyranny and the rampant corruption, one would think there was very little to complain about in Second Empire France. Syphilis, it must be conceded, seems also to have been a problem,[96] and it is likewise true that Piedmont's visiting king, Victor Emmanuel, expressed bitter dismay on hearing the

Weekday in Paris by Adolph von Menzel, 1869. Housed in the Kunstmuseum Düsseldorf (Wikimedia Commons).

price demanded by a courtesan who had caught his eye. But these were minor matters—the latter, in fact, was immediately resolved to the satisfaction of both parties when the emperor chivalrously offered to foot the bill.[97] Yet, for all the apparent good being done, the regime did not command broad-based support. Elections, though nominally democratic, were fixed in favor of official candidates.[98] Workers found that their bounty in wages failed to offset the long-term rise in prices. Industrialists objected to the free trade agreement concluded with Britain (1860), which increased the general prosperity but deprived them of the tariffs that had protected them against British competition.[99] On the left, republicans still pettily drew attention to the fact that some of their compatriots had been gunned down on the barricades during the *coup d'état* of 1851, and when their listeners remained impassive, they complained about the 25,000 others who had been jailed, exiled to Algeria or condemned to the miserable penal colonies (to which their listeners likewise remained generally impassive). The press alone seemingly offered no complaint—but it was operating under strict government censorship which above all else forbade complaining.

At the center of it all was the emperor—perpetually apprehensive for the security of his dynasty. Though hitherto his methods had been tyrannical, he did not possess the soul of a tyrant. Indeed, says his son's biographer, Katherine John, "If there was ever a more amiable man than Napoleon III, history has not recorded the fact."[100] We have seen him in the bell tower at Solferino bemoaning the brutality of war. At the birth of the prince imperial, his wife's labor pains found him pacing outside her chamber, weeping with compassion. (Later, he indulged the child terribly—apparently because he couldn't bear having the toddler feel cross with him.) Even the family dog took advantage of Napoleon's benign disposition by habitually jumping onto the couch with him and then nudging him towards one edge in a bid to usurp the most comfortable part of the cushion. (The emperor, we are told, invariably moved over without protest.)[101] He seems to have possessed sincere affection for the common classes. Says one historian, "he talked familiarly with artisans upon the boulevards; he drank healths to masons, carpenters, and plumbers…. He gloried in the appellation, 'emperor of the working man.'"[102] Alas, says another, "In his desire to win the favor of every class and of every party, [he] succeeded in winning the enmity of all."[103]

Ultimately, it was the Italian campaign that exposed the fault line in the imperial edifice. Catholics decried a policy that compromised the temporal authority of the pope, liberals vilified the abandonment of Piedmont at Villafranca, and nationalists condemned a plan gone so awry as to create a powerful new state on France's southeastern frontier.[104] As the decade of the 1860s opened, Napoleon attempted to curb the mounting disquiet with a program of liberalization. Pardons were extended to those jailed or exiled following the *coup d'état* of 1851. Restrictions on debate within the legislative chamber were eased and the ban on publishing its deliberations was lifted. Press freedoms were reinstated. Workers were given the right to form trade unions and even to strike (1864).[105] It was hoped that these measures would mollify the opposition parties, and moreover, make them share responsibility for those of his policies that might prove unpopular.[106] Sadly, these expectations were not realized. The reforms fell decidedly short of what was desired, and far from being praised for his liberality the emperor was pilloried for his ongoing sins by the unfettered opposition in the legislature and in the press.

Napoleon III, Emperor of France, portrait by Hippolyte Flandrin, 1861, Museum of the History of France (Wikimedia Commons).

Inevitably, he sought for a solution in foreign affairs. A chance to mend fences with liberals and Catholics alike was seemingly presented by a nationalist revolt against tsarist tyranny in Catholic Poland (1863). French sentiment had long been in favor of Polish liberty, and most Frenchmen bitterly resented the emperor's ensuing failure to act on Poland's behalf. But active intervention was deemed too risky, as it threatened to pit France against the combined might of Russia, Prussia and Austria—all of whom stood to lose if the Polish rebellion ended in success.[107] By this date, moreover, Napoleon had already hit upon what he deemed "the great idea of his reign"[108]—a bizarre colonial scheme that bade fair not only to unite the parties at home, but also to heal old wounds with Austria by providing that nation the opportunity to redeem her recent losses in Italy through an initiative further afield.

In distant Mexico, revolution had elevated the anti-clerical republican, Benito Juárez, to the presidential chair (1861). The preceding government of Mexico, backed by the church, had been corrupt, and Juárez now sought to salvage the nation's financial situation by confiscating all church property and renouncing the large foreign debt accrued by the toppled regime.[109] As France held a prominent place among Mexico's creditors, Juárez's policy provided Napoleon with an excellent pretext for intervention. Capitalizing on the distraction caused in the United States by the American Civil War, he embarked in 1862 upon an invasion of Mexico with the goal of carving out a puppet Mexican empire that would win the support of both Catholics and liberals at home by restoring the position of Mexico's Catholic Church and creating a new venue for commercial enrichment.[110] Ever the visionary, he seems also to have anticipated the creation of a canal across Central America with a new Constantinople adorning one of its shores as a standing monument to French enterprise.[111]

The invasion took place in early 1862. On May 5, it encountered a shock when the French expeditionary force was routed near Puebla. (The date—Cinco de Mayo—is celebrated in Mexico to this day.[112]) But reinforcements were sent, and in the ensuing campaign, Puebla succumbed to siege, Mexico City was occupied, and the Mexican throne was offered to Archduke Maximilian, brother of the Austrian Emperor, Franz Josef.

In the meantime, a separate initiative was undertaken to improve relations with the new kingdom of Italy. Since 1859, the presence of a French garrison in Rome had been a constant thorn in Franco-Italian relations. Indeed, by the mid–1860s, Italy had begun to look elsewhere—namely, to Prussia—in hopes of satisfying her peninsular aims. In a bid to reverse this current—and to regain his former status in Italian affairs—Napoleon offered to withdraw his troops from Rome by 1866 provided the Italians would guarantee continued papal jurisdiction in the city. Alas, the seeming step forward miscarried utterly—for no sooner did Napoleon withdraw his garrison as promised than he was forced to order its return to repel another attempt on the city by the indomitable Giuseppe Garibaldi. The ensuing victory over Garibaldi's forces at Mentana secured Rome but ruined the chance of a Franco-Italian rapprochement.[113]

The Seven Weeks' War: The Battle for German Hegemony

By this juncture, moreover, Prussia had changed the entire diplomatic equation. Since 1815, Prussia and Austria had been locked in a duel for German hegemony. Following the Revolutions of 1848, the conflict intensified. Initially, Austria held the upper hand, and on more than one occasion Prussia was forced to back down—the most notable instance being the "Humiliation of Olmütz" (1850), where an Austrian ultimatum sufficed to scuttle Frederick William IV's plan for a Prussian-led "Union of German

Princes." Long before this, however, Prussia had laid the groundwork for eventual victory in the contest by founding and assuming the leadership of the so-called *Zollverein*—a customs union that lowered tariffs between the various states of Germany in hopes of stimulating the industrial growth of all.

The idea was born of necessity. The Napoleonic Wars that ended at Waterloo in 1815 had reduced Prussia's public finances to chaos. According to the *Cambridge Modern History*, "The Prussian public debt in 1815 was 217,000,000 *thalers*, and the annual deficit was nearly 2,000,000 *thalers*."[114] (If one seeks for the derivation of the modern word "dollar," he or she will find it in the name of these obsolete German coins.[115]) Complicating the situation was the internal character of the Prussian kingdom. From its medieval beginnings as the Margraviate of Brandenburg, with its capital at Berlin, Prussia had taken form only gradually over the course of centuries through the periodic absorption of previously independent (or foreign ruled) provinces.[116] Nominally united under the ruling House of Hohenzollern (whose forefathers had purchased Brandenburg in 1417), the patchwork kingdom had never broken the fetters of its cultural and economic provincialism. Within its borders, says the *Cambridge Modern History*, "Innumerable tariff-walls impeded trade more effectively than they protected manufactures; there were sixty-seven tariffs in the old provinces of Prussia alone, and they affected nearly three thousand different articles." By 1818, the sorry fiscal situation mandated a change. It came in the form of a new Customs Law.[117]

Proposed and enacted by Prussia's director-general of taxation, Karl Georg Maaßen, the law abolished the existing tariff system, and transformed the whole of Prussia into a free-trade zone modeled on the teachings of Adam Smith. The neighboring states of the German Confederation perceived in this economic revolution a threat to their own financial traditions, if not to their autonomy. In this they were not wholly mistaken, for scarcely had the law been passed when Prussia—formerly so adept at increasing its territorial hegemony—embarked on the extension of its economic hegemony. Within a year, the principality of Schwarzburg-Sonderhausen became the first to enter into a customs agreement with Prussia (1819).[118]

Hoping to forestall the emergence of a Prussian economic colossus, several groupings of German states attempted to form rival customs unions. These attempts, encompassing more than a decade, were not successful. Indeed, thanks to the liberal terms of cooperation offered by Prussia, the involved principalities ultimately agreed to participate in the formation of the *Zollverein* (January 1, 1834), whereby the "Prussian" customs union became a "German" one, adhered to by most of the states of the German Confederation.[119]

In their apprehensiveness of the growing economic influence of Prussia, the German states had initially failed to apprehend what was now manifestly evident—i.e., that "in reality the [customs] law of 1818 was one of the earliest and greatest triumphs of the principles of Adam Smith."[120] Far from threatening the economic well-being of Prussia's neighbors, the growth of the customs union—and the gradual adherence to it of those self-same neighbors—proved a boon to commerce and a spur to industrialization throughout greater Germany.

There were as yet a handful of holdouts—most notably Austria. Engrossed in the task of preserving intact an empire of disparate and rival nationalities (many of which were hostile to the Germanic element), Austria held aloof from the German *Zollverein* and therefore did not share in its benefits. In consequence, by the mid–1860s, not only had Prussia supplanted Austria as the leader of Germany's economy, she had also developed her industrial strength to a much greater degree—particularly with regard to the military. In 1862, moreover, the new Prussian king, Wilhelm I, named as his prime minister the brilliant Otto von Bismarck. Born in the year of Waterloo, Bismarck won distinction during his youth "as a dashing fraternity-member and leader of beer-drinking contests." In 1847, however, his fortuitous marriage to a devout daughter of the landed aristocracy transformed him, allowing him to fix his considerable talents on what was to be his life's ambition—the unification of Germany under the leadership of the Prussian monarchy, not by discussion as in 1848, but by "blood and iron."[121]

He encountered the first obstacle to his policy at home, in the Prussian parliament, which steadfastly refused to grant the funds necessary for an expanded military. To surmount the impasse, Bismarck declared that since the budget could not be approved until the king and legislature reached an agreement, it was incumbent upon the former to take control of all interim expenditures lest government services grind to a halt.[122] Literally no one subscribed to this argument, yet it defied refutation since the spending of funds by the king without parliamentary consent was not expressly forbidden by the Prussian constitution. (Neither was such spending expressly allowed, but that was parliament's problem, not Bismarck's.) Having squared the economic circle, so to speak, Bismarck forged his new model Prussian army.[123]

He would find employment for it within the year. In 1863, the king of Denmark died without a direct heir. His nephew, Christian IX, was named to succeed him. Protesting the choice, Denmark's German duchies, Schleswig and Holstein, declared in favor of a rival pretender of German descent. On the pretext of protecting German rights, Prussia and Austria intervened militarily against Charles IX, with the Austrians occupying Holstein and the Prussians Schleswig (1864).[124]

In this venture, Bismarck was only feigning cooperation with the Austrians. Secretly he planned to use the proximity of the seized duchies to create an Austro-Prussian confrontation. First, however, it would be necessary to isolate Austria diplomatically. Russia could be counted upon. Prussia had been on good terms with her since the preceding year, when Bismarck allowed Russian troops to enter Prussian territory in pursuit of fugitives from the failed insurrection in Poland.[125] Likewise, the Prussian prime minister ensured the neutrality of Napoleon III by promising unspecified recompense to France. When, in April 1866, Bismarck obtained an alliance with Italy by offering to support her in the annexation of Venetia in return for combined action against Austria, his diplomatic maneuvering was complete. On June 7, Prussian forces occupied Holstein, using alleged Austrian abuses as a pretext. The action provoked the "Seven Weeks' War" (June–August 1866).

It was believed by most European observers that the Austrians would make short work of the upstart Prussians. Their army was larger, and they had excellent artillery and cavalry arms. Moreover, they began their mobilization almost a full month before the Prussians did.[126] But the Prussians had a few advantages of their own. First, their army was directed by a "general staff"—the first of its kind—thereby relieving the commanders in the field of training and logistical duties. Their officer corps was professional in both training and attitude—something that could not be said with confidence of their Austrian counterparts—and their new breech-loading rifle, the so-called "needle gun," could be reloaded not only more quickly than the Austrian muzzle-loader, but from a prone position, thus allowing the bearer to take cover during the process.[127]

Finally, Prussia held the moral high ground. To be sure, her occupation of Holstein posed a crisis of some magnitude, but it did not technically constitute Prussian aggression against Austria. Indeed, it was Austria that now initiated hostilities against Prussia (June 1866)—and in so doing it cast itself in the role of aggressor.[128] With war inevitable, Austria had not had a choice; the Prussians had modernized their rail and telegraph networks giving them a tremendous advantage in mobilization efficiency. In a calculated move, Bismarck let the Austrians get underway first, knowing that superior transport and communications would allow Prussia to field the bulk of its army before Austria could concentrate even half of its own.[129]

Approaching from the west, the Prussian First Army attacked the Austrians at Sadowa near the Bohemian city of Königgrätz on the morning of July 3, 1866. For more than eight hours the Austrians held their own, using their advantage in artillery to force the Prussians back along the entire line. However, as the day progressed, the Austrians became increasingly alarmed by a Prussian foray into the Swiepwald Forest on their right flank. Efforts to capture the position were repulsed owing to the murderous efficiency of the Prussian needle gun. Attempting to regroup as they fell back, the Austrian attackers encountered disaster—falling headlong into the path of the Prussian Second Army, whose unanticipated arrival from the north threatened the weary Austrians' right flank with envelopment.[130] In order to extricate themselves, the Austrians beat a hasty retreat, leaving 20,000 casualties on the field—including the bulk of the proud Hapsburg cavalry, which had sacrificed itself to allow the infantry to escape. Another 20,000 Austrians were taken prisoner, while Prussian losses numbered less than 10,000.[131]

With her main army in a shambles, Austria sued for peace. Wilhelm I was sorely tempted to demand the annexation of Austrian territory, but Bismarck had more

Cavalry engagement during the Battle of Königgrätz (Austrians in the light uniforms, Prussians in dark), by Alexander Ritter von Bensa (1820–1902), Heeresgeschichtliches Museum Wien (Wikimedia Commons).

important fish to fry, and convinced the king to sign a generous peace in return for an Austrian withdrawal from German affairs. Prussia's junior partner, Italy, could scarcely object. Not only was her army mauled at Custozza by a subsidiary Austrian army, but her navy sustained a reverse against the inferiorly equipped Austrian fleet in a clash of ironclads off the Adriatic island of Lissa. Despite this, Bismarck kept his word, and insisted that Austria relinquish Venetia to the kingdom of Italy. It was the only territorial concession that Austria was compelled to make.

The Seven Weeks' War effectively removed Austria from the affairs of both Germany and Italy. In the aftermath, Bismarck had no difficulty coaxing Germany's northern principalities into a North German Confederation dominated by Prussia. But the German states south of the Main River were, as yet, out of reach. Before Germany could be fashioned into a thoroughly Prussian Empire (and before Rome could take her rightful place as capital of Italy), one nuisance had still to be swept aside: the unsuspecting— and unready—Second French Empire.

The Franco-Prussian War and the Collapse of the Second French Empire

The pendulum of success that had brought luck to Napoleon III in his foreign endeavors had, by 1866, already expended its last momentum in delivering the dubious prizes of Viet Nam and Cambodia to French domination (1858–1867). By the time of Sadowa, French fortunes were swinging inexorably in the opposite direction. In April 1865, the American Civil War came to an end, giving the United States leisure to point out the discrepancy between the French emperor's Mexican adventure—"the great idea of his reign"—and the principles laid out in the Monroe Doctrine. Since war with the United States was not a viable option, it was inevitable that France must evacuate her troops in disgrace—a task that she began in January 1866 and completed in February of the following year. A chance for consigning the misadventure to distant memory was provided soon after by the opening in Paris of the famous *Exhibition Universelle* (World's Fair) on April 1, 1867. For a shining moment, France basked in a triumphant display of the latest in Western technology. Sad to relate, in the midst of the ceremonies, which were attended by the royalty of Europe, a dismal reminder of the Mexican affair arrived in the form of a telegram apprising the French government of the fate of Archduke Maximilian.[132] The well-meaning Austrian prince had remained at his post as "Mexican emperor" after the French withdrawal, while his wife, Empress Carlotta, sailed to Europe to beg further help from Napoleon (who could offer nothing but tears), and from the pope (who offered nothing at all).[133] The hapless Carlotta lapsed into insanity on receiving these responses, while across the ocean Mexican rebels seized Maximilian and executed him at Querétaro (June 1867).

The telegram announcing his fate arrived in secrecy on the day prior to the grand ceremony at which Napoleon was to distribute prizes to the Exhibition winners. It was confirmed just as the ceremony was opening, prompting the departure of the Austrian and Hungarian dignitaries.[134] It would have required sorcery to portray this finale in a positive light. As it was, the news added new fuel to the firestorm still raging in France over the Austrian defeat at Sadowa. Since that event, the emperor's detractors had berated him ceaselessly for doing "nothing" while a powerful German state was assembled on France's eastern frontier. By the time of Maximilian's demise, a propaganda campaign by the liberal opposition had Frenchmen convinced that the battle of Sadowa had been not an Austrian defeat, but a French one. Had France not lost her position as Europe's pre-eminent power?

In a bid to save face, the French emperor approached Bismarck about the unspecified compensation he had been promised for his neutrality in the Austro-Prussian conflict. Failure to settle this issue prior to the battle of Sadowa, however, had been a grave error. Napoleon asked if he might have part of the Rhineland. Bismarck demurred, as the population was largely German. The chancellor had no objection to a swath of Belgium. Alas, it was not his to give. An apparent compromise was reached on Luxembourg, which France was to acquire by purchase, but at the last moment the Prussian government withdrew its consent. Bismarck then delivered the *coup de grace* by leaking Napoleon's territorial desires to anyone who might be offended by them. England was dismayed to hear of the emperor's Belgian designs. His inquiry into the Rhineland had a far worse effect, for it frightened the south German states straight into Bismarck's back pocket.[135]

Napoleon III was now on the horns of a dilemma. If he were to pursue a course aimed at redeeming French pride, France would have to overhaul her armed forces. For one thing, the army was too small to stand up to Prussia. For another, its armaments were substandard. But the opposition in the Assembly was better at sounding the alarm than it was at producing funds for a rejuvenated military. While addressing the Chamber of Deputies, the war minister, Adolphe Niel, was rudely asked whether he hoped to convert France into a barracks. His curt reply—that if his detractors weren't careful, they would convert the nation into a graveyard[136]—was unavailing. The proposed improvements were shouted down. Nor could Napoleon count on his allies to bail him out. Austria had had its fill of fighting the Prussians, and following the French clash with Garibaldi at Mentana, Italy was more a Prussian than a French ally.

As 1870 dawned, Napoleon's declining prestige obliged him to make more substantive concessions to the growing cadre of liberals in the French Assembly. Viciously assailed by the republican elements in the chambers, he turned for support to the so-called "Third Party" headed by Émile Ollivier, which favored the establishment of a constitutional monarchy. In April 1870, on Ollivier's advice, the emperor put forward a new constitution, which allotted true legislative prerogative to the *Corps Legislatif* (or lower legislative house) while depriving the Senate (or upper house) of its power to block or approve amendments to the constitution, which were now to be subjected to plebiscite.[137] The emperor's ministers, formerly answerable only to himself, were now made responsible, in not quite parliamentary fashion, both to himself and to the legislature.[138] The emperor retained his right of appeal to the French people, who heartily approved the reforms in a national plebiscite by a vote of 7.5 million in favor versus 1.5 million opposed. Profoundly satisfied, Ollivier predicted that the emperor would retain his throne into "happy old age" and then pass it peaceably to his son.[139]

Alas, owing to external events, these happy prognostications were not to be realized. In 1868, Queen Isabella of Spain was dethroned for attempting to reinstate absolutism, and, after some slippery intrigues by Bismarck, her crown was offered to Leopold of Hohenzollern, a distant relative of the Prussian king. In 1866, Napoleon III had backed the candidacy of this prince's brother, Karol, in the latter's effort to become King of Romania, but whereas extension of Hohenzollern influence might have been tolerated, or even welcomed, in faraway Romania in that year, the militant liberals in the new French ministry would have none of it in neighboring Spain in 1870. Under pressure from the French press and from his liberal parliament, Napoleon insisted that Leopold's candidacy be withdrawn. The request was promptly granted, but French pride was not assuaged. The French foreign minister, Antoine Agénor, duc de Gramont, demanded that Wilhelm I also renounce all future Hohenzollern claim to the Spanish throne. Wilhelm, vacationing at Ems, answered that he had no further opinion on the matter, and suggested that the French government discuss it with his ministry in Berlin.

The apparent fizzling of the crisis was a great disappointment to Bismarck, who was bent on war and had been deliberately provoking the French in the Spanish matter. But he now saw an opportunity to stir up new trouble by editing the infamous *Ems Dispatch*—i.e., the telegram sent to him by the Prussian foreign office describing the interaction between Wilhelm and the French foreign minister. Whereas the actual interchange had been polite, Bismarck's official version made it appear that the principals had insulted one another. Moreover, by editing out Wilhelm's offer of further negotiations in Berlin, Bismarck gave the impression that the German king had issued a blunt refusal to Gramont's demand when this had not been the case. In sum, the Iron Chancellor had unfurled a "red rag upon the Gallic bull."[140] He would later boast that he had not added or altered a single word. True enough, but he omitted all the polite ones, and when the French press got hold of his edited account on Bastille Day (another nice touch by Bismarck), they declared there was nothing for it but war. Napoleon III—his army unready—sought to temporize and found support in the countryside. But Paris demanded a fight, and Paris spoke for France. Thus, "with a light heart,"[141] the overconfident French prime minister, Émile Ollivier, declared war on Prussia on July 19, 1870.

Disaster ensued. With the Prussian juggernaut looming on the horizon, the outnumbered French army could claim but one advantage: namely, their new rifle, the *chassepot*, which had twice the range of the Prussian needle gun.[142] Despite the fact that the emperor had once written a treatise on the subject, France had done nothing to improve her cannonry. She continued to rely on outdated bronze muzzle-loaders—an unfortunate choice, since the Krupp factories of Prussia were now turning out state-of-the-art breech-loading rifled artillery. The new ordnance had such superior range that it could pulverize the French guns with absolutely no threat of return fire.[143] Indeed, according to Charles Fair, it was scarcely sporting to pit the short-firing French artillery against the Prussian needle gun.[144]

Napoleon III only narrowly missed salvaging this situation when he commissioned an artillery officer named J.B. Reffye to design a new secret weapon: the *mitrailleuse*—a bulky precursor to the machine gun with a range of fire similar to that of the Prussian artillery. But the emperor had been an intriguer from his earliest days, and the new weapon was developed in such secrecy that at the outbreak of hostilities his officer corps hadn't the slightest inkling how to use it. It had been meant for deployment to the rear of the main dispositions, in the fashion of artillery, where the gunners would be unmolested by enemy rifle fire while taking advantage of their own weapon's superior range. But the French officer corps was resistant to the idea that a weapon that fired bullets should be treated as artillery, so they placed it in the front lines with the infantry. Reffye thought the decision appallingly stupid,[145] and he was right: ineptly deployed, the weapon proved useless since its operators could not protect themselves from the exasperating fire of the needle gun.[146]

The French High Command decided to concentrate its forces at Metz for a lunge into the Rhineland. Unfortunately, before it could get organized the Prussians delivered a pair of sharp reverses—forcing half the army to withdraw toward Paris under Marshal Patrice de MacMahon (who had distinguished himself in the Crimea), while the other half, led by Marshal Achille Bazaine (formerly commander of French forces in Mexico), clung indecisively to Metz with the fast-moving Prussians pressing around his flank. After fighting to a costly draw at the Battle of Vionville-Mars la Tour, where each side lost 16,000 men, Bazaine took up an excellent defensive position at Gravolette (just west of Metz).[147] There he awaited an attack by the Prussians, who were now behind him, blocking the road to Paris. When the attack came on August 18, the French made a good account of themselves, inflicting 20,000 casualties against their own 13,000. An attack on the well-entrenched French right flank in the Cemetery of Saint-Privat, accounted for 8,000 Prussian casualties in a twenty-minute span.[148] Further south, closer to Gravolette, a series of Prussian assaults were also murderously repulsed. But Bazaine failed to exploit either advantage. The hard-pressed troops at Saint-Privat were denied reinforcements, and finally had to give way, whereupon the vacillating French commander withdrew toward Metz, even though this meant certain encirclement.[149]

Meanwhile, Napoleon III—who had started out with Bazaine's army but was now with MacMahon's—decided to return to Paris to run the government while MacMahon established a defensive line for the city's protection. Unfortunately, Empress Eugénie and her zealous advisors forbade this course of action as tantamount to an admission of defeat, and all but ordered the emperor to proceed to Bazaine's rescue at Metz.[150] Ill with an infected kidney stone, and full of misgivings, the emperor yielded. A northerly

The Cemetery of Saint-Privat, by Alphonse-Marie-Adolphe de Neuville, Musée d'Orsay, Paris (Wikimedia Commons).

route, skirting the Belgian frontier, was chosen for the advance, but the army got no further than the fortress town of Sedan before the Prussians successfully boxed it in. Upon viewing their respective dispositions, Von Moltke exclaimed: "The trap is now shut, and the mouse is in it!" while on the French side, General Ducrot remarked bitterly that the army of France had marched itself directly into a "chamber pot."[151]

Whereas the obvious strategy was to withdraw again toward Paris before the trap was fully closed,[152] this was not done. MacMahon, who might have pulled it off, was grievously wounded in the initial skirmishes, and was replaced by General Emmanuel Félix de Wimpffen—a political appointee who promptly ordered an attack upon the very center of the Prussian line with the intention of breaking through to Metz. The plan was sheer folly. Apart from the fact that the Prussian center was impenetrable, says Charles Fair, the achievement of Wimpffen's object would leave an intact enemy force operating in his rear, where it could sever his supply lines and pounce upon undefended Paris.[153]

As events unfolded, the French were quickly surrounded, prompting Ducrot to attempt a cavalry breakout toward Paris. The attempt failed, but was carried out with such heroism that the Prussians allowed a body of horsemen who had advanced deeply into their lines to return to their army unmolested, saluting them as they withdrew.[154] Next came Wimpffen's attempted breakout in which 6,000 wretched infantrymen, raked by artillery fire, disappeared into a pall of smoke and explosion from which erupted a churning confetti of heads, torsos and other sundry body parts.[155] Across the field, men abandoned their rifles and knapsacks and made for the gates of Sedan, many being trampled to death in the stampede.[156] Hoping to save his dynasty by sacrificing his life, Napoleon III exposed himself to fire. The Prussians managed to hit everyone in the

Bismarck and Napoleon III at Sedan by Wilhelm Camphausen, 1878 (Wikimedia Commons).

vicinity except him. Unscathed, and unwilling to allow the slaughter to continue, the emperor surrendered with 80,000 men on September 2, 1870. Paris received the news from Napoleon himself in a dispatch on September 3: "The army has been defeated and is captive; I myself am a prisoner."[157]

It might be thought that the nation would have capitulated at this point, but instead it rallied. The empire was declared to be at an end. Napoleon III was blamed for the disastrous war he had never desired, and a provisional republican government was formed to continue the hostilities. The Prussians, meanwhile, advanced upon Paris. Leon Gambetta, the organizer of the continued resistance, escaped from the encircled capital by hot-air balloon (becoming thereby the war's first successful "aeronaut"[158]), and energetically recruited new levies in the countryside. He had hoped to liberate Metz and its 173,000 troops, but before he could march, the fortress capitulated (October 27). He sought, therefore, to break the iron ring around Paris. An attempt by the Paris garrison to coordinate plans with him went awry when the balloon delivering the requisite intelligence blew off course and landed in Norway.[159] Gambetta, meanwhile, managed briefly to drive the Prussians out of Orléans—an intoxicating triumph that was promptly undone by a Prussian counterattack. Still the Paris garrison fought on with desperate courage, mounting ineffectual sorties and sustaining a savage artillery barrage, while the populace subsisted on the meat of horses, domestic pets and even rodents.[160]

Things were much brighter on the German side. While the French capital starved, German unification became a reality. On January 18, 1871, with the sound of Paris being

Kaiser Wilhelm I (at top of stairs) proclaimed Emperor of Germany on January 18, 1871, in the Hall of Mirrors at Versailles, flanked by his similarly dressed son, Crown Prince Frederick (left) and son-in-law, Frederick I, Grand Duke of Baden (right). Bismarck stands near the center of the painting, dressed in a white uniform with Helmuth von Moltke standing next to him, facing the emperor. Painting by Anton von Werner (Wikimedia Commons).

bombarded in the background, the crown of the new "German Empire" was placed on the head of Wilhelm I during a ceremony held in the Hall of Mirrors at Versailles. Ten days later, the war came to an end. With Gambetta's forces defeated, Paris finally agreed to an armistice on January 28, 1871. By the Treaty of Frankfurt, Germany obtained Alsace and a portion of Lorraine (against the will, be it noted, of their respective populaces). The German border was advanced thereby from the Rhine River to the eminently more defensible Vosges Mountains.[161] In addition, an indemnity of five billion francs was imposed on France, with Prussian garrisons being stationed on French soil until the account was squared.

In actuality, the war had given unity to two nations—for in addition to Germany, Italy achieved *her* final unification. The forces of the Italian King, Victor Emmanuel, occupied Rome on September 20, 1870, after the city's French garrison withdrew to assist Gambetta in his bid for Paris. In a plebiscite, the city voted overwhelmingly in favor of union with the kingdom of Italy.

While the peoples of Germany and Italy cemented their bonds, France teetered on the brink of civil war. In February 1871, a new National Assembly replaced the Provisional Government that had succeeded the empire. As the nation at large desired peace and order—and did not trust the new republic to provide it—the voting had returned a majority of conservative monarchists. Paris, however, remained staunchly republican, and was aghast that the recent hardships she had suffered in the name of republicanism were to be given short shrift based on something so piddling as a fair and democratic election.

Despite the capital's discontent, the National Assembly, seated at Versailles, demanded that the populace disarm (March 1871). The request was problematic since the war had brought the city's commerce to a standstill, and most of those drawing any income at all were doing so on the basis of serving in the National Guard. As there was more grumbling than obedience, the Assembly decided to force the issue. On March 18, Versailles troops stole into Paris under cover of darkness in a bid to capture the National Guard artillery park at Montmartre. Seized the guns were, but the soldiers had not been supplied with enough horses to cart them away. Worse still, they hadn't been given breakfast prior to the raid, and as dawn broke and a crowd of onlookers (including members of the National Guard) began to gather, the hungry soldiers refused an order to fix bayonets, opting instead to fraternize with the crowd, or to wander off in search of food. Nor did their demeanor change when their commanding officer, General Claude Lecomte, was dragged away and executed by the increasingly hostile assemblage.[162]

The government's sortie was perceived as a treasonous act of aggression, and Paris responded by proclaiming a rival government. In a hastily arranged election, Socialists and Jacobins obtained the most votes, and on March 28, the "Paris Commune" was declared. For all intents and purposes, the French capital had seceded from France. A military showdown was now inevitable, but the Versailles government wanted no repetition of the events of March 18. New troops were recruited from the countryside—where anti–Parisian sentiment ran strong—and the natural prejudice of these conscripts was augmented by a campaign of outright lies. Their officers informed them that Paris had fallen prey to debauched interlopers from abroad, and that the only Frenchmen remaining in the capital were scofflaws, murderers and felons.[163]

None of it was true. The Communards were a diverse and not particularly cohesive group. While roustabouts and indigents were surely represented, so too were doctors,

Communards man a barricade at the intersection of Voltaire and Richard Lenoir Boulevards, photo by Bruno Braquehais, 1871 (Wikimedia Commons).

lawyers, workers and craftsman. During their short tenure, they reopened factories (closed since the Prussian siege) and placed them in the hands of workers' cooperatives. They coined their own currency, abolished nightshift work in bakeries, established an Artists' Federation and reformed women's education. (They also burned the Versailles government's brand-new guillotine and pulled down the Vendôme Column, crowned with a statue of the great Napoleon, which broke in pieces with the fall.)

Admirable as these endeavors might have been, the Communards would have done better to build effective barricades across Paris' newly widened boulevards—for, on April 2, the army of Versailles put the city under siege. On May 8 a bombardment of her fortresses commenced, and on May 21 she suffered irretrievable disaster. At the St. Cloud gate, a contingent of Versailles troops espied a man waving a white handkerchief. When they asked if he was surrendering, he said no—he just thought that they might like to know that no one was defending the gate. Within 24 hours, 80,000 government soldiers were inside the city.[164]

As the invaders made steady inroads, the reeling Communards published appeal after appeal begging them to fraternize: "Do as your brothers did on the 18th of March," went one manifesto. "Unite yourselves to the people of whom you are a part.... Quit your ranks and come to us; come to the arms of our families, and you will be received fraternally and with joy."[165] But the Versailles soldiers had been instructed to kill, and far from seeking out adoptive families, they seized prisoners and executed them without scruple. In grim retaliation, the Communards brutally executed hostages taken on suspicion of favoring the Versailles government (including the Archbishop of Paris), and burned several public buildings (most notably, the Tuileries). For seven days—the so-called

"Bloody Week"—handfuls of Communards held out in bitter street fighting. Their last stronghold was the Cemetery of Père-Lachaise. After it was taken, one hundred and forty-seven Communards were lined up against the cemetery wall and shot dead. The scene was repeated throughout the city as "suspects" were rounded up and gunned down by the hundreds—often with the *mitrailleuse*. In the end, twenty thousand of the city's defenders lost their lives as against one thousand government troops.[166] The bodies of the former were interred in mass graves with no attempt being made to identify them.[167] Of those Communards who survived, twenty-five thousand were arrested and sentenced to forced labor either in France or in her penal colonies.

Having fought under the red flag of socialism, the ill-fated Commune would live on in Marxist propaganda as the first meaningful effort to usher in a Communist revolution. Twenty years on, Karl Marx's collaborator, Friedrich Engels, remarking on the fear engendered by the term "Dictatorship of the Proletariat," would ask, "Well and good gentlemen, do you want to know what this dictatorship looks like? Look at the Paris Commune. That was the Dictatorship of the Proletariat."[168]

Victorian England in the Age of Peel and Palmerston

On June 20, 1837, Great Britain's amiable King William IV died. In the estimation of *Encyclopædia Britannica*, he had been "a genial, frank, warm-hearted man, but

a blundering, though well-intentioned prince."[169] Lampooned by the political satirist John Doyle as "a good sovereign, but … a little cracked,"[170] he had nonetheless served a useful tenure as Lord High Admiral during the reign of his brother, and as king had done the country a great service in facilitating the passage of the Reform Bill of 1832.

He left behind eight children. Alas, none of them was legitimate. Consequently, the throne passed to his eighteen-year-old niece, Alexandrina Victoria. Very little seems to have been expected of this young princess, who had slept, hitherto, in the same bedroom as her overbearing mother. But as her second act (the first being to choose "Victoria" as her regal name), the new queen decreed that she would sleep alone. On the selfsame day as this declaration of independence, she identified a congenial mentor in the Whig prime minister, Lord Melbourne (William Lamb), whom she affectionately nicknamed "Lord M."

The young Queen Victoria, 1842, portrait by Franz Xaver Winterhalter (Wikimedia Commons)

Two years into the reign, Melbourne's government resigned after a close vote in the House of Commons. Noting that the queen's ladies-in-waiting were all Whigs, Melbourne's would-be successor, Sir Robert Peel, insisted upon the introduction of two or three conservatives. The queen refused, and as Peel could not budge her, he announced that without her confidence it would be impossible for him to form a government. If his intention was to force the queen's hand, it failed utterly, for the impasse—known to history as the "Bedchamber Crisis"—provided Victoria with a happy pretext to summon Melbourne again.

Undoubtedly, in rallying to the queen and her chambermaids at this delicate hour, Melbourne and his ministers did good service toward the cause of chivalry. It was, however, a very imperfect example of the principle of constitutional monarchy.[171] Upon their resumption of office, the cry of favoritism went up and during a subsequent appearance on her balcony members of the crowd mocked the queen as "Mrs. Melbourne."[172] The government muddled on for two more years before resigning after losing a vote to reduce the tariff on sugar and fix the tariff on wheat (1841). Happily married by this time, and ably advised by her husband, Albert of Saxe-Coburg-Gotha (her maternal cousin and the love of her life), Victoria did not, on this occasion, contest Peel's accession as prime minister.

By now, the era of political reform seemed to have petered out. Surveying the House of Commons after four years' absence in India, Lord Macaulay quipped that "[George] Grote and his wife" constituted all that remained of the old radical party that had passed the Reform Bill of 1832. (Disgusted by the Whigs' lurch to the right, Grote himself retired from politics to finish his famed *History of Greece*, "declaring that it was not worth his while to continue to defend Whig conservatism against Tory conservatism.")[173] The time, therefore, seemed ripe for a return to Tory (or, as it was now known, "Conservative") government.

Peel, the Conservative leader, had first been elected to Parliament in 1809. He quickly rose to prominence, says *Encyclopædia Britannica*, with "a style of speaking which owed its force not to high flights of oratory, but to knowledge of the subject in hand, clearness of exposition, close reasoning, and tact in dealing with a parliamentary audience."[174] Obtaining a junior post at the War Office, he spoke so convincingly in the Commons in favor of Wellington's peninsular campaign that even the Whig opposition applauded (1811).[175] In 1812, he entered Lord Liverpool's cabinet as Chief Secretary for Ireland, becoming the Tory Party's leading spokesman against Catholic Emancipation during the decades of unrest following the 1801 Act of Union (which deprived Ireland of its own parliament while allowing only Irish Protestants to sit as the island's representatives at Westminster). His policy made him seem a mouthpiece for the obstinately anti–Catholic "Orangemen" of Protestant Ulster—enough so that the Catholic leader Daniel O'Connell derided him as "Orange Peel" in a battle of words that nearly ended in a duel.[176] In truth, Peel was not nearly so dogmatic as the Orangemen, and when the issue of Catholic Emancipation came to a head in 1829 with O'Connell's election to Parliament, he saw the necessity of reversing himself in order to promote the very thing he had argued so eloquently against. It was not the last time he would leave his own party and constituency feeling betrayed.

Famed for his reform of the legal code, his "sound money" program (whereby he transitioned English currency back to the gold standard after the Napoleonic Wars), and his Municipal Police Act of 1829 (which created his namesake police force of "Bobbies" or "Peelers"), Peel inherited his father's baronetcy in 1830, thus becoming "Sir" Robert. Two years later, the old Tory Party was reduced to a shambles by its dogged resistance to the Reform Bill of 1832, and Peel set about remolding the wreckage into a more broad-based "Conservative" Party. Hence, where the old Tories were inflexibly opposed to reform, fearing that the slightest concession would lead inexorably to the overthrow of their traditions and interests, Peel saw that the granting of prudent reforms could in fact preserve those traditions and interests by removing abuses, avoiding unrest and stealing the thunder of the radicals.[177] He had already provided an example in his shaping of the Catholic Emancipation Act, which allowed Catholics to hold office (thus righting an abuse), while imposing a property requirement that ensured the election of only middle and upper class candidates (i.e., those who were most likely to have conservative political leanings).[178]

Sir Robert Peel, portrait by Henry William Pickersgill, unknown date, National Portrait Gallery, London (Wikimedia Commons).

He took office in 1841 ostensibly as a protectionist. The Whigs had famously mismanaged the budget during their years in office. Just prior to the election, they sought to right their ship with the aforementioned bill to lower tariffs and amend the Corn Laws. Peel all but destroyed them in debate, asking, "Can there be a more lamentable spectacle than that of a Chancellor of the Exchequer, seated on an empty chest, by a pool of bottomless deficiency, fishing for a budget?"[179] But once again, he was to confound his own constituency. He had, in fact, been a convert to "free trade" principles for decades—something that he neglected to emphasize to his electors during the campaign. As Oman, notes, his outlook was an inevitable consequence of his pedigree, for "he was not a member of the old aristocratic Tory families but the son of a wealthy Lancashire millowner, a representative of the Conservatism of the middle classes, not of the old landed interest."[180] His budget for 1842 reduced tariffs on some 750 articles and likewise placed lower rates on corn so that in times of want it could be imported less expensively. His goals were to promote commerce, reduce the duties on raw materials needed in English factories, and increase the purchasing power of the poor by lowering prices (thereby mitigating a source for lower class discontent). At the same time, he expunged the Whig deficit by enacting a modest three-year income tax, applicable only to the well-to-do, so as not to burden the poor. By 1844, in which year Peel also obtained passage of a Bank Charter Act regulating the circulation of paper currency in line with his "sound money" principles, the government was showing a surplus.[181]

In the realm of tariff reform, however, repeal of the Corn Laws constituted the Holy Grail. Passed in 1815, these measures effectively excluded cheap foreign grain from the British market in the aftermath of the Napoleonic Wars, thus keeping domestic prices high and guaranteeing continued profits for Britain's landowning aristocracy. Indeed, the Corn Laws composed the cornerstone of the aristocracy's continued governmental influence in an era of increasing industrialization. The landowners argued that the tariffs were necessary to keep Britain self-sufficient in the production of food, but rapid population growth was rendering this argument untenable, adding the risk of food shortages to the burden of high prices.[182] Led by Richard Cobden, a Manchester calico printer, and John Bright, a mill owner's partner, opponents of the Corn Laws formed an Anti-Corn Law League[183] which lobbied nationwide on the single issue of repeal, using organizational and electioneering methods that would make it the forerunner of modern political parties in far greater measure than the contemporary Whigs and Tories.[184]

In touting their program, the League noted that abrogation of the Corn Laws would lower food prices for the working poor, thus raising their standard of living. Members of the manufacturing class offered the League their enthusiastic support. As Schapiro notes, "if foreign countries were permitted to send their food-stuffs free of duty to England they would buy more manufactured articles from her." The heightened demand would create more jobs at home—a process that might be accelerated by removing tariffs on imported raw materials, which in turn would lower the cost of finished goods, thereby raising demand further. (Among themselves, the manufacturers cited a less egalitarian benefit: a lower cost of living would allow them to lower employee wages.[185])

Among his electors, it was unthinkable that Peel should be a proponent of repeal, and the initial omens confirmed them in this belief. Peel had paternalistic views on political leadership and chafed at the League's methods of rousing public opinion with propagandistic pamphlets and speeches blaming a selfish aristocracy for the nation's ills. Never a democrat, he felt that the public was uneducated and easily misled. The role of government, he argued in 1831, was "to consult the interests of the people, not to obey the will of the people."[186] The Anti-Corn Law League had disparaged his modest adjustment of the Corn Law rates in the budget of 1842 as "insulting a starving people with a paltry concession."[187] But if he would not be bullied into abdicating what he believed to be the proper duty of government in serving Crown and country, he nonetheless believed that repeal of the Corn Laws was in the public interest—and a humanitarian calamity in Ireland now gave him the opportunity to pursue repeal without the appearance of bowing to an outside political interest group.[188]

Centuries of oppression had taken a pitiless toll on Ireland. The bulk of the land had been usurped by the English and was typically administered by absentee owners who gave no thought to their impoverished tenants apart from insisting that they pay their rent on time. Half of the Irish population lived in ghastly dirt-floor, single-room huts shared not just by entire families, but also by their barnyard animals. Worse still, the diet of the vast majority consisted solely of the potato—a crop that could be raised with a minimum of skill on tiny plots. People lived their entire lives without experiencing the taste of any other food.[189] By the early 1840s, even the British government admitted that the "Irish peasant is the most poorly nourished, most poorly housed, most poorly clothed of any in Europe."[190]

But the worst was yet to come. Beginning in 1845, a blight wiped out two Irish potato crops in succession. Observers noted that thriving potato fields wilted overnight to beget potatoes that were black with rot, shriveled and inedible.[191] Starvation swept the countryside. Towns were inundated with living skeletons begging for food. Says one eyewitness, "I have seen miserable creatures prick the cattle which they met on the road, and apply their lips to the wound, to appease their hunger by sucking the animal's blood."[192] The population of Ireland dropped by 25 percent in less than five years, with about half of this loss due to death and another half due to emigration, mostly to England and the United States.

Peel sought to alleviate this suffering (unavailingly as it turned out) by abolishing the Corn Laws in order to increase the supply of cheap food. The ensuing debate, supported by one up-and-coming "Peelite" Conservative, William Ewart Gladstone, and viciously decried by another, the flamboyant backbencher, Benjamin Disraeli, destroyed the Conservative Party Peel had worked so assiduously to build since the upheaval of 1832. In the end, he won the battle at the cost of his own political career. Says *Encyclopædia Britannica*, "The general election of 1841 had been mainly fought on the rival policies of protection and free trade. The country had decided for protection, and Sir R. Peel had done more than all his predecessors to give it free trade."[193] Although the repeal measure passed by a 98-vote margin, less than a third of Peel's own followers voted in favor—the margin of victory being provided by overwhelming Whig support.[194] He was voted out of office on the very day of the repeal, despite years of distinguished service to the Tory Party, which now disowned him (June 1846).[195] He has since enjoyed a reputation as a statesman for having placed the needs of the country before himself or his party. When he died four years later after a fall from his horse, the outpouring of public sentiment showed that he was already widely revered. His party, meanwhile, was riven into two factions—Peelites and Protectionists—who never forgave each other and never again joined forces, thereby conceding political predominance to the Whigs for the better part of three decades.[196]

Henry John Temple, Lord Palmerston, engraved by D.J. Pound from a photograph by Mayall, 1858 (Wikimedia Commons).

The departure of Peel allowed for the definite emergence of Lord Palmerston (Henry John Temple) as the dominant figure on the British political scene. Palmerston had gained his first political appointment at the age of 22, serving as one of six Junior Lords of the Admiralty during the premiership of Lord Grenville (1807). Defeated thrice for a seat in the Commons (1806–1807), he finally gained election as the Tory candidate for the rotten borough of Newport on the Isle of Wight—though the borough's possessive patron insisted as a precondition "that he would never, even for the election, set a foot in the place."[197] His first Commons' speech (quite apropos for a member serving simultaneously as Junior Lord of the Admiralty[198]) was in defense of the British Navy's seizure of the neutral Danish fleet in order to keep it out of the hands of Napoleon (1807). Two years later, he declined an offer to serve as Chancellor of the Exchequer in Spencer Perceval's cabinet because he did not feel that he had the requisite expertise in finance to debate the issue incessantly in the Commons.[199] He would not have another cabinet offer for nearly two decades. In the interim, however, he remained in government, holding a variety of subordinate posts including a prolonged stint at the War Office. (In his spare time, he gathered enough mistresses to warrant the moniker "Lord Cupid."[200])

Despite his modest political stature at this time, a lunatic retired soldier named Davies thought him important enough to warrant assassination. One day in 1818, as Palmerston mounted the stairs leading to his place of work, Davies fired a pistol at him. As fate would have it, Palmerston was accustomed to climb stairs at a run and the ball only grazed him.[201] Afterwards, in a charitable gesture, he paid the deranged assailant's legal expenses.[202] In 1827, he finally entered the cabinet as Secretary at War under George Canning. But Canning died within the year, and while serving afterwards under Wellington, Palmerston earned the ire of many prominent fellow Tories for supporting the cause of Catholic emancipation. He resigned his cabinet post in 1828, subsequently breaking with the Tories altogether on the question of political reform, which he saw as inevitable whether the Tories liked it or not.[203] When he again obtained a cabinet level post in 1830, it was as foreign secretary in a Whig ministry headed by Lord Grey. It was in this capacity that his reputation was made as a statesman willing to project British power abroad without regard to the irritation his policies might provoke in foreign courts.

For the next eleven years, serving first under Grey and afterwards under Melbourne, Palmerston would prove himself a dedicated servant of the British interest. Much of his labor during this period was expended in thwarting the foreign policy designs of the French king, Louis Philippe, whom he prevented in turn from gaining undue influence in newly independent Belgium (1831–1832) and from precipitating the collapse of the Ottoman Empire during the revolt of the French-sponsored Egyptian pasha, Mehemet Ali (1839–1840). In the latter episode, says *Encyclopædia Britannica*, Palmerston's successful repulse of Ali by the bombardment of Beirut and the capture of Acre caused him to be "regarded as one of the most powerful statesmen of the age."[204] For Palmerston, however, there was more to it than personal prestige or, indeed, the exquisite pleasure an Englishman feels after thwarting France. The territory that Mehmet Ali sought to dominate bestrode the land bridge to India—the "jewel in the crown" of the British Empire—and the foreign secretary could not abide its control by a French client.[205]

A more important aspect of Palmerston's foreign policy was his use of the British Navy to promote "free trade," particularly beyond the bounds of Britain's colonial empire—in Latin America, Africa and, more forcefully, in China. In this way, he opened new markets for British manufactures, thereby fueling the engine of Britain's industrial revolution and augmenting her already commanding position as the world's foremost economic power. With trade came influence, and as the policy progressed Britain bade fair to construct an "empire of trade" to complement her far-flung territorial empire. The methods were not always amicable. "The British," says Gregory Barton, "kicked the door of trade open if foreign governments did not open their markets willingly," but Palmerston also used force in more worthy causes—as when he sent naval patrols to the coast of West Africa to combat the slave trade.[206]

The accession of the Tories under Peel in 1841 put an end to Palmerston's first tenure as foreign secretary. Consequently, he took to the opposition benches in the Commons, roundly denouncing the foreign policy of his successor, Lord Aberdeen, who promoted a cordial relationship with France. Aberdeen took his revenge by putting his own signature to an Anglo-French anti-slave trade agreement that Palmerston had spent four laborious years negotiating prior to being turned out of office.[207] Palmerston's subsequent vociferous opposition to a treaty settling some of Canada's myriad boundary disputes with the United States (the 1842 Webster-Ashburton Treaty) ruffled feathers even within his own party forcing him to tone down his attacks.[208]

When Peel fell (1846), Palmerston regained his portfolio at the foreign office in a new Whig ministry headed by Lord John Russell ("Finality Jack" of the old Reform Bill days). His return coincided with a cooling of relations with France over the so-called "Affair of the Spanish Marriages" (1846). By gentleman's agreement between Lord Aberdeen and François Guizot (the French Foreign Minister), Spain's sixteen-year-old Queen Isabella II, and her younger sister, the infanta, Louisa Fernanda, were to marry princes from the House of Bourbon, provided that the sons of Louis Philippe (the Orléans branch) should not be eligible. Upon his return to office, Palmerston attempted to breach this agreement in favor of a prince of the House of Saxe-Coburg (which had ties to the British royal family). In response, Guizot held the gentleman's agreement to be null and void and arranged the marriage of the Spanish infanta to Antoine, Duke of Montpensier, a younger son of Louis Philippe. At the same time, Queen Isabella was betrothed to a husband who was not expected to father children, meaning that the heirs of Louis Philippe (i.e., via Antoine and Isabella) might one day be expected to inherit the throne of Spain. It was enough to cause a great deal of rancor between England and France, including charges that the latter was in breach of the 1713 Treaty of Utrecht, which ended the wars of Louis XIV.[209] The issue was rendered moot, however, by the overthrow of Louis Philippe at the outbreak of the Revolutions of 1848.

As revolution swept across the continent in that year, Palmerston's outspokenness in favor of the revolutionaries—most especially in northern Italy and Hungary—made him the darling of the British public, a concern to his own party and the Crown, and the bane of the nations of Europe. While he had no quarrel with Austria maintaining a strong position in central Europe, where it was an essential component of the continental balance of power, he declared that her rule in Italy, which she governed as though it were a "garrison town … has always been hateful."[210] He wanted the Austrians out, and favored the territorial enhancement of Piedmont-Sardinia so that the latter might serve as a barrier to both Austrian and French meddling in Italian affairs.[211] In 1849, he defied Russia and Austria by taking Turkey's side when the latter gave sanctuary to refugees from the failed Polish and Hungarian revolutions—among them, the Hungarian leader Louis Kossuth, whom he admired. (Indeed, he would have met with Kossuth when the latter visited England in 1851 had the cabinet not forbidden it.[212]) He gained further popular accolades at home for a riveting speech in defense of his actions in the so-called "Don Pacifico Affair" (1850), wherein he ordered a naval blockade of Piraeus to force Greece to pay reparations for harm done to British nationals on Greek soil. In actuality, the manhandling of the hapless Greeks had been far out of proportion to the alleged harm done to Don Pacifico and the other main plaintiff, George Finlay (a volunteer during the Greek War of Independence and author of a famous history of Greece). When the issue came before the House of Commons, Palmerston's very political life stood in jeopardy. On the whole, he was not a talented orator, but on this occasion he evoked cheers in the streets and put an end to all debate by declaring that "as the Roman, in days of old, held himself free from indignity when he could say *civis Romanus sum*; so also a British subject, in whatever land he may be, shall feel confident that the watchful eye and strong arm of England will protect him against injustice and wrong."[213]

By now, however, Queen Victoria, and more especially her husband, Prince Albert, were intensely distressed by the commotion Palmerston was causing in the capitals of Europe, and when, in the following year, the foreign secretary issued an unauthorized congratulation to then French President Louis-Napoleon Bonaparte on his 1851 *coup d'état*, it set the match to the powder keg. Prince Albert wrote a scathing letter to Lord Russell complaining that Britain's moderating influence in European affairs had "been rendered null and void by Lord Palmerston's personal manner of conducting ... foreign affairs, and by the universal hatred he has excited on the Continent."[214] Russell responded by dismissing Palmerston from office.

Palmerston was not long in turning the tables. Two months after his dismissal, he helped the Tory opposition topple Russell's government—an action that he characterized in a letter to his brother as "tit-for-tat."[215] By December 1852, he was back in the cabinet, serving in the unlikely capacity of home secretary in a Whig-Peelite coalition government headed by his old adversary, Lord Aberdeen. Here he presided over such reforms as the Penal Servitude Act of 1853, which ended the policy of transporting criminals (in large measure because Australia would no longer agree to take them) while establishing a parole system for eligible convicts at home; and the Smoke Abatement Act, passed in the same year, which sought to address the growing problem of industrial pollution.[216]

He had a very different attitude, however, when it came to political reform. As noted, he had seen the Reform Bill of 1832 as inevitable, but when the Aberdeen government contemplated a further extension of the vote in the early 1850s, Palmerston balked because it would enfranchise segments of the working class for which he had an abiding mistrust. (He was inordinately proud that he had personally commanded a platoon of special constables during the abortive Chartist uprising of 1848. In his view, the workers were too ignorant to make their own political decisions and would act as mere tools of the radical trade unions. "Can it be expected," he asked Aberdeen in a fit of hyperbole, "that men who murder their children to get 9£ to be spent in drink will not sell their vote for whatever they can get for it?")[217] In December 1852, he tendered his resignation, but the coming of the Crimean War convinced him to reconsider.

By 1850, Nicholas I of Russia was hated by the overwhelming majority of Englishmen owing, among other things, to his tyrannical suppression of Polish nationalism. In the lead-up to the Crimean War, Aberdeen adopted the pacific stance he had exhibited as foreign secretary under Peel in the 1840s. In contrast, Palmerston championed the bellicose sentiments of the people in demanding the dispatch of the fleet to the Bosphorus. In the end, of course, Britain went to war, but the disastrous initial campaign—in which dysentery, inclement weather and inept leadership did more injury to British arms than the Russians—led to the fall of Aberdeen's government. Queen Victoria now sought for anyone other than Palmerston to form a ministry only to find that there was no other choice.[218] Appointed prime minister, Palmerston presided over the victory in Crimea, which (by the Treaty of Paris, 1856) established the neutrality of the Black Sea and compelled the Russians to withdraw their fleet. In the estimation of *Encyclopædia Britannica*, "Never since Pitt had a minister enjoyed a greater share of popularity and power, and, unlike Pitt, Palmerston had the prestige of victory in war."[219]

In the ensuing years, he would not be less bellicose—using British naval power to force Persia to withdraw from the city of Herat (which it had seized from Afghanistan) and to punish China for seizing a small British sailing vessel (the so-called "*Arrow* Affair"). Far more celebrated, however, was his suppression of the famous Indian Mutiny of 1857.

The Mutiny had begun with a false rumor accusing the British of introducing a new rifle cartridge with casings greased in animal fat. The casings had to be bitten open prior to use, which the native Sepoy troops could only refuse to do, since the Hindus among them regarded the cow as sacred and the Muslims regarded the pig as unclean. As nothing could convince the Sepoys to load their rifles, their British officers contemptuously hurled eighty-five of them into the Meerut garrison stockade. But the Sepoys were deadly serious about their religious and dietary laws. Rather than breach them, they mutinied en masse. At Delhi, they murdered their British officers—some of whom managed to blow up the garrison magazine to keep it out of the mutineers' hands. The violence spread next to Cawnpore, where, after a spirited defense, the garrison surrendered on a promise of safe conduct only to be mown down with grapeshot.[220] Massacred separately, the women and children were cast into a well, where "their limbs were to be seen sticking out in a mass of gory confusion."[221]

Strained beyond limit in their attempt to manage the crisis, the local authorities appealed to the fleet to bring troops bound for China[222] to India instead. In addition, they enlisted loyal Sikhs and Gurkhas. The Sepoys, however, were well trained in British tactics. It took thirteen months to defeat them, and in the aftermath, they were made to suffer piteously. Some, says Churchill, were stitched into sacks of cowhide or pigskin,[223] while others "were fastened to the mouths of cannon and blown to pieces."[224]

With order restored, Palmerston decided to end the British East India Company's tenure as rulers of India and place the colony under a politically appointed secretary of state. Before he could do so, however, he was hoist on the petard of his own British chauvinism and cast out of office. In January 1858, the Italian radical Orsini made his attempt on the life of Napoleon III using bombs manufactured in England. Amid some very harsh remarks from the French ambassador, Palmerston introduced a "Conspiracy to Murder Bill" that, in the circumstances, was widely regarded as an act of appeasement towards France. Unwilling to "bow to French pressure" the Commons voted the bill down leading to Palmerston's fall. He was succeeded by Lord Derby, leader of the Protectionist Tories, who put through his own bill for the removal of the British East India Company. In the House of Commons, however, the Tories were in the minority. Derby's government could not long survive without a victory at the polls and this proved beyond achievement. New elections in April–May 1859 returned Palmerston to office.

It was to be his final ministry, and in foreign affairs it was not to be less adventurous. Although he maintained strict neutrality in the Franco-Austrian War of 1859, he spoke unabashedly in favor of Italian nationalism thereby gaining the plaudits of the British populace, who were similarly disposed. At the outbreak of the American Civil War, Britain's chief concern was her textile industry's dependence on Southern cotton. Palmerston promptly offended the North by declaring neutrality, which seemed to insinuate that the South had not simply rebelled but was a legitimate belligerent. When, in 1862, the U.S.S. *San Jacinto*, seized two southern emissaries—James Mason and John Slidell—from the British ship, *Trent*, Palmerston sent British troops to Canada, raising the specter of war, in order to force their release.[225] The following year, the North had its turn to demand reparations from England when England delivered to the South what was to become the famous Confederate raiding ship, *Alabama*. The ship would wreak havoc on Northern shipping until it was finally sunk in June 1864, and in the interim, it was determined by the British themselves that delivery of the ship had violated Britain's own Foreign Enlistment Act of 1819.[226] (The ensuing debate with the United States did not end until Britain finally paid reparations in 1872.)

Palmerston's last forays into foreign policy were not a success. Despite pro–Polish sentiment at home, he could see no means of providing material assistance to the Poles during their revolt against Russia in 1863. Then, in his last major foreign policy challenge—the Schleswig-Holstein Affair—he was badly outmaneuvered by Otto von Bismarck (1863–1864). Viewing Prussia and Austria as aggressors, he pledged Britain's commitment to Denmark's integrity in a House of Commons address (1863), declaring, "if Denmark were attacked, her assailants would not have to deal with Denmark alone."[227] Alas, as Bismarck had easily foreseen, in the moment of crisis, Britain was in no position to intervene in a land war against Prussia and Austria. Palmerston's position had been sheer bluff, and his bluff had been called. Says *Encyclopædia Britannica*, "the results to Britain were plain enough. She had been mighty in words and weak in deeds. It was no doubt open to her to contend … that the cause of Denmark was not of sufficient importance to justify her in going to war. But it was not open to her to encourage a weak power to resist and then desert her in the hour of her necessity."[228] In Trevelyan's estimation, "Palmerston's popular and jaunty diplomatic performances had had their day," and it was just as well that his predominance ended with his death the following year (1865), for if his methods had been of good service to Britain up until the Schleswig-Holstein Affair, they were ill-suited to the emerging era of *Realpolitik* and mechanized warfare.[229]

3

Societal Achievements,
1815–1870

On September 23, 1846, the planet Neptune—the existence of which had been predicted on the basis of unexplained "perturbations" in the movement of its fellow planet, Uranus—was discovered by the Berlin astronomer Johann Gottfried Galle. "Probably," says the *Cambridge Modern History*, "this one discovery had a greater effect in establishing the credibility of [the] scientific method in the civilized world at large than the far more important coordination of observation and hypothesis in the preceding fifty years."[1] Before the era we are now surveying was complete, the Russian chemist, Dmitri Mendeleev, would repeat the feat (after a fashion) by publishing his "periodic table" and correctly predicting that its empty positions must ultimately be filled by existing, but as yet unrecognized, elements.[2]

Human inventiveness was to make the 19th century a time of change unparalleled in history. Scientific advance, which had progressed slowly for millennia, underwent what can only be described as a revolution. "To get any adequate comparison with the nineteenth century," said the contemporary naturalist, Alfred Russel Wallace (who independently deduced Darwin's idea of "natural selection" prior to publication of the *Origin of Species*), "we must take, not any preceding century or group of centuries, but rather the whole preceding epoch of human history."[3] During the course of one hundred years, technology reduced the world to a fraction of its former size. The steam engine, invented to pump water out of the deep tunnels required for coal mining, was adapted to locomotion by the 1820s. Following upon the pioneering work of Richard Trevithick, George Stephenson, the son of a miner, developed a working steam locomotive to carry coal from the Killington coal mine to the local shipping port (1814). In 1825, he introduced the first locomotive to carry passengers and four years later introduced his prize-winning *Rocket* engine, which attained the unimaginable peak speed of 29 miles per hour on the new Manchester-Liverpool railway—the first bona fide passenger railway in history.[4] By 1848, Europe possessed 14,000 miles of railroad track, with England leading the way. By 1870, railway mileage almost quintupled to 65,000 miles.[5] Steam-powered rail travel reduced transport time in a way no previous invention had ever done—the same being accomplished for sea travel with the coming of the steamship.[6] In 1838, the *Great Western* became the first ship to cross the Atlantic entirely under steam power in a voyage lasting fifteen days (compared to anywhere up to six weeks under sail).[7]

Developments in communication were even more astounding. In 1814, the London *Times* began operating a steam-powered printing press capable of turning out over 1,000 printed sheets per hour at low cost. The economical method was soon adapted to book printing, greatly facilitating the dissemination of knowledge.[8] Two decades later, in 1832, Samuel F.B. Morse invented the telegraph, making communication across land instantaneous. The waterproofing of wire (by encasing it in gutta-percha, a rubber-like substance) made it possible to lay an underwater cable between Britain and France in 1851. Soon afterwards, the American financier Cyrus Field conceived the much greater project of a trans–Atlantic cable. Having convinced the governments of Britain and the United States to provide ships to sound out the route and transport the cable, Field launched the enterprise in 1857. Two ships, each carrying a spool of 1,250 miles of telegraph wire, set sail from Ireland in a convoy bound for Newfoundland.[9] Tragically, the cable snapped en route. Undeterred, Field made a second attempt, ruined by stormy weather, and a third, in which the cable was successfully laid, but then shorted out almost as soon as it was put to use. It was not until the fifth try, in 1866, that the trans–Atlantic project was brought to fruition (the cable being laid, incidentally, by the first of the era's massive iron steamships—Isambard Brunel's *Great Eastern*—driven by the efficient new "screw propeller" in addition to paddle wheels[10]). The passage of information between America and Europe, which had previously taken weeks under the best circumstances, could now be accomplished with immediacy.[11] Nor, indeed, was the communication revolution complete. Within a generation, Bell's telephone (1876) and Marconi's "wireless" telegraphy (1896) would make their appearance, putting standard telegraphy on the road to obsolescence.

What made the developments in travel and communication possible was an advance in the manipulation of materials. For centuries, iron smelting had relied upon wood charcoal, but in 18th-century England the supply of wood was becoming scarce. Thus, a new method of smelting, utilizing the intensely hot product of purified coal known as "coke," was adopted, and proved itself far superior to the former method. Advances continued through the 19th century when steel was developed using the Bessemer process—the blasting of hot air through liquefied pig iron contained in large vats (1856). The result was the creation of metals lighter in weight, but strong enough to support bridges, buildings and ships of a size never before contemplated.[12]

Power, too, underwent profound transformation. As H.G. Wells has noted, hitherto in humankind's history, if greater power was needed for a project it was obtained by recruiting more manpower—more slaves for the pyramid, more rowers for the galley.[13] It is poignant to note that the great engineering feat of the 1800s, the creation of the Suez Canal, began with thousands of Egyptian peasants toiling in mimicry of their ancient brethren, but ended beneath the strain of powerful earth-moving machinery.[14] The original concession made to the Canal's architect, Ferdinand de Lesseps (1805–1894), mandated that 80 percent of the Canal labor force would be composed of native Egyptian laborers, which the Egyptian ruler (or "khedive"), Said Pasha, undertook to provide. The fulfillment of this obligation resulted in a decided reliance on forced labor. England protested against the system and since Ismail (Said Pasha's successor) agreed, the labor pool was ultimately disbanded. Deprived of its manpower, the Canal Company requested the mediation of Napoleon III, who awarded an indemnity to the company that helped defray the cost of converting to modern means of excavation. In the view of *Encyclopædia Britannica*, "The abolition of forced labour was probably the salvation of the enterprise, for it meant the introduction of mechanical appliances and of modern engineering methods." The completion of the Canal in 1869, just prior to the collapse of the Second French Empire, was a culminating triumph of French engineering—cutting thousands of miles off the sea route from Europe to India by making it unnecessary to sail around Africa. Among the dignitaries on the first flotilla to pass through the Canal was Lesseps' second cousin, the Empress Eugénie.[15]

Steam remained the dominant energy source during this era, but in 1831 Michael Faraday laid the foundation for a new source of energy by developing an experimental "dynamo"—a machine that generated an electric current by using a hand crank to rotate a round copper plate between the poles of a horseshoe magnet.[16] The transmission of electric current by wire found its first successful practical application in Morse's telegraph. (Three decades later, in 1862, it found a somewhat less successful one in a nascent telephone invented by Philipp Reis of Hesse, whose method of opening and closing an electric circuit with each sound vibration transmitted consonant sounds well enough, "but not the vowels as yet in equal degree."[17]) In a similar anticipation of events, Étienne Lenoir patented a working (if inefficient) gas-powered internal combustion engine (1860), while the Frenchman Alphonse Beau de Rochas conceived the principle of the 4-cycle "compression" engine (1862) that was to make internal combustion practicable for wide use in the ensuing decades.[18]

In agriculture, the discovery that some crops consume nitrogen while others replenish it led to the adoption of the "crop rotation system" as a means of maintaining soil fertility. (In former times it had been necessary for farmers to let a portion of their fields lie fallow for an entire year.)[19] The era's most renowned chemist, Justus von Liebig (1803–1873), whose chemical researches had revealed nitrogen's agricultural importance, afterwards developed the first artificial chemical fertilizers, providing a further boon to agricultural output.[20]

Another chemist, Louis Pasteur (1822–1895), having staged experiments to solve the mystery of why beer, wine and milk were susceptible to spoiling, not only disproved the idea of "spontaneous generation" of organisms—i.e., the belief that organisms arose spontaneously in decaying matter—but also originated the "germ theory" of diseases. His process for preventing spoilage, patented in 1865, not only "inaugurated a new era in the brewing and wine-making industries" (to say nothing of milk), but also "rendered his name immortal" since the process came to be

Louis Pasteur, originator of the "germ theory" of diseases; photograph by Paul Nadar taken before 1895 (Wikimedia Commons).

known as "pasteurization."[21] Pasteur went on to develop vaccines against chicken cholera, anthrax and rabies by inoculating artificially weakened ("attenuated") strains of the causative organisms to produce immunity.[22] Such advances, say Wallbank and Taylor, created a sense of optimism in regard to "science" as had not been seen since the *philosophes* of the Enlightenment imbibed the panacea of Reason.[23]

At the outset of the period under study, there were two barriers to the emergence of modern surgery: the unbearable pain inflicted by the surgeon's scalpel and the mortifying rate of postoperative wound infection, often proving deadly even after minor procedures. To cope with the first of these barriers, surgeons emphasized speed over technique—many making their reputations on this basis alone (an approach, needless to say, that was fraught with danger for their patients, who might thus escape a moment's agony but not live to tell the tale).[24] This all changed on October 16, 1846, in the domed operating theater of the Massachusetts General Hospital. A trained dentist, William Thomas Green Morton, who was then attending the Harvard Medical School, had successfully put a patient to sleep with ether in order to extract a tooth, and afterwards convinced the hospital's chief of surgery, Dr. John Collins Warren, to let him administer the anesthetic during one of his operations. On the appointed day, Morton arrived late. Dr. Warren admonished him with the remark, "Well, sir, your patient is ready." With a gallery of spectators looking on, Morton put the patient to sleep and, turning to Warren, said, "Dr. Warren, *your* patient is ready."[25] The patient slept through the operation—the excision of a neck tumor—and emerged oblivious to what had occurred.

The solution to the second barrier to the emergence of modern surgery—postoperative wound infection and septicemia—was hit upon by the British surgeon, Joseph Lister, who believed that Pasteur's "germ theory" might explain the entire problem. To test the hypothesis, he developed a so-called "antiseptic" technique. He insisted on the use of fresh bandages, discarding those that were left over from previous operations, and donned a clean surgical apron for each procedure in an era when surgeons were accustomed to wear-

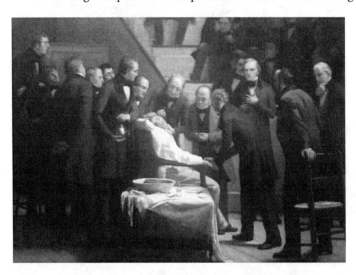

Ether Day, or the First Operation with Ether. **William Thomas Green Morton stands 6th from left. The patient is Gilbert Abbott. Dr. John Collins Warren wields the scalpel. Painting by Robert C. Hinckley (Wikimedia Commons).**

ing the same coat, unwashed, in surgery after surgery.[26] A chemical compound known as carbolic acid was used at the time to reduce the odor of sewage.[27] Lister adopted it as his antiseptic, cleansing his hands, his instruments and the part of the patient's body to be operated on with it, developing a steam-pump device to spray it into the surrounding air as the operation took place, and dressing the wound afterwards with bandages soaked in a solution containing it. Such antics were widely ridiculed, but the proof was in the results, which Lister published in *The*

Lancet in 1867. Formerly, one could march onto a modern field of battle with less mortality risk than attended a surgical operation. Lister's methods reduced postoperative mortality to less than five percent (and, incidentally, were used with profit to the wounded during the Franco-Prussian War).[28]

Greatly contributing to these strides in science and technology was the steady decline in interest rates that occurred in the decades preceding the industrial revolution.[29] The availability of cheap credit, coupled with the adoption of "limited liability" principles (which protected investors against loss beyond the value of their investments in the case of a failed business venture),[30] created enthusiasm among borrowers and investors alike at a time when the land, from which the bulk of society had obtained subsistence prior to 1800, could no longer provide work for a burgeoning populace. The easy credit allowed for the rise, at one end of the economic spectrum, of a new "capitalist" class, composed of those who became wealthy through investment in industry and technology, and, at the other end, of a working class—all too often exploited and wholly dependent for their livelihoods on arduous factory work that could, and often did, disappear at the next economic downturn. At a time when political power was still concentrated in the hands of the aristocratic landholding class, the rising capitalist and working classes clamored for a political voice of their own, impelling the nations of Europe towards democratic reform.[31] Indeed, in contemplating the period under study (which began with a discussion of the reactionary era following the Napoleonic wars), one may well appreciate the verdict of the eminent historian, Carlton Hayes, who wrote: "What finally determined the issue of the conflict between revolutionaries and reactionaries and the triumph of the ideas of Liberty, Equality, and Fraternity, was not a little revolutionary wave in politics, such as that of 1830, but a great revolution in industry—a revolution which threw all its strength and weight into the balance against the reactionaries."[32]

The economic and political changes were accelerated by demographic change. As money flowed into the technology sector, land flowed out of the hands of small farmers. This was particularly true in England where enclosure of farmland by aristocratic owners made agriculture more economical, but at the same time uprooted large numbers of agricultural laborers.[33] Over the course of several decades, significant population shifts occurred, as dispossessed farm workers flocked to the cities in search of factory jobs. But the transformation was not a smooth one. Working conditions were abysmal— the only pertinent regulations being those passed at the behest of capitalist financiers to prevent workers from forming combinations. Leaving aside the inhumane length of the workday—often 14 to 16 hours—factories operated without the slightest concession to health or safety. Dreadful injuries were sustained due to unsafe machinery with no compensation given to the victims.[34] Workers might be beaten for making minor errors.[35] Children harnessed to wagons hauled coal in the mines.[36] At home, clothing and nutrition were inadequate, and the unsanitary workers' slums were rife with disease. More than one historian has noted with a degree of irony that while anti-slavery sentiment in England imposed a nine-hour limit on the workday of slaves in the colonies at the outset of the industrial era, the factory worker at home—man, woman or child—was not thought to merit any protection whatever.[37]

In seeking a political voice, the bourgeois class enjoyed no little success, which it put to use in promoting free trade policies.[38] The working class, in contrast, remained without a voice. Indeed, at a time when technological advances were giving rise to an era of optimism, the outlook for the working class was pessimistic in the extreme. In the early 19th century, David Ricardo (1772–1823), a leading economic theorist, put forward his so-called "subsistence theory of wages" (later known as the "Iron Law of Wages"), which argued that under natural conditions, the worker could command a wage that would allow him to subsist and no more. Only during periods when capital was abundant and labor was scarce could the laborer demand a "market price" that would allow him to thrive. Alas, such periods—as brief as they were infrequent—contained the seeds of their own destruction; prosperity invariably spurred a population boom, ensuring that the growth of the labor pool would outpace the growth of capital and lead workers back to their subsistence wage.[39] Adding to the gloomy outlook was the so-called *Essay on Population* (1798), authored by the English clergyman-turned-economist, Thomas Robert Malthus (1766–1834), who predicted that population growth would always outpace the available food supply. The pessimism of Ricardo and Malthus—which included a belief that any attempt by government to ameliorate the situation of the poor would only magnify the problem by leading to further population growth—gained for the field of economics a reputation as "the dismal science."[40]

Deprived of parliamentary representation, the working class sought for an avenue of redress in popular agitation—first in England in the guise of Chartism, and later, as industry accelerated throughout Europe, in the form of socialism. The roots of the socialist movement were utopian. Imagining that society might be transformed simply by setting good examples, the first socialists established "model" working communities. Wales's Robert Owen (1771–1858), for example, created a factory city at New Lanark, where working conditions were humane, where educational facilities were provided, and where pay was, for that period, strikingly generous. Alas, attempts to reproduce Owen's results in other model communities proved elusive. Meanwhile, in France, the utopian socialist, Henri de Saint-Simon (1760–1825), accepted the existence of separate classes in society, but believed that the well-to-do bore some responsibility for the welfare of the less fortunate.[41] Although Napoleon III and Ferdinand de Lesseps were ultimately to be counted among his disciples, Saint-Simon died penniless after investing his lifesavings in projects to reform society for the benefit of the poor.[42]

The last in the line of utopian socialists was France's Louis Blanc (1811–1882), whose demand that government provide jobs for all eligible workers was made the subject of an experiment during the French Revolution of 1848. Alas, Blanc himself was not placed in charge of the program, which was carried out by hostile officials who saw to its failure. Indeed, it was the betrayal of the Paris working class by the bourgeoisie in that revolutionary year that handed socialism from the utopians to the Marxists—from those who favored peaceful social change by constitutional means, to those who argued for a forceful seizure of the means of production from the "untrustworthy" capitalists.[43] Karl Marx (1818–1883) laid down the battle lines in his 1848 *Communist Manifesto*. Industrial society, he argued, had become increasingly polarized into two opposing camps: a proletarian class of laborers whose tireless work was rewarded with but a pittance of

Opposite: **Illustration from page 11 of *Histoire Socialiste* published under the direction of Jean Jaurès, depicting from bottom left to top right, French Revolutionary proto-socialist, Gracchus Babeuf; 19th-century socialists Henri Saint-Simon, Robert Fourier, Karl Marx and Louis Blanc; anarchist Pierre-Joseph Proudhon; and conspiratorial socialist Louis Auguste Blanqui (Wikimedia Commons).**

Histoire

Socialiste

1789-1900

sous la direction de JEAN JAURÈS

PAR

JEAN JAURÈS *(Constituante ; Législative ; Convention jusqu'au 9 Thermidor)*;
GABRIEL DEVILLE *(Du 9 Thermidor au 18 Brumaire)*;
BROUSSE *(Du 18 Brumaire à Iéna)*;
HENRI TUROT *(D'Iéna à la Restauration)*;
VIVIANI *(La Restauration)*;
FOURNIÈRE et ROUANET *(Le règne de Louis-Philippe)*;
MILLERAND et GEORGES RENARD *(La République de 1848)*;
ANDLER et HERR *(Le Second Empire)*;
JEAN JAURÈS *(La Guerre franco-allemande)*;
DUBREUILH *(La Commune)*;
JOHN LABUSQUIÈRE *(La Troisième République (1871-1885)*;
GÉRAULT-RICHARD *(1885-1900)*;
JEAN JAURÈS *(Conclusion : le Bilan social du XIXᵉ siècle)*.

JULES ROUFF et Cⁱᵉ Éditeurs, 4, Rue La Vrillère, Paris

(Tous droits réservés)

what it deserved, and a bourgeois capitalist class which carried away all the profits. By constantly increasing the misery of the lower orders, the capitalist system must inevitably provoke a worldwide revolution yielding the collapse of capitalism and the rise of socialism—a new commonwealth in which the state would hold monopolies on the production and distribution of goods, and the proletariat (freed at last from the grasping hand of the capitalists) would garner the fruits of their own labor. With the new socialist order established and the age-old class struggle at an end, the state would cease to be necessary and would wither away. By 1889, Marxism had become the gospel of the "Second Socialist International"—a confederation of leading socialists pledged to prepare the world's industrial workers for the coming revolution.

Amid the struggle of classes and the strain of machinery, the idealistic romanticism of the early 19th century gave way to modern "realism"—a desire bordering on religious compulsion to reject façades in favor of a genuine depiction of reality. Photography—"the science and art of producing pictures by the action of light on chemically prepared … plates or films"[44]—first pioneered in France during the 1820s and 1830s by Nicéphore Niepce (1765–1833) and Louis Daguerre (1789–1851), was now well established, and artists of the so-called "academic" school had already mastered the skill of rendering with the brush what the camera could produce by the interaction of light and chemicals. But the preferred subject matter of the academic school reflected society's moral ideals rather than life's harsh truths—something that the spirit of the times

Luncheon on the Grass by Édouard Manet, 1863, Musée d'Orsay, Paris (Wikimedia Commons).

could not abide.[45] There arose in reaction a "realist" school that rejected heroic and idealized themes in favor of ordinary ones—portraying (with a shocking lack of embellishment) the reality that lay beneath the veil of middle-class moralism. Where the nymph of the academic school exalted the scene by her nudity, the unabashed nudes in Édouard Manet's *Breakfast on the Grass* and *Olympia* (1863) cannot in any wise be mistaken for nymphs. The nudity *sans* exaltation provoked a scandal in the art world. This did not, however, prevent Manet (1832–1883) from playing a key role afterwards in the advent of "impressionistic" art (evident in such works as *A Bullfight* [1864] and *The Death of Maximilian* [1867]), wherein minute inspection reveals only a cacophony of colorful swirls, but observation of the whole brings forth a cogent image. In an era of burgeoning technology, it has been argued that impressionism was itself a byproduct of scientific advance, for as Crane Brinton has noted, "Impressionists learned from physics that light was a complex phenomenon put together by the human eye from the prismatic reflections of nature. They proposed to break both light and shadow into their component colors and then allow the viewer's eye to reassemble them."[46]

Critics were certain that the new genre was a form of protest just as "realism" had been, but Manet denied this charge, saying that while such works might "resemble a protest … the painter has only thought of rendering an impression." His apology is sometimes credited with giving "impressionism" its name, although it is more generally attributed to the recognized master of the movement, Claude Monet (1840–1926), who titled one of his paintings *Une Impression*.[47]

Death of Maximilian, by Édouard Manet, 1867, Museum of Fine Arts, Boston (Wikimedia Commons).

In literature, the novel became for "realism" what poetry and drama had formerly been for romanticism.[48] In *Madame Bovary*, the Frenchman Gustave Flaubert (1821–1880) entraps his protagonist in the melancholy of ordinary life, and then allows her to self-destruct as her yearning for romantic escape leads first to ruinous adultery and finally to suicide. In England, the novels of Charles Dickens (1812–1870), though romantic in tone, served the cause of realism by exposing the plight of the underprivileged classes, while the prose of the Russian, Feodor Dostoevsky (1821–1881), explored human irrationality with such intensity as to anticipate the field of psychoanalysis.[49] Music was not so quick to surrender its romantic heritage, which flourished under the artistry of France's Hector Berlioz (1803–1869), Poland's Frédéric Chopin (1810–1849) and Russia's Pyotr Tchaikovsky (1840–1893). But the discipline came to be influenced heavily by the rising tide of nationalism, with national folk melodies influencing the music of the Hungarian, Franz Liszt (1811–1886), the German, Richard Wagner (1813–1883), and the Czech, Antonín Dvorják (1841–1904), while newly contrived national anthems and other patriotic music likewise contributed to popular nationalist fervor across Europe.[50]

Far from being limited to the arts, the transition from romanticism to realism was societal in scope. In politics, the failed revolutions of 1848 transformed the romanticism of the utopian socialists into the realism of the Marxists and anarchists. Nationalism underwent a parallel change. Liberals had tried to unite nations through legislation in 1848. After their failure, the nationalist movements were handed over to the likes of Bismarck who promptly uttered *Realpolitik's* most famed quotation: "Not by speeches and majority votes are the great questions of the day decided … but by blood and iron."[51]

Thus, the year 1848 proved a crucial turning point in the history of Europe. Metternich, the great enemy of nationalism, was cast from office just when sweeping changes in transportation and communication were making it possible to build truly modern nations. But at the same time, disillusionment over the year's failed revolutions delivered the torch of nationalism from the positivists and utopians to a more fanatical breed—men who put nations on a par with the gods, to be served in arms by the whole male citizenry of the state rather than by the mercenaries and dynastic armies of a bygone era.[52]

The current of change engulfing Europe seemed suddenly to achieve a culmination with the publication, in 1859, of Charles Darwin's *On the Origin of Species by Means of Natural Selection*. In it, Darwin argued that a Malthusian "struggle for existence" occurs within all species as their numbers outpace the existing food supply, ending inevitably in the "survival of the fittest"—i.e., of those possessing traits favorable to winning out in the struggle. These favorable traits are then passed on to succeeding generations through a process of "natural selection," while less favorable traits disappear with their less-fit owners, until gradually over time the species evolves. (The related problem of *how* hereditary traits were passed from generation to generation was worked out at about the same time by the Bohemian monk Gregor Mendel [1822–1884], whose experiments in crossbreeding different varieties of peas laid the basis for what we now call autosomal dominant and recessive inheritance. The significance of his discovery, however, was not appreciated until after his death.[53])

Darwin's theory was troubling enough in that it gave a definite alternative to the notion of Godly creation described in *The Book of Genesis*—something that doubters had been seeking since the Enlightenment and that the devout had hoped might never be devised.[54] More troubling, however, was the fact that Darwin's distinctly catchy phraseology had a knack for finding its way into fields in which it had no business—namely, the unrelated social problems of contemporary society. Hence, Herbert Spencer (1820–1903), a proponent of Darwin's views, espied a process of "natural selection" in competitive business pursuits wherein the poor lost out because they did not possess the requisite competitive traits. But even as Spencer deftly adapted Darwinism to the cause of unfettered *laissez faire* capitalism, Karl Marx applied it in an exactly opposite direction— claiming that the Darwinian "struggle for existence" within the realm of natural history was vindication in nature of his own dialectical "class struggle" theory, which was destined, in his view, to end in socialism.[55] The mischief wrought by Social Darwinism—the application of catch phrases like "survival of the fittest" and "natural selection" to the struggle between classes, races, peoples and nations— will become manifest in the ensuing chapters.

Portrait of Charles Darwin seated in a chair, line drawing from still photograph, in volume I of *Charles Darwin, Life and Letters* edited by his son, Francis Darwin (Wikimedia Commons).

Natural Selection:
The Nations Take Sides

The Domestic Affairs of France and Germany, 1870–1914

France: From the Ashes of Defeat

Adolphe Thiers, who headed the Versailles government during the bloody suppression of the Paris Commune, was old enough, at seventy-four, to have served as prime minister during the reign of Louis Philippe. Now, as president of the nascent Third French Republic, he displayed a degree of vigor surprising for his age—managing in just two years to put France back on its feet and pay off the entire five-billion-franc indemnity demanded by the German Empire.[1]

In normal times, he might have looked forward to a prolonged tenure in office on the basis of such an accomplishment. Alas, his elevation to the presidential chair had been an anomaly.

To better understand this, we must return to the National Assembly elections held on February 8, 1871, to replace the fallen government of Napoleon III. In these elections, republican candidates had been at a distinct disadvantage. In the aftermath of the battle of Sedan five months earlier, a provisional government had been proclaimed in the form of a "republic" with a mandate to carry on the war. Led by the patriot, Gambetta, it did so to the bitter end. Indeed, on learning that Bismarck was demanding Alsace and Lorraine as the price of peace, the most radical republicans announced their intention of fighting on even after the fall of Paris.

Alas, the occupation of the capital by Prussian troops on January 29 exposed the patriotic cause as a forlorn hope. By election day, the vast majority

Adolphe Thiers. Image from *History of the Third Republic, 1871–1897* by Pierre de Coubertin (Wikimedia Commons).

of Frenchmen perceived the necessity of peace—even on Bismarck's harsh terms—and they cast their votes accordingly, with the result that the first elected assembly of the "Third *Republic*" was composed overwhelmingly of *monarchist* (rather than *republican*) assemblymen.

Had the monarchists been of a single mind, they might have reestablished the monarchy as their initial act, but they were hopelessly divided into two rival factions—the so-called "Legitimists" favoring the Bourbon candidate, Henri, Count of Chambord (the grandson of Charles X), and the "Orléanists" supporting Philippe, Count of Paris (the grandson of Louis Philippe).[2] As neither faction could command a majority by itself, executive authority was conferred not upon Henri or Philippe as king, but on the liberal monarchist, Thiers, as president.

"Having become unexpectedly chief of the state at seventy-four," says *Encyclopædia Britannica*, "[Thiers] had no desire to descend again to the position of a minister of the Orléans dynasty which he had held at thirty-five." By degrees, possession of the presidential chair convinced him of the merits of republicanism, and by mid–1872, he was citing the divisions within the monarchist party as sufficient cause to adopt "the Republic as the form of government which caused the least division among Frenchmen."[3] Unconvinced by this line of argument, his erstwhile allies in the cause of monarchy maneuvered him out of office and replaced him with the famed soldier, Marshal Patrice de MacMahon, upon whom they could better rely (May 1873).

Three months later, the Count of Paris, who was but thirty-four, agreed to acquiesce in a Bourbon succession if his rival, the Count of Chambord, now fifty-three and without an heir, would designate him as his heir-apparent. The happy compromise opened the way to a Bourbon restoration, and in August 1873 the Assembly formally offered the throne to Henri, Count of Chambord.

Henri's response served as a ready demonstration that the Bourbon species had not evolved since its last representative was chased from the throne in 1830. In October, he announced that he would deign to accept the French Assembly's petition only if France abandoned the tricolor and restored the white *fleur-de-lis*—traditional flag of the absolutist *Ancien Regime*. Marshal MacMahon lamented that if the government were to acquiesce in this obnoxious demand, "the rifles in the army would go off by themselves."[4] Thiers, in mirthful sarcasm, hailed the Bourbon pretender as a new George Washington for the service he had rendered to the cause of French republicanism.[5]

In an effort to salvage the situation, the monarchists of the National Assembly prevailed upon MacMahon to remain in office as a figurehead president for a term of seven years—in effect, to stand guard over the throne until Henri should pass on to his reward and take the *fleur-de-lis* with him, leaving the crown and scepter to his Orleanist rival.[6] To promote this program, the monarchists passed a series of measures tailor-made for a constitutional monarch (1875). But monarchy—constitutional or otherwise—does not thrive when the throne is unoccupied, and in 1876, the republicans obtained a solid electoral majority in the Chamber of Deputies (i.e., the lower house of the new bicameral legislature). President MacMahon promptly dissolved the session, hoping that new elections would reverse the outcome (1877). As so often happens, the opposite occurred. Despite an intense propaganda campaign and a crackdown against the republican press, the republicans not only retained their majority in the Chamber of Deputies (1878), but also won the upper house or Senate (1879).

Defeated in his attempted electoral coup, MacMahon was forced to resign (1879).

His replacement was the staunch republican Jules Grévy, whose leading ambition was to transform the presidency into a ceremonial post so that a strong president might never again threaten the republic.[7] The chief personages in his government were Léon Gambetta (now president of the Chamber of Deputies), and Jules Ferry who, as prime minister, passed measures to solidify the regime's republican foundation—granting freedom of the press, legalizing trade unions, inaugurating a system of public schools (as an alternative to the monarchist-dominated clerical schools), moving the Chamber of Deputies back to Paris from Versailles, reinstating the *Marseillaise* as the national anthem and making Bastille Day a national holiday.[8]

Having firmly established his administration's liberal credentials, Ferry made a bid for conservative support as well by pursuing the newest trend in economics: imperialist colonial expansion— the surest avenue to new markets,

Georges Boulanger, photographed during the 1880s. Atelier Nadar; restored by Adam Cuerden, Gallica Digital Library (Wikimedia Commons).

raw materials and investment opportunities. The conservatives, however, would have none of it. They saw Ferry's colonial efforts as hijacking attention from the nation's prime directive—namely, avenging the disgrace of the Franco-Prussian War.[9]

The bulwarks of French conservatism at this time were the army and the church— the two most esteemed institutions in the state. Champions of the popular desire for revenge against Germany, they were, in domestic affairs, inextricably bound together by a shared sympathy for monarchism. Apprehending in these powerful royalist bastions a standing threat to the survival of the Republic, the government sought for a counterpoise. In January 1886, it elevated to the post of minister of war Georges Boulanger, a radical *republican* general—a rare find in the officer corps of the day—whose unblushing passion for revenge against Germany bade fair to steal the fire of his monarchist fellow officers. Though no orator, Boulanger was capable of thrilling crowds by posing as the heroic "man on horseback" whenever he appeared in public. On Bastille Day, July 14, 1886, he staged a pretentious military parade that transformed him into a national icon.[10]

Scarcely had Boulanger assumed the war ministry portfolio, however, before the government realized that it had let a genie out of the bottle. Fearing now that the man hailed by the mob as "General Revenge" might fan the embers of patriotism into the full flame of a premature war,[11] it sought to be rid of Boulanger—dismissing him from his ministerial post and reassigning him to the provinces. His charisma, however, had already gained him the support of both the radical left and the monarchist right, while the government was less popular than ever due to a domestic scandal in which President Grévy's own son-in-law was found to be handing out Legion of Honor awards in return for cash.

The frantic government now sought to curtail Boulanger's influence by relieving him of his military duties entirely. Alas, by law, this left him free to run for elective office. He announced his candidacy for the Chamber of Deputies in multiple constituencies—a not uncommon practice under the electoral law of the time—and was successful wherever he ran. From the floor of the Chamber of Deputies he declared that the cure to the nation's woes lay in a strengthened presidency. (One gets the distinct feeling that he had a specific candidate in mind in issuing this declaration.)[12] A growing clique of Bonapartists had now joined the others in rallying to him, and in January 1889, he put his popularity to the ultimate test by challenging the government's candidate for the metropolitan district of the Seine. For the first time, Boulanger sought to represent a constituency in Paris itself—the very citadel of republican sentiment. The result was a victory of stunning proportions. He defeated his rival by 80,000 votes. "Had he marched on the Elysée [i.e., the presidential palace] the night of his election," says *Encyclopædia Britannica*, "nothing could have saved the parliamentary Republic."[13]

But Boulanger's boldness in anti–German posturing was not matched by political guile. While his supporters bade him act, he retired for the night to the arms of his mistress.[14] The unexpected reprieve allowed his republican opponents to regain the initiative. A new ministry was formed under Pierre Tirard, the electoral law that had allowed Boulanger to run in more than one district was revoked, and plans were laid to summon the general to the floor of the Senate on a charge of treason. At the very mention of this last proceeding, Boulanger fled to Belgium, and with his flight "Boulangism"[15]— the autocratic movement of which he had been champion—vanished like a phantom. He lived but two more years, virtually forgotten, until, in the words of *Encyclopædia Britannica*, "the world was startled ... on the 30th of September 1891 by hearing that he had committed suicide in a cemetery at Brussels by blowing out his brains on the grave of his mistress, Madame de Bonnemains ... who had died in the preceding July."[16]

In the elections following Boulanger's flight, the monarchists and radical republicans who had rallied to his banner were roundly defeated. Yet the government still presided over a nation divided. Two of its most powerful institutions, the army and the church, remained citadels of anti-republicanism.[17] And now, the eruption of a new scandal stymied the Republic's bid for enduring popular support. Ferdinand de Lesseps, famed for his successful construction of the Suez Canal, had been engaged, during the 1880s, in an effort to replicate his engineering feat across the Isthmus of Panama. A "Panama Company" was duly formed and subscribed to by myriad investors, many of them being people of moderate means willing to entrust their life savings to a project that bore the trusted name of Lesseps. Alas, the engineering capacity of the company could not keep pace with the startling engineering requirements of the endeavor, nor indeed, with the vigor of the mosquitos who spread deadly plagues of malaria and yellow fever among the company's workforce.[18] In 1889, the company went belly up with a debt of $300,000,000. This was bad enough in its financial ramifications, but the ensuing court cases revealed that in an effort to stave off the inevitable, the company had bribed scores of French legislators to keep the truth from investors even as further subscriptions were collected in support of the project. The corruption scandal burst upon the public in 1892, causing a widespread loss of faith in the Republic.[19] If not for the folly of its detractors, the government could not have survived the blow.

The Dreyfus Affair

In 1885, a book entitled *La France Juive* ("Jewish France") was published in Paris, which was received with such acclaim that over the ensuing year one hundred editions scarcely managed to meet the demand.[20] Written by a journalist, Eduoard Drumont, the book bade fair to establish a new standard for literary success, and in the process of doing so, says the *Cambridge Modern History*, it did something else—it "created Antisemitism in France."[21]

In France as elsewhere, of course, Jew-hatred was a very old thing by 1885, but the term "anti–Semitism" had been coined just six years earlier as a label for its newest incarnation—agitated hostility toward the Jewish emancipation movement of the 19th century.[22] Drumont argued that this humanitarian movement—which sought to welcome Jews as full members of their respective societies—was grossly misguided, for it had taken no account of those characteristics—racial and moral—that rendered the Jew an eternal alien, neither amenable to assimilation nor capable of loyalty to the state.[23] In an era when nationalism ruled the spirit, these were serious (if fictional) deficiencies, and the better to guard against the inevitable machinations of a race widely believed to be bent on world economic domination (a kindred anti–Semitic canard that fit hand-in-glove with the notion of the "eternal alien"), Drumont established his own journal, *La Libre Parole* ("Free Speech"), as an organ of vigilance in the cause of French patriotism.

In order that the reader may acquire some sense of this journal's intellectual and literary achievement, we quote an excerpt from a piece, entitled *Jews in the Army*, published in the May 23, 1892, edition. It reads, "What would the kikes do in [the army's] ranks? … Beyond all religious consideration, there exists among the vast majority of military men a feeling of instinctive repulsion against the sons of Israel. One sees in them the usurer who completes the ruination of the indebted officer, the tradesman who speculates on the soldier's hunger, the spy who traffics without shame in the secrets of national defense…. Already lords of finance and administration, already dictating judgments to the courts, they will definitely be masters of France on the day they command the army. Rothschild will deliver the mobilization plans—and one can imagine to what end!"[24]

In their enmity to republican government, a multitude of odd bedfellows found a natural ally and guide in the new anti–Semitism. Says Carlton Hayes, "It appeared as a friend of the workingmen, telling them that their real oppressors were the Jewish capitalists who dominated Republican politics. It enlisted the support of many Catholics by blaming the irreligious and anti–Clerical legislation of the Republic upon the Jews. It adroitly appealed to national patriotism to rid the army of Jewish influence, insisting that the Jews … were in practice the secret agents of their German kinsmen. Thus, anti–Semitism became in France a rallying-cry whereby the Monarchists could draw to themselves numerous diverse elements and gather them into a single Nationalist party, bent upon the overthrow of the 'bourgeois and Jewish' republic."[25]

It remained only to collect the circumstantial evidence, and for readers of *La Libre Parole*, such evidence was myriad and manifest. "The revelations [regarding the Panama Canal Scandal]," notes *Encyclopædia Britannica*, "were in a large measure due to the industry of the *Libre Parole*; and they were all the more welcome to the readers of that journal since it was discovered that three Jews were implicated...."[26] That one of the three was a member of a Jewish banking family of German descent in no way hindered the anti–Semitic conspiracy theory that, among other things, blamed Jewish financiers for France's defeat in the Franco-Prussian War.

But the Panama revelations were small potatoes compared to what came next. In 1894, Captain Alfred Dreyfus, a Jewish officer in the French Army, was court-martialed on a charge of selling strategic information to the Germans. Convicted on the basis of a spurious handwriting sample, he was stripped of his commission in a humiliating ceremony in the courtyard of the *Ecole Militaire* in Paris amid chants of "Death to the Jews!" from a mob outside the gates.[27] Afterwards, he was exiled to the dreaded penal colony on Devil's Island where he was kept in solitary confinement with his ankles chained to his bedpost during sleep.[28]

Initially, the Dreyfus verdict was immensely popular in France, since it jibed so well with prevailing anti–Semitic theory and practice. But if the readers of *La Libre Parole* hoped to use Dreyfus' conviction to confirm their innate prejudices, fate had a cruel blow in store for them: Dreyfus, as it turns out, was innocent. Indeed, the case against him did not even rise to the level of "circumstantial." A discarded message salvaged from a trash bin in the German embassy identified a French traitor, referred to only as "the Scoundrel D." Dreyfus starts with "D," which was good, and Dreyfus was a Jew, which (in the army's view) was even better. But the spurious writing sample—known as the *bordereau*—purportedly serving as the main piece of evidence against him was judged by a handwriting expert from the Bank of France to have been written, very possibly, by someone else.[29]

Hoping for a different conclusion, the army solicited a second handwriting consultation—this time from Alphonse Bertillon. The son of an anthropologist, Bertillon had developed an anthropology-based system for tracking identifying characteristics on criminals with prior records. In the era before fingerprinting, his technique—known as "anthropometry" (or, alternatively, as "Bertillonage" after its creator)—was regarded as "state-of-the-art." The method

Alfred Dreyfus circa 1894, by Aaron Gerschel (1832–1910?) (Wikimedia Commons).

involved measuring the height and width of the head, the length of the middle finger (and of the distance from the elbow to the tip of the same middle finger) and finally of the left foot—"dimensions," says, *Encyclopædia Britannica*, that "...remain practically constant during adult life." Taken together, it was believed that they could render "every single individual ... perfectly distinguishable from others." Henceforward, French criminal records included Bertillon's prescribed measurements together with a mug shot—an imposing tool kit for future positive identification.[30]

One might wonder what all this has to do with handwriting. Well, after his success at police headquarters, Bertillon—who had no prior experience at handwriting analysis—posited that his methodology could be applied to human writing samples with no less facility than to the human skeleton.[31] A single evening of investigation sufficed for him to categorically identify the *bordereau* as being in Dreyfus' hand—a conclusion that was received with transports of joy at the war office (although his fevered explanation of his procedure convinced at least one listener that he was a fugitive from a madhouse).[32] Confronted with differences that even a layman might identify between the handwriting in the *bordereau* and samples obtained from Dreyfus during his interrogation, Bertillon contrived the theory (subsequently presented at trial) that as a means of plausible deniability in the event that he was apprehended, Dreyfus had cleverly *forged his own handwriting to look like a forgery of his own handwriting*.[33]

For a time, the miscarriage of justice went unrecognized. But on reviewing the case in 1896, the army's new chief of military intelligence, Colonel Georges Picquart, proved beyond reasonable doubt that the author of the *bordereau* was not Dreyfus, but a disreputable non–Jewish officer named Ferdinand Walsin-Esterhazy. Justice now hung in the balance, but to pursue it the Army must place its very reputation in peril. And this is where it got itself into trouble. Rather than reopen a case so tidily closed, rather than jeopardize its monarchist aspirations by surrendering the prize of a Jewish traitor supposedly allowed into the army by a republic manipulated by Jews, rather than risk exposure of the bigotry and ineptitude that had allowed an innocent man to be condemned while the actual traitor continued to pass classified materials to the Germans, the French high command exiled Picquart to a post in Algeria in order to silence him. And when the intelligence officer's integrity compelled him to remain obstinate, they dismissed him from his duties and placed him under arrest, while Esterhazy—now known at the highest levels to be guilty—was acquitted, after 3 minutes' deliberation,[34] in a mock court martial attended by patriotic hysteria.

Dreyfus, meanwhile, was left to waste away on Devil's Island until 1898, when the famed novelist, Émile Zola, publicized the scandal in an open letter to the government, entitled *J'Accuse*.[35] Published in Georges Clemenceau's newspaper, *L'Aurore*, on January 13, the thunderbolt proved too much to bear for a nation intent on hiding the truth from itself. Zola was charged with libel, and his trial was rigged so that the issue of Dreyfus could not be specifically addressed. On his way to and from the courtroom each day, the author was accosted by anti–Semitic mobs who shouted obscenities and set his effigy aflame.[36] After two weeks of testimony, he was condemned by a split jury and had to flee to England to avoid imprisonment.

But the case had been dragged into the open, just as Zola intended, and the attention of the world was now riveted on France. The French populace itself was bitterly divided on the issue—some aghast that the army's honor should be brought into question over an issue as trifling as justice, others appalled that justice should be trodden underfoot to save the army's trifling honor. While adherents of the former faction (composed of a coalition of Boulangists, clericals, monarchists and anti–Semites) were far more numerous, prominent politicians like Jean Jaurès (founder of the French Socialist Party) and Georges Clemenceau, who had once called for Dreyfus's execution,[37] were now active participants in the "Dreyfusard" (pro–Dreyfus) camp.

Exasperated by the perpetual disquiet, the newly appointed minister of war, General Godefroy Cavaignac (son of Eugene, the famed "butcher of the barricades"), appeared before the Chamber of Deputies on July 7, 1898, to cite specific documents, previously withheld from the public on a plea of national security, "proving" Dreyfus's guilt—one of them, an apparently damning correspondence between the German and Italian embassies that referred to Dreyfus by name. As he left the rostrum amid the applause of the deputies, it seemed that the matter was finally closed. Within forty-eight hours, however, the irrepressible Colonel Picquart had publicly denounced the incriminating document as a forgery.[38] Cavaignac, who sincerely trusted in its authenticity, sent a junior officer, one Captain Cuignet, to investigate. Surprisingly, Cuignet corroborated Picquart's charge. The memorandum had been pasted together from separate scraps, which was not out of the ordinary in the case of torn up documents recovered by French intelligence from the trash of foreign embassies. The problem in this case, Cuignet discovered, was that the component fragments were not from the same original sheet of paper, as was clearly demonstrated by the presence of discordant watermarks.[39] The document was indeed a forgery—traceable to Major Hubert Henry, an intelligence officer who had secretly fabricated it and had then presented it to his superiors in the guise of newly discovered authentic evidence in a bid to advance his own career. Pressured behind closed doors, Henry confessed to his crime. He was promptly escorted to prison, where, on the morrow, he committed suicide.

Sensing that the knock might come next at his door, Esterhazy fled the country, while the army's chief-of-staff, General Raoul de Boisdeffre (an accomplice to the cover-up), resigned. Once again, the "Affair" blared forth from the front page of every journal, and when it was learned in addition that a file of concocted "evidence" had been withheld from the defense at the original court martial,[40] the civil courts entered the fray, insisting that Dreyfus' conviction should be annulled and that he should be given a chance to clear his name in a new court martial (1899).

Unfortunately, when the new trial convened at Rennes, the military judges succumbed to their innate biases no less readily than their predecessors had done, refusing to admit evidence crucial to the defense—even after Dreyfus' attorney was wounded by a pistol-wielding fanatic outside the courtroom—while giving the Army's witnesses free rein to resurrect discredited arguments and to offer personal assurances of Dreyfus' guilt. With the world looking on, the tribunal shamelessly found Dreyfus guilty again, though it reduced his sentence to ten years and admitted that there were unspecified "extenuating circumstances." (The "extenuating circumstances," one presumes, were that the available evidence did not support the verdict.)

At this juncture, French President Émile Loubet intervened to pardon Dreyfus. On the pleadings of his wife, Lucie, who was certain that the ravages of Devil's Island had left him too weak to survive a second incarceration, Dreyfus reluctantly accepted. A pardon, however, did not address the question of Dreyfus's innocence. Indeed, it implied the very opposite. Nor did it address the larger question of whether the French Republic was to be a nation of laws equally applicable to all, or whether it was to remain in pawn to a monarchist army and church. The new Prime Minister, Pierre René Waldeck-Rousseau, was intent on addressing the second question, and now that republicans of all stripes—including the unruly socialists—recognized the autocratic danger, he was able to form a "Cabinet of Republican Defense."[41] To avert further street hysteria, the new ministry granted an amnesty to all parties involved in the Dreyfus Affair. At the same time, however, it appointed a republican minister of war, who purged the upper echelons of the army of monarchists while appointing avowed republicans in their stead.

It remained only to break the independent power of the church, which now stood alone as France's last bastion of anti-republicanism. A major advantage possessed by the church was its predominant position in the school system. Although Jules Ferry had sought to establish universal secular education at the elementary level during the 1870s, many French schools were still Church-run. Certain that these institutions were schooling the nation's youth in the "evils" of republicanism, the Republic (which, in the church's view, wanted to school that same youth in "atheism and immorality") embarked on a drastic course. In 1901, it decreed the dissolution of a Catholic monastic order known as the "Assumptionists," whose clerical newspaper, *La Croix*, had exhibited grotesque anti–Semitism and anti-republicanism during the Dreyfus Affair. All other monastic orders were required to apply for state authorization, and when fifty-four of them did so, they were rebuffed, meaning that their orders were likewise dissolved. There followed, in 1904, a law giving the state a monopoly on education, thereby depriving 16,000 monastic teachers of their livelihoods.[42] The *coup de grace*, however, was not delivered until a year later with passage of the Separation Law, which unilaterally abrogated Napoleon's century-old *Concordat* with the Pope—including the state obligation to pay the salaries of priests—and firmly established the separation of church and state (1905). Although there were scattered riots when the state claimed ownership of Church buildings,[43] the battle against clericalism (the notion that the church should have authority to intrude in non-religious matters) had been won.

Thus, did the Third Republic emerge triumphant. To many, the outcome seemed paradoxical. Between 1871 and the outbreak of the First World War forty-three years later, the republic was governed by no less than fifty different ministries—its predictable "instability" being the sole constant. But the French system, unlike the British or American, was composed of multiple parties, not just two. Hence, the fall of one ministry and the rise of the next did not entail the replacement of the sitting party by its archrival. Indeed, it need not even herald a change in policy. Frequently, it involved nothing more than an exchange of portfolios between a few sitting ministers—perhaps one or two individuals from one party leaving the coalition, while one or two from another stepped in as replacements. Under perpetual threat from powerful anti-republican forces, the Third Republic—even with its rapid rise and fall of governments—had now proved its resiliency.[44]

There remained but one item of business before it could finally lay anchor in a stormy sea—namely, remediation of the injustice that had brought matters to a head. In 1906, the Dreyfus case was heard for a third time—this time in civil court, and at last, the insipid guilty verdict was overturned. "Like the stories in popular novels," says J. Salwyn Schapiro, "all the heroes were rewarded and all the villains were punished. Dreyfus was restored to the army and promoted in rank. In the very courtyard where he had once been degraded, he was now given the decoration of the Legion of Honor."[45] Once again, a crowd stood outside the *Ecole Militaire* during a ceremony involving Dreyfus, but this time, cries of "Death to the Jews!" were replaced by entreaties to life: "Long live Dreyfus!" and "Long live Justice!" Simultaneously reinstated with the rank of general, Georges Picquart would rise to the office of minister of war in the years leading up to World War I. Émile Zola, who died tragically in 1902 when a faulty stove in his home leaked carbon monoxide, was interred with solemnity in the Pantheon. On the opposite side of the ledger, Edouard Drumont died penniless—his paper, *La Libre Parole*, having gone out of circulation.[46]

Germany Victorious: Bismarck's Reich, 1871–1890

While the fractious Third French Republic engaged in domestic squabbles, the new German Empire sought to forge a single nation out of twenty-six federated states. A constitution, promulgated in 1871, provided the framework by establishing an imperial dynasty hereditary in the House of Hohenzollern, whose seventy-four-year-old representative, Kaiser Wilhelm I, would reign to the age of ninety—playing the part well enough in the estimation of the *Cambridge Modern History*, to become "a venerable figure among the crowned heads of Europe, and a personality which strengthened the monarchic principle in the world."[47] The constitution empowered this living symbol of German unity to appoint an imperial chancellor (i.e., prime minister), to appoint imperial foreign ambassadors, to enter into treaties, and—as commander-in-chief of the army and navy—to declare *defensive* war.[48]

The power to embark on *offensive* war and to pass or veto laws, in contrast, resided in a two-house parliament consisting of an appointed upper house, or *Bundesrath*, and a popularly elected lower house, or *Reichstag*. While both houses possessed the power to pass legislation, each held veto power over the legislation of the other. Consequently, the lower house rarely availed itself of its law-making privilege, choosing instead to use its own threat of a veto to obtain desirable amendments to bills passed down to it from above. Two favorite *Reichstag* tactics were (i) to place a defined time limit on important laws, at the end of which a renewal vote would be required for them to continue in operation, and (ii) to veto efforts by the government to render itself financially independent of the *Reichstag* through permanent indirect taxes—such as those on tobacco and alcohol. (Many parliamentarians recalled only too well how Bismarck had collected and spent such revenues without the consent of the Prussian parliament in 1862.[49]) In this way, the Reichstag ensured its own relevance in the making of laws, and forced the emperor and his chancellor to strive for a working majority.[50]

The lower house's constitutional ability to block new taxes and military outlays under this system, together with its readiness to serve as a mouthpiece of popular opinion in its debating sessions, could be greatly irritating at times. One should not conclude, however, that democracy, or even a true parliamentary system, was intended by the forgoing arrangement. "The Fatherland," says J. Salwyn Schapiro, "was not formed by the absorption of Prussia into Germany, but by the absorption of Germany into Prussia: the part swallowed the whole."[51] This could scarcely have occurred without a proper weighting of checks and balances in Prussia's favor. As a starting point, it is useful to note that neither the kaiser nor his chancellor were responsible to the parliament. Hence, should a major piece of legislation fail to pass into law, the chancellor and his ministry would not fall as in Britain. Rather, it would remain unconcernedly in place.

Moreover, though the various non–Prussian states of the realm controlled 44 of 61 seats in the *Bundesrath*, and though these delegates were chosen by their respective princelings and bound to vote as they were told, this did not give them an equal say—even collectively—with Prussia. For if the chamber sought to pass a measure unfavorable to the chancellor's agenda, Prussia's seventeen delegates (who voted *en bloc* at the chancellor's pleasure) simply vetoed it—the number of votes constitutionally required for a veto being fourteen.

The lower house, or *Reichstag*, it is true, was elected in seemingly egalitarian fashion by universal male suffrage via secret ballot on the basis of "one man-one vote." This represented a tremendous departure from the Prussian Constitution of 1850 under which electoral votes were taken by voice while Prussian police stood by to keep tabs on the voters.[52] Though universal suffrage was nominally in force in the Prussia of that time, the electorate was stratified into three tiers based on tax payment, with each tier electing an equal number of representatives. At first glance, this may seem reasonable, but on closer scrutiny it becomes evident that the resulting system was patently designed to serve Prussia's wealthiest caste. Roughly speaking, in a given constituency, the great mass of ill-paid laborers commanded so little wealth that they all fit into a single tier, with a second tier encompassing the much smaller middle class, and a third, the rich (sometimes no more than a handful of individuals). Yet, despite the discrepancy in numbers, each tier wielded the same electoral clout. Thus, says Charles Downer Hazen, was universal suffrage in Prussia "most marvelously manipulated. The exercise of the right to vote was so arranged that the ballot of the poor man was practically annihilated."[53]

This system remained in effect for elections to the Prussian state legislature (or *Landtag*) during the imperial period, but was not used for elections to the imperial *Reichstag*, where, as stated, the system was truly "one man-one vote." Nevertheless, the Prussian tradition of false democracy was not abandoned under the empire. It was merely implemented differently: through a studied refusal to account for demographic change. As industrialization brought a flood of workers into the nation's cities between 1870 and 1914, creating for the first time a large and politically minded German working class, no attempt was made to realign parliamentary seats to conform to the population shifts. As cities grew, the number of *Reichstag* delegates representing them did not. Thus, even though the poor man's vote was technically equal in weight to that of his richer counterpart, he could not hope to command a representative number of Reichstag seats because the seats simply did not exist. It was, in effect, an entrenched system of "rotten boroughs" in which a "giant" urban constituency of 300,000 voters possessed no more electoral influence than a "dwarf" rural constituency of 15,000.[54]

An examination of the election results of 1907 is sufficient to demonstrate the unfairness of this system. Although more than three and a quarter million votes were cast for members of the socialist Social Democratic Party in that year as against one and a half million votes for the Conservatives, the former, being supported mostly by the poorer urban element, garnered just forty-three Reichstag seats, while the latter, with the backing of the agricultural aristocracy, gained eighty-three.[55] Despite howls of protest, no reform was undertaken prior to the fall of the Hohenzollern regime in 1918.

Nevertheless, it would hardly be correct to say that Germany was rife with discontent—far from it. By the dawn of the 20th century, political unification and the expansion of the railway and canal systems had transformed the kaiser's realm into an economic giant, second in vigor only to Great Britain. She had become the world's innovator in matters ranging from industry to music. With so much success, many Germans were more than willing to place nationalism ahead of democracy, and fealty to the Kaiser ahead of individual freedom. In the popular mind, the Sirens were beckoning Germany to assume her rightful place at the forefront of world affairs; and in order that Germany might pursue this "Teutonic Destiny," German individualism was willing to pay a steep—even exorbitant—price. In the words of one historian, the system was one of "autocracy by consent."[56]

The architect behind it all was Germany's "Iron Chancellor," Otto von Bismarck, who was appointed by the kaiser and responsible solely to him. Although Wilhelm took his own position seriously and did not consent to his chancellor's every policy, he considered Bismarck so indispensable that the latter could count on his firm support.[57] Indeed, the only question on which Wilhelm consistently overruled the great statesman involved whether the latter could resign if he didn't have his way, to which Wilhelm responded "No!" on every occasion until, becoming exasperated by the threat, he changed his answer to "Never!"[58]

The chief ambitions of Bismarck's policy were to keep France diplomatically isolated and thus incapable of embarking on a war of revenge, while consolidating the power of the Prussian monarchy within the newly unified German Empire. As regards the first issue, we shall have more to say in an ensuing section. As regards the second, we may begin by noting that the new empire did not possess the centralized administrative machinery enjoyed by nations with a long history of unity. "The unification of Germany," says *Encyclopædia Britannica*, "was not ended by the events of 1866 and 1871; it was only begun." The component principalities "retained their autonomy except in those matters which were expressly transferred to the imperial authorities."[59] With the exception of those few states that were directly annexed by Prussia for supporting Austria in the war of 1866—the most notable of these being Hanover—they likewise retained their reigning princelings (many of whom were jealous of their own prerogatives) as well as their old bureaucratic traditions and personnel.

In juxtaposition to this, the constitution bestowed upon Bismarck dictatorial authority over all seventeen Prussian votes in the *Bundesrath* and the power to propose legislation, execute existing laws and appoint imperial administrators.[60] Utilizing these powers, he oversaw the passage of a number of centralizing measures in the empire's first years. The minting of a new imperial coinage (bearing Wilhelm's image as a symbol of unity) to replace the varied currencies of the federated states served as a useful starting point, while the ensuing passage of an imperial banking act (1875) together with the creation of an imperial banking system—the *Reichsbank* (1876)—gave the central government the tools necessary to direct monetary policy.[61] Postal services were placed under imperial control, and though a uniform civil code proved elusive for two decades due to competing property statutes within the multitude of principalities, uniform commercial and criminal codes and standardized legal procedures were enacted throughout the empire by the late 1870s, superseding not only a tangle of local Germanic statutes dating as far back as the Middle Ages, but also Austrian law in Bavaria, Swedish law in Pomerania and French law west of the Rhine.[62]

While avoiding a formal takeover,[63] the railway systems of the various states were coordinated under an imperial railway bureau—not the least for military purposes in a nation where compulsory military service was the order of the day and the armies of the federated states were obligated to adopt Prussian drill and terms of service. It had been Bismarck's hope to obtain permanent funding for a standing imperial army with a peacetime strength equal numerically to one percent of the population. The *Reichstag* obtained an early victory over him by limiting military outlays for a term of seven years (or "*septennate*") before application had to be made for a vote of renewal.[64]

The *Reichstag*, indeed, was to serve as the amphitheater for the two major domestic trials of Bismarck's tenure—the *Kulturkampf* and the war on socialism. The German states south of the Main River,[65] which had been appended to the new empire at the end of the Franco-Prussian War, were—in contrast to the rest of the nation—predominantly Catholic. The withdrawal of the French garrison from Rome during that war, had allowed the kingdom of Italy to seize this natural capital of the Italian peninsula from the pope (1870)—something that German Catholics greatly resented—and when, in the same year, an ecumenical council declared the pope infallible in matters pertaining to faith and morals, Bismarck found himself presiding over a region divided in loyalty. Rather than adhere to the Prussian-led agenda of the empire that had just adopted them, the southerners rallied around a newly formed Catholic political party, which promptly captured 63 seats in the Reichstag. To Bismarck's discomfiture, this new "Center Party" (so-called because its 63 seats were located in the center of the assembly hall) soon became a magnet for all segments of society opposed to Prussian domination in Germany—included among whom were the Danes of Schleswig, the Poles of Posen and Silesia, the French in Alsace and Lorraine and the separatist Guelph nobility of Hanover (which had never accepted their principality's incorporation into Prussia).[66]

But the Iron Chancellor was not about to let an "infallible" pope use a Catholic political party to manipulate the secular affairs of Germany. Sermonizing against the government from the pulpit was declared a crime[67]; the Jesuits, allowed into Prussia by Frederick the Great, were expelled; and because religious matters were the constitutional prerogative of the states rather than of the empire,[68] the Prussian *Lantag* (i.e., state legislature—where Bismarck served simultaneously as prime minister) took the lead in passing the wide-ranging anti-clerical "May Laws" of 1873, 1874 and 1875. Whereas Pope Pius had issued a *Syllabus of Errors* (1864), which condemned civil marriage and secular education, the May Laws made civil marriage compulsory, established government control over the hiring and firing of clergy and decreed that clerical candidates must attend government high schools and universities.[69] Pope Pius declared the May Laws invalid, and bade the clergy defy them. Bismarck riposted with his famous phrase, "We shall not go to Canossa, either in the flesh or in the spirit"—a reference to the 11th Century Investiture Controversy, wherein the medieval German emperor, Henry IV, had gone to Canossa in supplication after attempting to defy Pope Gregory VII.[70]

Thus were the battle lines drawn for the crisis between church and state known to history as the *Kulturkampf,* or "struggle for civilization" (a name conjured by liberals and free thinkers who were convinced that the doctrine of papal infallibility and the *Syllabus of Errors* composed nothing less than a war on modernity). Bismarck waged the campaign with no less ferocity than he had waged his wars—hurling recalcitrant priests into jail and confiscating Church property. "So great was the severity with which these measures were enforced," writes Carlton Hayes, "that within a single year six Prussian bishops were imprisoned and in over 1300 parishes Catholic worship ceased."[71] Alas, far from yielding the anticipated result, Bismarck's "Diocletian persecution" merely steeled the resolve of the opposition. Imprisoned clergymen savored their role as martyrs,[72]

Zwischen Berlin und Rom.

Der letzte Zug war mir allerdings unangenehm; aber die Partie ist deßhalb noch nicht verloren. Ich habe noch einen sehr schönen Zug in petto!

Das wird auch der letzte sein, und dann sind Sie in wenigen Zügen matt — — wenigstens für Deutschland.

Kulturkampf caricature "Between Berlin and Rome." The caption reads: (*Pope:*) "The last move was certainly very unpleasant for me; but that doesn't yet mean the game is lost. I have one more very fine move up my sleeve!" (*Bismarck:*) "It will also be the last, and then you are mated in a few moves—at least for Germany." From the German weekly, *Kladderdatsch*, 16 May 1875. Wilhelm Scholtz (Wikimedia Commons).

while, with each passing election, Catholic Center candidates gained more seats in the *Reichstag*. By 1877, their deputation of ninety-two outnumbered any other single party.[73]

By 1878, it was manifestly clear that the *Kulturkampf* had borne poisoned fruit. "The government," says *Encyclopædia Britannica*, "had used all its resources; it had alienated millions of the people; it had raised up a compact party of nearly a hundred members in parliament."[74] And now, owing to the nation's accelerating pace of industrialization, there appeared on the horizon a more alarming menace in the form of socialist agitation among the working class—a problem that the Center Party bade fair to compound by flirting with socialist ideas on behalf of Catholic laborers (a reflection of the Church's traditional role as patron of the dispossessed).[75] Lest an unholy alliance arise between Catholicism and socialism, Bismarck decided that he must "go to Canossa" after all. The death of the headstrong Pope Pius IX (1878) and the accession of the amiable Leo XIII gave him his opportunity. The failed policy of repression was abandoned in stages (a process that consumed the better part of a decade) and cordial relations with the Vatican were restored.

The result was a dramatic reshuffling of the political deck in the *Reichstag*. Hitherto, Bismarck had derived his chief *Reichstag* support from the patriotic National Liberal Party, which had been willing to overlook the chancellor's shortcomings as a democrat and parliamentarian in order to join him in the quest for national unity. The bond with this party was an unnatural one for an authoritarian Prussian militarist. Moreover, the perception that he had become "the lackey of Liberalism"[76] had greatly eroded Bismarck's relations with Conservatives—the main bulwark of his support in the years leading up to the Franco-Prussian War.[77] Now, however, the outbreak of peace with the Catholic Center Party provided Bismarck with a chance to mend fences with the Conservatives. During the *Kulturkampf*, he had indulged the National Liberal's *laissez faire* economic policy as a matter of political expediency. But when French reparation payments ended in 1873, so, too, did the economic stimulus they provided. The result in German financial markets was the so-called "Panic of 1873."[78] From that moment forward *laissez faire* liberalism fell increasingly out of favor and Bismarck came under intensifying pressure from the industrial and agricultural communities to adopt a program of protective tariffs. Free trade, to be sure, had increased the flow of capital, but it had also flooded the market with cheap foreign imports, threatening many nascent domestic industries with stillbirth and driving down agricultural prices. In order that these myriad industries might take firm root on the one hand, and that he might recoup his support among the conservative *Junker* landed aristocracy on the other, Bismarck, in 1879, abandoned the free trade policy of the Liberals, whose support he no longer required, and adopted the program of protective tariffs favored by Conservatives, granting trade concessions only to those nations willing to reciprocate by importing German goods.[79]

It may well be argued that the shift to protectionism strengthened the state's economic foundation. Alas, it created a new specter in social terms. Under the imperial constitution, males over twenty-five years of age were entitled to vote in *Reichstag* elections. Consequently, as protectionism spurred the growth of German industry, urban workers came to encompass an ever-increasing fraction of the electorate—a fraction, moreover, which gravitated by its very nature towards the program of socialist agitators, whose Marxian outcry for an internationalized union of workers seemed the very antithesis of Bismarck's life striving for German national unity.[80] In 1877, socialist candidates secured an unprecedented twelve *Reichstag* seats, prompting Bismarck to gird himself for war with socialism even as he made peace with Catholicism.

Using as a pretext two anarchist attempts on the life of Wilhelm I (which he falsely attributed to socialists), Bismarck issued his opening salvo—convincing the *Reichstag* to pass the infamous "Exceptional Laws" of 1878, whereby socialist books, pamphlets, newspapers, associations and public meetings were placed, one and all, under the imperial ban. In various urban districts the government resorted to martial law, depriving socialist agitators of basic civil protections as police swept in to arrest them. "Practically," says one historian, "a mere decree of a police official sufficed to expel from Germany any one [sic] suspected or accused of being a Socialist.... 1400 publications were suppressed, 1500 persons were imprisoned, 900 banished.... One might not read the works of [the prominent socialist] Lassalle, for instance, even in a public library."[81] Ironically, at the outset of the imperial period, this same Ferdinand Lassalle had convinced Bismarck to adopt universal suffrage in *Reichstag* elections by arguing that "to inject a popular element into the government would mean the 'moral conquest of Germany.'"[82] The reward for accepting this sage advice was that even as Bismarck's reputation changed through twelve years of socialist persecution from that of a Prussian "Diocletian" (as the Catholics had once decried him), to that of a Prussian "Metternich" (as the socialists now did), the number of socialist seats in the *Reichstag* increased to thirty-five.

The realization that his policy was not prospering drove Bismarck to adopt a strategy that would result, paradoxically, in his being "considered the greatest *social reformer,* as well as the greatest diplomat, of his age."[83] In a bid to steal the fire of the socialists, he embarked on a program of benevolent reforms—passing measures to protect workers against illness and injury, and providing them with retirement pensions funded, in part, by the state. The retirement pension was his masterstroke. Bismarck knew that workers were unlikely to agitate against a government that provided them with security in old age. As he himself put it: "Give the workingman the right to employment as long as he has health, assure him care when he is sick, and maintenance when he is old…. [Then the socialists] will sound their bird call in vain; and as soon as the workingmen see that the government is deeply interested in their welfare, the flocking to them will cease."[84] He was, perhaps, not quite right in this estimation, as reflected in the *Reichstag* election returns, but as a means of rendering the workers less revolutionary and more favorable to the state, which (as opposed to, say, a genuine concern for the plight of the working class) was his ultimate motivation,[85] the program was a decided success. Furthermore, it transformed Bismarck's Germany into an unlikely model for social legislators in Britain and elsewhere who would soon seek to emulate the example.

One may marvel at such cleverness, but the fact remains that Bismarck had failed to win an outright victory in either of the domestic crises he faced in the twenty years after unification. And now he was to face a crisis that would end in his downfall. Kaiser Wilhelm I, with whom he worked so well, died in 1888, and was succeeded by his son, the liberal-minded Frederick III. Had Frederick lived, he might have rescued the German political system by making his ministers responsible to parliament in true parliamentary fashion. Alas, at his accession, he was ill with throat cancer sufficiently advanced that he could not speak.[86] He reigned for just three months before death brought his son, Wilhelm II, to the throne.

The new kaiser was just twenty-nine years old, but was strong-willed beyond his years. It was not long before he and his inherited chancellor butted heads. Owing to the results of the *Reichstag* elections of the preceding year, Bismarck could at last count on firm parliamentary support.[87] Unfortunately, in forging Germany's constitution two decades earlier, he had made himself responsible not to parliament, but to the emperor alone. The question of "whether the Hohenzollern dynasty or the Bismarck dynasty should reign,"[88] was thus in the hands of young Wilhelm, who was determined to "drop the pilot"[89] and embark on his own personal rule. When the Kaiser demanded his resignation in 1890, Bismarck had no choice but to submit. After three decades of service, he was asked to remit eleven days' pay—his quarterly salary having been paid on January 1 (for the period ending March 31) and his dismissal having come on March 20.[90] We must leave him now to the writing of his memoirs, which helped him to assuage his bitterness over this fate. We shall have occasion to meet him again, however, in the arena of his greatest triumphs when we examine the era's foreign affairs.

Kaiser Wilhelm's Reich

At Wilhelm II's accession, the German Empire was rapidly emerging as an industrial giant. Whereas more than half of the population had been employed in agriculture

"Dropping the Pilot." Kaiser Wilhelm dismisses Chancellor Bismarck, by John Tenniel (Wikimedia Commons).

at the end of the Franco-Prussian War, the trend had since moved decidedly in the opposite direction. By 1907, nearly fifteen million workers were engaged in industry and commerce as against less than ten million in agriculture.[91] During the 1890s, Germany surpassed Great Britain in steel production and achieved near parity in the production of coal.[92] While it is true that rampant intellectual property theft allowed German exporters to flood foreign markets with cheap facsimiles (sometimes with counterfeit British labels), Germany became so adept at rendering legitimate advances to industry through the application of science that the label "Made in Germany" became a mark of veneration in international trade.[93]

Concomitant with this burgeoning industrialization, Bismarck's anti-socialist legislation was allowed to expire (1890).[94] Free from the constraints of martial law, the socialist Social Democratic Party promoted the formation of trade unions, led the fight for improved working class conditions and lobbied for democratic constitutional reforms (such as responsible ministerial government).[95] In the elections of 1912, the Social Democrats would command 4.25 million votes—up from 1.5 million at the time of Wilhelm's accession[96]—a far higher total than any other single party, although as we have seen the empire's rigged voting system prevented this from being reflected fairly in the composition of the *Reichstag*. Moreover, as there were not less than fourteen political parties represented in the lower house in that year—most if not all of whom would have no truck with socialism—the Social Democrats found themselves perennially in the opposition in spite of their poll numbers.[97]

The party that tended to get its way in Wilhelm II's Germany was the Conservative Party, dominated by the Junker military aristocracy—a class devoted heart and soul to the person of the kaiser and opposed heart and soul to the notion of agricultural free trade (as this would drive down the prices of their produce). At the outset of the reign, it seemed that affairs might go against the Junkers, for Wilhelm fancied himself a champion of the working classes, whom he hoped to win over by expanding Bismarck's program of benevolent social legislation. Owing to the demand of the industrial classes for a reduction in food prices, Wilhelm's first chancellor, Leo Graf von Caprivi (served, 1890–1894), concluded a series of free trade agreements that allowed Russia, Austria-Hungary, Romania and Italy to flood the German market with cheap foodstuffs as

Kaiser Wilhelm II of Germany, 1902. Photographic portrait by court photographer Thomas Heinrich Voigt (Wikimedia Commons).

rapidly as German industrial products had been flooding in the opposite direction. The Junkers, however, riposted with the formation of an "Agrarian League" (or "League of Landlords") to lobby for its interests, and although it took the better part of a decade, a return to the policy of agricultural protectionism was ultimately achieved (1902).[98] (It did not hurt the Junkers' cause that by that date Wilhelm had come to regard the working classes as a "treasonable horde" owing to their increased support for the Social Democrats.[99])

Within the *Reichstag*, the Conservatives proved adept at shifting their party alliances to obtain their ends. In 1907, for example, they sided with the National Liberals to procure passage of a controversial colonial budget despite an ongoing uproar over German atrocities committed against natives in the colonies. Then, in the same year, they switched their alliance to the Catholic Center—whom they had all but denigrated as a party of papist internationalists during the colonial vote—to prevent passage of an inheritance tax that would have placed a heavy burden on landed interests. (To the chagrin of the commercially minded National Liberals, taxes were placed instead on banking, stocks and articles of consumption.)[100]

Towering above it all (or at least meddling in everything) was Wilhelm II—the very model of a modern German kaiser when it came to industry, the arts and scientific advance, but an utter anachronism when it came to government, which he regarded as a matter of personal rule by divine right. Experience changed this opinion not a whit. Twenty-two years into his reign, he declared, "I ... consider myself a chosen instrument of Heaven, and I shall go my way without regard to the views and opinions of the day."[101] Intelligent, but impetuously ill-mannered, he had a passion for public speaking, and a knack for impolitic pronouncements—as when he told England's *Daily Telegraph* in 1908 that while he, personally, was fond of Great Britain, his people were not. (The truth was something very like the opposite, as was shown by his repeated diplomatic provocations toward Britain and by the indignant domestic response when his musings about the sentiments of his people were published.) In the same interview, he "reminded" the British populace that he had provided their government with the strategy for victory in the Boer War.[102] (In point of fact, German sentiment—the kaiser's included—had favored the Boers.) But even if, as *Encyclopædia Britannica* notes, "there were obvious difficulties in ... controlling the utterances of a ruler, vigorous, self-confident and conscious of the best intentions, who was also the master of many legions, whose military spirit he could evoke at will,"[103] it remains hotly debated to this day how much impact he actually exercised over political affairs—some scholars branding him an overblown nuisance, others crediting him as a true practitioner of personal rule.[104]

In his own mind, he was the center of everything. From the time of his birth, he possessed a palsied left arm—the result of trauma to the corresponding nerve plexus during delivery—and the barbarity of his physicians in their useless attempts to reverse this injury only ensured that he would be scarred emotionally as well as physically. According to his biographer, J.C.G. Röhl, the prince was invited by these sage clinicians to while away the hours of his youth contorted into arm- and neck-stretching devices that would have occupied honored places in a medieval torture chamber.[105] To compensate for his deformity in later years, the kaiser accoutered himself in military regalia and identified himself time and again with the armed forces of which he was constitutionally commander-in-chief. "You are now my soldiers; you have given yourselves to me body and soul,"[106] he said on one occasion; and on another, "the soldier and the army, not parliamentary majorities, have welded together the German Empire—my confidence is placed in the army."[107]

His military chauvinism in no way impeded his despotic pretensions. It won the allegiance of the Junkers (from which class the officer corps was drawn) and of industrial titans like Alfred Krupp and August Thyssen (the chief producers of steel and armaments). At the grassroots level, most Germans shared Wilhelm's reverence for the army—in part, it cannot be denied, owing to the great victories of 1866 and 1870, but also, as H.G. Wells has noted, because "the German people was methodically indoctrinated with the idea of a German world-predominance based on might, and with the theory that war was a necessary thing."[108]

The cultural milieu seemed likewise to favor in the kaiser's despotism. In school, children learned four R's rather than three, with the fourth being Respect for authority.[109] To round it all out, the state, of which he was the living symbol, provided efficient, even paternalistic, government, while the inexorable advance of German science and industry bade fair to raise the "Teutonic Race" to its "rightful" position at the pinnacle of world affairs.[110]

The hard truth, however, was that the status quo was unsustainable. In denying a political outlet to the roiling social forces created by industrialization, Germany's ruling elite had pushed the German polity to the brink of being "ungovernable."[111] If revolution was not as yet in the air, there were strikes and street demonstrations from time to time[112]—clear evidence that the hard-put working classes would not forever be content to play the role of helots under a Spartan military regime.[113] The military build-up, moreover, which now included an aggressive naval program, was proving an expensive proposition that required perennial deficit spending. By 1913, the national debt stood at 490 billion marks despite the passage of a property tax in the preceding year.[114] While German citizens were left to ponder this number, an arrogant army officer created a public scandal by striking a disabled Alsatian shoemaker with his sword. The kaiser and the army took measures to whitewash this so-called Zabern Affair, but the attempt merely provoked further public indignation and a vote of censure in the *Reichstag*.[115]

Many authorities argue that Germany's ruling elite sought to avert further domestic crises by channeling discontent at home into patriotic forays abroad[116]—a theory that has the virtue of making it easy to blame Germany for the outbreak of the First World War. If so (and the notion has its modern skeptics[117]), the regime would have done better to continue with its domestic crises—for as we shall see Germany's military build-up and apparent hegemonic ambitions had driven her neighbors into a hostile alliance, raising the specter of a war on two fronts.[118]

5

Great Britain After Palmerston, 1865–1914

While the German government clung to authoritarianism, its counterpart in Britain entered upon a great era of liberalism and democratization following the death of the 80-year-old Henry John Temple—Lord Palmerston—who expired at Brocket Hall on August 18, 1865. Incapacitated by gout, Palmerston had retained his humor to the last—comforting his physician with the assurance, "Die? My dear doctor, that is the last thing I shall do."[1] In the realm of diplomacy, says Trevelyan, he had been "born to shine, and he shone with a lustre that no one can deny, though the amount of gold that went to make the glitter was then, and always will be a subject of agreeable controversy."[2] Although he had done much to suppress the slave trade and had championed the cause of oppressed peoples abroad, his liberalism at home did not extend beyond the commercial class. His attitude towards the workers never changed, and he opposed extending the franchise to them to the bitter end. Despite this, British laborers idolized him—in part because of his bravado in foreign affairs, but also because his well-known enthusiasm for sports and other amusements made him seem a kindred spirit.[3] When they came out eagerly to see him speak in the 1860 election cycle, John Bright hissed, "They rush to do honour to the man who despises and insults them."[4]

Faced with his intransigence, proponents of further franchise reform raised the flag of surrender and awaited the day that he should leave office. His death released them from their bondage.[5] By now the old division lines between Whig-Peelite "free-traders" and Conservative "protectionists" had given way to a new political order pitting Liberals (whose views would have been regarded as "radical" in the preceding era) against Conservatives (whose views had been tempered by two decades in opposition). Palmerston's government was succeeded by a new Liberal ministry with "Finality Jack" Russell as prime minister and William Ewart Gladstone as chancellor of the exchequer.

Gladstone had started his career as a thoroughgoing Tory, first rising to prominence as a disciple of Robert Peel. At one time, he had opposed further extension of the franchise more stridently than old "Finality Jack" himself, but both had now converted to the cause. For Gladstone, the crossing of the Rubicon came at the height of the American Civil War, when cotton imports from the South virtually ceased owing to the Union blockade. In Lancashire, England, thousands of millworkers were thrown out of work as their mills shut down for lack of raw material, but such was their commitment to the North's fight against slavery that they scarcely raised a voice in protest. Gladstone was astonished at this self-control and was convinced that those who possessed it should also possess the right to vote. His subsequent declaration that it was "a shame and a scandal that bodies of men such as these should be excluded from the parliamentary franchise"[6] greatly irritated Palmerston, who retorted that it would be no less absurd to enfranchise women.[7]

But Palmerston was gone now, and Gladstone seized the moment to put forward a moderate reform bill extending the franchise to a portion of the agricultural and urban working classes (February 1866). The bill did not prosper—being opposed not only by the Conservatives (who felt that it went too far), but also by many Liberals (who felt, with equal fervor, that it did not go far enough). Gladstone warned the House, "You cannot fight against the future,"[8] but the bill went down in defeat, and the Russell-Gladstone ministry went with it. The stage was now set for one of the most remarkable turnings of the political tables in modern British history—the passage of a reform bill by the Conservative Party at the behest of their long-time leader in the House of Commons, Benjamin Disraeli.

A master in the arts of oratory and political opportunism, Disraeli was born into the Jewish faith on December 21, 1804. When he was thirteen, his father had a falling out with the executive board of the local synagogue. So bitter was this rupture that the elder Disraeli instructed Benjamin and his other children to convert to Christianity, which they duly did. On completing his schooling, the young Disraeli entered upon a legal career, but finding his early experiences not to his liking, he turned to speculation, managing to lose everything he had and more in a South American mining scheme. He ventured next into journalism, obtaining financial backing to establish a newspaper "to rival the *Times*."[9] The rivalry lasted for six months before the paper went bankrupt.

He was now twenty-one years old. Before he was twenty-two, he would be famous. The medium of his success was his first novel, *Vivian Grey*, an "insolently clever"[10] instant best-seller made all the more mysterious in having been published anonymously (1826). Identified at last as the author, he became equally reviled as an upstart who dared to lampoon the ruling class[11] and the toast of high society—accepting invitations everywhere and arriving in the guise of a dandy, bedecked in jewelry (including rings worn on the outside of his gloves) to complement a wardrobe of gaudy attire and curly shoulder-length hair.[12] Lord Bulwer vividly records that in his first encounter with Disraeli the latter "wore green velvet trousers, a canary-coloured waistcoat, low shoes, silver buckles, lace at his wrists and his hair in ringlets."[13]

Alas, continuing financial troubles and the vitriol unleashed upon him by his literary and social critics led to a nervous breakdown that put Disraeli out of commission for an extended period.[14] At length, he sought solace in travels abroad, making it as far as Jerusalem while pursuing a generally successful literary career—though not successful enough to get him out of debt. He returned to England about the time of the Great Reform Bill of 1832 and mingled once more with society's elites, included among whom were several leading politicians. Giving thought to a political career, he attended a highly anticipated parliamentary debate featuring some of the best speakers of the day. He left the building utterly convinced that he could outshine the lot of them—so much so that he declared to the astonished guests at an exclusive dinner attended by Lord Melbourne that he would be prime minister one day.[15]

This bold prediction seemed very unlikely to be fulfilled. His initial forays into politics ended in failure. His flamboyance, his novels and his bourgeois origins marked him out as a radical, and he made multiple unsuccessful runs as an "independent" candidate before he hit on the winning formula. In 1837, on his fifth try, he sought and gained office as a Tory—having the subtlety to realize that his origins and viewpoints were a dime a dozen on the Whig benches, but would make him one of a kind among the aristocratic opposition.[16]

Peel thought him unimpressive, and on becoming prime minister in 1841, he refused Disraeli's request for a government office. Much aggrieved, Disraeli sought his own way forward. He fell in with a group of Cambridge-educated MPs who had formed a "Young England" movement. Their credo mixed nationalism with a belief that the ruling class had a moral obligation to ameliorate the plight of the poor (albeit through chivalrous paternalism rather than by extending the vote). In the ensuing years, he applied his literary skills to the cause, publishing three successful "political novels,"[17]—*Coningsby* (1844), *Sybil* (1845) and *Tancred* (1847)—to promote Young England's message. The group disbanded in 1845, but by then Disraeli was making a reputation for himself on the Tory backbenches by questioning Peel's trustworthiness as leader of the Conservative Party. Accusing the prime minister of being more Whig than Tory, he created much mirth in a February 1845 Commons address with the quip that Peel "had caught the Whigs bathing and walked away with their clothes," becoming thereafter "a strict Conservative of their garments."[18] When Peel proceeded to champion the cause of Corn Law repeal, Disraeli became more vitriolic. He accused the party leader of being utterly unprincipled—declaring that for decades he had "traded on the ideas and intelligence of others," and that his pilfering of the Anti-Corn Law League platform was only the latest example in a career of "political petty larceny."[19] His sarcastic and scathing denunciations elicited rousing cheers from those who felt betrayed by the prime minister and catapulted him to the forefront of the Protectionist opposition in the House of Commons.

For the time being, he ranked behind Lord Edward Smith Derby (the Protectionist leader in the House of Lords) and Lord George Bentinck (the Protectionist leader in the Commons). But in the elections of 1847, Baron Lionel de Rothschild won a seat for London, and the situation changed. As a Jew, Rothschild was ineligible to take his seat (the oath of office requiring a profession of Christianity). A measure was brought forward to remove this disability. Bentinck supported it, provoking such outrage among his fellow Protectionists that he resigned in disgust, leaving the party without a leader in the Commons. Notwithstanding the fact that he had also voted in favor (the only Protectionist other than Bentinck to do so), Disraeli was the inevitable choice to succeed to the position.

The matter was settled in 1852, when Palmerston's famous tit-for-tat brought down Lord John Russell's Liberal ministry. Queen Victoria promptly called on Lord Derby to form a minority Conservative government. For the post of chancellor of the exchequer, Derby chose Disraeli—formally elevating the latter to second in command in the Conservative Party and leader of the House of Commons. It was the first Conservative ministry since the fall of Peel, and when Derby tried to inform the aged and now nearly deaf Duke of Wellington of his cabinet choices, Wellington cried out repeatedly, "Who? Who?" at the unfamiliar names. The Whig opposition afterwards derided Derby's cabinet as the "Who? Who? Ministry."[20]

Disraeli had been protectionism's leading voice for years, but he well knew that there could be no turning back the clock. The era of Corn Law protectionism, he conceded to his confederates, was "not only dead, but damned."[21] His economic measures during this ministry included lowering the tariff on tea and the tax on malt—the former making the national beverage more affordable and the latter pleasing beer brewers and pub patrons alike.[22] His budget proposal for 1853, however, was a precarious hodge-podge aimed at maintaining free trade on the one hand and providing non-protectionist incentives to domestic agriculture on the other. Much to the delight of the old Peelites (one of whom offered the anti–Semitic comment that "Jews make no converts"[23]), the budget was voted down and the ministry fell.

The next six years were spent in opposition, but in 1858, Derby and Disraeli paired up again for a second try. On this occasion, Disraeli oversaw the belated passage of a Jewish Emancipation Bill (which finally allowed the perennially elected Baron Roth-schild to become Britain's first Jewish MP), and the Government of India Act, which ended the British East India Company's rule in that colony on the heels of the violent Indian Mutiny of 1857. It was during this ministry, as well, that Disraeli first attempted to pass a Conservative reform bill in order to avert the passage of a more radical measure by the Liberals.[24] The measure failed, and Derby's government resigned (1859).

Lord Palmerston's return to power at this juncture took reform off the table until his death in 1865, and when the Russell-Gladstone Reform Bill foundered in the face of Conservative and Radical opposition the following year, passion for reform intensi-fied throughout the country. Derby and Disraeli were now in office again and had only been there for a few weeks when London's workers were invited to attend a pro–Reform "mass meeting" in Hyde Park. The government forbade this assembly, sending police to lock the gates. Undeterred, the workers showed up in throngs (July 23, 1866). Accord-ing to the *Cambridge Modern History*, "The railings gave way before the pressure of the thousands who surged round them or hung upon them; and the demonstrators, a good-humoured laughing crowd, thus triumphantly took possession of the Park."[25] Der-by's government backed down and let them stay. Reform was now inevitable, and in the midst of the crisis, Disraeli perceived the opportunity of a lifetime—one that would allow him to "dish the Whigs" and make the Conservative party relevant in British pol-itics again after two decades in the wilderness.[26]

Hitherto it was taken as gospel that only the Liberals could bring about suffrage reform. But Disraeli held a different view. For if the Conservatives were now to pro-pose a reform bill similar to that just put forward by Gladstone, the chances of success would be significant. The Liberals simply could not oppose a measure that they had rec-ommended only months before. But if it passed now, all the credit would go to Disraeli and the Conservatives. Indeed, Disraeli's initial proposal to his fellow party members was to bring forth Gladstone's bill virtually unaltered, but now *under Conservative aus-pices*—outdoing even Peel in catching the Whigs bathing and walking away with their clothes.[27] Some of his fellow Conservatives failed to appreciate the humor in this sugges-tion, but Disraeli's mind was made up. When changes to the proposal failed to conciliate the leading naysayers in the cabinet (among them the future Lord Salisbury, then known as Viscount Cranborne), Disraeli let them resign in protest and moved ahead.

His draft bill was submitted to the House of Commons in March 1867. It was more moderate than Gladstone's, but it would not remain so. The dissatisfied Liberals pro-posed one amendment after another. Disraeli's only criteria for accepting these (whether he favored them personally or not) were (i) that they would command a majority in the upcoming vote; and (ii) that they were not put forward directly by his nemesis, Glad-stone.[28] (It is worth mentioning that John Stuart Mill suggested extending the franchise to women at this time—a progressive notion that the House received with hilarity. Dis-raeli dismissed the idea without comment.[29])

The final bill, which passed the House of Commons on July 16, 1867, was far more radical than initially envisaged, enfranchising all working-class heads of households (including working class renters paying more than £10 rent annually), while modestly reducing the 1832 voting qualifications for tenant farmers. The electoral rolls were thereby increased nationally from 1,353,000 to 2,243,000.[30] In retrospect, the increase hardly seems overwhelming, but at the time even Lord Derby described the granting of "household suffrage" as "a leap in the dark," while the famous (and alarmed) historian, Thomas Carlyle, likened it to "shooting Niagara."[31] Robert Lowe, an anti-reform Liberal who viewed democracy as being tantamount to "mob rule,"[32] issued the admonition that he and his fellow parliamentarians had now to "educate our masters."[33] Disraeli, however, was elated. By his "audacity and subtlety and resourcefulness," says Hazen, he had "succeeded in getting a very radical bill adopted by the very same legislators who the year before had rejected a moderate one."[34] His "supreme effort to win the masses to Conservatism" was now accomplished.[35] He may be forgiven if it failed of its purpose in the ensuing elections.

Seven months after the bill's passage, Lord Derby, crippled by gout, resigned as prime minister (February 1868). Queen Victoria promptly invited Disraeli to succeed him. Disraeli had already ingratiated himself with the queen. During the Conservative ministries of 1852 and 1858–1859, he had sent her daily reports from the House of Commons, which she likened to passages from his novels.[36] Moreover, during his most recent stint in opposition, he had spoken eloquently in favor of a lasting monument to her deceased husband, Prince Albert, whom he described as possessing "one of those minds which influence their age and mould the character of a people."[37]

Even as he assumed office, however, a crisis in Ireland was to hand the initiative to his archrival, Gladstone. The abuse of the Irish peasant had, if anything, grown more acute since the potato famine. Attempts by absentee British landlords to update farming methods on the island led to large scale evictions of uneducated, destitute peasants as people familiar with the new techniques moved in to replace them.[38] While Europe as a whole experienced unprecedented population growth, the population of Ireland continued to plunge, declining from 8,000,000 in 1845 to 5,600,000 in 1865 under the dual scourge of starvation and emigration.[39]

Amid the discontent, Irish radicals established the Fenian Brotherhood, a secret organization dedicated to Irish independence (1858). At the end of the American Civil War (1865), Irish expatriate veterans from the Union and Confederacy joined the movement in droves and its methods became more violent.[40] In June 1866, an armed band of Irish American Fenians crossed the Niagara River into Canada and made a bloody, if unsuccessful, assault on Fort Erie. In September of the following year, pistol wielding Fenians attacked a police van bearing two of their compatriots to prison in Manchester, killing one of the officers in the van's escort. In November, the Fenians set off a bomb at London's Clerkenwell Prison in a botched attempt to free one of their brothers. The explosion killed twelve and wounded more than one hundred in the surrounding community.[41] Michael Barrett, one of the perpetrators, was afterwards publicly hanged. (His was the last public execution in British history, for an Act banning public executions was passed later in the year.)[42]

The Russell and Derby governments responded to these outrages with repression—twice suspending habeas corpus in Ireland, while appointing a special commission to preside at the trials of apprehended Fenians (1866–1868). But the abiding inequity of

THE DERBY, 1867. DIZZY WINS WITH "REFORM BILL."

Mr. Punch. "DON'T BE TOO SURE; WAIT TILL HE'S *WEIGHED.*"

Cartoon by John Tenniel, for *Punch* of May 25, 1867. The leading jockey is Benjamin Disraeli; William Gladstone is close behind at left. The Reform Bill referred to ultimately became the 1867 Reform Act (Wikimedia Commons).

Protestant minority rule in an island of Roman Catholics (based, moreover, on a centuries' long policy of pitiless land confiscation by the British) could only produce an abiding discontent among the latter who lived, in Hazen's phrasing, as "a subject people in their own land" and "could not pass a day without feeling the bitterness of their situation."[43] Within weeks of Disraeli's assumption of the premiership, the matter came up for debate in the Commons. Hitherto, parliamentary discussion of the Irish plight had

VANITY FAIR. Jan. 30, 1869.

No 13. STATESMEN, No. 1.

"He educated the Tories and dished the Whigs to pass Reform, but to have
become what he is from what he was is the greatest Reform of all."

Caricature of Benjamin Disraeli in *Vanity Fair,* 30 January 1869. It appeared with the caption: "He educated the Tories and dished the Whigs to pass Reform, but to have become what he is from what he was is the greatest Reform of all." Carlo Pellegrini (Wikimedia Commons).

rarely led to practical solutions, but on this occasion, Gladstone boldly assailed the issue at its very root—calling for the disestablishment of the Anglican Church as the official church of Catholic Ireland. In so doing, says the *Cambridge Modern History*, he "altered in a moment the whole position of the Irish question."[44] His motion united those wings of the Liberal Party that had been divided on the question of Reform, while rallying Irish and non–Conformist MPs to the Liberal banner. Disraeli was caught entirely off guard and could only make a stumbling rebuttal.[45] An attempt to amend Gladstone's motion resulted in a defeat for the government, and when new elections were held in November 1868 with the question of disestablishment as the dominant issue,[46] the Liberals won an overwhelming victory—scoring particularly well among the newly enfranchised working-class voters whom Disraeli had sought to win over with his Reform Act.[47] Ironically, Gladstone lost his seat as MP for South Lancashire (which had not forgiven him for supporting Reform), but was returned for Greenwich, which, after the custom of the day, had also placed him on the ballot.[48] Rather than reconvening Parliament to submit his resignation, Disraeli resigned on the spot, thereby establishing a new precedent. In consolation for his loss, Queen Victoria offered Disraeli a peerage, and when Disraeli declined the honor in order to remain in the House of Commons, she created his wife "Countess of Beaconsfield" instead.[49] Victoria had occasion to miss him immediately, for when Gladstone appeared in audience for the traditional hand kiss, she found his sermonizing insufferable compared with Disraeli's charm.

William Ewart Gladstone, unknown author, from *Manchester Faces & Places,* Artistic Printing Company, 1901, p. 6 (Wikimedia Commons).

Gladstone and Disraeli shared the distinction of being the first leaders of their respective parties to be born in the 19th century. Likewise, they were the first to have entered parliament *after* the Great Reform Bill of 1832. Introduced for the first time at a dinner party in 1835, they took an immediate dislike to each other. Now they had risen to the forefront of their respective parties, and for the next twelve years, says Oman, Great Britain was "to be confronted by two rivals, one of whom offered it internal political reform, the other imperial greatness."[50] Their rivalry would be the predominant feature of British politics until death removed one of them from the scene.

Just as Disraeli's youth had not presaged his future as a Conservative, there was little in Gladstone's early life to suggest that he would become the era's great Liberal. Schooled at Oxford, he so distinguished himself in an 1831 address before the Oxford Union *against* the Great Reform Bill that Bishop Charles

Wordsworth foretold his future as prime minister.[51] In his first parliamentary run, he stood successfully as the Tory candidate for Newark, taking his seat as an MP in January 1833. His maiden speech cautioned against emancipating Britain's colonial slaves too precipitously. He likewise opposed labor reform and the removal of Jewish disabilities (citing in the latter case an alleged "theological unfitness of the Jews to sit in parliament"[52]). Deeply religious—he was a committed Anglican Evangelical who considered a career in the church before entering politics—he published a much-read (and criticized) tract in support of the established church, including its branch in Ireland, in 1838. But he also possessed a keen financial mind, and Sir Robert Peel was quick to recognize his potential. In 1841, the Tory prime minister appointed him vice-president of the Board of Trade, in which capacity Gladstone abandoned his former protectionist views and played a pivotal role in the tariff reforms of 1842. He resigned briefly over Peel's decision to conciliate Irish Catholics with a grant to the Roman Catholic College at Maynooth (1845), rejoined the cabinet in time to support Corn Law Repeal, and, after Peel's ouster, won election as MP for Oxford (one of Parliament's most coveted seats).

Siding with the Peelites after the breakup of the Tory Party, he was invited by Lord Aberdeen to assume the office of chancellor of the exchequer in 1853. Thus, says *Encyclopædia Britannica*, "he entered on the active duties of a great office for which he was pre-eminently fitted by a unique combination of financial, administrative and rhetorical gifts." His proposed budget for 1853, which contained strict economies and envisioned the eventual abolition of the income tax, "held the House spellbound," but his plans were overborne by the unexpected outbreak of the Crimean War.[53]

At this stage, his days as a Liberal still lay in the future. His attitude rather was that of a Christian missionary who approached politics as a "moral crusade." In 1849, he established a home for the redemption of prostitutes, and it was his somewhat peculiar habit to proselytize among London's prostitutes for their salvation when his workday in the Commons was done (all the more peculiar in that he was attracted to these women to the point of obsession—a fault for which he regularly scourged himself with a whip).[54] In 1853, he spoke against a National Education Bill proposed by John Russell out of concern that state control of the schools would entail their secularization.[55] Similarly, he opposed the Divorce Bill of 1857 on religious grounds. In 1852, and again in 1858, we find him giving serious thought to accepting a cabinet post in the Conservative governments led by Derby and Disraeli. Indeed, in 1859, he sided with Derby's government in the confidence vote that led to its fall.[56]

Ultimately, however, he remained in the Whig-Peelite coalition, serving again as chancellor of the exchequer during Palmerston's last ministry (1859–1865). From this point forward, he evolved those liberal attitudes that would mark his later career. Free trade had been his earliest Liberal opinion, and he had been its leading proponent since the days of Peel. Under Palmerston, he concluded the 1860 Commercial Treaty with France—for he believed that reciprocal trade agreements would promote harmony between nations by aligning their financial interests, and hoped to see the principle applied generally to lessen the chances of war.[57] Never a militarist, he criticized the raising of loans to fund Britain's military adventures, arguing that the British people would be less eager for a fight if they were made to foot the bill directly through increased taxation.[58] His budgets under Palmerston were a marvel of economy, reducing at one and the same time the public tax burden and the national debt. Commerce increased "by leaps and bounds" as barriers to free trade were removed.[59] Notably absent from his economic liberalism, however, was any notion of the modern welfare state. In Gladstone's view, it was incumbent on the individual to find his own way in the world. His financial measures, therefore, were aimed at providing increased economic opportunities, not handouts.[60]

His budgetary accomplishments brought him well-deserved plaudits, but his conversion to Liberalism in other venues—most notably on the questions of the Irish Church and franchise reform—cost him his Oxford seat in the election of 1865 and his South Lancashire seat in the election of 1868. Still, his star was undeniably on the rise. When Russell succeeded Palmerston as Prime Minister (1865), Gladstone became, for the first time, Liberal leader in the House of Commons. Two years later, on Russell's retirement, he became the avowed leader of the entire Liberal Party—and now, at age 59, the election of 1868 made him prime minister of England.

He would hold the office on four separate occasions over the next twenty-six years, carrying out much needed domestic reforms. The issue that obsessed him, however, was Irish emancipation. Directly upon assuming office, he disestablished the Anglican Church of Ireland (1869), abolishing the obligatory tithes imposed on Irish Catholics by a minority Protestant church establishment. (The issue of probity aside, the act remains memorable today for provoking an opposition movement that gave the English language one of its longest words—"antidisestablishmentarianism."[61]) The following year brought passage of the Land Act of 1870, which Gladstone hoped would curb unfair evictions of Irish tenants, while making it possible for them to purchase property from their landlords with government loans. Alas, eviction remained legal for failure to pay rent, and the landlords got around the bill by raising rents until undesired tenants were no longer able to pay.[62] Gladstone, who had previously declared that "My mission is to pacify Ireland,"[63] had instead to contend with a new outbreak of agrarian violence against the hated landlords, necessitating the passage of a "Peace Preservation Act" (1870) and the dispatch of British troops.[64]

At home, however, Gladstone was in the midst of what has been called his "Great Ministry" owing to a prolific program of reforming legislation. In 1870, the Prime Minister established competitive entry exams for civil service appointments, sweeping away the entrenched upper-class favoritism that had previously existed. The Forster Education Act of the same year did much to improve the nation's haphazard and woefully inadequate elementary school system that previously had left nearly half of British children with no schooling at all.[65] In 1871, religious requirements were removed from the universities, opening degree programs and teaching positions to all denominations (and, notably, to those who professed no religion at all). And in 1872, a landmark election law introduced the secret ballot, sharply curtailing the ability of electioneers to control votes through bribery or intimidation.

It was also during the "Great Ministry" that Gladstone's secretary of state for war, Edward Cardwell, enacted a series of long-overdue military reforms. The commander-in-chief of the army, formerly answerable directly to the crown, was now made accountable to the War Ministry and Parliament.[66] Flogging as a military punishment was outlawed in peacetime.[67] The lessons of Prussia's crushing victory over France in the Franco-Prussian War were taken to heart. The old system of 12-year enlistments was scrapped in favor of a Prussian-style model—requiring just seven years' active duty to be followed by five years in the reserve (1872).[68] More important, the notorious "purchase system" was abolished. Established by royal warrant in 1683 during the reign of

Charles II, the purchase system allowed retiring army officers to sell their commissions to the highest bidder, allowing incompetent but wealthy individuals to advance through the ranks while effectively denying promotion to talented but impecunious candidates. The system was found wanting during the Crimean War when the British officer corps distinguished itself by its ineptitude. Yet the system had remained in force. In 1871, Gladstone pushed an abolition measure through the House of Commons. The Lords promptly vetoed it—hardly surprising given that the purchase system had, in the words of Hazen, "rendered the army an appendage of the aristocracy" since scarcely anyone outside that class possessed the wealth to participate.[69] Undeterred, Gladstone petitioned Queen Victoria to abolish the system by royal warrant—just as it had been established by royal warrant. The queen obliged him (November 1871), but the proceeding was harshly criticized as extra-parliamentary, and Gladstone's popularity now began to wane. The Church, the aristocracy, the army and Irish Protestantism were now all arrayed against him, and in 1872, his public reputation was tarnished when he deferred to an international arbitration court to settle a dispute with the United States over damages inflicted during the American Civil War by the British-built Confederate raiding ship, *Alabama*. The court ruling was adverse, and Britain was obliged to pay £3,000,000 in compensation to the United States—an act that, in the view of many British citizens, made Britain appear weak.[70] (British inertia amid the rise of the German empire and Russia's violation of the neutrality of the Black Sea likewise contributed to this impression.)

In the same year, a bill put forward by radicals within his own party to prohibit the sale of alcohol did Gladstone no good at all—adding distillers, brewers, pub owners and publicans to the growing list of his adversaries and critics.[71] By 1873, when his attempt to endow a university for Ireland's Catholic population came to grief amid religious fervor, Disraeli was comparing Gladstone and his fellow reformers to "a range of exhausted volcanoes."[72] "The tone and tendency of Liberalism," the Conservative leader declared in a speech at Crystal Palace (June 24, 1872), "cannot be concealed. It is to attack the institutions of the country under the name of Reform and to make war on the manners and customs of the people under the pretext of progress."[73] In the Commons, Disraeli denounced the entire Liberal program as "harassing legislation."[74] Gladstone's Irish university endowment bill went down in defeat and in elections held the following January the Conservatives obtained a majority of fifty seats allowing them to form a majority government for the first time since the fall of Peel in 1846.

During the preceding six years in opposition, Disraeli had written a bestselling novel about the politics of the day (*Lothair*, published in 1870), endured the agonizing death of his beloved wife, Mary Anne (who succumbed to cancer in 1872), and weathered a short-lived attempt by a cadre of discouraged colleagues to oust him from the party leadership. He was now poised to embark on his own "great ministry." Intent on providing the nation with a respite from the "harassing legislation" of his predecessor, he nonetheless pursued beneficial social legislation, passing an Artisans' Dwellings Act to improve housing for urban workers, a Public Health Act to improve water quality and sanitation and an Agricultural Holdings Act compensating evicted tenant farmers for improvements made on their landlords' property (1875). By such measures he demonstrated that his "new Conservative Party" could rival the Liberals as a party of the people.

But it was in the realm of imperial affairs that Disraeli left his chief impress—capturing the public imagination with a bold assertion of British interests abroad and in the colonies. In November 1875, he achieved one of the most stunning coups of the century by purchasing 177,000 shares of interest in the Suez Canal (45 percent of the total) from the Egyptian Khedive, Ismail Pasha, who had managed to run up a considerable public debt through profligate spending, and who had had to put his own personal canal shares up for sale to cover the loss.

The completion of the canal in 1869 had proved a boon for Britain's commerce with her prize colony, India—reducing the burden of passage (which formerly entailed sailing around the southern tip of Africa) by literally thousands of miles. But the new route had the disadvantage of putting Anglo-Indian shipping at the mercy of France, since the latter nation—whose investors had after all financed the canal—held a controlling interest in the canal's stock company. Disraeli revolutionized this situation in the blink of an eye—making his offer by telegraph in order to get the jump on all potential competitors. The price was £4,000,000—the funds being advanced by the Rothschilds of London via back channels rather than being solicited publicly from the Bank of England lest word get out before the deal was complete.[75] The sale went through immediately, and to the delight of Queen Victoria and the chagrin of France, Britain obtained an imposing presence on the all-important waterway. To savor his achievement, Disraeli (who was soon afterwards created Earl of Beaconsfield[76] by the queen) passed a Royal Titles Bill proclaiming Victoria "Empress of India"—a title that became effective on January 1, 1877. By the following year, when he returned from the Congress of Berlin (which will be discussed in the next section), he stood at the height of his popularity. Had he called new elections at this juncture, he almost assuredly would have increased his majority in the Commons.[77] But he seems not to have recognized the opportunity and in the ensuing two years, costly military adventures in Afghanistan and Zululand exposed the downside of his imperialist policy.

Britain had already had an unhappy experience in Afghanistan. Suspicious of Russian meddling in that nation, a British army seized Kandahar and Kabul in 1839, and replaced the ruling prince with their own puppet. The Afghans would have none of it. By 1841, the entire country had risen in arms, and the Kabul garrison was expelled. The ensuing retreat was a disaster. Afghan snipers picked off the soldiers one by one as they withdrew through the treacherous mountain passes—the remnant of the force being slaughtered in a final stand at Gandamak. The lone survivor, a company surgeon named William Brydon, staggered back to Jelalabad with his wounds to deliver the devastating news. In a face-saving measure, a second British army crossed the border, defeated the Afghans and reoccupied Kabul. But it withdrew soon afterwards, and the entire enterprise was dropped.

The experience ought to have been enough to dissuade Britain from further involvement but renewed Russian meddling in 1878 caused her to repeat her mistake. In November, the British overthrew the ruling Amir and installed a puppet ruler in his place. Once again, the populace rose in arms, killing the British envoy in Kabul along with his attendants (September 1879). British troops commanded by Major-General Frederick Roberts fought their way into the city in October, and though they were able to fend off a desperate Afghan counterattack at year's end, the situation remained critical.

In the meantime, events even more alarming had transpired in South Africa. Founded by the Dutch as the "Cape Colony" in 1652, South Africa had been seized by the British during the Napoleonic wars, when Holland was a French satellite. At the Congress of Vienna (1814–1815), Britain decided to keep the territory permanently. Although her activities in the region were distressing to native tribesmen and Dutch colonists alike, the real turmoil commenced in 1878 when Britain attempted to intervene in a border conflict between the recently annexed Republic of Transvaal and neighboring Zululand.

The Zulus were the most formidable warrior tribe in the region, fielding an army of 50,000 whose appetite for war was kept ever at fever pitch by the strict enforcement of celibacy until a warrior had proven himself in battle. For attack, the Zulu soldier employed a short stabbing spear, and for defense a cowhide shield. In close combat, he would grapple the left side of his opponents shield with the left side of his own. Then pulling back with sudden force, he would twist his opponent to the right and finish him off with a spear thrust to the exposed armpit. The Zulu battle array was modeled on a stampeding buffalo—the center, or "chest" tying the enemy down, while the wings or "horns" enveloped its flanks. Behind the chest and horns, ready to deliver the decisive blow, were the "loins," a phalanx of warriors who were instructed to sit on the ground facing away from the action until they were needed, lest their zeal drive them to strike too soon.[78]

Opposed to this war machine was a British colonial force anchored by a nucleus of reliable regular troops. Unfortunately, these were few in number, and were supported by undisciplined irregulars and by native recruits who could not be counted upon at all.[79] In January 1879, this army advanced into Zululand in three columns, leaving behind a company of men to guard the crossing of the Buffalo River at Rorke's Drift. The middle column made camp ten miles east of the drift, near Isandhlwana Hill. Stationing 1,200 men there, the commander, Lord Chelmsford, advanced with 2,400 others to seek out the main Zulu force. The Zulus eluded him, however, and doubled back toward Isandhlwana. At first, there were only rumors and scattered sightings, but after some confused reconnaissance, a lone soldier, riding over a rise, saw below him the entire Zulu army. What is worse, it saw him. For a startled moment, they stared at one another, but then, the Zulus swarmed over the rise and on toward the British camp.[80] In the ensuing Battle of Isandhlwana, the native levies fled, leaving the 1st Battalion of the 24th regiment and a few auxiliaries to fight it out alone. They were massacred almost to a man. By the time Chelmsford returned with the main force, the Zulus had moved on to Rorke's Drift.

The company of soldiers in this latter position would not have been blamed had they abandoned their post. Indeed, mounted fugitives from Isandhlwana, who arrived just ahead of the Zulus, rode off again in such a panic that the company's native conscripts dropped what they were doing and ran off after them. But the company, roughly one hundred men in all, was charged with the supervision of a field hospital containing some thirty wounded soldiers who could not be transported at a pace sufficient to keep ahead of the Zulus. Consequently, the two lieutenants sharing command of the post, John Chard and Gonville Bromhead, ordered the construction of a makeshift fortress of mealie bags around the two buildings of their post and stood their ground against a Zulu force outnumbering them forty-to-one. Fighting with the rifle butt and bayonet when there was no time to load and shoot, the defenders were forced, more than once, to contract their perimeter. But their defense was so determined that the Zulus withdrew after what seemed an interminable series of attacks.

It was not until March that the British won a major victory over the Zulus at Kambula. But when they followed this with a second victory at Gingindhlovu a few days later, the Zulu King, Cetshwayo (a nephew of the famed Zulu chieftain, Shaka), asked

The Defence of Rourke's Drift by Alphonse-Marie-Adolphe de Neuville. Lieutenant Gonville Bromhead stands at the center of the painting pointing to his left. Lieutenant Chard, in pale breaches holding a rifle in his left hand, stands behind the barrier at far right. Art Gallery of New South Wales (Wikimedia Commons).

for terms. Chelmsford refused. News of the initial reverses had been badly received in the home country, and revenge was the only thing for it. Accordingly, the British commander embarked upon a second invasion of Zululand on May 31, 1879. By the following afternoon, his army had suffered a public relations disaster more dreadful than the defeat at Isandhlwana.

Accompanying Chelmsford's reinforcements was Prince Louis Napoleon Bonaparte, the son of Napoleon III. The late emperor had followed his wife and son into exile in Chiselhurst, England, after Bismarck released him from captivity in 1871. There he passed his twilight years (of which he was granted but two) designing an affordable stove for the poor. He died after a series of risky operations for his chronically infected kidney stones, leaving his son as pretender to the French imperial throne (1873).

The young prince was already an exuberant graduate of the Royal Military Academy at Woolwich, when he sought, and received, permission to travel to South Africa. His dash and bravado made him the toast of his brother officers, but his headstrong recklessness caused anxiety to those charged with his well-being. On the 1st of June, he set off with a small body of men to reconnoiter a previously scouted region from which the Zulus were known to be absent. Once away, however, the irrepressible prince convinced his fellows to proceed into hostile territory. This adventure proving most satisfactory, the men decided to dismount for a coffee break. Hardly had they done so before Zulus, too numerous to count, burst out of the surrounding thicket. Two troopers were immediately killed. The rest leaped atop their mounts and spurred them to a gallop—with the notable exception of the unfortunate prince, whose terrified horse, Percy, bolted, trampling over his right arm. As his comrades rode out of view, the prince drew his pistol and faced his attackers. He never turned away. When the British recovered his corpse, they counted seventeen wounds on the front of his body and none on the back.[81] The war ended a month later, when King Cetshwayo was defeated at the gates of his capital city (July 4, 1879).

Afghanistan and Zululand made for some very bad press back home—and at a most unfortunate time for Disraeli who was now beset by a constellation of domestic difficulties. In the House of Commons, he could get nothing done owing to Charles Stewart Parnell's emergence as leader of the Irish Party, which now demanded home rule for Ireland and incessantly obstructed government business in pursuit of that goal.[82] The economy, meanwhile, had been thrown into crisis by the failed harvest of 1879, causing hardship at all levels of society.[83] And, in the Scottish county of Midlothian, Disraeli's arch-nemesis, William Ewart Gladstone, was staging an impressive, and, what is worse, untimely, political comeback.

In the wake of his 1874 electoral defeat, Gladstone had virtually retired from public life, but the publication of a famous pamphlet, *The Bulgarian Horrors and the Question of the East*, in which he denounced the Ottoman Empire for atrocities committed in Bulgaria, brought him back into the public eye, selling over 200,000 copies in a matter of weeks (1876).[84] Deciding to run for Scotland's Midlothian seat in 1879, he embarked on a whistle-stop national campaign tour by rail—the first of its kind in British politics— condemning Disraeli's imperialism (and the "colonial oppression" that went with it) at every stop.[85] Crowds turned out to see him by the thousands.[86] The result was a stunning Liberal victory by a majority of 107 seats in the national election of 1880.

Too old now to hope for a return to office, Disraeli finished work on a new novel, *Endymion*, which proved a fantastic best-seller, and then began work on another in which a character clearly meant to represent Gladstone was irreverently lampooned. Alas, he caught a chill in March 1881 and died a month later from respiratory and renal complications at the age of seventy-six.[87] In the meantime, after exhausting all other options (and with the utmost reluctance), Queen Victoria invited Gladstone, whom she intensely disliked, to form his second ministry. Gladstone sought immediately to resume his program of Irish pacification and domestic reform. Over the loud protests of the Irish landlords, he passed the Land Act of 1881, which provided for the establishment of impartial courts to determine appropriate rents for tenant dwellings, with the rates decided upon to be fixed for a period of 15 years. No more would the landlords be able to raise rents with impunity in order to evict unwanted tenants.

Alas, the new measure was found wanting by the Irish themselves who were now absolutely intent on obtaining home rule. Forming a so-called "Land League," they embarked on a campaign of obstruction and violence across Ireland that included arson, murder, mutilation of cattle, and communal shunning of those who participated in unfair tenant evictions (a process that came to be known as "boycotting" in honor of its inaugural victim, Captain Charles Boycott).[88] Gladstone's government promptly clamped down, arresting the leading members of the League—chief among them, Charles Stewart Parnell. The League retaliated with a "No Rent Manifesto," which led to a cessation of rent payment throughout much of the island.[89]

Hoping to end the upheaval, Gladstone reversed gears—negotiating an agreement with Parnell for the release of the imprisoned Land Leaguers. The initiative—known as the "Kilmainham Treaty" after the prison in which Parnell was housed—came to naught within the week, however, when knife-wielding Irish assassins murdered Gladstone's secretary for Ireland, Lord Frederick Cavendish, and his under-secretary, Thomas

Henry Burke, in Dublin's Phoenix Park (May 6, 1882). In the wake of this atrocity (which was carried out "in broad daylight"),[90] the Commons passed a new "Crimes Prevention Act" (July 1882), but efforts to quell the Irish violence by force proved unavailing. Gladstone's Irish policy came in for a chorus of criticism, and it was soon compounded by nettlesome developments in foreign affairs.

Overseas adventurism held very little appeal for the Liberal leader. On taking office in 1880, he had been as anxious to extricate himself from entanglements abroad as his predecessor, Disraeli, had been keen to enter into them. Regrettably, foreign and colonial crises were to be the bane of his ministry. Scarcely a month into his tenure, British arms sustained a disastrous reverse at Maiwand in Afghanistan, suffering 934 killed out of a total force of 2,476, with the survivors taking refuge in Kandahar (July 1880).[91] In September, General Roberts retrieved the situation with a decisive victory after marching from Kabul to relieve the besieged Kandahar garrison, allowing Gladstone to withdraw from the country under "victorious" circumstances.

In South Africa, however, he was not so lucky. The Zulu War, though costly and fraught with misfortune, had been brought to a successful close under Disraeli. But the Zulus were not the only inhabitants of the Cape Colony to find Britain's presence objectionable. In seizing the territory from Holland during the Napoleonic Wars, Britain inherited a significant population of Dutch peasants. Finding that their own institutions were being supplanted, one after another, by English ones not to their liking, a large number of these peasants—or "Boers," as they were known, after the Dutch word for "farmers"—emigrated northward in the "Great Trek" of the late 1830s, to found two new Boer republics: The Transvaal and the Orange Free State.

The Zulu War had been preceded by a border war between the Transvaal and a Bantu tribe known as the Pedi (1876). The war ended in defeat—bankrupting Transvaal and reducing it to near anarchy. Britain, under Disraeli, promptly intervened, annexing the tottering republic to the Cape Colony—a policy favored by some of the Boer inhabitants, but despised by the majority (1877). Gladstone criticized this action bitterly during his Midlothian campaign, and was inclined to offer serious concessions after his election. The Boers, however, complicated the situation by taking up arms and annihilating a small British detachment at Bronkhorstspruit (December 1880). Reinforcements were dispatched forthwith under Sir George Colley, but far from restoring the honor of British arms, they sustained three consecutive reverses—at Laing's Nek, at the Ingogo River and most famously at Majuba Hill, where Colley's force of 550 men was decimated and Colley himself killed (February 27, 1881).

The necessity of restoring British honor was greater now than it had been after Bronkhorstspruit. But the concept was utterly lost on Gladstone. In the aftermath of Majuba Hill, says the *Cambridge Modern History*, he "decided to proceed with negotiations as if nothing had happened."[92] Transvaal was offered autonomy under British suzerainty; and when this was refused, Gladstone conceded full independence exclusive of the freedom to make foreign treaties without British approval.[93] In the estimation of the *Cambridge Modern History*, it was a course of action "apt to secure the maximum of discredit with the minimum of gratitude."[94] At home, the Conservative opposition castigated Gladstone for conceding independence without first avenging Majuba Hill, while the Transvaal Boers added further embarrassment by acting as though they had won the prime minister's concessions by force of arms.[95]

Scarcely was the affair closed before crisis erupted anew at the other end of the

African continent—in Egypt. Although Disraeli's unexpected stock purchase in 1875 had created a strain in Anglo-French relations, the two states were compelled soon afterwards to cooperate to protect their respective Egyptian interests. Even with £4,000,000 in his pocket, the khedive was not a man to put his economic house in order. By 1879, Egypt teetered on the brink of a bankruptcy that might have ruined British and French financiers alike. Flexing their diplomatic muscle, the two European nations assumed "dual control" of Egypt, compelled the khedive to step down, and forced his son and heir to reform Egypt's finances. While this averted bankruptcy, it also provoked a nationalist revolt against foreign domination that found a natural leader in Arabi Pasha (Ahmed Arabi)—an Egyptian army officer who, says *Encyclopædia Britannica*, "was a fluent speaker, and could exercise some influence over the masses by a rude kind of native eloquence."[96] His slogan was "Egypt for the Egyptians," and while his troops manned the fortresses of Alexandria, a mob took to the city's streets and murdered every European in sight (June 11, 1882).[97] To protect her financial interests—and the life and limb of her expatriates—Britain dispatched an army of occupation to quash the revolt. Led by Sir Garnet Wolseley, who had done good service in the Zulu War, it won a decisive victory at Tell El Kabir (September 11, 1882). Arabi was taken captive, and British influence alone prevented his execution at the hands of the khedive.

Because France had declined an invitation to participate in the campaign, Britain was now in a position to dictate Egyptian policy. Gladstone, however, had no desire to become permanently embroiled in the Turkish province and assured both France (now grown jealous) and Turkey that he intended to withdraw Wolseley's army at the earliest opportunity.[98]

The opportunity never came. Over the preceding half century, Egypt had reduced her southern neighbor, Sudan—a slave-trading desert wilderness commanding the Upper Nile—to the status of an unwilling dependency. The popular and eccentric British officer, Charles George "Chinese" Gordon, famed for a succession of heroic exploits in China during the days of Palmerston, had done much to suppress the slave trade while serving Khedive Ismail as governor-general of Sudan in the latter half of the 1870s. But Gordon resigned on the spot when Britain and France compelled Ismail to abdicate (1879), and his successor, Raouf Pasha, engaged in abject misrule of the Sudanese natives who promptly rebelled (1881). Led by Mohammed Ahmed, a religious fanatic who claimed to be the prophesied "Mahdi" who would conquer the world in the name of Islam, the rebels wrested whole swaths of Sudan from Egyptian control. Tewfik, who had succeeded his father Ismail as khedive, charged a British officer, Colonel William Hicks, with putting a stop to the matter, but Hicks was lured into the middle of nowhere and exterminated with 8,000 Egyptian troops (August 1883). At El Teb, six months later, another army of Egyptians, again with a British officer in command, timorously threw down their modern weapons on sighting the enemy and fairly allowed the spear-bearing dervishes to walk up and murder them.[99] Utterly unnerved, the khedive's remaining forces in Sudan made for the nearest citadels and bolted the doors behind them.

In order to save face, Britain dispatched "Chinese" Gordon to his former sphere of operations with orders to arrange the evacuation of these trembling souls. But, to the consternation of the Gladstone cabinet, Gordon (whom Trevelyan has described as "a single-minded hero fit for any service except initiating retreat") exceeded his orders and decided to resist the dervishes. He withdrew to Khartoum, the Sudanese capital, arranged its defense and refused to come back out—calculating that his popularity in

Britain would force the government's hand.[100] Gladstone had little inclination to exert himself on behalf of an officer whom he deemed insubordinate.[101] Beset by mounting criticism, he sought instead to salvage the fortunes of his ministry with a bold domestic initiative—passing the Reform Act of 1884, which at last granted suffrage to British agricultural laborers and redistributed parliamentary seats to provide more proportional representation.[102] Only when the radical Tory Randolph Churchill castigated him for his inertia, and frantic crowds took to the streets in support of Gordon's cause, did he consent to the dispatch of a relief expedition under General Wolseley. Unfortunately, it was now too late. After a protracted siege, the Mahdi's forces stormed Khartoum, massacring Gordon and ten thousand others just two days before Wolseley's vanguard arrived (January 1885).

"General Gordon's death," says *Encyclopædia Britannica*, "inflicted a fatal blow on [Gladstone's] government. It was thought that the general, whose singular devotion to duty made him a popular hero, had been allowed to assume an impossible task; had been feebly supported; and that the measures for his relief had been unduly postponed and at last only reluctantly undertaken."[103] Amid the ensuing uproar, Gladstone's budget bill for 1885 was defeated on the question of a proposed tax increase on beer and liquor, thereby prompting his resignation and the formation of a minority Conservative government under Lord Salisbury, pending new elections.

The balloting, held in November–December 1885, gave 335 seats to the Liberals and 249 to the Conservatives. But Parnell's Irish Nationalist Party held the balance with 86 seats (which, if added to the Conservatives, would have resulted in a drawn election).[104] Hence, in order to form a government, one party or the other had to woo the Irish MPs, whose platform continued to call for Irish home rule. Convinced that the only alternative was to commit to a policy of oppression and military rule, Gladstone took the plunge. In January 1886, he formed his third ministry with Parnell's support, and in April a bill proposing Irish home rule was placed before the Commons. By its terms, Ireland was to have autonomy in her own internal affairs. She would withdraw her delegates from the British Parliament (which, notably, would put an end to Irish obstructionism[105]), and establish her own legislature in Dublin. She would have no voice in the foreign or imperial policies of Great Britain (which was rather unfair since she would still be obliged to pay taxes in their support), but Gladstone did add a Land Bill, which would enable the Irish peasantry to purchase land from their landlords on an unprecedented scale with financial assistance from the British government.

The "Irish Government Bill" (known to history as the "Home Rule Bill") fractured Gladstone's Liberal Party. Whereas the prime minister saw the bill as consolidating the union with Ireland by alleviating grievances, many party members saw it as the first act of dissolution of the union. Led by John Bright, Joseph Chamberlain and Lord Hartington (i.e., Spencer Cavendish, the brother of the former secretary for Ireland, Frederick Cavendish, who had been murdered by the Phoenix Park assassins), these so-called Liberal Unionists formed an alliance with the Conservatives, enabling them to defeat the bill by a mere thirty votes. Consequently, Gladstone's ministry fell just six months after it had taken office.[106]

In the elections that followed, the Conservatives and Liberal Unionists obtained a combined 394 seats as against 270 for the Liberals and Irish Home Rulers. Led by Lord Salisbury, the government reverted to a policy of coercion in Ireland. "Apply the recipe honestly, consistently and resolutely for a period of twenty years," said the new prime

General Charles G. Gordon is standing on the stairs of his house about to be speared by dervishes. Etching by H. Dicksee after G.W. Joy, Wellcome Images, CC BY 4.0 *https://creative-commons.org/licenses/by/4.0/deed.en* (Wikimedia Commons).

minister, "and at the end of that time you will find that Ireland will be fit to accept any gifts in the way of local government or repeal of coercion laws that you may wish to give her."[107] The harshness of this approach was tempered by the passage of the Land Bill of 1891, which allowed 35,000 Irish tenant farmers to purchase the lands upon which they toiled with loans from the British government. The purchasers obtained immediate ownership of their property while entering into a 49-year mortgage that cost less annually than they had formerly paid in rent.[108] It was the first step in a Conservative strategy aimed at "killing Home Rule with kindness"—the government's hope being that in becoming owners of their own land, the Irish would come to desire peace and stability even in the absence of home rule.[109]

On the domestic scene, Salisbury continued Disraeli's policy of ameliorating the plight of the masses through social legislation, passing measures that established free elementary education (1891), extended new protections to female and child laborers and expanded working class housing. His ministry also presided over the passage of the County Councils Act of 1888, which removed local jurisdiction from aristocratic control and placed it in the hands of locally elected boards.[110] In foreign affairs, the prime minister signed important agreements with Germany, Portugal and France on the partition of Africa (1890), helping to ensure that Europe's "mad scramble" for colonies on that continent did not lead to a European conflict[111]; and, in a move fraught with implications for the future, he established the principle that Britain's navy must be as large as its two largest competitors put together.[112]

After six years in power, the Salisbury government was defeated on a no confidence vote, and for an unprecedented fourth time, William Ewart Gladstone became prime minister. Now aged eighty-two, the "Grand Old Man of the Liberal Party" sought to complete his life's work by giving Irish home rule one last try. With the support of the Irish Nationalists, he managed to get his bill passed in the House of Commons by a margin of 34 votes. Alas, the result was promptly overturned in the House of Lords by a decisive tally of 419 to 41. For Gladstone, this was the end. Before leaving office he spoke out against the upper house, whose membership was hereditary, for having interfered with the deliberations of the House of Commons, a body elected by the voice of the people.[113] He stepped down in 1894, and died four years later—his burial at Westminster Abbey being attended by 100,000 mourners.[114] His successor, Lord Rosebery, who had little enthusiasm for Irish home rule, let the issue drop, concentrating instead on the passage of an unpopular inheritance tax before resigning in June 1895.

Rent in twain by the Irish issue, the Liberal Party would not hold office again for a decade. The elections of 1895 gave the Conservatives and their Liberal Unionist allies a staggering 411 seats. (The odd bedfellows now formed an outright coalition—merging into a single "Unionist" party to emphasize their shared opposition to home rule and to deemphasize the oppositional Conservative and Liberal origins that had formerly separated them.[115]) Salisbury, as head of the government, embarked on his third ministry (1895–1902). The policy of Irish coercion was resumed, but, so, too, was the strategy of "killing Home Rule with kindness." A Local Government Act, passed in 1898, gave Ireland a measure of autonomy in local affairs, while a new Land Act, passed in 1903, allowed another 160,000 Irish tenant farmers to purchase their holdings on liberal mortgage terms.[116] Egged on by its Liberal Unionist members, the government also continued to pursue domestic social legislation—passing a Workmen's Compensation Act that obliged employers to pay compensation to workers injured on the job (1897).

It is, however, for imperial affairs that Salisbury's ministry is best remembered. It had been ten years since Gordon's death and the abandonment of Sudan to the Mahdi. In the interim, France had entered the arena as a regional contender in a bid to create a contiguous swath of colonial territory across the breadth of the African continent from French Congo on the west coast to French Somaliland on the east. Regrettably, this ambitious goal was at cross purposes with the aspirations of Britain—literally so, for the latter hoped to build a north-south railway from the Cape of Good Hope to Cairo over a *continuous stretch of British colonial territory*. It remained to be seen which colonial power would be able to fill in the territorial gaps necessary to its program, but for Britain the dilemma was further complicated by events in Abyssinia—a nation situated on Sudan's eastern border.

In the preceding decades, Italy, seeking her own African empire, had been thwarted by France in the race for Tunis (1881), and consequently had turned her attentions to Africa's Red Sea coast, where, in 1890, she established a colony in Eritrea, whose western border abutted Sudan and southern border abutted Abyssinia (Ethiopia). In 1893, acting on advice from Britain and Egypt, Italian Eritrea captured Kassala, Sudan (just across the Eritrean-Sudanese frontier) from the Mahdists. So far, so good, but in 1896, Italy stumbled into war with Abyssinia after an alleged treaty violation and, at Adowa, sustained a stunning reverse—her 20,000 troops being overwhelmed by 90,000 Abyssinian natives drilled in French tactics and supplied with French arms (1896).[117]

The Mahdists, meanwhile, had placed Kassala under siege in a determined effort to retake it. With the Italian forces barely holding on at Kassala (and ruing the day that they accepted Britain's counsel), and with British public opinion increasingly inflamed by rumors of cruel and oppressive rule by the Mahdi's successors in Sudan, the Salisbury government determined that the time had come to avenge the death of Gordon and re-impose Anglo-Egyptian authority in that lost province.[118] Accordingly, in March 1896, a mixed army of British and Egyptian troops under the command of Lord Herbert Kitchener started south along the right bank of the Nile, constructing a telegraph and railway line (and battling cholera and malaria) as it went. Thus commenced the famous "River War"—the history of which was chronicled by young Winston Churchill who served as an officer on the campaign.

By October 1896, victories at Akasha and Kerma had delivered Sudan's Northern (Dongola) province into Anglo-Egyptian hands. Although a Sudanese tribe wishing to defect to Kitchener was massacred by the dervishes in July of the following year, Kitchener's force made enough southward progress by Christmas Day 1897 to relieve the Italians of their burden at Kassala (which the latter were only too happy to be rid of).[119] A final showdown ensued at Omdurman, across the Nile from Khartoum, where, on September 2, 1898, a charge of 10,000 Mahdists was stopped cold by British gunfire. When the smoke cleared, it seemed that the victors had only to cross the river and enter the capital, but as they shouldered their rifles, 20,000 more dervishes suddenly appeared from nowhere and fell upon their rear. The charge took Kitchener entirely by surprise, and only the rapid deployment of the rearguard by Hector MacDonald, using a novel marching procedure, staved off disaster.[120] The enemy was again cut down in swaths, and by day's end, the Mahdists had been decisively defeated with the loss of 10,000 dead, 10,000 wounded and 5,000 taken prisoner as against 500 Anglo-Egyptian casualties.[121] In the battle's aftermath, the corpse of the Mahdi (who had died in 1885) was plucked from its tomb and thrown into the Nile—Kitchener claiming the severed head as a souvenir until popular outrage impelled its reburial in a Muslim cemetery.[122]

The charge of the 21st Lancers at Omdurman, September 2, 1898, by Edward Matthew Hale (1852–1924). Winston Churchill, then a 23-year-old subaltern, participated in the charge (Wikimedia Commons).

Two days after the victory of Omdurman, Anglo-Egyptian troops entered Khartoum and raised the flags of their respective nations. Before they could savor their victory, however, they learned that the French had raised a flag of their own at Fashoda, located 600 miles to the south along the Nile in Sudanese territory. It was part of the French quest for a coast-to-coast belt of colonial holdings across the breadth of Africa, and it simply could not be borne. Hence, Kitchener set out southwards again, arriving at Fashoda with a flotilla of five gunboats on September 19 to confront the French commander, Major Jean Baptiste Marchand. From Marchand's standpoint, this was likely just as well. His tiny force had already been attacked once by renegade Mahdists, and would likely not have survived the next onslaught, which was imminently expected.[123] Nonetheless, he refused to evacuate his troops. There ensued the so-called "Fashoda Incident," a tense six-week standoff—not so much, it must be confessed, for the principals on the scene, who merely exchanged courtesies over whiskey and soda while awaiting instructions from home,[124] but for their respective governments, which engaged in bitter recriminations and threats of war until France finally backed down in return for compensation elsewhere.

The British were thus free to resume their quest for a north-south belt of territory from the Cape to Cairo—and to experience the stumbling blocks that went with it. In 1884—just three years after the British defeat at Majuba Hill—gold deposits had been discovered in the Rand Mountain Range in Transvaal, triggering a great immigration of fortune seekers. The Boers observed with a jaundiced eye as Johannesburg grew into a bustling city of foreign "outlanders," the majority of whom were British. To keep the newcomers in their place, the Transvaal government denied them voting privileges, but compelled them nonetheless to pay taxes and to serve in the army.[125] The outlanders raised a cry of protest, and this proved the pretext for an astonishing bit of meddling.

The prime minister of the Cape Colony at this time was Cecil Rhodes, a quintessential imperialist and a leading originator of the elusive Cape to Cairo railway project.[126] As a director of the British South Africa Company (formed in 1889), Rhodes had

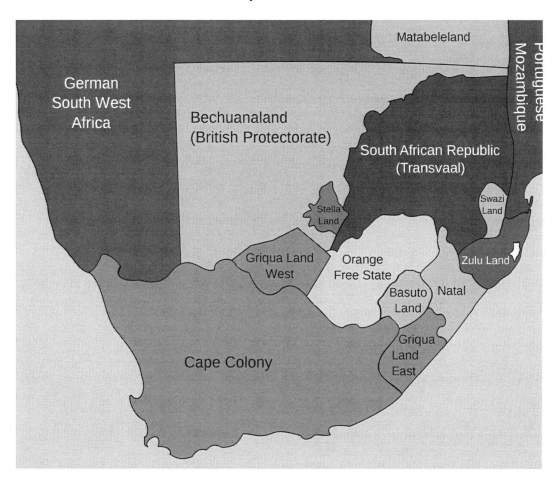

Map of South Africa showing the Cape Colony, the Orange Free State and the South African Republic (Transvaal) circa 1885 (Themightyquill, Kirkworld, Wikimedia Commons, CC BY-SA 3.0: https://creativecommons.org/licenses/by-sa/3.0).

helped expand South Africa's influence northward, skirting along the western border of Transvaal, into the future Rhodesia. By 1895, the benefits of returning Transvaal to British rule had become obvious to him—if not to the Transvaal Boers—and in pursuit of his idea, he fanned the flames of "outlander" discontent, providing them with money and arms to overthrow their government. In a final move, he allowed his administrator for Rhodesia, Dr. Leander Starr Jameson (formerly a highly reputed physician who had once counted Transvaal president, Paul Kruger, among his patients[127]) to proceed to the Transvaal border at the head of 500 men. Rhodes' intention seems to have been to have a force at hand to help swing the balance once the outlander uprising began, but Jameson took matters into his own hands, crossing the Transvaal border from Mafeking on December 29, 1895.[128] His incursion, known to history as the "Jameson Raid," came to immediate grief. The outlander uprising never occurred, and after advancing no further than Doornkop, Jameson and his filibusterers were intercepted and taken prisoner by the Boers.

The Transvaal populace was keen on seeing Jameson hanged, but in a gesture of either goodwill or contempt,[129] President Kruger handed him over along with his fellow

"The Rhodes Colossus": Caricature of Cecil John Rhodes after he announced plans for a tele-graph line and railroad from Cape Town to Cairo, by Edward Linley Sambourne (1844–1910), published in *Punch* (Wikimedia Commons).

ringleaders to be prosecuted in the British courts. Jameson received the light sentence of fifteen months imprisonment, of which he served but twelve, while Rhodes—whose complicity was laid before the world by the Boers who had intercepted and deciphered a coded message bearing his instructions[130]—was forced to step down as prime minister of the Cape Colony (although he received no other punishment).

The Boers were aghast at this leniency. Believing that the British colonial secretary, Joseph Chamberlain, had foreknowledge of Rhodes' intentions—a suspicion vindicated by history[131]—they were less inclined than ever to concede suffrage to the outlanders, whom they now regarded as a dangerous fifth column conniving with Britain to threaten Transvaal's independence. Having received a telegram of congratulation from Kaiser Wilhelm II on thwarting the raid "without appealing to the help of friendly powers,"[132] President Kruger adopted a policy of utter intransigence.

The British, for their part, viewed the affair as a test of their imperialist mettle. Sir Alfred Milner, sent as high commissioner to study the outlanders' grievances, reported to the home government that "the spectacle of thousands of British subjects kept permanently in the position of helots ... calling vainly to her Majesty's Government for redress, does steadily undermine the influence and reputation of Great Britain and the respect for the British government."[133] On Milner's advice, the British government doubled down on its demand for concessions. The British populace, which had never forgotten the embarrassment of Majuba Hill, gave its enthusiastic support.[134]

A last-ditch effort to reach an accommodation was made at Bloemfontein in a meeting between Milner and Kruger. But when Kruger learned that Britain was surreptitiously moving troops into the Cape Colony, and when Britain refused his ultimatum that these troops be withdrawn, the Orange Free State joined Transvaal in a declaration of war (October 11, 1899).[135] The ensuing "Boer War" (1899–1902) provided a shock to both participants. It began with an embarrassing series of British setbacks at the hands of the tiny republics. Using Krupp artillery purchased with funds awarded them after the Jameson raid,[136] the Boers successfully turned back British forces three times in a seven-day period that became infamous in Britain as "Black Week" (December 10–17, 1899). British garrisons at Ladysmith, Kimberley and Mafeking were held under siege, the last for seven months before British reinforcements, streaming in not only from Britain, but also from Canada, Australia and New Zealand, combined to turn the tide. (Among these reinforcements were a new commander-in-chief, Field-Marshal Lord Roberts, the hero of Kandahar, and a new chief-of-staff, Herbert Kitchener, the hero of Omdurman.) By September 1900, all the sieges had been broken, and the Transvaal and Orange Free State had been annexed to the British Empire.

This, however, did not end the matter. For the next two years, a bitter guerrilla contest was fought, in which the Boers cloaked themselves in civilian clothing and received succor from the civilian populace while carrying out deadly attacks on British forces. In retaliation, the British herded whole Boer families into concentration camps, where horrid conditions of starvation and disease carried away one-sixth of those confined.[137] Having thus provoked an international humanitarian outcry, Britain finally consented to end the fighting with the Treaty of Vereeniging (May 1902).

Fatigued by the burdens of office, the British prime minister, Lord Salisbury, tendered his resignation in July 1902. His foreign policy had always eschewed foreign alliances—an approach popularly known as "splendid isolation"—and that policy had now borne bitter fruit. Britain emerged from the Boer War without a single supporter among the nations of Europe. The jingoism with which the war had begun had given way to anxiety for the 350,000 troops who had left home to serve.[138] "Looking back today," wrote T.L. Jarman some sixty years later, "it may seem that the Boer War brought to an end the confident period of British imperialism."[139]

In contrast to the brutality of the war, the peace terms were sufficiently amicable (allowing for the loss of Boer independence) that by 1909, the two sides had forged a new Union of South Africa in which the rights of both parties, including the right of responsible self-government under British auspices, were constitutionally guaranteed. It is to be noted, however, that this did not come to fruition until the Liberals—many of whose leaders had not supported the war—returned to power; and, for now, the Conservatives were still firmly in control.

Salisbury was succeeded in office by his nephew, Arthur James Balfour, who presided soon afterwards over the passage of an Education Act that did much to improve secondary education throughout the country (1902). Despite this benefit, the act aroused a tremendous controversy, for its terms seemed to provide preferential treatment to schools run by the Church of England—providing them with funding without subjecting them to meaningful oversight by the supervisory local borough councils. The bill, says Hazen, "gave great offense to Dissenters and believers in secular education. It authorized taxation for a denomination of which multitudes of taxpayers were not members.... Thousands refused to pay

British Colonial Secretary Joseph "Joe" Chamberlain. Portrait by John Singer Sargent, National Portrait Gallery, London (Wikimedia Commons).

their taxes, and their property was, therefore, sold by public authority.... Many were imprisoned. There were over 70,000 summonses to court."[140] Despite the uproar, however, it was not the issue of education, or even the labors of the opposition party that finally broke the power of the Conservatives. Rather, it was a rift within the ranks of the party itself—a rift precipitated by the self-same question that had ruined Peel's Conservative Party sixty years before, and brought about by one of the most remarkable, and most polarizing, figures in Salisbury's (and now Balfour's) cabinet: the colonial secretary, Joseph Chamberlain.

Chamberlain had begun his career in business—earning enough from a screw-manufacturing concern in Birmingham to retire wealthy at the age of thirty-eight. Thereafter, he devoted himself to politics, gaining a reputation as a radical reformer.

In 1876, he won election as Birmingham's mayor, in which capacity he transformed the city by clearing out its slums, paving and lighting its streets, and municipalizing its water and gas supplies (the last improving sanitation and providing the city with a steady revenue stream). For his efforts, he came to be celebrated as "the father of modern Birmingham."[141] In 1878, the city repaid him by electing him to Parliament, where his championship of such policies as free education and a graduated income tax made him the avowed spokesman of the radical wing of the Liberal Party. Rewarded with a cabinet post in Gladstone's second ministry (1880–1885), he played a leading role in the passage of the Reform Bill of 1884, which enfranchised the agricultural working class.

"At this time," says *Encyclopædia Britannica*, "he took the current advanced Radical views of both Irish and foreign policy, hating 'coercion,' disliking the occupation of Egypt, and prominently defending the Transvaal settlement after Majuba."[142] But if he hated the use of coercion in Ireland, he nonetheless opposed Irish home rule as tantamount to dissolving the United Kingdom, and during Gladstone's third ministry, he resigned his cabinet post and voted against the Irish Government Bill. His defection to the new Liberal-Unionist Party was perhaps less momentous than that of Lord Hartington (who had been the Liberal leader during Gladstone's semi-retirement in the 1870s), but his was regarded as the greater betrayal, and, for it, Chamberlain was openly decried as a "Judas."[143] When Gladstone raised the issue of Irish home rule again during his last ministry (1893), Chamberlain lobbied against it so energetically as to be described as "the life and soul of the opposition."[144]

In 1895, Chamberlain accepted a cabinet position under Salisbury in the "Unionist" coalition government, this time as colonial secretary; and though he continued to advocate for liberal social reforms—successfully in the case of the Workers' Compensation Act of 1897, unsuccessfully in the pursuit of pensions for the aged—he was henceforth to make his chief contribution to history as an "imperialist." He took such a hard line against the Boers in 1899, that Salisbury referred to the ensuing Boer War as "Joe's War."[145]

Before that sobering conflict came to an end, Queen Victoria had died after a reign of sixty-four years (January 1901)—then the longest in British history. At the time of her accession, Britain had been the preeminent colonial power in the world and the unrivaled leader of the first industrial revolution. By the time of her death, Britain still reigned supreme as a colonial power, but Germany, France, Belgium, Portugal and Italy had entered into the scales of colonial rivalry in the "mad scramble" for Africa—and in so doing, they took advantage of Britain's free trade policy to dump cheap manufactures into British markets, while instituting protective tariffs against British goods in their own. Europe, moreover, was in the throes of a second industrial revolution—one in which steam-power and iron were replaced by internal combustion and steel—and this time England faced strong technological competition, particularly on the part of Germany (which was also embarking on a naval program meant to rival Britain's).[146]

It was in this milieu that Chamberlain began issuing appeals for the consolidation of Britain's colonial empire into a more unified whole for the purposes of mutual defense and preferential trade.[147] During the 1860s and 1870s, Britain's North American holdings had been fused into a federated Dominion of Canada. Provincial barriers to the building of railroads were thereby removed, and tracks were quickly laid across the breadth of the continent to yield rapid economic development. A similar federal system followed in Australia. Home rule was willingly conceded in both cases. Might not a similar federal system be applied to the empire as a whole? In 1897, Chamberlain raised the possibility at a meeting with the empire's colonial prime ministers, gathered together in London for Queen Victoria's Diamond Jubilee. The self-ruling colonies were too jealous of their autonomy to accept the scheme, but much understanding and goodwill resulted from the discussions.[148]

Another means to the desired end was the notion of an imperial *Zollverein* modeled on the old German system—featuring free trade inside the empire, but protective tariffs on foreign imports.[149] This, too, proved too strident an idea, but there was a less strident option, known as "imperial preference." Canada (which, unlike Britain, did have a protective tariff system) employed this option already—charging Britain a lower tariff rate than that imposed on outside countries. The roadblock for Chamberlain was that Britain had no tariffs at all, having been entirely committed to free trade for decades. In 1902, however, a nominal tariff was placed on (of all things) corn, with the proceeds going towards the war effort against the Boers. Here, in Chamberlain's view, was the opening he needed to make a start on an "imperial preference" system. With much support among imperially minded MPs, Chamberlain began lobbying for differential rates on this tariff—higher for foreign countries, lower for the colonies. To his great disappointment, however, Balfour's new chancellor of the exchequer, Charles Ritchie, dropped the tariff entirely from his 1903 budget.[150]

Despite being on otherwise excellent terms with Balfour, Chamberlain quit the cabinet because of this decision, and took the issue to the country in a series of speeches, arguing that British trade was beginning to lose ground to protectionist countries (particularly Germany and the United States), while touting the putative benefits of an "imperial preference" protectionist system—namely (as summarized by Carlton Hayes), "(1) the preferential agreement would cement the empire; (2) the tariff protection would stimulate British industry and allow British employers to pay higher wages; (3) the customs receipts would bring in revenue sufficient to enlarge the navy and accomplish expensive social reforms such as old-age pensions."[151] (It may be added, that with such a system in place, should a foreign power attempt to place commercial pressure on a British colony, Britain could protect that colony by implementing retaliatory tariff rates against the offending power.[152])

His campaign split the Unionist party—and the party suffered mightily in consequence. Beset by the struggle between diehard free traders and Chamberlain's "imperial preference" protectionists, by continuing opposition to the hated Education Act of 1902 and by a scandal over reports that Chinese laborers had been brought to South Africa to work in the mines under conditions bordering on slavery, Prime Minister Balfour resigned in December 1905. The ensuing elections, held in January 1906, brought the Liberals back to power in a landslide with 397 seats as against a paltry 156 for the Conservatives. Chamberlain, who was reelected to his Birmingham seat, was afterwards roundly denounced by his detractors for "having twice wrecked his party—first the Radical Party under Gladstone, and secondly the Unionist party under Mr. Balfour."[153] He suffered a devastating stroke in 1906 and, though reelected to Parliament afterwards, had to pass his political baton to his sons, Austen and Neville. Defeated in his own constituency, Arthur Balfour was transiently ousted from the House of Commons, but would later return to prominence and win a hallowed place in the consciousness of the Jewish people with the famous Balfour Declaration of 1917.

In the meantime, the newly empowered Liberal Party—far more radical than in the days of Gladstone—sought to inaugurate a new era of social and political reform. Unable to combat them in the House of Commons, the Conservatives relied upon their enduring majority in the House of Lords to veto any measures they deemed odious, heedless of the remonstrance given them more than a decade earlier by Gladstone against a hereditary body overturning the will of the people's duly elected representatives. For three years, the Lords' campaign of vetoes met with remarkable success. Among the vetoed legislation was a new school bill overriding the Education Act of 1902, which consequently remained in effect. But in 1909, the upper house overstepped itself by attempting to reject the government's budget, which sought to defray the costs of a naval expansion program and an Old Age Pensions Act (passed in 1908) with the institution of a graduated income tax and with increased taxes on investments and inheritance.[154] No one outside the House of Lords ever imagined that the unelected upper house had the right to reject the budget. In the House of Commons, Prime Minister Herbert Asquith declared that the very notion defied every principle of representative government. The Lords retorted that they had always possessed this right though they had never previously chosen to exercise it[155]—an interpretation that the Commons were not about to accept without a fight.

The unexpected and untimely death of King Edward VII (Queen Victoria's son and successor) in 1910 brought the issue to a head. Upon the accession of his son, George V, the Commons passed the Parliament Act of 1911, which denied the House of Lords veto power over money bills and granted only a "suspensive" veto on all other legislation. The Commons could override this "suspensive" veto by passing the involved bill three times provided that the king then appended his signature. After tense discussions with Prime Minister Asquith, George V agreed to combat any effort by the Lords to reject the Parliament Act by threatening to pack that House with newly created peers until the measure enjoyed a majority. This threat had worked once before—at the time of the Great Reform Bill of 1832—and it enjoyed equal success on this occasion. In August 1911, the Lords allowed the bill to pass into law.

Exultant over the outcome, the Liberals entered once more on a quest for Gladstone's Holy Grail—passing a new Home Rule Bill for Ireland, which not only invited the Irish to establish their own parliament, but also to retain a small number of seats in Britain's (April 1912). Ulster, the only Irish province in which Protestants were as numerous as Catholics, rejected the measure outright, declaring that they would not consent to Catholic ascendancy. Her populace made it known that they would resort to civil war if the law passed. The House of Lords obliged them by vetoing the bill, but the Commons passed it two more times, and the king signed it into law even as the Ulster party began mustering arms (September 1914).

Alas, before the bill could be acted upon, its implementation was indefinitely postponed by an unforeseen calamity.

6

Domestic Affairs of the Hapsburg Empire, Russia and Italy, 1870–1914

The Hapsburg Empire and the Dual Monarchy

In the wake of the Revolutions of 1848, the Hapsburg Empire reverted to a policy of reaction. Under Alexander Bach, the chief minister of the newly enthroned Emperor Franz Josef I, the temporary triumph of constitutionalism in Hungary and Austria was overturned and the aspirations of the empire's national minorities were suppressed. To enforce this system, revenues that ought to have gone towards improving the empire's industrial capacity and infrastructure, were used instead to support "a standing army of soldiers, a sitting army of officials, a kneeling army of priests, and a creeping army of informers."[1]

"For some ten years," says *Encyclopædia Britannica*, "the Austrian dominion groaned under one of the worst possible forms of autocratic government."[2] Yet the ruling autocracy did not thrive. During the Crimean War, Russia temporarily occupied Turkish Moldavia and Wallachia on the banks of the Danube, posing a threat to the free navigation of that river—a cornerstone of the Hapsburg empire's financial well-being. When the Russians withdrew, Austria took her own turn at occupying the principalities to guard against Russia's return. Her army remained mobilized for the duration of the war, incurring a financial burden that the empire could ill afford, while costing the Hapsburg regime the friendship of Russia, hitherto its one reliable ally.[3] In the ensuing war of 1859 against France and Piedmont, the empire found no support abroad and much less than it had counted on at home. Hungarian forces had long played an integral role in Austria's wars. But, under Bach, Hungary was shorn of her centuries-old autonomy. She was compelled instead to accept Austrian government officials and to conduct affairs of state in the German language.[4] In the midst of the war, many irate Magyars vented their rage by enlisting with Austria's enemies, and those who stayed and fought displayed very little zeal on the battlefield.[5] The resulting imperial defeat, which excluded the empire from Italian affairs (Venice excepted), showed once and for all that Hungary would have to be mollified for the empire to retain its status as a major power.[6]

Franz Josef responded with a pair of constitutional experiments, which he hoped might salvage the situation without compromising his prerogatives. The first of these—the so-called "October Diploma" of 1860—left all matters apart from finance and the military to the provincial diets. In its localism, the plan seemed to cater to the sentiments of the empire's varied nationalities, but its true purpose was to enlist the provincial aristocracies (who controlled the diets) as a bulwark against liberal reform. Finding the result unsatisfactory after a trial of just four months, however, Franz Josef suddenly reversed gears and sought—rather oddly—to enlist Austria's German liberals as a bulwark *against liberal reform.* Accordingly, the Diploma was superseded by the "February Patent" of 1861, which revoked the provincial powers granted in the Diploma, and bestowed them instead upon the favored political apparatus of the liberals: a centralized imperial parliament. In the emperor's view, such an assembly—if properly managed—might do his bidding collectively with no less efficiency than his former chancellor, Bach, had done individually.[7]

None of this, of course, did anything to address the concerns of the Hungarians, who disliked the first experiment most intensely, and the second more intensely still. In neither case did Hungary have her constitutional rights as an essentially separate nation within the empire restored. Rather, she was treated as a mere imperial province, on a par with all the others—something she would not abide.[8] The threat of a full-blown Hungarian uprising was now very real, but the emergence of a remarkable statesman retrieved the situation. Francis Deák was a Hungarian nationalist, but not a revolutionary. In negotiating on behalf of his people, he declared that forced unity would weaken the empire rather than strengthen it.[9] As an alternative, he recommended a partnership between Austria and Hungary that would leave Hungary independent in all matters of domestic policy, yet fully united to the empire—replete with continued fealty to Franz Josef as sovereign—in the realms of finance, foreign policy and military affairs. In this way, Hungary would regain its unique historical status within the empire, while the empire would retain its status as a major player in the halls of European diplomacy.[10] In the midst of the discussions, Austria sustained its calamitous defeat at Sadowa in the Seven Weeks' War with Prussia, resulting in the expulsion of the empire from German affairs—a devastating blow to Austria's Germanic ruling class. Utterly distraught, Franz Josef asked Deák what Hungary would now demand. "Only what she demanded before Sadowa," was the statesman's reply.[11] The result was a new constitution for the Hapsburg empire—the *Ausgleich,* or "Compromise," of 1867.

In accordance with this document, the empire was transformed into the Dual Monarchy of Austria-Hungary. Ruled by Franz Josef in the dual capacity of Austrian "emperor" and Hungarian "king," the two states were united solely with regard to three portfolios—war, foreign affairs and the finances pertaining to them.[12] In all else, they were completely separate and equal, possessing their own parliaments—the Austrian *Reichsrath* and Hungarian *Diet*—their own constitutions, their own ministries and their own official languages (German and Magyar, respectively). In order that both states might have equal say in matters of mutual concern, each of the parliaments nominated "delegations" of sixty deputies—meeting in Vienna one year and in Budapest the next—to debate foreign, financial and military policy. (The "delegations" actually met in separate halls so that they could employ their respective official languages in their deliberations. If the decisions reached were not in accord after three written consultations between the two bodies, they came together for a deciding vote, made in silence, without debate, so that the issue of language would not create tension.[13])

While Franz Josef's minister of finance determined the annual budget, the raising of taxes was left to the *Reichsrath* and *Diet,* not to the delegations. Tariff policy, issues of public debt and the percentage of taxes to be paid by each half of the monarchy were agreed for a ten-year term.[14] On a given term's expiration, the separate parliaments undertook to renegotiate—a procedure that frequently deteriorated into a festival of recrimination on such questions as whether Austria would really have to foot 70 percent of the imperial bill again (the answer being "yes" until the confrontation of 1907, when Hungary finally agreed to raise her own share to 36.4 percent), and whether Hungary, in addition to raising her own legions and appointing her own officer corps might also employ the Magyar tongue in conducting her share of the empire's military affairs (the answer being "no, they would have to use German"—at least until 1907 when the two sides decided not to address the issue at all).[15] From 1867 on, the contracting parties shared a single flag and a single currency—the union being consecrated with the coronation of Emperor Franz Josef as "King of Hungary" in Budapest (June 1867).

Thus was created a system of imperfect harmony between the empire's two dominant ethnicities—Germanic and Magyar—at the expense of all the others. The polyglot empire was, in fact, awash in minorities with unrealized aspirations: Czechs, Croats, Italians, Poles, Romanians, Ruthenians (Ukrainians), Serbs, Slovaks and Slovenes (just to take the main ones in alphabetical order). While nationalism served to unify Germany and Italy, it exercised a reverse effect within the Hapsburg dominion, wherein loyalty to the reigning dynasty served as the sole rampart against disintegration along nationalist lines. By 1910, the population of the Dual Monarchy stood at 51 million. Of these, there were but 11 million Germans and 10 million Magyars. Taken together, they could not muster a plurality,[16] much less a majority of the Dual Monarchy's population, yet theirs was the deciding voice in their respective parliaments.[17] A clause in the Austrian constitution granting full and equal rights to minorities, and in the Hungarian constitution allowing minorities to conduct education and government affairs in their own languages, were left in abeyance.[18] In Hungary, the undemocratic Magyars exploited their newfound freedom to suppress, by whatever means necessary, the nationalist ambitions of all other races in the state. Everything that had formerly irked them in their subjugation to Austria was now adopted as policy towards minorities in their own midst. Even outside their domains they labored to impede minority aspirations. When Bohemia's Czechs agitated for their own *Ausgleich* with a status equal to Hungary's, and Franz Josef was inclined to endorse the proposal (1871), the Magyars formed an alliance with the Germans of Austria and Bohemia in order to squelch the plan. (For some time afterwards, notes Carlton Hayes, the incensed Czechs boycotted the Austrian Parliament—and on their return, "they displayed much skill in throwing ink-bottles at the presiding officer and otherwise in provoking the wildest tumult."[19])

Within Hungary, a voting law passed in 1874 limited the suffrage to a mere 6 percent of the population, with the Magyar-controlled *Diet* being bitterly divided between a moderate majority (led by Kálmán Tisza, and later by his son, Stephen), which sought to conduct parliamentary proceedings in conformance with the *Ausgleich*, and a "Kossuthist" minority (named after Louis Kossuth, the iconic revolutionary of 1848, and led for a time by his son, Francis), which sought to disrupt those proceedings while agitating for complete Hungarian independence. Such was the enmity between these rival factions that their deliberations were wont to degenerate into riot and chaos. On one occasion, the Kossuthists ransacked the assembly hall (1903), and it became necessary to create a parliamentary police force to keep the peace. In the end, only a threat by Franz Josef to declare universal male suffrage in Hungary (tantamount to abolishing Magyar ascendancy) sufficed to halt the obstructionism (1906).[20]

At the time of the *Ausgleich*, Austria's German minority had every intention of emulating the hegemonic example of the Magyars. As regards the empire's myriad ethnicities, the chief Austrian negotiator, Count Friedrich Ferdinand von Beust, is said to have told his Hungarian counterpart, "You look after your barbarians, and I'll look after mine!"[21] The collapse of the Czech *Ausgleich* campaign in 1871 ushered in a period of German Liberal ascendancy in Austrian politics (1871–1879). Led by Prime Minister Adolf Auersperg, the Liberals insisted upon the use of German as the official language of state and pursued a policy of centralized rule from Vienna. Ever apprehensive about minority agitation—particularly on the part of the Czechs, who constituted the most formidable minority group—they suppressed Czech newspapers, dispatched police to disperse Czech patriotic meetings and passed an electoral law (1873) that gave town dwellers (predominantly German in ethnicity) roughly four times the electoral clout of their rural (predominantly Slavic) counterparts.[22]

In jurisprudence, the Liberals established the laudable principle of trial by jury.[23] In matters of religion, they displayed a distinct anti-clerical bias, passing laws providing for freedom of religion, civil marriage and secular education. (Pope Pius IX promptly denounced this legislation as "damnable and abominable," but to no avail.[24]) In economics, the Liberals favored *laissez faire* capitalism. Consequently, the Panic of 1873 dealt them a serious blow—all the more so when allegations of corruption forced the resignation of a member of Auersperg's cabinet. The lower middle class, who suffered mightily in the ensuing depression, abandoned the German Liberals in droves—many falling prey to conservative, aristocratic and clerical propaganda scapegoating "the Jews" for the party's financial missteps.[25]

Throughout the period of German Liberal ascendancy, Emperor Franz Josef never lost sight of the fact that though he might be German, he was no liberal. Having lost enthusiasm for a ministry which did not share his autocratic desire that he should have things his own way, and which, moreover, was now riven by internal conflict and generally unpopular, he withdrew his support from Auersperg in 1879, allowing for the emergence of a new government under Count Eduard Taaffe—a loyal friend since childhood, who possessed no higher ambition than to be "Minister of the Crown."[26] Backed by an "iron ring" of support from conservatives, clericals and Slavs—the opposition groups that had been driven into each other's arms by a shared hatred of the policies of the German Liberals—Taaffe would rule (or, as he termed it, "muddle through"[27]) for the next fourteen years, keeping the empire's competing factions "in a balanced state of mild dissatisfaction,"[28] while interpreting the Austrian Constitution's many "unsatisfactory clauses" in a manner that "rendered them tolerable even to those against whom they had been directed."[29] He sought "first of all," says *Encyclopædia Britannica*, "to govern by the help of the moderates of all parties … his watchword was 'unpolitical politics,' and he brought in little contentious legislation."[30] Nevertheless, he wrought positive benefits—providing the working class with sickness and accident insurance and extending the franchise to the lower middle class over the protests of the bourgeois German Liberals.[31]

While his exact contemporary, Kálmán Tisza, pursued a policy of Magyarization in Hungary, Taaffe abandoned the Liberals' program of Germanization in Austria—pursuing instead a policy of conciliation toward the subject races in return for loyalty to Franz Josef, and allegiance to the notion of Austrian unity. It was not always an easy policy. In order to show favor to the Poles of Galicia, for example, Taaffe had to abandon the Ruthenians (long the victims of Polish oppression). For a time, he managed to placate the Czechs—giving the Czech language parity in certain Bohemian affairs of state, splitting the German University of Prague into separate Czech and German academies (1882) and passing an electoral law that allowed Czech voters to secure majorities both in their provincial diet and in their imperial *Reichsrath* delegation.[32] Eventually, however, this encouraging legislation led to the emergence of an ardently nationalist "Young Czech" Party, which desired reforms of a more radical nature. In the elections of 1891, "Young Czech" candidates won a commanding majority of Bohemia's seats, provoking street clashes between Czech and German nationalists that ultimately forced the government to declare a "state of siege" in the city of Prague (1893).[33]

Taaffe now hit on the ingenious solution of proposing universal suffrage as a means of diluting nationalist tensions in a larger broth of social, economic and political rivalries. Alas, he neglected to prepare his ground and before he could embark on this noble venture, he found that he had shattered the "iron ring" that had formerly been the prop of his power. To be sure, his old enemies, the German Liberals stood to be ruined by enfranchisement of the increasingly socialist working class. But as *Encyclopædia Britannica* notes, "Not even the pleasure of ruining the Liberals was sufficient to persuade the Conservatives to vote for a measure which would transfer power from the well-to-do to the indigent." Nor, for that matter, were Galicia's Poles willing to jeopardize their privileged status by enfranchising the scarcely less numerous Ruthenians.[34] When Franz Josef refused to support the measure, Taaffe's long tenure came to an end (1893).

Emperor Franz Josef of Austria-Hungary, c. 1880, unknown photographer (Wikimedia Commons).

In the absence of Taaffe's temporizing hand, nationalist rivalries within the *Reichsrath* bloomed into full flower. When one of his successors, Count Kasimir Badeni, sought to settle the language issue in Bohemia in favor of the Czechs in order to get Czech support for the upcoming 10-year tariff and revenue renewal agreement with Hungary (1897),[35] the German delegates resorted to filibustering—one of their members speaking at the rostrum for twelve consecutive hours. When this failed to get the point across, the Germans threw inkwells at their Czech colleagues. A mental image of the *Reichsrath* president being forcibly pinned against the wall while ruffians of a rival faction tear his papers into shreds will give the reader some idea of parliamentary cordiality in this era.[36] Indeed, so acute did the obstructionism of the parties become that in order to get anything done at all between the years 1900 and 1904 Franz Josef had to invoke Article 14 of the Austrian constitution, allowing him to rule by decree.[37] (The fact that he rather enjoyed determining policy in this way did not change the fact that something was terribly amiss.)

In 1907, the tariff and revenue agreement between Austria and Hungary was due to be renegotiated—something that could not be achieved with two obstructed parliaments. A solution was necessary, and Franz Josef sought for it in the answer originally proposed by Taaffe: universal suffrage. The mere threat, as we have seen, induced the moderates and radicals of the Hungarian *Diet* to work together or witness the ruin of Magyar supremacy (1906). On the Austrian side, in contrast, the reform was actually carried out, with suffrage being extended to all males over twenty-four years of age. The *Reichsrath* was now to be composed of 516 delegates representing a like number of constituencies—each drawn, to the degree possible, along lines of nationality so as to dampen internal strife and allow matters of greater import to come to the fore. In the ensuing elections (January 1907), the nationalist parties lost ground to the economic parties of the newly enfranchised working classes. Soon afterwards, the newly published 12th volume of the *Cambridge Modern History* pronounced the measure a decided success. "There are still fierce national struggles, possibly more violent than heretofore," declared the monumental history, "but they are no longer able to impede the action of Parliament. Obstruction has become the weapon of the weakest sections, and in their hands it has lost its force. In decisive moments, the great parties, more especially the economic parties … have shown clearly and vigorously that they do not intend to allow the people's Parliament to be paralysed."[38] Alas, this triumphant assessment proved premature. The addition of class rivalry to nationalist rivalry within the *Reichsrath* allowed for the emergence of thirty competing parties, and a return to obstructionism was not long in coming. In 1911, new elections were held in a bid to break the impasse, but without success. Once again, the emperor and his prime minister resorted to Article 14 of the Constitution providing for rule by imperial decree.[39]

Given sufficient time, the Austrian empire might yet have solved its parliamentary conundrum, for it is by no means certain that nationalist agitation within the empire was equivalent to a desire on the part of the various ethnicities for full and separate independence.[40] Indeed, the year 1908 marked the 60th of Franz Josef's long reign, and his very longevity made him an object of reverence and a symbol of unity for his myriad peoples. He had, moreover, sustained several personal tragedies that made him an object of empathy—the execution of his brother, Maximilian, in the denouement of Napoleon III's Mexican adventure, the murder-suicide perpetrated by his son, Rudolf, and the assassination (at the hands of a deranged anarchist) of his beloved, careworn wife, Elisabeth—a captivating beauty renowned throughout Europe for her equestrian skill.[41]

Sadly, another such tragedy was still to come—one that would drag the monarchy down in its wake. It was ever a matter of embarrassment to Franz Josef that he had presided over Austria's expulsion from Italy and Germany in the wars of 1859 and 1866.[42] In due course, it occurred to him that he might make good on these losses in the Balkans. In 1878, Austrian forces occupied the Ottoman provinces of Bosnia and Herzegovina in the northwestern Balkans. In so doing, they elevated their domestic problem of nationalities to the international arena, setting in motion a ticking time bomb whose explosion awaited only the bullet of an assassin at Sarajevo.

Russia After Crimea: The "Tsar Liberator" and the "Peasants' Tsar"

Beholden to Russia for her part in quashing the Hungarian Revolution of 1848, Austria had repaid the debt poorly by her actions during the Crimean War. The death of Tsar Nicholas I in the midst of that conflict shifted the burden of admitting defeat onto the shoulders of his son and successor, Alexander II (ruled, 1855–1881). An enthusiastic champion of the reactionary "Nicholas System" while his father ruled, the new tsar realized that military defeat had rendered this inflexible policy untenable. In the ensuing months, restrictions on the press and academia were relaxed and myriad political prisoners—among them the survivors of the Decembrist Revolt of 1825—were set free.[43]

The most pressing evil, however, was Russia's archaic agricultural system, a bastion of feudal inefficiency and abuse that even Nicholas had favored reforming.[44] The average serf was illiterate and insular, leading a life of drudgery with reveries that extended no further than the horizon. He spent half his week laboring in the fields for his master, in return for which he was given a hovel for his family and a wisp of land on which to raise crops for their subsistence. His tools were antiquated and his methods obsolete. He married at the pleasure or dictation of his master. By law, he could not be sold from one estate to another, yet he was bound to the estate on which he served and was liable to corporal punishment at the hands of a landlord who could act as judge, jury and witness. The landlord, moreover, had authority to banish a serf to Siberia or to have him drafted into the army for disobedience.[45]

Tsar Alexander II of Russia, by Monogrammist V.G., 1888, Hermitage Museum (Wikimedia Commons).

In spite of these overblown prerogatives, the landlords found the system unprofitable by the mid–19th century, with many falling into debt and having to mortgage their estates. The backwardness of the system—if not its immorality—was widely recognized and was now being held forth as one of the contributing factors to the defeat in Crimea.[46] In the preceding decades, moreover, localized serf unrest had become commonplace, and there was spreading concern that the system would be violently overturned by the serfs themselves if something was not done to ameliorate their plight.[47]

Rather than tempt providence, Tsar Alexander decided to act. "Serfdom is doomed," he declared to a delegation of the Moscow nobility, "and it is better that this necessary reform [i.e., emancipation] should come from above, rather than from below."[48] Many members of the landed aristocracy did not agree, but the tsar stood firm, saying, "serf-dom was instituted by absolute power. Only absolute power can destroy it; and to do so is my will."[49] Accordingly, in 1861—a full two years, be it noted, before Lincoln eman-cipated America's slaves[50]—Europe's most ill-treated peasants were set free by imperial *ukase*. In all, some 48 million serfs were affected[51]—those on private estates being set free first (1861–1863), with those on crown lands following (1866).

Though well intentioned, the emancipation project seemed in some respects to pos-sess the attributes of a confidence scheme. The estate owners retained roughly half of their property (typically the better half). In return for the rest, they received from the state what might have been considered generous compensation had it been paid out in ready cash. Alas, it was paid instead in the form of interest-bearing government bonds and bills of exchange, leaving many debt-ridden landowners with so little liquid equity that they were scarcely able to meet their own estate mortgages, much less improve their remaining property or upgrade their equipment.[52]

The property impounded from the landlords was given, in turn, to the emancipa-ted serfs. This, too, might have been considered generous if the land had been free. But in the same breath that informed them of their emancipation, the serfs were told that freedom came with a forty-nine-year mortgage payable to the state (which thereby rede-emed in cash what it had paid out in bills and bonds). The average serf was a stoic fellow and bolstered by his Russian Orthodox faith and his belief in the goodness of his "little father," the tsar, he might have borne even this burden with equanimity had the parcel of land issued to him been sufficient to support a reasonable living. Sadly, in most cases it was not. He had lost access, moreover, to the landlord's pastureland for grazing his live-stock and to his forestland as a source of wood. Nor could he simply pack up and leave without permission from the government-supervised village commune, or *"mir,"* which was responsible for payment of all peasant-mortgages and held all deeds to the land pending redemption (including authority to confiscate or redistribute a given peasant's plot).[53] There is a reported instance of serfs greeting the explanation of the terms of their emancipation with peals of laughter,[54] and it was wryly said of their new status that they were now bound to the land as "serfs of the state" rather than of their former landlords.[55]

That being said, permission to leave the *mir* was typically granted to those peasants who requested it, since the *mir* was often happier to have the strip of land than the peasant who came with it. Indeed, in the decades to come, so many ex-serfs left their holdings to seek factory work that a cardinal, if unintended, achievement of emancipa-tion was a vast augmentation of the labor pool necessary for Russian industrialization.[56]

The dissatisfaction of the involved parties notwithstanding, Russia's intelligentsia embraced the efforts of the "Tsar Liberator," and had high hopes for further reforms. In this, they were not entirely disappointed. In the ensuing years, a revised legal code was adopted, applicable to all, without class prejudice. Trial by jury was introduced in cri-minal cases (though not in political ones). Local administration, formerly in the dicta-torial hands of the landlords, was handed over to elected local assemblies—known as *zemvstos*—within which all classes were represented. Organized at the county and pro-vincial level, the *zemvstos* levied taxes in order to finance hospitals, public sanitation, education, law enforcement, the courts, agricultural innovation and road and bridge maintenance. In addition, they sought to ease the inevitable antagonisms that arose bet-ween emancipated serfs and their former masters.[57] A revision of the tax on alcohol sales went somewhat awry—yielding a six-fold increase in public drunkenness without significant benefit to the treasury[58]—but the creation of a Russian State Bank at the outset of the 1860s provided the important service of making credit available for the expansion of railroads and industry.[59]

Yet, the chief hope and aspiration of the intelligentsia was not to be realized; namely, that Alexander might abandon autocracy in favor of parliamentary and constitutional government[60]—a necessary prerequisite, it was argued, if Russia was to close the gap with the rapidly modernizing states that had defeated her in the Crimean War. To the contrary, when he was not reforming things, Alexander was a dyed-in-the-wool autocrat—and events were now to confirm him in this prejudice. The death of Nicholas I, the defeat of Russia in the Crimean War, the amnesty granted to political prisoners by Alexander II at his accession (included among whom were a number of Polish patriots) and Italy's successful liberation war of 1859 had served in combination to reawaken Polish nationalism at the outset of the new reign. Enmity between Poland's feudal gentry and serfs had played a major role in the failure of the Polish uprising of 1831, and in a bid to rally the serfs to the cause of independence this time, Polish nationalists agitated for their emancipation.[61] Although Alexander had opened his reign with several liberalizing concessions to the Poles, he saw in this demand the seed of revolution. Consequently, he denied emancipation to the serfs of Poland at the time of his great *ukase*; and when, in the aftermath of this decision, the outcries of the Polish nationalists became more radical, he sought to conscript the leading agitators into the Russian army (January 1863).

This ill-considered expedient sparked an equally ill-considered revolutionary outbreak on the part of the Poles, whose woeful unpreparedness may be gauged by an early skirmish at Skala, in which the Polish patriot, Andrey Potebnia, met his death leading a charge of *scythe-bearing* Polish infantry.[62] Two weeks later, at Grokowiska, a three-day encounter between a few thousand combatants on either side ended in the defeat of the newly appointed Polish dictator and commander-in-chief, Marion Langiewicz, who fled across the Austrian border.[63]

Although France, Britain and, to an extent, Austria, sympathized with the Polish cause (and although thousands of foreign freedom fighters enlisted with the Poles—among them Giuseppe Garibaldi's son, who died in the fighting),[64] it rapidly became apparent that foreign intervention on Poland's behalf was not forthcoming.[65] The more moderate "white" Polish revolutionaries were now supplanted by the radical "reds," who instituted universal conscription, decreed emancipation of the serfs (with the penalty of death imposed on landlords who refused) and embarked on a reign of terror to prevent the faint of heart from accepting a conditional amnesty and counter-emancipation of the serfs offered by the tsar. Under the leadership of a new and energetic dictator, Romuald Traugutt, the Poles resorted to ambushes and guerrilla warfare. Both sides engaged in atrocities. But in April 1864, Traugutt was apprehended and hanged with his closest associates outside the gates of Warsaw, and with the subsequent capture and execution, at Podlasie, of the sole remaining guerrilla leader, Father Stanislaw Brzoska, the revolt came to an end.[66]

If the Polish uprising was not enough to dissuade the tsar from further reforms, the sequel settled the matter. On April 16, 1866, as Alexander returned to his carriage after his daily walk, a radical student named Dmitri Karakozov pressed through a crowd of onlookers and fired a pistol shot at him. The tsar owed his survival to an alert hatter's apprentice whose attempt to grab the shooter's hand deflected the shot. (A year later, a second assassination attempt was made by a disgruntled Pole, who shot at the carriage containing Napoleon III and the tsar during the latter's visit to the Paris Exhibition of 1867.)[67]

Karakozov's attempt provoked a change in Alexander's demeanor. He became sullen and withdrawn,[68] and now tended to agree with those of his advisors who said that his reforms had gone too far. In the ensuing decade, he suffered his regime to become more reactionary. Press censorship was reinstated. Political agitators—among them many university students—were apprehended by the notorious Third Section and sentenced without jury trials.[69] When the newly established *zemvstos* petitioned the government for constitutional reform, they were instructed to confine their debates to economic questions rather than to political ones. (For good measure, the electoral process was altered to make future *zemstvo* elections less democratic.)[70]

In parallel with these measures, the wheels of reform screeched to a halt, and the resultant inertia provoked a backlash from the once-friendly intelligentsia. Movements sprang to the fore ranging from "Nihilism"—whose devotees rejected all traditional ideas and institutions—to anarchism, which held that utopia could best be achieved by smashing the antiquated tsarist regime to pieces. During the 1870s, youthful Nihilist zealots (known as "Narodniks" for their policy of "going among the people") toured the countryside, explaining the evils of the existing system to Russia's simpleton peasants.[71] Taken aback by their appearance and odd ideas, the peasants were more inclined to assault these newcomers than to heed their advice. But the radicals would not be kept at bay, and when the government greeted their solicitations with suppression and arbitrary arrest, they adopted a more violent policy.

In 1879, a new movement, the "People's Will," became the modern world's first full-fledged terrorist organization. Sworn to destroy the tsarist regime, their repetitive acts of terrorism—which included the murder of the head of the Third Section and attempts to assassinate the tsar himself—first by bombing a train on which he was thought to be traveling and then by blowing up the dining room of the Winter Palace—compelled Alexander to summon the conciliatory Loris Melikoff to serve as his chief minister (1880). In a bid to steal the terrorists' thunder, Melikoff prevailed upon the tsar to return to a policy of political reform, and on March 13, 1881, Alexander agreed to a new program of measured democratization. As fate would have it, a bomb was hurled at his carriage that very afternoon.[72] Alexander was unhurt, and the man who hurled the bomb was immediately seized. Catching sight of him, the tsar remarked, "What that one? Why, he's nice looking."[73] Alas, this was no random act of terrorism. Three other assassins were lying in wait, and when Alexander attempted to go to the assistance of the wounded Cossacks in his escort, one of them threw a second bomb from just a few feet away. The explosion tore out Alexander's intestines and smashed his legs. He gasped to an attendant that if he must die, he would prefer that it be in the palace. He expired soon after being taken there.[74] The hope for meaningful reform in Tsarist Russia died with him.

His son and successor, Alexander III (ruled, 1881–1894), sought to alleviate the condition of the peasantry by eliminating the poll tax (widely considered "the last relic of serfdom"); by establishing a Peasants' Bank to provide credit at low interest; and by cancelling the peasants' land redemption payments in years of severe hardship. For these actions, he gained renown as the "Peasants' Tsar."[75] Towards the end of his reign,

The assassination of Alexander II, 1881, by Gustav Broling (Wikimedia Commons).

moreover, he appointed Sergei Witte as Minister of Finance and Commerce, and thereby brought Russia into the industrial era.

While serving as a government railroad official, Witte had distinguished himself by determining that a violent and mysterious derailment of the imperial train carrying the tsar and his family near Biorki, in 1888, had been caused by excessive traveling speed rather than by terrorism.[76] (In the aftermath of that harrowing episode, the robust six-foot-three tsar had used his back and shoulders to support the collapsed roof of the train's dining car, allowing his family to emerge unscathed from the wreckage.) Following his appointment, Witte attracted foreign industrial investment on a broad scale by drawing attention to Russia's cheap and abundant labor pool, her plentiful, and as yet undeveloped, natural resources, the state's protectionist tariffs (which minimized competition from foreign manufactures) and the promise of large government contracts for finished goods.[77] The result was a massive expansion in factories, mines and railways. At the outset of Alexander II's reign in 1855, for example, there were 650 miles of rail in the entire country (the majority composing the line between Moscow and St. Petersburg). By the time of his assassination in 1881, this figure had increased to 14,000 miles.[78] In contrast, at the end of Alexander III's reign just thirteen years later there were 40,000 miles of existing track, and work was well underway on the famous Trans-Siberian Railway, which was to open Russia's eastern expanse to settlement and industry.[79]

Beyond the economic realm, however, Alexander III was scarcely less reactionary than his grandfather, Nicholas I. Brusque and soldierly in bearing, inflexible and narrow-minded in intellect, the "Peasants' Tsar" was a convinced "Slavophile," who dressed in a peasant's blouse and believed in a unique Russian destiny that Western influences only served to corrupt. On ascending the throne, he announced that "The

Voice of God, orders us to stand firm at the helm of the government … with faith in the strength and truth of the autocratic power, which we are called upon to strengthen and preserve for the good of the people."[80] As chief minister, he chose his former tutor, the rabidly anti–Semitic Konstantin Pobiedonostsev, who equated freedom of the press with license to defame, and denounced representative institutions as arenas for the pursuit of private ambition at public expense.[81]

Acting on the motto, "One Russia, One Creed, One Tsar,"[82] the new regime carried out a program of "Russification" (i.e., the imposition of the Russian language and Orthodox Church authority) in the Lutheran Baltic Provinces and Catholic Poland. The government abandoned the liberalization project of Loris Melikoff; restricted the power of the *zemvstos* (and the number of those eligible to vote for them); suppressed liberal publications; purged the universities of radical students and professors; gave local authorities power to declare martial law; and promulgated the infamous "May Laws" of 1882, debarring Jews from public service and agricultural pursuits (lest they outperform the peasantry), while curtailing their educational opportunities and strictly enforcing their confinement to the Pale of Settlement in western Russia. A new innovation of the reign was the "pogrom," in which Jewish communities were subjected to wanton pillage and murder at the hands of bigoted mobs while officialdom did nothing to intervene. By these persecutory measures, Pobiedonostsev seems to have hoped to induce a third of Russian Jewry to emigrate, another third to convert to Russian Orthodoxy, and the last to perish in the ghettos.[83] A wave of Jewish emigration (if not conversion) ensued with 300,000 fleeing the country in 1891 alone—mostly to the United States and England.[84]

To enforce the regime's reactionary policies a veritable "police state" was erected by the new "Director of State Police," Vyacheslav von Plehve, whose ubiquitous constables and spies hounded terrorists unto their deaths "with a vigor so great and a success so terrible," says Carlton Hayes, "that the reign of Alexander III was marked by a seeming lull in revolutionary propaganda."[85] Despite pleas for clemency, including one from the famed novelist, Leo Tolstoy, the reign opened with the execution, by hanging, of the assassins of Alexander II (the female mastermind, Sophia Perovskaya, among them). Six years later, Alexander Ulyanov, the elder brother of the future Soviet ruler, Vladimir Ulyanov (better known as "Lenin"), was likewise executed after being apprehended in an assassination plot.

But the quietude achieved by the policy of repression was more apparent than real. It came, moreover, at the cost of isolating the regime. For his own protection, the tsar relocated his residence to the walled palace at Gatchina—thirty miles removed from St. Petersburg—with a veritable army of Cossacks stationed outside.[86] Here he might spend time with his wife and family, to whom he was admirably devoted. Here, too, he might maintain his rigid belief system. Beyond the walls of the palace, however, and beyond the collective imagination of the regime, industrialization was unleashing changes in Russia that police chains could not bind—including a small but politically minded middle class and an abused and malcontent urban proletariat.[87]

The Last Tsar

In 1894, Alexander III died of nephritis with the façade of tranquility still intact. The storm would break upon his son. Nicholas II did not want to be tsar and tearfully admitted as much to those around him upon his father's death.[88] Nothing had been done to prepare him for the office. At the insistence of Count Witte—and over the protests of his father who thought him too naïve—Nicholas was appointed president of the Trans-Siberian Railroad Commission during the early 1890s. Given sage guidance, he discharged this duty competently, but he was given no other official responsibilities.[89] As hesitating as his father was domineering, the new tsar repeatedly showed deference to the decisions of his overbearing mother—a habit that provoked his newlywed bride, Alexandra (formerly Princess Alix of Hesse, a granddaughter of Queen Victoria), to remind him that a tsar must speak for himself.[90]

The new tsar's coronation, which was delayed until May 1896, had an inauspicious beginning and a tragic end. In the midst of the solemnity, the chain necklace holding the venerated Order of Saint Andrew somehow came loose from the tsar's neck and rattled onto the floor of the Cathedral of the Assumption. The evil augury thus foretold came to fruition three days later at the traditional handing out of souvenirs on Khodynka Field. As a half million attendees crowded onto the campus from the surrounding avenues, rumor announced that the supply of souvenir teacups bearing the Romanov double-eagle emblem was insufficient. There ensued a mad rush toward the kiosks from which they were being dispensed. Alas, a series of unseen trenches intervened—the handiwork of Russian military engineers, who normally used the field for their training exercises.[91] The mounted Cossacks standing guard at the site were carried backward as if by a tidal wave. Pressed inexorably from behind, throngs of unfortunates toppled into the trenches and were buried or trodden over by those who came after them.[92] The number of dead reached 2,000, with many others maimed.

Distraught by the news, the tsar proposed hastening to the site to assist the injured, or barring that, withdrawing to a monastery for prayer. His powerful uncles bade him instead to keep up appearances by attending an imperial ball scheduled for that evening. His mother protested, but his wife, now her bitter rival, cast the deciding vote in favor— not out of spite, but out of superstition that it would be unlucky to cut short the coronation festivities on such a tragic note.

If ever there was an occasion when Nicholas ought to have listened to his mother rather than to his wife, this was it. Faced with conflicting advice, however, the tsar resorted to his one unfailing talent—the ability to make the wrong decision. The dance went forward as planned, creating a most regrettable impression among the people.[93]

"It was soon realized," says Schapiro, "that Nicholas resembled neither his father in strength of purpose nor his grandfather in liberality of spirit...."[94] On the occasion of his accession, the *zemstvo* of the district of Tver expressed hope that the new tsar might establish a national representative assembly to assist him in good governance. In a reply dictated by Pobiedonostsev (who was retained as chief minister) they were informed that such musings were but "senseless dreams."[95] "I shall preserve the principles of autocracy as firmly and unswervingly as my late father of imperishable memory," the new tsar declared.[96] His program included the "Russification" of the hitherto autonomous Grand Duchy of Finland, which had possessed its own constitution, currency, postal system and military since its incorporation into Russia in 1809. The revocation of their constitution provoked the Finns to declare a day of mourning. Within the week a petition of protest attracted a half million signatures—each and every one to no avail. The reactionaries of the Russian autocracy thought the existence of a constitutional province a very poor example for the country.

In pursuit of autocracy at home, the censors banned John Richard Green's *Short*

History of the English People, which presented rather too rosy a picture of life under Britain's constitutional monarchy. "What [the government] enforces," mourned the contemporary Russian historian, Paul Vinogradoff, "is obedience to order, not to law, and its contempt of law is exemplified in every way." Police supervision of the universities was redoubled. During a single year, it was estimated that twenty percent of the student body at the University of Moscow was sentenced to Siberia or driven into foreign exile.[97] Under the tutelage of holdovers like Pobiedonostsev and Plehve, the antiquated system of Alexander III (perhaps it would be more apt to say "of Nicholas I") was elevated to peak efficiency in the first decade of the new reign. While the state was cracking down, however, a great accomplishment was in process that was carrying Russian society beyond the capacity of even the most sophisticated police apparatus—for the economic policy of the finance minister, Count Witte, had finally borne fruit.

By the turn of the century, Witte had attracted a fortune in foreign investment with his program of protective tariffs and his provision of industrial transport at bargain rates on Russia's ever-expanding state-owned rail system. So fast did factories appear during his tenure that they were likened unto "mushrooms."[98] The populations of Moscow and Saint Petersburg surpassed one million[99] as penniless peasants flocked from the countryside to the cities to become factory laborers—some turning to industry in order to supplement their meager agricultural earnings during the offseason, others forsaking rural life altogether as the rate of population growth outstripped the supply of primitively-cultivated arable land.

In addition to protecting nascent industry, Witte's tariff system made it cost-effective for investors to exploit Russia's vast untapped natural resources. "Between 1886 and 1899," says the *Cambridge Modern History*, "the national output of iron was more than quadrupled, till it exceeded that of France."[100] Hitherto, it had been cheaper to import such essentials as coal, iron and oil; but with branch connections now running from the main rail lines to areas rich in raw materials, coal from the Donetz basin, iron from Krivoy Rog, oil from the Caucasus, cotton from central Asia and timber and minerals from Siberia became the lifeblood of Russian industry.[101]

If, in spite of this trend, the nation remained overwhelmingly agricultural, there emerged for the first time in Russian history an abused proletarian class composed of several million souls—many of whom labored up to 18 hours a day and slept in their workrooms.[102] Abysmal as this may have been, conditions in the countryside were frequently worse. To support the growth of industry and the maintenance of the Russian army and navy, the tax burden on the peasantry perpetually increased. "It may be said without exaggeration," says Vinogradoff, "that for the majority of the Russian peasantry the primary object of life is to earn enough to pay the taxes, everything else is accident."[103] The state raised money, too, by exporting such vast quantities of grain at discounted prices that there was scarcely enough left over to meet domestic needs. Hence, when the harvest failed in 1891 across a broad swath of the country, all the grain reserves from prior harvests had already been sent abroad. The severity of the resulting famine may be gauged by the occasional use of the word "cannibalism" in otherwise polite conversation.[104] Even the "good" times were bad. Speaking in 1902, Vinogradoff noted that "In some districts of the province of Samara, which counts among the granaries of Russia, there have been years when one-third, and even one-half of the population have been turned into mendicants."[105]

Despite the mounting hardship, the regime's intricate police network effectively muzzled opposition to the autocracy throughout the 1890s, while its centralized civil service—composed of a half-million functionaries drawn from the aristocracy and professional classes—presided over state policy from the capital at St. Petersburg to the hithermost regions of the realm.[106] It has been said that the tsarist regime was scarcely more than "a police department writ large." Yet the system was not without flexibility, for the civil service was so poorly paid and consequently so susceptible to bribery that the resultant apparatus has been dubbed "a despotism tempered by corruption."[107]

Reigning over the whole was his majesty, Tsar Nicholas II. But if it appeared to contemporaries that Nicholas occupied the apex of a power pyramid, it would be truer to say that he was seated atop a volcano. Still smarting from the abolition of serfdom, the aristocracy resented the emphasis the government was now placing on commerce and industry, whose leadership, in turn, was perturbed by the absence of a political voice to match its growing share of the national wealth. The disenfranchised professional classes and intelligentsia were similarly restless, while the empire's myriad national minorities—most especially the Finns and Poles—writhed and strained beneath the yoke of Russification.[108]

At the lower echelons of society, unrest sometimes found expression in violence. When, for example, failed harvests resulted in a recurrence of famine in 1897, the peasantry ran riot—burning manors, killing landlords, slaughtering livestock and senselessly destroying rural infrastructure established over the course of decades by the *zemvstos*. In the same year, tens of thousands of textile laborers staged mass strikes in St. Petersburg.[109] There ensued the formation of Russia's first Marxist political organization—the "Workmen's Social Democratic Party"—which found a willing audience for its propaganda among the proletariat in Russia's overcrowded factories (1898). Three years later, a "Socialist Revolutionary Party" emerged in the countryside promising to confiscate the great landed estates for redistribution among the peasantry.[110]

These Marxist movements were as yet small, and the police were sometimes surprisingly imaginative in countering them. Beginning in 1902, the head of the Moscow *Okhrana* (secret police), Colonel Sergei Zubatov, began recruiting workers into technically "illegal" trade unions controlled clandestinely by his own agents. These, in turn, orchestrated outcries for improved working conditions—at times to the point of strikes—but carefully avoided any mention of Marx or revolution, thereby averting radicalism by sleight of hand.[111] Alas, the agrarian Social Revolutionary Party lay beyond Zubatov's purview. Moreover, it possessed a "combat section" that was now to embark on a series of assassinations that would invoke the specter of its precursor, the "People's Will." The first of its celebrated victims was the minister of the interior, Dmitry Sipyagin, who was shot dead in the foyer of the Mariinsky Palace by a 20-year-old radical student on April 2, 1902. Sipyagin's successor in the post was none other than the notorious former director of the state police, Vyacheslav Plehve, who was everywhere hated, but especially so in Lithuania, Finland and Poland owing to his central role in the "Russification" of those provinces.

Within a year of assuming office, Plehve helped engineer the dismissal of the regime's one enlightened voice, the finance minister, Count Witte, whose industrialization policy he staunchly opposed "on the ground that it involved the existence both of a dangerous proletariat and of a prosperous middle class equally inimical to the autocracy."[112] Under Plehve, a campaign of rigid intolerance was pursued, with the arrest and exile of even moderate anti-government agitators. Roving bands of reactionary hooligans, known as the "Black Hundreds," were unloosed upon the nation's dissenters, and, more especially upon the Jews, who were victimized in vicious pogroms as part of a purposeful government-inspired, anti–Semitic revival aimed at distracting attention from the woeful state of the nation.[113] In 1903, a pogrom against the Jews of Kishinev provoked a worldwide uproar as men, women and children were gruesomely murdered while local authorities refused to act.[114]

Plehve's reactionary program was characterized, too, by the use of *agents provocateurs* who incited would-be terrorists to violence and then tipped off the police in time to preempt their activities and carry out arrests. The most extraordinary of these agents was Yevno Azev, who managed to get himself appointed head of the terrorists' own "combat section" where, to quote Schapiro, "he was very energetic in organizing groups and then secretly betraying them to the police."[115] What the government did not know about Azev was that in order to maintain appearances he let the assassins finish their tasks from time to time. In 1904, for example, he let them kill Plehve. (The assassin, Yegor Sazonov, hurled a bomb at the interior minister's carriage on Izmailovsky Prospect in St. Petersburg leaving Plehve dead, the boulevard strewn with debris and the carriage reduced to a skeleton chassis with its four wheels miraculously intact.[116])

The Russo-Japanese War and Its Aftermath

For a few years, the assassinations, betrayals, arrests, hangings, manor burnings and strikes proceeded apace; but a tipping point was ultimately reached in 1905 owing to an unfortunate military foray involving one of the great imperial playgrounds of the 19th century. We speak, here, of the Far East, where, for centuries, the vast empire of China had existed in splendid isolation—that is, until the 1830s, when Britain finally convinced the reclusive nation that Western Civilization had something to offer. It was called "opium," and the Chinese—or at least a few Chinese—could not seem to get enough of it. Hopes for an East-West entente based upon the opium trade were rudely dashed, however, when, in May 1839, Chinese authorities at Canton Harbor seized and destroyed the latest smuggled shipment of the illegal drug. Britain reacted with outrage. She retaliated with a declaration of war (although she had first to identify a pretext that did not involve opium, which caused a delay of six weeks).[117]

After the initial skirmishing went Britain's way, China offered to cede Hong Kong to Her Majesty's Government and to pay an indemnity of six million dollars. Britain, however, was intent on obtaining more. Relying on superior weaponry to inflict roughly one hundred casualties for every one sustained,[118] her troops advanced from Canton to Nanking where they imposed the Treaty of Nanking (1842), securing not only twenty million dollars in indemnities and possession of Hong Kong (which Britain had occupied at the outset of the struggle), but also trading privileges in five of China's busiest ports—among them, Canton and Shanghai.

A decade after this so-called "Opium War," a similar "invitation" to liberalize trade policy was extended to Japan by Commodore Matthew Perry at the head of a conspicuously well-armed United States naval squadron (1853). The reactions of the two eastern nations to the forcible opening of their ports differed markedly. China remained withdrawn from Western culture insomuch as this was possible, whereas Japan (after some heated discussion and an unavoidable, if anachronistic, Samurai uprising) avidly adopted Western scientific and economic principles. In the course of a single generation (1867–1900), Japan abolished feudalism, built factories and railroads, adopted a

Prussian-style constitution and conscripted a Prussian-style army, thereby transforming itself into a modern state.

All she lacked now were new sources of raw materials for her factories and new markets for her goods. And for these, she resorted to another Western precedent— namely, imperialism. In 1894, she secured her markets and materials by occupying the "hermit kingdom" of Korea and Chinese Manchuria. Aghast, China mobilized a vast army with which to drive the odious little "dwarfs"[119] back to the island whence they had come. But China's outmoded forces were annihilated, and Japan emerged from the contest in possession of Port Arthur, a valuable warm water anchorage located on China's Liaotung peninsula.

Scarcely had this "Sino-Japanese War" ended (1895), however, before the major European powers, spearheaded by a jealous Russia (which desired Manchuria and Port Arthur for itself), intervened to undo the Japanese triumph on the pretext of protecting Chinese independence. As was soon apparent to all, the Europeans posed a greater threat to Chinese autonomy than had her recent conquerors. To be sure, the Japanese were sent packing, but in their place Russia, France, Germany and England each established their own "spheres of influence" on Chinese soil.

This would have been bad enough merely on the grounds of intrusiveness; but according to Hazen, the "really vital religion" of the Chinese for many centuries had been "ancestor worship," and the intruding Europeans had an unfortunate knack for building new railroads over sacred burial grounds—a habit that, in Schapiro's phrasing, "aroused popular fury against those who violated the sanctity of ancestral tombs."[120] Chafing at this and other acts of despoliation, the Chinese populace embarked upon the "Boxer Rebellion" of 1900—so-called because the most fanatical rebels belonged to the "Society of Righteous and Harmonious Fists," a group of martial arts experts ridiculed in the European press as "the Boxers." In the ensuing months, the Boxers received overt assistance from the Chinese government and army in a bid "to drive the foreign devils into the sea."[121] Foreign nationals were set upon by Chinese mobs, Peking's Legation Quarter was placed under siege, and the German ambassador was gunned down in cold blood. In the end, the rescue of the assailed Peking embassies required a joint military expedition by Japanese, Russian, French, German, American and British soldiers. The Boxers were subdued, and at the insistence of the allies, hundreds were executed, while the Chinese government was burdened with a huge indemnity and made to suffer the establishment of foreign military outposts on its soil.

To the great consternation of Japan, the European intervention enabled her neighbor, Russia, to obtain, for the first time in its long history, a warm water port—namely, the self-same Port Arthur from which the Japanese had just been evicted. Worse still, Russia began extending her hegemony over the adjacent Asian coastline—a policy that bade fair to cripple Japan's economy by separating her from her markets on the mainland.[122] (In the midst of it, the Japanese seem not to have been fooled by an influx of Russian soldiers dressed as lumbermen in search of timber.[123])

In sum, everything seemed to be going Russia's way. But to obtain the myriad concessions it had received at Chinese expense, the tsar's government had loaned China a great deal of money. China, in turn, had passed the larger part of these funds along to Japan to satisfy the large war indemnity imposed after the Sino-Japanese War. And Japan had used these same funds to embark on a massive military build-up.[124] Hence, when Russia refused to redress Japan's grievances via diplomacy, a refurbished Japanese army, financed indirectly by Russian rubles, invaded Korea (February 1904)—opening the hostilities with an unscrupulous surprise attack on the Russian fleet in Port Arthur Bay two days *prior* to her declaration of war (a procedure which may sound vaguely familiar to American readers).

Over the next six months, Japanese forces severed Port Arthur's rail connection with Siberia, and subdued two Russian fleets—i.e., those of Port Arthur and Vladivostok.[125] Beleaguered Port Arthur was then besieged, bombarded and stormed repeatedly until the Japanese captured it in January 1905 at a cost of 60,000 casualties. Afterwards, the scene of operations shifted to Mukden in Manchuria, where the Japanese engaged Russia's remaining forces in a bloody two-week showdown (March 1905). It was the largest contest on a field of battle to date, involving over 600,000 troops.[126] It was also another Russian defeat. The tsar's forces lost 90,000 men, the Japanese 70,000.

Russia, of course, had massive reserves in manpower, but they were located, for the most part, thousands of miles to the west in European Russia, with only the single artery of the Trans-Siberian Railway available for transport. (The railway, moreover, was not sturdy enough for sustained carriage of heavy artillery.)[127] Russia's last throw was a forlorn hope. In October 1904, she dispatched her Baltic Fleet to sail around Africa and India to the theater of war. It finally arrived in the China Sea, half a world away, in May 1905—which is to say, four months too late to relieve Port Arthur. Bound for the Russian Pacific port of Vladivostok, its commander, Admiral Zinovi Rozhdestvensky, made the ironic decision (after so long a voyage) to pursue a short-cut—steaming into the Straits of Tsushima between Japan and Korea, rather than taking the longer but less foreboding route around Japan.[128] There, in the Straits, on May 27, his fleet was cornered by the Japanese navy, and sent to the bottom, carrying Russia's remaining war hopes into the deep.

When the fate of the Baltic fleet became known, the tsar was at leisure on the imperial tennis court. He paused long enough to hear the news and went back to his game.[129] By this time, there was unrest throughout the country. In many cases, soldiers ordered to the Manchurian front had to be prodded aboard the transport trains with bayonets, while reservists fled to Austria or Germany rather than report for duty. It was common knowledge that the nation's military leadership was incompetent, and that war profiteers were diverting materials meant for the army to the black market.[130] Menacing throngs appeared in the streets of Moscow and Saint Petersburg calling for the overthrow of the autocracy—a situation that was greatly exacerbated on January 22, 1905, when a certain idealistic priest (and sometimes government agent), Father Georgy Gapon, advised striking workers at the St. Petersburg Putilov factory to seek redress for their grievances by marching on the Winter Palace to petition the "little father," Tsar Nicholas, himself. So good did this idea seem, that some 200,000 souls decided to participate in the procession. Unfortunately, the sight of so many marchers converging on the Winter Palace created a rather different impression than Father Gapon had intended, and before any worthwhile petitioning could take place, the alarmed Palace Guard fired several volleys of warning shots directly into the crowd, killing hundreds. (For good measure, says the *Cambridge Modern History*, "in the Alexander Garden a volley from the troops brought down some of the urchins who had climbed the trees."[131]) By an odd coincidence, the tsar was not even present. He and his family were away at Tsarskoe Selo.

Far from forcing the discontent underground, the volley-fire of "Bloody Sunday" unlocked the floodgates. In February, Grand Duke Sergei, the sadistic Governor of Moscow, fell victim to a bomb. In June, the abused sailors of the Black Sea fleet's prized warship, *Potemkin*, mutinied—killing their officers before putting in at Odessa, where, quite by coincidence, revolutionaries were engaged in violent street fighting with tsarist troops. (In his masterful 1929 film version of the event, famed Russian director Sergei Eisenstein portrayed the mutineers as joining hands with the insurgents. In truth, they only fired a few badly aimed artillery shells into the city before abandoning the street fighters to their bloody fate. With the remainder of the Black Sea fleet in pursuit, *Potemkin* steamed for the Romanian port of Costanza, where the sailors scuttled it and took asylum ashore.[132] The fleet reached Odessa two days later.)

Amid these disturbances, the disastrous war with Japan could not be indefinitely prosecuted. Mercifully, the Treaty of Portsmouth, mediated by Theodore Roosevelt, ended hostilities in September 1905. But in the following month, Russia's domestic discontent reached unmanageable proportions. Mob disorder in Moscow and Saint Petersburg blossomed into a general strike that paralyzed the nation's transport system just as famine was provoking peasant riots in the countryside. Laborers in the factories, mines and postal service soon threw in their lot with the striking rail and telegraph workers; and when the gas and electric plants followed suit, the nation's cities went dark as pitch in the night.[133] (A similar general strike in Finland forced the tsar to restore the old Finnish constitution at this time. It was later revoked again.)

To cope with the crisis, Nicholas recalled Count Witte to serve as prime minister.[134] Witte suppressed the uprisings forcibly, but convinced Nicholas to issue an official *ukase*, known as the "October Manifesto," proclaiming freedom of speech, association and conscience, and granting the establishment of a "Duma," or representative assembly (October 1905). The ensuing elections, held in March and April, gave 185 seats to the "Constitutional Democrats"—"Kadets" for short—who were bent on establishing a true constitutional monarchy in Russia. Social Democrats captured 14 seats and a peasant party, the so-called "Labor Group," took 100. Another party, the "Octobrists," who were content that the Duma should be no more than a consultative assembly, as spelled out in the October Manifesto, obtained a mere 40 seats.[135] Before the new parliament opened its first session, however, the government had taken measures to limit its powers by adding an upper house—the Council of State—half of whose membership was elected, and half appointed. For a measure to be brought before the tsar, it had first to pass both houses. If, on the other hand, the lower, popularly elected, house, proposed a hostile budget, the tsar could seek one more to his liking from the upper house.[136]

Now that the violent unrest in the cities and countryside had been put down, Witte found that he could no longer influence the tsar. He therefore tendered his resignation (April 1906). His successor, Ivan Goremykin, promptly pronounced the existence of a body of so-called "organic laws," subject to the tsar's authority alone, which the Duma was not allowed to violate.[137] In defiance, the Duma called for investigations into the handling of the Russo-Japanese War and into the government's role in the pogroms against the Jews (which were still ongoing). Additionally, it called for the abolition of capital punishment and amnesty for political prisoners, while supporting the "Labor Group" in its call for the dissolution of large rural estates for redistribution among small peasant proprietors. Finding its measures vetoed, it demanded that the tsar's ministry be made responsible to the Duma, and when this was refused it tried to bring its case directly to the people. Nicholas responded by dissolving the assembly and calling for new elections (July 1906).[138]

Despite government meddling in the electoral process, the ensuing elections resulted in another victory for the Kadets, while also giving fully 100 seats to the overtly

Marxist Social Democrats and Social Revolutionaries (March 1907). The second Duma was thus even more radical than its predecessor, and after locking horns with a new, strong-willed prime minister, Peter Stolypin, for scarcely 100 days, it, too, was dissolved—this time with several of its leading members being arrested on trumped up charges of revolutionary conspiracy.[139]

In order to obtain the election of a body that would do its bidding the government now resorted to what was effectively an electoral *coup d'état*—sharply reducing the number of delegates representing the national minorities, while, in the words of *Encyclopædia Britannica*, employing a procedure of "indirect election, through a series of electoral colleges … [that handed] effective power to the propertied classes without ostensibly depriving any one of the vote."[140] The result of these machinations was the election of the third—or "Landowner's"—Duma,[141] which opened its session in November 1907 and would serve until the end of its allotted five-year term in 1912. For all but the last year, the dominant figure in the government was Peter Stolypin who continued in the post of prime minister.

Though staunchly conservative, Stolypin embarked on a program of reform, which he characterized as "a wager on the strong and sober"[142]—providing state disability insurance to workingmen, expanding elementary education and streamlining local government. His rural policy greatly increased the nation's agricultural output by cancelling peasant redemption dues still outstanding from the 1861 emancipation edict, abolishing communal ownership of property by the *mir*, and reanimating the Peasant Land Bank in order to allow enterprising peasants to purchase viable plots of land on which to pursue a better life. Stolypin seems to have hoped that his program would create a class of small landowners loyal to the autocracy.[143]

Before instituting these reforms, Stolypin declared open war on the anarchy of the preceding years. His motto was "First pacification, then reform," and in this policy, he was not without support, for the nation was exhausted from its recent trials. In 1906–1907, more than 4,000 policemen, government officials and innocent bystanders were killed or wounded in acts of terrorism.[144] Stolypin struck back in a resolute campaign—staying the course even after his own summer home was bombed leaving more than twenty dead and two of his children badly injured (1906).[145] Between 1906 and 1908, more than two thousand terrorists were executed[146]—enough to make "Stolypin's necktie" a euphemism for the hangman's noose[147]—while thousands more were dispatched to Siberia or hounded into foreign exile for political crimes. With order restored, the Duma was suffered, on occasion, to assert itself in the name of necessary reforms. At the behest of its leadership, the tsar's powerful uncles were removed from command of the navy (which had performed so badly under their stewardship during the Russo-Japanese War) and the Old Believers were allowed to pronounce their heresies without censure.[148] Stolypin's forbearance in such matters was sufficient to render him as hated among reactionaries as he had been hitherto among revolutionaries. He was assassinated by pistol shot at point-blank range on September 1, 1911, at the Kiev Opera House in full view of the tsar's imperial box. The assassin, fittingly enough, was the Socialist Revolutionary-turned-police agent, D.G. Bogrov, who presumably had his choice of two pretexts—radical right or radical left—on which to pull the trigger. (Bogrov was executed for his crime before anyone thought to ask him in which capacity he had acted.)[149]

Thus died Stolypin, the last best hope of the tsarist regime, leaving Russia without a capable hand at the rudder when Europe blundered into a cataclysmic war three years later.

The Kingdom of Italy, 1870–1914

While pleas for responsible ministerial government went unheard in Russia, the newly unified state of Italy attempted to produce a true parliamentary system based on the British model. While the Italian king appointed his ministers, they were answerable to a two-house parliament in which the lower, popularly elected chamber held the leading voice.

Despite vehement protests from Pope Pius IX, who regarded the unification of Italy as a "Sardinian" usurpation, the Italian government moved its capital from Florence to Rome in 1870. Mindful of international sentiment,[150] it simultaneously confirmed the pontiff's status as spiritual leader of Catholicism and offered generous compensation for his temporal losses. Pius refused these terms, but the Italian parliament overruled him by promulgating the *Law of Papal Guarantees* (May 1871), which recognized papal sovereignty over Rome's "Leonine City" district. Within this tiny realm (encompassing the Vatican, Lateran and Castle Gandolfo), Italian officials were to have no jurisdiction—their very entry being prohibited without a papal invitation. The pope was to possess his own diplomatic service. His spiritual powers were again confirmed, and he was to receive a generous annual pension as restitution for the loss of the Papal States.[151] Predictably, Pius refused to consent to the law, but he had no power to combat it other than the passive tactics of declaring himself "prisoner of the Vatican," spurning his pension and refusing to tread on the usurped soil of his former domains. He remained on the Vatican grounds until his death in 1878 (and so did his successor, Leo XIII, who died in 1903). As one of his last acts, however, Pius did send his own father confessor to the deathbed of King Victor Emmanuel II, who predeceased him by one month.[152]

To promote the cause of national unification, the government's ruling conservative faction centralized the administrative apparatus of the state, redeemed Italy's railroads from foreign (mostly French and Austrian) investors, and conscripted a national army.[153] The government assumed all debts held by the peninsula's former principalities. These amounted to a formidable sum, and it took six years and the passage of several unpopular taxes before the government books were balanced (1876).[154] Old boundary lines were purposefully erased by the introduction of a new provincial system modeled on the "departments" of France. "Italy is made," declared one enthusiast. "Let us now make Italians."[155]

Alas, it was easier to express this sentiment than to fulfill it. Northern Italy was industrialized and advanced, southern Italy agricultural and backward. The southern aristocracy chafed at the loss of their former ruling prerogatives. The peasantry chafed at the "foreign" political machinery and heavy taxes imposed by the "Sardinian" king and his parliament. Unrest was so rife at the outset of the unification period that half the Italian army had to be stationed in the south to keep the peace.[156]

In the elections of 1876, leftist candidates swept the conservative faction out of office with promises to extend the suffrage, to make education compulsory and, above all, to repeal the hated "grist" (grain) tax—decried throughout the peninsula as "the tax on hunger."[157] The culmination of this electoral revolution was less than satisfactory. To be sure, an initial reduction in voter qualifications enlarged the electorate from 628,000 voters to 2,050,000 (1882).[158] But a law on compulsory education was not enforced, and the grist tax, though abolished in 1884, was replaced by a tax on corn that effectively nullified the benefit.[159] High tariffs, moreover, did more harm than good—at one point provoking the termination of trade relations with France with the consequent loss of lucrative French investments (1887).[160]

To maintain its hold on power amid so much disappointment, the left abjured normal parliamentary procedure in favor of *transformismo*—a process of "transforming" political reluctance into political enthusiasm by means that were rather difficult to distinguish from flagrant bribery.[161] In the estimation of one historian, the left's first great leader, Agostino Depretis (1813–1887), "practiced political corruption unparalleled in the history of the monarchy and inaugurated a system of government by factions and sectional interests which long disgraced Italy."[162] Building upon this foundation, Depretis' successor, Francesco Crispi (1819–1901), "proved himself a master at the game of managing elections,"[163] while ruling as a virtual dictator. Discredited in an enormous financial scandal involving the Bank of Rome, Crispi purged the voter rolls by more than 25 percent in order to maintain power in the ensuing elections (1894).[164] He was cast from office two years later, however, when the vaunted Italian army—product of the government's overbearing tax policy—was spectacularly defeated at Adowa in Italy's ill-fated colonial venture in Ethiopia.

The Italian peasantry and proletariat were, by this juncture, at the end of their tether. The tax burden in proportion to income was higher in Italy than in any other European state.[165] Millions of laborers—mostly peasants from the south—had already emigrated to South America or the United States in search of a better life. Before leaving office, Crispi, a native Sicilian, declared martial law in Sicily in order to put down rioting agricultural laborers (1893–1894).[166] Fresh from its defeat at Adowa, the army won a discreditable victory over civilian bread rioters in Milan (1898), whom they suppressed with a ferocity not seen since the era of Austrian rule.[167] For two years (1898–1900), the army dominated the government under the premiership of Luigi Pelloux—a former army chief-of-staff, who filled out his cabinet with generals, admirals and monarchists. Arrests and violent repression became the order of the day. The leftist opposition fought back by obstructing all business in the Chamber of Deputies: shouting chaotically, knocking over ballot boxes and—when all else failed—singing Garibaldi's hymn.[168]

In July 1900, Pelloux resigned despite a favorable election return to make way for a "ministry of conciliation." Four weeks later, an anarchist fatally shot King Humbert I in his carriage in broad daylight. His death, and the accession of his son, Victor Emmanuel III, marked the transition away from repression. A new minister of the interior, Giovanni Giolitti, assumed a neutral attitude in labor disputes, allowing trade unions to flourish. In 1901 alone, there were more than 1000 industrial and more than 600 agricultural strikes. A railroad strike in 1902 threatened to shut down the nation's transport. (As an alternative to armed suppression, the government drafted the railway workers into the army and ordered them back to duty.[169])

The workers ultimately overplayed their hand with a general strike that effectively shut down the entire industrial north (1904). The ensuing elections witnessed a conservative backlash—including a high participation rate by Catholic voters (who were released by Pius X from a longstanding papal ban on political engagement following the strike).[170] In 1905, state ownership of the railways was reinstituted after years of privatization.[171]

Despite the unrest, Italy's industrial output increased by leaps and bounds between 1897 and 1913, with the silk and cotton industries leading the way. Italian exports tripled and the nation's merchant marine surpassed 1000 ships. The government, in the meantime, passed workers' legislation, providing for accident and sickness insurance, old age pensions and a mandatory day off per week (1898–1908).[172] In 1912, Giolitti, who had emerged as the era's leading politician, presided over the passage of a new electoral law, extending the vote to all males over twenty-one who were either literate or had served in the army. Under the new criteria, the number of eligible voters increased from less than 3,000,000 to an estimated 8,635,000.[173] The law was tantamount to a grant of universal male suffrage, since universal conscription was in force, and educational reform had reduced the national illiteracy rate to twenty-five percent. (In comparison, scarcely twenty-five percent of Italians *could read* at the time of unification—in Naples and Sicily, the figure being less than ten percent.[174])

In the very year of the election bill, Italy seized Tripoli from Turkey, thereby assuaging the memory of Adowa. Still in the exuberance of youth, the nation believed itself to be destined for great things. Despite the rancor of its early history, the very nationalism that had wrought unification in the 1860s, continued to exercise a potent effect—creating, in the words of Carlton Hayes, "a yearning in the breast of every loyal modern Italian to emulate the ancient Romans in culture and in prowess."[175] Innate to the Italian spirit of the day was *Irredentism*—the belief that there were Italian regions that must yet be reunited with the motherland (most especially Austrian-held Trentino and Trieste). For this reason, the populace bore its heavy tax burden with equanimity and accepted the government's increasing annual military expenditures (which nearly quadrupled from $35 million in 1871 to $136 million in 1913[176]) with a sense of pride. For this reason, too, Italy would repudiate a longstanding "Triple Alliance" with Austria and Germany, and cast her lot with France, England and Russia in the First World War.[177]

7

International Affairs, 1870–1914

*Countdown to Collision: The Eastern Question
and the European Alliance System
from the Breakfast War to the Balkan Wars*

Having reviewed at some length the domestic evolution of the European states between 1870 and 1914, we must now turn to the relations between them. At the outset of our story, as the reader may recall, we found the representatives of the Grand Alliance gathered in Vienna for the purpose of restoring Europe to the "serene equilibrium" that existed before the French Revolution. The dual contagion of liberalism and nationalism was condemned to extinction, and a defensive cordon erected around France whence the plague had arisen. The map of Europe was redrawn, not in accordance with the self-determination of peoples, but merely for the fulfillment of these ends, and a Quadruple Alliance of the great powers—England, Austria, Russia and Prussia—was forged to guarantee the settlement (1815).

Metternich, the mastermind behind it all, came away with all his objects achieved. Russia was thwarted in its aspiration to obtain all of Poland, the realization of which would have allowed that nation to intrude into Austria's sphere of influence in central Europe. Similarly, Prussia was thwarted in its desire to obtain all of Saxony, thereby preserving Austria's predominance in greater Germany. Finally, by extricating the Hapsburg Empire from the Austrian Netherlands (i.e., Belgium)—the only imperial territory contiguous with France—Metternich transferred the responsibility for initial defense against French aggression to others, while compensating his emperor for the loss with the annexation of Lombardy and Venetia.

To be sure, cracks soon appeared in the edifice. England, under Castlereagh, would not remain party to an alliance of governments against the aspirations of peoples. The Belgians would not suffer the rule of the hated Dutch, nor the French of the reactionary Bourbon, Charles X. Metternich himself would be chased from Vienna during the Revolutions of 1848. Yet even at that late hour the foundation of his work remained intact. The 1848 revolutions in Austria, Bohemia, Hungary and Italy all ended in failure. Hence, Austria emerged with her empire in one piece. The German revolution likewise succumbed, leaving greater Germany weak, and—for a time—under Austrian domination.

But in the ensuing twenty-two years, Bismarck and Cavour remade the map of Europe anew, and Metternich's Concert of Europe was definitively overthrown. A united Germany emerged, unannounced and unexpected, with Bismarck at the helm, seeking not to restore an old equilibrium, but to preserve one that he had brought into being. With German unification achieved, there was little to gain through aggressive war and everything to lose.[1] Bismarck wished now to keep the peace and with it all that he had obtained for the German empire. Above all, he wished to prevent France from embarking on a war of revenge.

By the annexation of Alsace and Lorraine at the conclusion of the Franco-Prussian War, and by the imposition of a five billion franc indemnity, Bismarck had hoped to render France incapable of retaliation for fifty years.[2] Alas, as we have seen, France displayed a hitherto unrecognized economic strength—paying off the entire indemnity in two years—while the loss of her prized provinces along the Rhine guaranteed that she would desire revenge not for fifty years, but if necessary, for five hundred. The latter fact imperiled Bismarck's program; for, to quote the *Cambridge Modern History*, "from the very outset the new structure of the German empire was burdened as it were by a French mortgage, since every foreign foe could henceforth reckon unconditionally on French support."[3]

Bismarck decided, therefore, that Germany should have no foes, and the European milieu seemed—almost providentially—to favor his design. In surveying the continent, it appeared to the German chancellor that only the papacy, which had lost its temporal powers, could rival France in unhappiness over Europe's new status quo. The Catholic bond might certainly draw France and the papacy together, but the pope (as Stalin would later famously observe) possessed no legions. Hence, a papal alliance with France was not to be feared—unless Austria, also overwhelmingly Catholic, were also to adhere to it.[4] Austria, however, had received seemingly generous terms from Prussia after the devastating Seven Weeks' War of 1866. Had she desired revenge, she could have intervened on France's behalf in the Franco-Prussian War, but she had not done so—a decision that many regarded as incomprehensible.

Further to the east, autocratic Russia made an even less likely bedfellow for republican France. Apart from the divergence in political philosophy, Russia had reaped a strategic advantage from France's defeat. At the end of the Crimean War, at the insistence of Britain and France, the Black Sea had been declared a neutral body of water, off limits to all European naval vessels. The clause had been directed against Russia—the defeated party in that war—and Russia had been greatly vexed by it, for it left her Black Sea ports, chief among them Odessa, without naval protection. Although the treaty also barred Turkish warships from the Black Sea, the Turks had the supreme advantage of being able to keep their navy in the nearby Aegean. They could thus strike rapidly into the Black Sea in time of war, while the nearest Russian squadrons would have to come from the Baltic.[5]

While grappling with France in 1870, Bismarck gave tacit approval to Russia's unilateral repudiation of the offensive clause. He knew that Britain would disapprove, and that Russia's action would thus distract both Russian and British attention from the Franco-Prussian War, sharply reducing the likelihood of intervention by either of them on France's behalf.[6] He knew also that if Britain wished to oppose the Russian move, she would have to act alone, for France could not, and Austria and Prussia would not, help her. Unwilling to assume this risk, Britain agreed to defer the matter to an international conference held in London in 1871. There it was decided that the involved parties would acquiesce in the repudiation of Black Sea neutrality in return for Russia's adherence to the "London Declaration," which specifically affirmed that under international law, "no power can liberate itself from the engagements of a treaty, nor modify the stipulations thereof, [without] the consent of the contracting powers by means of an amicable arrangement."[7] In other words, Russia's breach of the Treaty of Paris (1856) was to be condoned provided that Russia endorsed a self-evident tenet of diplomacy that it had just violated with impunity. Although Russia would have opportunity soon enough to apprehend the full implication of this agreement, it seemed at the time a very good deal, and the tsar had Bismarck's benevolent neutrality to thank for it. Moreover, he still felt gratitude toward the German chancellor for his assistance in quashing the Polish uprising of 1863.

In sum, Bismarck's subtle beneficence toward his eastern neighbors had created goodwill—the increasingly cordial relations being confirmed at a meeting in Berlin in September 1872 attended by Austria's Emperor Franz Josef, Russia's Tsar Alexander II and Germany's Kaiser Wilhelm I. By October of the following year, an informal *entente* had come into being—the so-called "Three Emperors' League"—pledging their majesties to confer on all issues that might jeopardize the peace. (The natural prejudices of a "monarchical" league, moreover, would tend towards the further isolation of republican France.[8])

There remained only Italy and Great Britain. Of these, the former still resented Napoleon III's abandonment of the Italian cause in 1859—no less, indeed, than it still revered Bismarck's assistance in obtaining Venetia from Austria in 1866. Germany's *Kulturkampf*, moreover, mirrored Italy's own ongoing conflict with the papacy. Hence, the likelihood that Italy would join France in an alliance against Germany seemed extremely remote.[9] Similarly, there was no natural source of enmity between Germany and Great Britain—and Bismarck intended to keep it that way by remaining aloof from the European drive for colonies, while faithfully acknowledging Britain's status as "mistress of the seas." (For complex reasons, he would reverse his views on the colonial question during the 1880s, only to find, after amassing an empire, that his initial prejudices had been correct—namely that the burdens of colonialism outweighed the benefits.[10])

All things remaining equal, then, Bismarck's system was entirely secure. Alas, it took no more than a speculative article in the Berlin *Post* to demonstrate the fragility of the equilibrium. The article, published on April 8, 1875, and entitled "*Is War in Sight?*" raised the alarm over France's rapid recovery, both economic and military, since the defeat of 1871, and suggested a preventive German military strike as the appropriate antidote—the opinion being seconded by the German Army's chief-of-staff, Helmuth von Moltke, and by at least one talkative German diplomat who sought to explain the merits of the argument to the French ambassador in Berlin.[11] Amid the ensuing hue and cry, the British and Russian governments contemplated the potential response to such an attack upon France—which, as it turned out, might very well be an Anglo-Russian alliance against Germany.[12] (So much for placing faith in the "Three Emperor's League.")

Bismarck quickly disavowed any intention of attacking France, while reproving those among his colleagues who favored a program so manifestly dangerous.[13] But in maintaining peace and good relations with his neighbors, there were also factors beyond Bismarck's control. Chief among these was the "Eastern Question"—that restrained phrase relating to the anticipated collapse of the Ottoman Empire and the competition for the spoils that would surely result.

In Bismarck's view, the issue was "not worth the bones of a single Pomeranian grenadier."[14] That the other Great Powers did not share this opinion would soon become apparent—for in the very year of the "war in sight" crisis, an insurrection broke out against Turkish rule among the overtaxed, ill-treated Christians of the province of Herzegovina. Aided by fellow Christians from Serbia and Bulgaria, the rebels routed several local detachments of Turkish soldiers and murdered every Turkish official they could get hold of. In retaliation, the Turks carried out a ruthless suppression—most notably in Bulgaria where a terrifying force of irregular troops known as Bashi-Bazouks massacred some 12,000 men, women and children. Brandishing rags drenched with kerosene, the Bashi-Bazouks incinerated fully one thousand of these unfortunates alive in the Church of Batak (April 24, 1876).[15] At Panagurishte, Bulgarian babies were flung in the air and caught on the points of Turkish bayonets.[16]

News of these atrocities was slow to reach Europe. In England, Disraeli dismissed the initial reports as mere "coffee house babble."[17] But it was clear that the turbulence was getting worse not better, and as it did, alarm began to mount—particularly in Russia (which shared the Orthodox creed and Slavic ethnicity of the Christian rebels) and Austria (which dreaded Slavic unrest anywhere as a potential spark for separatist rebellion among its own Slavic population). When, in the midst of it all, Turkey announced that it could not meet the interest payments on its public debt, the bondholders of Europe also chimed in with an opinion.[18]

Tremendous foreign pressure now came to bear on the Turkish government (or "Porte") to get control of the situation before it endangered the peace (and economy) of Europe. Sweeping reforms were demanded in the treatment of non–Muslims. Unfortunately, at one and the same time, the Porte was being pressured by the Muslim faithful at home to crush the rebels and to resist the meddling of "foreign infidels." Bankrupt and led by incompetents, the Porte took no effective action in either direction. Consequently, matters spiraled out of control. On May 7, 1876, Muslim fanatics murdered the French and German consuls at a mosque in Salonika. In response, the rulers of the "Three Emperors' League" issued the "Berlin Memorandum" (May 13) demanding an end to the fighting and the adoption by the Porte of meaningful reforms within two months (with the veiled threat that "*further action could be taken*" if these demands were not met).[19] France and Italy endorsed this note. Disraeli, who had not been consulted, flatly refused, while dispatching the Mediterranean fleet to Besika Bay near the entrance of the Turkish Straits as a warning to the signatories against precipitate action.

A crisis point was reached on May 30, when a riotous mob of religious students in Constantinople deposed the reigning sultan, Abdul Aziz, for allegedly kowtowing to foreign pressure. His nephew, Murad V, though terrified and unwilling, was named to succeed him. The reign of this new sultan proved exceedingly short. Four days into it, he was informed that his deposed uncle was dead—purportedly by suicide, though his wounds suggested otherwise. Thereafter, Murad passed his days in a state of catatonic stupefaction,[20] certain that he would share his uncle's fate. He was deposed after a reign of three months on the pretext of insanity (albeit without bodily harm). His half-brother, Abdul Hamid II, took his place.

By this time, Serbia and Montenegro had declared war on their Turkish suzerain (June–July 1876), and Russian volunteers were pouring into the Balkans to support the Christian rebels. In England, Benjamin Disraeli saw the moment rapidly approaching when he must intercede to uphold the integrity of the Turkish empire (this being the traditional British policy in the Near East since a Turkish collapse might jeopardize Britain's trade routes to India). Before he could so much as summon his cabinet, however, he found his hands irrevocably tied. In July, a British diplomat, Walter Baring, had been sent to Bulgaria to investigate the incessant reports of Turkish atrocities. On September 1, 1876, he delivered his report, confirming the burning of Batak's church along with its parishioners. He went on to say, *inter alia*, that "In the streets at every step lay human remains, rotting and sweltering in the summer sun," and that on exiting the village, he encountered "more than 60 skulls in a little hollow, and it was evident from their appearance that nearly all of them had been severed from the bodies by axes and yataghans."[21]

Nor was this the end of it. Later in the same month, William Ewart Gladstone issued from retirement his famous pamphlet, *The Bulgarian Horrors and the Question of the East*, in which he called upon the Turks to clear out of Europe, "one and all, bag and baggage."[22] Within weeks, the pamphlet sold 200,000 copies, provoking a wave of popular indignation throughout the country. Disraeli, whose policy was now hopelessly compromised, pronounced the pamphlet so "ill-written" as to be "of all the Bulgarian horrors, perhaps the greatest...."[23] Nonetheless, he could scarcely come to Turkey's defense amid the public uproar.

Meanwhile, back in Turkey, Sultan Abdul Hamid II was experiencing better luck than his recent predecessors. His soldiers, imbued with newfound Islamist zeal in the wake of Constantinople's religious uprisings,[24] fought with sufficient fervor to send the Serbs and Montenegrins reeling in defeat even as Gladstone sold his pamphlets. Far from securing the Ottoman position, however, these victories raised panic in Europe that the Turks would reprise their atrocities in the newly defeated provinces.

Tsar Alexander II was now under such intense pressure from his countrymen to intervene on the rebels' behalf that, on November 2, he informed the British ambassador that the Balkan situation could no longer be borne, and that "unless Europe was prepared to act with firmness and energy, he should be obliged to act alone."[25] He reiterated the point publicly in a speech to Moscow's dignitaries on November 11.[26] To forestall this outcome, Britain proposed a conference of the Great Powers in Constantinople for the purpose of devising a settlement that would ensure necessary reforms in the Balkans while maintaining the integrity of the Ottoman empire.[27] The conference convened in November and issued its recommendations the following month. Hardly had it done so, however, when the artillery of Constantinople fired a thundering salvo to announce the unexpected promulgation of a new constitution by the sultan himself. The terms of this document were more liberal than those put forward by the Powers. But the sultan could afford to be more liberal, for he wasn't being sincere. He had no intention of putting his new charter into effect, and had merely promulgated it to provide himself with a pretext to reject the recommendations of his diplomatic guests.[28]

It was an extremely clever charade, flawed only in that it fooled no one—least of all Alexander II, who now began preparing for war. On January 15, 1877—three days before Abdul Hamid formally rejected the proposals put forward by the Great Powers in Constantinople—the tsar completed the secret "Budapest Convention" with the Austrian emperor, Franz Josef, securing Austria's benevolent neutrality by conceding to that nation the right to occupy Bosnia and Herzegovina. (Russia promised additionally that its troops would not enter Constantinople, that it would establish no Balkan protectorates and that a European Congress would have the last say in any peace terms.[29])

The winter snows in the Balkan Mountains prevented any immediate action,[30] but by the spring Russian troops were massing on the Ottoman frontier. The sultan directed his subjects in Romania—the northernmost of his Balkan provinces—to prepare their defenses. Instead, the Romanians declared themselves independent of the Ottoman empire.

The Turks might have seen it coming. Composed historically of two separate principalities, Moldavia and Wallachia, which were ruled autonomously by Christian officials under Turkish suzerainty, the Romanians had effectively merged their territories into a unified province in 1859. The Turks had banned such a union, but the Romanians had defied them with an ingenious stratagem: electing the same individual—Colonel Alexander Couza—to the post of *hospodar*, or governor, in both principalities. Domineering and progressive, Couza liquidated Romania's land-wealthy monasteries and liberated her serfs (each of whom received a grant of 7.5 to 15 acres of farmland).[31] In so doing, however, he alienated the Romanian aristocracy. Consequently, in 1866, he was deposed in favor of a foreign aristocrat—Prince Karol of Hohenzollern. For the Turks, this was scarcely an improvement. Possessing a military background, Karol spent the ensuing decade reforming the Romanian army, providing it with modern Prussian munitions and a capable Prussian officer corps.[32] By the mid–1870s, independence alone was lacking, and Turkey's mounting difficulties finally provided the Romanians with a suitable occasion to proclaim it. On April 16, Karol signed a convention with Tsar Alexander, promising safe passage to the tsar's troops and the services of his own army in return for recognition of Romania's independent status.[33]

The tsar's preparations were now complete, and on April 24, 1877 (the anniversary of the Batak massacre), he declared war. His troops embarked on a two-front invasion: striking southward into the Balkans to rescue Russia's "little Slav brothers," and traversing the Caucasus on the eastern shore of the Black Sea to invade Turkish Georgia and Armenia. Thus was inaugurated the Russo-Turkish "Breakfast War"—so-called because it was avidly followed in the morning papers by an enthralled audience of European breakfasters.[34]

By early June, the Russian forces had traversed the whole of Romania and arrived at the Danube. On the 22nd of that month, they pushed across the river into the Bulgarian Dobrudja. The Turks fell back to Trajan's Gate where they established a defensive line only to find that they had been duped; for the abandonment of their initial positions allowed a much larger Russian force to cross the Danube unopposed near Sistova on June 26.[35] Bypassing a strongly garrisoned quadrilateral of Turkish fortresses in northern Bulgaria, the Russians raided deep into Turkish territory, capturing the Shipka Pass (i.e., the main corridor through the Balkan Mountains). But on reaching the well-armed fortress of Plevna, which sat astride Russia's intended line of communications through Bulgaria, the advance suddenly ground to a halt.[36] An initial effort to reduce this citadel by storm was thrown back with staggering losses in July, and a larger attempt in September fared even worse with 15,000 Russian and Romanian troops being cut to pieces beneath the redoubts. Osman Pasha, the local Turkish commander, was hailed throughout the Ottoman empire as Osman "Ghazi"—"the Triumphant."[37] For the Russians, there was no choice but to place the stronghold under siege, and to ensure success, they called the old master, Todleben of Sebastopol, out of retirement. Todleben took charge in late September and, working his usual miracles, had the Turks at their last gasp within three months.

After failing in a desperate effort to break Todleben's encirclement (December 10), Osman Pasha capitulated with 43,000 men, of whom a scant 15,000 survived the trek into Russian imprisonment.[38] The tsar's forces had been held at bay for 143 days, but they

A scene from the Breakfast War: Taking of the Grivitsa redoubt by the Russians during the Russo-Turkish War of 1877–1878. A few hours later the redoubt was recaptured by the Ottomans and finally fell to the Romanians on the 30th of August 1877 in what became known as the "Third Battle of Grivitsa." Capturing of the Grivitsa redoubt. Painting by Nikolai Dmitriev-Orenburgsky. Artillery Museum, Saint Petersburg (Wikimedia Commons).

now forged ahead through mountains and snow to within seven miles of Constantinople—the last stretch of conquest being denied them by word that a British naval squadron had entered the Sea of Marmora. With his army in a state of exhaustion and the sultan now suing for peace, the tsar chose not to call the British bluff.

On March 3, 1878, the Treaty of San Stefano put an end to the fighting. By its terms, Russia obtained the Bulgarian Dobrudja. It intended to trade this strip of land to Romania in return for Bessarabia, which it had lost at the end of the Crimean War—an exchange that would bring the Russian border forward to the Danube and the Pruth. In the Caucasus, the Russians annexed Batoum, Kars and Ardahan. Additionally, the sultan was compelled to recognize the complete independence of Montenegro, Serbia and Romania. ("King" Karol celebrated this last clause by assuming a crown forged from the metal of a Turkish gun seized at Plevna.[39])

All this, the European powers might have allowed. But the Russian plan for the remainder of Turkish Europe—namely, that it be fused into a single "autonomous" Bulgarian state—was bitterly contested. Believing (correctly) that the so-called "Greater Bulgaria" was meant to be a Russian satellite replete with warm water anchorages in the Aegean for the Russian fleet, the British and Austrians balked at the proposal. Austria, indeed, had reason to feel that it had been swindled. Evicted from Italy and Germany in the wars of the preceding decades, the Dual Monarchy saw expansion into the Balkans as the surest means to obtain recompense. *Drang nach Osten*—"Movement to the East"—she called her program, and it encompassed the rather unrealistic design of reaching the Aegean coastline at Salonika.[40] Indeed, for this reason, Austria had insisted upon a pledge from Russia prior to the war guaranteeing against the emergence of a state formidable enough to serve as a barrier.[41] A "Greater Bulgaria" was precisely what Austria did not want.

For her part, Britain showed every appearance of preparing for war. With the Russian army practically at the gates of Constantinople, the British public had utterly reversed itself and taken the side of the Ottomans, viewing them no longer as the *perpetrators* of Balkan atrocities but as the *victims* of Russian aggression—the change in sentiment being echoed in British music halls with a song lyric that ran, "We don't want to fight, But *by jingo* if we do, We've got the ships, we've got the men, and we've got the money, too!"[42] Amid this "jingoism" (a new word in the English lexicon), Benjamin Disraeli obtained a £6,000,000 military grant from Parliament, sent additional ships to the Mediterranean, called up the army reserves and began transporting Indian Sepoy troops to Malta via the Suez Canal.[43]

In point of fact, Britain could scarcely fight Russia alone—for the tsar's forces were concentrated on land while her own were at sea. Had she attempted to do so, as Bismarck wryly noted, it would have been akin to "a fight between an elephant and a whale."[44] War, however, did not prove necessary. Instead, the Russians were hoisted on their own petard by the Austrian government, which declared that any change in the status of the Balkans was tantamount to a revision of the Peace of Paris (1856) and must by international law, be referred to a congress of the Powers bound by that treaty.[45] The Russians found that they could not wriggle free of this demand, for they had thrice bound themselves to the principle of mediation—first, in signing the Peace of Paris; second, in their 1871 "bargain" under the "London Declaration," wherein their breach of the Peace of Paris' Black Sea neutrality clause was condoned in exchange for acknowledgment that treaties could not be unilaterally revised; and third, in her secret promise to the Austrians in January 1877 that should Russia engage in a Turkish war, she would submit final peace terms to a European Congress.

The result was the famous Congress of Berlin (1878), attended by an array of dignitaries to rival their forebears at the Congress of Vienna. Bismarck himself served as president in the putative role of "honest broker." Disraeli and Salisbury (who had recently replaced Lord Derby the Younger as foreign secretary) represented Britain. Prince Alexander Gorchakov, the tsar's foreign minister, was chief negotiator for Russia, and Gyula Andrássy for Austria-Hungary. France, Italy and Turkey were also represented. So, too, were Romania, Serbia, Montenegro and Greece, although their delegates were given no vote in the decisions that bore so heavily on their fate.[46] By the time the Congress convened, several issues had already been decided by secret negotiation—the most important being that the new Bulgarian state should not extend to the Aegean coastline, and that, in return for the right to occupy the island of Cyprus and the Porte's promise to improve the lot of Christians remaining under Ottoman rule, Great Britain would guarantee Turkey's possessions in Asia Minor against further Russian encroachment (something that was within the British interest in any event, since maintaining stability along the trade routes to India was ever at the forefront of her policy).

Out of deference to Disraeli, Bismarck opened the Congress with an address in English. Disraeli intended that his own address should be given in French, but certain that his limited facility with that language would not create the desired impression, his retinue convinced him that the other delegates would be distraught if denied the opportunity to hear the English language's greatest orator in his own tongue.[47] In the ensuing deliberations, the independence of Romania, Serbia and Montenegro was confirmed, albeit with less generous borders than were promised under the Treaty of San Stefano. In the Caucasus, Russia was confirmed in its possession of Kars, Batoum and Ardahan.

Congress of Berlin, 1878, by Anton von Werner. The six individuals in the foreground at far left are (left to right) Baron Haymerle, Count Károlyi, Count de Launay, Prince Gorchakov, William Henry Waddington and Benjamin Disraeli. In the foreground at right are (left to right) Count Andrássy, Otto von Bismarck and Count Shuvalov. Central State Archive, Bulgaria (Wikimedia Commons).

The provision of the San Stefano Treaty ceding Romanian Bessarabia to the tsar in exchange for the Doburdja was retained, as was the secret pre-war agreement authorizing Austria-Hungary's occupation of Bosnia and Herzegovina, which was now carried into effect on the pretext of "preserving order" in these provinces (which were to remain nominally under Turkish rule).[48]

The moments of highest drama, however, were reserved for the Bulgarian settlement. No matter what ulterior motives she might have had in doing so, Russia had delineated the borders of her proposed "Greater Bulgaria" along ethnic lines.[49] The Congress of Berlin reversed this admirable result. Prior to the war, the Ottomans had protested that they had no familiarity with the word "Bulgaria," for the area on the map about which so much complaint was being made was known to them as "Rumelia." On being pressed, they allowed that they might have heard the term "Bulgaria" used in reference to a region north of the Balkan Mountains.[50] The European governments had treated this self-evident imposture with contempt at the time, but at Berlin they concluded that the Turkish claim was substantially correct. Consequently, like ancient Gaul, Russia's "Greater Bulgaria" (Turkish "Rumelia") was divided into three parts: North of the Balkan range, a "Lesser Bulgaria" came into existence—nominally still part of the Ottoman empire, but garrisoned by Russian troops and governed autonomously and constitutionally under its own prince, Alexander of Battenberg (a nephew of the tsar). South of the Balkan Mountains, a second territory, ruled administratively by a Christian governor, but in all other respects still under Turkish dominion, was christened "Eastern Rumelia" (mainly to promote the illusion that it was not "Bulgarian"—even if everyone who lived there was). The last partition, stretching from the Black Sea to the Aegean, was dubbed "Macedonia" and remained wholly under Turkish authority. As A.J.P. Taylor has noted, there was in fact no Macedonian ethnicity at the time—the term *Macedonian* being universally regarded as a euphemism for a *Bulgarian abandoned to the mercy of the Turks*.[51] (There were, however, also a large number of Greeks, Serbians and even Romanian "Vlachs" within its borders.)

In vain did Russia attempt to salvage the fruits of victory. Seeing that "Greater Bulgaria" must be partitioned, Gorchakov sought to deny Turkey the right of garrisoning the fortresses of Eastern Rumelia. Bismarck broached the topic with Disraeli. Hitherto, the two statesmen had gotten along famously. "The old Jew—he is the man!" Bismarck

Map of the Balkans to illustrate the Treaty of Berlin by J.F. Horrabin (Illustrator), from H.G. Wells' *Outline of History*, **1923 (Wikimedia Commons).**

declared of the Congress' most distinguished guest. In lighter moments, he assured the prime minister that socialism did not stand a chance in Britain since the upper and lower classes were irrevocably bound by a shared love of horseracing.[52] But when he raised the question of Eastern Rumelia's fortresses, he received a brusque response. Not only did Disraeli refuse Russia's petition, but he demanded that Bismarck render his own judgment on the spot. Caught off guard, Bismarck asked if the prime minister was issuing an ultimatum. Disraeli affirmed that this was so and announced further that the British delegation was prepared to depart by train that very day if Bismarck's answer was adverse.[53] Unwilling to see his splendid congress come to nothing, Bismarck acquiesced. All was now decided, leaving a bitterly disappointed Prince Gorchakov to grumble that "We have sacrificed 100,000 picked men and 100 millions of money, for an illusion."[54]

Disraeli returned home to public accolades, telling the throngs that came out to greet him at Charing Cross that he had attained "peace with honor." But Salisbury, who stood at his shoulder, would ultimately conclude that, in backing Turkey, Great Britain had "put her money on the wrong horse."[55] Propped up once more by British support, the Turks failed to deliver on promised reforms in her treatment of minorities—most ominously in Armenia—and she emerged from the war so enfeebled that she failed to maintain her hold on Eastern Rumelia even in the absence of foreign intervention.

Because the decisions taken at Berlin were designed to limit Russian influence rather than to serve the nationalist aspirations of the peoples involved, the Balkans remained a hotbed of discontent.[56] Britain boasted that by thwarting the emergence of "Greater Bulgaria," she had confined Russian influence to the region north of the Balkan Mountains,[57] but the same and more might have been achieved had she done nothing, for anti–Russian sentiment in the Balkans was strong and growing. Romania would never forgive Russia for demanding the cession of Bessarabia (a province peopled by fellow Romanians) in return for the Dobrudja (a barren wasteland peopled by Bulgarians and Turks)—even if the latter provided her with a very serviceable port on the Black Sea at Costanza. At the Congress of Berlin, she protested that her sons had fought and died at Plevna in order that Romania might pay the price of Turkey's defeat.[58] Bulgaria was satisfied neither with the territory allotted to her nor with Russia's attempts to treat her as a mere satellite, while the two Serbian states, Serbia and Montenegro, were incensed by the fate of Bosnia and Herzegovina—home to their ethnic kinsmen, and now occupied by Austria-Hungary. Novibazar, a strip of territory separating Serbia from Montenegro (much of which had been awarded to Montenegro at San Stefano), was likewise garrisoned by Austria, blocking the anticipated path for an all-Serbian railway from Belgrade, the Serbian capital, to the Montenegrin port of Antivari on the Adriatic, thus leaving landlocked Serbia dependent upon Austria for an outlet to the sea.[59]

Apart from angering the peoples of the Balkans, the Treaty of Berlin spelled the end of Bismarck's Three Emperors' League, setting Europe on course for the divisions that would lead to World War I. Russia felt betrayed by both of her League partners. In response to the Treaty of San Stefano, Austria-Hungary had concentrated troops in the Carpathians whence they could strike the flank of the Russian supply lines and reverse the verdict of the war.[60] Moreover, where Russia had been denied the fruits of victory after a costly campaign, Austria-Hungary had obtained her fruits without a fight. The two nations were now manifest rivals in the Balkans—Russia as the champion of Slavic nationalism, Austria-Hungary as the unyielding opponent. (Indeed, henceforth, Russia would promote pan-Slavic propaganda among Austria's Slavs.)

Russia's sense of betrayal was stronger still in the case of the German empire. The Russians received Bismarck's decision to play the role of "honest broker" with "astonishment and indignation," says *Encyclopædia Britannica*. "What they expected was not an impartial arbiter but a cordial and useful friend in need." Bismarck's decision to support the British position was seen as nothing short of perfidy. Prince Gorchakov summed up the situation in a letter to the Russian ambassador in Vienna: "Needless to say, that in our eyes, the Three Emperors' Alliance is practically torn in pieces by the conduct of our two allies."[61]

Bismarck spent the remainder of his tenure as German chancellor attempting to repair the shattered system he had erected to keep France in isolation. With Russia estranged, he sought first to strengthen the bond with his remaining ally, Austria-Hungary. In 1879, he forged a secret alliance with the Dual Monarchy providing for joint action if either nation was attacked by Russia. (The alliance was not binding in the setting of a war with France, unless Russia joined the conflict as a French ally.) In 1881, he contrived to further isolate France by advising Jules Ferry, the French prime minister, that Germany would not object to a French seizure of Tunis, knowing full well that the small North African state was the lynchpin of Italy's colonial designs. France swallowed the bait, incurring the wrath of Italy and distracting her own attention and resources from a potential war of revenge against Germany in a single stroke. Irate over the French action, Italy appended her signature to the German-Austrian Alliance (despite the fact that this entailed a pact with Austria, her traditional enemy[62]) thereby creating the "Triple Alliance" that would endure until the outbreak of the First World War. The pact was a boon to Austria, for it guaranteed that in the event of an Austro-Russian war, Italy could not attack her from the rear in a bid to seize *Italia Irredenta* (i.e., those Italian-speaking communities—especially Trentino and Trieste—still retained by the Austrian Empire).[63]

From Bismarck's perspective, however, the situation was still fraught with risk; for the fact remained that Russia might solve her evolving diplomatic isolation by forming an alliance with France, thus presenting Germany with the prospect of a two-front war should hostilities erupt. To forestall this threat, Bismarck sought to mend fences with Russia. His initial scheme called for the resurrection of the Three Emperors' League. He achieved some semblance of it in 1881, when the three emperors agreed that should any one of them go to war with a fourth power, the remaining two would maintain a benevolent neutrality. The agreement was renewed in 1884, but it fell to pieces the following year when events in Bulgaria so inflamed the Balkan rivalry between Russia and Austria-Hungary that further rapprochement between the two became impossible. Forced once more to change course, Bismarck forged a secret bilateral "Reinsurance Treaty" with Russia (1887), whereby each party agreed to maintain neutrality if the other went to war. (The agreement was not binding in the case of a German attack on France or a Russian attack on Austria-Hungary.)

On the basis of these entanglements, Bismarck kept his diplomatic system intact until he fell from power in 1890. Without his guiding hand the edifice would tumble to ruin. Despite frantic entreaties from the Russian diplomatic corps,[64] Kaiser Wilhelm II opted not to renew the expiring Reinsurance Treaty when he assumed command of policy (1890). Russia, at this juncture, was poised to begin work on the Trans-Siberian Railway and likewise wished to expand her industrial and mining output. These enterprises required capital, and as fate would have it, much of this capital was supplied in the form of loans from French entrepreneurs. Consequently, despite the incompatibility of their political systems, warm relations began to grow between the two isolated nations. When a French fleet put in at Kronstadt, near Saint Petersburg, in 1891, French sailors fraternized with their Russian counterparts and Tsar Alexander III stood reverently for a performance of the Marseillaise.[65] Secret negotiations ensued, which culminated in the signing of an equally secret "Dual Alliance" between the French republic and the tsarist autocracy (1894).

For twenty years, Bismarck had kept France in isolation. By allowing the Reinsurance Treaty to lapse, Kaiser Wilhelm accomplished the reverse in an instant while simultaneously throwing away the last chance for an amicable bond with Russia. The distressing diplomatic revolution was not brought to completion, however, until Wilhelm ruined another piece of Bismarck's painstaking diplomacy—the cordial relations with Britain. In 1896, the Kaiser achieved an initial affront to British sensibilities by sending a congratulatory telegram to the Boer leader, Paul Kruger, in the aftermath of the failed Jameson Raid. To follow up on this promising beginning, he (i) sold munitions to the Boers in the lead up to the Boer War (receiving in return funds paid to the Boers by Britain in reparation for the Jameson Raid[66]); (ii) invested in the Berlin-Baghdad Railway—a projected overland rail link between Berlin and the Persian Gulf meant to supplant the Suez as a thoroughfare to the East (which Britain ruined by convincing the Sheikhdom of Kuwait to block the railway short of the Gulf)[67]; and (iii) obtained passage of bills in 1898 and 1900 for an aggressive expansion of the German navy.

A surer means of provoking British animus could scarcely be imagined than this last measure. A decade earlier, Lord Salisbury had established the principle that Britain's navy must be as large as its two largest competitors combined.[68] The danger now was not solely that the kaiser's program might violate Salisbury's venerable axiom, but that it would constitute a commercial challenge of the first rank. By the dawn of the 20th century, Germany's state-of-the-art industrial infrastructure was superior to Britain's. Though still eclipsed in total industrial output, Germany was the world's leading innovator in the chemical and electrical industries, she was far ahead of Britain in the production of steel, and she was catching up in iron and coal.[69] The addition of a German fleet capable of making Britain think twice before resorting to naval action would allow Germany to compete for commerce and colonies, fulfilling the kaiser's quest for an imperial "place in the sun" at Britain's expense.[70]

From Britain's standpoint, the timing of it all was rather inconvenient. For decades, her naval predominance had allowed her to live in "splendid isolation," free of encumbering continental alliances. The Boer War, however, proved such a public relations disaster as to leave her merely in "isolation" with no happy adjectives attached. With Germany poised to challenge her on the high seas, France competing with her colonially and Russia encroaching relentlessly on her sphere of influence in Asia (Russia's riposte to British obstructionism in the Balkans and the Straits[71]), the abandonment of a policy that had left her alone and vulnerable seemed only prudent. In 1902, she took an initial step by signing an accord with Japan aimed at reining in Russia's expansion in Asia. Alas, ostracized for her treatment of the Boers and in open rivalry with the continent's leading powers, there seemed very little likelihood of accomplishing more.

Her dilemma was solved, unexpectedly, by the decisive diplomacy of the French foreign minister, Théophile Delcassé, and by the affable charm of her own new monarch, Edward VII (ruled, 1901–1910). Delcassé was intent on recovering Alsace and Lorraine from Germany, and believed that the establishment of good relations with England would be a distinct advantage in pursuit of that end. Conversely, continued colonial rivalry with England would be a distinct distraction—diverting necessary resources from the army to the navy.[72] For a time, France seemed unable to decide which battle it wished to fight, but for Delcassé the choice was clear—for he knew that the beating heart of France required the recovery of Alsace and Lorraine. Moreover, the outset of his tenure at the foreign office coincided with the Fashoda Incident—an event that exposed the notion of a colonial war with Britain as sheer folly. Back down France must, for she could not win. But Delcasse's decision to do so gracefully was strategic—laying the initial groundwork for an Anglo-French *rapprochement*.[73] A waiting game ensued, lasting five years, before the royal visit of Edward VII to France in May 1903 helped to achieve a breakthrough. Arriving to catcalls (for neither Fashoda nor the Boer War was yet forgotten), King Edward effused such jovial affection towards his hosts and their country as to earn wild ovations by the time of his departure.[74] He returned to England with a reputation as "Edward the Peacemaker,"[75] leaving the door open for Delcassé. Within a year, a joint understanding—the *Entente Cordiale*—was achieved (April 1904). An array of issues was addressed in this agreement, settling virtually all outstanding colonial disputes, but the clause of greatest import involved North Africa where Britain conceded Morocco to be within the French sphere of influence in return for recognition of her own precedence in Egypt.

The outbreak of the Russo-Japanese War in the self-same year put the new accord to an immediate test. While neither *Entente* power was directly involved in that distant conflict, they were allied to opposing sides: France to Russia, Britain to Japan. Far from precipitating an Anglo-French rift, however, the crisis merely exposed the ineptitude of Russia, making France all the more eager to widen her circle of friends.[76] Determined that France should have no friends at all, Kaiser Wilhelm challenged the French position in Morocco, calling for the maintenance of the little state's independence and an "open door" trade policy with all nations. He seems to have believed that his stance would cause England to renege on her *Entente* obligations, but at the ensuing "Algeciras Conference" (held in Algeciras, Spain), England stood by France, and the *Entente* emerged stronger than ever. Thwarted in Morocco, the kaiser attempted to drive a wedge between France and her other ally by hoodwinking his cousin, Tsar Nicholas II (with whom he was vacationing in the Baltic), into signing a Russo-German defensive alliance. The tsar happily appended his signature, but the initiative came to naught, for on returning home, the Russian ruler learnt from his ministers that the so-called "Treaty of Björko" constituted a flagrant violation of Russia's Dual Alliance with France and could not be implemented.[77] To the contrary, indeed, it soon dawned on Britain and Russia that with the former in accord with France and the latter in alliance with her, there was little reason not to pursue harmonious relations with each other. In 1907, the two powers reached an understanding on respective spheres of influence in Asia and the contention between them came to an end. (Following her costly defeat in the Russo-Japanese War, Russia was scarcely fit to challenge Britain in Asia in any event.[78])

Hence, to the apparent benefit of the concerned parties, the Dual Alliance and the *Entente Cordiale* were amalgamated into a "Triple Entente"—an understanding between Britain, France and Russia. All the while, Kaiser Wilhelm seems to have imagined that his unending stream of challenges and provocations would render Britain so aware of her isolation as to sign an alliance with him (presumably marking the first time in the annals of diplomacy that one nation had ever made an ally of another through cease-less annoyance). Instead, he found his own nation hemmed in, east and west, by British allies. He complained aloud that his uncle, Britain's King Edward VII, had contrived a hostile encirclement of Germany.[79] But the truth was very much worse, for Europe was now polarized into two opposing camps with the Triple Alliance of Germany, Austria and Italy pitted against the Triple Entente of France, Russia, and Britain. A European powder keg had been brought into existence and lacked only a fuse to set off. The fuse, as it turns out, was the Eastern Question.

Domestic Developments in the Balkan States

Romania

The Congress of Berlin had liberated 11 million people—Romanian, Greek and Slav—from Turkish rule, but had satisfied very few of them.[80] Newly independent Romania not only chafed at the loss of Bessarabia to Russia, but also believed it had claims on Austrian Bukovina and Hungarian Transylvania where Romanian majorities toiled under the foreign yoke.[81] At home, the small farms Prince Couza had distributed among the liberated serfs in the 1860s proved insufficient to support the families cultivating them. In 1889, the state lands were parceled out to the peasantry, providing them with a modest increase in acreage. But even with the introduction of modern farm machinery their lot remained untenable. In 1907, they staged an insurrection so violent that 150,000 soldiers had to be mobilized to pacify it.[82] In the aftermath, the government reduced the agrarian tax burden, and established banks to provide peasants with loans at low rates.

In industry and mining the state enjoyed better success, for it possessed large deposits of oil, minerals and coal. The rail system was expanded, the economy was placed on the gold standard and the army became the largest of any Balkan state.[83] Through it all, the foreign-born royal couple, King Karol and Queen Elisabeth, remained popular—the latter gaining fame, under the pseudonym "Carmen Sylva," as the author of poetry on traditional Romanian themes. But the regime was malicious in its treatment of the Jews. Despite a pledge undertaken at the Congress of Berlin to establish equal treatment of all religions in the newly independent state, the Jews of Romania were denied citizenship and openly discriminated against. Many decided to emigrate, with the majority going to the United States.

Greece

At the opposite end of the Balkan Peninsula, Greece had been the first of the Balkan states to obtain independence (1830) and also the first to be dissatisfied with her boundaries. Thessaly, Epirus, southern Macedonia (with the port of Salonika) and the Aegean Islands—all inhabited predominantly by Greeks—lay outside the nascent state. In 1832, a Bavarian prince, Otto I, was established on the throne and ruled as the nation's first sovereign for nearly three decades. Disliked for his tyrannical methods, but most especially because he acquired no territory even when the outbreak of the Crimean War seemed to offer an opportunity,[84] he was ousted by a popular uprising in 1862. His successor, George I, a son of the Danish king, ensured his popularity within a year of his accession by granting a new constitution providing for a single house legislature elected by universal manhood suffrage (the so-called *Boulé*). Britain, too, did its part to secure the new dynasty by ceding the Ionian Islands, a souvenir from the Congress of Vienna (1815)—the Greek kingdom's first accretion of territory since gaining independence.[85]

At the Congress of Berlin, Greece was promised a "rectification" of her boundary with Turkey, and though it took three years before this promise was fulfilled, Abdul Hamid II ultimately agreed to the cession of Thessaly (1881). The sultan failed to follow through, however, on a pledge of reform for those Christians remaining under Ottoman rule, and in 1896, the hard-pressed Greek inhabitants of Crete fomented a rebellion. Swept up in a popular outcry demanding intervention, the Greek king declared war on behalf of the rebellious island. The Turks, however, had refurbished their army with help from Kaiser Wilhelm (whose ever-active mind had now lit upon the idea of building a railway from Berlin to Baghdad). The Greeks were defeated in three successive battles in Thessaly before taking refuge in the famed pass at Thermopylae. The "Thirty Days' War" thus ended ignominiously with Greece suing for peace and Crete still in Turkish hands. But the European Powers were not oblivious to the cause of the Cretan uprising. At their insistence, Crete's Christians were granted autonomy under a "High Commissioner" answerable to the Powers, but still subject to the Sultan's suzerainty. (The post was awarded to Prince George, a son of the Greek king—a virtual admission that the Greco-Cretan attempt at union was just.)[86] The Greeks, moreover, discovered a Cretan patriot of remarkable ability, Eleuthérios Venizélos, whom they subsequently invited to Greece as an advisor on Cretan liberation. By 1910, Venizélos had become prime minister of Greece, in which capacity he carried out necessary economic and military reforms, while ensuring "by deft diplomacy ... that in the next war against Turkey, Greece should not fight hopelessly alone as in 1897 but with united support of Bulgaria and Serbia."[87]

Bulgaria

If the hopes of any Balkan state had been raised and then shattered at the Congress of Berlin it was Bulgaria. The Treaty of San Stefano had promised boundaries stretching from the Black Sea to the Aegean, but the famed Congress had delivered a truncated rump. In 1878, a Russian commissioner, Prince Dondukoff-Korsakoff, had been appointed to guide this "lesser Bulgaria" in its transition towards autonomous rule. To ensure the continuing need for Russian oversight, he promulgated a constitution providing for a single-chamber legislature (the so-called *Sobranje*)—elected democratically by universal manhood suffrage—and a ministry and ruling prince (Alexander of Battenberg) that were not responsible to it. In the view of the commissioner, the two branches—one democratic, the other authoritarian—would be ever at each other's throats, necessitating the referral of all crucial policy decisions to the tsar. In seeming fulfillment of this prophecy, Prince Alexander locked horns with the *Sobranje*, altered the constitution in an authoritarian direction and called in Russian advisors to serve as his leading ministers (1881).

But if the average Bulgarian and the ruling prince were willing to follow the Russian lead in foreign policy, neither was willing to be treated as a mere tsarist subject in his own homeland.[88] In 1883, Prince Alexander rebelled against Moscow's heavy-handedness, sacking his two leading Russian advisors and joining forces with the nationalist majority in the *Sobranje*. The move was greatly resented in Moscow, where plans were laid to reassert Russian authority. But in 1885, these machinations received a severe setback when East Rumelia ousted its Turkish governor and declared for union with Bulgaria-proper. The step seemed rather bold to Prince Alexander, but the leaders of the *Sobranje* insisted upon his endorsement, giving him "the choice of advancing to Philippopolis [the East Rumelian capital] or retiring to Darmstadt [the ancestral home of the Battenbergs]."[89] Acceding to the *Sobranje's* demand, the "Prince of Bulgaria" saw his title increased to "Prince of the Two Bulgarias."

"Such is the shortsightedness of the ablest diplomatists," notes the *Cambridge Modern History*, "that, when the union of the two Bulgarias came … it was the British Government that supported and the Russian that condemned it."[90] In the British view, a Bulgaria doubled in size and independent in spirit could serve as a useful buffer between Russia and the Ottoman empire. Reaching the same conclusion, but with far less mirth, Russia broke off diplomatic relations with Bulgaria and recalled her officers from the Bulgarian Army, leaving it without a soldier ranking higher than captain.[91] Jealous that Bulgaria should exist at all as a rival claimant to the Ottoman inheritance,[92] Serbia declared war in response to the union with East Rumelia. Within two days, Serbian forces had approached to within twenty-two miles of Sofia, the Bulgarian capital, where it met a Bulgarian army led by Prince Alexander himself. There ensued the three-day battle of Slivnitsa (November 16–19, 1885), where, against all expectation, the Bulgarian army and its officer corps of captains emerged triumphant. The Serbs fell back in disarray, leaving the road to Belgrade open. Vienna, however, was as unwilling as ever to suffer the emergence of a "Greater Bulgaria," and invited Prince Alexander to arrest his march or face war with the Hapsburg empire.

Acquiescing in the Austrian ultimatum, Prince Alexander was received in his capital as a military hero. Of German extraction, he now set about reorganizing his army along Prussian lines. In this endeavor, he encountered the resistance of certain officers who were still attached to the Russian drill, and who found themselves, in consequence, passed over for promotion.[93] In the meantime, the Russian tsar had become increasingly vexed by the "Bulgaria for the Bulgarians" attitude at Sofia. Still intent on having Bulgaria for the Russians, he had his agents recruit a cabal of the disaffected "Russian drill" officers (chief among them the Bulgarian minister of war and the commandant of the military academy[94]) to do Moscow's bidding. On August 21, 1886, the recruited mutineers burst into Prince Alexander's bedroom. Young and fleet of foot, the prince eluded them and fled into his garden only to find more conspirators awaiting him with fixed bayonets.[95] Forced to sign his abdication "with loaded revolvers [pointed] at his head," Alexander was spirited out of Sofia and ushered into exile that very night.[96]

The conspiracy, however, did not prosper. Led by the speaker of the *Sobranje*, Stefan Nicolas Stambuloff, and supported by regiments loyal to the prince, the nationalist party reasserted its authority within the week. After 12 days in exile, Prince Alexander reentered his capital amid cheering throngs. But the experience had broken his will. Fearing another Russian intervention, he appealed to the tsar to sanction his return, and when the latter refused, he abdicated again even as his countrymen entreated him to remain.[97]

In this, Bulgaria's hour of need, Russia helpfully dispatched a new commissioner to "restore order," but Britain and Austria let it be known that the reestablishment of Russian predominance would not be tolerated. The ensuing elections to the *Sobranje* produced only thirty pro–Russian delegates as against 470 nationalists,[98] with Stambuloff emerging as the leading political figure. Dubbed the "Bulgarian Bismarck" by British pundits,[99] Stambuloff ousted the pro–Russian party, and frustrated all attempts to challenge the rule of Prince Alexander's successor, the Austrian aristocrat and soldier, Ferdinand of Saxe-Coburg. In foreign affairs, Stambuloff aligned himself with Bismarck's Triple Alliance, Great Britain, even with the sultan (still Bulgaria's nominal suzerain) to thwart further Russian meddling.[100] In domestic policy, he oversaw the expansion of railroads, manufacturing and commerce, improvements in agricultural methods and education, and the transformation of "the capital, Sofia, a dirty, wretched Turkish village … into one of the attractive capitals of Europe."[101]

For seven years he exercised a free hand, but his methods became increasingly tyrannical until, at length, Prince Ferdinand, who had now learnt the language and customs of his adopted country, withdrew his support and dismissed him from office (1894). Rather ignominiously, Stambuloff was deprived of his property and left to the mercy of his enemies, four of whom accosted him in the streets of Sofia on July 15, 1895, severing his hands and leaving him mortally wounded.[102] He was but forty-one years old and is said to have departed life with the words "God save Bulgaria."[103]

Prince Ferdinand had as yet enjoyed little support in Europe owing to the adverse attitude of Russia. He therefore sought reconciliation with Moscow—achieving it by having his son baptized into the Orthodox faith with a proxy of Tsar Nicholas II serving as godfather. (Ferdinand, himself, was Catholic.) That Bulgaria would subsequently have to choose between Russia and Germany may be left to a later discussion.

Serbia

Serbia, Bulgaria's foe and neighbor to the west, meanwhile, had bankrupted itself by the war of 1885. King Milan, an Austrian pawn despite the anti–Austrian prejudices of his people, had overseen the spiraling of his nation's debt from 7 million to 312 million francs.[104] In 1889, he promulgated a liberal constitution, but it was not enough to preserve his throne. He abdicated two months later in favor of his twelve-year-old son, Alexander, the last of the Obrenovic line. There ensued a five-year regency marked by political chaos, but on coming of age, Alexander called his father home from exile to advise him and resorted to autocratic rule.

To this point, relations with Austria-Hungary had been friendly, and so they remained for six more years as firm government put an end to domestic strife. But in 1900, Alexander took a Bohemian wife, Draga Mashin (a former lady-in-waiting to his mother, and ten years his senior), and quite inexplicably switched his allegiance to Russia. In a bid to obtain popular support for this peculiar program, he promulgated a new constitution, establishing a free press and a two-house legislature.[105] The move availed him little. His policy and his wife, who bore him no children, were widely hated—a situation made worse by persistent rumors that Alexander planned to designate one of Draga's brothers as heir to the throne. Attacked in both parliament and press, and dogged by secret intelligence that a military conspiracy was afoot, the king toyed with the notions of divorce and another policy reversal.[106] Before he could act, however, troops stormed the palace and dragged the royal couple from their refuge in a wardrobe closet (June 10, 1903).[107] "The last Obrenovich," says the *Cambridge Modern History*, "fell, clasping his wife in his arms, while the ruffians who profaned the name of officer stabbed and outraged the body of the Queen."[108] Afterwards, the corpses of the royal couple were cast from a palace window.

On the morrow, the church bells are said to have sounded in celebration at the news, and the denizens of the capital were seen dancing in the streets, as "Belgrade proved to the world that she was still, after a century of practical freedom, inhabited by thinly polished barbarians."[109] The crown (for the regicides had thought ahead) was conferred on Peter Karageorgevic, grandson of that Black George who had raised the flag of rebellion against the Turks in the first decades of the preceding century. In contrast to the aristocratic Obrenovics, the Karageorgevics were the party of popular patriotism. Consequently, the 1903 revolution brought about a flowering of the so-called "Great Serbian Idea"—the belief that Serbia, Montenegro, Novibazar, Bosnia, Herzegovina and northwestern Macedonia (the various areas of predominantly Serbian ethnicity) should all be united into one great Serbian state.[110] Rather than remain dependent on Austria-Hungary (the occupiers of Bosnia and Herzegovina) for an outlet to the sea, the new regime reached a commercial accord with Bulgaria for the use of the latter's Black Sea ports.[111] The Dual Monarchy answered this provocation with a tariff war, known afterwards as the "Pig War" (1904–1905), because Serbia's pigs (her prime export) were excluded from Hapsburg markets. The Serbs countered by spreading "Greater Serbia" propaganda in Bosnia and Herzegovina, causing Vienna much chagrin and apprehension.[112]

The Ottoman Revolution

And so matters stood when suddenly in 1908, revolution broke out in a most unexpected quarter. On July 23 of that year, a party of revolutionaries in Salonika known as the "Young Turks" sent a telegraphic message to Sultan Abdul Hamid II proclaiming the restoration of the defunct Turkish Constitution of 1876—the very document that the sultan himself had promulgated as a ruse to thwart the diplomacy of the Great Powers prior to the Russo-Turkish War.

In days past, this impudent summons would have been answered with the sword. But coming from Salonika, a predominantly Greek city in Turkish Macedonia, the declaration held ominous significance. The city was the headquarters of the 3rd Army corps. Inadequately equipped,

Sultan Abdul Hamid II of the Ottoman empire. Library of Congress (Wikimedia Commons).

inconsistently paid and stationed in a chaotic province where Greeks and Slavs clashed with Muslims and with each other, day in and day out, year after year, the army was known to be on the brink of mutiny. Months earlier, a general sent to restore military discipline had been shot down in cold blood.[113] Now, in conjunction with the Young Turks' declaration, the sultan was advised that not just the 3rd Army corps, but also the 2nd Army corps stationed at Adrianople, were prepared to march on the capital in support of the revolutionaries.

"From 1880 to 1908," says the historian William Stearns Davis, "Turkey was governed under a stark tyranny worthy rather of the ninth than of the nineteenth century." Abdul Hamid himself was known throughout Europe as the "Red Sultan" for his cruelty (the moniker being conferred upon him for the massacre of innumerable thousands of Armenians in eastern Anatolia between 1894 and 1896).[114] But he had nowhere near the number of reliable troops needed to fend off two army corps. Consequently, on the advice of his chief religious scholar, his leading ministers and his astrologer, he acceded to the Young Turks' demand for a parliamentary system of government under the charter he had issued and abrogated so many years before (July 24, 1908). To make the best of a bad situation, he comported himself as though he had done so out of magnanimity and toured the streets of the capital to the cheers of the multitude.[115]

The "Young Turks" who had brought about this unanticipated revolution were a hodgepodge of liberals and nationalists held together by a belief that the nation had been brought to wrack and ruin by the incompetence and corruption of the existing regime. Schooled for the most part in Western Europe, where they had taken refuge from the Sultan's tyranny, they prescribed the adoption of Western-style constitutionalism as the surest avenue to achieving reforms needed to compete in the modern world.[116] Above all, they wished to substitute nationalism for fanatical religion as the motive force of the state, and thereby "induce their compatriots to forget religious differences in a spirit of national patriotism—that 'fraternity' of allegiance to a common flag."[117] As Major Enver Bey declared on hearing of the sultan's capitulation, "Henceforth, we are all brothers! There are no longer Bulgars, Greeks, Rumanians, Jews, Moslems; under the blue sky we are all equal: we glory in the name of being Ottomans!"[118]

The sentiment was a fine one, but it contained an inherent flaw, for what Enver Bey was describing was not "nationalism" in the European sense of the word. Rather it was a concept called "Ottomanization"—the idea that the Ottoman Empire would come together as a multiethnic, religiously diverse assortment of peoples fanatically devoted to the idea of the Ottoman state. It had not yet dawned upon the authors of this program (though the Hapsburg empire stood as a ready example) that true "nationalism" would exert a divisive rather than a unifying effect in such a milieu. Put another way, if one was to make an appeal to "nationalism" in the Ottoman Empire of 1908, the subject peoples were far more likely to desire separation and independence than they were to desire a "'fraternity' of allegiance to a common flag."

Nonetheless, in the heady days and weeks after the revolution, there was much fraternization between the various religions and ethnicities in the streets of the capital— enough, indeed, to raise concern that the Turkish Empire might stir back to life rather too energetically. "The success of the Young Turks," says *Encyclopædia Britannica*, "created a serious situation for the statesmen of Austria-Hungary and Bulgaria. A regenerated Ottoman Empire might in time be strong enough to demand the evacuation of Bosnia and Herzegovina, and to maintain or extend the nominal suzerainty over Bulgaria which the sultan had exercised since 1878."[119] Consequently, on October 5, 1908, Bulgaria became the first of the "Ottoman" provinces, to exercise the principle just discussed—declaring its full independence from the sultanate and conferring the title "tsar" upon its ruler, Prince Ferdinand. Two days later, Crete announced the dissolution of her ties with Turkey in favor of a union with Greece. Not to be outdone, Austria-Hungary converted her "occupation" of Bosnia and Herzegovina into full-fledged annexation—a breach of the Treaty of Berlin that did not go unnoticed in the courts of Europe. (Kaiser Wilhelm, however, supported the Austrian move—stating that "if his 'august ally' were compelled to draw the sword" in defense of her action, "a knight 'in shining armor' would be found at her side."[120] Hence, for the moment, the other powers simply shelved the issue.)

The forces of reaction in the capital blamed these territorial losses on the revolutionaries, who, in their view, were corrupting the state with ideas imported from the infidel West.[121] Abetted by the sultan, they staged a counter-revolution in the name of traditional Islam, seizing control of Constantinople in April 1909, while Mohammedan fanatics carried out a new massacre of Armenians in the countryside. But at Salonika, the Young Turk revolutionaries boasted a loyal army of 25,000 men, which promptly marched on the capital. After a brief bombardment, the army entered the city on April 25, deposing Abdul Hamid (who was allowed a comfortable retirement in Salonika) in favor of his long-sequestered, dissolute brother, Mehmed V. To the revolutionaries, who sought a mere figurehead, there could be no better recommendation than this new prince's admission that he "had not read a newspaper in twenty years."[122] Confirmed in power, the Young Turks' ruling "Committee of Union and Progress" discarded the veil of Ottomanization (with its promise of ethno-religious liberties in return for loyalty to the empire) and pursued an open program of chauvinistic Turkish nationalism or "Turkification." Where the former was egalitarian, it must lead inevitably to the empire's dissolution. Where the latter was bigoted, it alone (or so the thinking went) could maintain the empire's integrity.

Accordingly, the Turkish language was imposed on minorities. Schools advanced a dogmatic Turkish curriculum. Muslim colonies were established in Turkish Macedonia to teach Turkish ways and keep the Christian minorities (who were to be disarmed) in check. Public meetings and minority agitation were forbidden. Under the old regime, the empire's religious minorities had paid a tax for the privilege of living apart in the enjoyment of their own religion and customs (subject, of course to the occasional visit from rampaging Bashi Bazouks). Under the new program of "equality for all," this privilege was not to be expanded, as some had been led to expect by early propaganda, but rather done away with.

In sum, those inhabitants of the empire who had formerly been pushed about for *being* Greek, Slav, Armenian, Albanian, Arab or Jew were now to be pushed about (rather more roughly, truth be told) for *not being* Turks. And as this realization began to dawn on its intended victims, they came to fear "the liberty and equality of the 'Young Turks' far more than they had the tyranny of the old Sultan."[123] As the British ambassador pithily put it, "'Ottoman' inevitably means 'Turk' and [the] present policy of 'Ottomanization' is one of pounding the non–Turkish elements in a Turkish mortar."[124]

The Tripolitanian War and the First Balkan War

Much resistance was encountered and much discontent spawned in the implementation of this policy, and in the midst of it all, the folly of the premise upon which it was based—i.e., that it would maintain the empire's integrity—bloomed into full flower. In 1911, Italy invaded the Turkish province of Tripoli. The pretext for this bald-faced aggression (aimed at satisfying Italy's desire for a North African colony after France beat her to Tunis in 1881) was the "imperiled" safety of Italian merchants living in the province. The landing of Italian troops achieved something very like the opposite, for the Arabs of the hinterland responded to the invasion by declaring a jihad.[125] Finding their progress stymied beyond a few coastal strongholds, the Italians seized the Dodecanese Islands in the Aegean (including the major island of Rhodes) in order to force the Turks' hands. Faced with a simultaneous insurrection in Albania, Turkey relinquished Tripoli in return for peace.

"The great significance of this war," says Charles Downer Hazen, "did not lie in the fact that Italy acquired a new colony. It lay in the fact that it began again the process, arrested since 1878, of the violent dismemberment of the Turkish Empire; that it revealed the weakness of that Empire, powerless to preserve its integrity...."[126] Ten days before the signing of the Treaty of Lausanne ended the "Tripolitanian" War (the name given to the war between Turkey and Italy), the Balkan nations of Montenegro, Serbia, Greece and Bulgaria invaded Turkish Macedonia to ignite the First Balkan War.

In the preceding months, the four Balkan states had taken increasing note of Turkish weakness. Although they were not on particularly friendly terms with each other, they could not but recognize the opportunity open before them—particularly with a portion of the Ottoman army tied down in Tripoli.[127] Using as a pretext the pleadings of Christian refugees who had fled persecution and massacre in Turkish Macedonia amid the continuing government-sponsored influx of Muslim colonists,[128] they formed a series of alliances aimed at driving the Turks out of Europe for the benefit of their ethnic brothers in Macedonia and, more especially, for their own territorial aggrandizement.

Hostilities began on October 8, 1912. Declaring a "holy war against the cruel and infidel Turk,"[129] the Montenegrins struck first, pushing south into Albania towards Scutari. By early November, a multi-front offensive by the Balkan allies had successfully cleared Macedonia of Turkish forces. The Serbs took Novibazar and Monastir in northwestern Macedonia and then turned west to capture Durazzo on the Adriatic. Greece seized Salonika and regions beyond in southern Macedonia, while her navy occupied a number of Aegean islands and blockaded enemy ports.[130] Of all the armies, however, Bulgaria's performed with particular distinction—taking on the main Turkish field forces in Thrace (the hinterland to the west of Constantinople) and inflicting stunning defeats on them at Kirk Kilissé, and Lulé Burgas where over three hundred and fifty thousand soldiers were engaged.[131] In the latter battle, the Turks made a determined stand, but starving and short of munitions by the morning of the fourth day, they gave up the struggle and soon "the whole of the great army of the sultan was fleeing in a rabble from the field of disaster: artillerymen forsaking cannon to ride off on the horses: infantrymen dropping rifles that they might run the faster. The flight ceased not until the Turks were behind the Tchatalja forts just beyond which lay Constantinople."[132] Left behind in Thrace to fend for themselves were a few isolated citadels—Adrianople chief among them.

On December 3, a preliminary armistice was declared. Peace talks ensued in London, where ambassadors of the Great Powers informed the Turks that they supported a Bulgarian demand for the surrender of Adrianople. Concerned that the liberal grand vizier, Kamil Pasha might consent (for he was still a believer in the constitution and the idea of multi-ethnic brotherhood), members of the Committee of Union and Progress led by Enver Bey burst in upon him with pistols drawn, demanding his resignation and gunning down his minister of war to show they were serious.[133] The coup was unavailing. The fighting resumed and Adrianople fell to a combined army of Bulgarians and Serbs on March 26, 1913.[134]

Abortive Peace and the Second Balkan War

Had it not been for the meddling of Austria-Hungary, the Balkan conflagration might now have come to an end with the Ottoman empire virtually expelled from Europe. But fearing that the 7.3 million Serbs in her own dominions would be incited to nationalist agitation if Serbia and her 3.3 million Serbs[135] emerged from the conflict with too much prestige, the Dual Monarchy intervened in the London talks to deny the landlocked Serbian state the outlet she had won on the Adriatic (and which had been promised to her under the Balkan alliance formed before the war).[136] With Italian support, the Austrians insisted on the founding of an independent "Albania" in the coastal regions captured by the Serbs (Treaty of London, May 30, 1913). Bitter was Serbia's disappointment, but with Germany also backing Austria, she could do nothing. She merely requested that in compensation, she be allowed to annex a portion of Macedonia promised to Bulgaria before the war, but ultimately captured and occupied by her own troops. The Bulgarians, however, had borne the brunt of the fighting in the recent war without reaping the lion's share of the territorial spoils. They refused Serbia's demands, and treated Romania (which hadn't even fought) and Greece with equal contempt when they, too, attempted to negotiate for more territory. Far from acquiescing, Bulgaria asserted her own counterclaims upon territories that had been occupied by her allies in violation of pre-war agreements.

An end to the debate proving elusive, Bulgaria took the ill-advised step of attacking Serbia, thereby inaugurating a Second Balkan War (June 1913). It was a colossal blunder. Greece, Montenegro and Romania joined forces against her, and the Turks seized the moment to attack from the south and retrieve some of her European holdings. Adrianople had to be abandoned by its Bulgarian garrison. In July, Turkish cavalry led by Enver Bey reoccupied the city without resistance.[137] Beset by enemies on all sides, Bulgaria submitted to the Treaty of Bucharest (August 1913), losing much of what she had gained in the First Balkan War.

Seeds of Armageddon

"In these two wars," writes William Stearns Davis, "about 348,000 men were killed or wounded, and about $1,200,000,000 in treasure expended by all the combatants together: figures small indeed compared with the awful sacrifices of Armageddon, but compared with previous wars no trifling price to pay even for very great changes upon the maps."[138] While it was reassuring that a general European conflagration had not erupted during the Balkan Wars, the region remained a storm center of conflicting interests between European powers great and small. Particularly acute was the bitterness between Austria and Serbia. As early as 1875, the Austro-Hungarian Foreign

Minister, Count Gyula Andrássy, had voiced the sentiment that if ever the Turks lost control of the Balkans, the pandemic of Slavic nationalism would defy containment, and "we should be ruined and should ourselves assume the role of 'Sick Man.'"[139] Of all the Balkan states, Serbia was perceived as the chief threat. Austria had possessed a frenzied enmity for her little neighbor to the south dating to 1903, when Serbia's pro–Austrian Obrenovic dynasty was overthrown in favor of the pro–Russian, ultra-nationalist Karageorgevics. Indeed, the goal of Austria-Hungary's 1908 annexation of Bosnia-Herzegovina—a region overwhelmingly populated by Serbs—was not merely to prevent Turkey from reclaiming it at some future date, but also to forever deny it to Serbia, and thus guarantee that her diminutive Balkan neighbor would remain landlocked and weak.

By the end of the Balkan Wars, Austria-Hungary's hostility toward Serbia knew no bounds, and it is safe to say that the feeling was mutual. Since the Hapsburg annexation of Bosnia-Herzegovina, the Serbs had been conducting vitriolic anti–Austrian propaganda among the Dual Monarchy's south Slav (Serbian and Croatian) populations—a process that intensified when Austrian diplomacy robbed Serbia of the outlet on the Adriatic she had won in the First Balkan War. Notwithstanding Austria's action, Serbia had emerged from the Balkan Wars with double the territory she possessed at their outbreak. In so doing, she not only placed a geographic barrier in the way of Austria's wished-for expansion towards Salonika (now little more than a pipedream), but also elevated her reputation among south Slavs living in the Hapsburg empire,[140] thereby raising the specter of perpetual and irrepressible Pan-Slav separatist agitation.

Deeming the situation an existential threat, Austria's principal military leaders proposed that south Slav unity should be achieved within an enlarged empire *at the cost of Serbian sovereignty*, rather than in an independent Serbia *at the cost of the empire's dissolution*.[141] No longer content merely to thwart her southern neighbor at every turn, Austria-Hungary was now bent on dealing Serbian prestige a mortal blow—a crushing military defeat that would expose the aspiration for a "Greater Serbia" as a mirage. The tricky bit was to identify a convincing pretext. "And then," says William Stearn Davis, "from clear heaven came a gift of the gods! An outrageous crime, which shocked the world, which gave the Austrians ample excuse in their own eyes for picking a quarrel with Serbia...."[142]

This crime will make a very good starting point for our next chapter. Suffice to say here, that the same force propelling Austria to war against Serbia—i.e., Pan-Slavism—must necessarily draw Russia into the conflict in its defense. Lacking the means to fight Serbia and Russia on her own, Austria must have support from Germany. Germany, however, could not come to her support without drawing in France under the terms of the Dual Alliance, thereby placing herself between the hammer and anvil of a two-front war.

Better for everyone, then, that this cascade should never be set in motion. Better that the rival alliance systems, which were after all defensive in nature, should serve as a deterrent rather than as an impetus to war. Except for one thing: Germany had a plan—a plan that would allow her to defeat France rapidly before Russia had a chance to mobilize. France defeated, she could then turn all her attention to the East. In other words, instead of fighting a single two-front war, she would fight a pair of single-front wars in succession. Brilliant (or apparently so) in conception, the plan was predicated on the existing status quo. In 1914, Russia did not possess an adequate rail network to set her army in timely motion and she lagged far behind Germany in industrial capacity

The Balkan States after the Wars of 1912–1913 by J.F. Horriban (Illustrator), from H.G. Wells'
Outline of History, 1923 (Wikimedia Commons).

and in the quantity and quality of her armaments (most especially in artillery). Aware
of these deficiencies, however, Russia had embarked on a four-year plan to close the gap
in armaments and to create a strategic railway network—the completion date being projected for 1917. Thus, Germany's window of opportunity would soon close. If it must
come to war, the time to strike was now.[143]

8

Societal Achievements, 1870–1914

On September 15, 1864, a 37-year-old English adventurer was partridge shooting on the outskirts of Bath, when he happened upon a stone wall. In negotiating this obstacle, he found it necessary to put down his rifle. On reaching back to retrieve it, he grasped it by the muzzle: a fatal decision—for as he raised it towards himself, the weapon discharged, inflicting a mortal wound. On this account a very interesting debate scheduled for the following day at the geographical section of the British Association was destined never to occur. The topic was the source of the Nile, and the deceased—John Hanning Speke—was the man who had found it. In so doing, says *Encyclopædia Britannica*, he solved a "problem that had baffled all previous efforts—extending over 2000 years...."[1]

Prior to the last decades of the 19th century, very little was known about the interior of Africa. The Boers, it is true, had moved inland somewhat during the Great Trek of the 1830s; and the Mediterranean coast was familiar enough. As for the rest, European settlements had been limited to coastal trading stations. The interior—with its mountains, deserts, jungles, impassable rivers, malarial mosquitos, deadly tsetse flies and strange inhabitants—simply did not beckon when all necessary commerce (including, regrettably, the slave trade) could be accomplished on the coast.

Even the maintenance of coastal ties often proved onerous. After outlawing the Atlantic slave trade in 1807, for example, the British fell into conflict with the slave-trading Ashanti kingdom, which was attempting to encroach on the coast of what is now Ghana (then inhabited by the friendly Fanti tribe). At Essamako (1824), 10,000 Ashanti warriors overwhelmed a British force of 500 under the local governor, Sir Charles McCarthy, whose "skull was afterwards used at Kumasi [the Ashanti capital] as a royal drinking cup." (By one account, it had not helped the cause of the outnumbered British that their quartermaster had accidentally dispatched them to the front with crates of vermicelli rather than bullets.)[2]

The British eventually got the upper hand in this struggle, but war broke out anew in 1863 upon Britain's refusal to surrender a fugitive slave. After a pair of defeats in the new struggle, a House of Commons Select Committee proposed the abandonment of all enterprises on the West African coast, apart from Freetown in Sierra Leone (which had been established as a haven for liberated slaves).[3] The proposal was not adopted, but even after a British force under Sir Garnet Wolseley burnt Kumasi and imposed terms (1874), the trouble was not put to rest; for King Mensa, who now assumed the Ashanti throne, would not honor the peace terms, pay the specified indemnity, or curb the tribal practice of human sacrifice. Renewed fighting in 1895–1896 and 1901–1902 ultimately led to Britain's annexation of the kingdom.[4]

If difficulties like these tended to dampen official enthusiasm for the "Dark Continent," there was as yet some well-meaning (if culturally conceited[5]) missionary interest in saving the "heathen." Among those who went for this purpose was the decidedly not conceited, humanitarian Scottish physician, David Livingstone, who arrived at Port Elizabeth, Cape Colony, in 1840. Unlike most missionaries, Livingstone was not content to remain in one place—for, as *Encyclopædia Britannica* notes, he "regarded himself to the last as a pioneer-missionary, whose work was to open up the country to others." Early in his travels he was well-nigh eaten by a lion, escaping with a crippled left arm, but this did not stop him from being the first white man to chart the Kalahari Desert (which he traversed from south to north) and to lay eyes on Lake Ngami in Bechuanaland (Botswana) some 1300 miles from the coast (1849).[6]

Photographic portrait of David Livingstone circa 1870, author unknown, published by the London Missionary Society (Wikimedia Commons).

The continent's natural routes of exploration were not overland, however, but along its four great rivers: the Nile, Niger, Congo and Zambezi.[7] Between 1854 and 1856, Livingstone crossed south central Africa from Portuguese Angola on the west coast to Mozambique (likewise Portuguese-controlled) on the east. En route, he charted the course of the Zambezi, discovering (among other things) the Victoria Falls (1855). In 1856, he returned to England, where he published an account of his travels, before returning to the mouth of the Zambezi for a new expedition—this one lasting six years (1858–64).

While Livingstone resumed his travels, another pair of explorers, John Speke and Richard Burton, resumed theirs. Veterans of an expedition to Somaliland (cut short by a slight scuffle with the locals wherein the former sustained eleven wounds and the latter had both cheeks pierced by a javelin[8]), Speke and Burton set out from Zanzibar on the African east coast to search for three great inland lakes which were rumored to exist. Burton, a lover of Arabic who had once made it to Mecca in the guise of a Mohammedan on pilgrimage, wished to explore Lake Nyasa, furthest to the south, but his Arab hosts barred the route. Consequently, in June 1857, the party set out for the middle one, Lake Tanganyika, which they reached in January 1858. On the return trip, Burton fell ill, and Speke took the opportunity to go in search of the northernmost lake—Lake

Henry Morton Stanley, newspaper reporter, explorer and tireless self-promoter, was hired by the *New York Herald* to find the missing Livingstone in 1871, winning himself wealth and reputation. His trusty rifle-bearer is named Kalulu. Smithsonian Institution Libraries (Wikimedia Commons).

Nyanza (afterwards known as Lake Victoria)—which he theorized to be the source of the Nile. His journey was rewarded on August 3, 1858, when a creek he had been following brought him within view "of a lake extending northward to the horizon."[9] Burton, however, was not impressed with the unscholarly theories of his junior partner, and the party returned to Zanzibar without further exploration.

Intent on proving his hypothesis, Speke returned to Lake Victoria in 1861, accompanied by J.A. Grant. Despite much annoyance from the local natives, their exertions culminated in the discovery of the Nile's point of origin on July 28, 1862[10]—the triumph being announced to the world by telegraph from Khartoum. Speke then returned to England, where he suffered his unfortunate hunting accident prior to the scheduled debate with his former superior, Burton. Burton had been rather malicious in defending his own view that Lake Tanganyika was the Nile's source. On hearing of Speke's death, he burst into tears, certain that his criticism had driven his erstwhile friend to suicide.[11]

By this time, David Livingstone had completed his second expedition, during which he sailed up the Shire River (a tributary of the Zambezi) and discovered Lake Nyasa—the southernmost of Burton's and Speke's three great lakes (1859). Along the way, he was mortified to discover a bustling slave trade in central Africa run by Arab and Swahili traders and disgracefully abetted by the local Portuguese authorities.[12] Returning to London (1864), he became acquainted with Speke's discoveries, which he found intriguing, but unsatisfactory, since they did not answer the riddle of the legendary "fountains of the Nile" described by the Greek historian, Herodotus (2:28). It was in search of these "fountains" that Livingstone set out on his last expedition (1866–1873). Abandoned along the way by some of his porters (who subsequently reported him dead), he arrived at Nyangwe on the Lualaba River (which he mistook for the upper Nile) in March 1871. While he was there, Arab slavers attacked the town, murdering hundreds of women who were attending the town market, and carrying others into slavery. In his own words, his "first impulse was to pistol the murderers." Instead, he prepared a report of the incident to send back home, which ultimately "roused indignation in England to such a degree as to lead to determined … and successful efforts to get the sultan of Zanzibar to suppress the trade."[13]

The man who bore Livingstone's report to England was Henry Morton Stanley. Just four months after the Nyangwe massacre, Stanley, a journalist and adventurer who had been sent in search of Livingstone by the *New York Herald*, found him on the banks of Lake Tanganyika. After issuing his famous greeting ("Dr. Livingstone, I presume?"), Stanley presented the explorer with an abundance of supplies, which he had brought courtesy of the *Herald's* publisher, J.G. Bennett. He would remain with Livingstone for four months, during which time they explored Lake Tanganyika to its northern bank, proving that it made no contribution to the Nile. On parting company, Livingstone returned to the Lualaba to resume his search for the "fountains of Herodotus." Alas, he was carried away by dysentery on May 1, 1873.

Convinced that it simply wouldn't do to bury him in the middle of nowhere, Livingstone's devoted African companions dried his corpse in the sun to preserve it, carried it 1,000 miles to Zanzibar, and then took ship to England where Livingstone was interred at Westminster Abbey in April 1874.[14] At the funeral, Stanley, who held his former host in reverence, acted as one of the pallbearers. So, too, did Jacob Wainwright, a rescued slave who had helped carry Livingstone's body out of the jungle. Of all the African explorers, Livingstone distinguished himself by his altruism. "In all the countries through which he travelled," says the *1911 Encyclopædia Britannica*, "his memory is cherished by the native tribes who, almost without exception, treated Livingstone as a superior being; his treatment of them was always tender, gentle and gentlemanly. By the Arab slavers whom he opposed he was also greatly admired, and was by them styled 'the very great doctor.'"[15] His work on the Lualaba was completed by the subsequent explorations of Lieutenant Verney Cameron (who first surmised that the river was actually the Congo rather than the Nile)[16] and the irrepressible Stanley, whose monumental expedition of 1874 through 1877, charted the circumference of Lake Victoria and then followed the course of what was indeed the Congo from Nyangwe to its outlet on the Atlantic.[17]

Livingstone's dying testament was that the ongoing central-African slave trade might be abolished: "All I can add in my solitude is may Heaven's rich blessing come down on everyone, American, English or Turk, who will help to heal this open sore of the world."[18] He even pointed the way—calling for implementation of the "'3 Cs': Commerce, Christianity and Civilization."[19]

The first to take up his mantle—with motives (and results) that were rather less noble than Livingstone's—was Leopold II, King of Belgium. Leopold's life dream had been the possession of an African empire.[20] In 1876, at a conference attended by Europe's premier explorers and geographers, whom he had summoned to Brussels, Leopold inaugurated "The International Association for the Exploration and Civilization of Africa," ostensibly pledged to the eradication of the slave trade and the spread of civilization.[21] Its initial activities were directed to the region of Lake Tanganyika; but on reading Stanley's accounts from the Congo, Leopold recognized that his long-sought opportunity had arrived. He invited the explorer to Brussels and engaged him as his agent for a new "International Association of the Congo." In so doing, he stole a march on the other European powers—particularly Great Britain, which had not acted on Cameron's or Stanley's initial reports of the region's commercial potential.[22]

Returning to the Congo basin on Leopold's behalf, Stanley established a number of stations along the river—most notably, Leopoldville, located above the rapids at a widening in the river called Stanley Pool. "A more difficult task," notes *Encyclopædia Britannica*, "was the making of a road through the cataract [waterfall] region and the carrying over it in sections of four small steamers, all of which were launched on the middle river."[23] In these various undertakings, Stanley showed himself to be "a man of inflexible will, who having conceived a vast design carried it to its conclusion regardless of any obstacles, sparing neither himself nor his associates, and, if opposed prepared to shed blood to attain his object."[24] An extremely facile writer, Stanley described his adventures in several best-selling books—most notably, *How I Found Livingstone* and *In Darkest Africa*—which thrilled European audiences, if failing to impart much empathy for the many natives he mistreated along the way.[25]

By the time Stanley's labors in the Congo were complete (1884), much else had occurred in Africa. France, for example, had taken Tunis; Britain had occupied Egypt; the explorer Pierre Savorgnan de Brazza had established a French claim to the north bank of the Congo River; and Portugal (supported by Britain) had put forth a claim to both banks of the Congo River at its mouth (which, after all, Portuguese navigators had discovered in the 1480s). In short, the "Scramble for Africa" had begun. By the time it ended two decades later, the European powers had laid claim to 90 percent of the continent, with only Abyssinia (Ethiopia) and Liberia retaining their independence.[26]

The reasons for this astonishing activity were legion, ranging from the strategic

(Britain's occupation of Egypt to secure her interest in the Suez Canal) to the grandiose (Cecil Rhodes' scheme for a Cape to Cairo rail system); from missionary concerns (spawning the notion of the "White Man's Burden," replete with its noble aspirations and racist assumptions) to hopes for economic exploitation (as in the ivory trade and in the mining of gold and diamonds); from the need for raw materials important to industry (rubber and palm oil) to trade in exotic spices (cocoa and Zanzibar clove); everything, indeed, from the decline of Ottoman power in coastal North Africa to capital investment opportunities in an era of protectionism to nationalist fervor to popular enthusiasm to mere fear of missing out.[27] (We may add a timely demographic contribution. In 1800, Europeans accounted for twenty percent of the global population—a figure that rose to twenty-five percent by 1900 in the milieu of rapid industrialization. This trend would not be sustained in the ensuing century—but for a fleeting moment, Europe had population to spare.[28])

Facilitating the continent's division, and contributing in no small way to its timing, were the period's myriad scientific and engineering achievements, among which we may give special mention to medical advances (quinine for malaria), the capacity to press into the interior with rail and telegraph lines, improvements in steam-powered shipping, and the sheer technological advantage held over Africa's native populations by the colonizing powers, particularly in military terms.[29] It was hoped by the partitioning powers that expansion into Africa would provide an economic boon, but for the most part, the expected profits did not materialize. Indeed, the imperialist nations were to learn that empire building was as likely to burden the national economy as to strengthen it. This is not to say, however, that riches were not to be had by those willing to play fast and loose with the rules—Leopold's Congo being a case in point.

As the "scramble" picked up steam in the mid–1880s, King Leopold became increasingly anxious to secure recognition of his status in the Congo. Consequently, in 1884, a conference was convened in Berlin to establish internationally accepted procedures for laying claim to new territories. The setting of rules tended rather to increase than to decrease the overall chaos; for in settling upon "effective occupation" as the means of establishing claims, the "Berlin Conference" (1884–85) spurred the rival powers to race each other all the more feverishly to create requisite facts on the ground.[30] From Leopold's standpoint, however, the conference had done good service—for it had confirmed him as sovereign of the "Congo Free State" on the conditions of "free navigation of the Congo, free commerce, the suppression of slave-trading, and the protection of missionaries, scientists, and explorers...."[31]

In its initial years, the colony operated at a substantial loss, with Leopold funding the difference from his own private fortune. In 1890, the state of Belgium chipped in with an interest-free loan of 25 million francs. But in 1891, at Leopold's instruction—and in direct violation of the terms of the Berlin Conference's charter, which specifically forbade monopolies—the Congo Free State secretly assumed sole control of the rubber and ivory trade in all "vacant lands" (i.e., lands deemed property of the state because they were not directly "lived upon or 'effectively' cultivated" by the natives).[32] To exploit these rich resources, concession companies were formed "in which the state had a financial interest either as a shareholder or as entitled to part of the profits," while King Leopold himself was awarded a personal estate, or "crown domain," ten times the size of Belgium.[33]

When all was said and done, says Schapiro, "The government was administered solely in the interest of the stockholders, and the natives were reduced to virtual slavery.

To make them collect as much rubber as possible they were subjected to cruel treatment, to whipping, torture, and death."[34] For an extended period, the truth was hidden from the public view behind a philanthropic façade embodied in the person of the king. But in 1900, a review of the state's financial records by the Liverpool shipping clerk, E.D. Morel (whose employer, Elder Dempster Shipping Lines, handled all transport between the Congo and Antwerp), revealed that while rubber and other commodities were flowing out of the Free State in large amounts (the rubber exports alone being valued at $8.2 million annually by 1902),[35] very little, apart from military stores, was flowing back in. In other words, the native population was living under military rule and wasn't profiting one iota.[36]

As evidence of atrocities and maladministration mounted—and as international and domestic pressure increased in proportion—King Leopold agreed to the formation of a commission of inquiry (1904). Its report, issued in October of the following year, prompted a University of Brussels professor to declare that "the Congo Free State is not a colony in the proper sense of the term: it is a financial speculation.... The colony is administered neither in the interest of the natives nor even in the economic interests of Belgium; the moving desire is to assure the sovereign king the maximum of pecuniary benefit."[37] In the attendant scandal, Leopold surrendered sovereignty over the colony (though not without being generously compensated), which on November 15, 1908, was annexed to Belgium "without ceremony of any kind,"[38] to be known, henceforth, as the "Belgian Congo."

At the time of the Congo Free State inquiry, an episode of surpassing brutality transpired in the German colony of South West Africa. In 1904, the Herero people—victims of every form of colonial indignity—rebelled against their German overlords. The Germans made short work of them in the Battle of Waterburg, and then harried the survivors into the neighboring Omaheke Desert. Stragglers were gunned down or thrust through with bayonets on sight, and those who tried to escape the unforgiving sand dunes through surrender were shown no quarter. We read of women being raped just prior to their murder, of infants being tossed in the air and caught on the points of bayonets, and of prisoners being flogged so brutally that their skin was torn away.[39] Over eighty percent of the tribe was exterminated—the majority dying of exposure in the desert while German troops fortified the border zone to prevent their escape.[40] Afterwards, a tour of the desert revealed that the victims had dug forty-foot holes in the sand with their bare hands, but had not found water.[41] The affair was the work of the German commander on the scene—General Lothar von Trotha—and not clearly a direct policy of the home government,[42] but it is just as well that Germany's days as a colonial power were numbered.[43]

It is beyond the scope of a section entitled "societal achievements" to follow in detail the remarkable surgery performed on the African continent by the European Powers. Nor would it be appropriate, under such a heading, to chart the history of the various colonies thus formed (for which the infamous examples of the Congo Free State and German South West Africa must suffice). Perhaps the best that can be said of Europe's colonial adventure was that it was mercifully short. As J.M. MacKenzie has noted, "Many Africans were born before the partition occurred, and were still alive when Europe departed in the early 1960s."[44] Nevertheless, we may tidy up a loose end or two by noting that (i) Britain's longed-for continuous stretch of territory from the Cape to Cairo was ultimately derailed by Germany's establishment of German East Africa; (ii)

France's dream of a continuous stretch of colonial territory across North Africa between Senegal and French Somaliland was thwarted by the intervening Sudan; and (iii) Portugal's like desire for a continuous swath across south-central Africa from Angola in the west to Mozambique in the east was foiled by Cecil Rhodes' founding of Rhodesia.

Imperialist interests (and atrocities) aside, the partition of Africa was an object of popular fascination, encompassing the penultimate age of exploration—*penultimate* because at the dawn of the 20th century there was as yet another frontier to be charted: the North and South Poles. The last decades of the 19th century had witnessed multiple attempts at reaching the North Pole. All of them fell short—and the realization of failure en route frequently led expeditions to adopt the alternative goal of getting closer than anyone else had, thereby achieving a new "farthest north." In 1881, a United States expedition led by Adolphus Greely achieved the latter object by reaching 83°24′N. Alas, the party became stranded without supplies on the return journey, and by the time their

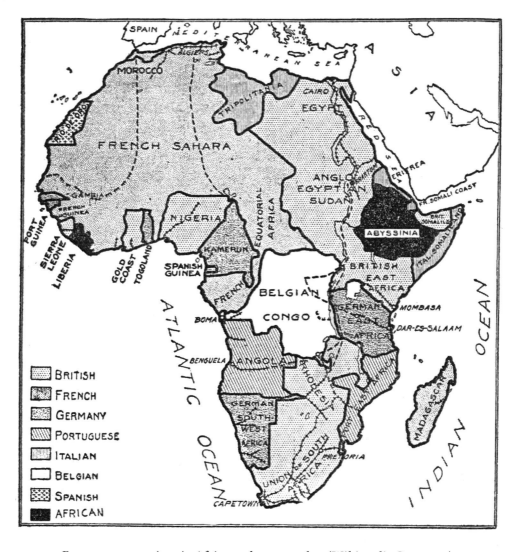

European possessions in Africa, unknown author (Wikimedia Commons).

rescue was effected one team member had been executed for stealing food and multiple others had died of starvation (including one who had been secretly eating those of his chums who had succumbed before him).[45]

In the ensuing years, some truly imaginative methods of reaching the Pole were devised. Fridtjof Nansen, a Norwegian innovator in arctic sledding and skiing who had been the first to cross Greenland (proving en route that it was entirely covered in ice [1888]), had determined from his studies "that there was a general drift [of arctic ice] across the polar basin and perhaps across the Pole."[46] He designed a ship, the *Fram*, for the purpose of being intentionally trapped in the ice at a particular point, with the idea of hitching a ride on the drift to the Pole and then onward back to navigable water. The *Fram*, says *Encyclopædia Britannica*, "was specially built of immense strength and peculiar form, being pointed at bow and stern and having sloping sides, so that the ice–floes, pressing together, should tend, not to crush, but merely to slip beneath and lift her."[47] Nansen's plan nearly worked, but the ice drift's direction shifted slightly before reaching the Pole, forcing him to abandon the ship and set off by sled. He achieved a new "farthest north" of 86°14′ before being forced to turn back (1893–1895).[48]

Two years later, the Swede Salomon August Andrée attempted to reach the North Pole by hot air balloon. Unfortunately, the balloon sustained damage at takeoff and crashed after a journey of 220 miles. The party of three attempted to return on foot, crossing the ice to a previously uncharted island before perishing—possibly owing to trichinosis infection after eating a polar bear without being able to cook it sufficiently.[49]

Ultimately, it was the American naval engineer Robert E. Peary (whose wife had borne him a daughter in the Arctic when he took her there on a previous expedition) who claimed success in reaching the Pole in April 1909, accompanied by Matthew Henson (a black companion who had once been his valet) and four Eskimos.[50] A controversy arose at the time due to a rival claim put forward by another explorer, F.A. Cook (later found to be unsubstantiated), and this was followed by further controversy owing to doubts about Peary's navigational accuracy and the record speeds that would have been required to achieve his reported timetable. (The dispute remains unsettled to the present day.)[51]

If Peary, in fact, did not reach the North Pole, the honor may belong to the Norwegian explorer, Roald Amundsen, who overflew the Pole in a dirigible piloted by Umberto Nobile on May 12, 1926, three days after the American, Richard E. Byrd, claimed to have done the same in an airplane. (Byrd is now thought to have miscalculated his position.) Amundsen, however, is best remembered for his accomplishments at the other end of the world in a famous race against the Royal Navy's Robert Falcon Scott. On a previous expedition to the Antarctic, Captain Scott had set a "farthest south" of 82°16′ (1901–1904). One of the members of his party, Ernest Shackleton, subsequently shattered this record on his own expedition, coming tantalizingly close to the South Pole at 88°23′S before lack of food and altitude sickness forced him to turn back (January 9, 1909).[52] The final 97 geographical miles to the Pole eluded his team when their last surviving pack pony (which they had intended to shoot and eat) slipped into a crevasse and could not be retrieved. As *Encyclopædia Britannica* laments, "its loss meant so much less food, and as far as can be judged, this alone made it impossible for the party to reach the Pole."[53]

On September 13, 1909, Robert F. Scott announced his intention of rectifying this deficiency by undertaking a second expedition. On reaching Australia, he received an unwelcome telegram from Amundsen advising him that he, too, was setting out for the South Pole. Amundsen had borrowed the *Fram* from Fridtjof Nansen with the initial intention of reaching the North Pole by the latter's method of lodging the ship in the Arctic ice drift, but hearing of Peary's presumably successful expedition, he turned about and headed in the opposite direction.

Scott established his base at Cape Evans and Amundsen his at "Framheim" in the Bay of Whales, at opposite ends of the Ross Ice Shelf. After much preparatory work, including the establishment of an advance supply depot (which had to be placed short of where he wanted it owing to bad weather), Scott set out with his party on October 11, 1911. Amundsen was aware that Scott had brought motorized sledges, which he feared would give the British party the upper hand in the race, but the sledges proved a failure, and much of Scott's journey was accomplished by man-hauling, while Amundsen and his party—expert in the use of skis and dog-hauled sledges—consistently made 15 miles a day. When Scott's party reached the Pole on January 17, 1912, they found that the Norwegians had preceded them, leaving behind a tent and flag. Pausing for a photograph (in which their disappointment is palpable), Scott's party set out on its return journey. Alas, their tragedy had only begun. Inexplicably, Scott had allowed an extra man to accompany the team on the last leg of the expedition, which meant that supplies meant for four men would have to suffice for five. On the way back, the weather turned intensely hostile. One member of the group, Edgar Evans, collapsed and died. Another, L.E.G. Oates,

Robert Falcon Scott's Pole party of his ill-fated expedition, from left to right: Lawrence E.G. Oates (standing), Henry G. Bowers (sitting), Robert Falcon Scott (standing in front of Union Jack flag on pole), Dr. Edward Adrian Wilson (sitting), Edgar Evans (standing). Bowers (1883–1912) took this photograph at the South Pole, using a piece of string to operate the camera shutter (Wikimedia Commons).

left the team's tent and wandered off into the wilderness, hoping to leave the others sufficient food to reach their supply depot alive. But Scott's failure to establish his supply depot far enough south ultimately proved fatal. The surviving members of the team met their death in a blizzard eleven miles shy of it. A search party located their tent in November 1912. In it were found the bodies of Scott and his two remaining companions, Henry Bowers and Edward Wilson, along with their journals and a last message from Scott saying, "Had we lived, I should have had a tale to tell of the hardihood, endurance and courage of my companions which would have stirred the heart of every Englishman. These rough notes and our dead bodies must tell the tale...."[54]

The Second Industrial Revolution

Prior to the age of polar exploration, the completion of the Suez Canal had been counted a monumental accomplishment (1869). But it would not have had the impact that it did were it not for technical advances that came afterward—most especially in steam-powered shipping. Isambard Brunel's *Great Western* and other early steamships required so much room for fuel that there was little left over for cargo. Consequently, most freight had still to be carried under sail—and sailing ships were not suitable for passage through the Suez Canal because the winds of the Red Sea were not reliable. Hence, when the Suez Canal opened, sailing ships—and the cargo they carried—still had to sail around the whole of Africa. As luck (or necessity) would have it, however, the 1870s witnessed the invention of the parsimonious "triple-expansion" marine engine, which greatly reduced fuel consumption while providing greater horsepower, making steam-powered freight shipping practicable for the first time—and with it the exploitation of the short route to India via Suez.[55]

The first large ship to be fitted with a triple-expansion marine engine—the SS *Aberdeen*, launched in 1882—displaced 3600 tons and traveled at 12 knots (13 miles per hour). Before the century was out, Charles Parsons would revolutionize marine engineering again by introducing a powerful, low-vibration marine "turbine" engine. In 1897, he demonstrated its capability with his own 44-ton yacht, *Turbinia*, which made an unannounced appearance at Queen Victoria's Diamond Jubilee, where it turned heads by achieving a speed of 34 knots (or 39 miles) per hour.[56] By 1910, the Parsons engine could turn an ocean liner's massive propeller one hundred and fifty times per minute making it possible to cross the Atlantic in five days, and to schedule a reasonably accurate "arrival hour" in advance.[57] The ill-fated *Titanic*, powered by a Parsons turbine engine with two reciprocating triple-expansion engines in support, traveled twice as fast as the *Aberdeen* though it displaced 14.5 times its tonnage.[58]

By the 1880s, steel had begun to replace iron in the hulls of oceangoing vessels—a trend that was accelerated by a new advance in steel production. Henry Bessemer's eponymous process, developed in the 1850s, had been regarded as a "miracle" due to its simplicity, but it had been predicated on the removal of *carbon* impurities from pig iron. When he attempted to export the process to the European continent by the sale of licenses, the resultant steel proved worthless. The problem, as Gavin Weightman relates in his book, *The Industrial Revolutionaries*, was that most of the iron ore mined on the continent (in contrast to that mined in Britain and the United States) contained an additional impurity—*phosphorus*. In Germany, Alfred Krupp got around the problem by purchasing iron deposits in Spain, where the phosphorus content was low, but the rest of the continent awaited Sidney Thomas' discovery that crushed dolomite binds phosphorus. The impurity could thus be extracted by lining the internal surface of steel furnaces with this mineral, thereby producing high quality steel.[59] After extensive experimentation, Thomas published his results in an article entitled "The Elimination of Phosphorus in the Bessemer Converter," co-written by his cousin, P.C. Gilchrist, a Welsh iron works chemist (1879).[60] With the adoption of the new process, says Schapiro, "the steel supply of the world was greatly increased."[61]

The advent of steel-framed building construction, meanwhile, allowed for the emergence of the first "skyscrapers" in crowded cities like New York and Chicago—an eye-catching example of which was Manhattan's landmark "Flatiron" (Fuller) Building, built in 1902. As H.G. Wells famously observed at the time, "There are people who sneer at this kind of progress as being a progress in 'mere size,' but that sort of sneering merely marks the intellectual limitations of those who indulge in it. The great ship or the steel-frame building is not, as they imagine, a magnified version of the small ship or building of the past; it is a thing different in kind.... In the old house or ship, matter was dominant—the material and its needs had to be slavishly obeyed; in the new, matter has been captured, changed, coerced."[62]

As the skyscrapers went up, revolutionary changes in power were occurring in the streets below. Pioneered by Lenoir and Rochas in the early 1860s, internal combustion came to fruition in the hands of Nikolaus August Otto and Eugen Langen, who won a gold medal for a more fuel-efficient version of the Lenoir's engine at the Paris Exhibition of 1867, and patented the first working 4-cycle "compression" engine (based on Rochas' theory) in 1876.[63] For nearly a decade, internal combustion motors were used exclusively to power small industrial machines, but thereafter they were adapted to other uses—most notably, the automobile. In 1885, Edward Butler of Great Britain built the earliest known internal combustion powered vehicle—a benzoline-powered tricycle. In the same year, Gottlieb Daimler of Germany applied a petroleum-powered internal combustion engine to a bicycle, thereby inventing the motorcycle. Shortly thereafter, Daimler and Karl Benz independently produced prototype cars—Benz's being a three-wheeler, which he called a "motorwagen." But the first to perfect a transmission system that would come into standard use was the Frenchman, Émile Levassor, who put a Daimler engine in a novel position—up front—engaging it with a clutch to transmit its rotational power (or "torque") to a geared transmission apparatus that turned the wheels.[64] (The invention was given a boost by the nearly coincidental invention of the pneumatic tire by a veterinary surgeon named John Boyd Dunlop, who hit upon the idea while trying to improve the performance of his son's tricycle so the latter could outrace his schoolmates.[65])

For centuries, horse-drawn vehicles had dominated the urban landscape. But between 1899 and 1909, there was a veritable explosion in the use of the new motorized vehicles. In the former year, France possessed a combined 1,672 motor vehicles for pleasure and industry. By the latter year, it possessed 46,000. Britain greatly eclipsed these numbers with 74,038 vehicles already registered by 1905, and 154,415 by 1908.[66] In the ten-year period beginning in 1903, the number of motorized buses on the streets of London rose from 13 to more than 3,500, while the number of horse-drawn buses fell from 3,623 to 142.[67] Across the pond, in the United States automobile production rose from a paltry 600 cars in 1899 to 114,891 in 1909.

In the same interval, motorized air flight became a reality when Orville and Wilbur Wright accomplished the feat at Kitty Hawk, North Carolina on December 17, 1903. As *Encyclopædia Britannica* notes, the rapid advances achieved in flight from that date until the outbreak of World War I were owed in great measure to improvements in automobile engines, which "provided the designers of flying machines with what they had long been looking for—a motor very powerful in proportion to its weight."[68]

Progressing in tandem with petroleum-based internal combustion was an alternate energy source: electricity. In 1876, Alexander Graham Bell (1847–1922), a Scottish-born professor of vocal physiology at Boston University, produced the first commercially patented telephone. The device converted sound into pressure-induced vibrations on a membrane, which in turn produced an electric current of variable intensity—the intensity being proportional to the vibrational changes. The current was then transmitted by wire to a distant receiver, where it was converted back to vibrations on a membrane and thus to sound.[69] A year later, Thomas Edison (1847–1931), utilizing the principle of "variable resistance," added the improvement of a microphone transmitter, thus producing a louder sound that could travel a greater distance.[70] Edison, however, is better remembered as one of the inventors—along with England's Joseph Swan—of the incandescent light bulb, consisting of two platinum electrodes connected by a carbon filament contained within a glass-vacuum bulb (1878–1879). (A vacuum was necessary to remove oxygen, which otherwise would have undergone combustion.)[71]

Before we leave the subject of electricity, two additional aspects bear mentioning. First, unlike steam or internal combustion, which must be utilized where they are produced, electric power can be generated at one site and transmitted over wire "as water is sent along a pipe," to be employed at a distance.[72] Werner von Siemens of Germany was among the first to employ the principle in powering the first electric elevator (1880)[73] and the first commercially successful electric tram (1881).[74] Edison, meanwhile, established the first public electric supply station, located on Pearl Street in New York City. *Encyclopædia Britannica* has noted that "By the end of the 19th century every large city in Europe and in North and South America was provided with a public electric supply for the purposes of electric lighting."[75] We may, however, cite a notable exception in Constantinople, where the Red Sultan, Abdul Hamid II, had gotten it into his head that he might be killed by dynamite (Alfred Nobel's nitroglycerin-based explosive), and deduced phonetically that the "dynamo" employed in electricity must be related in some way. "He prudently prohibited *both*," says W.S. Davis, "to be on the safe side."[76]

The second of electricity's fascinating aspects was Heinrich Rudolf Hertz's discovery of a "method of producing electric waves in space."[77] In scientific terms, we actually speak of "electromagnetic" waves—the combined nature of which had been proven mathematically in 1864 by the Scotsman, James Clerk Maxwell (1831–1879). The idea of generating such waves experimentally was first proposed in 1883 by Ireland's George Francis Fitzgerald. Hertz succeeded in the task in 1888. Four years later, Édouard Branly invented a device for detecting Hertz's waves (1892), and four years after that Guglielmo Marconi (1874–1937) utilized an electromagnetic wave generator and detector to create wireless telegraphy (1896).[78]

The new advances found immediate application in the military sciences. The Parsons turbine engine, for example, allowed for the development of a revolutionary new class of battleship: the "dreadnought," or ship that "feared nothing," since it was faster (at 21 knots), better armored and more heavily gunned than all existing classes. Built in the aftermath of Russia's shocking defeat at Tsushima,[79] the class took the name of its prototype—the *HMS Dreadnought*, launched in 1906 at the behest of Britain's First Sea Lord, John Fisher. Its appearance has been credited with accelerating the naval arms race between Britain and Germany—although most of the spending increases were on the part of Britain, whose outlays rose from £11 million annually in 1909 to £18 million annually by 1914 while Germany's remained flat in the £10-£11 million range.[80]

While developing his famous method of producing steel, Henry Bessemer made a less well-known attempt to invent an automatic machine gun. In 1854, he got far enough to obtain a patent, but his gun did not prove practical, and its production was not pursued.[81] For the next thirty years, the only operative machine guns—the multi-barreled French *mitrailleuse* and the Anglo-American "Gatling," both dating to the 1860s—required the turning of a hand crank. What Bessemer had hoped to do was to use the force of the explosion inside the cartridge not just to fire the bullet but also to eject the spent cartridge and load a new one. Hiram Maxim (1840–1916) eventually solved the problem by utilizing a different power source—the "recoil" produced by the bullet's forward momentum. In Maxim's gun, the firing pin strikes the primer at the rear of the cartridge setting off the internal powder explosion that launches the bullet. The bullet's forward momentum is accompanied by an equal and opposite recoil of the breechblock. As the breechblock recoils, it pulls in a new cartridge from the ammunition belt and drops it into the chamber as the old cartridge drops out. Then, in springing back to position, the breechblock pushes the new cartridge into the barrel and ejects the spent

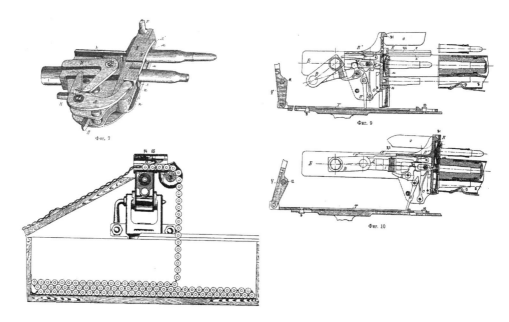

Maxim machine gun mechanism. Top left, breechblock. Bottom left, face-on diagram of cartridge belt feeding into the gun. Top right, breechblock in recoil position: a fresh cartridge has dropped into position to be thrust into the barrel, and the spent cartridge has dropped into position for ejection through the ejection tube. Bottom right, breechblock in firing position: A new cartridge is being grabbed from the belt for the next recoil. The fresh cartridge has been thrust into the barrel and the spent cartridge is being ejected through the ejection tube. *Brokhous and Efron Encyclopedic Dictionary* (Wikimedia Commons).

cartridge through an ejection tube located underneath the barrel in one and the same motion (see figure). As long as the trigger remains pulled, the cycle repeats, firing up to 600 rounds per minute, one cartridge after another. Maxim (who nearly beat Edison and Swan to the incandescent light bulb) also invented a smokeless powder for his cartridges, modestly naming it "maximite"—a mixture of nitroglycerin, tri-nitrocellulose and castor oil. (It is believed that Bessemer's machine gun failed because the smoky black powder of the day tended to build up and jam the gun.[82])

For artillerists, "recoil" had forever been a problem, not a solution. Until the 1890s, the firing of an artillery shell sent the entire gun reeling backwards, the gunners having to stand clear to avoid being bowled over. The crew had then to rush back to the gun, push it back into position, reload and re-aim before the next round could be fired. In the 1890s, however, a working "gun-recoil system" was invented that allowed the gun to slide backwards within a cradle while the carriage on which it was mounted remained fixed in position. A hydraulic brake gradually absorbed the recoiling force to halt the gun's backward motion in the cradle, whereupon it was returned to its starting point by compressed springs or compressed air. The gunners could then reload and fire again without the other intervening steps. Since the gunners no longer had to stand clear, moreover, shields could be mounted on the gun carriage to protect them from enemy fire.[83]

Another artillery innovation of the period was the "time-fuse" shrapnel shell, which allowed the detonation of a shell filled with metal projectiles (i.e., shrapnel) to be delayed until it reached the vicinity of the enemy, whereupon the projectiles would be jettisoned with explosive force across a wide area. (The name derives from its inventor, Lieutenant Henry Shrapnel of the Royal Artillery, who first introduced a shell containing projectiles in 1784.)[84]

Compulsory military service, meanwhile, had made armies larger (and rail expansion had made their deployment more rapid) than ever. By the turn of the 20th century, armies were so advanced that devastation undreamed of as late as the Franco-Prussian War had become a sobering reality. It—or at least the financial outlay it entailed—was

The Krupp 26 cm (10.2 inch) gun was exhibited at the World Fair in Vienna 1873 and it was featured in the *Scientific American* on August 22, 1874, accompanied by this illustration. Unrecognized signature (lower left). *Scientific American*, 1874 (Wikimedia Commons).

enough to provoke Tsar Nicholas II of Russia to summon an international peace congress in 1898.[85] In his written rescript, the Tsar stated that "The economic crises … [related to the] massing of war material, are transforming the armed peace of our days into a crushing burden…." He proposed that the congress "should seek 'without delay *means for putting a limit to the progressive increase of military and naval armaments.*'" In addition, it was to seek revision of the laws governing the conduct of war and provide a means for settling international disputes by arbitration.[86]

The congress opened its deliberations at The Hague on May 18, 1899. As to the limitation of armaments, it made very little headway. When the onus of rising military costs was raised, a German delegate, who seems to have missed the spirit of it all, assured the congregation that "The German people is not crushed under the weight of charges and taxes,—it is not hanging on the brink of an abyss; it is not approaching exhaustion and ruin. Quite the contrary; public and private wealth is increasing, the general welfare and standard of life is being raised from one year to another." On the question of arbitration, the German delegation was again lukewarm, arguing that it "'*must be injurious to Germany,*' since she could mobilize faster than any other nation—an advantage she would lose if her enemies could simply invoke arbitration as a ruse to buy time."[87]

Amid such protestations, the conference was able to accomplish little prior to adjourning on July 29, 1899. Nevertheless, it did (i) establish a Permanent Court of Arbitration at The Hague to which nations might refer their disputes on a purely voluntary basis; (ii) outlaw "the dropping of projectiles from balloons and the use of asphyxiating gases and 'dumdum' bullets" (i.e., hollow-tipped bullets which flatten on impact creating a wound of greater diameter); and (iii) affirm the procedure for treating wounded soldiers outlined in the 1864 Geneva Convention.[88] In 1907, Theodore Roosevelt joined the Tsar in summoning a Second Peace Conference at The Hague, which counted among its accomplishments the establishment of a convention "requiring a formal declaration of war before the opening of hostilities."[89] (One imagines the Russian delegates giving their Japanese counterparts a rather stern look amid the ayes and nays.)

When all was said and done, the practical effect of the peace conferences was nil. Between 1912 and 1913, Germany enlarged the size of its army by 30 percent, achieving a troop-strength of 665,000. France responded by increasing the term of military conscription from two years to three, while Nicholas II approved a plan for a 40 percent increase in the size of the Russian army. Hence, says one historian, "Europe by 1914 was experiencing a spiralling arms race…."[90] When war came, moreover, the ban on poison gas was ignored and projectiles were dropped freely from airplanes.

Science, Medicine and Culture

In science, thought, literature, art and medicine, trends from the preceding era had, by the dawn of the new century, entered into full blossom. In 1871, Charles Darwin produced his second revolutionary work, *The Descent of Man*, which argued that humankind had descended from the same common ancestor as the monkey and the ape. "We must … acknowledge, as it seems to me," he wrote, "that man with all his noble qualities … still bears in his bodily frame the indelible stamp of his lowly origin."[91] The argument was enough to provoke complaint even from those who had previously defended his *Origin of Species*—but sadly, not enough to bring discredit upon Social Darwinism, whose adherents were now employing the catchphrase "survival of the fittest," to justify racism, imperialism and war.[92]

By 1900, Darwin's theories had come to exercise a pervasive influence. "What Galileo and Newton were to the seventeenth century," says Bertrand Russell, "Darwin was to the nineteenth."[93] In formulating the tenets of psychoanalysis, Sigmund Freud argued that "inherited dispositions are residues of the acquisition of our ancestors." These include—and pit against one another—the innate drives contained within the *id*, and the restrictive cultural-societal norms imposed (rather severely, if one may venture a criticism) by the *superego*. It is left to the *ego*—the psyche's odd man out—to steer a rational course between these *unconscious* forces (a veritable Scylla and Charybdis in hiding) or succumb to maladjustment in the form of *neuroses*. The task must be accomplished, moreover, while the unconscious continues to run amuck in the shadows, with the *ego* scarcely suspecting "that it is not even master in its own house."[94]

In philosophy, Friedrich Nietzsche railed against Christianity, democracy and socialism as irrational creations that defy nature by elevating "the weak" over "the strong"—the very reverse of natural selection.[95] "I am opposed to parliamentary government and the power of the press," went one of his aphorisms, "because they are the means whereby cattle become masters."[96] He envisioned as preferable the emergence of a ruling class of "supermen"—a notion that was seized upon and perverted by the Nazis during the 20th century. In 1888, Nietzsche went mad while rescuing a horse from a ruthless beating and remained catatonic until his death twelve years later—a fate that some, including his doctors, attributed to syphilis[97] (though we may note, in keeping with our line of discussion, that inheritance might have played the critical role, since his father went mad before him).

In literature, Émile Zola produced a twenty-volume series tracing the "natural history" of a fictional French family during the reign of Napoleon III.[98] His approach created a new literary movement, "naturalism," wherein his protagonists' innate passions and instincts (psychological inheritances as evocative of the lower animal kingdom as the "bodily frame") conspire with external circumstances to determine each character's fate as assuredly as a laboratory experiment or a law of nature might do. Zola's epic, say the editors of a recent translation, was "intended to follow out scientifically the effects of heredity and environment on one family,"[99] and as *Encyclopædia Britannica* notes of all modern naturalist philosophy, "Life and mind ... take a secondary place; the cosmical mechanism determines *them*, while they are powerless to modify it."[100]

The naturalist movement was an offshoot of "realism" (which sought to portray subject matter dispassionately, without embellishment). So, too, was the new dramatic genre called the "problem play," made famous by the Norwegian playwright, Henrik Ibsen, whose works laid bare one or another of society's ills with unforgiving objectivity (typically without deigning to suggest a remedy). When one of his plays raised a hue and cry of protest, he answered with a satirical new "problem play"—*An Enemy of The People*—wherein the "people" are exposed as their own worst enemies as they ostracize the one rational voice in their midst: a fellow who is merely trying to point out that the town bath's defective drainage system poses a health hazard and ought to be fixed.[101] In Russia, another group of literary realists, the novelists Turgenev, Dostoevsky and Tolstoy, assumed the prohibited roles of "press, parliament and pulpit" in exposing the injustices of the tsarist autocracy.[102]

In art, impressionism continued as the leading genre—even insinuating its way into sculpture and music. Auguste Rodin's sculptural masterpiece, *The Thinker*, exudes "larger than life" emotional power but is left unfinished in detail—thereby leaving the eye something to "fill in" just as impressionistic painting does.[103] Similarly, in music, Claude Debussy (1862–1918) juxtaposed dissonant chords to produce an "oscillating" sound quality, hoping thus to "express the constant change of emotion or life" in the same way that impressionist painters used divergent light and color to create "the sense of a passing moment held in paint."[104]

Although in time Rodin (1840–1917) would be revered as the "father of modern sculpture" and Debussy as the "father of modern music," their work was initially dismissed as "incomprehensible" and "formless."[105] Lack of clarity had been impressionism's abiding paradox, and the impressionist painter's trick of forcing the eye to reconstruct dabs of color and light into a coordinated whole had begun to wear—never mind importing it into other mediums.[106] The puzzle was solved (fittingly enough, in "an age of progress") when Paul Cézanne (1839–1906) found an analogy in mathematics—determining that "everything in nature adheres to the cone, cylinder or cube."[107] Armed with this geometric axiom, he set himself the monumental tasks of enhancing clarity without abandoning the impressionists' advances in color and light, and of depicting multiple planes in space without resorting to the constraining technique of Renaissance perspective.[108] His solution was the "constructive" brushstroke—still broken up like that of the impressionists, but composed of carefully arranged blocks of color rather than haphazard dabs, thus simplifying detail and enhancing geometric shape. At the same time, he was able to create a novel multi-dimensional effect simply by juxtaposing contrasting colors or changing the angle between one set of uniform brush strokes and another.[109] "His work," says Arthur May, "marked the culmination of French painting in the nineteenth century and served as the point of departure for more bizarre and restless techniques" of the twentieth, such as "Cubism."[110] (It was a remarkable achievement for anyone with an eye for such things. But George Eastman, of Eastman-Kodak fame, must have wondered what all the fuss was about, having already invented a portable "box camera" and a practical roll of film to put in it by 1888.[111] With no more tripod or unwieldy plate, why not simply take a picture?)

In the medical sciences, Pasteur's "germ theory" proved as revolutionary in its influence as Darwinism did in society at large. Having received a microscope as a gift from his wife, the German physician (and Pasteur disciple), Robert Koch (1843–1910), became a veritable bacterial "botanist"—developing methods of growing bacteria on culture media as well as chemical stains to enhance their microscopic appearance.[112] His labors have been credited with establishing the fields of bacteriology and immunology,[113] "but [his] epoch-making advance," says Sir William Osler, who has christened him a "medical Galileo" (an allusion, no doubt, to a vision of Koch peering into his microscope as Galileo did into his telescope), was to demonstrate that he could produce a given disease in an animal by inoculating it with the corresponding bacterium grown on a culture plate in his laboratory.[114] In so doing, he established beyond doubt the tie between the specific bacterium and the disease (not to mention the validity of Pasteur's germ theory).

In 1882, Koch isolated the causative organism of tuberculosis—reproducing the disease in a guinea pig by inoculation. His continuing work on the disease gained him the 1905 Nobel Prize in medicine and physiology. In the meantime, he isolated the comma-shaped bacterium responsible for cholera and determined that it was transmitted in public water supplies (1883)[115]—a discovery that helped intensify the drive toward

Pyramid of Skulls by Paul Cézanne, The Yorck Project (Wikimedia Commons).

public sanitation, since it was now understood that the battle against disease was being fought against "a living contagion which found in poverty, filth and wretched homes the conditions for its existence."[116] In Britain—and afterwards throughout Europe and America—measures were undertaken to provide clean water, sewage systems and garbage disposal. Indeed, much of Europe's population growth after 1870 was attributable not to an increase in births, but to improved public health and a decline in deaths.[117] On this basis, Osler has placed sanitation "among the great modern revolutions...."[118]

Rudolf Virchow (1821–1902), a colleague of Koch's at the famed Charité Hospital in Berlin, was one of the 19th century's most extraordinary figures. No less adept than Koch with the microscope, he characterized the human body as a "cell-state, in which every cell is a citizen."[119] Hailed as the "father of modern pathology,"[120] he gave the first description of leukemia, determined that tumors are composed of cells (and that their growth is the result of constant cell division),[121] elucidated a famous triad of microscopic changes that occur with thrombosis (pathological blood clotting) that still bears his name, founded his own medical journal (after another journal rejected some of his articles) and authored several medical textbooks—the most famous being *Cellular Pathologie*.

A harsh drillmaster, Virchow heckled unprepared students in the classroom and lecturers at the podium with whom he disagreed.[122] But his interests and accomplishments extended well beyond medicine. During the Revolution of 1848, he helped build barricades in Berlin—an escapade that resulted in temporary dismissal from his post at Charité. In 1862, he obtained a seat in the Prussian *Reichstag*, which he held until 1893, tirelessly opposing Bismarck on the budget and almost everything else. (He has been credited with coining the term *Kulturkampf* for Bismarck's war on Catholicism.[123]) During the Franco-Prussian War, he distinguished himself by establishing an army ambulance corps and field hospital. An avid anthropologist, he was, for a time, president of the Berlin Anthropological Society. In 1879, he accompanied the famed archaeologist, Heinrich Schliemann, to what they thought (erroneously) to be Troy.[124] He also served on the Berlin Municipal Council where he enacted sanitary reforms that, in the estimation of *Encyclopedia Britannica*, transformed it into "one of the healthiest cities in the world from being one of the unhealthiest."[125] That he rejected the validity of Pasteur's germ theory, Koch's work on toxins and Darwin's theory of evolution remains an ironic footnote to a fascinating career.[126] He died of complications from a hip fracture on attempting to exit a moving tram at the age of 81.[127]

The advances made by Koch and Virchow in bacteriology and sanitation facilitated a tremendous engineering feat at the outset of the 20th century. In the 1880s, Ferdinand de Lesseps' French Canal Company had failed miserably in its attempt to construct a canal across Panama. Financial corruption aside, the failure of the endeavor had been preordained by disease. In 1885, *177 canal workers out of every 1,000* succumbed to contagion. Dysentery and typhus played their role in this travesty, but the chief culprits were malaria and, more especially, yellow fever.[128]

Malaria, common in swampy areas, had long been attributed to (and had derived its name from) "bad air"—in Italian, "*mal aria.*" In 1880, Alphonse Laveran, a French army surgeon serving in Algeria, identified a parasitic organism in the red blood cells of a patient afflicted with the disease. It was a good start, but the discovery that the parasite was borne by mosquito would not come until 1897, when Ronald Ross, a British army surgeon stationed in India, isolated the same parasite, first from the stomach, and afterwards from the saliva, of a species of mosquito called *Anopheles*. Quinine had been available as a treatment for malaria since the early 17th century, but the new discovery allowed for a sanitation-based approach to its eradication: namely, the drainage of the swamps and stagnant pools of water that compose the *Anopheles* mosquito's habitat.[129]

Death from malaria subsequently plummeted in India, Africa and Italy where it was most prevalent. Alas, neither the eradication measures nor quinine had an impact on yellow fever, which continued to make the Panama region the "white man's grave." (Despite the moniker, there was no actual race predilection on the part of the contagion. The disease was simply so ubiquitous in afflicted regions that it was universally contracted in childhood—an age group in which it manifests as a mild disease, conferring immunity thereafter. People native to the region—often nonwhite—thus seemed to be unaffected, whereas workers from abroad—mostly white Europeans—suffered devastating morbidity and mortality.)[130]

The solution came of necessity after the USS *Maine* went up in a puff of smoke in Havana harbor in February 1898. The cause of the explosion is still not known with certainty, but it served as a very good pretext for the United States to declare hostilities against Spain. The United States emerged victorious from the ensuing "Spanish-American War"—seizing Cuba and the Philippines in the process.

The war's outbreak had been greatly facilitated by the propaganda of warmongering "yellow journalists"—most prominently, William Randolph Hearst and Joseph Pulitzer.

Although "yellow journalism" bears no relation to "yellow fever" in its etymology, the occupation of Havana by American soldiers had every relation to that disease. If the Americans were to stay, they simply had to get to the bottom of things, for the average case mortality ranged as high as 80 percent.[131]

In 1900, a commission headed by Dr. Walter Reed, a professor of bacteriology at the Army Medical School, arrived to study the problem. Following up on a report from 1881 by a certain Dr. Carlos Finlay implicating the mosquito, his team identified the culprit "vector" (or carrier) in the mosquito species *Aëdes ægypti*. Identifying the actual causative organism proved rather more difficult, but Reed and his team did determine that it was infinitesimally small, for it could pass through a Chamberland porcelain filter—impervious to most known bacteria. The riddle would not be solved for a quarter century, when the organism was found to be a virus (a class of contagion that cannot reproduce without residing in a living host—a characteristic that has led some to regard viruses as only "half alive"). In the meantime, however, Reed's discoveries solved the different riddle of why malaria eradication efforts had had no effect, for unlike the swamp-dwelling *Anopheles* mosquito, the *Aëdes ægypti* resides preferentially in cities.

Tragically, in the midst of the investigation, Reed's colleague, Dr. Jesse Lazear, sustained a fatal bite. He died within the fortnight, heroically assisting the team to the last.[132] But now that the truth was known, firm action was undertaken. The Army's chief of sanitation in Havana, Dr. William Gorgas, embarked on a program of house-to-house inspections—oiling the surface of all stagnant water puddles (as a repellant), installing mosquito-proof screens on the quarters of afflicted persons (to prevent mosquitos from biting them and spreading the contagion), fumigating areas of infestation and fining residents who had not taken proper precautions if mosquito larvae were found on their property. The measures were initiated in February 1901, and by the next year not a single case arose in the city.[133]

With the battle won in Havana, Gorgas was dispatched to Panama. In 1904, the United States decided that it would try its hand at the Panama Canal project, which had previously been brought to ruin by the scourge of yellow fever. The death rate in the year after Gorgas' arrival (1905) was as high as 71 per 1,000 American workers per month, and there was some concern that the enterprise might fail. But Gorgas organized another effective campaign, and by the end of 1905, says William Osler, "the total mortality among the whites had fallen to 8 per thousand, but among the blacks it was still high, 44."[134] Osler did not explain the discrepant death rates. It was known from the experience in Havana, however, that infected mosquitos "fed" only at night.[135] Consequently, daylight labor was safe, but nighttime precautions were essential—and herein lies the wretched answer to the puzzle; for, in contrast to the sleeping quarters provided to white laborers, those provided to blacks were either not outfitted with proper protections against mosquitos or were located in areas where eradication measures had not yet been undertaken. The following year, however, the disease was eradicated by Gorgas' sanitation measures. There were no more cases for the duration—the canal being completed in 1914.[136]

Other medical advances were also in train. By 1900, London's Harley Street had become the preferred office district for myriad physician "specialists" to whom general practitioners could turn for consultation—establishing a consultative tradition that continues to this day.[137] At about the same time, the Johns Hopkins Hospital (1889) and Medical School (1893) opened their doors in Baltimore, Maryland (funded by a bequest from the Quaker entrepreneur, Johns Hopkins). Led by a pair of outstanding clinicians, the

Canadian-born William Osler (later knighted) and the American, William Halsted, the institution all but revolutionized medical teaching and training. Osler was universally revered for his abilities as an educator. His *Principles and Practice of Medicine* would remain the standard medical textbook for decades. Halsted, the era's preeminent surgeon (despite a secret morphine addiction), developed landmark surgical techniques—most famously the "radical mastectomy" for the treatment of breast cancer—and introduced a novel "residency" training program that became the model for the entire country. He is chiefly remembered, however, for the introduction of the rubber surgical glove, which he commissioned from inventors at the Goodyear Rubber Company after his chief nurse developed a skin reaction to antiseptics used in the operating room. Sterile operative conditions were thereby greatly enhanced. (And the story has a romantic ending—for the nurse, Caroline Hampton, afterwards became Halsted's wife.)[138]

In 1902, the Dutch physiologist, Willem Einthoven, invented a method of recording the electrical activity of the heart—providing physicians with the so-called electrocardiogram or EKG. Physics, too, made its contribution. During the late 19th century William Crookes of England developed a vacuum tube (subsequently named the "Crookes tube" in his honor), which produced a fluorescent stream of light (called a "cathode ray") when an electrical discharge passed between two electrodes. In 1897, the British physicist, Joseph John Thomson, discovered that these rays were actually composed of particles *smaller* than the atom—hitherto thought to be the smallest particle in existence. (The particles are now known as electrons.)

Not surprisingly, Crookes' tubes became the rage with physicists everywhere. Wishing to block out the light from a Crookes tube he was tinkering with in his darkened laboratory, one of these experimenters, Wilhelm Konrad Roentgen of Wurzburg, Germany, encompassed it with black cardboard. Despite seeing no light when he applied voltage to the electrodes, he afterwards noted a glow emanating from a piece of chemically treated paper located elsewhere on his workbench. He surmised that some sort of invisible ray had traversed the black cardboard surrounding the Crookes tube and reached the paper to produce this effect. He repeated the experiment placing various items between the Crookes tube and a similarly treated piece of paper, applying an electric discharge each time, and he found that items of greater density cast a correspondingly darker shadow when the paper fluoresced. One of these items was a hand-held piece of lead—the shadow produced being cast not only by the metal, but also by the bones of the hand that held it. Being rather less romantic than William Halsted, Roentgen summoned his wife to his laboratory and bade her place her hand against a photographic plate while he exposed it to his invisible ray for a quarter of an hour.[139] The developed plate subsequently revealed a perfect "X-ray" image of her hand (the term X-radiation being chosen to denote its enigmatic nature).[140] Happily, Mrs. Roentgen survived the experiment (no thanks to any precaution taken by her husband), while Roentgen's new X-Ray became the marvel of the medical world where it found unceasing application.

Social Undercurrents: The Women's Movement, Socialism, Syndicalism and Anarchism

On June 4, 1913, King George V of England escorted Queen Mary to the races at Epsom Downs, Surrey, where their horse, Anmer, was set to compete with fourteen others in the day's third race. With thousands of enthusiasts lining the inner and outer portions of the track, the race got underway with Anmer's jockey, thirty-two-year-old Herbert "Bertie" Jones, clearly visible in the king's colors. By the midpoint of the race, it was evident that it was not to be their day. Rounding Tattenham Corner into the final straightaway of the horseshoe-shaped track, Jones and Anmer were in third from last place. And then suddenly, amid the thundering hoof beats, there was a collision that threw horse and rider head over heels. Laying in their wake was the unconscious, twisted body of a woman. A disbelieving throng rushed onto the track, seeking to lend assistance. Bertie and Anmer would survive. The woman, aged forty, remained in a coma, dying four days later. Her name was Emily Davison. She was a suffragette.[141]

The period between 1871 and 1914 has sometimes been characterized as "the era of the benevolent bourgeoisie."[142] In these years, the capitalist middle class exercised an inescapable influence on society, from the arts and sciences to economics and politics. And, in many respects, society became more altruistic in consequence. Class privilege, still entrenched at the outset of the industrial revolution, was now (at least in theory) a relic of the past—the bourgeoisie having striven for and obtained constitutional liberties and equality before the law, irrespective of class, in nearly every European country. From the 1860s onwards, the general tendency in European politics had been towards increased democracy—often culminating in universal male suffrage. "State socialism" had become a definite part of the political landscape with the passage of regulations to improve working conditions, compensate for work-related injury, provide public education, improve public housing and sanitation, and (in Germany and England) provide old age pensions. England's Fabian Society, whose adherents included such middle-class luminaries as George Bernard Shaw and H.G. Wells, engaged in constant skirmishing for liberal reforms with the intention (as reflected in their *nom de guerre*) of wearing down the opposition little by little, just as Fabius "Cunctator" had done to Hannibal in the Second Punic War.

Those who weren't bourgeois in body, notes Carlton Hayes, were often so in spirit.[143] Some members of the old aristocracy, finding the income from their estates no longer sufficient to their needs, entered enthusiastically upon business pursuits (which their class had formerly disdained) and joined the chorus advocating for legislation in support of industry and commerce. The peasantry and urban proletariat, in spite of their hardships, were not averse to investing their meager savings (if they were lucky enough to possess any) in the stock market—and even those who were not so lucky seemed to understand at some level "that the livelihood of all was in fact contingent upon the prosperity of the bourgeoisie."[144] Nationalism, too, tended to erase class distinctions, for the patriot at the pub could glory in the nation's achievements as readily as the imperialist at the breakfast table. Even the Catholic Church—so often a target of bourgeois secularist attack—chimed in with *Rerum Novarum*, a papal encyclical published in 1891 by the "working man's Pope," Leo XIII, calling for harmony between capital and labor.[145]

It was all quite rosy … except when it wasn't. At the dawn of the 20th century, a third of Belgian working class families lived in single room abodes. A Vienna bricklaying company of the same period housed its workers in dormitories with multiple families *in the same room*.[146] It does not require a sweeping imagination to comprehend that subsistence under such Malthusian conditions falls short of utopia. Similarly, universal male suffrage loses some of its luster if one's vote is not weighted the same as another or if there is no provision for proportional representation.

And it loses more luster still if one is not male. Although feminism got off to a comparatively early start in England—perhaps dating to the publication, in 1697, of *Serious Proposals to Ladies* by Mary Astell, in which the author made the case for equal educational opportunities for women—the cause had not made much headway. Nearly a century later, in 1792, Mary Wollstonecraft expanded upon the idea in *A Vindication of the Rights of Women*, in which she lobbied not only for equal opportunity in education but also for economic self-sufficiency and female suffrage. For her efforts, she was scorned as a "hyena in petticoats."[147] She lived but five years after the publication of her manifesto, dying tragically of childbed fever at the age of thirty-eight, ten days after the birth of her daughter, Mary (who would marry Percy Bysshe Shelley and gain lasting fame herself as the author of the horror classic, *Frankenstein*).

During the industrial revolution, as women entered the labor force on a large scale (at substantially lower wages, be it noted, than their male counterparts), the question of female emancipation arose anew. John Stuart Mill championed the cause, proposing in 1867 that the electoral Reform Bill of that year should apply to women as well as men. Although, the suggestion provoked a great deal of laughter on the parliamentary benches, fully seventy-three forward-thinking MPs voted in favor. At roughly the same time, a number of "suffragist" societies came into being. Mill's wife, Harriet Taylor, and stepdaughter, Helen Taylor, were active in the movement. Another participant was Florence Nightingale (1820–1910), who had had to travel to Germany to obtain training as a nurse (sitting in with a group of reformed female prisoners for the purpose) in her own fight for female emancipation in the 1840s, and who gained fame during the Crimean War as the "Lady of the Lamp" for her nighttime lantern rounds in the hospital at Scutari (an overcrowded, unventilated death house when she arrived, which she and her crew of thirty-seven nurses, ministering to thousands, intrepidly transformed— decreasing the death rate from 40 percent to two percent).[148] By 1870, petitions encompassing 200,000 signatures in favor of female suffrage were being presented annually to parliament. John Bright, George Trevelyan and Joseph Chamberlain all came out in favor. Gladstone stood opposed to the last,[149] but the "Grand Old Man" retired for good in 1894, and after a decade of uninterrupted Conservative rule, expectations were raised by the return to power of the Liberal Party under new leadership in 1906.

Alas, the Liberals failed to act, and in consequence the suffragist movement resorted to a policy of "deeds, not words." Led by Emmeline Pankhurst (1858–1928), founder of the Women's Social and Political Union, the militant suffragists—or "suffragettes"—disrupted sessions of Parliament from the gallery, accosted government ministers, burst in upon church services, smashed store windows (sometimes using metal balls on which the word "bomb" had been inscribed[150]), cut telegraph lines, set fire to mailboxes and defaced museum exhibits. Police answered this campaign of "direct action" with excessive brutality. Thrown in prison, suffragettes went on hunger strikes, which their jailers used as a pretext for further chastisement—holding them down and forcing tubes down their throats through which they administered involuntary feedings.[151] Among the women brutalized in this fashion was Emily Davison.

Ms. Davison studied English Literature at Oxford where she attained first class honors but no degree, since women were not eligible to earn them. Obtaining a living as a teacher, she joined the Women's Social and Political Union in 1906. Three years later she committed herself full-time to the movement, establishing herself as a fervent militant. She was jailed for her actions on several occasions—most notably after attacking a

Baptist minister whom she mistook for David Lloyd George. What she had intended to do at the Epsom Derby continues to be a puzzle. After the eight lead horses had galloped past her position on the inner rail, she ducked onto the track and allegedly grabbed at the bridle of the first two horses she encountered. Both eluded her. The king's horse hit her straight on, but Bertie Jones later stated that she seemed again to be reaching for something. It has been surmised on this basis that she had not intended to make herself a martyr through suicide, but merely wished to attach a suffragette banner to the king's horse to draw attention to the cause. But it was as martyrdom that her act was received, with 6,000 of her suffragette sisters marching in her funeral procession, and 30,000 more waiting at the burial site.[152] Her tombstone bore the suffragette motto, "Deeds, not words."[153]

There was, however, much outrage over her action as well. Consequently, women's suffrage remained elusive for several more years until Emmeline Pankhurst heeded a suggestion from David Lloyd George and led her suffragettes into the munitions factories during the First World War to make shells for the war effort. A parliamentary bill of 1918 rewarded this action by enfranchising women over 30 who owned property. Suffrage on equal terms with men (i.e., at age 21 or older) came a decade later.[154]

The Women's Movement was not alone in resorting to "deeds." It has been said that in fashioning his economic interpretation of history Karl Marx "did for social science what Darwin did for natural science."[155] But in the period 1871 to 1914, Marx had competitors. His principle maxim had been that a single fact was "common to all past ages; namely the exploitation of one part of society by another."[156] In 1864, Marx organized his minions into the International Working Men's Association, which preached his canon that "The history of all hitherto existing society is the history of class struggles"[157]; that the current "capitalist" society has evolved from those class struggles that preceded it; and that—since all capital derives from labor, and labor receives in return scarcely any of the capital thus derived—a struggle must ensue between capital and labor that will usher in a new social order in which the means of production are owned collectively and goods are distributed equitably.[158]

As one prominent historian notes, "this does not mean, as is popularly supposed, confiscating private property and dividing it equally among all

Miss Emily Davison, circa 1905. LSE Library (Wikimedia Commons).

THE DAILY MIRROR, Thursday, June 5, 1913

OUR 3,000th NUMBER—MANY SPECIAL FEATURES.

The Daily Mirror

THE MORNING JOURNAL WITH THE SECOND LARGEST NET SALE.

24 Pages

No. 3,000.   Registered at the G.P.O. as a Newspaper.   THURSDAY, JUNE 5, 1913   One Halfpenny.

WOMAN RUSHES ON THE DERBY COURSE AND SNATCHES AT THE BRIDLE OF THE KING'S HORSE, INJURING HERSELF AND THE JOCKEY.

The Derby of 1913 proved the most dramatic in the history of the famous race, and was marked by an exciting incident which is entirely without precedent. As the runners were rounding Tattenham Corner a woman rushed from beneath the railings and made a snatch at the bridle of Anmer, the King's horse, which struck her with its chest and turned a complete somersault. The woman was seriously injured, while Jones, his Majesty's jockey, was thrown from his mount and badly hurt. The photograph shows Anmer after its fall, with Jones and the woman on the ground. Her hat was flung several yards away. The woman's clothing was marked "E. W. Davison," and suffragette flags were found pinned under her jacket.—(*Daily Mirror* photograph.)

Front Page of *The Daily Mirror* showing the Emily Davison tragedy (Wikimedia Commons).

the people…. People will continue to possess private personal property, such as clothes, houses, books, and furniture, but not industrial property, such as factories, mines or railways, which will be State monopolies."[159] Although the "First International" vanished into oblivion in the mid–1870s owing to a combination of inadequate funding, internal dissension and government repression in the aftermath of the (Marxist-venerated) Paris Commune,[160] the ensuing decades witnessed a steady increase in the popularity of Marxist Socialism at the polls. As we have seen, Bismarck's efforts first to suppress and then to steal the fire of the socialists in Germany did nothing to halt the emergence and growth of the Social Democratic Party (whose share of the vote rose from 125,000 in 1871 to 1,427,000 in 1890—the year of his retirement).[161] In England, the Fabian Society, founded in 1884, became the harbinger of the socialistic Labor Party, which came into being in 1900. France, Italy, Austria, Belgium and Sweden likewise experienced an increase in the socialist vote.[162]

By 1889, a "Second Socialist International" was founded—Marxist in its ultimate goal of collective ownership of the means of production, but willing to proceed along parliamentary lines to obtain piecemeal reforms until the moment should be ripe for revolution. The new strategy was codified by Germany's Social Democrats in the "Erfurt Program" of 1891, and subsequently adopted by socialist parties throughout Europe. To be sure, the program necessitated glaring compromises, but this was scarcely a matter for concern. For, as Marx had argued in the *Communist Manifesto*, the ultimate outcome was inevitable: In addition to exploiting the proletariat, capitalist competition pitted one capitalist against another. In time, so many would be ruined and cast penniless into the ranks of the proletariat that the latter class must bear the system away as if by tidal wave. In Marx's catchy phrasing, "Capitalism produces above all its own grave diggers."[163]

Despite this comforting sentiment, not everyone was content to sit on their hands until the balloon went up. One could literally die waiting (as Marx himself had proved in 1883). Moreover, those counting heads could not help but note that the number of capitalists seemed to be increasing, not shrinking. The realization drove some socialists (most notably Jean Jaurès of France, who we last encountered as a defendant of Alfred Dreyfus) to the heresy of "Revisionism"—the idea, first promulgated by the German socialist, Eduard Bernstein, that the socialist revolution might never come, and that consequently socialists should actually cooperate with bourgeois parties in pursuit of needed reforms.[164] The very idea put socialists at one another's throats.[165] Amid their quibbling, however, there was also another response—one that manifested in outcries for "direct action." And the loudest chorus of these outcries emanated from the adherents of a rival and irreconcilable philosophy: "Anarchism."

Prior to the publication of the *Communist Manifesto* in 1848, the Frenchman Pierre-Joseph Proudhon (1809–1865) issued a manifesto of his own entitled *What is Property?* (1840). To this question, he answered, "Property is theft!" It is theft because "it appropriates the value produced by the labor of others without rendering an equivalent."[166] Proudhon's solution was not collective ownership by the state, but the eradication of the state entirely. In its place would be nothing but voluntary contracts between individuals. There was to be no governance from above: "No more parties, no more authority, absolute liberty of man and citizen." It must be so, he argued, because "all parties, without exception, in so much as they seek for power, are varieties of absolutism, and … there [will] be no liberty for citizens" until "the renunciation of authority should have replaced faith in authority."[167]

Proudhon believed in the goodness of humankind and imagined that the transformation to non-authoritarian society might come about peaceably. But after the revolutionary failures of 1848, such utopian romanticism was on the way out. Seated among the delegates of Marx's First International was the anarchist Russian exile, Mikhail Bakunin (1814–1876), who was perhaps more than anyone else responsible for the organization's demise. Where Marx and his followers sought state ownership of the means of production, Bakunin and his fellow anarchists argued, "The only revolution that can do any good to the people is that which utterly annihilates every idea of the State and overthrows all traditions, orders and classes…. Our task is destruction, terrible, total, inexorable and universal." What was to come afterwards, the anarchists helpfully suggested, was "the business of future generations."[168] But first things first—and to achieve the desired destruction of everything, the anarchists called for "direct action," or as they preferred to put it, "propaganda of the deed."

Bakunin was expelled from the First International in 1872, and when his disciples followed him into the wilderness, the schism left that organization mortally wounded. Henceforth, socialism and anarchism went their separate ways—the one *seeking collective ownership through government action*, the other *seeking the abolition of government through direct action*.[169]

Despite the focus on tearing things asunder, anarchist thinkers did have a conception of what might be accomplished in a positive sense by their program. For example, Bakunin's successor and fellow Russian exile, Prince Peter Kropotkin (1842–1921), formerly a prominent member of the Russian Geographical Society (of which he declined an offer to serve in the prestigious capacity of Secretary[170]), imagined the establishment of what he termed "Anarchist-Communism" whereby, for example, a large city might guarantee to all its inhabitants "dwelling, food and clothing to an extent corresponding to the comfort now available to the middle classes only, in exchange for a half-day's, or five hours' work…" while "all those things which would be considered as luxuries might be obtained by every one if he joins for the other half of the day all sorts of free associations pursuing all possible aims—educational, literary, scientific, artistic, sports and so on."[171]

An Anarchist congress held in Pittsburgh, Pennsylvania, in 1883, developed a six-point program as to how something of this nature might come to pass: "*First*, Destruction of the existing class rule by all means, i.e., energetic, relentless, revolutionary and international. *Second*, Establishment of a free society, based upon a co-operative organization of production. *Third*, Free exchange of equivalent products by and between the productive organizations, without commerce and profit-mongery. *Fourth*, Organization of education on a secular, scientific and equal basis for both sexes. *Fifth*, Equal rights for all without distinction of sex or race. *Sixth*, Regulation of all public affairs by free contracts between the autonomous (independent) communes and associations, resting on a federalistic basis."[172]

The last five of these strike one as rather noble—even ahead of their time in their notions on race and sex. But point one—indeed, its first word, "Destruction"—had a way of putting people off before they gave the other five so much as a passing glance. Nor is this the worst of it, for despite the endless labor that the anarchist *thinkers* of Pittsburgh must have expended on their highbrow blueprint, anarchist *doers* never seem to get past that first word either. Had they set off to establish their own community on the basis of points two through six, and then showed the rest of us how well it worked, they might have deserved plaudits. Instead, they threw a bomb at Alexander II (whom the reader may remember as the tsar who freed the serfs).

In the minds of anarchist *doers*, the hypothesis that humankind would be better off with no governing apparatus at all could best be tested by bringing down the entire existing edifice at once by some inspiring act.[173] Their favored methodology was terrorism, and a martyr for the movement was duly identified in the French anarchist,

Ravachol. Guillotined for murdering defenseless bourgeois spinsters and setting off a pair of bombs in Paris in 1892, Ravachol attained his status by bellowing "*Vive l'anarchie!*" from the scaffold in his last moments. Even before his trial was concluded, the restaurant where he was arrested on a tip from a waiter had been bombed in revenge, and other such acts were to follow.[174]

Distraught that he could not afford to feed his family, another anarchist, Auguste Vaillant,lobbed a homemade bomb from the gallery of the Chamber of Deputies into the midst of the parliamentarians below (1893). (There were no deaths, as Vaillant meant to protest, not to kill, and had constructed a device of low concussive force.) He, too, was guillotined (despite being defended by Dreyfus' attorney, Labori), and he, too, was avenged—first with the bombing of a French café by Emile Henry (who, confronted at trial with the fact that he had murdered innocents, declared, "There are no innocent bourgeois") and then with the assassination in Lyons of the French president, Sadi Carnot, who was assailed in his open carriage by a knife-wielding Italian anarchist.[175]

Such acts, complained Peter Kropotkin in his 1911 *Encyclopædia Britannica* apologia for anarchism, "created in the general public the impression that violence is the substance of Anarchism...." In consequence, "violent prosecutions were directed against them," to which "the Anarchists retaliated by acts of violence which in their turn were followed by more executions from above, and new acts of revenge from below."[176] This, of course, turns logic on its head. "Violent prosecutions," were not carried out in response to "impressions" of violence, but to bona fide "acts" of violence. At one point, a Parisian police officer made the mistake of bringing a bomb discovered at a miner's strike back to his station for further study. Upon his arrival, it detonated, killing him and five of his fellow officers. Convinced that the police had become a target, many Parisians refused to go near them for weeks for fear that they would become collateral damage when the next bomb went off.[177] In 1898, an Italian anarchist stabbed Franz Josef's tormented wife, Empress Elisabeth, in the chest with a sharpened file while she was visiting Geneva. Not realizing the extent of her injury, the doomed woman insisted on continuing her afternoon walk before loss of blood caused her to faint. She died shortly afterwards.[178] In 1900, another Italian anarchist, this one from Paterson, New Jersey, assassinated Italy's King Humbert (a kindly monarch known popularly as "Humbert the Good") who is said to have had just enough time to give his murderer a very disapproving look before expiring.[179] Nor was the United States immune. In September 1901, a Polish-American anarchist shot President William McKinley in Buffalo, New York. McKinley died eight days later.

A major barrier to the prevention of such acts was the tendency for lone individuals to engage in them. There was, however, a kindred movement that was quite collective in its approach: namely, "syndicalism" (the term being derived from the French word "*syndicat*," meaning "trade union"). While syndicalism was not beneath resorting to violence, mostly in the form of "sabotage" (a term derived from "sabot," a worker's shoe sometimes used to jam machines at the dawn of French industrialism), its chief tactic was the "general strike."[180]

The movement envisioned the organization of workers into industry-wide labor unions so that when the union went on strike an entire industry would be paralyzed. The goal was to compel radical societal change by obliterating the industry's profitability and denying society necessary services (such as transport, communications or food supply).[181] Here was a startling divergence from socialism's Erfurt program, which sought to promote change indirectly through government action. Syndicalism would have no truck with government, which it utterly disdained as corrupt and exploitative, promoting instead direct action by workers against their employers in order to topple the capitalist system. In 1911, a general strike was actually tried by the workers of the French railroad industry, albeit with the more modest goal of obtaining a wage increase. The French Premier, Aristide Briand, quashed it by drafting the involved workers into the army and ordering them to report to work or face military discipline.[182] (The tactic, which had been used successfully against railroad strikers in Italy in 1902, must have been particularly grating since syndicalism had long regarded the army as "a tool of the capitalists," and regularly preached against military service.[183])

The following year, anarchism gave assassination another fling with the shooting death of the Spanish premier José Canalejas in Madrid. But, still, the existing order did not collapse. And then, quite unexpectedly, in the faraway Balkans, a pistol-wielding, fanatical nationalist achieved what all the efforts of anarchist assassins and syndicalist strikers had not. By the time the smoke finally cleared, the 19th century had experienced its death throes (having survived in a figurative sense until 1914) and four European empires had been reduced to dust.

Survival of the Fittest: The Nations Collide

The First World War and the Treaty of Versailles, 1914–1919

On June 28, 1914, Archduke Franz Ferdinand, heir to the Hapsburg throne, made a tour of Sarajevo in recently annexed Bosnia, despite being advised that Bosnian hostility to Hapsburg rule made such an undertaking perilous. Proceeding in an open car with Archduchess Sophie at his side, the Archduke quickly became the target of an assassin's bomb. The explosion missed its mark, leaving a member of his entourage and several onlookers wounded in the street. After a brief stop for discussion at city hall, where the archduke asked pointedly whether there would be more attacks, the unfortunate decision was made to continue with the tour.[1] Alas, on setting out, the Archduke's driver turned down the wrong street. Even worse, on being apprised of his mistake, he halted the vehicle directly in front of one of the conspirators— the nineteen-year-old Bosnian student, Gavrilo Princip. Princip stepped forward and fired his pistol. Seeing blood issue from her husband's mouth, Archduchess Sophie asked in alarm what had happened. She then collapsed, for she, too, had been shot. With his last gasps, the archduke entreated her not to die.[2] Neither survived long enough to obtain medical attention. It was their 14th wedding anniversary—and, more ominously, the 525th anniversary of Medieval Serbia's catastrophic defeat at Kossovo.[3]

News of the assassination was transmitted by phone to Franz Josef

Archduke Franz Ferdinand, his wife, Sophie, and their three children (left to right), Prince Maximilian (age 6), Prince Ernst (age 4) and Princess Sophie (age 7), photograph in the *New York Tribune*, 8 November 1908 (Wikimedia Commons).

on the morning of June 29, 1914,[4] and was announced to the world in Austria's *Wiener Montags Journal* later in the day.[5] Although the emperor had not seen eye to eye with his heir (who had been challenging his policies for years), he was shaken by the tragedy. In contrast, his foreign minister, Count Leopold Berchtold, and Army chief-of-staff, Franz Conrad von Hötzendorf, saw in the assassination a heaven-sent opportunity. The empire's ruling clique had been searching for a magic bullet to solve the problem of nationalist separatism since the *Ausgleich* with Hungary in 1867—and it believed it had finally found one in the fatal shot fired at Franz Ferdinand, for it could be used as a pretext to strike a decisive military blow against the Slavic bogeyman, Serbia.

The evidence for Serbian complicity in the archduke's murder was abundant if circumstantial. Serbia had been a veritable font of anti–Hapsburg agitation since the annexation of Bosnia and Herzegovina in 1908. Within hours of the killings, it was learned that Gavrilo Princip was of Serbian descent. The Serbian press, moreover, had boasted in most impolitic fashion that the conspirators had hatched their plot in the Serbian capital of Belgrade.[6] Had the Hapsburg monarchy taken immediate military action against Serbia, it would likely have encountered substantial international sympathy, for the assassination had provoked revulsion throughout the world.[7] In this milieu, the conflict might even have remained localized.

Before acting, however, Austria wished to be certain of German support. On July 5, in a private audience with Kaiser Wilhelm II, the Austrian ambassador, Count Ladislas Szögyény, asked whether Germany would stand by Austria in an attack on Serbia even if Russia were to declare war in response. The kaiser answered that Austria "could count on Germany's full support." He added that she should act without delay since Russia would be taken unprepared by rapid action and, consequently, "would think twice before it took up arms."[8]

In effect, Wilhelm had handed Austria a "blank check," but he had done so on the assumption that Serbia would act expeditiously while international sentiment was on her side and before Russia could get her bearings. Sadly, for herself and for the world, Austria did not comprehend the immediacy.[9] Instead of acting, she dispatched a foreign ministry official to Sarajevo to find proof of Serbia's complicity. His investigation, completed on July 13, found nothing definitive, concluding, "On the contrary there are grounds for believing it quite out of the question."[10]

History may give this finding an honored place among its many ironies, for without the Austrians knowing it, the Serbians actually *were* to blame—the plot having been perpetrated by none other than the Serbian Army's chief-of-intelligence, Dragutin Dimitrijević, a fanatical proponent of the Greater Serbia idea,[11] and director (during his spare time) of a Serbian terrorist organization known as the Black Hand, which hoped to destabilize the Austro-Hungarian empire through acts of terrorism. (Serbia, so the thinking went, might then step in to unite the Slavs as Piedmont had united the Italians and Prussia had united the Germans.[12]) It was no coincidence that the Black Hand chose Franz Ferdinand as its target, for it was well known that upon his accession, the archduke intended to steal the fire of the Serbs by granting his Slavic subjects some form of autonomy within the empire—an insufferable notion to Serb ultra-nationalists who were counting on the empire's Slavs to rebel and join in the creation of a Greater Serbia.[13] Even the Serbian prime minister had advance knowledge of the plot. But fearing international embarrassment or violent reprisal from the Black Hand conspirators, he failed to warn the Austrians—his only action being to propose through an intermediary that the archduke cancel his trip.[14]

Notwithstanding these facts, the Austrian investigation had come up empty. It had now been more than two weeks since the assassinations, and the world's moral outrage had begun to subside. (The kaiser, indeed, had left Berlin for a vacation cruise to Norway.) Only now did it occur to Austria that Serbia's guilt or innocence was of little account. From the outset, it had not been Austria's purpose to obtain a diplomatic victory. She had had such victories in annexing Bosnia and Herzegovina in 1908 and in denying Serbia an outlet on the sea after the First Balkan War (1912). But these victories had done nothing to curb Slav separatist agitation.[15] Consequently, Austria's purpose was to go to war. A quick humiliating victory over her southern neighbor was what was required—one that might destroy the notion of a "Greater Serbia" forever and render the empire's Slavs amenable to achieving their nationalist aspirations inside rather than outside the Hapsburg realm.

In pursuit of this panacea, Count Berchtold, the Austrian Foreign Minister, issued a condemnatory ultimatum to the Serbians, which could not have been accepted without making a mockery of Serbia's independence.[16] It was delivered on July 23—twenty-five days after the events in Sarajevo—by which time the world at large assumed that the crisis had passed. A response to the ultimatum was demanded within forty-eight hours. Unenthused with the prospect of fighting her powerful neighbor, Serbia did her best to accept most of the points in the Austrian ultimatum, but requested, in the interests of her own autonomy, that the most compromising demands be submitted to international mediation (July 25).

Returning from his cruise on July 28, Wilhelm would pronounce Serbia's response, "A brilliant performance for a time limit of only 48 hours! A great moral success for Vienna, but with it, all reason for war is gone…."[17] Without firing a shot, Austria had battered Serbia's prestige, but Serbia's answer had left her very little cause to declare war. Pity that Austria seems not to have noticed either result. She answered Serbia's effort to appease her by mobilizing her army.

In the present crisis, the Russian foreign minister had been given no forewarning of the Austrian ultimatum—an insulting slight. But even in the absence of insults, Austria cannot have imagined that Russia would simply stand by while her sworn enemy attacked her chief Balkan ally. (Indeed, had Russia not been crippled by her defeat in the Russo-Japanese War, she would likely have gone to war over Austria's annexation of Bosnia and Herzegovina in 1908.)[18] The situation was now grave in the extreme. The following day (July 26), Britain's foreign secretary, Sir Edward Grey, proposed a conference among the uninvolved powers—Britain, Germany, France and Italy—to mediate the issue. Germany declined almost as a reflex.

Understandable hesitations now set in. Hardly had Germany rebuffed Britain's suggestion before she sent a secret note to Vienna asking whether the Austrian government might be willing to negotiate on the basis of Serbia's concessions (July 27).[19] Blank check in hand, Austria did not deign to answer. To the contrary, she declared war on Serbia (July 28). There ensued a frantic exchange of missives between the kaiser and the tsar (which the royal cousins respectively signed "Willy" and "Nicky") in which they implored each other to do what they could to preserve the peace. With Austrian gunboats already shelling Belgrade from the Danube,[20] however, the tsar came under intense pressure from his advisors to mobilize. In a forlorn bid to avoid a clash with his cousin, he approved a partial mobilization against Austria alone on July 29, only to be informed that the Russian plan of deployment did not allow for such a contingency.[21] Reluctantly, he acceded to a general mobilization order the following day.

The reader need not be reminded that, since 1894, the European alliance system had divided the continent into two opposing camps, pitting the Triple Alliance of Germany, Austria and Italy against the Dual Alliance of France and Russia (the latter being expanded into a "Triple Entente" in 1907 by the adherence of Great Britain). It may, however, have escaped the reader's notice how truly unfortunate this circumstance was—for Russia's mobilization was now to unleash a series of war declarations that could not be avoided amid the tangle of confederacies.

By terms of the Triple Alliance, Germany was obliged to support Austria in the event of an attack by Russia. On August 1, Germany met this obligation by declaring war on Russia (her ambassador in St. Petersburg breaking down in tears moments after handing Germany's declaration to the Russian foreign minister).[22] In the event of an attack by Germany, however, the Dual Alliance obliged France to come to Russia's assistance. France had consistently reaffirmed her pledge to do so. (Indeed, in 1912, her president, Raymond Poincaré, had specifically stated that Russia could count on French support even if the war arose over strife in the faraway Balkans.)[23]

The kaiser did not wait for the inevitable French proclamation. On August 1, he issued an ultimatum giving France 18 hours to declare whether she intended to remain neutral. After receiving the reply that "France would act in accordance with her interests,"[24] he impatiently declared war on her on August 3. Hence, in the course of a week, the existing alliance system had transformed an unnecessary and isolated conflict between Austria and Serbia into a general war involving Germany, Austria, France, Russia and Serbia. Though party to the Triple Alliance, Italy declared herself neutral, pointing out that Austria had provoked Russia's attack on her by waging an offensive war against Serbia, and that the Italians were therefore not bound to support her. Britain, too, wrestled with the option of remaining aloof, as she was not specifically obliged to intervene on the basis of the 1907 Triple Entente with France and Russia. She had spent the preceding week lobbying furiously (if unsuccessfully) for a peace conference. On August 3, there was still a chance that she would remain neutral.

This chance evaporated on August 4, however, because Germany's mobilization plan, which we are about to discuss, called for an invasion of France by way of Belgium and Luxembourg—a particularly unfortunate scheme if the Germans hoped to avoid a British declaration of war. Britain had been committed by international treaty to the defense of Belgian neutrality since 1839 (not, it should be mentioned, out of any particular affection for the Belgians—delightful as those fine people might be—but because Belgium contained ports on the Channel coast which would best be kept out of more powerful hands). German troops crossed Luxembourg's frontier on August 3 and Belgium's on the following day. Through diplomatic channels, Britain demanded that the advance come to a halt. The demand was ignored. The Germans were incredulous that the British were working themselves into a tizzy over a "scrap of paper" from 1839. After all, Prussia (now Germany) had signed the same treaty and was now violating it without the slightest compunction. At midnight, Britain declared war on Germany to Sir Edward Grey's solemn lament: "The lamps are going out all over Europe; we shall not see them lit again in our lifetime."[25]

1914: *Tannenberg and the Marne*

In nine situations out of ten, the events described above would have been cause for alarm. But Germany's chief-of-staff, Helmuth von Moltke (the Younger), had the situation well in hand—so much so that he had secretly counseled Austria against nego-tiation on July 31 while Germany's chancellor was officially doing the opposite.[26] To begin with, the timing could not have been more propitious. Russia had just embarked on a military rebuilding program that would have placed her on a par with Germany by 1917. As matters stood, however, Germany held a significant advantage both in artil-lery strength and in the ability to move her forces by rail. More than this, she had a plan that would allow her to avoid the dreaded prospect of a two-front war by fighting two single-front wars in succession.

Known as the "Schlieffen Plan" after its originator, Count Alfred von Schlieffen (Moltke's predecessor), the scenario called for a delaying action on the Russian front while Germany's main resources were thrown against France. With the direct route into France guarded by a network of fortresses that could not be overrun without cat-astrophic losses, the plan envisaged an indirect itinerary through neutral Belgium. (In defense of this crime, the German chancellor, Theobald von Bethmann-Hollweg, would state emphatically, if not very convincingly, that "Necessity knows no law!"[27]) In six weeks, according to the timetable, German troops would be marching victoriously through the Arc de Triomphe—presumably, en route to the Paris train station, whence they would board the trains for the Russian front to repeat the procedure against the Russians.

According to the old adage, if something sounds too good to be true, it isn't. But to say so in this case would be to ignore the ineptitude of the French High Command. France had desired revenge against Germany since 1871, but in all the intervening years, the notion of a German strike through the Low Countries had occurred to only one member of her supreme war council (General Victor-Constant Michel) and he had been sacked forthwith for mentioning the possibility.[28] Faced now with the reality of German troops pouring into Belgium, France's military experts convinced themselves that the thrust was merely a diversion and moved ahead with their own strategy—"Plan 17"—which called for an eastward lunge into Alsace and Lorraine (i.e., the territories that had been usurped by Germany in the Franco-Prussian War).

The blueprint was so obvious that the German High Command had wagered every-thing on France adopting it. With the French advancing eastwards, the Germans could stampede through Belgium and pounce upon Paris—thus dealing a mortal blow to the enemy's morale (and to his communications). This done, they had merely to follow in the footsteps of the main French Army and attack it from behind.[29] Truly, the war in France *would* be over in six weeks.

It was brilliant in conception, but it was destined to fail. The crucial flaw, as the eminent military historian, John Keegan, points out, was that the operation called for so great a mass of men that there could be no hope of getting them to their objectives on time. Once the German rail system ended at the Belgian border, there simply were not enough roads on which to march.[30] On his accession as chief-of-staff in 1906, Moltke unwittingly "solved" this problem, but in the wrong way and for the wrong reason. Believing that Schlieffen's original dispositions left the defense of Alsace and Lorraine (i.e., on the German left) too vulnerable in order to build up the all-powerful right wing, Moltke strengthened the former at the expense of the latter.[31] This was an extraordinary blunder. Schlieffen had purposefully left the Alsace-Lorraine sector weak in order to bait the French into the trap, and Moltke's puttering did no more than to make it doubt-ful that the right-wing strike-force would have enough men to accomplish its task.

But there was trouble long before Paris. Indeed, things went awry as soon as the Germans crossed into Belgium where, to their utter dismay, they learned that King Albert had mobilized his quaint little army, and that his soldiers, clad in their amusing top hats, were actually intending to resist. Incensed that the Belgians would dare to stand their ground, the Germans hurled waves of men at the fortress network around Liège. As the world stood by in amazement, they were thrown back by artillery and machine gun fire with great loss of life. With no alternative, the Germans held up their timetable while huge siege guns were transported to the front.[32] Once these arrived, however, the antiquated forts were reduced to rubble. By August 16, all had capitulated.

On August 20, German forces entered Brussels. Describing the scene to the London-based *News Chronicle*, the American correspondent Richard Harding Davis reported that three soldiers on bicycles were the first to arrive. "What came after them, and twenty-four hours later is still coming, is not men marching, but a force of nature like a tidal wave, an avalanche or a river flooding its banks ... when hour after hour passed and there was no halt, no breathing time, no open spaces in the ranks, the thing became uncanny, inhuman."[33] Namur fell two days later.

While the Belgian Army fell back on Antwerp (which was bombed by a German zeppelin on August 25),[34] civilian patriots attempted to slow the German advance by acting as snipers, and by destroying bridges, railroads and telegraph lines. Outraged by these guerrilla tactics, the Germans gunned down innocent civilians by the hundreds—men, women and children—in the town squares of Aerschot, Tamines and Dinant.[35] At Louvain, confused German units accidentally began shooting at each other in the darkness, and their internecine mêlée could not be brought to a halt until the city, along with its library of priceless medieval documents, had been burnt to the ground.[36] When the international community howled in protest, the Germans argued that the Belgians had brought it on themselves by carrying out guerrilla actions in violation of international law. (Of course, if "international law" had been a priority for the Germans, they would not have invaded Belgium.)[37]

Despite the ghastly German "reprisals," the drive through Belgium was taking longer than expected. The French, meanwhile, were making their expected attack into Lorraine, wearing their bright red pants and blue jackets. Unlike the rest of the armies of the world, which had adopted drab uniforms to make their soldiers less conspicuous, the French remained dazzlingly colorful in a misguided effort to overawe the enemy with a show of élan.[38] The result was intensely unpleasant. By August 21, the smartly dressed (but easily seen) French had been hurled back with some 300,000 casualties.[39]

The "Battle of the Frontiers" had exposed the extreme folly of "Plan 17." By now it was apparent that the main German thrust was indeed aimed through Belgium. Attempting to restrain the tide, the British Expeditionary Force (BEF) saw its first action at Mons on August 23. Smaller but more experienced than any army in the field, the BEF had a core of veterans who had fought in the Boer War where they had learned the value of entrenchment against massed attack.[40] Thus, when the battle commenced, they were already dug in, and the Germans, advancing against them shoulder-to-shoulder as stupidly as the French had done in Lorraine, were miserably gunned down.

Unfortunately, by day's end the French forces guarding the BEF's right flank had been driven from their position, and the British were compelled to fall back with them. Unhinged by his allies' failure to hold their ground, the British commander-in-chief, Sir John French, announced that he would retire with his army until he was out of harm's

French infantry charge, 1914. Agence Rol (Wikimedia Commons).

way. Only a direct appeal from the British Minister of War, Lord Kitchener, who rushed from London to Paris, convinced him to halt. Still the relentless German onslaught proved too much for the Allies. They were soon in headlong retreat, and Joseph Joffre, the French commander-in-chief, was not sure he could regroup before reaching the Seine.[41] The French government abandoned the capital for Bordeaux. It appeared that France would fall as quickly as it had in 1870.

Victory was staring Germany in the face—and, if the Russians had been anywhere near as slow in mobilizing as the Schlieffen Plan counted on them to be, victory might have been achieved. But against all expectations, two Russian armies reached the East Prussian frontier in mid–August. The first of these, marching north of the Masurian Lakes, under the command of Pavel Rennenkampf, was charged with tying down Germany's undermanned East Prussian defenders from the front, while the second, under Aleksandr Samsonov, was to sneak around the lakes from the south to fall upon the enemy from behind.[42] Encountering the Germans much earlier (and further east) than anticipated, Rennenkampf fought a successful skirmish and then came to a dead halt quite out of Samsonov's reach. Nevertheless, Samsonov, prodded by his superiors, continued to forge blindly ahead.

Apprised of Samsonov's advance (and smarting from his losses in the clash with Rennenkampf), the German commander, General von Prittwitz, informed his own superiors that he intended to withdraw behind the Vistula River—a course that would cede all of East Prussia to the Russians. His Deputy Chief of Operations, Colonel Max Hoffmann, urged him instead to redeploy against the advancing Samsonov, and offered several excellent reasons for doing so—the most compelling being that if the Germans made for the Vistula now, Samsonov, who was very much closer, would get there ahead of them.[43]

Moltke agreed that retreat was undesirable, and replaced the timorous Prittwitz with Field Marshal Paul von Hindenburg, a veteran old enough to have served at Sadowa

(1866). Sporting the antiquated blue uniform that he had worn into retirement three years earlier,[44] Hindenburg set out for the East accompanied by General Erich Luden-dorff, the rising star of the German officer corps, who was to serve as his chief-of-staff. On August 25, Moltke decided to reinforce them with troops drawn from the Western Front—a move that was not only fatal to the Schlieffen Plan, but was entirely unnecessary, since Hindenburg and Ludendorff were content with the forces already at their disposal. Indeed, the new German commanders did not wait for these reinforcements but marched immediately against Samsonov—the exact course that Colonel Hoffman had urged upon Prittwitz before the latter was removed from command.

The hapless Samsonov, who was still pressing ahead in the expectation of cooperating with Rennenkampf, blundered into the advancing Germans at Tannenburg, just west of the Masurian Lakes. Before he knew what he was in for, the Germans had turned both his flanks in a devastating "double-envelopment" reminiscent of Hannibal's celebrated tactics at Cannae in 216 BC. As the magnitude of the disaster became apparent, a distraught Samsonov walked into the woods and shot himself. His soldiers were cut to pieces—many drowning in flight in the surrounding swamplands (August 26–30).[45]

Credit for the magnificent victory should have gone to Hoffmann, or if not to him, to Ludendorff. Least deserving was the senescent Hindenburg, but since he was nominally in command, popular acclaim went to him. (As Barbara Tuchman relates, Hoffmann exacted a wry revenge later in the war. Giving tours of the battlefield, he made sure to point out to visitors where Hindenburg slept—not only before and after the battle, but during it.)[46] In any event, with reinforcements pouring in from the Western Front, the Germans followed up their victory with another—routing Rennenkampf's army in early September at the Battle of the Masurian Lakes. (Rennekampf managed to foil a Prussian attempt at envelopment, but afterwards fled in his staff car to Kovno inside the Russian frontier—saving his own skin while his abandoned army suffered 125,000 casualties.)[47]

Although the Russian offensive had been decisively repulsed, Moltke's decision to transfer troops to the Eastern Front had created a crisis of numbers for the forces driving on Paris. One of the corps sent to the East had been taken from the German 2nd Army,[48] which now came under counterattack from the French at Guise. The 2nd Army commander promptly requested assistance from the German 1st Army, under General Alexander von Kluck.[49]

Deployed on the extreme right of the German line, von Kluck's 1st Army had been tasked with sweeping southwestwards to envelop Paris. But von Kluck was concerned that his own forces were becoming overextended by the continued march toward the French capital. Furthermore, he was convinced that there was no viable enemy force to his front—meaning that the Allied left flank was dangling unprotected and could be pounced upon. He therefore made the momentous decision to forget Paris and the siege that capturing it would entail, and wheel his army eastwards—in part to honor the 2nd Army's request for assistance, but more especially in a bid to win the war at a blow by enveloping the exposed Allied left flank.[50] When Moltke approved the decision, von Kluck's army pivoted eastwards—its lead divisions crossing the Marne thirty miles north of Paris.

General Joseph Gallieni, the Military Governor of Paris, was busy trying to mold the motley forces at his disposal[51] into a serviceable defensive force when air reconnaissance revealed von Kluck's eastward turn. At first, he refused to credit the report.[52] His staff, however, greeted the news with something bordering on pandemonium[53]; for in executing his inward wheel, von Kluck had exposed his own right flank to a counterattack by the French forces being assembled in Paris. Without a moment to lose, Gallieni went on the offensive—mobilizing the city's fleet of 600 taxicabs to help ferry men to the front. While the French forces piled in, five to a cab,[54] the French Commander-in-Chief, General Joseph Joffre, issued desperate orders to the rest of the army, insisting that the collective Allied retreat stop, and that soldiers stand their ground even if it meant death.[55] Still executing his eastward wheel, von Kluck was forced to halt and pivot back toward Paris to meet the attack of Gallieni's troops on his flank. What followed was the "Battle of the Marne" (September 6–12).

At the outset of the affair, the Allies had a chance for outright victory. Von Kluck's latest turnabout had opened a gap between his own army and the adjacent German 2nd Army that he had ostensibly been attempting to assist. Sir John French's British Expeditionary Force was well positioned to drive through the opening, but Sir John had only barely agreed to take part in the counter-offensive after an impassioned plea by Joffre, and now moved too slowly to take advantage of an opportunity that might have ended the war.[56] As a result, the Germans were able to withdraw in good order.

Nevertheless, the Battle of the Marne remains one of the decisive encounters of the First World War. The Schlieffen Plan lay in ruins, and as the Germans fell back to entrench behind the Aisne River, a despondent Moltke is said to have informed the kaiser that the war was lost.[57] Still, there were some in the German High Command who perceived one last hope for rapid victory in a push westward to outflank the Allies in Flanders. In the ensuing "Race to the Channel," they did not achieve their goal. A brave holding action by the Belgians at Antwerp slowed their progress, affording the French and British time to plug the remaining gaps.[58] In desperation, the Germans attempted to force their way through the Allied line at Ypres, but without success and at a staggering cost of 130,000 casualties[59] (including enough young German reservists for the battle to be remembered in German lore as "the Massacre of the Innocents").[60] British troops drawn from India—Sikhs and Gurkhas—served with distinction defending the British line.

The only race now was that of building entrenchments. The British were unequivocally on the worst ground for this type of activity, for in Flanders where they had taken up position one could not dig deeper than 18 inches without hitting water.[61] As an unenviable alternative, the soldiers built breastworks above ground while under fire from German snipers. By year's end, the opposing entrenchments would stretch from the Channel coast to the Swiss border. A stalemate had been reached on the Western Front that was to last for four years.

Almost forgotten in the midst of the greater carnage was the little conflict that had set everything in motion: the war between Austria and Serbia. It began on a sour note for the Dual Monarchy when she learned that Russia was mobilizing to attack her more rapidly than expected. This necessitated the transfer of her reserves to the northern front in Galicia, and denuded her southern army. The latter sought to invade Serbia anyway, crossing the Sava and Drina Rivers on August 12. Assailed by Serb *komitadji* (irregulars), the Austrian forces retaliated with savage atrocities—carrying out summary executions of civilians at Sabac and Lesnica.[62] The Serbs put up a fierce resistance, and then counterattacked, inflicting a sharp defeat on the Austrians at the Battle of Cer (August 16–19). On August 24, the Austrians fell back across the border in panicked flight having sustained 40,000 casualties in the 12-day campaign.[63]

By this time, the Russians had made their aforementioned foray into East Prussia, prompting Germany to demand an immediate Austrian offensive against the tsar. But when the Austrians attempted to oblige, their outmanned and outgunned soldiery were taken in flank and horribly routed near Lemberg by Russian forces under General Alexei Brusilov. On September 11, they limped back across the River San, having suffered over 300,000 casualties.[64]

Despite this catastrophe, the Austrians attacked Serbia again in early November, and on December 2, they occupied Belgrade. This, however, was the highpoint of the campaign. On December 3, the Serbs unleashed a desperate counterattack, recovering their capital and hurling the Austrians from their territory for a second time by mid-month.

The disastrous setbacks suffered by Austria were partially offset by Turkey's entry into the war on the side of the Central Powers (November 1914). Since the Berlin-Baghdad Railway scheme of the 1890s, the Ottoman-German tie had been a close one. So much so, that at the outset of the war, Turkey allowed two fugitive German warships to take refuge in the Black Sea. She ought, by this action, to have forfeited her neutrality, but immediate hostilities with the Allies were forestalled by the bogus claim that Germany had "sold" the two cruisers to the Turks and were merely delivering them to their new owners.[65]

Surprisingly, the ruse worked—but only too well in the German view, because the Turks continued to avoid commitment to the Central Powers for months afterwards. Tired of waiting, the German crews aboard the two "Turkish" vessels set course for the Russian Black Sea ports of Odessa and Sevastopol and, on October 28, bombarded them without authorization from the Turkish government (albeit with the connivance of the Germanophile Turkish War Minister, Enver Pasha).[66] Since the ships were officially the property of Turkey, this action prompted a declaration of war by Russia on the Ottoman empire. Like it or not, the Turks were now formally allied to the Central Powers.

The development was fraught with menace for the Allies, but not because the Turkish Army was an

German troops photographed alongside their machine gun in a trench on the Western Front (Bowden Postcard Collection Online, Miami University Libraries, Wikimedia Commons).

awe-inspiring fighting force. Indeed, its shortcomings were abundantly displayed in its first offensive effort—a haphazard thrust into the Russian Caucasus in December 1914 that was hurled back with 80,000 casualties (50,000 killed on the field of battle, and another 30,000 frozen in their mountain encampments).[67] No, the issue was not one of fighting capacity, but rather one of strategy, for the Turkish alliance placed the Straits leading to the Black Sea in hostile hands, and thus left the French and British with no short route to Russia by which to reinforce or deliver munitions to their ally.[68] Still worse, the Suez Canal was placed in jeopardy, and with it the crucial short route to India and Australia whence Britain hoped to draw supplies and reinforcements.[69] Early in 1915, the Turks attacked Egypt in an effort to gain control of the Canal. Luckily, they fared no better here than they had in the Caucasus.

Defeated on two fronts, the Turks turned their wrath on their own Christian Armenian population. The Armenians had inhabited historic Armenia—overlapping the borders of Turkey, Russia and Iran—for three thousand years, but had long been a conquered people. The Turks denied them basic civil rights, and subjected them to violent persecution. The worst episode had occurred during the 1890s, when Turkish soldiers and Kurdish bandits carried out a massive pogrom. Men, women and children were chased from their homes and put to the sword. At Trebizond, Armenian innocents jumped into the Black Sea to escape the marauders. The Muslims gave chase in boats, and dashed out their brains or pushed them under the water to drown.[70] Over 100,000 Armenians lost their lives in these proceedings.

But the new campaign was far worse, for now the Turkish aim was nothing short of genocide. Having presided over the loss of extensive territory in the Christian Balkans prior to the First World War, the "Young Turks" were determined to "Turkify" everything that remained of their dominions. The Armenians resisted. Thus, following the failure of the Turkish drive into the Caucasus (in the heartland of historic Armenia), they were accused of aiding and abetting the enemy, and targeted for extermination. In what was termed "resettlement," entire villages of Armenians were robbed of all their lands and possessions, and driven like cattle into the desert wastelands of Mesopotamia and Syria. En route, they were set upon by Kurdish horsemen, who slaughtered them without regard to age or sex, and with full complicity of the Turkish authorities. Children were murdered for sport; women were raped and then hacked in pieces.[71] Those who did not die by violent hands succumbed to hunger and thirst on the march. When they sought to draw water from the Euphrates, they were shot down. Witnesses saw despairing mothers handing their children to the passing Bedouins in hopes of saving them.[72] By mid–1917, 700,000 Armenians were already dead,[73] yet the carnage continued for another six years claiming in excess of one million lives. Even after the war, when Turkey was defeated, there was no effective intervention by the major powers. It was the Turks' most successful "campaign" of the war, and one that has earned them eternal infamy. And there is a disturbing epilogue—for, to this day, it remains the official position of the Turkish government that the Armenian genocide never occurred.

1915: *Neuve Chapelle, Gallipoli, Champagne and Loos*

On Christmas Day, 1914, at various points along the Western Front, soldiers from the opposing trenches ventured into No Man's Land to fraternize with one another—exchanging liquor, chocolate and souvenirs in an implausible display of cama-raderie. Burial parties were allowed to gather up the dead, and at some points the com-batants serenaded each other with Christmas songs. Such behavior was immediately outlawed by the higher ups.[74]

Confronted with stalemate along the entire Western Front, the opposing High Commands grasped for alternative strategies—the Germans lighting upon the idea of applying the Schlieffen Plan in reverse. They would sit tight in a defensive posture in the West and attempt to cast the Russians out of the war with a concentrated effort in the East where the vast open spaces seemed to offer the opportunity for mobile war-fare. While they pondered this plan, the BEF surprised them with an attack at Neuve Chapelle, opening the affair with an artillery barrage directed squarely at the German trenches (March 10, 1915). According to Alan Clark, men, earth and gun emplacements were blown into the air repeatedly. Then, as the British infantry moved forward, the area beyond the German trenches was bombarded to impede the enemy from bringing up his reserves.[75] The town fell immediately. Nor was any opposition encountered beyond it. The British, it seemed, had achieved a breakthrough.

Alas, no one had prepared for such an eventuality. Nor did it prove possible to improvise on the fly. Surprised by their own success, the British High Command dashed off memorandums to one another, the delivery of which took in excess of an hour each.[76] Instead of pressing ahead, the commanders thought it prudent to halt their lead battal-ions until their flanks had been secured. They neglected, however, to halt those com-ing up behind, and soon the frontline became a jumble of entangled units. By the time the confusion had been sorted out, the Germans had plugged the gap, and no further advance was possible.[77]

Convinced that further offensives on the Western Front would be futile, Lord Kitchener, the British War Minister, adopted a plan promoted by Winston Churchill, First Lord of the Admiralty, aimed at capturing the Turkish Straits leading to the Black Sea. Should the stroke be successful, the Western Allies could establish a direct lifeline to Russia. In February and March 1915, a preliminary effort to force the Straits was made by sea. To get through, it was necessary to knock out the coastal fortresses at the entry to the Straits, sweep the minefields beyond and then take on a second series of fortresses at the "Narrows" leading to the Sea of Marmora.[78] The venture had an auspicious begin-ning. The outermost fortresses were put out of action, and by the middle of March, the fleet was confident that it had cleared out the mines on the approach to the Narrows. But the Turks secretly laid new mines just prior to the main assault, and though the Allied ships managed to deliver a devastating bombardment to the fortresses on the morn-ing of March 18, they found themselves steaming back and forth through mined waters without knowing it. Just before 2 o'clock, the French ship, *Bouvet*, became the first to make the discovery. A mine ignited her ammunition stores, and sank her in two min-utes, with all but 66 of her crew being lost.[79] Two British battleships followed her to the bottom and another, badly damaged, had to be towed to shallow waters before the after-noon was over. To the great relief of the Turks (who were nearly out of ammunition), Admiral de Robeck, commanding the fleet, declined to press the assault. The abortive naval strike thus served only to eliminate all hope for surprise when the British finally adopted an alternative plan—this one involving an amphibious landing on the Gallipoli Peninsula at the entrance to the Dardanelles.

For the new campaign, seventy-five thousand Australian and New Zealand troops

Western Front 1915–1918 by J.F. Horrabin (Illustrator) from H.G. Wells' *Outline of History*, 1923 (Wikimedia Commons).

(known as Anzacs) were entrusted to Sir Ian Hamilton. On the first day (April 25, 1915), they attempted to establish a series of beachheads on Cape Helles. At the main landing site, Sedd-el-Bahr, at the southern tip of the peninsula, a hostile current slowed the progress of the boats. By the time the Anzacs managed to establish a foothold, the beach was littered with corpses, and the lapping waters were red with blood. In the sea beyond, landing craft drifted aimlessly, filled with dead marines who had been cut down by Turkish machine gun fire during the approach.[80] Those ashore took cover where they could, serenaded by the rattle of machine guns and the shrieks of their wounded comrades, whom they were powerless to help.[81]

At the subsidiary landing sites, things went better. At either extremity of Cape Helles, troops landed almost without opposition. Had they advanced inland they might have achieved a decisive breakthrough. Instead, they sat inert without orders while the opportunity slipped through their fingers. At a separate landing site—Anzac Cove on the western shore of the peninsula—the Australians and New Zealanders also got ashore with a significant numerical superiority over the defenders. Unfortunately, in the pre-dawn darkness, they had hit the beaches a mile off course with nearly impassable terrain leading inland. Despite an extraordinary effort, they got bogged down in the scrub just long enough to be beaten to the high ground by Mustapha Kemal, the determined commander of the local Turkish reserves, who coldly told his soldiers that they must hold fast to each centimeter of ground even if it cost them their lives. Thanks to Kemal's efforts, the Turks had time to stabilize their defenses before the British organized themselves for an inland drive.[82]

While the Dardanelles gamble was pursued, Britain waged economic warfare against Germany with a tightening naval blockade. The superiority of the British surface fleet had made itself apparent by the end of 1914, and after some minor skirmishes, the German fleet took refuge in the Kiel Canal.[83] With command of the water secured, the British were able to intercept and seize ships bearing goods to Germany. Germany answered by unleashing a U-boat campaign in February. Three months later, without issuing a warning, they torpedoed and sank the Cunard liner *Lusitania*, killing some 1200 civilian passengers. Over 100 of these victims were American, and the terse reaction from President Wilson convinced the Germans to be more sporting (at least in the short term). Over the next several months, German submarines would surface, issue warnings, and allow their prey to abandon ship before launching torpedoes.

Back on land, the Germans had embarked upon their new strategic initiatives for 1915. In April, they withdrew a large contingent of forces from the western sector for duty in the East, covering their departure with a diversionary attack at Ypres.[84] The attack (known as the Second Battle of Ypres) was made infamous by the introduction of poison gas. Released from cylinders in front of the German lines, it formed a yellow-green cloud, wafting forward on the strength of a favorable wind. At first, its intended victims found its appearance mesmerizing. But soon enough, the chlorine vapor swept into the trenches to wreak asphyxiation—sending men and horses into coughing, suffocating flight.[85] Left behind, according to German eyewitnesses, were darkened corpses tinged with yellow residue— their fists clenched as though they were still enduring torment.[86] A breach four miles wide was opened in the Allied line, and was only meagerly reinforced during the ensuing days.

Now it was the German turn to waste a golden opportunity. Because the attack had been nothing more than a diversion, no extra troops had been deployed to exploit a possible breakthrough.[87] Still, the British High Command managed to make a bad situation intolerable by improvising foolhardy counterattacks to regain lost ground. With insufficient artillery support, British troops were gunned down by the thousands—more often than not within a stone's throw of their own trenches. Those who advanced further were treated to a new cloud of gas, against which they had no protection.[88]

On April 26, 1915, one day after the initial Anzac landings on Gallipoli, Italy agreed to enter the war on the side of the Allies. Less than three weeks earlier, she had offered to join the Central Powers in return for Trentino and Trieste—known to Italian nationalists as *Italia Irredenta* or "unredeemed Italy" (i.e., ethnically Italian regions still under Hapsburg rule). Austria had refused. Now, with Allied troops ashore in Gallipoli, a French diplomat quipped, "The Italians are rushing to the aid of the victors."[89] On May 23, Italy declared war on Austria. Over the course of the year, Italian troops made repeated forays into the inhospitable mountains in the South Tyrol and along the Isonzo River. All were thrown back with devastating loss—the only redeeming aspect of these futile efforts being that they tied down a fair number of Austrian troops.

Meanwhile, on the Western Front, Marshall Joffre hurled the French Army against Vimy Ridge near Arras (May 9). The British attempted to lend support by attacking Aubers Ridge, to the front of their position at Neuve Chapelle. Bagpipers sent forward at the head of one of the British charges were cut down by German machine guns.[90] The costly attacks achieved nothing—failing even to make Joffre think twice before planning those to follow. In September, new offensives were unleashed by the French in Champagne and by the British at Loos. At the former, the French purchased two miles of rubble at very high cost, while at Loos, the British commanders managed to gas their own troops when the wind suddenly changed after they had opened their cylinders. Despite this mishap, the British soldiery—some of whom were seen kicking a soccer ball as they crossed No Man's Land[91]—continued their advance and broke through on either flank of the attack front. But now the High Command failed them again—stupidly reinforcing the stalled areas in the center, while the Germans patched the holes on the wings.[92] As the fight wore on, the British commander-in-chief, Sir John French, was urged by his subordinates to commit a large body of reserves, but adamantly refused stating that the troops were too inexperienced and that they were unfit for duty after three days on the march.[93] By the second day of battle, the chance for a breakthrough had been lost. In the aftermath, French was relieved of command. His replacement was Sir Douglas Haig.

For the soldier in the trench, this change promised no great advantage. Haig had once consulted a séance medium for the purpose of asking military questions.[94] At Loos, he had been among the most insistent in calling on Sir John French to commit the reserves. And when, on the second day of the battle, French finally relented, Haig ordered them forward into open country against German machine-gun emplacements. The German defenders were amazed by the stupidity of this tactic, which produced a casualty rate of 80 percent among the hapless attackers. At first the German troops waxed triumphant, but the useless butchery soon sickened them, and when the attack finally faltered and the British began to withdraw, they ceased their fire and did not put finger to trigger for the remainder of the day.[95] The site was afterwards known to the Germans as the "*Leichenfeld von Loos*" (i.e., the "Corpse Field of Loos")."[96]

By this time, the Gallipoli offensive had also ended in disaster. Since no headway could be made from the British beachheads at Cape Helles and Anzac Cove, the battle bogged down into trench-style warfare similar to that on the Western Front. On August 6, a surprise landing of reinforcements was effected at Suvla Bay, just to the north of Anzac Cove, but owing to the dithering of its commander, General Frederick Stopford, no attempt was made to seize the surrounding high ground on the first day when it was literally there for the taking. On the following morning, the Turks arrived in force, whereupon a series of British assaults were thrown back. Further south, British troops staging a simultaneous attack from Anzac Cove, seized the heights of Chunuk Bair, from which they could see the Straits in the distance. But four days later, Mustapha Kemal retook the heights in a dawn bayonet charge in which an entire battalion of green British recruits was put to slaughter. All hope of reaching the Straits died with them.[97] By month's end, it was evident that the Gallipoli Campaign had failed.

The impact of this defeat was disastrous. No sooner had the British failure become manifest, than Bulgaria entered the war on the side of the Central Powers.[98] The Gallipoli debacle had convinced her that the Allied cause was doomed. Besides, Bulgaria still had a bone to pick with Serbia dating to the Second Balkan War. Accordingly, in

October, she invaded Serbia from the east, while German and Austrian troops pressed in from the north. Under simultaneous attack from two directions, the Serbian front crumbled. A vain attempt was made to hold out while the British and French landed 80,000 troops at Salonika (in Greece) in order to come to their assistance. Alas, the Greek king, Constantine (a brother-in-law of the kaiser), refused his cooperation and no meaningful help could be rendered. Serbia was defeated overwhelmingly. The vestiges of her army fled through freezing snowdrifts and biting winds to the Albanian mountains—there to be rescued by the British fleet and transferred to Corfu.

Owing to Bulgaria's entry into the war, the Central Powers now controlled a continuous swath of territory from the Baltic Coast to Mesopotamia. Instead of the Allies establishing a line of supply to Russia, the Central Powers had established one with Turkey. The attendant rise in Turkish resources spelt doom for the Gallipoli venture,[99] and in December, the British Government finally decided to withdraw on the advice of General Sir Charles Monro who had been sent from the Western Front to render an opinion. (He decided on withdrawal within a day, prompting Churchill's wry comment, "He came, he saw, he capitulated.") Surprisingly, the evacuation went without a hitch—being carried out without a single casualty, whereas rates as high as 30 to 40 percent had been anticipated.[100]

While the Allies suffered one setback after another in 1915, the Central Powers achieved striking successes—most especially on the Eastern Front, where two German armies (one in the north commanded by Hindenburg, and one in the south under August von Mackensen) opened a two-prong offensive against Russia beginning in early May. In the South, Mackensen's forces, cooperating with the Austrians, pierced the enemy front between Gorlice and Tarnow. By June, the Russians had been driven out of Galicia—relinquishing the fortress of Przemysl, which they had captured at great cost in March. There followed a great pincer attack in the north led by Hindenburg and Ludendorff, which delivered all of Poland and Lithuania into German hands. Warsaw, Kovno, Bialystok and Brest-Litovsk were occupied in rapid succession in August. In September, Vilna, Lithuania was likewise taken. The industrially backward Russians were so plagued by a shortage of munitions in these contests, that they sent unarmed soldiers into battle with orders to procure rifles from the hands of their fallen comrades.[101] In all, they suffered over a million casualties, with an additional million lost as prisoners.[102] An effort by the retreating Russians to leave a scorched earth to the invaders merely clogged the roads eastwards with millions of civilian refugees.[103] In the midst of the carnage, the tsar decided to assume command of the army, supplanting the able Grand Duke Nicholas. The result of this misguided decision was that the growing disaster at the front came to be associated with the person of the tsar.

1916: Verdun and the Somme

By the beginning of 1916, the Eastern Front seemed sufficiently subdued to allow Germany to make another attempt to end the war with a single devastating push in the West. Chosen as the point of attack was the French fortress network at Verdun—a stronghold important not only because its strategic heights along the Meuse blocked the road to Paris, but because it was an historic symbol of French glory and sacrifice in war.[104] Its loss would be doubly disheartening and possibly decisive; and even if it did not fall, the French could be counted upon to "bleed themselves white" in its defense. In fact, the twisted, secret design of the German commander-in-chief, Erich von Falkenhayn, was to manufacture a stalemate at Verdun for the very purpose of exsanguinating the French Army in a months-long battle of attrition.[105]

On February 21, 1916, the Germans unloosed an artillery barrage, unprecedented in its magnitude, along a narrow front east of the Meuse. "High explosive shells fairly obliterated the French first line trenches," says the historian, Carlton Hayes. "Groves which might have afforded shelter to the French artillery were wiped out of existence, trees being uprooted and shattered into splinters…. Then, while the German guns lengthened their range so as to place a 'curtain of fire' in the rear of the French trenches, cutting off supplies and reinforcements, the German infantry … occupied the ruined French first line."[106] Any remaining pockets of resistance were wiped out with the help of Germany's latest innovation—the flamethrower.[107] Within a week, Fort Douaumont, reputedly the most formidable citadel on earth, fell to German raiding parties, one of which formed a human pyramid in order to slip into an unguarded gun turret.[108] The fortress was largely empty. The Verdun sector had been so quiet since the opening weeks of the war that many of its men and guns had been removed for service elsewhere. Moreover, the fate of Belgium's forts in 1914 had convinced most military thinkers that forts were not defensible.[109] Taken by surprise, the undermanned French line wavered and fell back, but ultimately held—often defended by groups of soldiers fighting from shell craters in the pockmarked landscape.[110]

While this transpired, says Winston Churchill, Joseph Joffre was living a carefree

French soldiers leave their trench for an attack during the Battle of Verdun, 1916. Collection DocAnciens/docpix.fr (Wikimedia Commons).

life at his Chantilly headquarters. Indeed, when a subordinate came to him seeking permission to travel to Verdun to assess the evolving situation, he found the French commander-in-chief asleep. Once aroused, Joffre granted the request, remained awake long enough to declare that retreat was not an option, and then got back into bed.[111]

Verdun's defenses were tottering, but the arrival of reinforcements and a new commander, General Philippe Pétain, helped to stiffen the garrison's resolve. In order to meet supply needs, Pétain organized a massive truck convoy—the first ever used in war—along the "Sacred Way," a two-lane, dirt road that served as the only link between Verdun and the interior. Additionally, he instituted a system of rapid rotation of troops in and out of the line of fire in an effort to prevent battle fatigue and maintain morale—this being an absolute necessity since no one could long tolerate such bitter fighting. The fortresses still in his possession, though not sufficient to withstand frontline attack, nonetheless did excellent service as rearward artillery stations.[112] Indeed, the battle largely deteriorated into one of artillery against infantry, as the tiny salient around Verdun played host to an unprecedented concentration of shellfire. The terrain quaked and roiled beneath the onslaught. Men were buried alive or blown to oblivion before they knew the enemy was upon them.[113] The strain of the unceasing bombardment drove soldiers insane or left them benumbed. In the trenches, living men went about their tasks with partially exposed corpses encased in the walls next to them. "One eats, one drinks beside the dead, one sleeps in the midst of the dying, one laughs and one sings in the company of corpses," wrote Georges Duhamel, a French military doctor serving at Verdun.[114] One French position came to be known as the "Trench of Bayonets" after an entire squadron of men was buried alive by a sudden shift of the exploding earth. The only indication that they had been positioned there was the gruesome spectacle of their rifle barrels protruding out of the earth with bayonets still fixed.[115]

The heavy action at Verdun earned the fortress network a new moniker: "the meat grinder." In early June, the Germans captured Fort Vaux, which had been under intense fire for three months. In a final bid for relief, the fortress garrison sent out its last carrier pigeon. Though ailing from an earlier gas attack, the pigeon delivered its message. Its bravery was rewarded—posthumously—with the Legion of Honor, for it died of exhaustion on arrival.[116] Under unrelenting attack, Verdun seemed on the verge of collapse. But the German advance was eventually halted, even thrown back—and though the French had adopted Pétain's battle cry, "They shall not pass," it was not French valor alone that held the line. Action in other theaters also played a hand.

Conducting her war against Italy without aid from the Germans, Austria was scarcely able to cope. In a bid to turn the tide, she transferred troops from Galicia, on the Russian Front, to the northern Italian theater. It was a fateful decision, for coincidentally the Russian commander, Alexei Brusilov, was planning a major strike in the very sector that the Austrians had denuded.[117] When the blow fell, it smashed the Austrian line in pieces,[118] leaving Falkenhayn no choice but to interrupt his operations at Verdun, in order to send reinforcements to the threatened sector.

Brusilov's drive ultimately ground to a halt with catastrophic losses. In fact, it had only been meant as a diversion to draw in the enemy's reserves while the main blow was delivered further to the north opposite Vilna. Tragically for Brusilov and his men, General Alexei Evert never launched the planned assault despite having two million men and most of the campaign's resources sitting idle under his command.[119] Consequently, ten days after halting at Verdun, Falkenhayn was satisfied that the crisis was over, and made ready to resume his push. The French, however, had used the respite afforded them by Brusilov to restore their defenses. Indeed, after a German attack came up short on June 23, the French seized the initiative and counterattacked. By August, the failure of Falkenhayn's strategy was manifest. Having lost more than 300,000 men—almost as many as the French whom he had sought to "bleed white"—he was sacked in favor of Hindenburg and Ludendorff.

Nor was Verdun Germany's lone setback. In February, Portugal declared in favor of the Allies—sending reinforcements to the Western Front, and seizing German ships in her harbors. Then, on May 31, 1916, the German navy emerged from its base at Kiel for the first time since 1914, in a bid to lure the British fleet, or a portion thereof, into a waiting ambush of submarines.[120] A sharp exchange between the vanguards of the two fleets ensued at Jutland off the Danish coast, during which the Germans inflicted roughly 6000 casualties as against just 2500 of their own. The difference in numbers was owed in part to the disagreeable propensity of certain British ships to explode into oblivion when struck by a single shell—the result of inadequate ammunition storage precautions.[121] Still, it was hardly a strategic victory for Germany. The U-boats failed to intercept a single ship, and the German fleet was more than once placed in mortal danger of being cut off from its haven at Kiel. Only the coming of night allowed the Germans to slip into the clear and retire. Nor would they again seriously challenge British control of the sea. Germany would remain hostage to the British naval blockade of her shores for the remainder of the war, much to the hardship of her populace.

A week after the clash at Jutland, Lord Kitchener, the British War Minister, was killed crossing the North Sea en route to Russia, when his ship the *Hampshire* struck an enemy mine off Scapa Flow and went to the bottom.[122] Back on land, the British had amassed a huge army with the help of a new conscription law. Thus equipped, they commenced their own great land campaign for 1916 on a twenty-five-mile front astride the Somme River Basin. The offensive, launched on July 1, a month after Jutland, was originally to be more French than British. Indeed, Joffre had chosen the site, not Haig. But with the French Army pinned down at Verdun, the Battle of the Somme became a predominantly British affair.[123]

One could hardly have chosen a worse piece of real estate to contest. Churchill doubted that better enemy entrenchments existed anywhere,[124] and Haig himself conceded in his dispatches that the German defenses were virtually "impregnable."[125] This did not, however, dissuade him from attacking them.

The offensive kicked off exactly as planned, beginning with a weeklong artillery bombardment at the end of June. The soldiers in the trenches had been assured that the sheer intensity of this barrage would suffice to decimate the barbed wire in No Man's Land and pulverize the German trenches, eliminating defenders and machine guns alike. There would be nothing for the infantry to do except to stroll over and occupy the enemy trenches.[126]

The British soldiery would have done better to consult General Haig's séance medium than to place their trust in this rosy prophecy. To be sure, says Hayes, German "parapets crumbled beneath the impact of the shells, cover hitherto thought bomb-proof was crushed and destroyed, and the garrisons of the enemy's works, sorely shattered in morale, were driven down into the deepest dugouts to seek shelter from the pitiless hail of projectiles."[127] But by this point in the war, the Germans were able to take refuge from such bombardment in underground labyrinths as deep as mineshafts, dug to a depth of

General Haig (second from left) makes a point with British minister of munitions David Lloyd George (right), while Marshal Joffre (standing between them) looks on, 12 September 1916. At left is French undersecretary for munitions, Albert Thomas (Wikimedia Commons).

30 feet below the surface where Allied shells could not penetrate—and they carried their machine guns with them.[128] Thus, the prolonged shelling did little more than announce the intended offensive to the very people who would best have been kept in suspense. And had the final crescendo not been enough to alert the defenders that the assault was imminent, they had only to peer through their dugout periscopes to espy the ubiquitous steel helmets jutting above the British parapets as the attackers positioned themselves to emerge from the trenches.[129]

When the British guns at last fell silent, the Germans emerged, weapons in hand. Consequently, the British infantrymen—bogged down with 60 pounds of accouterments, and marching line abreast as though they were on a parade ground[130]—walked, not to their objectives, but to their deaths in a hail of exploding shells and machine-gun fire. And there was yet another surprise in store: Those who made it as far as the enemy barbed wire were aghast to find it largely intact! Soldiers were shot dead in front of these impassable barriers by the score, having run the gauntlet of No Man's Land in vain.[131] One battalion that attacked on that day, the 6th Royal Warwicks, sustained 100 percent casualties with 316 wounded out of the 836 who went over the top, and the rest—520 soldiers—killed to a man.[132]

Despite these obstacles, many of the German first-line trenches were taken. Unfortunately, the objectives for the day also called for an assault on the second line, to be covered by artillery barrages delivered on a preset schedule. Needless to say, this schedule—which was based on the time it would take a man to *stroll* to his objective—did not jibe with the readiness of the troops to press ahead.[133] By nightfall, nearly half of the 120,000 British soldiers engaged had become casualties—the worst single day's carnage ever sustained by British arms.[134]

Nevertheless, the British High Command decided to continue the offensive—and two weeks later a daring tactic nearly produced a breakthrough. On the night of July 14, the British left their trenches along a limited front under cover of darkness. Guided by white tape laid by advance scouts, they proceeded en masse across No Man's Land to within a stone's throw of the enemy line. Then, after a brief but intense artillery bombardment at dawn, they sprang up and stormed the enemy trenches from close range, capturing them at a blow. Haig thought the moment had finally come to throw his cherished cavalry into the breach, but he was too slow in doing so, with the result that the horsemen merely made an exotic target for the German reserves who rushed forward to plug the gap. By the next evening, German counterattacks had erased the British gains.[135] The Somme Offensive dragged on until November, attaining a maximum penetration of seven miles.[136] Before it was over, a new weapon—the tank—had made its appearance, but it performed poorly, and did nothing to alter the outcome. From beginning to end, the campaign had been a dreadful miscarriage, destroying the finest part of the British Army without tangible benefit.

Meanwhile, in August, little Romania—wooed and cajoled by both sides since the outbreak of the war—finally cast her fortunes with the Allies. Unfortunately, her long deliberation had not imbued her with a propitious sense of timing. Had she made her decision in June, her army might have cooperated with Russia during the Brusilov

"Tankdrome" was a muster zone for tank squadrons on the Western Front, circa 1917 (© Everett Collection/Shutterstock).

offensive. But it was not until late August that she mobilized, and by this time Brusi-lov had been defeated.[137] Undeterred, the ill-equipped Romanians struck through the Carpathians toward Hungary, hoping to seize Transylvania. Hardly had they made this westward lunge, however, before they were forced to halt and divert all their reserves to the south to deal with an attack by Bulgaria. When this was followed by an Austro-German counterattack on the Carpathian front, the Romanian Army reeled into retreat, and scarcely stopped until they had reached the River Sereth, leaving most of their country and all of their oil and wheat in enemy hands. Bucharest, the capital, fell on December 6. Four months after entering the war, Romania was effectively out of it.

1917: Revolution in Russia, Mutiny in the French Army, Passchendaele

On November 21, 1916, Emperor Franz Josef, who had ruled Austria continuously since the Revolution of 1848, died at 86 years of age. His successor was his great-nephew, Karl I, who inherited an overextended army, a tottering economy and widespread civilian food shortages. Married to a French wife, Zita, he began to seek for a way out of the war through secret negotiations with the Allies. The talks proved unsuccessful.[138] In December, the British prime minister, Herbert Asquith, fell from power—a political casualty of the failed Somme Offensive. David Lloyd George succeeded him at the head of a coalition government. Known as the "People's David" for his championship of the "People's Budget" of 1909, which led to the constitutional showdown between the Commons and Lords, Lloyd George had already solved critical supply problems for the army as Minister of Munitions. He would now do the same for the home front—instituting a convoy system to protect vital shipping over the protests of the admiralty (which had argued that grouped shipping would be even more vulnerable to submarine attack), and introducing efficient food production and rationing programs that eliminated growing food queues and left "Britons ... better fed during the war than before or after."[139]

In Russia, changes of even greater moment were afoot. By staying at the front—though too far to the rear of the fighting to identify with the plight of the troops[140]—Tsar Nicholas II had transformed himself into the very symbol of Russian military futility. Even worse, his wife, Alexandra, had engulfed the regime in scandal. A mystic in her own right, Alexandra had developed a trance-like devotion to a dissolute monk, Gregory Rasputin, whom she believed capable of aiding her hemophiliac son during life-threatening bleeding crises. Rasputin was a notorious drinker and womanizer, and it was not long before rumors tied him sexually to the tsarina. The slander wasn't true, but the effect on the monarchy was ruinous, all the more so because the "mad monk" had parlayed his power over the tsarina into an overbearing influence at court—impeding the workings of a government that was already teetering on the brink of collapse. In December 1916, when the situation had already deteriorated beyond the point of redemption, a cadre of aristocrats led by a certain Prince Felix Yusupov lured Rasputin to a private party where they attempted to poison him with cyanide. Shocked to find him immune to its effects, they shot him several times with a pistol and then bludgeoned him repeatedly only to find that he was still alive. Despairing of success, they overpowered him and threw him into the River Neva before congratulating one another on their perseverance in a most difficult enterprise. Yet, had Rasputin been able to swim, they might have had to start over, for at autopsy the cause of death was found to be drowning.[141]

Rasputin's demise came too late. The Russian economy was in a state of ruin, and in February 1917, severe bread shortages led to a general strike in Petrograd (the new de-Germanized name for St. Petersburg). The government attempted to quell the uprising by ordering the army to fire on the street crowds. Instead, the soldiers gunned down their officers, transforming the strike into a revolution.[142] On March 11, the tsar attempted to dissolve the Duma (which had demanded greater powers in order to deal with the crisis). In response, the Duma declared itself a provisional government.

Advised by his closest confidantes that the situation was beyond remedy, Nicholas agreed to abdicate—doing so in the name of his son as well. At first, there was hope in the Allied camp that under more competent leadership Russia's military capacity might actually increase. By May, the new government had come to be dominated by a socialist lawyer and orator named Alexander Kerensky, whose domestic reforms were reasonably well received. Alas for the Allies, his enthusiasm for a renewed offensive was to prove rather less popular.

Nicholas II of Russia with the family (left to right): Olga, Maria, Nicholas II, Alexandra Fyodorovna, Anastasia, Alexei and Tatiana. Livadiya, Crimea, 1913. Portrait by the Levitsky Studio, Livadiya. Today the original photograph is held at the Hermitage Museum, St. Petersburg, Russia (Wikimedia Commons).

Despite these foreboding developments, Britain and France soon had cause for optimism, for in April, the United States Congress declared war on Germany. Relations between Germany and America had cooled considerably since January 31, 1917, when the former announced the resumption of unrestricted U-boat warfare in a bid to starve England out of the war. Matters did not reach the freezing point, however, until the end of February, when the British government intercepted and published a telegraph message sent by the German foreign office to the government of Mexico. This so-called "Zimmermann Telegram" invited the Mexicans to join Germany (and potentially Japan) in a war on the United States if the latter attempted to embroil herself in Europe. In the event of victory, Mexico was to receive her former territories in the American southwest—Texas, New Mexico and Arizona. While the United States pondered this shocking memorandum, the Germans began to sink U.S. merchant ships (March 16). This proved the last straw. On April 2, 1917, Woodrow Wilson asked Congress for a declaration of war against Germany. On April 6, his request was granted with enthusiasm.

The reservoir of manpower and resources that America could bring to the Allied cause was admittedly astounding, but mobilization would be slow, and the impact would not be immediate. In the meantime, the French and British High Commands had big plans of their own. Although the successful defense of Verdun was in truth the fruit of General Pétain's cautious strategy, all the laurels had gone to the brash tactician, General Robert Nivelle, whose tactical innovations had been instrumental in retaking ground captured by the Germans in that offensive. Claiming that he possessed "the formula" for victory, Nivelle was absolutely convinced that his new techniques could achieve a breakthrough on the Western Front.[143] His swaggering optimism soon infected the entire nation—catapulting him into the position of commander-in-chief in succession to Joffre.

Nivelle's plan for 1917 called for a massive offensive over a broad front utilizing the tactics he had employed at Verdun. Specifically, he proposed a strike across the once scenic *Chemin des Dames* ("Ladies Road") between Soisson and Rheims that would ensnare the Germans in an exposed salient, stretching northwards to Arras. After destroying the enemy's entrenchments, guns and barbed wire with a preliminary bombardment, the infantry would advance, cloaked by a "creeping barrage" of shellfire, falling first just beyond their own front lines and proceeding bound by bound toward the enemy.[144] Victory would come, in Nivelle's estimation, within forty-eight hours. Zero hour was set for April 16, 1917.

Unfortunately, by that date the target of Nivelle's attack had ceased to exist. Seeing the French mass against them on a thirty-mile front, the Germans decided to abandon the exposed salient in February—carrying out a strategic retreat to the heavily-entrenched Hindenburg Line some twenty miles to the rear. As they withdrew, they destroyed roads, razed buildings, toppled trees, set booby traps and fouled wells.[145] By early April, they were fully established on the new line, housed in defensive works extending to a depth of ten miles in some areas, protected in front by a buffer zone of charred earth and ruins.

The utter disruption of his entire strategy seems not to have fazed Nivelle. His wager was one of tactics not strategy, and if the former wrought the devastation anticipated of it, the latter might take care of itself. Besides, he could still trap the Germans, even on the Hindenburg Line, if he could only breach the *Chemin des Dames*.

Unfortunately, he could not—for the Germans were poised to receive his attack with a novel tactical deployment of their own known as "defense in depth." Under the new alignment, the front trenches were only lightly defended. Behind them, in the broken, ascending terrain, were a series of machine gun emplacements blessed with an excellent line of sight. Finally, well to the rear and out of reach of the Allied artillery, were the main German reserves, standing at the ready to counterattack as soon as the French had committed themselves.[146]

Any residual faith in Nivelle's scheme ought to have been nullified on April 6, when a nocturnal raid by the Germans resulted in the capture of a French officer bearing detailed plans for the offensive. Nivelle was duly informed of the catastrophe but remained supremely confident.[147] Ignoring the fact that, since January, the Germans had increased the number of divisions in the targeted sector from a paltry nine to a robust forty,[148] Nivelle cited the example of Arras, where a diversionary British attack on April 9 utilized his new tactical procedures to good effect. Although the British attack bogged down after the first day, it was all the proof Nivelle needed. On April 16, he raised the curtain on the main show.

Sir Edward Spears, an observer of the opening assault, later wrote that two minutes prior to zero hour, "a sudden great hush fell over the battlefield … it gave the impression of Death, a finger to his lips."[149] From the first, nothing went as planned. The lengthy French bombardment played to a near-empty house, falling on the lightly manned zones up front.[150] Then, the creeping barrage outpaced the attacking infantry, leaving the German machine gun crews time to recover and get in place.[151] The affair was an unmitigated disaster. The French were scarcely out of their trenches before being pinned down. For ten days Nivelle pressed the attack, even though its futility had been exposed from the opening hour. In the end, his army suffered an estimated 200,000 casualties out of 700,000 men engaged.[152]

Even with failure staring him in the face, Nivelle refused to reconsider the offensive. So his army reconsidered for him. The first mutinies came on April 29. Men moving up to the front began bleating like sheep.[153] Entire regiments refused to advance, and soldiers rotated to the rear for rest ignored the call to return. Some announced their willingness to take up their positions and defend their country, but only if the useless attacks against the enemy's entrenched positions came to a halt.[154] To cope with the situation, the Army High Command resorted to severe measures. Officially just forty-nine mutineers were executed before order was restored, but there seem to have been a number of unofficial executions as well, with many of the victims being chosen by lot. (Afterwards, apologists for the French Army noted that the "lot method" had been a venerable tradition in France dating to Roman times.) How far things actually went we will never know, but a haunting (albeit unsubstantiated) rumor speaks of mutineers being marched to remote areas of the front where their own artillery opened fire on them, tearing them to pieces.[155]

Blaming everyone but himself, Nivelle was removed on May 15 in favor of Philippe Pétain who had been his superior at Verdun, and who had been against the offensive from the first. Pétain visited soldiers at the front, seeing to their comfort, and promising them that no further offensives would be undertaken until the Americans and the new tanks could be brought to bear.[156] Had the Germans known about the mutiny, they might have attempted to pierce the French line. But the French Army maintained the episode in such secrecy that even the British did not know. (Pétain eventually informed Sir Douglas Haig, the British commander-in-chief, who was counting on French support for a new offensive in Flanders, but the British prime minister, David Lloyd George, remained in the dark until June.[157])

The disaster threw the French government into turmoil and brought Georges Clemenceau to the prime minister's post where he would remain for the duration of the war. In a career spanning four decades, Clemenceau had been a perennial dissenter, earning the moniker "the Tiger" for his ceaseless diatribes against the policies of the Third Republic.[158] Though seventy-six years old at his accession, Clemenceau showed that he had lost none of his former energy, urging the nation to "total war," and each citizen "to cleave to the soldier, to live, to suffer to fight with him."[159]

With his allies dropping like flies and the Americans still an ocean distant, Sir Douglas Haig decided he would have to win the war on his own. His plan was to pierce the German line in Belgium, and then to press on to the Channel coast to seize Germany's U-boat bases. Building upon his time-honored tactic of hurling men against machine guns, Haig apparently hoped to confuse the Germans by attacking over ground that would have been difficult to negotiate even if the enemy had not been there to defend it: the oozing mud-fields of Flanders.

Despite the odds, Haig's push began on a singularly positive note with the capture of Messines Ridge, commanding the southern flank of the Ypres salient (June 7). British engineers had tunneled beneath it and blown up the German defenses with 19 mines— their simultaneous detonation being heard by Mr. Lloyd George in distant London.[160] The Ypres salient had long been a suicidal precinct. Vulnerable to enfilading fire, its British defenders had suffered roughly 7,000 casualties per week even in "quiet" periods.[161] Ultimately, they had either to seize the high ground or withdraw, and Haig was hardly the type to do the latter. The mining operation had been the idea of Second Army commander, Sir Herbert Plumer, and had taken the better part of two years to complete. To get beneath the boggy subsoil, and to avoid detection by German countermining parties—an unpleasant occurrence that typically degenerated into underground butchery—the tunnels had been dug at the extraordinary depth of 80 to 120 feet.[162] In the end, all but one mine escaped detection. Their explosion was devastating. Countless Germans were blown to smithereens. Others were killed by the shock wave—their corpses being found in placid poses, as though still alive, when British infantry occupied the position.[163]

The Messines stroke, constituting one of the few instances in the war where munitions were expended in preference to lives, went off brilliantly.[164] But it was nothing a new dose of stupidity couldn't fix. As prelude to the Third Battle of Ypres, a ten-day bombardment destroyed the drainage system of the intended battlefield, turning it into something very like breakfast porridge.[165] Torrential downpours served to exacerbate the situation. Men, struggling forward in the mud, fully exhausted themselves just getting into position for the assault. Pack animals laden with munitions lost their footing on the plank-board roads and vanished—swallowed whole into the morass.[166]

The condition of the ground notwithstanding, British infantry were ordered forward in a series of attacks beginning on July 31. In a rain-drenched campaign lasting four months, soldiers plodded through the muck under fire, often unable to fire back because their rifles were jammed with mud.[167] Advancing soldiers took turns pulling each other out of the mire or were machine-gunned while transfixed in it.[168] The wounded took refuge in shell holes with water deep enough for swimming, and then drowned as the rains brought the level over their heads.[169] Corpses sucked beneath the slime in one attack were disgorged by shellfire in the next,[170] while tanks, sent into a situation for which they were entirely unsuited, gurgled to a stall, leaving their occupants with the nightmarish choice of remaining inside as sitting ducks for the German artillery, or of climbing out in the face of machine-gun fire.[171]

None of Haig's strategic objectives were met, but like Nivelle before him, he refused to call off the offensive. The final pushes, in still more rain, were the most horrible, coming to an end at last with the early November capture of the town of Passchendaele. Taken on a tour of the battlefield at the end of the offensive, Lieutenant General Sir Launcelot Kiggell broke down and wept—lamenting that men had been sent to fight on such ground. He was duly informed that he had not yet seen the worst of it.[172] The grim campaign, netting a few miles of barren, mud-soaked real estate, nearly broke the spirit of the British Army, which had suffered the loss of some 300,000 men as compared to roughly 200,000 Germans.[173]

Disastrous as the British and French attacks were, Russia's 1917 effort fared even worse. In July, the Kerensky government embarked on Russia's last offensive of the war. Led by General Brusilov, the "Kerensky Offensive" achieved an initial breakthrough along a forty-mile front in Galicia. But even as the army advanced, Brusilov's

Soldiers of an Australian 4th Division field artillery brigade on a duckboard track passing through Chateau Wood, near Hooge in the Ypres salient, 29 October 1917. The leading soldier is Gunner James Fulton and the second soldier is Lieutenant Anthony Devine. The men belong to a battery of the 10th Field Artillery Brigade. Australian War Memorial collection number E01220. Photograph by Frank Hurley (Wikimedia Commons).

ill-equipped soldiers began to desert, and when the Germans counterattacked, the trend became universal. Officers attempting to call their men back to their duty were murdered in cold blood.

Behind the lines, the radical wing of the Russian Socialist Party—known as the Bolsheviks—sought to capitalize on the evolving chaos. Their leader, Lenin, had been in exile in Zurich for years, but had returned to Petrograd in April, crossing German territory in a sealed train ("like a plague bacillus," says Churchill)[174] with the full complicity of Ludendorff who was counting on him to wreak havoc once he arrived. Adopting the popular slogan "Peace, land and bread," Lenin denounced the war policy of the Provisional Government, challenging its very right to rule with the cry, "All power to the Soviets!"—i.e., the radical "councils" of workers, soldiers and peasants that were everywhere springing into existence. The threat of arrest briefly drove the Bolshevik leader back into exile—this time to Finland. But in September, the Provisional Government fairly imploded. Seeing anarchy all around him, Kerensky secretly plotted with the army's new commander-in-chief, Lavr Kornilov, to restore order by force. As the scheme matured, however, Kerensky became convinced that Kornilov meant to seize power for himself, and ordered him to relinquish his command.[175] Whether or not Kornilov had actually been planning a coup, he now tried to carry one out, only to find that his soldiers had come under the sway of Bolshevik agitators and would not heed his orders.

Kerensky did not profit by this outcome, for the so-called "Kornilov Affair" had revealed the incapacity of the provisional regime. The door was now open to the Bolsheviks, and on November 7, 1917, the conspiratorial little party staged its own coup—seizing control of Petrograd's communication and transportation systems. Kerensky promptly fled—the rest of his government withdrawing to the Winter Palace, which was stormed by "Red Guards" (Bolshevik militia) and mutinous sailors from the naval base at Kronstadt later that night. At the war ministry, a lone loyalist officer had secretly taken refuge in the attic, telegraphing pleas for help throughout the day. Learning that the Winter Palace had fallen, he emerged from his sanctuary, walked downstairs with an air of nonchalance and left the building before anyone became the least suspicious of what he had been up to.[176]

The "October Revolution" (the Russian calendar was two weeks behind the rest of Europe) gave power to the Bolsheviks, but the survival of the new regime was by no means assured. Within a month, tsarist officers had raised counterrevolutionary armies in the provinces, and Finland and the Ukraine had rejected the revolutionary takeover. (Both would declare their independence in the coming months.) Nevertheless, Lenin controlled Petrograd. In December, when elections to a Constituent Assembly gave the Bolsheviks only 168 out of 707 seats, he simply dissolved it. In the meantime, he sought to end the war.

The mayhem in Russia left the Central Powers free to concentrate their efforts on other fronts. On October 24, 1917, a combined Austro-German force broke clean through the Italian Front at Caporetto, tearing a hole fifteen miles wide in the Isonzo Line. The Italians fell back in confused retreat. Nearly 300,000 were captured—many cheering the arrival of their captors whom they treated as deliverers from the agony of trench warfare. Desertion became rife. Luigi Cadorna, commanding the Italian forces, attempted to regroup behind the Tagliamento River, but the advancing enemy quickly breached this barrier, forcing him to fall back to the more formidable Piave. Here the line held while the shattered army was pieced back together.

For the Allies, the last months of 1917 were the bleakest of the war. The French and British offensives had ended in catastrophe leaving both armies demoralized. The Italians had been pushed to the brink of collapse and the Russians over it.[177] Desperate for good news from any quarter, they received a small morsel on November 20, when, at Cambrai, tanks were used in a massed attack over suitable ground for the first time in the war.

The tank had been conceived independently by Winston Churchill and Colonel E.D. Swinton in 1915 as the key to breaking the stalemate on the Western Front.[178] Few in the army took the notion seriously, so Churchill used his position at the Admiralty to nurture the project—using public monies, but keeping the matter secret from the rest of the government, whom he knew to be hostile.[179] Designed as a motorized, armored tractor capable of breaching barbed-wire, crossing trench-works, and neutralizing enemy machine-guns while infantry was brought up in support (and Churchill proposed protecting the infantry with hand-held, bullet-proof shields, though this idea was never adopted[180]), the tank had been used in too small numbers on the Somme and on impossible ground at Passchendaele. Finally, at Cambrai, the British High Command consented to using it in the manner for which it had been intended—in a mass strike on a limited front of solid terrain. Although the gains of the battle itself were quickly lost to German counterattacks, and many of the tanks broke down, the new weapon had finally demonstrated its potential. The key to unlocking the stalemate on the Western Front had at last been found.

Still it was clear to both sides that they were now involved in a footrace. The Allies were reeling, and the Americans had not yet arrived in force. If the Germans could deliver the deathblow quickly, they could win the war before the Americans had time to tip the balance.

1918: *The Ludendorff Offensive, Allied Victory*

On October 31, 1917, Australian troops commanded by General Sir Edmund Allenby staged a cavalry charge that swept away the Turkish lines guarding Beersheba in Palestine. On November 2, the British Foreign Secretary, Arthur Balfour, issued the famous "Balfour Declaration," pledging British support for "the establishment in Palestine of a National Home for the Jewish people." Of the myriad considerations leading to this declaration, not the least were strategic—for Britain hoped that its pledge might rally the Jews of Russia to press for a continuation of the war,[181] while also providing Britain with an ally in the environs of the Suez Canal once victory was attained. But after so much carnage on the Western Front in the preceding year, the moral factor was perhaps transcendent—for the Balfour Declaration gave Britain an opportunity to bring the self-determination of peoples to the fore in the midst of the fight. As Barbara Tuchman has put it, "The Balfour Declaration, sounding over the roar of the guns, seemed like a tocsin of peace and of a better world," in effect, terminating "the oldest of national tragedies."[182] On December 9, 1917, General Allenby learned that the Turks had evacuated their troops from Jerusalem. He made his own entry into the city two days later.

On January 8, 1918, Woodrow Wilson issued his celebrated "Fourteen Points," outlining the requisite terms for a just peace at the end of the war. Included among them were an end to secret treaties, the evacuation of occupied territories, the self-determination of peoples, freedom of the seas, equality of trade conditions for all nations and "the formation of a general association of nations ... for the purpose of affording mutual guarantees of political independence and territorial integrity to great and small states alike."

By this time, the notion that the Jews of Russia could keep that nation in the fight on the basis of the Balfour Declaration had been exposed as a chimera. On November 8, 1917, Nikolai Lenin issued a "Decree of Peace"—the text of which he read aloud to a cheering throng in Petrograd.[183] On November 27, Leon Trotsky, now Russia's "commissar of foreign affairs," published the texts of the various secret treaties the tsarist regime had signed with its allies during the course of the war delineating a division of the spoils in case of victory.[184] The effect, as Trotsky had intended, was to create a scandal for the other signatories (Britain, France and Italy), thereby undermining popular support for the war (hence, Wilson's admonition against secret treaties in his Fourteen Points). Then on December 15, 1917, the Bolshevik government signed a temporary truce with Germany and entered into formal peace talks at Brest-Litovsk.

Initially, the negotiations went smoothly. The phrase "peace without annexations" crept into the German vocabulary—surely a positive sign. But when the two sides got down to brass tacks, the Russians found that Germany intended to keep all territories she had occupied since the outbreak of hostilities—i.e., Latvia, Lithuania and most of Poland—arguing that they could scarcely say "no" if the involved populaces espoused a desire for incorporation into the German empire (as was likely with Russian Bolshevism standing as the sole alternative). Shortly after articulating this principle, Germany and Austria granted recognition to the Ukraine, which had declared for independence.[185] In a fit of pique, Trotsky, heading the Russian delegation, announced that if the Germans would not make an honorable peace, then Russia would neither treat with them nor fight. In response to this empty threat, the Germans resumed their offensive, meeting essentially no resistance (February 17, 1918). By month's end they had driven beyond Minsk in the north and Kiev in the south—an advance of hundreds of miles. Territory was taken so easily that General Max Hoffmann called the campaign "comical."[186]

Despite fierce argumentation, Lenin now insisted on capitulation in order to obtain "breathing space" for the revolution—assuring his obstinate colleagues that the combatants would ultimately destroy one another, "and we shall then start a second socialist revolution on a world scale."[187] By the terms of the Treaty of Brest-Litovsk, signed on March 3, 1918, huge amounts of territory, containing 65 million people and vast resources—including everything that the Germans had seized in the new offensive—passed into German hands. More importantly, forty-four German divisions were freed up for transfer to the Western Front. Consequently, on March 21, 1918, the Germans were able to launch their largest Western offensive of the war—and their first on that front since Verdun. Their strategic plan was to overwhelm the Allies in France before American soldiers arrived in sufficient numbers to alter the scales. The first German thrust was delivered near St. Quentin at the easternmost extent of the Somme River. The site, roughly midway along the front between Verdun and Ypres, was chosen because it was there that the British line ended and the French line began. Ludendorff planned to hew them in twain, and then to harry the British Army all the way to the Belgian coast where it would be annihilated.[188]

Despite their new preponderance in numbers, the Germans did not plan to achieve their goals sheerly by mass effect. New tactics were imported from the mobile warfare of the Eastern Front. Preliminary shelling was carried out by "hurricane bombardment"—lasting hours rather than days—sufficient in intensity to throw the Allied defenders into disorder, but affording them no time to alter their dispositions or summon reserves before the enemy was upon them. In addition to high explosives, the Germans fired shells containing poison gas—tear gas at first, to provoke the victimized soldiery to remove their masks, followed by phosgene gas to asphyxiate them.[189] The bombardment, moreover, was directed primarily against the Allied artillery, thereby allowing the German attackers to get into position without being harassed by return fire.[190] Directly this was accomplished, small squads of "storm troops" would advance, under cover of a creeping barrage, to probe for weak points in the Allied line. Once a vulnerable spot had been identified, they would force a breach, and reserve troops would pour in after them. Strongly held positions were simply to be sidestepped. It would be easy enough to eliminate them after the initial penetrations had been exploited.[191]

Helped by a covering fog, the German attacks both north and south of St. Quentin achieved near total surprise (March 21). But Ludendorff now committed a mortal blunder. He had meant for the northern strike against Arras to be decisive. Instead, it was the southern strike which sent the Allies reeling and opened a breach, while the northern blow hammered itself to a stop against stronger defenses on less passable terrain. Convinced that a breakthrough in the north was essential, Ludendorff persisted in fruitless attempts to force the British out of Arras for a week while prohibiting his left wing from pouring through the opening it had forged.[192] When he finally realized his error and began funneling troops to the south, the opportunity had passed. After an advance of forty miles, the drive petered to a halt outside Amiens, partly because of mounting Allied resistance, and partly because the Germans stopped to loot. Having been deprived of luxuries for as long as they could remember, the attackers reacted with a mixture of awe and disbelief as they overran the rich supply depots in the Allied rear. They had been told that the U-boat campaign was starving the Allies into submission. Now, by virtue of their lightning advance, they were undeceived. According to an eyewitness, German soldiers donned surplus British boots, marveled at waterproof raincoats (which their own army lacked), and staggered about drunk on wine. Some, indeed, were still inebriated when ordered back into battle the next day.[193]

Had the Germans been able to capture Amiens—a critical transport and communications center—they might have driven an impenetrable wedge between the armies of Britain and France.[194] As it was, they had been able to bring forward three newly forged, long-range artillery pieces—the so-called "Paris Guns"—which proceeded to shell the French capital from a distance of seventy-four miles, inflicting more than 250 casualties.[195] The shock forced the Allies to overhaul their command structure. To this point in the war, their armies had practiced only a loose cooperation. Realizing that they must unify their actions, they promoted General Ferdinand Foch to the newly created post of "Allied commander-in-chief."

Meanwhile, Ludendorff delivered his next blow. It fell in Flanders where the British line ended and the Portuguese line began (April 9). The Portuguese fled as fast as their legs could carry them. Stampeding into a battalion of bicycle-mounted British infantry, they stole the bikes in order to enhance the nimbleness of their desertion.[196] The British fell back, abandoning Passchendaele and Messines. But the line held, so Ludendorff switched the theater of action once more—this time to the forty-mile front of the *Chemin des Dames*, the scene of General Nivelle's ill-fated 1917 offensive. Again the Germans achieved surprise. Despite the decision to adopt a German-style "defense-in-depth" everywhere else on the front, the French commander at the *Chemin des Dames* had crammed every last man into the frontline trenches. The German artillery made mincemeat of them.[197] Those who survived took to their heels. Three days later, they were still on the run—yelling to the American troops coming up to relieve them that the war was lost.[198] In four days (May 27–31) the Germans advanced forty miles, reaching the Marne for the first time since 1914. Nonetheless, they had yet to achieve a clean breakthrough, the newest attack bogging down at Chateau-Thierry where American troops stemmed the tide. For the next three weeks, German infantry duked it out with United States Marines in the nearby Belleau Wood. When it was over on June 25, the Germans had been driven out. It was the most significant contribution by American forces to that point in the war. The Germans made two last pushes—on June 9 near Compiègne and on July 15 at Rheims. The latter attack brought them across the Marne, but it achieved nothing of strategic importance. The Allied line—now organized as a true "defense-in-depth"[199]—remained intact. Paris was still free. And there were now more than a million American troops on the Western Front.[200]

The first Allied counterblow came just three days later. On July 18, French and American troops surprised the entrenched Germans between the Marne and Aisne rivers. With the help of 330 Renault tanks, the French advanced five kilometers on a forty-five-kilometer front, driving the Germans back across the Marne.[201] The German sojourn on the far bank of that river had lasted but seventy-two hours.[202]

In preparation for the next blow, the Allies spirited 2000 artillery pieces and over 400 tanks into the region around Amiens—the Royal Air Force masking the din of the deployment by creating a "noise barrage" above the German lines.[203] On August 8, the tanks, supported by infantry, emerged from a covering fog to strike terror into the enemy. Confronted by a weapon that moved forward relentlessly despite machine gun fire, some Germans threw down their rifles and fled in panic, while others surrendered *en masse* to single tanks.[204] Although the Allied attack began to stall by the second day with a quarter of the behemoths destroyed and many others damaged,[205] German morale had suffered a devastating blow. Reserves earmarked for offensives elsewhere had to be rushed to the scene to halt the Allied drive. Ludendorff summed up the catastrophe in a phrase, calling August 8 "the black day of the German army."

Having long dismissed the utility of the tank, Ludendorff at last perceived its import. At one and the same moment, he lost all hope for winning the war. At a meeting of the High Command on August 11, he told the Kaiser that military victory was no longer feasible, and that a negotiated settlement was the only alternative.[206]

But peace was not to be had. With the Allied attack bogging down in front of Amiens, Foch unloosed the Americans in their first independent action—a pincer drive into the St. Mihiel salient south of Verdun. Alert to the danger, the Germans were already withdrawing when the attack came. Plowing through their rearguard, the Americans (commanded by such future luminaries as Brigadier-General Douglas MacArthur, Colonel George C. Marshall, and tank commander, Lieutenant-Colonel George S. Patton) flattened out the salient and took more than 15,000 prisoners (September 1918). On the heels of this action, the French and Americans launched a joint attack between the Argonne Forest and the River Meuse, just west of Verdun. Alas, the attack here met with stiff resistance, and although slow progress was made throughout the course of October, the Americans paid in blood for every mile gained. It was in the midst of this offensive that an American battalion was mistakenly ordered to press forward into the dense Argonne woodlands even though its supporting forces had been repulsed on either flank. Cut off for nearly a week, the "Lost Battalion" was, in turn, surrounded by the Germans and pounded by the Allies' own errant artillery fire. Nevertheless, it clung tenaciously to its exposed position. When finally relieved, less than 200 men out of an initial force of 550 were still alive.[207] Overall, the Americans suffered more than 100,000 casualties in the Argonne.

Given an opportunity to fight, American soldiers had acquitted themselves admirably. But for the many thousands of black soldiers who had crossed the Atlantic as part of the American Expeditionary Force, the opportunity to fight was denied owing to nothing more than the color of their skin. Undeterred by this blatant prejudice (which scarcely jibed with the idealism of Wilson's Fourteen Points), many black units forged their own path to the front—serving alongside the French who happily embraced them.[208] The only soldiers Marshal Foch found contemptible were the Germans—and he continued to pound away at *them* relentlessly. Soon after the Argonne offensive got underway on the German left, he had Haig throw British, Belgian and French forces against their right in Flanders (September 28). With the Germans tied down on both flanks, Foch delivered his *coup de grâce*: On October 8, Anglo-French forces launched an attack that smashed clean through the center of the Hindenburg line between Cambrai and St. Quentin.[209] By October 16, the Germans had been wrenched from the Belgian coast as well. The enemy was in full retreat!

Germany's allies were likewise crumbling. In late September, French and Serbian forces, striking out of Salonika, shattered the Bulgarian army. The Bulgarians acknowledged defeat, and were granted an armistice on September 29. King Ferdinand sealed the agreement by abdicating in favor of his son, Boris, but the latter was chased from the throne within a month.[210] The Turks also suffered decisive setbacks. After seizing Jerusalem, General Allenby struck northwards to Megiddo in September, ensnaring 70,000 Turks. In this campaign, the 38th through 42nd battalions of the Royal Fusiliers—composed of Jewish volunteers and remembered collectively as the "Jewish Legion"—fought under Allenby. Arabs commanded by Emir Faisal and T.E. Lawrence—a.k.a. "Lawrence of Arabia"—likewise participated, entering Damascus in early October. On October 31, the Ottomans acceded to an armistice, allowing Allied occupation of strategic points and opening the Straits to Allied naval vessels.

As these events unfolded, Austria-Hungary likewise suffered catastrophe. In June, her demoralized army had been repulsed in an effort to cross the Piave. The soldiers called it the "bread offensive," because they did not even possess adequate rations to sustain themselves.[211] On October 27, the Italians counterattacked, piercing the front at Vittorio Veneto. The setback was decisive. Austria-Hungary capitulated on November 4, ceding *Italia Irredenta* to Italy, surrendering her major armaments, and granting passage to Allied troops. (Germans stationed within Hapsburg territory were given fifteen days to get out.) Unable to bear the weight of this defeat, the Austrian empire collapsed. Czechoslovakia and Hungary declared independence, and in Austria proper, revolution drove the last Hapsburg emperor from his throne.

Amid these crises, the overtaxed Ludendorff became psychologically unhinged, denying his own culpability for Germany's predicament and shouting accusations at members of his staff as the fancy took him (September 28, 1918). As his tirade reached a crescendo, he suddenly fell silent, crumpled to the floor and frothed at the mouth.[212] On reviving, he told the Kaiser that peace was a necessity. He then launched his last successful campaign of the war—convincing the nation that all fault lay with the politicians. This charade was to have appalling repercussions—giving rise to the anti–Semitic "stab in the back" slur that was seized upon later by the Nazis.[213]

On October 26, Ludendorff was sacked. On October 29, the German navy was ordered out of Kiel to fight the British for the honor of Germany. Rather than obey this senseless order, the sailors mutinied. Their action set off a revolution that would engulf all Germany in the coming week. Bavaria's King Ludwig III fled amidst the unrest, and Bavaria became a republic. On November 9, the kaiser himself abdicated, taking refuge in Holland, and when his sons abjured the throne, the whole of Germany became a republic.

Though falling back in all sectors, the German Army was still fighting and, if forced to do so, might bitterly contest an Allied advance into their homeland. Her citizenry had not yet had to face the reality of total defeat as would occur when foreign troops marched into their cities and towns. Alsace and Lorraine, moreover, remained in German hands, and to win them on the battlefield, the Allies would have to launch new offensives stretching into 1919.[214]

On the other hand, German military defeat was certain and her new leadership, facing the specter of social revolution at home, was desperate for peace. On November 8, 1918, a German armistice delegation met with Marshal Foch in his railway car in Compiègne Forest. Foch did not negotiate, but rather dictated terms. Alsace and Lorraine were to revert immediately to France; Germany was to surrender the bulk of her armaments and withdraw from all occupied territories (including those she had taken from the Russians at Brest-Litovsk); and the Rhineland (i.e., German territory on the west bank of the Rhine) was to be placed under Allied military occupation pending fulfillment of final treaty obligations.[215]

In sum, as Hew Strachan has noted, Foch sought, as the price of a ceasefire, to obtain on the spot what would have taken months to wrest from Germany by force of arms.[216] Haig, who had been among the first of the Allied commanders to believe that victory could be attained in 1918,[217] but whose supply lines were now overstretched, ardently supported the armistice. Charles Mangin, Foch's subordinate, argued vehemently against it, stating (presciently) that if the Allies did not win their gains on the battlefield and occupy Germany, the Germans would never admit to themselves that they had truly been defeated. Another war would thus become inevitable.[218] Mangin was overruled. The terms of the armistice being accepted by the despondent German delegation, Foch decreed that the fighting should cease at 11 a.m. on November 11, 1918. (Alas, in the trenches, some soldiers on both sides kept shooting—and killing—until the final second.[219]) News of the armistice was greeted with frenzied celebration in the Allied capitals. In London, the delirious celebrants created so much disorder that, after three days, the bobbies had to be called in.[220] Even David Lloyd George was a little undignified, running about on Downing Street shouting joyously that the war was to end at 11 o'clock.[221]

The Peace of Paris

Delegations from the victorious nations met in Paris in January 1919 to work out details of the peace. The defeated nations were not invited to attend. They would be notified when the terms had been decided and the treaties were ready for signature. Although several plenary sessions were held, attended by all thirty-two invited delegations, the cacophony of competing interests mandated that the chief decision-making be undertaken by the so-called "Big Four"—Woodrow Wilson of the United States, Georges Clemenceau of France, David Lloyd George of Great Britain and Vittorio Orlando of Italy.

Wilson had reached Paris in December 1918, fully intending to orchestrate a peace based on his now famous "Fourteen Points."[222] The twin pillars of his program were the "self-determination" of peoples (which was to "make the world safe for democracy") and the League of Nations (which, by arbitrating future conflicts, was to make World War I "the war to end all wars"). Cheering throngs greeted Wilson everywhere he went, convincing him that "the people" supported his idealistic program.[223] Tellingly, however, the midterm elections of the preceding month in his own United States had delivered a majority to the opposing Republican Party.

Representing France was the seventy-seven-year-old premier, Georges Clemenceau. Old enough to have served as a foreign correspondent during the American Civil War,[224] the "Tiger" harbored bitter memories of France's humiliation in the Franco-Prussian War of 1870 and saw the victory of 1918 as the chance to obtain retribution at last. To him Wilson's idealistic rhetoric seemed like the banter of a German sympathizer.[225] He complained that the American president spoke like Jesus Christ, behaved like Lloyd George, and outdid the Lord by issuing fourteen points rather than ten.[226] Nor did Clemenceau lack support. The cheering Parisian throngs whom Wilson had assumed were on his side were aligned to a greater degree with their own premier—as was reflected in the composition of the postwar Chamber of Deputies, which included enough wounded war veterans to obtain the moniker "the one-legged chamber."[227]

Apart from revenge, Clemenceau's chief concern was to secure France against renewed German aggression. He was acutely aware that in spite of the Allied victory, France had emerged from the war in a strategically compromised condition, for she had lost her Russian ally. Germany was no longer threatened by a major power on her eastern frontier and in a future conflict could concentrate her entire might against France.[228] Germany, moreover, had a significantly larger population, and her industrial base had not been destroyed in the fighting, as the mining and manufacturing centers of northern France had been.[229] The answer, in Clemenceau's view, was to push the German frontier back to the Rhine, divesting her of the Rhineland (which would become an independent buffer state under French protection) and the coal-producing Saar Basin (which would be ceded outright to France). He was opposed in these designs, however, by Wilson and Lloyd George who believed the permanent separation of ethnically German territories from Germany would create "an Alsace-Lorraine in reverse."[230]

That said, the British view towards defeated Germany was hardly less vindictive than the French. In December 1918, David Lloyd George's coalition government had won reelection by a landslide on the campaign slogans "Hang the Kaiser" and "Make Germany Pay."[231] His constituents were now counting on the British prime minister to make good his exaggerations. In the phrasing of Britain's First Lord of the Admiralty, Eric Geddes, Lloyd George was to put the screws to Germany "until the pips squeaked."[232] More pragmatic than many of his supporters, Lloyd George understood that for her own economic well-being Britain must reestablish world—and, more especially, German—markets for her exports. But when he exhibited a tendency towards leniency on this basis he received a concerned telegram from 370 MPs reminding him of his campaign promises.[233] The harsh treaty terms that he was now to play a role in fashioning would ever remain the object of his regret—his subsequent efforts to amend them gaining him repute as the earliest of Germany's "appeasers."[234]

Of the Big Four, Vittorio Orlando was the least influential—in no small measure because he was the only one who was not fluent in English, the language in which the discussions were held. By the secret "Treaty of London" (1915), which had lured Italy into the war on the Allied side, Trentino, Trieste and portions of the Istrian and Dalmatian coastlines had been promised to Italy as spoils of war. Orlando was now intent on seeing the London terms fulfilled. But he also sought something else. Until World War I, Austria-Hungary had been Italy's great rival for Adriatic hegemony. The defeat of the Hapsburgs had driven them from the Adriatic coastline, but had raised up in their stead a potentially powerful "Kingdom of the Serbs, Croats and Slovenes" (subsequently to be known as Yugoslavia). On the coast of Istria lay the prized port of Fiume—the possession of which might allow Yugoslavia to seize the mantle of Austria-Hungary's lost Adriatic influence. After so much sacrifice, Italy would brook no such rival. Therefore she must have Fiume for herself.[235]

Alas, it had not been promised to her, and as many times as Orlando demanded the strategic seaport, Wilson refused. The first of his Fourteen Points had called for "open covenants … openly arrived at," and the president could scarcely bear having to honor the existing terms of a "secret" treaty, never mind adding to them. Even as it stood, the Treaty of London violated the principle of self-determination—placing hundreds of thousands of Germans and Slavs under Italian rule in the annexed territories. While the port of Fiume had an Italian majority, the surrounding district was predominantly Slav.[236] In the end, Wilson appealed directly to the Italian people, imploring them to disavow Orlando's Fiume claim. The Italian leader promptly stormed out of the proceedings—leaving the remainder of the terms to be hammered out by what were now the "Big Three."

For Clemenceau, Lloyd George and Wilson, the fate of Germany—economically and territorially—loomed as the key point of contention. Sixty-five million soldiers had been mobilized worldwide during the course of the war. Of these, an estimated 1 in 5 had been killed and another 1 in 3 wounded. The overall economic cost was reckoned at $337 billion, ranging from $5 million per hour early in the war to $10 million per hour in the final year.[237] Greatly in debt to the United States, France maintained that the entire cost of the war should be borne by Germany. Lloyd George's chief economic advisor, John Maynard Keynes, regarded this notion as absurd, estimating that Germany might muster 3 percent of this total at most.[238] Wilson—who was adamant that his Allies honor their wartime debts to the United States—wanted to set reparations at a level commensurate with Germany's ability to pay, so that on receiving said payments France and Great Britain could meet their own debt obligations to Washington.[239] Consequently, a compromise formula, devised by the American delegate, John Foster Dulles, obliged Germany to pay the entire cost of the war in the case of Belgium (whose neutrality it had so wantonly violated), but in all other cases to pay only the cost of "civilian" damages, while bearing "moral" (but not "economic") responsibility for the rest. Fulfilled to the letter, this proposal would have afforded Great Britain very little in the way of reparations since her territory had not been invaded. Lloyd George, therefore, lobbied successfully for the inclusion of merchant shipping losses as well as veterans' and survivors' pensions.[240]

When the German delegation was finally summoned to Trianon Palace on May 7, 1919, to receive the final peace terms, they expected a treaty based on Woodrow Wilson's Fourteen Points.[241] They got one more closely resembling their own Treaty of Brest-Litovsk. When they had taken their seats, Georges Clemenceau stood to address them, saying, "You have asked for peace. We are ready to give you peace."[242] Discerning from the opening remarks that Germany was to bear full responsibility for the war, Count Ulrich von Brockdorff-Rantzau, chief of the German delegation, issued a petulant and long-winded protest, the chief effect of which was to help David Lloyd George appreciate why French people so exquisitely despise Germans.[243] Clemenceau's sole reaction was to comment on Brockdorff-Rantzau's rudeness in not having the courtesy to stand up while speaking.[244]

Following this inauspicious start, the German delegation was given three weeks to examine the text of the treaty. There would be no oral argument. Any grievances must be tendered in writing. On May 29, the Germans submitted their objections in detail. After due consideration, the Allies offered some minor revisions on June 16, allowing five days for Germany's final reply. After four days had elapsed, they instructed Marshall Foch to invade Germany if no answer was received within the ensuing 72 hours. Despite mass protests throughout Germany, the newly elected German National Assembly accepted the terms.

Refusing to append his signature to the treaty, Brockdorff-Rantzau resigned. After a frantic search (for few, indeed, were those who *were* willing to sign), two members of the German cabinet—Hermann Müller and Johannes Bell—were deputed to sign in his stead. Hence on June 28, 1919, five years to the day since the assassination of Franz Ferdinand in Sarajevo, Müller and Bell left their Paris hotel, harangued by stone-throwing mobs,[245] to attend the signing ceremony in the Hall of Mirrors at Versailles—the self-same room where the victorious Prussians had proclaimed the German Empire in 1871.

The Treaty of Versailles, along with its sister treaties (which together composed the "Peace of Paris"), remade the map of Europe. Poland reemerged from oblivion, Czechoslovakia obtained independence, and Serbia—the nucleus of the nascent Yugoslavia—obtained Bosnia and Herzegovina, providing her at long last with an outlet on the Adriatic. On the surface, it might have been mistaken for a glittering fulfillment of Wilson's dream of self-determination for Europe's minorities. But in order to purchase Allied support for his vaunted League of Nations, the American president had had to make stark compromises.

By Article 231 (the so-called "war-guilt" clause), the Treaty of Versailles obliged Germany to bear full responsibility for the war. Whereas Alsace and Lorraine were justifiably returned to France, German territory was also ceded to Denmark, Belgium, Poland and Czechoslovakia. Thus, at the stroke of a pen, millions of German nationals became dissatisfied minority subjects under foreign rule. Danzig, a Baltic port with a predominantly German population, was taken out of German hands, and designated a "free" city, while a strip of territory leading to it—known subsequently as the Polish Corridor—was handed over to the Poles to provide them with an outlet on the Baltic (a solution that created a very disagreeable geographic separation between East Prussia and the rest of Germany).

The German Army was limited to 100,000 men. Her tanks and airplanes were confiscated, and her navy was limited to thirty-six surface ships—submarines being strictly forbidden. Rather than surrender the remainder of their ships to the Allies, the Germans

The Signing of Peace in the Hall of Mirrors, Versailles, 28th June 1919. In the foreground, Dr. Johannes Bell (Germany) signs the treaty with Herr Hermann Muller leaning over him. Seated opposite them (left to right): General Tasker H. Bliss, Colonel Edward M. House, Henry White, Robert Lansing, President Woodrow Wilson (United States); Georges Clemenceau (France); David Lloyd George, Andrew Bonar Law, Arthur Balfour, Viscount Milner, G.N. Barnes (Great Britain); The Marquis Saionji (Japan). Standing in the background (left to right): Eleuthérios Venizélos (Greece); Dr. Afonso Costa (Portugal); Lord Riddell (British Press); Sir George E. Foster (Canada); Nikola Pachitch (Serbia); Stephen Pichon (France); Colonel Sir Maurice Hankey, Edwin S. Montagu (Great Britain); the Maharajah of Bikaner (India); Vittorio Orlando (Italy); Paul Hymans (Belgium); General Louis Botha (South Africa); W.M. Hughes (Australia). Painting by William Orpen (Wikimedia Commons).

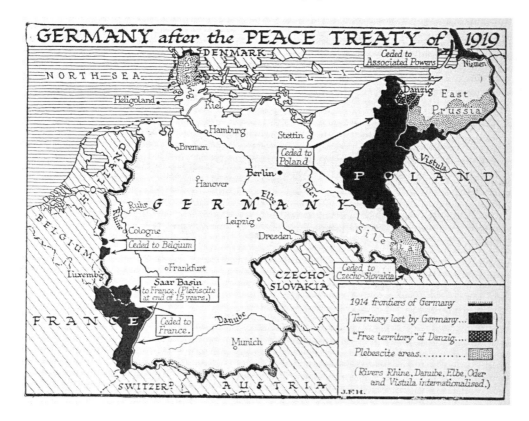

Germany after the Peace Treaty of 1919 by J.F. Horrabin (Illustrator), from H.G. Wells' *Outline of History,* **1923 (Wikimedia Commons).**

defiantly scuttled them at Scapa Flow under the very noses of the British fleet. The east bank of the Rhine River was declared a perpetual demilitarized zone to a depth of fifty kilometers. Germany lost all of her colonies, and was ordered to pay an initial installment of 5 billion dollars to the Allies, who would present her with a full reparations bill within twenty-four months. (Having raised expectations among their home constituencies to an impossible level, Lloyd George and Clemenceau had either to admit to their unrealistic exaggerations on reparations or continue the façade by deferring a final decision in the hope that domestic pressure would abate in the interim.[246])

To make Germany sign, the Allies kept her under economic blockade, reducing her people to starvation. And to keep her hostage to the terms, they stationed troops in the Rhineland and placed the Saar Basin under League of Nations jurisdiction (allowing France free exploitation of its coalmines), both for a projected period of fifteen years. In the Rhineland, staged withdrawals would begin at five years provided Germany was fulfilling her treaty obligations.[247] The Saar would remain in League hands for the full fifteen-year term, whereupon a plebiscite would give the populace a choice of continuing under League jurisdiction, becoming part of France or rejoining Germany. If the inhabitants opted for the last, Germany would be obliged to repurchase the coalmines from France before the territory reverted to her.

In return for abandoning his demand for permanent separation of the Saar and Rhineland from Germany, Clemenceau obtained treaties obliging the United States and

Great Britain to come to her assistance in the event of renewed German aggression. The United States Senate, however, never confirmed the American obligation, rendering it void.[248]

In all, the Treaty of Versailles divested Germany of 13 percent of her territory, 8 million of her inhabitants, 75 percent of her iron stores (primarily from Alsace and Lorraine) and 33 percent of her coal reserves (primarily from the Saar and Upper Silesia).[249] It is only fair to point out, however, that during its retreat from northern France, the German army had systematically flooded the majority of France's coalmines and destroyed much other private and industrial property.[250]

Peace had now to be made with the other belligerents. On September 10, 1919, Austria signed the punitive Treaty of St. Germain. By its terms, her centuries-old empire was dismantled. The union with Hungary was dissolved. Bohemia, Moravia and Ruthenia were delivered to Czechoslovakia, Galicia to Poland, and Bosnia and Herzegovina to Serbia. All that remained now of the once sprawling, multi-national empire was an impoverished, landlocked remnant. Again the argument of self-determination had been invoked, but the redrawn borders told a different story. In the Hapsburg empire, Germans had composed a ruling elite. In the successor states, many of them would have to live as minorities dominated by other peoples. A little tinkering with the borders might have kept many of these Germans in Austria, or handed them to Germany, but such was the desire to keep both states weak that the effort simply wasn't made. Moreover, although Austria's remaining population was predominantly German, the Treaty of St. Germain expressly forbade her from being incorporated into Germany without unanimous League approval, even if she could not remain solvent on her own. (The Allies did not want Germany to have access to Austria's manpower—and to deprive her of it they were willing to violate their own principle of self-determination by prohibiting a future merger between the two states.)[251] Nor, indeed, was Austria likely to remain solvent. During the Hapsburg era, the Danube basin had been commercially united. Now that the empire had been fractured into separate nations, trade barriers slowed Austria's commerce to a crawl.[252]

Hungary fared no better. The victors turned a deaf ear to her complaint that the treaty foisted upon her would make unwilling Romanian subjects of one and a half million Transylvanian Magyars. The nation's fledgling democracy toppled under the weight of this provision, and was briefly succeeded by a Communist regime under Béla Kun who tried to defy the Romanians, with the result that Romanian troops occupied Budapest.[253] On June 4, 1920, the Hungarian delegation signed the Treaty of Trianon, accepting the status of a truncated state.

Bulgaria, too, was punished for throwing in her lot with the Central Powers. By the Treaty of Neuilly, her Aegean coastline was taken from her and given over to Greece, leaving her without access to the Mediterranean. She did, however, retain an outlet on the Black Sea.

Of the Central Powers, Turkey alone managed to defy the terms imposed on her. The Treaty of Sèvres, signed in the exhibition room of the National Porcelain Factory on August 10, 1920, partitioned the Ottoman Empire—shearing away all her Arab lands, creating an independent Armenia in eastern Anatolia, and establishing Greek, Italian and French protectorates along much of Anatolia's Mediterranean coastline. Its signing by representatives of Sultan Mehmed VI, however, provoked a Turkish nationalist rebellion at Ankara.

Led by the war hero Mustapha Kemal (of Gallipoli fame), the nationalists disavowed the treaty. In an effort to force compliance, the Allies supported a Greek invasion of the Anatolian hinterland. In May 1919, Greek forces had established themselves at Smyrna—a predominantly Greek city on the Anatolian coastline. Emboldened by visions of a restored Byzantine empire, they now embarked on an inland drive toward Ankara, the epicenter of the nationalist uprising.[254] Successful at first, the invasion ground to a halt after a monkey residing in the Greek royal menagerie became agitated and bit King Alexander, bringing sepsis and death to the twenty-seven-year-old sovereign. The tragedy returned the throne to Alexander's predecessor—that same King Constantine who had refused passage to Allied forces at Salonika during the war. Although Constantine was more than willing to continue the effort against Turkey, the Allies would not support him—their desire to obtain retribution for his wartime behavior being greater than their desire to defeat the Turks.[255] Consequently, the Greeks rapidly exhausted their munitions, while the Turkish nationalists under Kemal's leadership procured enough armaments from France and Russia to inflict decisive defeats on the invaders on the banks of the Sakarya River, less than 150 miles from Ankara (where Kemal obtained the title "*Ghazi*" or "Conqueror") and at Dumlupmar in August 1922. By the following month, Turkish forces had reoccupied Smyrna—much of which was burnt to the ground as the Greek Army and much of the Greek populace fled by sea.[256] The whole of Anatolia was again in Turkish hands.

The victories provided Mustapha Kemal with sufficient leverage to unseat the last of the Turkish sultans (November 1922) and to forge his own agreement with the Allies. The Treaty of Lausanne, signed on July 24, 1923, provided for the exchange of one million Greek subjects living under Turkish rule for a half-million Turks residing in Greece. All of Anatolia was restored to Turkish sovereignty, as was eastern Thrace (including Adrianople), which had been denied to Turkey by the Treaty of Sèvres. She did, however, surrender hegemony over her Arab provinces, which (to the great disappointment of the Arab peoples) were divided into a collection of so-called "mandates"—distinguishable from colonies only in that they were subject to the oversight of the League of Nations with a putative goal of *eventual* independence.[257] Accordingly, Syria and Lebanon became French protectorates, while Palestine (which, according to the Balfour Declaration of 1917, was to have been the site of a new "Jewish National Home"), joined Iraq and Egypt as British protectorates. All had hoped for immediate independence—a status imparted only to the Hejaz (i.e., modern Saudi Arabia).

In forging these various agreements, the victors have been accused of "decorating a vindictive peace with lofty principles."[258] Whereas the Congress of Vienna (1815) had remade the map of Europe in the name of "legitimacy," the Paris peacemakers remade it—at least nominally—in the interest of "self-determination."[259] The idealistic Wilson believed that autocratic scheming had brought about the war and that if power were vested in the people lasting peace would ensue.[260] By establishing boundaries on the basis of self-determination, he hoped to extinguish the flame of nationalist conflict in perpetuity.[261] To some degree, his purpose had been achieved, as evidenced by the rise of the new states of Eastern Europe. In rare circumstances, as in Upper Silesia, final boundaries had been determined democratically on the basis of plebiscites.

But to a greater degree, the peace had come up short. At times, this resulted from technical factors—for ethnicity and geography did not always align in a tidy way. At other times it was owed to a lack of expertise. ("Who are the Slovaks?" Lloyd George asked at one meeting. "I can't seem to place them."[262]) But a desire for revenge and lingering fears of resurgent German militarism were ever-present motives. Consequently, cutting the Central Powers down to size took precedence over the greater purpose of jump-starting the European economy, which lay moribund after four years of war. The restoration of prosperity for victors and vanquished alike was the true key to a lasting peace. But despite constant remonstrations from John Maynard Keynes (who left the talks in despair to write his damning indictment, *The Economic Consequences of the Peace*), the point was lost on the peacemakers. Roused by popular hysteria, press propaganda and personal animus, they imposed a Carthaginian settlement, burying German and Austrian finances in a quagmire that would ultimately consume them all.[263]

In the coming years, the seeds sown at Paris would reap a ghastly harvest of economic depression, totalitarianism, appeasement and renewed warfare. For now, however, Wilson believed that all could be set right by establishing his cherished League of Nations—an international deliberative body pledged to discuss world problems and advise on peaceful solutions. At his insistence, the League Covenant had been incorporated as a preamble to all of the treaties. His belief that such an entity could right the wrongs done in Paris through sober discussion and consensus building ought to have been belied by the experience of the preceding months. The Big Four, after all, had nominally been on the same side, yet Orlando had walked out over Fiume, Clemenceau had called Lloyd George a liar (and had proposed a duel to settle the issue when the latter protested)[264] and even Wilson himself had threatened to sail home and make a separate peace with Germany if Clemenceau ever again raised the issue of the Saar.

None of this dissuaded the American president while in Paris, but on returning home his hopes received a mortal blow—for the United States Senate refused to ratify the Treaty of Versailles or the League of Nations Covenant. The Senate's isolationist Republican majority—whose leadership had not been represented at the talks—would not countenance an agreement that virtually guaranteed American entanglement in future European conflicts.

In an attempt to reverse this decision, Wilson resorted to every expedient, including coercion. Time and again, he argued that the League would correct any injustices in the treaties. His efforts were unavailing. Even some members of his own party withheld their support, saying that "an unjust peace meant an unjust League—the one would enchain the other."[265] In the view of one historian, Wilson failed to understand that the Treaty was the "substance" of the peace, and by wagering all on the League, "he gave up the substance for the shadow."[266] Campaigning night and day in favor of the treaty, Wilson suffered a series of strokes that impaired his ability to lead the nation. His incapacitation heralded the end of the fight. In November 1919, the Senate voted down the treaty. America would not be party to the League of Nations.

Domestic Affairs Between
the Wars, 1919–1939

The Bolshevik Regime and Russian Civil War

On August 30, 1918, after delivering an address at a Moscow munitions factory, the speaker of honor paused to converse with members of the throng that had come out to see him. At that moment, three shots rang out, two striking home—wounding the speaker in the neck and left shoulder—the third striking a bystander. Apprehended near the scene, in possession of a pistol, was a visually impaired female member of the now outlawed "Social Revolutionary Party." Her name was Fanya Kaplan. Her intended victim's name was V.I. Ulyanov—better known to history as "Lenin."[1]

Born on April 22, 1870, Vladimir Ilyich Ulyanov was the son of an esteemed middle class school superintendent. Embarking on a career of revolutionary agitation in his teens after his brother was hanged for a plot against the tsar (1887), he assumed the name "Lenin" (not "Nikolai Lenin" as is often supposed; for when he signed his writings "N. Lenin" the "N" actually stood for "no one," indicating a fictitious identity).[2] In 1897, his seditious activity resulted in his arrest and exile to Siberia. Liberated three years later, he helped found and edit *Iskra* (*The Spark*), the newspaper of the Marxist "Social Democratic Party," in which he now became a formidable force. At the party congress of 1903, which opened in Brussels before being harried to London, his insistence that the party's leadership be centralized and dictatorial (rather than decentralized and democratic) fractured the party into rival wings—his own followers being known afterwards as "Bolsheviks" (i.e., "the majority"), his opponents as "Mensheviks" (i.e., "the minority"). These were, however, misnomers, for the Bolsheviks were actually outnumbered—having won the vote on party leadership only after Lenin's domineering methods caused many of his rivals to storm out of the congress in protest.[3]

A master of political intrigue and secret correspondence (he was, for example, expert in the use of vanishing ink),[4] Lenin lived in foreign exile from 1900 to 1917—returning only briefly in 1905 to participate in the abortive revolution of that year. Otherwise, he lived an ascetic life abroad in the company of his wife and fellow revolutionary, Nadezhda Krupskaya, spending hours daily in the hallowed libraries of Europe—most especially in the famed Reading Room of the British Museum, where he imbibed works on politics, economics and the art of insurrection.

At the outbreak of the First World War he bade his minions to infiltrate the army and spread defeatism; for defeat would bring chaos and with it the opportunity for revolution.[5] Greeted by cheering throngs on his return from exile in the famous "sealed" train (April 16, 1917), he rejected all cooperation with the Provisional Government—adhering to a long-held tenet that the party must remain "revolutionary" and at no time collaborate in a bourgeois regime.[6] In June, at an "All Russian Congress of Soviets," he provoked laughter by suggesting that the Bolsheviks (then in a distinct minority) were ready to assume power. Kerensky, present in the same assembly, shouted him down to the cheers of the other delegates, but the proletarian gallery shouted for Lenin—for he promised them "peace, land and bread."[7]

On the basis of this and his other seemingly populist slogan "All power to the Soviets!" his party seized power with a semblance of popular support when Kerensky's authority disintegrated in November. Establishing his headquarters at Petrograd's Smolny Institute, Lenin instituted a "dictatorship of the proletariat" directed by a so-called "Council of People's Commissars"—a necessity, he claimed, until the populace at large had obtained adequate instruction in the ways of communism.[8] The new ruling council promptly decreed state ownership of banks, industry and farmland; repudiated all government debt; replaced the courts with "revolutionary tribunals" (a harbinger of the Terror to come); outlawed all titles apart from "Comrade"; and adopted the Western calendar, thereby moving the date forward by two weeks and transforming the Bolshevik "October Revolution" (as dated by the old calendar) into a November one.[9] Within weeks, however, elections for a Constituent Assembly belied the Bolshevik claim to a ruling mandate—awarding the rival Social Revolutionaries (the revolutionary party of the peasantry), more than 58 percent of the 41 million votes cast as against 24 percent for the Bolsheviks.[10] On January 18, 1918, crowds thronged the streets of Petrograd to

Lenin harangues the crowd in Piazza Sverdlov in Moscow during the Russian Civil War, 1920. Standing on the stairs at right is Red Army commander and fellow revolutionary Leon Trotsky. Photograph by Grigory Petrovich Goldstein (Wikimedia Commons).

welcome the assembly's elected delegates, but after an inaugural session—during which the Bolsheviks hooted down every speaker before staging a dramatic walkout[11]—the assemblymen found themselves barred from the meeting hall by distinctly unfriendly Bolshevik soldiers.

On the same day, the German delegation at Brest-Litovsk finally unveiled a map outlining their intended peace terms. There followed Trotsky's six-week charade of refusing to fight or sign the terms, during which time the Germans advanced ever further into Russian territory. By March 3, 1918, when the Russian delegation finally appended its signature, thereby (in Lenin's parlance) obtaining "breathing space for the revolution," German forces had pressed into Estonia, within striking distance of Petrograd. Citing security concerns, Lenin relocated the seat of government to the Kremlin in Moscow two weeks later.[12]

Although the Treaty of Brest-Litovsk was nullified by Germany's defeat in November 1918, Russia's premature withdrawal from the war made her a loser in spite of the Allied victory. Finland, Estonia, Latvia and Lithuania were carved from her northwestern frontier, Bessarabia was awarded to Romania and Russia's former Polish domains were incorporated into the new Poland. Nor could the Bolsheviks contest these changes, for they were simultaneously engaged in a bitter civil war with the so-called "White Army"—a disparate collection of forces ranging from reactionaries to constitutionalists bonded together by little other than a shared hatred of Bolshevism.[13] Because the Bolsheviks had sought to spread their revolution abroad and had renounced the tsarist regime's war debts (totaling some ten billion dollars), the Allies also intervened militarily against them—supporting the "Whites" with troop landings in Siberia, the Crimea, Odessa and Murmansk in a bid (as Churchill put it) "to strangle Bolshevism in its cradle."[14] The first of these troops landed while World War I still raged, but their mission was not clearly defined, and many of them simply took control of Allied munitions depots on Russian soil and waited on events.

Complicating the picture was a marooned force of 35,000 elite Czechoslovakian troops who had defected to Russia during the war in order to fight Austria-Hungary in the name of Czech independence. When the Bolsheviks withdrew from the war, they offered the Czechs free passage by rail to Vladivostok where the Allies were to evacuate them. Once they had entrained, however, they were told that they must surrender their arms. Rather than do so, they forged an alliance with the White forces in Siberia, under the tsarist admiral Alexander Kolchak. Turning around, they advanced westwards to within 400 miles of Moscow, gaining control of most of the Trans-Siberian rail system en route (August 1918). In the same month, American and British troops descended from their base at Murmansk to seize Archangel.

In November 1918, Admiral Kolchak assumed overall command of the White armies, declaring, "I will not go down the path of reaction, nor the ruinous path of party politics … my main goal is to produce a battle-ready army, attain a victory over Bolshevism, and establish law and order so that the people may without prejudice choose for themselves the manner of government which they prefer."[15] The Bolshevik position, already tenuous in the extreme, worsened considerably the following spring, when the White armies embarked on a three-pronged offensive. While Admiral Kolchak drove towards the Volga from Siberia, a second White army struck out of Estonia toward Petrograd under General Yudenich, and a third, under General Denikin, drove northwards from the Crimea, to besiege Tsaritsyn (the future Stalingrad, a pivotal link in

Moscow's grain supply), Kiev and Orel, a scant 200 miles from Moscow.[16] The Bolsheviks now controlled scarcely ten percent of the country, consisting predominantly of Petrograd, Moscow and the surrounding environs.[17]

To deal with the escalating crisis, the Bolsheviks instituted a "Red Terror" in the summer of 1918, directly after the attempt on Lenin's life by Fanya Kaplan. Led by the "saintly executioner," Felix Dzerzhinsky, who had once hoped to become a priest,[18] a secret police force known as "Cheka" (an acronym for "Extraordinary Commission to Combat Counter-Revolution, Speculation and Sabotage") carried out arrests and executions with essentially no supervision—accomplishing its task so efficiently, says Schapiro, that when it was disbanded in 1922, "there were no more counter-revolutionists to apprehend."[19]

On July 17, 1918, the tsar and his family, imprisoned at Ekaterinburg, were escorted to a dingy basement where they were informed that, in light of the attacks on the government by their supporters, they were to be shot. Nicholas and Alexandra were quickly killed in a flurry of pistol fire. In the ensuing silence, however, the children showed signs of life. The assassins therefore, resumed their task. The tsarevich, Aleksei, was promptly dispatched, but the daughters seemed to defy death, no matter how many bullets were fired at them.[20] The killers resorted next to the bayonet. When this, too, proved unavailing, the chief executioner coldly ordered the victims to be shot in the head. Later, when the bodies were stripped, it was discovered that the girls had sown the royal jewels into their dresses in the forlorn hope of smuggling them out of the country. Instead, the jewels had acted as a shield to the bullets and bayonets, thus prolonging their grisly suffering.[21] Ten days later, when White forces captured Ekaterinburg, they learned that the victims' bodies had been cut in pieces, doused with sulfuric acid and set on fire before being deposited in a mineshaft.[22] (The family's pet spaniel, Jimmy, had likewise been executed.[23])

The civil war proceeded in most uncivil fashion. Prisoners and civilians on both sides were murdered indiscriminately in simultaneous "Red" and "White" Terrors. The Cheka impaled priests on stakes or crucified them.[24] The Whites carried out pogroms, murdering as many as 100,000 Jews.[25] A typical incident reported by an eyewitness describes Whites fleeing over a cliff into the Dneiper River only to be machine gunned from shore by the pursuing Reds. A month later, the scene was replayed with the roles reversed.[26]

Having promised "peace, land and bread," Lenin had delivered starvation, tyranny and civil war.[27] In a policy known as "War Communism," state ownership of factories and farmland came to be synonymous with the conscription of unwilling workers into the labor force and the requisition of produce from peasant farmers (leaving behind scarcely enough to feed their families).[28] All resources were focused on provisioning a five-million-man army, newly organized by the Bolshevik commissar-of-war, Leon Trotsky.

The son of a Jewish peasant, Trotsky was born Lev Davidovich Bronstein, but by the time of the revolution he had already served multiple prison terms as a political detainee, and had taken the name of a former jailor—Trotsky—as his alias. The tsarist government grew so weary of his ceaseless revolutionary activities, that it finally exiled him to the wastes of Arctic Siberia, a thousand miles from the closest railhead. He escaped on a reindeer sleigh hidden in a bale of hay.[29] Without missing a beat, he continued his anti-government agitation, rose in the ranks, reconciled himself with the theories of Lenin (with whom he had long been at odds), and served as a key figure in the October Revolution. He now worked tirelessly to build an efficient Red Army. He became a great motivator of men—mostly by threatening to shoot them if they did not obey. Units displaying cowardice in the field were subjected to Roman-style decimation. Soldiers attempting to flee in the midst of battle were machine-gunned by "battle police" stationed in the rear.[30] To ensure that his officers—many of them former tsarist commanders forced to serve against their will—toed the party line, he appointed political commissars to every battalion. Retreat against orders meant death—both for the commissar and for the officer.[31]

While the population at large experienced insufferable privations, Trotsky's new legions reversed the tide of battle. Although the Whites had the better generals, they did not act in unison. The Reds, in contrast, enjoyed the advantages of greater numbers, interior lines of communication, an extensive rail network radiating outwards from Moscow (allowing for rapid reinforcement of threatened fronts) and inflexible obedience rigidly enforced from above. Whereas the Whites could not consistently define what they were fighting to achieve, the Reds were ever facile with a popular, if disingenuous, political slogan to stir the troops—and where that didn't suffice, they had less scruple about employing terror.[32]

By late 1919, Yudenich had been hurled back into Estonia. In January 1920, Kolchak was captured and executed at Irkutsk after the Czechs deserted him in return for a Bolshevik assurance of free passage to Vladivostok. Finding the ground too frozen for burial, the executioners cut a hole in the ice of the Ushakovka River and slipped Kolchak's corpse underneath.[33] Shortly thereafter, Trotsky's Red Cavalry outflanked Denikin's army on the heights overlooking the Don River,[34] driving the rebel general into flight toward the Crimea, where he took refuge with the Allies.

By this time, however, a new threat had become manifest. At the Peace of Paris, a revivified Poland had come into being—its eastern boundary tentatively established along the ethnically demarcated "Curzon Line," first proposed by Britain's Foreign Secretary, Lord George Curzon, in December 1919. Alas, the projected line fell far short of the boundary desired by Roman Dmowski, head of the Polish delegation in Paris. As leader of Poland's formidable National Democratic Party, Dmowski was determined that the new Poland should encompass the same territory as the old—extending eastward to the pre-partition border of 1772 to include much of Lithuania, Belorussia and the Ukraine. An unrelenting Polish chauvinist and vocal anti–Semite, Dmowski envisioned a state in which all ethnic minorities would be compelled to adopt the Polish language and conform to Polish institutions.

Dmowski, however, was not Poland's most popular political figure, a distinction that belonged instead to the Polish war hero and chief-of-state, Józef Piłsudski. Piłsudski had a different vision for Poland. Born in Russian Lithuania in 1867, he spent his youth as a socialist agitator—rising to the leadership of the Polish Socialist Party, editing its newspaper, *Robotnik* ("*The Worker*"), and serving terms in exile—both in Siberia and abroad. Twice he escaped from political imprisonment, and on a third occasion, he avoided jail altogether by convincing his captors that he was psychotic so that they committed him to a madhouse instead.[35]

Ultimately, Polish patriotism determined that Piłsudski should forsake socialist "internationalism" to pursue a career as a freedom fighter. In the years leading up to World War I, he moved to Austrian Galicia where ethnic Poles enjoyed greater cultural freedoms than in Germany or Russia. Once arrived, he organized a network of "Rifle-man's Unions"—nominally for purposes of sport, but ultimately trained in full military drill (with the state's blessing). At the outbreak of the war, the "unions" were incorporated into the Austrian army as two fully formed "Polish Legions." Piłsudski's goal, as their commanding general, was to help defeat Russia and thereby win the support of Germany and Austria-Hungary for an independent Poland. The Central Powers paid abundant lip service to this wish, but when they issued an imperious demand for an oath of loyalty from his troops in 1917, Piłsudski grew suspicious and refused, prompting his removal from command and imprisonment for the duration of the war. He emerged from captivity in 1918 as the national hero of a reborn Poland, being named to the posts of chief-of-state and commander-in-chief of the army.[36]

Unlike the chauvinistic Dmowski, Piłsudski believed that Poland would not be able to sustain an independent existence between the hammer and anvil of her powerful neighbors, Germany and Russia—especially if the latter emerged from her civil war in possession of Belorussia and the Ukraine.[37] His proposed solution—known as the "Jagiellonian Idea" (after the medieval Polish-Lithuanian Commonwealth ruled by the Jagiellon dynasty)—was to create an eastern European commonwealth of independent states bound in a coalition of mutual security under the stewardship of the Polish Republic.[38] Poland, Lithuania, Belorussia and Ukraine would compose the nucleus of the commonwealth, which might ultimately expand to include all eastern European states from Finland in the north to the Balkans and Caucasus in the south.[39] The territorial extent would exceed that of Dmowski's unitary Poland, but (in theory, at least) there would be no imposition of Polish hegemony on the other members of the confederacy.

In one of the ironies of history, Piłsudski's elder brother, Bronisław, had been a co-conspirator with Lenin's elder brother, Alexander, in the 1887 plot against Tsar Alexander III.[40] There were no ties of affection, however, between the younger siblings; for despite being embroiled in civil war, Lenin was already laying the political groundwork to reclaim the provinces Piłsudski hoped to recruit for his democratic federation. Indeed, the Bolsheviks intended to conquer Poland itself—believing that its overthrow would serve as the harbinger of a worldwide proletarian revolution that would topple the bourgeois regimes of the West like dominoes.

Consequently, after Germany's defeat in the First World War, the withdrawal of German forces from the territories obtained at Brest-Litovsk set the stage for an inevitable clash between the new Polish Republic and Bolshevik Russia. Taking advantage of the ongoing Russian Civil War, Piłsudski was able to strike the first blows. On April 18, 1919, Polish cavalry surprised the garrison of Vilna, clattering through the streets of the historical Lithuanian capital to the cheers of its Polish inhabitants.[41] In July, Polish forces occupied Lvov in the Ukraine, in August, Minsk (capital of Belorussia), and in January 1920, Dvinsk, a predominantly Jewish city in Latvia (which was duly handed over to the Latvians in a show of ethnic magnanimity).

Everywhere victorious, Piłsudski had nonetheless placed Poland in a strategically vulnerable position, nearly doubling the length of the border shared with Russia—an enemy with far superior manpower potential.[42] Worse still, Vilna was a Polish city engulfed in a Lithuanian hinterland, Lvov a Polish city engulfed by Ukrainians—a clear set up for ethnic tensions between Poland and her putative confederates.

By the spring of 1920, the Bolsheviks had turned the tide of their civil war. Yudenich had been hurled back on Estonia, Kolchak had been captured and executed and Denikin sent reeling towards Crimea. To forestall a Russian counteroffensive before it could develop, Piłsudski sought to deliver a decisive blow. On April 25, 1920, he invaded the Ukraine accompanied by Symon Petliura, an officer and politician of Cossack lineage who aspired (with Piłsudski's support) to head the government of an independent Ukrainian Republic. On May 6, their forces occupied Kiev, which had last been in Polish hands in the 1600s.

Unable to stem the onslaught, the Russians simply withdrew with their forces intact, while Piłsudski issued a manifesto announcing the Ukraine's liberation. Alas, Petliura was unable to rouse his fellow countrymen, and there was no strategically defensible boundary upon which Piłsudski could consolidate his gains. On May 27, the Bolsheviks launched a counterattack—the First Red Cavalry Army commanded by Semyon Budenny attempting to storm the entrenched Polish forces at Kuratov, south of Kiev. The initial onslaught was repulsed, but thereafter the Poles were driven back by the converging armies of Mikhail Tukhachevsky in the north and Budenny in the south. The former crossed the Berezina to capture Minsk on July 11, took Vilna on July 14 and Grodno on the River Niemen (just east of the "Curzon Line") at month's end.[43] The Poles fell back on both fronts, stumbling all the way back to Warsaw, where they dug in for a last stand. Believing that the Polish working class would rally to the Red Army, Tukhachevsky arrived at the gates of Warsaw expounding his theory of the "permanent offensive," whereby he would advance through all the states of Europe, recruiting new armies of proletarians as he went without need for reinforcements from home.[44]

Budenny, in contrast, never reached Warsaw. Along with Joseph Stalin, his assigned political officer, he had gotten bogged down in the siege of Lvov, 200 miles to the southeast. Consequently, Tukhachevsky's advancing armies had no protection on their southern flank—a situation that set the stage for Piłsudski's so-called "Miracle on the Vistula." Between August 6 and August 12, Piłsudski secretly assembled a strike force to the southeast of the enemy front line. On August 16, this force struck northwards against Tukhachevsky's flank, cutting his lines of communication, and threatening his army with encirclement. Thrown into disarray when they thought the battle was won, the Russians panicked and fled leaving behind 100,000 casualties in killed, wounded and captured. (Polish casualties are estimated at 40,000.[45])

Too late, Tukhachevsky had summoned Budenny's First Red Cavalry Army to his support—and with equally catastrophic consequences. Lured forward into a vulnerable position, Budenny's saber-wielding cavalry were defeated at Komarów (Zamość) by Polish lancers commanded by Colonel Juliusz Rómmel in Europe's last clash of cavalry armies (August 31, 1920).[46] Three weeks later, on the northern front, Tukhachevsky suffered another defeat at Grodno, forcing his retreat from the banks of the Niemen. As the Russians abandoned their positions, Lithuania laid claim to Vilna, but Piłsudski, having spent a portion of his youth there, would not be without it. With his winking consent, a "mutinous" portion of his army seized the city—"liberating" its Polish and Jewish inhabitants while providing the Polish Republic with plausible deniability of its usurpation before a frowning international community. (The citizenry of Vilna later voted for inclusion in the Polish Republic.)[47]

The slaughter of the Polish-Soviet War ended with the Treaty of Riga, signed by the exhausted combatants in March 1921. The terms advanced the Polish frontier two hundred miles beyond the ethnographic "Curzon Line" proposed at Versailles—a hollow victory, for it did not bring Piłsudski's vaunted commonwealth into being. Thus, it failed to render the Poles secure against future attack while arousing a burning desire for revenge on the part of the Soviets. In the last analysis, Piłsudski's victory came closer to Dmowski's vision for Poland than his own.[48]

Meanwhile, with quiet restored on the Polish front, the Bolsheviks were able to destroy the last remnants of the White Army under Baron Wrangel, and put a halt to their civil war. But even though they were now firmly entrenched in power, their problems weren't over. War Communism had been an abysmal failure. State control of the means of production bred inefficiency. By 1921, the relentless printing of paper money had caused the value of the ruble to drop below the value of the paper and ink used to print it.[49] Industrial and agricultural production fell to a fraction of pre-war levels, while famine and epidemic (typhus and the Spanish flu) compounded the misery. Peasant farmers, tired of having their surplus produce confiscated, refused to farm beyond their own needs. Starving millions ate hay, brewed tree bark for tea, and consumed animals that were themselves dead or dying from starvation.[50] Bread made from clay and leaves became a staple,[51] while ravenous souls raided cemeteries and cannibalized human remains.[52] By 1921, disease, famine, terror and civil war had claimed as many as 14 million Russian lives,[53] and the regime had had to appeal to the Allies for charity.

At length, the Krondstat naval garrison, famed for its heroic role in the October Revolution, rebelled against these privations, demanding the restoration of freedoms promised at the outset of the revolution. Although the uprising was violently suppressed, it induced Lenin to abandon War Communism in favor of a New Economic Policy (NEP) allowing capitalist ventures in agriculture and industry on a limited scale. The change gave rise to a capitalist class of farmers known as *kulaks* in the countryside, and to a successful merchant class of "Nepmen" in the cities. Lenin covered this tactical retreat by arguing that the situation was not yet ripe for rigid Marxism, leaving compromise as the only alternative. Under the NEP, the economy showed signs of recovery.

Domestic Affairs of the Major Powers Between the World Wars

Russia and the Advent of Stalinism, 1924–1938

The name "Lenin" is sometimes erroneously translated as "Man of Iron." In actuality, the Russian word "len" means "flax"—the material of which linen is made. If his name meant anything, then, it meant "Man of Linen." He died at fifty-three in 1924 after a series of strokes, leaving Leon Trotsky as heir apparent to the party leadership. Trotsky, however, allowed himself to be outmaneuvered by a rival member of the Politburo (i.e., Russia's executive committee). The rival was Joseph Stalin.

Joseph Djugashvili, later "Stalin"—the "Man of Steel"[54]—was born of peasant stock in tsarist Georgia in 1879. Web-toed, scarred by smallpox, and bearing a partially withered left arm—the result, according to some authorities, of being run over by a horse-drawn carriage at age eleven—he was beaten as a boy by his brutish alcoholic father, and probably on this account developed into a brutish survivalist himself.[55] Although his mother, Ekaterina, looked very much like a nun in her traditional Georgian attire, she might have borne her son adulterously, for she has been linked to more than one prospective lover.[56]

Paranoia was added to the list of young Joseph's bad qualities perhaps as early as age fourteen when he entered a seminary school where students were encouraged to spy on each other. He was drawn to Marxism while still in his teens—so neglecting his seminary studies thereafter as to be expelled from school just months prior to graduation. His pre–Revolution activities have been the subject of controversy. Indeed, it is believed by many that, despite his apparent Marxist enthusiasm, he was actually an undercover police informer.[57] After meeting Lenin in 1905, however, he obtained a bona fide niche among the Bolsheviks: plotting robberies to help provide the party with funds. The most spectacular of these escapades was a handheld bomb attack against a horse-drawn carriage bearing 340,000 rubles to the Imperial State Bank in Tiflis' Yerevan Square (1907). The explosions left nearly 100 dead and wounded in the street—among them the horses pulling the carriage, which were blown to smithereens.[58]

During the Russian Revolution and Civil War, Stalin distinguished himself by exporting the regime's Red Terror to besieged Tsaritsyn—the city that would eventually be renamed "Stalingrad." Appointed to Lenin's cabinet as "people's commissar for nationalities," he crushed the autonomy of his native Georgia with Red Army troops in 1921. A year later, his tireless pursuit of the party's grunt work convinced Lenin to appoint him to the office of secretary-general of the Communist Party—a post that, unfortunately, carried with it the right to appoint his own lackeys to key bureaucratic positions. From this point forward, Stalin's efforts were directed toward increasing his own power within the party, while undermining that of his rivals. His first quarry was the intellectual Trotsky. The two agreed on nothing—not even the fundamental question concerning the proper milieu for Communism. Trotsky, having seen the industrial might of the West while living in exile, believed that a worldwide revolution was necessary for Marxism to succeed. Stalin thought "world revolution" was a pipe dream, and favored the more parochial notion of "socialism in one country."[59] Because Trotsky's intellectual snobbery offended other leading Bolsheviks, Stalin was able to enlist the support of prominent party members—most notably, Lev Kamenev and Grigory Zinoviev—in a bid to push Trotsky out of power when Lenin's health began to fail.

Lenin suffered three strokes in all between 1922 and his death in 1924. Increasingly infirm, he found himself doted over by Stalin who had been appointed by the Central Committee to assist in his "recuperation." With the bearing of a tender parent, Stalin lessened the strain on the stricken man by withholding vital information from him regarding governmental affairs and by making sure no one else told him anything either.[60] Lenin was not fooled by this maddening charade, and in his last will and testament he recommended that Stalin be removed from his post as secretary general. Although the document was read aloud in front of the Central Committee after Lenin's death, no one was willing to act on it. Undoubtedly, fear played a role, but Stalin also had a way of disarming his attackers, no matter who they might be. By avoiding direct confrontation and allowing others to make his attacks for him—interjecting only to temper their zeal—he was able to present himself as moderate, even harmless.[61] At the reading of Lenin's testament, he remained silent and allowed Kamenev and Zinoviev (who greatly needed his backing against Trotsky) to argue successfully in his defense. Once their testimony had rendered his position secure, he offered to resign, but "reluctantly" agreed to stay at his post at the unanimous insistence of the Central Committee.

Trotsky had been far from the capital convalescing from an illness at the time of Lenin's death, and was not informed of the leader's demise until it was too late to attend the funeral. By contrast, Stalin served as a pallbearer, and further proved his putative reverence for the dead leader by insisting (over the protests of Lenin's wife) that his mummified corpse be exhibited in perpetuity in a glass sarcophagus in Red Square.[62] He subsequently accumulated abundant political capital from the grisly icon—time and again justifying his policies in the name of preserving Lenin's revolution just as he had preserved Lenin himself.

By 1928, Trotsky had been hounded into exile, Kamenev and Zinoviev had been brushed aside, and Stalin had emerged all-powerful. The dictator was now in a position to embark upon his own program for Russia—"socialism in one country." The first step in the process was the overthrow of Lenin's New Economic Policy (NEP). Limited capitalism had brought industrial and agricultural production back to pre-war levels,[63] but promised to do no better—not to mention the fact that the program made a mockery of the socialist ideal. The fundamental problem from an economic standpoint was that Russia was still a nation of peasants. In order to become a modern industrial state, she would have to mechanize agriculture, freeing up the bulk of the peasantry for work in factories and mines.[64] Towards this end, Stalin instituted a series of "Five Year Plans" aimed at agricultural collectivization and rapid industrialization (1928).

In the countryside, collectivization was fiercely resisted. Rather than surrender their hard-earned produce for a pittance as the government demanded, the agricultural capitalist class (or *kulaks*) withheld their wares from the market.[65] In retaliation, Stalin liquidated the entire *kulak* class—and much of the recalcitrant peasantry besides. The unwilling peasants fought back by destroying harvests and livestock, hoping to render Stalin's collectivization program a failure. They were made to suffer pitiably for their defiance. Red Army troops descended upon rural villages, killing those who resisted along with multitudes of innocents. Survivors were dispatched to far off factories and mines for forced labor.[66] By 1936, ninety percent of the countryside would be collectivized, and lost production would be partly recouped by modern tractors and other farm machinery.[67] But the yields were expropriated for Stalin's own purposes. In the Ukraine, where collectivization had met its fiercest resistance, millions of peasants perished from starvation. Those left behind subsisted on such delicacies as rodents, insects, tree bark or horse manure mixed with weeds,[68] while Stalin hoarded grain in state warehouses, to be sold abroad to help finance his industrial policies.[69] Horrified by rumors of cannibalism emanating from the countryside (and by the knowledge that her husband had engineered the man-made famine), Stalin's wife, Nadezhda, committed suicide in 1932. American journalist William Stoneman attempted to expose the truth about the famine in the *Chicago Daily News* (as did Malcolm Muggeridge in Britain's *Manchester Guardian*), but in one of the most stunning examples of journalistic malpractice in history, the *New York Times'* Stalinist Moscow correspondent, Walter Duranty, whitewashed the affair with stories parroting the Soviet party line.[70] Years later, Stalin admitted to Winston Churchill that, between those who starved to death and those who were executed, some ten million Russians lost their lives during the period of collectivization.[71]

Simultaneous with these events, Stalin inaugurated his first five-year industrialization program, supervised by a managerial class that stood above the masses. Ordinary workers received wages based on individual production. To spur them on, propaganda made national heroes of supposed prolific workers—most notably, Alexei Stakhanov, who was absurdly credited with mining over 200 tons of coal in a single day.[72] The masses were encouraged to emulate such "heroes" with the promise that their collective effort would bring a better life. Novels such as Ostrovsky's *How the Steel Was Tempered* and Gladkhov's *Cement* (about a cement factory) became the "must reads" of the day,[73] and Stalin's crash literacy program, which raised the national literacy rate from 40 percent to 95 percent,[74] ensured that people could "enjoy" them. In no time, zealous "Stakhanovites" appeared in the factories, working at a feverish pace in delirious celebration of Alexei Stakhanov and the "Great Leader," Stalin. (Not a few were murdered by their irate fellow workers for raising production expectations.[75])

Rather less fanfare attended the regime's "gulags" or slave labor camps, where millions of outcasts toiled, usually until they dropped dead, to build railroads and to exploit mines. In a statistical sense, the five-year growth in productivity was astounding, but in every sphere, quantity was given precedence over quality. In order to meet quotas, factories spewed out inferior machinery—much of which broke down at the first use. Although some of these quality problems were corrected in the second Five Year Plan (1933–1938), emphasis remained entirely on the manufacture of materials needed by the state, while consumer production fell far short of providing the most basic necessities for private citizens. Hence, even as Russia emerged as a modern industrial colossus, her people were left to wallow in starvation and want.[76]

In the midst of it all, Stalin embarked on a series of paranoid purges of the Communist Party—known collectively as the "Great Terror"—in which he exterminated anyone who might rival him on the basis of popularity or position, even if they were dedicated to his policies. The initial pretext for these killings was the assassination of fellow Politburo member Sergei Kirov in Leningrad on December 1, 1934 (which itself was likely carried out at Stalin's order).[77] Among the first to perish in consequence were Lev Kamenev and Grigory Zinoviev, who were framed for orchestrating Kirov's murder in a putative "Trotskyite" plot to overthrow the communist regime. Eight nonentities (four of them NKVD secret police agents) cheerfully signed confessions stating that they had acted on the two men's behalf in the killing. All of them had been promised immunity once they had fulfilled their roles, but at trial's end, they were escorted out and shot along with their celebrated co-defendants.[78]

Though entirely innocent, Kamenev and Zinoviev had likewise confessed—a standard requirement of all accused persons since Comrade Stalin could not be made to appear unjust. No matter how implausible the crime, purge victims routinely admitted guilt—some induced by threats (or acts) of retribution against their families, others by being kept awake for days in ceaseless interrogation until they caved in.[79] The accused were often made to fabricate their own supposed "crimes" before pleading guilty to them.[80] Of the millions condemned in these proceedings, an estimated 750,000 were executed. The rest were sent to die in the gulags.[81] The most prominent victims were made to deliver rehearsed confessions (in which other innocents were invariably implicated) at a series of three great "show trials" in the late 1930s. Political rivals were the chief targets in these judicial shams, but there were other classes of victims, too. Industrial officials, for example, were convicted of industrial sabotage as a facile explanation for the deficiencies of the Five Year Plans,[82] while a great purge of the Red Army officer corps (1937) removed the nonexistent danger of a military coup, while throwing the army into disarray just in time for World War II. (It would be incorrect to say that Stalin decimated his corps of generals. Rather, he did the opposite—leaving only 10 percent alive. Colonels fared better at 20 percent.[83])

Among the myriad defendants at the show trials, only one mustered the requisite nerve to deny the charges against him in court, but after a short recess, he confessed, too.[84] Most of the condemned wretches were quickly dispatched by pistol shot to the head, delivered in a prison basement at the order of Stalin's head of secret police—a position held first by Henry Yagoda, then by Nikolai Yezhov (who betrayed Yagoda), and finally by Lavrenti Beria (who betrayed Yezhov). Kamenev and Zinoviev were among the first to disappear in this way (1936); Marshal Tukhachevsky, hero of the Polish War (1937), and the loyal, but too popular, Nikolai Bukharin (1938) were among the last. No one was immune to retribution. Indeed, this was the point Stalin had set out to make. He even silenced Lenin's widow by informing her that if she didn't cease her recriminations, he would find a new "Lenin's widow" to take her place.[85]

Outside the dock, reality itself was assailed. Leon Trotsky, who had once characterized Stalin as "the outstanding mediocrity of the party,"[86] never ceased to be the object of Stalin's venom. Official photographs from the revolutionary period were altered to remove Trotsky's image, and the history books were rewritten to exclude his achievements. For Stalin, however, Orwellian erasure did not suffice. In 1940, he sent an assassin to Mexico, who killed the exiled bogeyman by piercing his skull with an ice pick.

The result of it all was a totalitarian state in which individuals believed what they were told to believe, thought what they were told to think, and felt what they were told to feel. The Soviet press, as one newspaper editor noted, did not buy into "the bourgeois notion of facts." The news consisted of that which promoted the cause of Stalinism and nothing else. Art, literature and theater were strictly censored. Religion was suppressed. Information from abroad never penetrated the frontier. On every street and at every gathering, informants were certain to be present listening for a wayward phrase—at times even within one's own household. As often as not, informants were recruited against their will, but like other workers they were expected to meet their quotas. Consequently, neighbors informed on neighbors, friends on friends and children on their own parents.[87]

Such was the achievement of Stalinism and "socialism in one country."

Italy and the Advent of Fascism, 1919–1938

If Stalin wanted no foreign ideas to enter his country, the rest of the world wanted no Bolshevist ideas to exit it. The Western Powers viewed communism as a contagion requiring quarantine,[88] and Soviet foreign policy since the October Revolution of 1917 had done nothing to change this perception. In early 1919, Lenin launched the Communist Third International (or "Comintern") in hopes of spreading the revolution beyond the borders of Russia—or, failing that, of keeping the Western powers so busy fighting communist agitation inside their own countries, that they would have no opportunity to attack the Soviet Union.[89] Even from its earliest days, the campaign was not wholly unproductive. Communist parties, ready to take their cues from Moscow, sprouted up throughout Europe.[90] Hungary had a communist regime for a few months in early 1919, while in the industrial north of Italy, workers responded to unemployment and inflation by seizing factories and running them as Marxist collectives. The factory owners were outraged, and when Italy's central government failed to intervene, the owners formed an unholy alliance with the region's ardently anti-communist nationalists.

Bitter that Italy's 600,000 casualties in the Great War had not been better rewarded at the peace table, the disgruntled nationalists were spoiling for a fight. In 1920, the renegade nationalist, Gabriele D'Annunzio, seized the coveted Yugoslavian port of Fiume, arriving by chartered boat[91] with a band of black-shirted toughs who staged impressive parades and adopted a one-armed salute to pay homage to their leader. Under international pressure, the Italian government ousted D'Annunzio, but his methods soon took sprout in Italy itself, where roving bands of black-shirted hoodlums began perpetrating acts of violence against communist agitators. Led by Benito Mussolini—himself a former socialist—they called themselves "Fascists," having adopted as their emblem the *fasces*, an ancient Roman symbol of authority.

Between 1920 and 1922, clashes in the streets between Fascists and socialists claimed as many as 2,000 lives, with police and civilian bystanders counted among the victims.[92] Incompetent to deal with the crisis, the government offered Mussolini a cabinet post. He refused saying, "Fascism will not come into the government by the service entrance."[93] Then, in October 1922, after threatening to seize power by force at a huge rally in Naples, Mussolini and his thugs marched on Rome—or more accurately, his thugs marched on Rome, while Mussolini went to Milan by train to wait on events. Luigi Facta, the sitting prime minister, wanted to declare martial law to combat the hooligans. Had King Victor Emmanuel III signed the necessary orders, the army could have dispersed them with relative ease. But many leading members of society including industrialists, landowners, Catholic prelates, journalists and politicians (among them, the famed former prime minister Giovanni Giolitti) were convinced that the Fascists would restore order by quashing the socialists, and that the party and their leader could be controlled once co-opted into the government.[94] Hence, rather than declare martial law, the king phoned Mussolini in Milan, and offered him the premiership. Mussolini promptly boarded another train. He arrived in Rome on October 29.[95]

Born in 1883, Mussolini began his professional career as a schoolteacher, following in the footsteps of his mother. His father had been a blacksmith by trade but had spent most of his time pestering anyone who would listen—including young Benito—about the merits of socialism.[96] The propaganda made an impression on the son who soon abandoned teaching to pursue a career as a socialist agitator. By 1913, his résumé included five arrests, flight to (and subsequent expulsion from) Switzerland and Austrian Trentino, a reputation for provocative political writings and fiery oratorical harangues, and a case of syphilis.[97] It was enough to catapult him to the editorship of Italy's premier socialist daily, *Avanti* ("Forward")—which, to his credit, quadrupled its circulation within months (1912).[98]

The outbreak of World War I, however, utterly changed his politics. Hitherto, he had been a staunch anti-militarist, famously lambasting the government for embarking on its colonial aggression against Libya in 1911. But the events of August 1914 exposed the myth of international working-class solidarity while at the same time revealing the power of nationalism to intoxicate the masses. Losing faith in socialism's ability to achieve revolutionary ends (but not in war's ability to sow the ground for social revolution),[99] he now became a staunch interventionist. For this heresy, he was ostracized from the Italian Socialist Party and removed from his editorial position at *Avanti*. Undeterred, he started his own paper, *Il Popolo d'Italia* ("The Italian People"), which propagandized for Italy's entry into the war. He was drafted in August 1915 and served with distinction on the Isonzo Front—rising to the rank of corporal before being severely wounded when a "state-of-the-art" trench mortar exploded during an introductory demonstration, killing five bystanders.[100]

Seeking a new political vehicle after the war, Mussolini founded the Fascist party at a small rally in Milan in March 1919. Its initial platform, which sought to rival socialism in its appeal to workers, proved an abysmal failure,[101] but Mussolini soon found a niche for it in perpetrating violent acts against the party that had expelled him, thereby winning him the support of anti-socialists of varying stripes—and ultimately, the chance to form a government.

On assuming office in 1922, he received emergency powers to deal with the mounting chaos—which mostly entailed reining in his own putative followers. Accordingly, the *squadristi*—or squads of Fascist bullies who were responsible for most of the violence—were organized into a formal militia with centralized leadership, while regional Fascist party leaders (hitherto largely independent) were conscripted into a Fascist Grand Council, where Mussolini could keep a closer eye on them.[102] Likewise, he appointed Fascists to serve as provincial governors or "prefects."[103] This accomplished, he set to work on his first major piece of legislation, the "Acerbo Law" of 1923 (named after its author, Giacomo Acerbo), which proposed the allotment of two-thirds of the seats in parliament to the party receiving the most votes in a general election. With armed Fascist militia looking on from the gallery, the measure passed by a comfortable majority. In the ensuing elections, however, it proved superfluous. With armed Fascist militia offering helpful advice at the polls, Mussolini and his minions actually received 66 percent of the vote.[104]

Despite this result, Mussolini did not yet possess dictatorial authority—a fact that became abundantly clear in 1924 when Giacomo Matteotti, a respected and vocal critic of Fascist methods and corruption, was found dead at the hands of Fascist henchmen. Mussolini seems not to have given an express order for this heinous act (although the same might be said of Henry II in regard to Becket). Nevertheless, the public backlash might have forced him out of office had leading political figures (the king included) not continued to support him out of fear that if the Fascists were ruined and cast out, the socialists might step into the void.[105]

Aghast that he was allowed to remain at his post, opposition MPs stormed out of the chamber of deputies in what became known as "the Aventine Secession" (an allusion to the secession of the plebs from Rome in 494 BC). Their defiance, however, only made it easier for Mussolini to pursue absolute power.[106] Declaring the secessionists' seats forfeit (1926), he obtained authority to rule by decree, outlawed all opposition parties, censored the press, assumed control of the military, revoked parliament's right to initiate legislation (henceforth, it would serve as a rubber stamp for his own) and appointed Fascists to the mayoralties of Italy's towns and cities.[107]

Preferring, henceforth, to be known as *il Duce*, Mussolini supervised the establishment of a so-called "corporate state"—organizing capital and labor into thirteen national "syndicates,"[108] coordinated and controlled by a "ministry of corporations" headed by himself. Strikes and lockouts were outlawed. Capital and labor were compelled to settle their quarrels peacefully without resort to work stoppages. Irreconcilable disputes were adjudicated by one of sixteen labor courts whose decisions were not subject to appeal.[109] The enforced collaboration, in theory, was to benefit employers and workers alike. In practice, it tended rather to benefit the former—but the chief beneficiary, was the state, which obtained absolute authority over industry.

New election laws, passed in 1928 and 1938, removed all pretense of democracy from Italian elections. The 1928 law gave syndicates the power to nominate 800 candidates for the Chamber of Deputies (400 chosen by the employers, 400 by the employees), with an additional 200 nominated by other state agencies. Of this total—1,000 nominees in all—the Fascist Grand Council chose a list 400 candidates, whom voters were to accept or reject *en masse* by a vote of "yes" or "no." Suffrage was limited to male syndicate members, taxpayers, state employees and pensioners and approved clergymen. Women were debarred—as were an estimated three million males who had been eligible to vote under the old law. In the election of the following year, the official list was approved by more than 98 percent of eligible voters. (The 1934 election was not so hotly contested—the "yes" vote being even higher.) In 1938, the system was again overturned, this time in favor of a new legislature—the Chamber of Fasces and Corporations—whose 700 delegates were appointed directly by Mussolini without any voter input at all.[110]

Amid it all, social order was reestablished, faith was restored in the currency, a favorable war debt agreement was reached with the Allies, the marshes around Rome were drained and cleared of mosquitos and the longstanding conflict between the kingdom of Italy and the pope was amicably resolved (1929).[111] But apart from winning soccer's World Cup twice (1934 and 1938),[112] the regime's successes were more apparent than real. With the number of unemployed often above one million, poverty was still ubiquitous. Italians were simply no longer allowed to say so. Obsessed with increasing the nation's industrial and agricultural output—a matter of Fascist pride that took little account of individual living standards, particularly among the small farmers of the rural south[113]—the government fixed wages and prices, imposed high tariffs on foreign imports, increased the domestic tax burden, and (in a bid to make the state self-sufficient in wheat) pressured Italians to reduce their spaghetti intake.[114] "Condemned to a life of perpetual enthusiasm" (as Arthur J. May puts it[115]), Italians suffered "less" from the Great Depression than their counterparts in the European democracies mostly because their government said they did. (Though one may also cite their relative economic backwardness when it began.)[116]

On the pretext of combating illiteracy, the government made elementary education compulsory—and then used the schools to indoctrinate the nation's youth "in a healthful spirit of Fascism," beginning on day one with the pledge, "Let us salute the flag in the Roman fashion; hail to Italy; hail to Mussolini."[117] An oath of allegiance was likewise required of all educators from the elementary to the university level.[118] When Italy drew close to Nazi Germany in the late 1930s, the nation's 70,000 Jews were excluded from commercial, professional and educational opportunities and from intermarriage with putative "Aryan" Italians. In 1938, Jews who had immigrated to Italy since the Great War were stripped of their citizenship (if previously granted to them) and expelled from the country.[119]

In pursuit of these myriad policies, the government resorted to arbitrary and violent methods. Those opposing them had no avenue of redress, and if they spoke out anyway, they had castor oil forced down their throats or something very much worse. Thus did Mussolini establish three of the four pillars of modern fascism (as delineated by Robert Freeman in *The InterWar Years*): single party rule, abolition of civil freedoms and corporate-state economy. As to the fourth—military aggression—preparations were well underway with a massive buildup of land, air and naval forces.[120] As an accompaniment to his puffed-up posturing on the balcony overlooking the Palazzo Venezia, the Duce required that Italy achieve "autarchy"—or national economic self-sufficiency—not because he regarded this as an economic ideal, but because it would give him the freedom to embark on his true purpose: the establishment of a modern-day Roman empire through territorial conquest (without the encumbrance of economic dependence on other nations).[121]

Germany and the Advent of Nazism, 1919–1934

Germany, too, had a flirtation with communism in the immediate aftermath of the Great War, when the so-called "Spartacus League" staged an uprising that threatened to topple the provisional government. In Berlin, workers went on strike in the Spartacists' support, prompting a terrified Chancellor Friedrich Ebert to recruit unofficial armed bands—the so-called "*Freikorps*"—to stamp out the flame. The Communists were gunned down with impunity, and the Sparticist Revolt ended in the brutality of "Bloody Week" (January 6–11, 1919), during which the movement's leaders, Karl Leibknecht and Rosa Luxemburg, were executed (or in the parlance of the times, "shot while trying to escape."[122]) Three months later, Communists seized control of Bavaria's provincial government, but after three weeks in power they, too, were violently overthrown.

On August 11, 1919, the provisional government, holding its session in Weimar to avoid the contentiousness of Berlin, approved the so-called "Weimar Constitution," providing the new German republic with an impressive bill of rights (including female suffrage), a figurehead president (who could, however, assume emergency powers under certain conditions), and a chancellor, whose ministry was, for the first time in Germany's history, to be responsible to the *Reichstag*—still the lower, but now the more powerful, house of a two-house legislature.

It would have been problematic enough to sell such ideas to a people weaned on autocracy, but there were other, more formidable, obstacles standing in the way of success. The Weimar government was handicapped from its inception by popular hostility to its acceptance of the Treaty of Versailles, with its cession of German territory and its insistence that Germany bear full responsibility for the outbreak of the war. With seemingly intact armies returning from the front, the German masses questioned the very notion of defeat, preferring instead to believe Ludendorff's revisionist theorem that politicians and financiers—the so-called "November criminals"—had stabbed the army in the back, ending the war for their own profit.[123] (Nor did the politicians necessarily help their own cause. In December 1918, Chancellor Ebert had welcomed returning troops on parade in Berlin with the salutation, "I salute you who return unvanquished from the field of battle."[124])

Matters came to a head in March 1920 when the government attempted to disarm the *Freikorps* in compliance with the Treaty of Versailles.[125] Rather than surrender their arms, the *Freikorps* staged the so-called "Kapp Putsch"—an armed attempt to elevate the reactionary monarchist, Wolfgang Kapp, to the chancellorship. Sporting swastikas on their helmets,[126] they entered the capital and put the government to flight. But Berlin's trade unions would not stand for it. They staged a general strike, bringing services to a grinding halt, and the putsch collapsed. (Ironically, when the workers concluded that the next logical step was socialist revolution, the government had to enlist the *Freikorps* again to suppress their agitation.[127])

The polarization towards fanaticism on the left and the right was reflected in the *Reichstag* elections of June 1920. At the time of the National Assembly elections of the preceding year, the parties of the middle—i.e., the Social Democrats, the Democratic

Party and the Catholic Center—had obtained a combined 73 percent of the vote. They now garnered only 43 percent. Henceforth, the Weimar Republic would be ruled by fractious, and generally short-lived, coalitions.[128] The chief point of contention was the peace treaty—now widely denounced as the "Versailles *Diktat*." Resentment over the terms, already rife, rose by an order of magnitude in May 1921, when the Allies tendered their final reparations bill, totaling an astounding 132 billion marks (about 33 billion dollars). Divested, at Versailles, of a portion of her territory and population, her colonial empire, her Saar mines and the port of Danzig—in short, of the necessities for a profitable economy—she was now saddled with a debt far beyond her means to pay.

Almost immediately, there were acts of violence. In August 1921, Matthias Erzberger, who had headed the delegation that accepted the "stab-in-the-back" armistice terms of November 1918, was shot dead while vacationing in the Black Forest. Several months later, Walther Rathenau, the Jewish foreign minister and prime mover of the German war economy, met a similar fate. Their assassins were treated with kid gloves by courts sympathetic to the nationalist outcry.[129] The mood of defiance was especially strong within the army, whose commander, Hans von Seeckt, evaded the provisions of the Versailles Treaty via a secret agreement with Russia allowing for military training and joint tank and airplane development on Russian soil.[130]

It is unclear whether the Weimar Government could have adhered to the reparations schedule even had it so desired, but it hardly put forth an effort. In retaliation, France and Belgium sent troops into the industrially active Ruhr Valley, and announced that they would collect overdue deliveries of coal by force (1923). The policy was a disaster. Germans were unanimous in their hostility to the occupation and opposed it with a campaign of passive resistance. Indeed, it was widely joked that, apart from Bismarck, Raymond Poincaré (the French prime minister and architect of the occupation) had done more than anyone to unify Germany.[131] The cost of the enterprise to French taxpayers easily outpaced the value of the renewed coal shipments. Britain, moreover, refused to support the occupation, since she no longer adhered to the French view on German recovery. France still had a vested interest in keeping her neighbor weak. If Germany rebounded economically, she might also rebound militarily, creating an immediate threat to France. But with the German navy dismantled, and with the U-boats gone, no such concerns were felt in Britain. In her eyes, a revived German economy was desirable, for it would create a robust market for British exports. The differing outlooks strained Franco-British relations.[132]

While the Allies quibbled, Germany delivered an unexpected counterstroke. She devalued her own currency into oblivion, hoping to make the question of reparations meaningless. The result was runaway inflation. One-billion-mark notes were used in daily transactions. By the end of 1923, a bus ticket cost 150 billion marks—more than the entire reparations bill.[133] The worthless paper notes were used as kindling for stoves.[134] Cynical Germans joked that they went to the grocery store with a basketful of money and came home with a wallet-full of food.[135] Life savings were wiped out. Workers' salaries could not buy a loaf of bread. The only winners in this economic circus were the large corporations, which bought out the ruined small proprietors who had formerly been their competitors.[136]

While it all made for a hilarious practical joke on the French, it could not go on forever. Prior to the war, the German mark had sold at 4.2 to the dollar. By November 1923, it was selling at 2.5 trillion to the dollar,[137] and the government, which had been paying the workers of the Ruhr to stay home, could no longer afford to do so. With no alternative, it announced an end to the passive resistance campaign, whereat an obscure nationalist fanatic, Adolf Hitler—head of the fledgling National Socialist or "Nazi" Party, and a fervent subscriber to the "stab in the back" theory of defeat—sought to topple the government from a Munich beer hall. Interrupting a political meeting being held by the Bavarian state commissioner, the chief of police and the province's ranking general, he leaped atop a chair and fired a pistol at the ceiling. Announcing that Nazi militia (the so-called "*Sturmabteilung*" or "Storm Detachment"—"*SA*," for short) had surrounded the building, he convinced the attendees that the revolution was already under way and that the time had come to strike back at the "November criminals." The Bavarian officials had been planning a coup of their own, but with pistols being waved at them, they decided (at least nominally) to play along. The next day, followed by 2,000 or so of the Nazi faithful, Hitler attempted to emulate Mussolini's "March on Rome," parading arm-in-arm with no less a celebrity than Erich Ludendorff. Hardly had they set out, however, before the Munich police put an end to the so-called "Beer Hall Putsch" with a volley of carbine fire. Sixteen marchers fell dead. The rest dispersed helter-skelter, while Hitler, who dislocated his shoulder toppling to the ground, staggered into a waiting motorcar and sped away. He was arrested two days later.[138]

The survival of a government whose monetary policy had rendered its entire citizenry bankrupt was no mean feat. Erring on the side of prudence, however, the new foreign minister, Gustav Stresemann, decided against an encore—choosing instead to do something to end Germany's inflationary spiral in hopes of gaining more lenient terms from the victors. Consequently, he announced that Germany was willing to make a good faith effort to meet her reparations obligations. There followed the issuance of a new unit of currency, the *Rentenmark*—later renamed the *Reichsmark*—valued at the prewar level of 4.2 to the dollar and backed by a real estate mortgage on the whole of Germany.[139]

Much relieved, the Allies sought to cooperate. The result was the Dawes Plan of 1924 (named after General Charles Dawes who chaired the responsible commission). To get the German economy rolling again, it was decided that loans—mostly originating in the United States—would be made to Germany, who would use the funds (or at least some of them) to pay reparations installments to Britain and France. The two Western Allies would then hand the money back to the United States to pay off their war loans.[140] The whole affair sounds like a flawed attempt to square the circle. Round and round the money went, and though Germany was now receiving a good deal more in loans—which, by the way, she never paid back—than she was paying out in reparations, there seems not to have been so much as a raised eyebrow.[141] (According to Ruth Henig, the figures for the years 1924 through 1929 were 16 billion *Reichsmarks* received as against 7 billion applied to reparations.[142])

To this day, the enigma of this absurd policy is how it could possibly have worked as well as it did. The loans revitalized German industry, reparations payments were made, and a trade upsurge ensued which lasted for nearly five years. With money again flowing, an effluvium of goodwill swept across Europe. In France, Raymond Poincaré, who had engineered the costly French occupation of the Ruhr, was thrown out of office, and a more conciliatory ministry was formed which included, as foreign minister, the future Nobel Peace Prize winner, Aristide Briand. In October 1925, the newfound sense of international brotherhood culminated in a conference at Locarno, Switzerland, out of which flowed seven separate treaties involving such diverse signatories as Great Britain,

France, Germany, Italy, Belgium, Poland and Czechoslovakia. The most important of these agreements guaranteed the French and Belgian borders with Germany and the continued demilitarization of the Rhineland. Four others—signed by Germany with France, Belgium, Poland and Czechoslovakia, respectively—guaranteed that all future disputes between Germany and her neighbors would be settled by arbitration.

Germany thus emerged with her signature on five of the seven Locarno treaties—eclipsing France by one. But France wasn't done. At Locarno, she had signed special treaties of guarantee with Czechoslovakia and Poland. The following year, she reached a similar arrangement with Romania, and a year after that with Yugoslavia. When one considers that Czechoslovakia, Romania and Yugoslavia had already signed dual alliances with one another—forming themselves into a so-called "Little Entente" (1921)—with an additional pledge to "consult" with Poland from time to time, France may fairly be said to have entangled herself in so many treaties that if Germany ever again went to war France could not help but be pitted against her.[143]

Luckily, there seemed little chance of that. In 1926, Germany was admitted to the League of Nations and Aristide Briand and Gustav Stresemann shared the Nobel Peace Prize. The following year, Briand, proposed a Franco-American initiative "mutually outlawing war."[144] In 1928, the blueprint came to fruition as the "Kellogg-Briand Pact," which repudiated war in the conduct of international relations. It was signed by sixty-three nations. A year later (1929), the Allies withdrew their forces from the Rhineland (five years ahead of schedule), and then agreed to the "Young Plan," which lowered the German reparations bill to $8 billion, payable over 58.5 years—which (not coincidentally) precisely equaled the term for outstanding Allied war debt payments to the United States.[145]

In this climate, even some Germans—though, admittedly, not many—were beginning to admire the Weimar government. Alas, such enthusiasts were greatly outnumbered by the regime's detractors—chief among them, the rabidly nationalist parties of the *Reichstag*, whose unrelenting insistence that Germany should aspire to greatness (rather than prostrate herself for the privilege of making reparations payments for the next sixty years) did little to encourage further Allied concessions.[146]

And then, the coming of the Great Depression brought the merry-go-round to a halt. While the European economy languished in the post-war years, the United States had enjoyed unparalleled prosperity—a trend that was reflected in increased trading on the Wall Street stock market. Amid the general euphoria, it was little noted that much of this trading was done on margin. Buyers paid only a small fraction of the face value of a stock, then behaved as if they owned the entire value and reinvested it, sometimes several times in succession, buying on margin at each step. Great amounts of stock were thus being traded without funds to back them up. The United States Federal Reserve Bank was the first to blink—raising interest rates to rein in profligate trading in August 1929.[147] The measure worked rather better than was hoped. With higher loan rates, the entire economy began to contract. In October 1929, astute investors discerned the risk of this situation and began to sell, thereby initiating a panic. On Black Thursday, October 24, 1929, thirteen million shares changed hands, and the lack of actual cash available to pay out these securities came home to roost.[148] Investors, big and small, were ruined. Industry ground to a halt, banks failed, people lost their life's savings, and millions of workers were laid off.

The phenomenon did not affect the United States alone. Throughout the 1920s, American loans (and investment) had kept European governments solvent, stimulated the European economy and encouraged European peoples to buy American products. By 1930, however, the United States was no longer in a position to extend these loans. Indeed, despairing of selling U.S. products abroad once the loans ceased, Congress decided to protect U.S. domestic industries from foreign competition by enacting the so-called "Hawley-Smoot Tariff." Hence, at one and the same time, Europe became the recipient of a double-blow: losing its primary financier and having its exports largely excluded from the American market.

In an effort to keep afloat, Germany and Austria sought to form a customs union. France immediately protested, claiming (with some justification) that the political implications of such a merger violated Article 88 of the Treaty of St. Germain forbidding Austro-German unification. This hostile reaction exacerbated the growing economic crisis in Austria and Germany, and helped precipitate the failure of the *Kredit Anstalt*—a major Austrian banking house (1931).[149] Panic seized the European banking industry, spreading first to Germany where the influential DANAT Bank closed its doors on July 13th. Then, as investors withdrew funds from the London Money Market, it ravaged England, which was forced to abandon the gold standard amid rioting over salary reductions for government workers. Within a year, Great Britain—long the champion of free trade—had resorted to a policy of high tariffs like the Americans.[150]

The results were predictable. Without capital to sustain them, European factories and mines failed by the score causing widespread unemployment. Hoping that balanced budgets might revive the prosperity that buying on margin had ruined, the United States and European governments cut spending. It was exactly the wrong policy. The decrease in spending only worsened the deflationary cycle. In Germany, hordes of disaffected, jobless citizens began flocking to the banner of political extremists. The Nazi Party, formerly a fringe group controlling just twelve *Reichstag* seats, won an impressive 107 seats in the September 1930 elections.

Chancellor Heinrich Brüning, meanwhile, had lost patience with the fractious legislature. In July, he prevailed upon President Paul von Hindenburg to invoke the emergency powers available under the Weimar Constitution so that the cabinet's proposals could be enacted by presidential decree. In addition to setting a very bad precedent, the move did nothing to improve the economy. As foreign investors withdrew their investments, the *Reichsbank's* gold reserves declined by 41 percent in just 3 weeks (June 1931). Unemployment, already at 2 million in 1930, rose to 6 million (30 percent of the workforce) in 1931.[151] After two years in office, Brüning was being disparaged as the "Hunger Chancellor."[152] Not one to let a crisis go to waste, he announced that Germany could no longer meet her reparations obligations under the Young Plan.

Amid the chaos, the Nazi Party continued to gain support—so much so, that Adolf Hitler challenged Hindenburg for the presidency in 1932. He was defeated, but he garnered an impressive 13 million votes (36 percent of the those cast). Soon thereafter, Hindenburg named Franz von Papen to replace Brüning as chancellor. In the ensuing *Reichstag* elections, however, the Nazis won 230 seats, and the Communists 89. Together they controlled more than half of the total (608), leaving Papen unable to form a majority without the cooperation of one or the other. Hitler insisted upon the chancellorship as the price of Nazi participation in the government, but after meeting with him, an astonished Hindenburg absolutely refused this demand, saying privately that Hitler was fit, at best, to be postal minister (which, as Churchill notes, would have left him responsible for licking postage stamps with pictures of Hindenburg on them).[153]

With Papen unable to piece together a coalition, the reins were turned over to Kurt von Schleicher, a scheming army general, who fared no better. Still the Nazis might have been kept at bay. At no time did they command a *Reichstag* majority on their own, and their failure to gain power in mid–1932 alienated many of those who had supported them. Gregor Strasser, a high-ranking party official, bolted the party. Campaign contributions fell off markedly, and members of the *SA*, the 400,000-man Nazi gangster army, had to act the part of panhandlers—taking to the streets with tin cans to beg for funds.[154] By the time Schleicher took office, new elections had decreased the Nazi contingent in the Reichstag to 196 seats. Clearly, their popular support was on the wane, leaving their ability to interfere with the workings of government as their main bargaining chip.[155]

Nonetheless, it was at this juncture that Hitler was sworn in as Germany's chancellor (January 30, 1933)—not on the basis of democratic votes, but as part of a behind-the-scenes conspiracy hatched by Franz von Papen, who hoped to regain power for himself. With the Nazis effectively blocking the formation of a *Reichstag* majority, Papen convinced Hindenburg to name Hitler chancellor, boasting that he would keep the Nazi leader on a short leash.[156] ("In two months," as Papen assured one skeptic, "we'll have pushed Hitler so far into a corner that he'll squeal."[157] It was, to say the least, a gross misjudgment.)

Born in Austria in 1889, Hitler was the son of a customs clerk named Alois Hitler. (Alois was the natural son of Johann Heidler—or Hitler. Until 1876, when his father took legal action to legitimize him, Alois went by his mother's maiden name, "Schicklgruber."[158]) Alois' son, Adolf, failed as a schoolboy, as an artist (his application to the Vienna Academy of Art was twice rejected) and even as a vagabond before finding his niche as an enlistee in the German Army at the outbreak of World War I. Though twice decorated with the Iron Cross, he achieved no rank higher than corporal. When the armistice was signed, he was recovering in an army hospital after being temporarily blinded by poison gas. He wept at the news. Subscribing wholeheartedly to the "stab in the back theory" of defeat, he continued in the service of the army after the war. In 1920, he joined the German Workers' Party (soon to be renamed the National Socialist, or "Nazi," Party) as an army spy, only to find that its platform fit in well with his own ideas. His fierce nationalism, rabid anti–Semitism and talent for extremist oratory soon gained him the party leadership.

By 1923, he believed himself ready to become master of all Germany, but the outcome of the Munich Beer Hall Putsch temporarily disabused him. The farce did, however, make him something of a national celebrity. Sentenced to a five-year prison term, he ultimately served less than a year—just enough time to begin work on his autobiography and testament, *Mein Kampf* ("My Struggle"), which told of his amusing plan to reunite all Germans living in the Eastern European successor states to the fatherland, and then to seize Poland and the Ukraine in order to provide them with living space. For the time being, no one paid much attention.

In the same year that Hitler maneuvered himself into the chancellery, the American public elected Franklin Delano Roosevelt to succeed Herbert Hoover as president of the United States. During this time of economic calamity, both rulers asked for and received emergency powers. But whereas Roosevelt used his powers to initiate a massive public works program to give jobs to the millions of unemployed, to provide financial relief to America's beleaguered farmers, to provide affordable energy to the Tennessee

Valley through the establishment of the Tennessee Valley Authority (which supervised the building of a series of dams), to initiate federal social security, disability and pension programs and to stabilize the nation's tottering banking system, Hitler used his to establish a totalitarian state. Just before Germans went to the polls in March 1933, a Communist simpleton, Marinus van der Lubbe, attempted to set fire to the *Reichstag*. He failed miserably, but the Nazis knew of his plan in advance, and showed up the same night to set a much more admirable fire of their own, burning the *Reichstag* to a cinder. They then apprehended van der Lubbe at the scene and denounced the fire as a Communist plot.[159] In the national elections six days later, the Nazis obtained 44 percent of the vote and their nationalist allies an additional 8 percent, thus providing Hitler with a working majority.

Using the fire as a pretext, Hitler obtained passage of a so-called "Enabling Act," which granted him dictatorial powers for four years. During this time, the German economy improved markedly. Unemployment plummeted, particularly after 1935, as a massive rearmament program was undertaken. As in Italy, a government-controlled corporate-state economy was erected featuring forced cooperation between capital and labor, and a ban on strikes and lockouts. Domestic production and consumption was strongly encouraged. Wherever possible, international trade was carried out under a barter system wherein German manufactures were exchanged abroad for raw materials that were scarce at home. (As it happened, the foreign market could bear only so many German razor blades and harmonicas, and on one occasion, a German concern had to convince a foreign creditor to accept a hippopotamus to settle a debt.)[160] As in Italy, the goal of the corporate state was "autarchy"—or complete self-sufficiency—so that foreign aggression could be undertaken without commercial pressure from abroad.[161]

In an effort to eliminate all opposition forces within the state, civil rights were abolished. Books deemed antithetical to Nazism were burned in massive bonfires, contrary professors were purged from the universities, the media was utterly suborned as a propaganda tool by Hitler's lackey, Joseph Goebbels, and those suspected of hostility to the regime were either killed outright or became early inmates of the concentration camps (for these had begun to make their appearance immediately after Hitler's accession). With financial backing from the nation's industrialists, the regime terrorized Socialists and Communists—beating, imprisoning or even killing them. Despite abundant evidence that he could not have acted alone, van der Lubbe was convicted for the *Reichstag* fire, and sent to the guillotine.[162] (The death machine, which would claim almost as many lives in Hitler's Germany as in revolutionary France, had been modernized with a spring loaded mechanism that provided a short forceful stroke of the blade, thus allowing for a compact instrument that could be employed indoors and out of sight.)[163]

Nazi racial theories became a cornerstone of the educational system. Early marriage was promoted in order to boost the "Aryan" birthrate. Conversely, a mandatory sterilization law was passed in January 1934 for carriers of certain hereditary diseases.[164] In July 1933, Hitler dispatched Franz von Papen to sign a new concordat with the pope, which seemingly provided for separation of church and state. In practice, the Nazis forbade the Church from interfering in German politics while divesting it of many of the prerogatives it thought it had maintained. The state likewise sought control over the nation's Protestant sects—forcing unity upon them, and pressuring them to construe the Nazi revolution as a manifestation of Divine will. The most extreme of the Führer's "German Christian" advisors wished to abolish the crucifix and Old Testament, amend the New Testament to deny the divinity of Jesus and compel all Protestants and Catholics to enroll in a single national church. The Rev. Martin Niemöller—the recipient of an Iron Cross for his service as a U-boat commander in the First World War—led the resistance to such policies. The regime dispatched him to a concentration camp in 1938.[165]

During this same period, Hitler took his first actions against the Jews—the agents, in his delusional imaginings, of a vast, international Judeo-Bolshevist conspiracy that supposedly lay at the root of all Germany's ills. Department stores throughout Germany were branded as "Jewish" and ransacked by Nazi mobs.[166] Jews were beaten in the streets, and when this sparked international protest, prominent German Jews were forced to write public letters claiming that the reports of anti–Semitic violence were false.[167] The new regime banned Jews from public service and the professions, targeted them with economic boycotts and then, by the Nuremberg Laws of 1935, stripped them of their citizenship outright. Hitherto, the vast majority of German Jews were entirely assimilated, considering themselves more German than Jewish. But in accordance with the new Nuremberg Laws, they were told that they were not Germans at all, simply Jews residing on German soil—"subjects," not "citizens," of the Reich.[168]

Having quashed their putative domestic enemies, the Nazis turned on one another. On June 30, 1934, Hitler authorized an overnight bloodbath to wipe out "enemies" within the party. The main target was the unofficial Nazi Army, Ernst Röhm's *SA*, which, to the infinite discomfiture of the Regular Army, aspired to be Germany's main fighting force. There were now several million of the brown-shirted thugs, and with Röhm at the helm, they were pressing Hitler to carry out a social revolution in which the wealth of the privileged classes would be seized by the state. National "Socialist" or no, this simply wasn't on Hitler's agenda. Rumors already abounded that Hindenburg would enlist the support of the Army to overthrow the Nazi regime if something wasn't done about Röhm's posturing and the mounting terror.[169] Consequently, in what has come to be known as the "Night of the Long Knives," Röhm and his chief supporters were rousted from their beds in the dead of night and shot—many shouting "Heil Hitler" to prove their loyalty even as their murderers took aim.[170] Nor was the festival of slaughter deemed complete until a number of Hitler's political opponents had also been butchered. Among the dead were Kurt von Schleicher, Hitler's predecessor in the post of chancellor, who was grotesquely murdered along with his wife for alleged double-dealings with Hitler during the latter's rise to power; Gustav von Kahr, the Bavarian state commissioner who had withheld his support during the Munich Beer Hall Putsch of 1923; and Gregor Strasser, the former high-ranking Nazi who had abandoned the Party two years earlier. Thankful for the liquidation of the *SA*, and believing itself safe from further political meddling, the German Army consented to having its soldiers pledge personal allegiance to the Führer.

Very soon afterwards, a temptation to foreign aggression presented itself in neighboring Austria where an attempt was made by the outlawed Austrian Nazi Party to topple the government (July 1934). We shall have more to say of this conspiracy in our discussion of foreign affairs. Suffice to say here that Hitler wanted to intervene but chose not to when Mussolini (who opposed his design) moved troops to the Austrian frontier. It was perhaps the last prudent decision he would ever make. One week later, on August 2, 1934, President Paul von Hindenburg died at the age of 86. Afterwards, his office was merged with the chancellorship by government decree—meaning that Hitler now occupied both posts. In an ensuing plebiscite, 88 percent of Germany's 43 million voters approved the decision. The last hindrance to Nazi totalitarianism was thus removed.

Great Britain

In 1918, David Lloyd George had assured British soldiers returning from the front that their efforts would be rewarded, and that Britain would be rendered "a land fit for heroes."[171] The expectation was that the massive industry rallied to the cause of war would now be rallied to the cause of peace. Industrial and agricultural output would continue at wartime levels to ensure adequate housing and material comforts for all.

Nothing of the sort happened. After a short-lived postwar boom, commerce underwent a dramatic slowdown in mid–1920. With Europe's economy reeling from the costs of the war, the continental market for English goods ran dry. To compound the problem, Lloyd George, faced with mounting government deficits, had to raise taxes and slash spending. With speculators and financiers pursuing their own profits without regard for those who had made wartime sacrifices, unemployment rose to a peak of 2.5 million in mid–1921.[172] An expansion of unemployment insurance offered only incremental relief. In the same year, a miner's strike threatened to encompass multiple industries in a nationwide general strike. The crisis was averted at the last moment when the railway and transport industries withdrew their support—a "betrayal," known afterwards as "Black Friday," that became infamous in the eyes of the working class. Amid it all, distraught combat veterans placed a wreath at the British war memorial bearing the epitaph, "From the living victims—the unemployed—to our dead comrades who died in vain."[173]

Commerce faltered within the empire as well, owing in part to native discontent. Indian nationalists asked why they had not been included in the Versailles discussions on self-determination, when thousands of their brethren had served on the Western Front. Rather than debate the point, Britain passed the Rowlatt Acts, extending the imperial government's wartime emergency powers as a means of suppressing all dissent. Provoked by these "Black Acts," the people of the Punjab rioted for three days running (April 10–12, 1919), killing several Europeans. In retaliation, the local British commander, Brigadier General Reginald Dyer, intruded upon a peaceful rally in the walled-in Jallianwallah Garden at Amritsar, sealed the garden exit and ordered his men to open fire with machine guns on the 10,000 unarmed men, women and children in attendance. Speaking to the House of Commons, Winston Churchill reported that the surprised victims "ran madly this way and the other. When the fire was directed upon the centre, they ran to the sides. The fire was then directed upon the sides. Many threw themselves down on the ground, and the fire was then directed on the ground. This was continued for 8 or 10 minutes, and it stopped only when the ammunition had reached the point of exhaustion."[174] A total of 1,600 civilian casualties were sustained in what came to be called the Amritsar Massacre (April 1919). Although the British government inaugurated some modest reforms in the aftermath of the atrocity, they were not nearly enough to satisfy an emerging Indian nationalist movement headed by Mohandas K. Gandhi.

Nor was India the only source of distress—for the simmering question of Ireland had burst once more into full flame. The last prewar general election, held in December 1910, had resulted in the narrowest of victories for the Liberals over the Conservatives. To secure a majority in the Commons, the Liberals required the cooperation of the Irish Parliamentary Party. In obtaining it they incurred a debt that could only be repaid by the promulgation of a new Irish Home Rule Bill.[175] The bill ultimately passed (1914), but the outbreak of the Great War and the threat of civil war between Protestant Ulster and the rest of Ireland deferred any further action.

Deeming "home rule" insufficient in any event, the more radical of Ireland's nationalists sought to capitalize on the outbreak of the war to obtain full independence—"England's adversity," it was said, "was Ireland's opportunity."[176] Unlike the men of the Ulster provinces, who went off to war as the 36th "Ulster" division (subsequently suffering heavy casualties on the Somme), the men of the south faced official objections to the use of the designation "Irish" for their two divisions—the 10th (which was badly mauled at Gallipoli) and the 16th.[177] This slight was greatly resented, and as Irish deaths at the front continued to mount, the discontent burst into plain view in the Easter Rebellion of 1916.

Famous in the annals of Irish nationalism, the uprising was nearly aborted before it began. Sir Roger Casement—a former British diplomat who had helped expose Belgian brutality in the Congo Free State before devoting himself to the cause of Irish nationalism[178]—had gone to Germany to negotiate the purchase of arms for the Irish rebels. The British, however, had been tracking his movements, and no sooner did he debark in Ireland from a German U-boat than he was taken into custody.[179] The ship carrying the arms had to be scuttled offshore on the same day to avoid capture by the Royal Navy.[180] The twin fiascos resulted in the issuance of a "stand down" order on Easter Sunday (the day designated for the uprising), but the following day the rebel rank and file decided to forge ahead—seizing the Government Post Office in Dublin and proclaiming the establishment of an independent Irish Republic. There ensued five days of bitter urban warfare, with many civilians being caught in the crossfire and much of the city being reduced to flaming ruins before artillery and machine gun fire finally settled the issue in the government's favor. When it was over, several of the rebel ringleaders were convicted of treason and executed.

It may be noted that much of the country had not supported the uprising, abetted as it was by the German enemy, while their sons, brothers and husbands risked their lives for "King and Country" as volunteers at the Front. Nevertheless, far from restoring calm (if that was the intent), the execution of the rebellion's ringleaders provoked widespread outrage, driving much of the populace into the arms of the radical republican Sinn Fein Party. Led by Eamon de Valera,[181] a staunch nationalist who had once been a mathematics professor, Sinn Fein won surprising victories in several by-elections over the ensuing two years. When Britain sought to extend its conscription law to Ireland in panicked response to the Ludendorff Offensive in April 1918, the tide became unstoppable. In the postwar "khaki" elections of December 1918, Irish voters gave the party an overwhelming majority outside of Ulster.

The Irish Revolution was now proclaimed. Rather than take their seats at Westminster, the new Irish Sinn Fein MPs formed their own parliament in Dublin, declaring the establishment of an independent Irish Republic under the presidency of de Valera (1919). There ensued a bloody Anglo-Irish War—also called the "Irish War for Independence"—in which a newly constituted Irish Republican Army staged repeated attacks on the Royal Irish Constabulary, the chief enforcers of British authority in Ireland. Although the constabulary was composed mainly of local Irishmen, the IRA branded them as traitors, boycotted them, and, not infrequently, killed them in their homes or at the local pub when they were off duty.[182]

Thrown onto the defensive, but hesitant to employ regular army troops against fellow citizens, the government in London recruited a special "police force" composed mostly of unemployed army veterans to reinforce the constabulary.[183] Known as the "Black and Tans" (owing to their improvised dark green and khaki uniforms), the new recruits locked horns with the IRA in a pitiless campaign of attacks and reprisals, culminating in the events of "Bloody Sunday" (November 21, 1920), wherein a special squad of gunmen led by IRA intelligence chief Michael Collins assassinated more than a dozen British undercover agents in Dublin, and the Black and Tans savagely ran amuck during an ill-considered raid on a Dublin soccer stadium in the midst of a match, killing a like number.[184] One week later, at Kilmichael in County Cork, the IRA ambushed a convoy of so-called "Auxiliaries" (a specialist force that was even more notorious than the Black and Tans), killing 16 and leaving a lone survivor paralyzed.[185]

Soon afterwards, a pair of agreements emanating from London added the burden of civil war to the existing mayhem. Towards the end of 1920, the British Parliament passed a new "Government of Ireland Bill" partitioning the island into autonomous "Northern" and "Southern" provinces. "Northern Ireland"—governed from Belfast and composed of six out of the nine historic counties of Ulster—received the most expansive boundaries consistent with a durable Protestant majority (although Catholics were more numerous in two of the included counties).[186] The remainder of the island was dubbed "Southern Ireland."

Catholics of all stripes regarded the partition as anathema—most especially those left behind in Northern Ireland, who would now constitute a minority in a Protestant land. It was an agonizing inversion of the situation that had faced Protestant Ulster at the time of the Home Rule Act of 1914.[187] While the South would not consider the proposal, the Protestant leaders in Ulster accepted it. Consequently, in May 1921, "Northern Ireland" came into being as an autonomous province of the United Kingdom. The result was a sectarian civil war, with IRA fighters moving north to carry out attacks on the new regime, while a new "Ulster Special Constabulary" carried out reprisals that included widespread intimidation and violence against its own Catholic minority. A plea for peace from King George V, who traveled personally to Belfast in an attempt to soothe passions, proved unavailing. The train bearing his cavalry escort to Dublin was ambushed the following day, resulting in the death of four men and eighty horses.[188] Soon thereafter, however, the IRA suffered a major reverse in Dublin, where the Auxiliaries captured more than one hundred IRA fighters after the latter set fire to the Customs House.

In London, Lloyd George was coming under increasing pressure to put an end to an unpopular and economically burdensome conflict that seemingly could not be won. He offered a truce and, employing his "Welsh Wizardry" at negotiation, struck a compromise agreement with an Irish delegation headed by Michael Collins and Arthur Griffith, who had been deputed by Eamon de Valera to attend talks in London. The accord provided for the establishment of a virtually independent "Irish Free State" nominally tied to the British crown by a figurehead governor-general. Northern Ireland would remain separate, but a boundary commission was to redraw its borders, returning much of the Catholic minority to the Irish Free State.

The agreement had much in its favor, but de Valera adamantly opposed it, citing the provision for a separate Northern Ireland (boundary commission or no) and the failure to create a full-fledged Irish republic. In spite of his objections, the Dublin Parliament approved the Treaty by a margin of seven votes. The result was a second civil war, in which Collins, as head of the new Irish Free State, was compelled to shell rebel strongholds in Dublin with artillery supplied by the British government. The rebels retaliated by blowing up the Public Records Office, destroying documents that were hundreds of years old.[189] Before the unhappy conflict came to an end, the populace had shown its support for the treaty in new elections, but Collins had been shot dead in ambush.

Lloyd George had extricated his government from a conflict that, in the words of Richard Bennett, "the English have struggled to forget and the Irish cannot help but remember."[190] But the British economy was floundering. The number of unemployed adult males in Britain was now consistently above one million and the prime minister's "land fit for heroes" was nowhere in sight.[191] The Anglo-Irish War had been waged at great economic cost, and Lloyd George's subsequent threat to declare war on Turkey after the Greek defeat at Smyrna (1922) proved his undoing. The Conservative Party withdrew from his coalition government, forcing the prime minister to step down and summon new elections.

The ensuing two years were politically calamitous. Running on their own merits, the Conservatives, led by Andrew Bonar Law, emerged triumphant in the election of November 1922. However, after condemning the French occupation of the Ruhr, Bonar Law had to resign due to throat cancer. His successor, Stanley Baldwin, wished to give home industry a boost by introducing tariffs on foreign imports, but felt he could not do so without a popular referendum. Hence, in December 1923, elections were again held with the Conservatives winning a plurality, but not a majority, of seats.[192] The Liberal and Labor parties were therefore able to oust them by forming a coalition government under the Labor Party leader, Ramsay MacDonald.

It was the first Labor ministry in British history, and it was not a success. Despite repeated assurances that his party "never had the least inclination to try short cuts to the millennium,"[193] MacDonald was suspected of favoring radical measures. Consequently, even as unemployment continued to rise, the Liberal opposition within his own cabinet blocked his attempts at social legislation. In foreign affairs, the prime minister successfully promoted the Dawes Plan, but his government's recognition of the Soviet Union, and its desire for a trade deal with that nation, provoked accusations of Bolshevism and caused the Liberals to quit the coalition after a tenure of just nine months.[194]

The ensuing elections were rocked by scandal when the London *Daily Mail* published a clandestine letter implying that Britain's ongoing negotiations with the Soviet Union were meant to spread Bolshevism to the United Kingdom.[195] The letter—penned (allegedly) by the prominent Soviet official, Grigory Zinoviev, and addressed to the British Communist Party leadership—was a forgery, but Labor did not survive the blow. On October 29, 1924, Stanley Baldwin returned to office with a greater than two-thirds Conservative majority in the House of Commons.

With his own party divided on the question of protective tariffs, Baldwin introduced a program entitled "safeguarding employment" in which specific industries were empowered to petition parliament for "safeguarding duties" against foreign competitors in order to preserve domestic jobs. In the matter of coal, however, the problem was simply too big. Oil, diesel and hydroelectric power were now major alternative energy sources. Domestic demand was low, and with Germany being forced to supply coal to France under the Treaty of Versailles, the demand abroad was even lower.[196]

The problem was exacerbated in 1925, when Baldwin's Chancellor of the Exchequer, Winston Churchill (newly recruited to the Conservative Party after a long tenure with the Liberals), placed the British economy back on the gold standard in hopes of restoring the nation's bygone economic primacy. The economist John Maynard Keynes vilified the decision in a booklet titled *The Economic Consequences of Mr. Churchill*.[197] Far from accomplishing its stated aim, Churchill's policy priced Britain out of the export market by raising the value of the British pound with respect to other currencies.[198] British coal now cost more abroad than coal from competing producer states. The British coal industry reacted by demanding longer hours and lower wages for its workers so that prices could be reduced. The workers objected, and when the existing wage contract expired on May 1, 1926, the Trades Union Congress called a general strike in their support encompassing multiple industries, including steel and transport.[199]

The main outcome of the General Strike of 1926—transiently crippling though it was—was to remove the right of the unions to stage such a strike ever again. The government was able to provide essential services by enlisting non-union workers, and nine days into the strike the Trades Union Congress withdrew its support. Although the coal miners themselves remained on strike for months forcing the country to import coal from abroad, the promise of Miner's Federation Secretary Arthur J. Cook—"Not a penny off the pay, not a second on the day,"[200]—proved beyond fulfillment. When the strike ended in November, the workers returned on worse terms than had been offered to them at the outset of the strike.[201] A few months later, Parliament passed the Trades Unions and Trades Disputes Act of 1927 making general strikes illegal.[202]

This was not, however, at all the same thing as solving the nation's economic woes. Much of Britain's industrial infrastructure was antiquated in comparison to that of the United States, Japan and Germany, and the balance of imports and exports continued its adverse trend. By mid–1928, nearly 30 percent of British coal miners were unemployed, with the number of unemployed shipbuilders and steel workers being only marginally lower.[203] In the midst of it all, the nation held new general elections (1929). In 1924, the Liberal Party had been reduced to a paltry 40 seats. Lloyd George proposed to return it to power with a platform featuring a national public works program to solve unemployment. The electorate, however, chose to give another chance to Ramsay MacDonald and Labor.

Unfortunately for MacDonald, he took office just in time for the Great Depression. Over the ensuing two years, the number of unemployed rose to nearly 3 million, and the cost of the dole threatened to bankrupt the treasury. MacDonald sought a 10 percent decrease in the dole budget, but much of his own party refused to support him.[204] In a surprising riposte, he turned out the cabinet and formed a new National Coalition government with Conservative support. (Labor denounced him as a traitor for it and ousted him from the party.[205]) In short order, the new government passed a finance bill decreasing payments to the unemployed and cutting the salaries of government workers. The measure provoked widespread protests and, in some cases, full-scale riots. Nervous foreign investors withdrew their funds from the Bank of England causing Britain's gold reserves to decline sharply. The exchequer responded by dropping the gold standard and allowing the British pound to undergo devaluation (September 1931). In new elections held the following month, National Coalition candidates, headed by MacDonald but composed mostly of Conservatives, trounced Labor by a margin of ten to one.[206] The pillar of their economic program was the imposition of protectionist tariffs, which, though controversial, seemed to stabilize the economy.[207]

MacDonald remained prime minister for three more years, but his mental faculties had begun to decline. His speeches in Parliament became increasingly incoherent—one witness remarking that "nobody knew what the prime minister was going to say in the House of Commons, and, when he did say it, nobody understood it."[208] He stepped down at the age of 70, in June 1935, and died two years later.

Stanley Baldwin now returned as prime minister for the third and last time. From a domestic standpoint, his final ministry is remembered chiefly for the succession crisis following the death of King George V in January 1936. The crown passed to the king's eldest son who took the throne as Edward VIII. A playboy and Nazi sympathizer (so much so that the British Foreign Intelligence Service began monitoring his activities),[209] Edward was in thrall to Mrs. Wallis Warfield Simpson, an American who was in the midst of seeking a divorce from her second husband. Once she was free, Edward intended to marry her. Although the people of Britain and the empire were not sure if Mrs. Simpson should not be queen because she was an American, or if she should not be queen because she had been twice married and divorced, they were agreed that she should not be queen.[210] Secretly, the cabinet members informed Baldwin that if Edward did not break off the romance, they would resign, which must inevitably create a constitutional crisis pitting the king against parliament, whether in forming a new cabinet (if there were enough willing participants to support Edward's cause) or in holding new elections in which the king's impending "improper" marriage must be the principal issue.

Told that the current cabinet would not support him, Edward announced that he would abdicate, but then changed his mind, stating that he would pursue a morganatic wedding with Mrs. Simpson that would preclude her from being recognized as queen—a solution that, in his view, would render the issue moot. Informed that the cabinet and the dominions would not approve even a morganatic marriage, Edward suggested that he take the question to the people in a radio address—a move that Baldwin rejected as unconstitutional. Checkmate having been achieved, the king abdicated on December 10, 1936.[211] (The following October, in his new capacity as "Duke of Windsor," he brought Wallis to Germany, where the happy couple had pictures taken with Hitler.[212]) His younger brother—now George VI—succeeded him. In May 1937, Baldwin retired in favor of his chancellor of the exchequer, Neville Chamberlain—soon to be notorious in our story. We must, however, leave that topic to our discussion of international affairs.

France: National Bloc, Left Cartel and Popular Front

On returning from Versailles in 1919, Georges Clemenceau successfully championed a bill to limit the workday to eight hours. Then, to finish out his venerable career, he took the obvious step of standing for the presidency in the elections of January 1920. He didn't win. Hailed as the "Father of Victory," at the end of the war, he was, at the end of the peace, denounced as the "Squanderer of Victory"[213]—ostensibly for being too *lenient* on the Germans at Versailles. Stepping down as prime minister of the "Sacred Union" (the coalition government that had been formed during the war), he withdrew form public life bitterly resenting his fate. Ironically, Paul Deschanel, who defeated him in the presidential election, had to resign before the year was out after leaping from a moving presidential train in a fit of lunacy and wandering about in his pajamas until the authorities retrieved him.[214]

Control of the Third Republic was now contested between two rival coalitions: the conservative National Bloc and the liberal Left Cartel (*Cartel des Gauches*). Emerging from the war with 13,000 square miles of its industrial north reduced to ruins and nearly 1,600,000 dead (indeed, 30 percent of all French males between the ages of 18 and 28 had perished),[215] France was in no mood for the high taxes and moderate foreign policy favored by the latter. Consequently, the National Bloc emerged from the "horizon blue" elections of 1920 (named in honor of the color of the French infantry uniform) with a 70 percent majority in the Chamber of Deputies.

The national temperament dictated that German taxpayers—not French—must pay the cost of rebuilding the ravaged north. On top of the war debt already owed to the United States and Great Britain, Raymond Poincaré, the National Bloc's dominant political figure, required new loans for national reconstruction. To fund these debts without raising taxes, the collection of reparations from Germany was absolutely essential. It was for this reason that Poincaré invaded the Ruhr in 1923,[216] but as we have seen the policy ended in disaster. The German campaign of passive resistance spawned an inflationary whirlwind, ruining the value of the mark, and threatening to drag the franc after it. To the rest of the world, moreover, France had appeared obdurate in her policy toward Germany—and to top matters off, she needed another international loan to stabilize her economy. She obtained it, but at the price of abandoning her reparations policy.[217] In the elections of 1924, Poincaré was ousted from office, and the Left Cartel formed a ministry under Édouard Herriot. By supporting the Dawes Plan (1924) and Locarno treaties (1925), Herriot brought a satisfactory end to the reparations imbroglio, obtained collective security for the nation and restored France's international reputation. But the Left Cartel's economic policy was unsound.[218] Government expenditures regularly outpaced revenues, and as it did, the franc declined to a tenth of its prewar value—worth a mere 2 cents when it had been worth 20.[219] People living on fixed incomes fell into penury, and the Left Cartel's insistence that the economic woes of the state necessitated increased taxes on the wealthy (a class with prodigious skill at tax evasion) only worsened the crisis by provoking an exodus of capital as nervous investors moved their assets abroad.[220]

Herriot's ministry foundered on the question of taxes (April 1925). It was followed in the ensuing year by a half dozen other failed ministries. The political turmoil came to an end only with the formation, in 1926, of an emergency "National Union Ministry," led by Poincaré, but including several former prime ministers—among them Poincaré's erstwhile rivals of the Left, Herriot and Aristide Briand. Known to be incorruptible (if flawed in other respects), Poincaré was allowed to rule by decree in economic matters.[221] Thus empowered, he brought the inflationary trend to a halt through strict economies—cutting expenditures and raising taxes, even on the wealthy, who deigned to submit to his modest requirements since they knew him to be a conservative rather than a radical.[222] Formerly derided as "Poincaré la Guerre" and "Poincaré la Ruhr" for his intransigent foreign policy,[223] the resurrected statesman was now revered as the "savior of the franc" for stabilizing its value at a fifth of its pre-war level—which is to say at 4 cents. It was not, however, primarily the middle or lower class that lavished him with this praise. Beneficial as the prime minister's intervention may have been to industrialists, property owners and the government itself, it sharply diminished the value of the average Frenchman's savings.[224]

When Poincaré retired in 1929, the French economy (if not the average Frenchman) was on firm footing. More agrarian and self-sufficient than other industrialized states, France at first avoided the worst effects of the Great Depression—even managing to enact a workmen's insurance program.[225] But the panic attendant on the collapse of

Austria's *Kredit Anstalt* bank in 1931 had profound reverberations on the French stock exchange. Amid the crisis, Great Britain and the United States abandoned the gold standard and allowed their currencies to undergo devaluation—a move intended to buttress their export trade. But after the crisis of the preceding decade, France absolutely refused to follow their lead. The franc, consequently, became expensive in relation to other currencies, effectively pricing French products out of the export market—a market, incidentally, that was already contracting since France dealt mostly in luxury items that were not sought after in the throes of a depression.[226]

Thus, the world economic calamity finally struck home—and when it did, the political situation deteriorated again, with ministries being cast out of office almost before they took their seats. Because of the multiplicity of French political parties, the ruling ministries of the Third Republic were composed of fragile coalitions that were apt to dissolve at the drop of a hat. Between 1870 and 1940, 110 separate ministries ruled France—34 of them between 1917 and 1937.[227] In this milieu, inept government policy was taken for corruption—most vociferously by *Action Française*, a royalist organization with fascist (not to mention anti–Semitic) leanings. In December 1933, the impulse gained momentum owing to a pair of major scandals. Early in the month, a bond scam run by the director of the Bayonne municipal pawnshop, Serge Alexandre Stavisky, went belly up, costing thousands of citizens their life's savings. Six hundred million francs were lost in all.[228] As the police closed in on him, Stavisky—a fraudster who had ties to some of France's leading politicians—shot himself. Rumor, however, said that the police had been in on the scheme, and that they had shot Stavisky so he couldn't squeal on the corrupt politicians. The subsequent mysterious death of a judge who had granted Stavisky nineteen trial postponements on a previous indictment confirmed many Frenchmen in the belief that those "who knew too much" were being rubbed out.[229]

Hot on the heels of this so-called "Stavisky Affair," a major rail accident at Lagny resulted in two hundred fatalities at the height of the Christmas season. Despite allegations of railway safety negligence, the government did not aggressively probe the issue.[230] Certain that corruption was the only explanation, protestors ran riot in Paris. Unable to contain them, the police called in mounted auxiliaries (the Mobile Guards) and firemen—the latter employing their fire hoses to disperse the angry throngs when all else had failed.[231]

The largest of the demonstrations occurred on February 6, 1934, when an assortment of agitators from the extreme right and the extreme left of the political spectrum took to the streets. Among the participants were the veteran's organization *Croix de Feu* ("Cross of Fire"), the royalist diehards of *Action Française* (accompanied by their well-educated, but nevertheless juvenile delinquent youth organization, the *Camelots du Roi*, or "King's Henchmen"—France's version of Mussolini's "black shirts"),[232] and hardline Communists, who, in accordance with the dictates of Moscow, were willing to cooperate even with arch political rivals if it afforded them the chance to strike a blow at the bourgeois republic.[233]

The intent of the mob seems to have been to storm the Chamber of Deputies and chase the legislators from their seats. According to the eyewitness, William Shirer, *Croix de Feu* agitators, advancing down the lightly defended Rue de Bourgogne, could have accomplished the task with ease. But their commander, uneasy about the repercussions, prudently ordered them to stand down.[234] On the Place de la Concorde the situation was otherwise. Police there were pelted with rocks or thrown into the Seine while attempting to fend off *Action Francaise* and the Communists.[235] Recognized exiting the Palais-Bourbon (the Chamber of Deputies' meeting place), Édouard Herriot was seized by the mob and bullied toward the Seine. He protested that as the longtime mayor of Lyons, it would be more appropriate to throw him into the Rhone. The police saved him before the crowd could render a final decision.[236]

At 10:30 p.m., the violence escalated as a crowd of 10,000 rioters staged repeated charges against a defending force of policemen, firemen and mounted Mobile Guardsmen on the Place de la Concorde. As Shirer describes the scene, the defenders were at their last gasp and would have given way at the next charge, but in the nick of time 500 gendarmes under the command of a certain Colonel Simon arrived to reinforce them. Their countercharge put the rioters to flight, leaving 16 dead and many hundreds wounded in the street. The police themselves suffered one fatality and more than 1,600 injured.[237] Amid threats that the riots would be renewed the following night, Prime Minister Édouard Daladier sought to declare martial law, but found that most members of his own cabinet would not support him. Seeing no alternative, he resigned.[238]

The riots persisted for the better part of a week. In the aftermath, Daladier's replacement, Gaston Doumergue, sought to strengthen the constitutional position of the prime minister and cabinet relative to the Chamber of Deputies, hoping thus to render the government less prone to the dissolutions that transpired with such maddening regularity. In violation of precedent, he bypassed the contentious Chamber and brought his proposed reforms directly to the people in a series of radio broadcasts.[239] When he demanded, however, that the Chamber of Deputies approve, without debate, a budget proposal that he would not let them see, even the cabinet balked. Several members resigned, causing Doumergue's fall from power in November 1934 with his constitutional program in ruins.[240]

In the ensuing two years, France would be ruled by three separate ministries, which between them managed to increase taxes, to reduce state salaries and pensions and to do nothing at all as German troops marched into the Rhineland. By the time the next general elections were held in 1936, fascists and royalists were roaming the streets, chanting, "Take France from the politicians and give it back to the French people!" Setting aside their perennial differences, the parties of the left—Socialists, Radical Socialists and Communists—formed a so-called "Popular Front," answering the slogans of the right with their own promise to "break the power of the two hundred families who control the economic life of the nation."[241] Although Léon Blum, the Jewish humanitarian leader of the Socialist Party, was unable to campaign after being beaten up by royalist thugs,[242] the Popular Front came out on top.

With a broad-based leftist government now in charge, the working class decided its moment had arrived. The Popular Front assumed ministerial authority amid a wave of "sit-down" strikes across multiple industries, as workers showed up at the workplace but refused to do their jobs. In effect, employers found their factories under hostile occupation. All production ground to a halt. (The workers kept vital services such as food and transport up and running so as not to alienate public sympathy.[243]) As the government would not use force against the very workers who had just voted for them,[244] the employers were forced to negotiate. In June 1936, they sat down with Prime Minister Blum and a deputation of trade union officials at the Hotel Matignon (Blum's official prime ministerial residence). The result was the so-called "Matignon Agreement," whereby the working class obtained wage increases, the forty-hour workweek and the right to collective bargaining with compulsory arbitration of refractory disputes. They also obtained something altogether new—paid vacations (although their subsequent invasion of the hallowed retreats of the bourgeoisie was greeted with upturned noses).[245]

By the same agreement, the Bank of France (the putative vehicle of "the two hundred families who control the economic life of the nation") was brought under government control.[246] In the ensuing months the salary reductions imposed on state workers in 1935 were reversed, and a public works program was inaugurated. In fine, the Popular Front had accomplished all things save balancing the budget.[247] It was enough to provoke a new "flight from the franc," as investors, fearing what the government might do next, once again moved money abroad. To stem the tide, Blum was forced to place a moratorium on further reforms and to commit the cardinal sin of devaluing the franc (in violation of solemn campaign promises).[248] In June 1937, he sought power to rule by decree in economic matters, including in matters of currency exchange. His bid was defeated, and he resigned. The Popular Front fell with him.

The Radical Socialists now formed a ministry and, under pressure from financial conservatives, reversed the forty-hour workweek. Labor rightly felt betrayed, and the latter months of 1938 witnessed a new wave of strikes—many of them violent. The simmering class conflict was cut short, however, by events abroad.

11

International Affairs
Between the Wars, 1919–1939

The End of the Versailles System
and the League of Nations Covenant

Of the Big Four at Versailles, France alone retained her devotion to the perpetual containment of Germany. Her chief ally, Great Britain, was too interested in the reestablishment of a healthy export market in Germany to share France's interest in keeping her neighbor weak. The United States had refused to ratify the Treaty of Versailles precisely because she wished to avoid the political and military entanglements it might entail, while Italy, angered by the paltry gains awarded to her at Versailles, was intent on an expansionist foreign policy that was more likely to conflict with French and British ambitions than German.[1] The promise of international harmony created by the Locarno Treaties and the Kellogg-Briand Pact of the mid–1920s, moreover, had gone up in smoke with the advent of the Great Depression and the disappearance of American loans. And now, the rise of Hitlerism in Germany had rendered French anxieties all the more acute.

In 1932, a World Disarmament Conference was convened under League of Nations' auspices in Geneva, Switzerland, with the stated goal of reducing international armaments on the basis of military parity. In April 1934, the conference proposed the establishment of parity between France and Germany, with their respective armies being limited to 300,000 soldiers. Noting that this meant disarmament only for France, and *rearmament* for Germany (whose armed forces had been limited by the Versailles terms to 100,000 men), the French Foreign Minister, Louis Barthou, withdrew from the conference, declaring that in the future France would "assure her security by her own means" (April 1934).[2]

In Barthou's view, everything depended upon Eastern Europe, where he hoped to forge closer ties with Soviet Russia and the Little Entente powers (i.e., Czechoslovakia, Romania and Yugoslavia). In September 1934, he took an initial step by helping to orchestrate the Soviet Union's acceptance into the League of Nations. At the same time, he sought to promote a so-called "Eastern Locarno," whereby Germany was to enter into agreements with Russia, Poland, Czechoslovakia and Romania guaranteeing the existing borders of the Eastern European states. Not surprisingly, Hitler refused outright (September 1934).[3]

Undeterred, Barthou pressed ahead. Seeking to smooth over relations between two potential allies—Italy and Yugoslavia—he invited Yugoslavia's King Alexander to Marseille for discussions (October 1934). Alas, the visit was ill fated. Formerly known as the

"Kingdom of the Serbs, Croats and Slovenes," Yugoslavia was a hotbed of ethnic dis-content—most particularly between the Serbs, who favored centralized rule under their own ascendancy, and the Croats, who favored decentralization with autonomy for the nation's minorities. The parliament, or *Skupshtina*, consequently, became a great arena of name-calling and physical violence. On more than one occasion, the police had to be summoned to separate the disputants—and to little avail, for wild hysteria remained the order of the day. In June 1928, the violence culminated in a Serbian deputy opening fire with a pistol on the Croatian delegation—mortally wounding the famed Croatian orator and party leader, Stefan Radich.[4] Amid Croatian threats of secession, parliamentary rule now collapsed. In response, King Alexander assumed dictatorial authority—changing the name of the state from the "Kingdom of the Serbs, Croats and Slovenes" to "Yugosla-via," and bidding his people to unite in the name of their shared Slavic heritage. But even after the promulgation of a new constitution in 1931, it was patently clear that Alexander intended to pursue a pro–Serbian policy at the expense of everyone else.

It was in this milieu that Alexander traveled to Marseille where enthusiastic crowds greeted him at the dock as a boat tendered him to shore from a Yugoslavian naval vessel. Louis Barthou was there to meet him, and after a short walk, the two entered the back-seat of an open motorcar in preparation for a gala parade through the city. Scarcely was the procession underway, however, when a Macedonian member of the Croatian ter-rorist organization, *Ustacha*, jumped onto the automobile's running board and shot the two statesmen from point-blank range.[5] Both died within minutes, while police, joined by irate bystanders, seized the attacker, threw him to the ground and kicked and tram-pled him to death.

For France, the loss proved irreparable, for no one else in the French foreign min-istry possessed Barthou's breadth of vision regarding French security. Germany, mean-while, had already withdrawn from the League of Nations over the issue of armaments (October 1933) and had embarked on an aggressive rearmament program—concentrat-ing first and foremost on air power (which was forbidden to Germany by the Treaty of Versailles) and including the construction of a large number of bombers. The program was an open "secret," designed (as Ruth Henig notes) to deter France or anyone else from taking preemptive military action against Germany while the latter expanded her other armed service branches.[6]

In reacting to Germany's rearmament, Great Britain, France and Italy stumbled over one another's toes in a tragicomedy that might have been written by the ancient Greeks. Just prior to a planned visit to Germany by British foreign secretary, John Simon, Britain published a White Paper calling for a substantial increase in military expenditures—an action taken, it should be noted, out of concern that Germany was secretly rearming (which Germany was). Pretending, to the contrary, that Germany was the imperiled party, Hitler announced the implementation of compulsory military ser-vice with the intent of enlarging the German army to 500,000 men.[7] In so doing, the Nazi leader correctly wagered that none of the European powers would call his bluff, and when, despite the conscription announcement, Simon proceeded with his visit, Hit-ler took matters a step further by revealing that the Luftwaffe was already equal in size to the Royal Air Force—all the while cheerfully expressing his willingness to enter into "arms limitations" talks.[8]

The German threat was now deemed so acute that French Prime Minister Pierre Flandin and British Prime Minister Ramsay MacDonald personally traveled to Stresa on the shore of Italy's Lake Maggiore to enlist the support of Benito Mussolini. The picturesque location inspired the three leaders to agree to a united front against any attempt to alter the terms of the Treaty of Versailles by force—"an impressive display of words," says A.J.P. Taylor, "though rather late in the day when so much had been changed already."[9]

And now came the missteps. In May 1935, France offended Great Britain and Italy by concluding a limited mutual assistance pact with the Soviet Union, which her two partners still regarded as a pariah—Italy, because Mussolini hated communism, Britain, because it feared Soviet encroachment in Asia.[10] The following month, Britain did the French one better by signing an agreement with Hitler that limited the size of Germany's navy to one-third the size of Britain's. Inasmuch as this covenant allowed Germany to violate the naval restrictions imposed on her by the Treaty of Versailles (so much so, indeed, that Germany could have kept her shipyards operating at full capacity for a decade without reaching the new limit[11]), it was taken as something of an affront by the other two Stresa signatories, who, after all, had just undertaken with Britain to *prevent* rather than to *abet* such infractions.[12]

It was now Mussolini's turn to offend, and the Italian dictator did not disappoint. Before we embark on that story, however, a brief digression is necessary in order to explain why Great Britain could have been so diplomatically ham-fisted as to sign a naval agreement with Germany just two months after the formation of the "Stresa Front."

As it turns out, her decision had very little to do with European affairs, and everything to do with imperial affairs in the Far East. When last we encountered China, she was struggling with modernization, and as we return to her at this point in our story, she is struggling with it still. During the previous century, she had clung tenaciously to her ancient traditions. But the humiliation wrought by Europe's imperialist exploitation and by defeat in the Sino-Japanese War (1894–95) sparked a nationalist movement whose proponents favored Westernization as a means of reclaiming the nation's dignity and independence.

The Manchu Dynasty, which had ruled the nation in feudal fashion for three centuries, stubbornly refused to adopt the nationalist program. By 1911, however, it could no longer resist the growing unrest. In that year, a young reformer named Sun Yat-sen led a revolution, overthrowing the child emperor, P'u Yi, and establishing a republic. In China's decentralized vastness, however, Sun's Nationalist Party (the "Kuomintang") encountered opposition from local warlords and from former units of the imperial army. The fragmentation of authority led ultimately to the establishment of rival capitals— one in Canton controlled constitutionally by the Kuomintang, the other in Peking, still dependent on foreign loans and therefore beholden to foreign influence (1917).[13]

In the midst of the chaos, Japan capitalized on the outbreak of World War I to seize Germany's concessions in China's Shantung Province. China demanded that the Japanese depart. Japan responded with the so-called "Twenty-One Demands," which, if accepted, would have transformed China into a virtual Japanese protectorate (January 1915). China was saved from this predicament by the protests of the European powers and the United States whose own treaty rights stood to be infringed by the Japanese ultimatum. Nevertheless, Japan emerged from the quarrel with important railway and economic concessions in the important northern province of Manchuria—home to abundant raw materials (with the railroads to carry them) and *entrepôt* for one-third of

China's exports and one-fifth of her imports.[14] At war's end, moreover, Japan's delegation lobbied successfully in Paris for recognition of her claims to the captured German concessions in Shantung Province (mostly because France and Great Britain had promised these concessions to her when she agreed to enter the war in 1914).[15]

The nationalists of the Kuomintang never recognized Japan's various aggressions. In the wake of Russia's Bolshevik Revolution, communism had obtained a wide following in China, and in a bid to consolidate his control over the country Sun enlisted the communists' support against the warlords and the Peking government (1924). The following year, Sun succumbed to cancer, whereupon his former secretary, Chiang Kai-shek, commandant of the military academy, assumed leadership. By 1928, Chiang had captured Peking and established a new national capital at Nanking. But he had also broken with the communists, whom he hated with a passion, and whose numbers seemed to be multiplying exponentially—especially in rural areas—under the leadership of Mao Tse-tung (one of the founders of the Chinese Communist Party).[16] The result was further civil warfare.

By 1931, however, China faced a more formidable threat. To counter ongoing Japanese interference in Manchuria, China had built new railways (to rival those that had been under Japanese concession since the days of the Twenty-One Demands) and had veritably flooded the province with immigrants from other parts of China. Then in the summer of 1931, the Chinese imposed a national boycott against Japanese trade,[17] striking a blow at Japan's cotton export industry just when tariffs and world depression were obliterating her commerce in silk.[18]

At the height of the crisis, the Japanese military, if not her government, contrived a novel solution to the nation's growing economic woes. They would invade war-torn China and commandeer her resources and labor for the benefit of the Japanese economy.[19] The scheme had been dreamed up by Japan's aristocratic military caste, which had very little difficulty carrying it into effect since it had the ear of the Japanese emperor and had been silencing political naysayers by assassination for a decade.[20] By 1931, all was in order. Without consulting the civil government, the Japanese Army invaded Manchuria—using as a pretext the explosion of a bomb (likely set off by themselves[21]) on the Japanese-controlled South Manchurian Railway. By year's end, Japanese troops had occupied the entire province, declaring it to be an "independent" state, to be known henceforth as "Manchukuo." A veneer of "legitimacy" was given to this aggression by the appointment of P'u Yi, the ousted Chinese Manchu emperor, as nominal leader of the puppet Manchukuo government.

The League of Nations was slow to protest the action, since many of its member-states feared the decline in trade that an outright break with Japan would entail.[22] Britain, however, had an additional reason to proceed cautiously, since a breach with Japan might imperil her own Far Eastern colonial interests, particularly in Shanghai, Hong Kong and Singapore.[23] Eventually, the League did condemn the Japanese conquest (February 1933). Japan answered this censure by withdrawing her delegation from the League of Nations while continuing her invasion of Manchuria. When the League failed to retaliate, its fecklessness was exposed to the world.[24] From the British standpoint, however, the problem was even worse. Although she had avoided an open breach with Japan, Britain now found herself facing a new dilemma, potentially more costly than the old—for Japan's military action in China carried with it a desire to exceed the limits imposed on the size of the Japanese Navy by the 1922 Treaty of Washington (which set the British-American-Japanese tonnage ratio at 5:5:3) and the 1930 Treaty of London (which liberalized the ratio to 10:10:7 for certain classes of ships). The Royal Navy was barely able to defend Britain's far-flung colonial empire adequately as matters stood, and with her economy tottering, she was in poor position to fund an expansion of her navy if the Japanese decided to embark on a naval arms race with her.[25] And if Germany were to embark on a naval arms race with her at the same time, the strain on the British economy could scarcely be borne. Consequently, when Hitler offered to limit the size of Germany's navy at half the ratio it had possessed relative to Britain at the outbreak of World War I, Britain fairly leapt at the chance.[26]

The British decision, as the English historian Alfred Cobban has noted, sparked an animated debate in France as to whether the British were duplicitous or asinine.[27] Mussolini, however, saw it as an opportunity to embark on a prized project of his own. At the Stresa Conference, the Duce had volunteered to read aloud the joint statement of the assembled leaders regarding their "complete agreement in opposing ... any unilateral repudiation of treaties which may endanger the peace of Europe...." As Churchill relates in his war memoirs, the British delegates in attendance (perhaps even the doddering Ramsay MacDonald) could not help but notice that Mussolini had accentuated the words "of Europe" in what was otherwise a quite lovely rendering of the text.[28] If they had any doubt as to what meaning the Italian leader sought to impart by this special emphasis, Mussolini did not long keep them in suspense. In October 1935, he embarked on the invasion of Abyssinia (Ethiopia), which, as a careful glance at a map of that era will show, was not part *of Europe*.

The logical syllogism concocted by Mussolini in order to begin forging a "new Roman empire"—to wit, "I am pledged to the peace of Europe; Ethiopia is not in Europe; Therefore, I am free to make war on Ethiopia"—contains a material fallacy that the Romans of old used to call a *"non sequitur."*[29] Notwithstanding this error, the Duce found a ready pretext for his Ethiopian design in a violent border clash at Walwal on the country's ill-defined border with Italian Somaliland.[30] Employing tanks, planes, machine guns and poison gas, his legions made steady inroads against Ethiopia's turban-clad cavalry and barefoot, rifle-bearing infantry before mountainous terrain and a lack of roads slowed their progress.[31] Adowa, site of Italy's humiliating colonial defeat in 1896, was bombed from the air and captured within 72 hours. (Italian troops festooned the ruins with a cenotaph to memorialize their victory.)[32]

Ethiopia's emperor, Haile Selassie, promptly appealed to the League of Nations, which was obliged, under Article 10 of its charter, to defend the sovereignty of all member states against wanton attack. It did not help matters that the League's two most powerful members, Britain and France, were also the world's leading imperialist powers, and therefore in poor position to lecture Italy on the ethics of colonial aggression.[33] Nevertheless, the League responded by invoking Article 16 of the charter—providing for the imposition of economic sanctions against aggressor nations. "Thus," says Walter Consuelo Langsam, "began the first 'great experiment of the coercive powers' of the League."[34]

The experiment was not a success—largely because, on the one hand, the sanctions, which took effect on November 18, 1935, did not ban the sale to Italy of the one resource that was truly imperative (i.e., oil)[35]; whilst on the other, Britain left the Suez Canal open to Italian shipping when barring passage would have made continuation of the war impossible.[36] In the meantime, behind the scenes, British and French "diplomacy" could do no better than to contrive the secret "Hoare-Laval Pact" (December 1935)—a plan to bribe Haile Selassie with an outlet to the Red Sea via a corridor through British Somali-land provided that he would peacefully cede to Mussolini the vast areas of his country already occupied by Italian forces. (It may be added that the corridor offered to Selas-sie was decrepit enough to be derided in the *Times* as a "corridor for camels."[37]) When the pact was leaked to the press, it created a scandal from which the League never recov-ered. In Britain, Hoare was sacked as foreign secretary. Nevertheless, relations with Italy remained under strain—and, worse still, the germ of appeasement had entered into European diplomacy.

Concerned over the breach with Italy, the French Chamber of Deputies finally got around to ratifying the 1935 Franco-Soviet Pact on February 27, 1936. The squab-ble between the signatories of the Stresa Agreement had now reached a level sufficient to distract their attention from their original objective—the containment of Nazi Ger-many. Consequently, Hitler seized the moment to drop his next bombshell. Loudly con-demning the Franco-Soviet Pact as a breach of "the spirit of Locarno" and a threat to peace, he ordered German troops to reoccupy the Rhineland on March 7, 1936.[38] It was the most flagrant violation of the Treaty of Versailles to date.

In an effort to confound world opinion, the Führer proposed, on the morning of the occupation, a pact guaranteeing the demilitarization of the Rhineland for a period of twenty-five years if France would likewise demilitarize her own side of the frontier. (This was two hours before his troops marched.[39]) Additionally, he offered to sign non-aggression agreements with the various states on Germany's borders. Such chican-ery was not without effect amongst those who still hoped desperately to count Hitler a peaceable man.[40] France, however, could not help but see Hitler's offer for the sham it was. To demilitarize her own side of the frontier, France would have to abandon her famed Maginot Line defenses,[41] while Germany's "concession" in return would be to have her obligation to keep the Rhineland demilitarized *shortened* from perpetuity (as required by her signature on the Treaty of Versailles) to a mere twenty-five years!

Declaring that he would not tolerate the presence of German guns on the outskirts of Strasbourg,[42] Albert Sarraut (the newest in the ongoing succession of French prime ministers) sought the counsel of his generals. Their response tempered his bellicosity. To reverse the *fait accompli*, they told him, would require all-out war.[43] His generals, how-ever, were wrong. If opposition had been encountered, the German High Command fully intended to retreat behind the Rhine.[44] Sarraut had no way of knowing this, and since France did not have a promise of support from England, the German move was not countered. Hitler's troops were free to dig in.

Britain, meanwhile, had grown so tepid in her opposition to Mussolini as to ask him whether it would be an imposition if the League cut off his oil supplies. Naturally, he said yes, and, after Hitler's occupation of the Rhineland, Britain did not dare ask again. (Indeed, Britain argued *against* oil sanctions at the next League session.)[45] Prompting these misguided decisions was the belief on the part of France and Britain that Musso-lini was needed as a counterbalance to Hitler. The rightness or wrongness of Italy's inva-sion of Ethiopia was strictly secondary in importance to this overriding concern. The League must do nothing that might alienate Mussolini from the Western democracies. In such a setting, the outcome of the Ethiopian War was a forgone conclusion. The Ital-ians captured Addis Ababa, the Ethiopian capital, in May 1936. Driven into exile, Haile Selassie addressed the League in a special session, but to no avail. After contemplating his speech, the League voted to lift its sanctions against Italy.[46]

Thus did the League of Nations and the Treaty of Versailles sustain mortal wounds at the hands of hesitation and indecision.

The Spanish Civil War

While the Western democracies' track record in enforcing the provisions of the Treaty of Versailles was one of consistency, it was not one of success. The democracies had not made Germany pay her reparations, they had not forced her to abide by the limitations placed on her armed forces, and they had not prevented the re-militarization of the Rhineland. Their intervention in Manchuria via the League of Nations had been fruitless, and their actions on Ethiopia had been a disgrace—serving to alienate Mussolini while catering to his aggression. Increasingly disdainful of Britain and France, Nazi Germany and Fascist Italy now drew closer to one another. Three agreements signaled the metamorphosis. In October 1936, Italy and Germany agreed to consult each other on matters of foreign policy, thus forming the so-called "Rome-Berlin Axis," around which, in the view of the signatories, the future course of world events would "rotate."[47] A month later, Germany and Japan signed a so-called Anti-Comintern Pact, aimed at combating communism. Finally, after visiting Hitler in Munich in 1937, Mussolini completed the triangle by adhering to the Anti-Comintern Pact.

To oppose this anti-democratic tide, two "Popular Front" governments came to power in Europe: one in France, the other in Spain. As we have seen, the French Popular Front, led by Léon Blum and composed of radicals, socialists and communists, enacted long overdue labor reforms, establishing the 40-hour workweek and the right to collective bargaining. Her parallel government in Spain, however, had no such luxury—she went immediately to war.

Until 1931, Spain was still ruled by the Bourbon dynasty. Nominally, the government was a constitutional monarchy based upon a charter of 1876, but the franchise was limited to the clergy, the military caste and the aristocratic landowners (composing 1 percent of the population but possessing 50 percent of the arable land,[48] which it used preferentially for the grazing of sheep rather than for the employment of the peasantry[49]). Industry, such as it existed, was mostly concentrated in the north and northeast, particularly in the province of Catalonia—and more particularly still in its capital, Barcelona, the scene of repeated proletarian strikes over poor working conditions and insufferable taxation.[50]

Although Spain remained neutral during the First World War, the army possessed machine guns, which it employed, from time to time, against the unruly strikers of Barcelona. It employed them, too, but with less success against the Berber tribesmen of colonial Morocco. Indeed, in July 1921, Spain's colonial forces suffered a catastrophic defeat in the Moroccan Rif at the hands of the Berber chieftain, Abd-el-Krim, with the loss of 12,000 men.[51] As it turns out, King Alfonso XIII had personally ordered the army into the mountainous Rif against the advice of his war minister (whom he derided as an "imbecile").[52]

To forestall publication of a damning parliamentary report on this national humiliation that might have toppled Alfonso from his throne, Genralissimo Miguel Primo de Rivera declared martial law (1923).[53] For the next seven years, Primo ruled as a tyrant in the name of the king, attempting without success to placate the masses with modest reforms and a program of public works. The economy did not thrive, however, and the Great Depression finally brought about Primo's downfall. He resigned in 1930 and died in French exile a few weeks later.

Alfonso XIII now attempted to re-establish a personal regime with a constitutional façade based upon the traditional parliamentary system known as "rotativism," wherein Liberal and Conservative ministries alternated with one another on a secretly agreed basis, with elections being held solely for appearances' sake.[54] The popularity of this arrangement may be judged by the fact that between 1896 and 1921, no less than ten Spanish prime ministers were assassinated.[55] The people had little to gain either from the reinstitution of this system or from a sports-minded king who was wont to close the state motorway for his racecars while his people lived in penury.[56] In 1931, mounting civil unrest and adverse election returns convinced the king to flee. His departure prompted the proclamation of a republic under the presidency of Niceto Alcalá Zamora.

The new regime—part liberal, part Marxist in composition—took power in the midst of anti-republican riots on the right, communist and anti-clerical riots on the left and separatist agitation in Catalonia and the Basque Region. Martial law proved necessary to restore a modicum of calm.[57] By December 1931, a new constitution had been promulgated, and with it a series of reforms that seemed rather to crystallize than to soften the chasm between the ruling elite and the deprived masses. To the dismay of the devout—rich and poor—Catholicism lost its standing as the state religion. The Jesuit Order was dissolved and its property confiscated. The clergy was angered by revocation of their state salaries and by secularization of the schools; the army by the cashiering of various high-ranking officers and by the seemingly unpatriotic grant of autonomy to the separatist province of Catalonia; and the rural population by a land reform bill that provoked the landlords by attacking their property rights without significantly benefiting the peasants. No one was satisfied. To the old elites the reforms went too far, to the masses not far enough. The result was more turmoil. In August 1932, General José Sanjurjo attempted an abortive military coup. In January 1933, Barcelona staged another of its ubiquitous strikes.[58] Both had to be put down by loyal army troops.

Amid the unrest, the first national elections under the new constitution were held in November 1933. The result was an unexpected swing to the right with the largest number of parliamentary seats going to CEDA, a confederation of right-wing parties—the most formidable of which was Gil Robles' pro–Catholic, fascist-leaning Agrarian People's Party. In the fall of 1934, CEDA delegates obtained the cabinet portfolios for Labor, Agriculture and Justice. Seeing in this the specter of corporate fascism and a threat to their hard-won reforms—many of which were indeed being repealed—the parties of the left called a general strike.[59] The strike itself was unavailing, but it was followed by a violent miners' insurrection in the Basque province of Asturias, which the government quashed by dispatching Moorish auxiliaries and foreign legionnaires to shoot down the agitators (a task these dutiful soldiers continued to perform even after the miners had capitulated). Assisting them in this labor was the Civil Guard—a trigger-happy national police force clad in ridiculous matador-style hats, whose barracks had been targeted by the miners earlier in the uprising with several guardsmen being lynched.[60]

By 1935, the political situation was one of increasing hysteria. Radicals on the left insisted that the government must either press ahead with far-reaching reforms or succumb to fascism and reaction. Radicals on the right insisted with equal fervor that the government must resist reform or succumb to Bolshevism.[61] In the elections of February

1936, the parties of the left formed a Popular Front ticket to keep at bay the reactionary threat represented by CEDA and the smaller, but overtly fascist, Phalanx (Falange) Party founded by Jose Antonio Primo de Rivera (son of the former dictator).

The balloting gave a narrow victory to the Popular Front. But the Front had been formed for electoral purposes only. Led by Francisco Largo Caballero—upon whom *Pravda* had bestowed the exalted, if misleading, nickname "the Spanish Lenin"[62]—the socialist, communist and syndicalist deputies refused to serve in a "bourgeois" cabinet. The ministry, therefore, consisted solely of centrist and leftist republicans, and though the Marxists promised to support the new cabinet from the sidelines, they instead denounced its policies (which were reminiscent of the platform of 1931–1933) as being entirely too tepid. The government, therefore, found itself assailed both on the left (which it had not expected) and on the right. Amid mounting tensions, radicals on both sides staged ostentatious parades that often degenerated into deadly street violence.[63] In Madrid, Falangist thugs gunned down political adversaries in drive-by shootings,[64] while radical leftists staged strikes and ransacked churches. Rather than await reforms from above, peasant revolutionaries seized countryside estates—President Zamora's among them.[65] (In the village of Yeste, the Civil Guard shot the offending peasants dead.[66])

Fearing that the army would capitalize on the disorder to stage a coup, the republican ministry sacked a number of high-ranking officers and exiled others to the colonies. Additionally, it revoked the pensions of retired military men who had espoused reactionary political views.[67] These measures, taken to preempt a military coup, helped instead to precipitate one. The spark was provided by a pair of murders in Madrid—one of a republican police lieutenant, the other of a popular reactionary politician. Speciously blaming the government for the latter, Spanish troops stationed in Morocco staged a mutiny (July 17, 1936). The following day, as the uprising spread to most of the army units on the Spanish mainland, a light airplane reached Morocco from the Canary Islands. Aboard was Francisco Franco, the former head of the Spanish Foreign Legion, who had been banished to the Canaries by the government, and who would soon assume leadership of the insurrection.

It was assumed by the mutineers that they would have an easy time of things. Instead, a gruesome civil war ensued in which neither party took prisoners. Wherever one side was victorious, those suspected of supporting the opposition were summarily executed. Neither camp can be considered blameless in this lamentable business. At the official level, however, Franco's insurgents tended to sanction such atrocities, while the Republican government increasingly took measures to forestall them.[68]

At the outset of the fighting, the Republican government and its ragtag army of leftists and liberals received an apparent boon. In contrast to the insurgent army, the Spanish navy remained loyal, stranding Franco's Moroccan troops in Africa. Franco appealed to the Axis Powers for assistance. Hitler and Mussolini promptly intervened— first with airplanes that taxied insurgent forces across the Straits of Gibraltar in small groups,[69] and later with ships chaperoned by bombers. By August 1936, Franco's troops had arrived in sufficient numbers to press into the interior. At the end of the month, they captured Badajoz, where, in a stunning atrocity, they herded 2000 Republican partisans into the city bullring, and gunned them down in cold blood.[70] On September 27, they reached Toledo, relieving a force of fellow insurgents who had been besieged in the Alcazar for ten weeks. During the siege, the Republicans had cruelly executed a fourteen-year-old boy—the son of the Alcazar commander. In retribution, the insurgents shot captured Republicans and threw live grenades into a hospital filled with Republican wounded.[71]

The reeling Republic now appealed to France for support. Léon Blum, the French premier, was disposed to help and sent some initial aid. He felt, however, that he could not fully commit without British backing. Alas, Britain's Prime Minister, Stanley Baldwin, was quite unwilling to get involved—all the less so amid reports that the Republic could not even rein in its own followers. Across the country, fanatical Socialists and Anarchists burst into churches to loot and kill while the government stood by powerless to stop them. Over 6000 priests and nuns were murdered in these proceedings, prompting international outcries against the "godless Republic."[72] In Catalonia and other regions, the putative adherents of the Republic had begun collectivizing farms, factories and transport without the government's permission. Anarchists and "Trotskyite" Marxists insisted that this "workers' revolution" must continue. Liberals and Communists—who, with Soviet backing, would soon gain the upper hand—said it must cease, at least until the war was won.[73] During the "May Days" of 1937, the two sides clashed openly in the streets of Barcelona, apparently oblivious to the raging civil war with Franco.

The mayhem caused British financiers to fear for their investments in Spain. Likewise, even though official American sympathies lay with the legitimate Spanish government, the Texaco and Standard Oil Companies preferred doing business with avowed capitalists. True to this principle, their tankers put in at insurgent ports.[74] Consequently, despite the pleadings of the Spanish government, Britain and France would do no more than propose a "Nonintervention Pact" which forbade the sale of arms to either side. Germany, Italy and Russia happily appended their signatures. They did not intend to comply, but they were more than happy to have a signed agreement committing the British and French to do so.

Ultimately, the legitimate government forces, or "Loyalists," received assistance from Russia, mostly in the form of armaments. They also received an influx of some 40,000 volunteers from around the world, who enlisted to combat fascism, and were organized into "International Brigades" with oversight from the Comintern. Among the enlistees was George Orwell, who joined the anti–Stalinist Marxist militia, POUM. The Loyalists relied most especially, however, on homegrown recruits, many of them from the labor unions. Women also volunteered—most famously the Communist politician, orator and fighter, Dolores Ibárruri, known popularly as *la Pasionara* ("the Passion Flower") who provided the Republicans with their war cry, *¡No Pasarán!*—"They shall not pass!"[75]

Though strongly favored by devout Catholics, the insurgent forces, or "Nationalists," were less popular overall and had to rely more heavily on foreign assistance. Thousands of Moorish fighters from Spanish Morocco enlisted with Franco, as did 70,000 Italian and 16,000 German "volunteers"—the latter bringing with them tanks, planes and artillery, courtesy of the Axis Powers, while their Loyalist counterparts, in many cases, were lucky to have a rifle.[76]

In order to pay lip service to the Nonintervention Pact while all this intervention took place, the signatories agreed to carry out naval surveillance of the Spanish coast, with the Axis powers taking responsibility for most of the Republican coastline, and France and England overseeing the Nationalist. Significantly, no one was assigned to the coast of Portugal, whose dictator, António Salazar, allowed the free flow of materiel

An impression of the fighting during the Spanish Civil War, entitled *El Frente* ("The Front"), by Republican artist Aurelio Arteta, 31 December 1937 (Wikimedia Commons).

bound for Franco's Nationalists.[77] Hence, the rightful Loyalist government had great difficulty obtaining outside aid (although they were entitled to it under international law), while the rebel Nationalists (who by law ought to have received none) enjoyed access to a steady supply.[78]

Despite the odds, Loyalist forces held the line in Madrid against a determined Nationalist onslaught between November 1936 and March 1937. The surprising set-back convinced Hitler that the war would not soon end, and that his soldiers in Spain—known collectively as the "Condor Legion"—might as well take advantage of the convenient battleground to rack up some combat experience. Accordingly, in the Spring of 1937, German planes bombed the undefended Basque city of Guernica in a trial run of the Luftwaffe's new bombing tactics.[79] Franco was not informed that the attack was to take place, but was forced in its aftermath to state publicly that the Germans "had not been involved."[80] The raid reduced Guernica to ruins, leaving behind a terrified popu-lace and thousands of civilian casualties—many of whom had been machine-gunned from the air as they scrambled for safety.[81] The horror of the event was subsequently immortalized in the painting *Guernica* by Pablo Picasso.[82]

By the end of 1937, the Condor Legion's shock tactics had subjugated the entire Basque region. Far from increasing aid to the Loyalists in this crisis, Stalin delivered only those munitions for which the hard-pressed Loyalist government could pay with gold and silver—and then never enough to win, just enough to keep the fascist pow-ers busy on a front far from Russia.[83] After Munich, he saw little purpose in supplying even this much and the cause became hopeless.[84] The end was not long in coming. By April 1938, the Nationalists had ruptured the Loyalist front, isolating Barcelona from the rest of the peninsula. When, in January of the following year, Barcelona itself fell, some 400,000 Spaniards fled to France to preserve their lives—among them the Span-ish president, Manuel Azaña. (George Orwell, who sustained a bullet wound to the face during the conflict, narrowly made it out by this route to write his war memoir, *Hom-age to Catalonia.* As a member of the allegedly "Trotskyite" POUM, he had been in more peril from the Stalinists in the Republican camp than from the victorious National-ists.) Madrid, the lone remaining Loyalist stronghold, fell in March 1939, giving victory to the insurgents. The war had cost the nation 600,000 lives. In its aftermath, no quar-ter was shown to those who had stood by the government—an estimated two million being executed, imprisoned or herded into concentration camps for their Republican sentiments.[85]

The Rape of Nanking

While the Germans and Italians busied themselves in Spain, the Japanese pressed on in China. Their initial seizure of Manchuria had done nothing to dissuade Chiang Kai-shek from pursuing his campaign against the Chinese Communists. In 1934, Chiang cornered a huge Communist force at Juichin in southeastern China. The Communists managed to escape but were pursued afterwards in a relentless 12-month, 6000-mile chase known as the "Long March." The odyssey—in which fully 80 percent of them per-ished—eventually took them to the safe haven of Yenan in barren north-central China.[86] Chiang would have pursued them even there had his own forces not kidnapped him and forced him to attend to the Japanese (December 1936).[87]

In July 1937, using an armed clash at the Marco Polo Bridge (near Peking) as a pre-text, Japan extended the scope of its invasion. By mid–December, they had driven as far as Chiang's capital, Nanking, where they committed some of the worst atrocities in the sullied annals of warfare. Cornered in the city, Chinese soldiers surrendered by the tens of thousands under a false promise of leniency. Once disarmed, they were shackled together and machine-gunned or blown to bits with grenades. Japanese soldiers honed their bayonet skills on unarmed victims or poured petrol on them and incinerated them alive.[88] In a single day's butchery, some two thousand victims were harried to the banks of the Yangtze River and beheaded—the corpses being thrown into the water at bayonet point by those doomed to follow.[89]

Eyewitnesses state that as Japanese troops occupied the city, they shot civilians out of hand.[90] Iris Chang, author of *The Rape of Nanking*, the best English language account of the six-week atrocity, tells of victims being crucified, buried alive, torn apart by ravenous dogs, and used as fodder for decapitation contests. Babies were skewered on bayonets in full view of their parents. In all, at least 260,000 noncombatants lost their lives.[91] Women were gang-raped by Japanese soldiers and then killed—some being used as target practice as they attempted to run, others bleeding to death after being stabbed in the genitalia. Tens of thousands met this fate. (Amid international outcries, the Japanese would later adopt more subtle methods—secretly abducting Korean and Chinese women to serve as so-called "comfort women" in Japanese military brothels where the policy of rape could be carried on less conspicuously.)[92]

Meanwhile, the fighting continued. Far superior in tactics and materiel, the Japanese captured all of China's major Pacific seaports, then drove deep inland to seize Hankow, which had become the provisional capital following the loss of Nanking.[93] Ultimately, however, China proved too large to swallow. Chiang's government withdrew to Chungking, in central China, while the Communists continued to control Yenan. Japanese brutality notwithstanding, there would be no rapid conclusion to this conflict, which was, in actuality, the opening scene of the Second World War.

Anschluss

Scene two was about to burst upon Europe. Anschluss—union with Germany—had been a subject of contention in Austria since the Peace of Paris. Reduced to a rump state of 32,000 square miles and 7 million inhabitants (1.8 million of whom lived in Vienna),[94] the former heartland of the Hapsburg empire emerged from the Great War in a state of economic collapse. The imperial raw materials upon which Austrian industry had hitherto depended now lay abroad in the Hapsburg successor states or in territory usurped by the victors—separated from the Austrian market not only by boundary lines, but also by customs barriers. The source of most of Austria's food supply was likewise alienated from her—and as she could not pay to import an adequate supply, much of the populace simply starved.[95]

Seeking relief by any means, Austria's postwar provisional government pronounced the establishment of a "German-Austrian" republic—nominally independent, but federated (at least commercially) within a greater Germany (February 1919). In September, this pronouncement was rendered a dead letter by the Allies' imposition of the Treaty of St. Germain, which forbade any union between Austria and Germany without League of Nations approval. Two of Austria's nine provinces—Tyrol and Salzburg—promptly voted for union anyway. Styria and Upper Austria prepared to do the same. The Allies forbade it on threat of military intervention.[96]

In the meantime, the economic situation continued to worsen. Prior to the war, Austria's unit of currency—the "crown"—was valued at five to the dollar. By the winter of 1920–1921 it had fallen to 3,000 to the dollar, and by 1922 to 77,000 to the dollar.[97] Subsisting in large measure on international charity, Austria appealed to the League of Nations, which responded with the "First Geneva Protocol" (1922), providing $130 million in loans, payable over twenty years, while reiterating that Austria must not enter into a union with Germany.

The influx of currency created a degree of economic stability, but the political situation was one of deep divisions. In Vienna and its environs, the industrial proletariat elected Social Democrats to leadership. Secular and socialistic, the party assumed ownership of Vienna's municipal transport system, power grid and water supply; built schools and medical clinics; set strict rent controls; cleared out slums and erected massive apartment buildings for the working class—the most celebrated being the *Karl Marx Hof*, a complex nearly two-thirds of a mile in length. Adorned with arches, towers, balconies and a central courtyard (graced by a statue of Marx), the complex cost $4 million dollars to build and housed 2,000 working class families.[98]

The remainder of the country—traditionalist, agricultural and devoutly Catholic—reviled such policies and the taxes that went to pay for them in what remained a weak economy. Their support went to the Christian Socialist and Pan-German parties, which generally desired either a union with Germany or a return to monarchy. In the latter half of the 1920s, the nation's political rivalry deteriorated to the point that the radical right and radical left organized their own paramilitary forces—the reactionary *Heimwehr* boasting 60,000 recruits; the overtly socialist *Schutzbund*, 90,000. By the Treaty of St. Germain, the official Austrian Army was limited to 30,000 men. The task of keeping the peace was therefore next to impossible. In one notorious incident, rioting workers in Vienna burnt down the venerable Palace of Justice after three *Heimwehr* members were acquitted (underhandedly it was believed) of murdering a socialist during a street clash. By the time the Vienna uprising was suppressed, the boulevards were littered with dead and wounded (July 1927).[99]

This occurred, it should be noted, when the economy was reasonably good. Two years later, the coming of the Great Depression put a quarter of the Austrian work force on the dole. Germany, as we have seen, was likewise suffering and the two states attempted to form a Customs Union (1930). The rest of Europe would not allow it, declaring it a violation of the Treaty of St. Germain. Consequently, the project was dropped. Within a year, *Kredit Anstalt*, Austria's chief banking house, collapsed, sparking a wave of bank failures throughout Austria, Germany and Eastern Europe. By 1932, the treasury could no longer support the cost of unemployment payments. The League of Nations offered another loan—this time $42 million dollars payable over twenty years—provided Austria would forswear union with Germany for the entire term. The Pan-German Party virulently opposed this stipulation, but the loan agreement (known as the "Lausanne Protocol") passed the Austrian Parliament by a margin of two votes thanks to the lobbying of the Christian Socialist Chancellor, Engelbert Dollfuss.[100]

Known as the "Millimetternich" (he was but 4 feet 11 inches tall), Dollfuss had formerly favored Anschluss with Germany, but Hitler's ascent to power, and the corresponding growth of a bullying Nazi Party in Austria, turned him into a staunch Austrian nationalist. His methods were dictatorial. Having prorogued parliament after a contentious debate elicited the simultaneous resignations of the speaker and two deputy speakers (one of whom, by law, had to be present to officiate at every parliamentary session), he obtained authorization from the president to rule by decree and declared the formation of a "Fatherland Front" devoted to the maintenance of Austrian independence.[101] On February 11, 1934, he declared the dissolution of "all" political parties (by which he meant the rival Social Democratic and Nazi parties—for the Christian Socialist Party and *Heimwehr* remained the chief bulwarks of his support). The Social Democrats were targeted first, sparking a four-day civil war that culminated in the bombardment of the working-class quarter of Vienna—the *Karl Marx Hof* being the site of extensive death and destruction. In the aftermath, Dollfuss signed a concordat with the pope and promulgated a new constitution establishing a fascist regime on the Italian model (both occurring on May 1, 1934).

In these proceedings, Dollfuss had the backing of Mussolini who was not yet the ally of Hitler and who had a keen interest in preserving Austria's independence. France had always been the most ardent opponent of Austro-German union, for the resulting state would have been larger than France and would have possessed 1.75 times the population. But Italy ran France a close second. German control of Austria would pose a greater threat to her northeastern frontier than Italy had ever faced at Hapsburg hands—an issue that could easily become acute in light of Italy's annexation of ethnically-German South Tyrol at the end of World War I.[102]

Austria's Nazi Party, meanwhile, had spent the year sowing mayhem with a campaign of anti-government violence and destruction. With the socialists out of the way, Dollfuss moved to suppress them. Emboldened by Hitler's "Night of the Long Knives" (June 30–July 2, 1934), however, the Austro-Nazis attempted to beat him to the punch. On July 25, 1934, Austrian Nazi conspirators clad in stolen *Heimwehr* uniforms strolled past the unsuspecting guards at the chancellery, broke into a cabinet meeting, and shot Dollfuss at point-blank range. The victim survived for several hours, begging for a priest—a request that was denied by his murderers, who instead announced his "resignation" over Vienna's radio.[103] But now the coup came apart. The plotters were besieged in the chancellery by loyal Austrian troops. Although Hitler wanted to intervene, Mussolini (who, by painful coincidence, was playing host to Dollfuss' wife and family when the events unfolded) thwarted him by dispatching Italian troops to the Brenner Pass, promising to make it "bristle with bayonets" if Germany so much as blinked.[104] Hitler did not see this as a bluff. He disavowed the conspiracy, and in the absence of his support, it collapsed. For Hitler, it was a rare show of prudence. He was, however, merely biding his time. Anschluss was part and parcel of the program he had outlined a decade before in *Mein Kampf* (a book that Mussolini had characterized a few months earlier as too "boring" to read).[105]

The fallen Dollfuss was succeeded by his minister of education, Kurt von Schuschnigg, who had overseen the recapture of the chancellery—convincing the Nazi plotters to surrender on a promise of safe-conduct to the German border. (The promise was not honored. The plotters were arrested, and several of them were hanged.[106]) Schuschnigg pressed ahead with Dollfuss' Christian Socialist dictatorship, but seems ultimately to have envisioned a Hapsburg restoration.[107] Austria's Nazis and Social Democrats remained under the ban.

The European situation, however, shifted beneath his feet. Hitler's unopposed reoccupation of the Rhineland (March 1936) exposed the inconstancy of the Western democracies, while Mussolini, desiring German support for his imperial aggression in Ethiopia, was beginning his drift into the Führer's orbit. Hoping to forestall future troubles, Schuschnigg agreed to meet with Hitler in July 1936. The talks appeared to bear fruit—Schushnigg providing a secret guarantee of amnesty for incarcerated Austrian Nazis in return for a promise from Hitler that Germany would honor Austria's independence.[108]

The worth of Hitler's promise was soon made evident. The reprieved Austrian Nazis wasted no time in manufacturing a crisis at Berlin's bidding. By 1937, a new Nazi campaign of terrorist bombings and rioting was in full swing in Austria, affording Hitler ample opportunity to voice false concerns for the safety of Austria's German populace.[109] Schuschnigg was invited to Berchtesgaden to discuss the matter in February 1938. Rather than converse, however, Hitler unleashed a raving diatribe, threatening military action unless Austria's Nazi Party was legalized and prominent cabinet posts were given to its members. Certain that Hitler's ultimate aim was Austria's annexation, Schuschnigg appealed to his people—organizing a plebiscite that he hoped would show Austrian opposition to being devoured. Hitler was not willing to gamble on the outcome. On March 11, 1938, just days before the plebiscite was to be held, German forces invaded Austria on the pretext of "restoring law and order."

Had there been opposition, the operation might have failed. Rushed into action, many German vehicles broke down and had to be abandoned on the Austrian roads. But Austria had no means of resisting, and by day's end, the triumphant Wehrmacht had occupied Vienna. Schuschnigg was arrested. (He would spend the war imprisoned in concentration camps—first Sachsenhausen, then Dachau.) After a triumphant ride through Vienna, standing upright in the open back seat of a touring car on streets lined with cheering throngs (to whom he gave the Nazi salute), Hitler authorized his own plebiscite—the result of which was 99 percent approval for Austria's incorporation into Germany. There were immediate widespread arrests and the frontiers were closed to prevent flight.[110] The Jews, in particular, were targeted for brutal persecution. With mocking crowds looking on, they were rounded up and made to scour streets, sidewalks and public latrines.[111] Their homes were plundered. Thousands were imprisoned. Many others attempted flight only to find that the S.S. border guards were apt to refuse passage even after accepting exorbitant bribes for the purpose. Under international pressure, the Nazis permitted the emigration of Sigmund Freud, then elderly and dying of cancer. Before allowing him to depart, however, they insisted that he write a letter stating that he had been treated well. In point of fact, he had not been, so he closed the epistle with the sarcastic comment that he could "most warmly recommend the Gestapo to everybody."[112]

Munich

Hitler's aggression was another crucial opportunity for the Western democracies. And it was another opportunity lost, for England and France did nothing. Indeed, the British Prime Minister, Neville Chamberlain, convinced himself that Hitler's grievances to this point had been reasonable. In view of the harshness of the Treaties of Versailles and St. Germain, perhaps it was only fitting that Austrian Germans should join their brethren in the Reich. Nor was he alone in this opinion. In 1936, for example, the Nazi apologist, Lord Lothian (Philip Henry Kerr), had remarked that Hitler's reoccupation of the Rhineland was only a matter of the Germans "going into their own back-garden."[113]

But Hitler was far from satiated, and with Anschluss scarcely accomplished, he was already eyeing his next quarry. Czechoslovakia was now enveloped by German territory on three sides. Along her western marches was a C-shaped rim of territory known as the Sudetenland. Home to the Skoda armament works, the region also housed three and a half million Germans. Nazi propaganda falsely accused the Czech government not only of abusing this minority (which had composed an elite class during the Hapsburg period) but also of kowtowing to Soviet Russia in a bid to propagate the Comintern's "Semitic communism" throughout Europe.[114] To the contrary, Czechoslovakia was the most democratic state in Eastern Europe. Its constitution, modeled on that of the United States, provided for the separation of powers, ministerial responsibility and a presidency possessing the power of suspensive veto. The state's founding father, Thomas Masaryk, a former college professor, had an American wife, and had spent the war years lobbying abroad for Czech independence. Indeed, the Czech Legion, sent to Russia to fight alongside the Allies during the war (and subsequently trapped in Russia after the Bolshevik Revolution), had been his brainchild.[115]

The landlocked state that Masaryk declared independent in October 1918 was 600 miles in length from east to west and as narrow as 50 miles in width (its widest point being 125 miles). Not particularly defensible, it nonetheless had much going in its favor. By the terms of the 1919 peace treaties, it enjoyed guaranteed access to the Baltic ports of Hamburg and Stettin and to the Adriatic port of Trieste. It possessed the lion's share of the former Hapsburg empire's industrial infrastructure as well as great resources in coal, iron and arable land (enough, indeed, to make it self-sufficient in food). In 1919, the Catholic Church and the old German and Magyar elites owned most of the land in the form of large estates, while the holdings of small farmers were often too meager to support a living. As a remedy, the nascent government instituted a land reform program that broke up all estates exceeding 375 arable acres and sold them to the peasantry in parcels of 37.5 acres or less. Aimed at creating an agricultural middle class, the policy was anathema to the dispossessed landowners,[116] but this was hardly the leading source of discontent within the state, for the population was a patchwork of competing ethnicities. Of its 15 million inhabitants, Czechs composed 45 percent, Slovaks and Germans 22 percent each, Magyars 5 percent, and Ruthenians (Ukrainians) 4 percent. Each of the minorities desired (and agitated for) local cultural and political autonomy, which, in the case of the Slovaks and Ruthenians, was granted during the late 1920s. Alas, the domestic pacification that might have resulted was, in large measure, ruined by meddling from outside. Under the Hapsburgs the Hungarian Magyars had enjoyed ascendancy in Slovakia and Ruthenia—an ascendancy they wished to reassert through annexation. Further north, the Teschen mining district, awarded to Czechoslovakia by the Paris Peace Conference, was coveted by Poland.[117]

The problem that trumped all others, however, was the German problem. From 1919 to 1938, the Czech Sudetenland with its large German population formed the frontier with Austria to the south and with Germany to the north and west. Owing to its strategic location, the granting of autonomy to Sudeten Germans was impracticable. President Masaryk seemingly solved the riddle by promoting Sudeten German participation in the Czech government, but the coming of the Great Depression and the subsequent rise of Hitlerism in Germany spelled the end of this period of harmony.

By 1935, the *Sudetendeutsche Partei*, subsidized from Berlin and led by the avowed Nazi, Konrad Henlein, had become the Sudetenland's predominant political party. Henceforth, all attempts at accommodation proved fruitless. Henlein's sole guiding principle was to "demand so much that we can never be satisfied." Accordingly, no matter what concessions the Czech government might offer, Henlein, taking his instructions from Hitler, simply declared them insufficient, raised the ante and demanded more.[118] In the meantime, Henlein stoked the flames of Sudeten discontent. A cause for grievance was found in every Czech action and broadcast to the world by German propaganda. At times, the effect was convincing. When Czech police forcibly dispersed a *Sudetendeutsche Partei* rally at Tarnice-Sanov in October 1937, for example, the Czech government was subjected to international opprobrium.[119]

Anschluss transformed the situation. Czechoslovakia had been a perennial opponent of Austro-German union, for its achievement would create a strategic nightmare—leaving the Czech nation encircled by German territory on three sides (north, west and south). Its consummation by Hitler in March 1938 posed an existential threat. Should war ensue, the fortifications on Czechoslovakia's western frontier could be circumvented by a strike from the south (i.e., from the territory of the former Austria, now incorporated into the Reich).

Anschluss was followed immediately by increased ethnic agitation in the Sudetenland. By May 1938, fraudulent reports from the Goebbels' Propaganda Ministry in Berlin were falsely portraying the Sudeten Germans as victims of a "Czech Terror" aimed at crushing Sudeten aspirations for autonomy.[120] In fact, under pressure from Britain and France (who were bent on appeasement), the Czechs were making every effort to be conciliatory.[121] Henlein's minions answered the government's olive branches with staged riots.[122] And now, amid the escalating chaos, reports reached the Czech government of German troop movements along the border. Convinced that Hitler planned to use the Sudeten disturbances as a *casus belli*, the Czechs mobilized their army to their western frontier (May 20, 1938). Warned by Britain and France that any offensive action by Germany against Czechoslovakia might escalate into a general European war, Hitler was forced to issue an assurance that no hostile action was contemplated.

The so-called "May Crisis" thus ended as quickly as it had begun. But in spite of the apparent fortitude of Britain and France, Czechoslovakia was in greater danger than ever. From this point forward, Hitler was obsessed with gaining revenge for Czechoslovakia's mobilization, which (in his psychologically unbalanced view) constituted a brazen attempt to humiliate him. Within the week, he had secretly informed his generals that "Case Green"—the invasion and destruction of Czechoslovakia—was to go forward no later than October 1, 1938.[123]

Although the Czechs possessed a formidable army, they would be hard pressed to hold their own if it came to war with Germany, for as we have seen the Czech fortification line was now outflanked from the south. Outside assistance would therefore be essential—and on paper, Czechoslovakia seemed to possess a guarantee of it. In 1935, the Czech foreign minister, Edvard Beneš, had forged a mutual defense pact with France, obligating the latter to come to Czechoslovakia's assistance in the event of a German attack. Soon afterwards, Russia signed a pact with France stating that *if France fulfilled her obligation*, Russia would likewise provide military support to Czechoslovakia.

Alas, since that time, France's domestic turmoil had caused her to defer increasingly to Great Britain in matters of foreign policy. Consequently, she was hesitant to meet her obligation to the Czechs without British support—and Britain, as it turns out, was not inclined to offer it. As early as March 1938, during a speech in the House of Commons, Neville Chamberlain had stressed the fact that Britain was not obligated to support France in the defense of Czechoslovakia against German aggression.[124] In response, the French premier, Édouard Daladier, traveled to London to forewarn his British counterpart that Germany's putative concern for Sudeten German self-determination was an imposture (April 1938). Hitler meant to conquer Czechoslovakia, Poland and Romania and then, bolstered by the resources appropriated from those countries, to turn against the Western democracies. The time to stand up to Hitler was now, before Germany grew too powerful.[125]

The British prime minister did not find this line of argument convincing. Son of Joseph Chamberlain, the famed turn-of-the-century British colonial secretary, Neville Chamberlain had neither been drawn to, nor groomed for, a career in politics. After studying metallurgy and engineering, he had been sent to the Bahamas at the age of twenty-two to make his fortune in the growing of sisal. The fact that the reader has likely never heard of sisal (a fibrous crop used in the making of rope) should provide an indication of the success of this unfortunate venture, which cost the family an estimated £50,000.[126] Returning to England at twenty-seven, he spent another ten years in business pursuits before trying his hand at politics after all. In 1915, he was elected lord mayor of Birmingham as a champion of progressive social policies. In 1916, Lloyd George named him director of national services (although, as a student of phrenology, he reportedly did not fancy the contour of Neville's head).[127]

Neville did not thrive under Lloyd George's tutelage. He resigned his post the following year. But in 1922, Andrew Bonar Law appointed him postmaster general and his career began to take off. Over the next decade, he would distinguish himself first as minister of health (in which capacity he passed a prolific amount of social legislation), and then as chancellor of the exchequer (wherefrom he balanced the budget and obtained passage of an Import Duties Bill that promised to fulfill his father's dream of an "imperial preference" system). While such labors gained him well-deserved plaudits, his demeanor remained sufficiently rigid and aloof as to invite unfavorable comparisons with the rolled-up umbrella that he carried.[128] Upon Baldwin's retirement in 1937, George VI invited him to assume the office of prime minister. It would be the most fateful premiership since Lord North's at the outset of the American Revolution.

In the aftermath of Daladier's visit to London, Chamberlain's foreign secretary, Lord Halifax, assured Berlin that the British government had not made any new military commitments to France, and that it had advised the Czechs to meet all reasonable Sudeten demands.[129] Despite Britain's willingness to join France in warning Hitler of the risk of war at the time of the May Crisis, Chamberlain had no intention of being drawn in. Although he had allotted funds for the expansion of the Royal Air Force, he had done nothing to rebuild the army, which remained undermanned and underequipped, possessing just two battle-ready divisions. Having lost a favorite cousin in the Great War, Chamberlain could not even contemplate a return to the trenches. Britain would concentrate on deterrence alone—deterrence by air and sea.[130]

On May 22, two days after the Czech mobilization, Halifax reminded the defeatist French foreign minister, Georges Bonnet, that if France went to war over Czechoslovakia she had no assurance of British support.[131] Bonnet promptly undercut his own premier

(Daladier) by arguing that Edvard Beneš (now president of Czechoslovakia) had jeopardized the peace by mobilizing. The proponents of appeasement in both Britain and France loudly parroted this argument.[132] Off the record, Chamberlain was quoted as suggesting that Czechoslovakia should cede the Sudetenland to Germany "in the interest of peace."[133] (In a letter to his sister, he argued that Germany wanted nothing more for the Sudetenlanders than what the British had wanted for the Outlanders in the lead up to the Boer War.[134]) Lord Walter Runciman—foisted upon the Czechs as a special envoy to help negotiate a settlement—accomplished very little other than to hobnob with the Sudeten aristocracy.[135]

All the while, Czechoslovakia was placed under increasing pressure from her supposed allies to meet the demands of the Sudetenlanders. It was clear to Edvard Beneš that Britain and France had fallen for the propaganda that Hitler only desired self-determination for the Sudeten Germans. In a bid to expose this chimera, he summoned the Sudeten negotiators to his office on September 4, 1938, and offered them a blank sheet of paper on which to inscribe their demands, promising to grant them, sight unseen. When they declined, he invited them to state their terms so that he could write and sign them. In doing so, he called their bluff, for they had never wanted the Czech government to meet their demands. Indeed, they required the very opposite—continued Czech rejection, for that alone could serve as a pretext for German military intervention. Although they left the office with a paper bearing Beneš' signature granting the Sudetenland autonomy under a totalitarian government headed by Henlein, they were mortified by the prospect of a negotiated settlement. The following day, they broke off all discussions over an alleged clash between Czech police and Sudeten agitators at Moravska-Ostrava.[136]

Beneš had exposed the Sudetenlanders' insincerity. Unfortunately, no one had been paying attention. The whole of Europe was fixated instead on Hitler's upcoming address at the 1938 Nuremberg Rally, scheduled for September 12, in which it was anticipated that the Führer would make a definitive statement on the Czech question (very possibly a declaration of war). In the run up to the speech, Hermann Goering had set the tone—telling the regimented hordes in attendance that the Czechs were a "pygmy race" controlled by the Jews. Hitler, however, stole the show, railing against Czechoslovakia's tyrannical treatment of the "martyred" Sudeten minority and Beneš's supposedly purposeful attempt to humiliate him during the May Crisis.[137] Although he stopped short of declaring war, his words brought the crisis to a head.

As recently as September 8, Édouard Daladier had told the British Ambassador, Eric Phipps, that if Germany invaded Czechoslovakia, France intended to honor its commitment to come to Czechoslovakia's assistance. But just as in the Stavisky Riot crisis of 1934, Daladier could find no one to support his firm stand. His military generals bemoaned the prospect of facing 50 to 60 German divisions should French forces cross the frontier. (They were off by a factor of ten. If Germany attacked Czechoslovakia, she would have only 5 frontline divisions to spare along the Rhine. Everything else would have to be thrown at the Czechs.) The head of the French Air Force told him that the Luftwaffe would obliterate France's outmoded fleet of planes within the first two weeks of hostilities.[138] On the morrow of Hitler's Nuremberg address, Daladier found his cabinet hopelessly divided. The foreign minister, Bonnet, was nearly hysterical in professing the need for peace. Seeing no alternative, Daladier phoned Chamberlain, imploring him to do what he could to prevent a German attack on Czechoslovakia.[139]

Chamberlain responded with his own secretly predetermined initiative—code-named "Plan Z."[140] He telegrammed Hitler, offering to fly to Germany to confer with

Neville Chamberlain holding the paper containing the resolution to commit to peaceful methods signed by both Hitler and himself on his return from Munich. He is showing the piece of paper to the crowd at Heston Aerodrome on 30 September 1938. Later that day at 10 Downing Street before another cheering crowd he said, "My good friends, for the second time in our history, a British Prime Minister has returned from Germany bringing peace with honour. I believe it is peace for our time" (Wikimedia Commons).

him directly. Hitler issued an immediate acceptance, and on September 15, Chamberlain boarded an aircraft for the first time in his life, flying to meet the Führer at Berchtesgaden. In the ensuing talks, held on September 16, Hitler insisted that the Sudeten Germans could not continue to live under foreign tyranny and persistently threatened the use of force to bring them under the protection of the Reich. After issuing a protest that there could be no further discussion if Germany was intent on war, Chamberlain "negotiated" Hitler's agreement to refrain from hostilities, at least for a time, in exchange for his own promise to lobby for the peaceful surrender of the Sudetenland to Germany in the name of self-determination.[141]

It may be noted that the question of ceding the Sudetenland to Germany was entirely new. Henlein had only demanded it of the Czechs that very morning. Hitler was certain, moreover, that the Czechs would never agree, since loss of the Sudetenland would leave the nation utterly defenseless against further German aggression. From a strategic standpoint, the number of Germans living in the region was not the main item of significance, for it also housed Czechoslovakia's entire network of mountain fortresses (the equivalent of France's Maginot Line) and her highly productive Skoda armaments factory, whose output was nearly on a par with Britain's.[142]

Departing with the impression that "In spite of the hardness and ruthlessness I thought I saw in [Hitler's] face, I got the impression that *here was a man who could be relied upon when he had given his word*,"[143] Chamberlain returned to London and obtained the support of the cabinet (September 17). The following day, he unveiled the plan to Daladier and Bonnet. Daladier still held the opinion that Hitler intended to swallow the whole of Czechoslovakia (and Romania after that) before turning on France and England. Chamberlain replied that he had asked Hitler if he intended to conquer all of Czechoslovakia and that Hitler had assured him that the Czechs were not wanted in the Reich. He would make no demands beyond the Sudetenland. Receiving no support from Bonnet, Daladier gave in. The proposal to be put to Czechoslovakia demanded the session to Germany of all Sudeten areas in which Germans composed more than 50 percent of the population. Additionally, Czechoslovakia was to abrogate her defense pacts with France and Russia. In return, the Czechs would receive an international guarantee for the integrity of her remaining territory against unprovoked aggression.[144]

The Czechs, who knew nothing of these discussions, had meanwhile devised a plan for Sudeten autonomy that would have satisfied all reasonable demands if only their "allies" had not been in such a rush to appease Hitler.[145] Presented with a *fait accompli* by those whom they had taken to be their friends, they initially refused. Britain and France countered by sending their ambassadors to awaken Beneš at 2 a.m. to inform him that if Czechoslovakia withheld its assent, and if war with Germany resulted, the onus would be on the Czechs. Neither France nor Britain would come to their assistance. In a state of stunned disbelief, Beneš convened his cabinet that very morning and obtained their despairing acceptance (September 21).[146]

On September 22, 1938, Chamberlain returned to Germany to finalize the agreement with Hitler at Godesberg. On arriving, however, he was astounded to learn that "after the events of the last few days" Hitler had found it necessary to increase his demands, and that the terms reached at Berchtesgaden were "no longer any use."[147] After a flimsy protest, Chamberlain returned to England with Hitler's new "Godesberg" demands, which required an immediate Czech evacuation of the Sudetenland. On presenting them to the cabinet, he could not even command Halifax's support.[148] Hitler's new demands were rejected.

Anxiety in the West immediately rose to fever pitch. While Hitler unleashed new verbal tirades against the Czechs in a Berlin speech at the Sportpalast, wherein he claimed that the Sudetenland composed "the last territorial claim which I have to make in Europe" (September 26),[149] France ordered a partial mobilization of her army, and Britain of her fleet. It appeared that Europe must go over the brink. At the eleventh hour, however, several high-ranking generals in Hitler's own army secretly offered the Allies a way out of the cataclysm. Convinced that Germany could not prevail in a major war, they promised to overthrow Hitler if the Western democracies would only make a steadfast resolution to oppose him in Czechoslovakia.[150] The democracies could also count on the support of Soviet Russia, which had given abundant assurances that it would uphold its treaty obligation to assist Czechoslovakia in the event of foreign invasion, provided that France did so, too.

Rather than seize on these initiatives, Chamberlain addressed the nation by radio on the evening of September 27, lamenting, "How horrible, fantastic, incredible it is that we should be digging trenches, and trying on gas masks because of a quarrel in a far-away country between people of whom we know nothing!"[151] The same night, he received an unexpected message from Hitler saying that he would defer to the British prime minister's judgment as to whether further diplomatic efforts were worthwhile. Chamberlain responded by suggesting a summit meeting to include Britain, France, Germany and Italy. At the same time, he wrote to Mussolini, beseeching the Italian leader to use his influence to get Hitler to agree. The following day, during an address to the Commons, Chamberlain received Hitler's response in mid-speech. After a dramatic pause, he announced to the House that Hitler had agreed to four-power talks in Munich. The House erupted in bedlam. It was reported that MPs openly wept for joy.[152]

Later that day, just prior to embarking on his third flight to Germany in two weeks, Chamberlain remarked that as a "boy, I used to repeat, 'If at first you don't succeed, try, try again.' That is what I am doing." What followed invited the wry lampoon, "If at first you don't concede, fly, fly again."[153] The Munich Conference was held on September 29, 1938. Mussolini opened the discussions with a proposal (purportedly his own, but actually written for him by Goering and other leading Nazis) that essentially made Hitler's Godesberg demands the basis of discussion.[154] The ensuing twelve hours of "negotiation" resulted in the so-called "Munich Agreement," whereby Hitler got the Sudetenland (with more generous borders than previously discussed), and Chamberlain got Hitler's signature on a joint statement professing "the desire of our two peoples never to go to war with one another again," and pledging that "consultation shall be the method adopted to deal with any other questions that may concern our two countries."[155] The Czechs had not even been allowed to attend the discussions. The Munich decision was simply thrust upon them. (Indeed, Chamberlain reportedly yawned several times when two Czech delegates, apprised of the outcome after cooling their heels in an adjoining room all day, attempted to voice their concerns.[156])

The British prime minister returned to England with his joint statement clasped firmly in hand, announcing, that he had achieved "peace for our time."[157] Flying back to Paris and seeing a massive crowd at the airfield below, Daladier was noticeably less jubilant. Certain that he would be hanged on the spot, he instructed the pilot to circle the airfield several times before agreeing to land. When he realized the throng was applauding, he was shocked. Turning to a confidante, he remarked, "The imbeciles—if they only knew what they were acclaiming."[158] Chamberlain, too, received a deliriously happy reception. Appeasement seems anathema to us now, but in England and France in the late 1930s, the prospect of war only conjured up visions of the ghastly trench battles of World War I. The popular desire for peace was pervasive. England's leading newspapers were unanimous in endorsing the policy.[159] Speaking before parliament, Winston Churchill delivered an isolated rebuke. "We have sustained a defeat without a war.... And do not suppose that this is the end.... This is only the first sip, the first foretaste of a bitter cup which will be proffered to us year by year unless, by a supreme recovery of moral health and martial vigour, we arise again and take our stand for freedom as in the olden time."[160] His remarks were interrupted by howls of protest.[161] (The preceding day, he had remarked to a colleague that given a "choice between war and dishonor," Chamberlain "chose dishonor, and he will get war anyway."[162])

On October 5, President Beneš of Czechoslovakia resigned from office and took refuge in England, saying that he would leave it to history to pronounce judgment on the Munich Agreement.[163] Within five months, history had spoken. In March 1939, Hitler, with great suddenness, occupied the Czech provinces of Bohemia and Moravia. Nazi troops marched unopposed into Prague, the Czech capital. (Goering had informed the new Czech president, Emil Hácha, that the city would be bombed to a smoking ruin if resistance was encountered. The very threat caused Hácha to faint.[164]) The remainder of the country was partitioned—Hitler proclaiming the establishment of an independent state in Slovakia, confirming Poland in its ownership of the Teschen mining district (treacherously seized from a prostrate Czechoslovakia in the aftermath of Munich) and ceding the rest of the state to Hungary. As an afterthought, he telegrammed Mussolini to let him know that Czechoslovakia had ceased to exist. Highly irritated over not being forewarned, Mussolini grumbled to his son-in-law, "every time Hitler occupies a country he sends me a message."[165]

The Polish Corridor and the Nazi-Soviet Pact

Chamberlain and Daladier had fallen for a bluff. Unbeknownst to them, Hitler's generals did not believe, in September 1938, that the German army was strong enough to breach the Czech fortifications in the Sudetenland. In the event of war, the Czechs could have brought 35 battle-ready divisions to bear.[166] These were now lost to the Western democracies—an injury that was compounded by insult when Hitler devoured Bohemia and Moravia, exposing to the entire world that Britain and France had been duped. Hitler's purpose had never been to obtain fair treatment for German minorities living under foreign "tyranny" as he had previously insisted. He was bent on hegemonic expansion eastwards—the very blueprint he had outlined in *Mein Kampf*. His latest aggression was greeted with angry outbursts in the British House of Commons.

But Hitler's provocations had scarcely begun. Within the week, he issued an ultimatum to Lithuania for the surrender of Memelland—a region in southern Lithuania that had been detached from East Prussia by the Treaty of Versailles. On March 22, 1939, German forces occupied the vital port city of Memel, presenting Lithuania with a *fait accompli*.[167] On the same day, an ultimatum was delivered to Poland for the cession of the port of Danzig and the establishment of an extraterritorial German highway and railroad across the "Polish Corridor." Poland refused.

No longer harboring illusions about Herr Hitler, Neville Chamberlain addressed the House of Commons on March 31, saying: "In the event of any action which clearly threatened Polish independence and which the Polish Government accordingly considered it vital to resist with their national forces, His Majesty's Government would feel themselves bound at once to lend the Polish Government all support in their power. They have given the Polish Government an assurance to this effect. I may add that the French Government have authorized me to make it plain that they stand in the same position in this matter."[168] Józef Beck, the Polish Foreign Minister, is said to have been informed of this guarantee while tapping the ashes from a cigarette, and to have accepted it, between one tap and the next.[169]

The resurrected state of Poland had had a storied history between the wars. In the aftermath of the Polish-Soviet War (1919–1921), the nation was shaken by political deadlock and spiraling inflation. Ethnically, the population was 69 percent Polish, but for the preceding one and a half centuries, the new *majority* had lived a dispersed existence as *oppressed minorities* within three culturally different empires. Working harmoniously after so many years of separation proved difficult. When the first *Sejm* (or lower house of parliament) convened under Poland's new constitution in 1922, it contained 31 separate political parties.[170] Two days into his tenure as the nation's first president, Gabriel

Narutowicz was shot dead by a fanatical adherent of the National Democratic Party, which had been unable to secure the office for its own candidate.

The effort to weld the state into a unified whole was further complicated by the inclusion within its borders of sizeable minority populations. At the Paris Peace Conference, Poland had been required to sign a treaty guaranteeing the political and civil rights of her minorities, particularly with regard to religious freedoms and the use of native languages. Ardent Polish nationalists resented this agreement and sought to abrogate it, while its putative beneficiaries complained that the promised protections were inadequate and inconsistently enforced. Bitter over their enforced separation from Germany, the German inhabitants of the Polish Corridor and Upper Silesia (4 percent of the population) chafed at the imposition of Polish institutions and the unceasing influx of ethnic Poles. Similarly, the Ukrainians of Galicia expressed resentment over the government's "endeavor to colonize the Polish soldiery on … expropriated lands in preference to the local peasantry," and "the flooding of the region with new, inexperienced, and inefficient administrators."[171] Composed of 17 percent of the population, the Ukrainians had aspired to independence or autonomy in 1918. Seeing their hopes dashed, the more radical elements resorted to terrorism and underground warfare, leading to harsh government reprisals and further deterioration in inter-ethnic relations.[172]

Caught in the middle of everything were the nation's Jews who composed the remaining 10 percent of the population. Finding in them a convenient scapegoat for all the nation's ills, the bigoted National Democratic Party (or *Endecja*) subjected them to a virulent anti–Semitic campaign,[173] depicting them, as the occasion dictated, as profiteers, Bolshevists, eternal aliens, unpatriotic pro–German conspirators or—for the benefit of the parish priests and devout peasantry—"Christ-killers."[174] So many anti–Semitic outrages occurred during the early years of the republic (including pogroms at Lvov and Kielce in 1918 and a mass execution at Pinsk in 1919) that Great Britain and the United States felt compelled to dispatch investigatory commissions to probe the matter. In 1925, the Polish government issued the conciliatory "Declaration of Warsaw," guaranteeing civil and religious liberties to the beleaguered minority, which thus enjoyed a relative respite until the onset of the Great Depression and Hitler's rise to power in Germany stimulated a new wave of anti–Semitic vitriol and persecution.[175] It was in this latter period that the Primate of Poland, Cardinal August Hlond, issued his infamous pastoral letter (1936) demonizing Jewish character and condoning anti–Jewish boycotts. (To his extremely limited credit, he did condemn outright acts of violence.[176]) Despite their persecution, Poland's Jews distinguished themselves in law, medicine, academics and the arts throughout the interwar period.[177]

Amid these challenges, the value of the Polish mark fell from 9.8 to the dollar in 1918 to 5 million to the dollar in 1923.[178] Economic measures taken to reverse the situation, including the introduction of a new unit of currency, the *zloty*, failed utterly owing to a ruinous harvest in 1924 and an ill-timed tariff war with the hostile Stresemann regime in Germany (which included a German boycott against coal imports from Upper Silesia—a disputed region unwillingly ceded to Poland by Germany after a plebiscite in 1921).[179] Although Poland was overwhelmingly agricultural, one-third of Polish farms were less than 5 acres in size—scarcely large enough for their own subsistence.[180] Land reform was essential, but the bickering politicians were at loggerheads. Industrialization, too, was necessary, but there was no money to invest in it.[181]

By the mid–1920s, calls for stronger, more efficient governance had become increasingly strident. Józef Piłsudski, widely regarded as the "father of the country," who had gone into brooding seclusion in 1922 rather than accept what he viewed as a constitutionally watered-down presidency, now reemerged to lead the chorus of outcries. In May 1926, his political nemesis, Wincenty Witos, formed a new ministry. The two men engaged one another in venomous denunciation. In the midst of it, the government branded Piłsudski a "calumniator," and threatened him with judicial action.[182] Rather than wait on events, he marched on Warsaw with three regiments of soldiers. President Stanisław Wojciechowski confronted him on Poniatowski Bridge declaring his exploit unconstitutional (May 12, 1926). "For me," Piłsudski answered, "the legal road is closed." There ensued a three-days' running battle in the streets of Warsaw that claimed nearly 400 lives.[183] Government troops attempting to descend on the capital found pro–Piłsudski railway workers unwilling to transport them.[184] Enjoying support from nationalists, leftists, disaffected minorities and the army, Piłsudski emerged triumphant. President Wojciechowski and Premier Witos resigned, to be succeeded, respectively, by Piłsudski's trusted adherents, Ignace Mościcki and Kasimir Bartel, while Piłsudski contented himself with the post of war minister.

For the ensuing nine years until his death from liver cancer in 1935, Piłsudski was the effective head of state—engaging the Sejm in a constant battle for constitutional reform aimed at strengthening the executive branch of government. Despite increasingly dictatorial methods—which included vote rigging, intimidation, press censorship, arrests of political opponents (including Witos) and the passage of an authoritarian constitution after the opposition had defiantly walked out of the Sejm in the middle of the debate (1934)—Piłsudski retained his popularity by distancing himself from specific policy-making. His supporters in the Sejm were organized into a "Non-Party Bloc" committed to collaborative governance and "cleaning up" (*Sanacja*) corruption and obstructionism in the halls of government.[185]

Although the ministries of the period were sufficiently populated by military men as to be derided as "Cabinets of Colonels,"[186] the interval was not lacking in accomplishment. Owing to the conjunction, in 1926, of a sound harvest, the opening of the British market to Silesian coal (during that year's British coal strike), and the wholesale adoption of economic reforms recommended by Princeton Professor Edwin W. Kemmerer, the Polish economy stabilized until the coming of the Great Depression threw it into disarray again.[187] A Land Reform Act, passed in December 1925 after years of bickering, helped to alleviate the agrarian crisis by mandating the redistribution to the peasantry of a collective half million acres of land taken annually from the nation's large estates for a period of ten years.[188] Piłsudski sought improved relations with the state's ethnic minorities—facilitating Jewish and Ukrainian assimilation, while promoting cultural autonomy for the latter (a program that was sabotaged by Ukrainian fanatics and Soviet raiders who terrorized those Poles and Ukrainians who sought reconciliation.[189]) The working class benefited from social legislation and low-income housing,[190] and, under Piłsudski's immediate successors, a start was made on industrializing the region between the Vistula and San Rivers using newly established hydroelectric power stations.[191]

Despite these measures, prosperity proved elusive—the standard of living being well below that of the Western European states—and so, too, did security. At the outset of the interwar period, Poland had signed an alliance with France (1921). The value of this alliance, however, had been called into question by the French fiasco in the Ruhr (1923), and by the failure of the Western democracies to demand, at Locarno (1925), that Germany sign a guarantee of her eastern border with Poland and Czechoslovakia, as she had been obliged to do in the West with France and Belgium.[192] By the early 1930s, the progress of Nazism in Germany had rendered Polish anxieties more acute. Piłsudski decided, therefore, to pursue a novel foreign policy by signing nonaggression pacts first with the Soviet Union (1932), and then with Hitler (1934).[193] In so doing, the Polish leader hoped to neutralize the threat on either border by achieving a "balance" between them.[194] Instead, he placed Poland on a tightrope between Scylla and Charybdis. Surveying the situation at the time, the novelist, historian, and prophesier, H.G. Wells, predicted that Poland and Germany would be at war by 1940.[195] Indeed, Piłsudski himself doubted that his nation had obtained more than four years' respite.[196]

Germany posed the most acute danger. At the time of the 1934 nonaggression pact, Hitler viewed Piłsudski (erroneously) as a potential ally in his plan for eastward expansion.[197] (He would continue to harbor such illusions about Poland until 1939.) But the nonaggression pact had failed to address the two chief items of contention between the signatories: namely, the Polish Corridor and Danzig (Gdańsk). In 1919, it had been reckoned by the Paris peacemakers that providing Poland with an outlet to the sea outweighed the importance of Germany's territorial contiguity. A strip of German territory running along the course of the Vistula River to the port of Danzig on the Baltic Sea was therefore ceded to Poland. Alas, the cure proved quite as bad as the disease. Germany took great umbrage at the establishment of this "Polish Corridor" (which created a geographic separation between Germany-proper and the province of East Prussia). The choice of Danzig as a "Polish" maritime outlet was likewise problematic, for the city's ethnic make-up was overwhelmingly German. In an attempt to address this issue, the Paris peacemakers determined that Danzig should be a "free city" under League of Nations' sponsorship, to be ruled by its own two-house legislature under its own constitution in all matters other than foreign relations and commerce—authority in these last spheres being allocated to Poland. The result was interminable conflict between the "free city" and the Polish state.[198]

Tiring of Danzig's antipathy (perhaps, indeed, to exact a measure of revenge for it), the Poles began work on their own port along an adjacent strip of coastline at the tip of the Polish Corridor. Called Gdynia, the port welcomed just 24 ships in its first full year of operation (1924). However, with each succeeding year the number grew exponentially until more ships were landing at Gdynia (7,200 per year) than at Danzig itself.[199] The Poles were enormously proud of this accomplishment—boasting, at every opportunity, that the port had been "built at American speed."[200] The Danzigers, in contrast, were enormously vexed by the diversion to Poland of commerce and customs receipts that (in their view) rightfully belonged to them. It was a time of great tension, for the year was 1933, and Danzig's legislative elections had produced a Nazi majority in both houses. But the following year, Hitler and Piłsudski signed their nonaggression pact, and Danzig and Poland were able to reach an agreement stipulating that Gdynia should receive no more than 55 percent of the combined commerce of the dueling ports.[201]

And so matters stood (more or less) until March 1939, when (i) Hitler issued his demand for the repatriation of Danzig and an extraterritorial railroad and highway across the Polish Corridor; (ii) Poland refused these demands; (iii) Britain and France offered to guarantee Poland's territorial integrity in the setting of unprovoked German attack; and (iv) Józef Beck accepted this guarantee between one flick of his cigarette ashes and the next.

The true purpose behind Hitler's ultimatum to Poland was embodied in the term "*Lebensraum*" ("living space").[202] Previously, the problem had been too many Germans living as oppressed minorities under foreign rule. Now that Germany had provided a haven for all her brothers, she needed to supply them with room to live. (Hitler's mind had lit upon the Baltic States and Ukraine as logical choices in conformance with the longstanding plans he had outlined in *Mein Kampf.*) Having supported the Poles in the seizure of Teschen from Czechoslovakia in October 1938, the Führer hoped that Poland might willingly participate in his intended program.[203] Indeed, in submitting his demands to the Polish government in March 1939, he had simultaneously proffered a guarantee of Poland's existing borders and had invited Poland to become a member-in-good-standing of the Anti-Comintern Pact alongside Germany, Japan and Italy. (The latter was a clear intimation that Poland might expect territorial compensation at Soviet expense in return for cooperating with Germany's ultimatum.)[204] The approach, however, had not worked. Consequently, Hitler adopted a policy of "no more mister nice guy"—abrogating the 1934 Polish-German Nonaggression Pact, and ordering his generals to prepare for "Case White": the invasion and destruction of Poland.

A propaganda campaign no less virulent than the one employed against Czechoslovakia vis-à-vis the Sudetenland was now unleashed upon the Poles, accusing them of mistreating ethnic Germans in the Polish Corridor.[205] There were those in the West who still believed that appeasement was the answer. Among these was Walter Montagu Douglas Scott (Lord Buccleuch), the Lord Steward of King George VI's Household, who traveled to Germany in April 1939 hoping to attend Hitler's 50th birthday celebration. A gentle protest from the king convinced him to find a pretext to return to Britain before the big day; but on his return, Buccleuch wrote to Chamberlain and Halifax, emphasizing that *compared to his treatment of Czechoslovakia and Austria*, Hitler's demands upon Poland had been "very reasonable."[206] *Compared to his treatment of Czechoslovakia and Austria*, this was undoubtedly true; for compared to *that*, most things in life are "very reasonable." But Chamberlain was finally on to Hitler's game, while, in France, Daladier (notwithstanding his participation in the Munich fiasco) had been on to it all along.

Alas, being awake to the threat posed by Hitler was not the same as being in a position to confront it. Britain and France were woefully behind the German pace of rearmament. To compensate, they attempted (belatedly) to forge an alliance with Russia. The resulting talks proved unproductive—not the least because the democracies approached them without urgency, or even enthusiasm (a byproduct of their aversion to Bolshevism). Had they been more attentive, notes William Shirer, they might have realized what fate had in store for them.

In the aftermath of the Munich Agreement of the preceding year, the French ambassador, Robert Coulondre, had gone to the Russian foreign office in Moscow to discuss the rationale behind France's abandonment of Czechoslovakia (October 4, 1938). There to receive him was Vladimir Potemkin, who listened attentively for a few moments, then asked, "My poor friend, what have you done? You have opened the way to a fourth partition of Poland."[207] Stalin, it seems, had viewed the Allied policy of appeasement—most particularly, the betrayal of the Czechs—as evidence that the democracies could never be trusted. Indeed, an alliance with the West might mean that Russia alone would have to bear the brunt of any war against Germany.[208] The democracies had not rallied to the cause of Spain, Austria or Czechoslovakia (never mind Abyssinia). Why would they help Russia if she attempted to oppose the German juggernaut? Would they not benefit to a greater degree by sitting on the sidelines while Germany and Russia destroyed one another?[209]

During the talks with Britain and France, Stalin demanded clear-cut guarantees of military action from both powers in case of war with Germany (with specific details spelled out), as well as free passage for his troops through the threatened states of Eastern Europe (the very notion of which was anathema to Poland and the Baltic States).[210] When these guarantees were not forthcoming, Stalin stunned the world by signing a ten-year "non-aggression pact" with Hitler (August 23, 1939).

France and Britain were taken aback. Hitherto, Germany and Russia had been mortal enemies, and Hitler had been wont to characterize Stalin as a "blood-stained sub-human."[211] By setting aside their feelings long enough to sign the Nazi-Soviet Pact, however, Stalin gained time to rebuild his military (after liquidating most of its officer corps during the Great Purge of 1937–1938), while the Führer effectively isolated the Western democracies from the only major European power that might have supported them. Although it was not known until the opening of the German archives after the war (and was denied even then by the Soviet Union), the pact's secret provisions effectively partitioned Poland between the signatories, while giving Germany license to seize Lithuania and Russia license to do the same with Finland, Estonia, Latvia and Romanian Bessarabia (a province that had belonged to Russia prior to the Peace of Paris).[212]

Hitler now felt free to press ahead with his designs upon Poland, secure in the belief that France and England would continue in their policy of irresolution. It was his first great miscalculation, for the Allies would not cater to further aggression. On August 31, Hitler's SS staged a sham provocation to serve as a pretext for the Nazi invasion of Poland. A dozen German criminals dressed in Polish army uniforms were murdered by lethal injection. Their corpses were then riddled with bullets and deposited outside a German radio station near the Polish border.[213] Claiming, on this contrived basis, that she had been attacked, Germany declared war on Poland and sent her army across the border on September 1, 1939.

Although they were in no position to render timely assistance to the Poles, Britain and France declared war on Germany on September 3, 1939. Addressing his nation by radio at 11:15 a.m., Neville Chamberlain somberly announced, "This morning the British Ambassador in Berlin handed the German Government a final note stating that unless we heard from them by 11 o'clock that they were prepared at once to withdraw their troops from Poland, a state of war would exist between us. I have to tell you now that no such undertaking has been received, and that consequently this country is at war with Germany."[214]

It was now Hitler's turn to be stunned. Although he was fond of threatening Britain and France with war, he neither desired nor expected them to take up the gauntlet.[215] On being informed of Chamberlain's decision, he is said to have sat momentarily transfixed, and then, "with a savage look," to have asked Ribbentrop, "What now?"[216]

For some time afterwards, the Führer tried to convince himself that it wasn't actually true. According to Albert Speer, he told his sycophantic retinue that the Allies might threaten to fight, but that they would never actually do so. It was merely a cover for their diplomatic embarrassment.[217] Reality, however, has a way of spoiling even the most steadfast delusions—and an impending change in the British cabinet would soon show that the Allies meant business. Shortly after Chamberlain's radio address on the morning of September 3, the air raid sirens sounded across London. Prominent among those shuffling into the city's various shelters was the consummately prepared Winston Churchill who reported to his assigned cellar carrying "a bottle of brandy and other appropriate medical comforts."[218]

World War II:
Axis Blitzkrieg, 1939–1942

Blitzkrieg in Poland: The Second World War Begins

On September 1, 1939, a modern German army, boasting an array of mechanized and armored vehicles, crossed the Polish frontier. Against this onrushing tide, the Poles mustered an assortment of outmoded implements of war, the most mobile of which were the Polish Lancers—the finest horse cavalry to be found in 1939 Europe. To avoid destruction on the ground, Poland's obsolete air force had to be dispersed to a plethora of clandestine airstrips in the rear. Although Polish fighter squadrons fought skillfully and heroically—shooting down 42 planes at a cost of 38 in the skies over Warsaw in the first days of the war—the Polish Air Force was outnumbered 5 to 1, leaving the *Luftwaffe* to dominate the skies from the first hour.[1] Everything else in Poland's arsenal was committed to the defense of her western frontier—a region which possessed neither fortifications nor defensible barriers, but which could not be abandoned without sacrificing the nation's essential industries and vital agricultural land.[2]

With control of the skies, the Germans knocked out Poland's railroads and communications. Convoys of Polish soldiers were bombed before they could reach the front. Those who were already in position were encircled as Hitler's motorized forces thrust in simultaneously from the north (East Prussia), south (Czechoslovakia) and west (Germany proper). According to a longstanding myth, Polish Lancers, trapped in the Corridor on the first day of fighting, hurled themselves against German tanks in a desperate effort to break through and link up with their comrades. The survivors were allegedly astonished to find that the German tanks were real as they filed past them into captivity—having been assured prior to the charge that they were made of cardboard or canvas rather than of armor.[3] In actuality, this was a German fabrication, designed to portray the Poles as valiant but dimwitted, and (more importantly) to hide the fact that the Polish cavalry performed not only admirably but, in many instances, successfully during the course of the war.[4] In the episode that gave rise to the myth, for example (the Battle of Krojanty, September 1, 1939), the involved horsemen actually stormed into German *infantry*, putting them to panicked flight with their sabers before machine gun-firing armored cars arrived to inflict a score of casualties and force their withdrawal.[5] At Mokra, on the same day, dismounted cavalrymen who had ridden to their positions with infantry weapons (including anti-tank rifles and horse-drawn artillery) drove back repeated panzer attacks. At one point in the battle a Polish cavalry unit, caught in the fog of war, accidently *did* canter into a column of German panzers, but the horsemen were not so rash as to charge with sabers drawn.[6]

Southwest of Warsaw, Poland's best infantry divisions caught the Germans in flank near the Bzura River, inflicting substantial casualties, but with the *Luftwaffe* holding uncontested control of the skies, the attack was foredoomed to defeat. The only remaining hope lay in timely intervention by the Allies, but this was not forthcoming. Direct air support was out of the question since there were no intact Polish airfields on which to land. (The Allied planes, moreover, would have had to run a gauntlet of German fighter aircraft in order to get there.)[7] That said, Britain had sworn to undertake a bombing campaign *against Germany itself* in the event of an attack on Poland. But now that the moment had arrived, she seemed very little disposed to fulfill this oath. (As we shall see, she would be chary to risk her newly minted planes even for the sake of France in 1940. Britain had invested disproportionately in her air force in the late 1930s out of fear that her cities would be bombed in time of war. Deployment abroad was at odds with the primary object of home defense.)

This left the option of a rapid ground attack across the Franco-German border, where the Allies (though they didn't know it) held a massive advantage in strength—110 fighting divisions versus 23. At the very least, an attack in this theater would have forced Hitler to divert substantial forces from Poland to his western frontier (if it did not win the war outright).[8] Prior to the German invasion, France had promised Poland that it would launch such a campaign by the 15th day of fighting.[9] Like Britain, she balked when the moment came. Asked by his government when a major offensive could begin, the French commander-in-chief, Maurice Gamelin, replied with perfect sincerity that, if all went well, he hoped to complete his preparations by 1941 or 1942.[10] For appearances sake, a few French divisions did advance into the Saar Basin, but when the weaker German forces opposite them staged a feeble counterattack a few weeks later, the High Command ordered an immediate withdrawal—much to the detriment of army morale.[11]

By that time, gallant Poland had already fallen. Without effective assistance from the West, Warsaw (led by its legendary mayor, "Stefan the Stubborn"[12]) resisted as long as it could. Two weeks into the fighting, however, Russia attacked Poland from the east on the pretext of safeguarding the beleaguered state's White Russian and Ukrainian inhabitants.[13] Bereft of hope, the Polish government fled into exile. On September 28, 1939, Poland ceased to exist. Her forces had sustained 200,000 military and untold civilian casualties—the latter due to *Luftwaffe* bombing and strafing as well as other forms of indiscriminate killing. The *Wehrmacht*, however, had paid a heavier price than is sometimes realized—losing as many as 50,000 dead or wounded and hundreds of tanks and planes.[14] (In invading from the east, the Russians suffered less than 1,000 killed.[15]) Despite the odds against them, the Polish soldiery had fought with courage and determination. When matters became hopeless, more than 100,000 of them escaped across the border, mostly to Romania. From there, they made their way to France and England by a thousand different routes in order to form a Polish Army-in-exile that would distinguish itself in every major campaign undertaken in the West for the duration of the war.[16]

For those left behind, however, the agony was only beginning. On the first day of fighting, Polish postal workers in Danzig had held out briefly against a German attack. On surrendering, they were harried out of the post office and shot down in cold blood. It was a portent of things to come.[17] Throughout the fighting and afterwards, German death squads lined up Polish patriots in front of pits and shot them dead. Jews were rounded up and crowded into ghettos in Warsaw and Lodz. Thousands of Polish intellectuals—men and women—were arrested and murdered. Mussolini was shocked enough by the barbarity to leak his inside information of it to the Allied press.[18] Further east, the luckless Poles were treated to a dose of Soviet savagery. Thousands of Polish officers, taken prisoner by the Russians, were slaughtered and buried in the Katyń Forest. (The Germans stumbled upon their mass graves in 1943, and publicized the atrocity in a desperate effort to stimulate anti–Russian sentiment in the West as their own fortunes waned.)

Entering Warsaw on October 6, Hitler crowned his victory with an insulting olive branch—arguing that France and Britain had gone to war over Poland, and since Poland no longer existed, there was no longer a reason for war.[19] Whatever may be said of the Allies' performance to this point, they at least managed not to dignify this "offer" with a response. Desultory or no, the war would go on.

The Russo-Finnish "Winter War" and the German Conquest of Denmark and Norway

The fighting, however, would switch to a surprising arena: Scandinavia. At issue was Swedish iron ore—the source of seventy percent of the iron used in the German armaments industry.[20] At the outset of the war, the German navy was supreme in the Baltic Sea, and during the summer months, the ore could be shipped through these waters directly from Swedish ports. The winter, however, was another matter. At that time of year, Sweden's ports were icebound, and the precious metal had to be transported overland to the Norwegian port of Narvik and then shipped down the Atlantic seaboard to the Baltic and Germany.[21]

The first hint of trouble for this two-tiered supply route came from the east. The rapid defeat of Poland had convinced Russia to establish protectorates over the Baltic States (Latvia, Estonia and Lithuania) before Germany beat her to the punch. For the time being the states remained "independent," but under threat of force, they acquiesced in the establishment of Russian garrisons and airfields at strategic points along the Baltic coast. Thus, the Russian colossus reappeared on the Baltic shoreline for the first time since the Treaty of Brest Litovsk.

This did not, of itself, pose an immediate threat. But as an extension of her new Baltic policy, Russia demanded the cession of territory from Finland. As matters stood, Russia's great northern port of Leningrad (formerly St. Petersburg) was within artillery range of the Finnish frontier. To ease anxieties in the Kremlin, the Finns would have to scoot back—and while they were at it, they could lease to Russia the island of Hangö commanding the approaches to the Gulf of Finland (at whose apex Leningrad sits). To soften the blow of these aggressive demands, the Russians offered to compensate Finland with a slice of frontier territory further to the north.[22] With a measure of trepidation, the Finns informed Stalin that they could not accept his government's magnanimous ultimatum. In reply, Stalin sent an army of a half-million men across the Finnish frontier to assault the Mannerheim Line—a series of entrenchments guarding the Karelian Isthmus, which separates southern Finland from Russia.[23]

Despite intense fighting and heavy casualties, the Russians made no headway. Consequently, they switched their offensive to the northern shore of Lake Ladoga, hoping to isolate and outflank the Mannerheim defenses. Here the result was even worse. Amid freezing temperatures and snowbound roads, their advance slowed to a crawl. Entire convoys stalled, and were annihilated by armed Finnish ski-patrolmen, who gained the appellation "the White Death"—a reference to their bleach-white coveralls, which afforded excellent camouflage in the snowy landscape.[24] (The Russians, in contrast, stood out clearly against the snow during the day and by campfire light at night—easy targets for Finnish snipers and machine-gunners.[25]) A Russian division entrapped near the town of Suomussalmi sought to escape over an ice-covered lake only to drown horribly when Finnish planes shattered the surface with bombs.[26] Possessing precious little artillery, the Finns fended off Russian tanks with incendiary glass bottles filled with gasoline (which they nicknamed "Molotov Cocktails" in honor of Russia's hated, propagandist foreign minister).[27] By February 1940, the northern approaches had to be abandoned, and Russia's entire weight was thrown once more against the Mannerheim Line.

Britain and France, who had stood by idly while the nations of eastern Europe were overrun by Germany, now declared that they could not suffer the bullying of a smaller state by a larger one, and announced plans to succor the Finns by dispatching an expeditionary force to serve on the Mannerheim Line. On the surface, it appeared a noble gesture—though a little exasperating when one considers that the French and British were supposed to be fighting the Germans, not the Russians. But a closer examination unmasks an ulterior motive. To achieve their philanthropic purpose, the Allies had first to get their expeditionary force to its destination. Since Germany controlled the Baltic, the only possible route lay across Norway and Sweden.

To this point, the Nazis must have been amazed at how easily their adversaries could be distracted. But the potential seriousness of the situation now dawned on them. Were the Allies to provide assistance to Finland via the Scandinavian Peninsula, they would have to seize the very routes by which Sweden's iron ore reached Germany—and this, as it turns out, was the true object of the Allied intervention scheme.[28] To avert catastrophe, plans were laid hastily in Berlin to preempt the Allied landings by seizing the major ports of Norway and Denmark.

In the meantime, sad to say, the valorous Finns collapsed beneath the strain. In March 1940, the Soviet horde finally broke through their Mannerheim defenses, forcing their surrender. Estimates place the number of Finnish dead anywhere from 25,000 to 48,000 and Russian dead at 127,000 to 250,000.[29] As the end to hostilities left the Allies with no alibi for moving troops into Scandinavia, they undertook the lesser step of mining Norway's coastal waters in an effort to disrupt German shipping. One day later, on April 9, 1940, Hitler attacked Denmark and Norway. Hapless Denmark fought a brief skirmish outside the Royal Palace in Copenhagen, but with German bombers circling overhead, it was thought best to capitulate. Norway proved more determined—in part because her King, Haakon VII, threatened to abdicate if his government accepted the German summons to surrender.[30] Unfortunately, by the end of the first day of fighting, the Germans had seized all of Norway's major ports and airfields. At Narvik, German commandos seized the harbor after emerging unexpectedly from "Trojan horse" merchant vessels, which had been sitting idle at the port for a week, allegedly waiting to load cargo.[31] Allied attempts to succor the Norwegians were badly bungled. After a valiant but forlorn attempt at resistance, King Haakon fled to England on June 7.

The Battle for France Begins

The only war left to fight in Europe was on the Western Front where all had been unnervingly quiet since the Allied declaration of war on September 3, 1939. While

Blitzkreig, a war of movement, wrought destruction in Poland and Scandinavia, Sitz-kreig, a war fought on the seat of one's pants, held sway in France. From the German point of view, this respite—derided in the worldwide press as the "Phony War" or "Bore War"—came of necessity. At the outset of the fighting, the entire German Army had been mobilized against Poland. There simply weren't any first line units available to fight in the West save a flimsy force left behind as a screen. A determined Allied attack in September 1939 would have spelled disaster for Hitler. Yet, this attack never came.

There had never really been any chance that it would. If France had learned anything from the mutiny of her army in 1917, it was that she should not throw away French lives in ill-conceived offensives. During the interwar period, she constructed a string of impregnable fortresses along the Franco-German frontier, connected to each other by underground rail, and manned by the flower of the French Army—fully 60 percent of her active fighting force.[32] The complex was known as the Maginot Line, and its presence precluded a direct attack on France via this sector. The only alternative open to the Germans—at least as the French saw it—was another end run through the Low Countries.

What to do in this circumstance was problematic. A pre-emptive strike against Germany along this part of the frontier was out of the question since the Allies were unwilling to violate Dutch and Belgian neutrality. Nor were the French willing to abandon the Low Countries to the Germans by extending the Maginot Line to the Channel coast and sitting tight behind their defenses. To do so would be to grant the Germans free passage to the Franco-Belgian border, whence their long-range artillery could pulverize Lille and the other industrial centers of northeastern France, regardless of the presence of fortifications. No, France would simply have to wait for Germany to make the first move, and then defend Lille and the industrial northeast by advancing into Belgium and Holland to combat the invaders far from their own soil.[33]

As events played out, the Germans did indeed make their preliminary attacks through the Low Countries. Unfortunately for France, it was all part of a much larger deception.

On May 10, 1940, Neville Chamberlain stepped down as Britain's prime minister after a scathing attack in the Commons by David Lloyd George. He hoped the king would name Lord Halifax to succeed him, since the only possible alternative was Winston Churchill, whose insistence on taking the war seriously alarmed almost everyone. Halifax's chances, however, were hampered by the fact that he was a member of the House of Lords, none of whom had held the office of Prime Minister since before the First World War when the Lords had abused their privileged status in an effort to undermine democratic reforms. As Churchill's principal secretary, Jock Colville, tells the story, Chamberlain attempted to paint Churchill into a corner by asking if he would object to a member of the House of Lords being named to head the government. Since he could not say "yes" without handing the premiership to Halifax and could not say "no" without appearing self-serving, Churchill said nothing at all.[34] The king called him to form a coalition government later in the day.

Born on November 30, 1874, to the renowned parliamentarian, Lord Randolph Churchill, and the beautiful American socialite, Jennie Jerome, Winston began life as an indifferent schoolboy who craved the attention of a father who seems scarcely to have noticed him.[35] Chancing upon the boy while he was playing with an impressive collection of toy soldiers one day, Lord Randolph inquired whether he might consider a military career. Winston assumed that the patriarch wished him to take up the mantle of their great fighting ancestor, John Churchill, Duke of Marlborough, and answered yes. Only later did he learn that his father doubted whether he possessed the intellect for anything better.[36]

Attending the British military academy at Sandhurst, Winston finished an impressive eighth out of a class of 150.[37] Posted to Cuba as a military observer at the age of twenty-one during that island's rebellion against Spain (1895), he came within inches of death when a bullet pierced his hat, killing a horse standing next to him.[38] Before he was twenty-five, he had fought his way out of a whirling ambush in India's mountainous Swat Valley (1897), participated in a gallant cavalry charge at Omdurman in Sudan (1898), lost his first bid for parliament and published *The River War*, a best-selling history of the Omdurman campaign. Along the way, he led his regiment's polo team to the 1898 All-India championship.[39]

After a short tenure back home, he traveled to South Africa to cover the Boer War as a correspondent. Captured on patrol with British soldiers, he thrilled the home country by staging one of history's most dramatic escapes—being pursued relentlessly before reaching safe haven in Portuguese East Africa after an odyssey of hundreds of miles (1899).[40] Returning to a hero's welcome in England, he was elected to parliament as a Conservative in 1901, but his championship of his father's policy of restraint in military spending, together with his opposition to Joseph Chamberlain's imperial preference tariff project (Winston supported free trade), quickly put him at odds with the party leadership. Ostracized, he bolted to the Liberal Party in 1904, becoming the friend and protégé of David Lloyd George. In 1908, he entered the cabinet, serving first as president of the Board of Trade and later as home secretary, in which capacities he championed social reforms for the working class.

By 1911, however, the kaiser's increasing bellicosity (most particularly, in the Agadir Crisis of that year) caused him to reverse his former opposition to military expenditure and to become so strident an advocate for armaments as to be named First Lord of the Admiralty. By the outbreak of World War I in August 1914, he had modernized the fleet, converted it from coal to oil (thus making it possible to refuel at sea) and placed it on a war footing with a neatly timed "practice mobilization" in June 1914.[41] He remained in this post until the disastrously executed Gallipoli Campaign of 1915 forced his resignation.

Soon afterwards, he went to the Western Front on active service, obtaining command of a battalion—the Sixth Royal Scots Fusiliers—with the rank of lieutenant colonel. Serving in the trenches, he cut a curious figure in his French "Adrian" helmet (which he preferred to the standard British issue) while displaying courage under fire and a keen interest in the welfare of his men. In 1917, David Lloyd George brought him back into the cabinet as minister of munitions in which capacity he greatly improved the efficiency of munitions supply and played a continuing vital role in the development of the tank.[42] Capitalizing on his training as an aviator (obtained during his time at the Admiralty), he flew daily to the Front in order to acquire firsthand information. (Not the most gifted of pilots, he had his aeronautical privileges revoked by his wife, Clementine, after crashing twice in the same afternoon.[43])

Following the elections of December 1918, Lloyd George made him minister of war and placed him in charge of demobilization. Aghast that Russia had succumbed to what he characterized as the "baboonery of Bolshevism,"[44] Churchill argued for the immediate dispatch of a British expeditionary force to assist Russia's anti–Bolshevik White

Army. But the British people had had their fill of carnage by this time, so Lloyd George transferred Churchill to the colonial office, thereby depriving him of further say on the subject.

As colonial secretary, Churchill remade the map of the Middle East—creating Iraq and the emirate of Transjordan out of territory conquered from the former Ottoman empire.[45] Closer to home, he played a crucial part in forging the Anglo-Irish Treaty that ended the Irish Rebellion and established the Irish Free State. (During the negotiations, the chief Irish negotiator, Michael Collins, rebuked Churchill for having put a £5,000 bounty on his head during the uprising, to which Churchill replied that he had at least offered a good price—the Boers having only asked £25 for his own after his 1899 escape.[46])

On David Lloyd George's fall from power in 1922, Churchill switched his allegiance back to the Tories. Though much criticized for having "ratted" twice, he received a handsome reward when Stanley Baldwin invited him to become chancellor of the exchequer (1924).[47] He assumed office in the self-same robe worn by his father at *his* investment as chancellor, and continued in the role for five years, delivering annual budget addresses that are said to have rivaled those of Gladstone in oratory and concision. Alas, his tenure is best remembered for his ill-advised decision to return to the gold standard, thus exacerbating the nation's economic stagnation and provoking John Maynard Keynes' polemic, *The Economic Consequences of Mr. Churchill* (the title of which implied that Churchill's monetary policy was for England what the "Carthaginian" Versailles settlement had been for Europe).

Cast out of office upon Baldwin's defeat in 1929, he spent a decade in the wilderness, as the nation remained deaf to his warnings about Hitler and the need for rearmament. When not being hooted down in Parliament for his unpopular opinions, he spent his time at the family estate at Chartwell painting landscapes (an avocation at which he displayed admirable talent), building walls with brick and mortar (which he could do with the skill of a professional) and—most importantly— writing. It was during this time that he finished *The World Crisis* (a five-volume history of the First World War) and *Marlborough: His Life and Times* (a biography of his illustrious ancestor, the famous victor of Blenheim). The former of these contained passages

Winston Churchill—British statesman, army officer, and writer (1874–1965). Central Office of Information (Wikimedia Commons).

defending his wartime record, prompting Arthur Balfour to quip, "Winston has written an enormous book about himself and called it *The World Crisis*."[48]

Although his stance against self-rule for India (1935) and his impolitic support for Edward VIII during the "abdication crisis" (1936) tarnished his image, he slowly attracted noteworthy supporters for his campaign against Hitler—many of them visiting him at Chartwell where he formed an unofficial "government in exile."[49] (Lady Astor, a Hitler apologist and an American-born MP, was certainly not a member. She once told Churchill in jest that if they were married, she would poison his coffee. He answered that if they were married, he would drink it.[50])

Even as late as Munich, when his rebuke to Chamberlain was shouted down in the Commons, the majority still favored appeasement, but Hitler's subsequent march into Czechoslovakia finally caused the pendulum to swing. Recognized at last for his prescience, Churchill was offered his old position as First Lord of the Admiralty on the day that Britain declared war. He accepted the job with relish, and when Chamberlain resigned in May 1940, Churchill was invited by the king to succeed him as prime minister.

It was at nearly the same moment that Hitler inaugurated the war in the West by invading Holland, Belgium and Luxemburg. On the night of May 9–10, after a week of false alarms, the border patrol stations of the Low Countries reported to their respective governments that they could hear the unmistakable sound of rumbling motors and marching boots in the darkness.[51] The first blow, however, was delivered in silence. At 4:00 a.m. on May 10, four thousand German paratroopers descended from the sky to secure key bridge crossings deep within Holland. The ground forces following in their wake were thus able to drive through the country so rapidly that the Dutch gave up after just five days of resistance. A merciless air bombardment of defenseless Rotterdam presaged the final surrender.

In neighboring Belgium, a German glider force landed on the roof of Eben Emael (the fortress upon which the nation's defenses hinged)—forcing its capitulation by casting hand-held bombs into its turrets and air ducts.[52] Because the Germans had only a few hundred airborne troops still available for action after taking the bridges in Holland, they confused the Belgians by dropping hundreds of dummy paratroopers at various points, while their real paratroopers secured crossings over the Albert Canal—another key to the small nation's defense.[53] The Belgians appealed to Britain and France for help, and Allied troops poured into the Low Countries, certain that the main attack was coming their way. It was not. While they lurched forward into Belgium, the key thrust was being delivered elsewhere—through the supposedly impassable Ardennes Forest, where the Maginot Line ends and Belgium begins.

When General Erich von Manstein first conceived a blow through the Ardennes, the German High Command rejected the idea out of hand. But when Germany's foremost tank expert, General Heinz Guderian, answered Manstein's queries by saying that the supposed impassability of the forest was a myth, Manstein brought the plan directly to Hitler. The Führer was so impressed that he insisted that the strategy be adopted despite the High Command's reservations.[54] Thus, on the very day of the attack on the Low Countries (May 10), an immense assemblage of tanks and motorized infantry entered the Ardennes.[55] Two days later they emerged on the French frontier, opposite the weakest point in the Allied line. The French defenders made a desperate attempt at resistance but were overwhelmed. The Allied front had been pierced a mere ninety-six hours into the "Battle for France."

On hearing of the breakthrough, General Alphonse Joseph Georges, commander of French forces in the northeastern sector, gave an appropriate, if not very useful, response by starting to cry in front of his staff.[56] While they tried to console him, Churchill traveled to France to confer with Maurice Gamelin, the French commander-in-chief (who, no doubt, was still working feverishly on his much-anticipated major offensive for 1941 or '42). Churchill suggested that the French commit their strategic reserve at this critical juncture, then listened in disbelief while a distraught Gamelin explained that France possessed no strategic reserve.[57]

The German armor was now free to race westward toward the English Channel and wasted no time in doing so. Indeed, opposition was so slight that the tank commanders were seen waving to passersby as they sped down the roads.[58] In their wake came motorized infantry, charged with the task of holding key positions along the line of advance as the spearhead dashed forward. Although the German flank was exposed during this drive, French attacks against it were undermanned and ineffectual—the most notable of them being at Laon, led by Charles de Gaulle who had just been promoted to general. Despite making some initial headway, de Gaulle was forced to retreat, owing in part to a total lack of air support.[59] Thus, just eight days after emerging from the Ardennes, the first German units were already in place on the Channel coast (May 20).

Dunkirk

The Allied troops in Belgium were now isolated with enemy troops to their front and rear. Breakouts to the south were attempted but proved ineffectual, since few men could be spared from the ongoing battle with German troops advancing from the North. Harried from two directions, the Allies fell back toward the Channel coast. By May 24, only a fraction of them had reached the sole open port of significance—Dunkirk, located just south of the Franco-Belgian border. By contrast, German armored units were already present outside neighboring Calais, and were thus in a position to reach Dunkirk in force before the bulk of the Allied army could hope to get there. Encirclement seemed imminent.

But it was prevented by a direct order from the Führer, who absolutely forbade the commanders on the scene to proceed to the beleaguered port, arguing that the marshy ground would take too great a toll on the German tanks, and thereby jeopardize the forthcoming campaign in France.[60] As a result, the panzers sat motionless on the outskirts of Calais for forty-eight hours while the Allies solidified their defensive perimeter around Dunkirk. When the engines finally started up again, the discouraged Germans found that they could make scarce headway against these revitalized Anglo-French positions. At Le Paradis and Wormhout, German SS troops murdered Allied POWs. (In the latter instance, says Andrew Roberts, a British sergeant and sergeant major jumped on grenades thrown into their midst in a bid to save their men.)[61]

Although Allied concern over maintaining an open port had momentarily subsided, a fresh crisis immediately presented itself. On May 24, a new German thrust in the north breached the defensive line of the Belgian Army at Courtrai, placing the forces of King Leopold in a disastrous position. As a result, the King notified the Allies that he intended to surrender. Strictly speaking, he could not do this on his own initiative since Belgium was a constitutional monarchy and her parliament wanted to continue the war.

Nonetheless, on May 28, Leopold directed his troops to capitulate unconditionally—an action that laid bare the British left flank.[62]

With the route back to France blocked by the panzers and their left flank dangling in imminent jeopardy, the British decided to evacuate their forces from the Channel coast. The French were not, at first, made privy to this decision. Nor was there any assurance that the enterprise could be carried out successfully. Indeed, the planners of the operation anticipated that there would be two days, at most, to get the men seaborne before enemy bombardment made further embarkation impossible, and that no more than 45,000 men could be brought out in so short an interval.[63] There was every expectation that the *Luftwaffe* would annihilate those left behind in a matter of days.

In the event, however, "Operation Dynamo" (so-named because the evacuation command post was located in a hollowed-out portion of the Dover cliffs where a navy "dynamo" generator had once been[64]) continued for nine full days. Cloudy weather and the RAF's matchless effort to provide air cover did much to confound the German air attacks and to produce a much happier outcome than had been anticipated. Churchill whimsically gives some credit, too, to the nature of the terrain, claiming that the yielding sand on the beaches so dampened the explosions of German bombs and artillery shells that the soldiers soon grew contemptuous of them.[65]

By sacrificing their equipment, the besieged soldiery managed to crowd into a motley collection of vessels, many of them captained by British civilians who had braved the Channel in private boats. Some of the evacuees were taken directly off the beaches, but the majority reached safety by traversing the East Mole, a concrete pier, capped by

Dunkirk 26–29 May 1940. **British troops line up on the beach at Dunkirk to await evacuation. Imperial War Museums. Unknown author (Wikimedia Commons).**

a wooden walkway, that terminated a full mile from shore.[66] At the far end, ships were able to moor in relatively deep water. In all, some 340,000 men—roughly two-thirds of them British, the other third French—were rescued. British casualties have been estimated at 68,000 dead, wounded and captured.[67] Of these, 2000 were sustained at sea, including 639 in one ship. (Another vessel managed to stay afloat after being breached at the water line by moving her cargo and passengers to the opposite side, so that she listed enough for the hole to tilt up out of the water.)[68] French losses were undoubtedly much higher.

The "Miracle of Dunkirk" greatly cheered the British populace—so much so that Churchill felt constrained to remind the country in a speech to the Commons on June 4, 1940, that "Wars are not won by evacuations." It was also in this speech, however, that he uttered some of the most stirring phrases in the history of English oratory: "Even though large tracts of Europe and many old and famous States have fallen or may fall into the grip of the Gestapo and the odious apparatus of Nazi rule, we shall not flag or fail. We shall go on to the end, we shall fight in France, we shall fight on the seas and oceans, we shall fight with growing confidence and growing strength in the air, we shall defend our island, whatever the cost may be, we shall fight on the beaches, we shall fight on the landing-grounds, we shall fight in the fields and in the streets, we shall fight in the hills; we shall never surrender...."[69]

Questions still remain regarding Hitler's intentions in stopping his tanks at Calais. Some believe that he overestimated the Luftwaffe's ability to prevent the evacuation. Others say that he knew France would be subjugated, and felt that kind treatment to the men at Dunkirk might help facilitate England's surrender as well. He would simply be chivalrous and allow the British to escape, thus allowing them to give up with their honor intact.[70] Whether or not this was his purpose, his orders contributed greatly to the Allied escape, and did nothing to raise sentiment for capitulation in Britain. Eight years later, General Ritter von Thoma, one of the tank commanders on the scene, was still unable to contain his anger over the halt order. In an interview with B.H. Liddell Hart, he insisted that victory had been within Germany's grasp and that Hitler's meddling had ruined everything.[71]

France Defeated

Despite the Dunkirk miracle, conditions deteriorated rapidly for France. In desperation, Maxime Weygand, who had now succeeded Gamelin as French commander-in-chief, attempted to forge a new defensive front—the so-called "Weygand Line"—in hopes of halting the Germans on the Somme before they could occupy Paris. Abandoning the traditional concept of linear defense, he instituted a system of strongholds arrayed in checkerboard fashion along the army's various lines of communications. Each bastion was designed to act as a self-subsisting unit—its defenders prepared to direct fire in any direction should the panzers break through and cut them off. The plan—a marked departure from the tactics used thus far in the campaign—represented the earliest birth pangs of the so-called "defense-in-depth" which would prove its mettle against German blitzkrieg tactics later in the war.[72]

Unfortunately for France, the best-equipped French divisions had perished in Belgium, leaving those still available hopelessly outclassed. Although the Germans were made to pay a much steeper price than they had for previous gains of similar or greater magnitude, Weygand's "hedgehog" defenses were rapidly breached, causing the French commander to order a general retreat to the line of the Seine just seventy-two hours into the fighting. On June 10, the French government abandoned the capital for Tours. (By the 14th, it would withdraw to Bordeaux, much further south.) That same day, Mussolini made the culminating mistake of his career by entering the war on the German side. Over the ensuing days, his ground forces would be stopped cold in the Alpine passes. (In the air, however, his flying aces would prove as adept as any *Luftwaffe* pilot in strafing civilian refugees as they fled the battle zones.[73]) On June 11, 1940, Paris was declared an open city. Sixty percent of the population fled, choking the roads leading to the south.[74] Three days later, columns of German troops marched down the *Champs Élysées* with scarcely a Frenchman in sight. As a culminating insult, they paused along the route to adorn the Arc de Triomphe with a Nazi flag.

Hoping to rally the nation for a final effort, Paul Reynaud, the French prime minister, turned to the hero of World War I, Marshal Philippe Pétain. Alas, Pétain was not nearly as helpful in the Second World War as he had been in the First. Indeed, in some respects, the current *débâcle* was of his own making. Between the wars, there had been much discussion about extending the Maginot Line westwards past Sedan to the point where the River Meuse crosses into Belgium. Had this been done, the German thrust through the Ardennes, which had decided the entire campaign, would have been inconceivable. But Pétain's pontifications about the forest's well-known "impassability" led to the measure's defeat. Thus France, in her mortal peril, placed herself at the feet of the very man whose debating skills were chiefly responsible for her abysmal predicament.[75]

To Reynaud's dismay, the aging marshal had no practicable strategy to offer, insisting instead that surrender was the only viable course. Weygand—now an ardent defeatist—agreed without reservation, predicting that Britain would be throttled like a chicken in three weeks.[76] Desperate to keep his ally in the war, Churchill flew to France on June 11. Given Britain's evacuation at Dunkirk and her refusal to place her air force at French disposal, the French High Command was not impressed. General Weygand pointedly asked Churchill what *he* would do if one hundred German divisions *invaded Britain*. Churchill replied that, while he was not a specialist in such matters, he believed that drowning them in the Channel might be effective, and that if any got across safely, a sharp blow to the head would likely suffice.[77] As the French had no further questions, the prime minister returned to England the following day.

Still, a few powerful figures in the French government wanted to continue the fight—among them, the nation's prime minister, Paul Reynaud, and the president, Albert Lebrun. In a final attempt to prop up their cause, Churchill chivalrously offered to form an "indissoluble union" between Britain and France—forging the two states into a single nation with reciprocal citizenship granted to their respective inhabitants.[78] Sadly, this lofty offer did not produce the desired result. On June 16, the French cabinet voted in favor of an armistice. Reynaud promptly resigned in disgust. He was replaced by Pétain. Lebrun, however, stayed at his post and laid plans to form a government-in-exile, with the idea of continuing the war from French North Africa. Before he could act, the government fell prey to a defeatist propaganda campaign orchestrated by Pierre Laval—a former prime minister who hoped to resuscitate his defunct political career by collaborating with the enemy once France had capitulated. Laval accused Lebrun and his supporters of cowardice for "conspiring" to leave French soil during the country's greatest crisis. A true patriot, he asserted, would remain and share the fate of the nation.[79]

In the midst of Laval's harangue, the *Luftwaffe* bombed Bordeaux, despite the fact that the new seat of government was defenseless and had been declared an open city (June 19, 1940). The raid claimed hundreds of victims, and it has been conjectured that the traitorous Laval may have been complicit in it.[80] Stunned by the attack, Lebrun hesitated and lost his chance to move the government into exile. Two of his closest supporters, having already made their way to North Africa, were arrested on trumped-up charges of treason as Laval and the defeatists gained the upper hand.[81]

On June 21, Pétain's government opened negotiations with Germany. An armistice, dictated by the Germans and not open to serious negotiation, was signed the following day in the self-same railway carriage where the Germans had made their own appeal for an armistice in November 1918. By terms of the Treaty, German forces occupied northern France and the whole French Atlantic seaboard. Italy obtained a strip of territory from Nice in the south to the Swiss border at Geneva and the Franco-Italian frontier was demilitarized. What remained of the country became known as Vichy France and was nominally independent.

Despite the abrupt collapse, the French soldiery had fought with courage. In Belgium, properly equipped French units had proven that they could hold their own against the Nazi horde. At Dunkirk, they had manned the defensive perimeter with steadfast determination even though many of them viewed the British, clambering aboard their ships, as being little better than deserters.[82] Afterwards, during the campaign inside France, individual soldiers fought bravely despite being tactically and strategically overmatched.

The decisive factor was the mindset of the French High Command who had never shaken off the ghost of the First World War. Despite the lessons offered by Germany's annihilation of Poland the preceding year, they thought in terms of fixed linear defenses, with troops held in reserve to plug the gaps in the "unlikely" event that the enemy broke through. Only when it was too late did they perceive that breakthroughs were the rule rather than the exception in Germany's new mobile "*blitzkrieg*" form of warfare, and that reserves would have no means of making their way into the breach with dive-bombing Stukas roaming freely above them to wreak havoc with communications and transport.[83]

While the French placed their stock in fixed fortifications and in heavy artillery pieces that could be moved with extreme difficulty—if at all—once combat had commenced, the Germans not only advanced their guns at a motorized pace, but relied heavily on their Stukas, which could double as a mobile, airborne "artillery" force, capable of striking wherever they might be needed, practically at a moment's notice.[84] Germany massed her tanks in the van of her army whence they could pierce the enemy front and carry out a rapid exploitation. France dispersed hers amongst the infantry so that both arms could advance together.[85] In World War I the latter tactic had been effective. In 1940, it deprived the French Army of firepower and mobility, converting its men and materiel into slow moving fodder—easy prey for the *Luftwaffe*.

Yoked to a fatally outdated strategy, the French did not begin to perceive the problems they would face once battle was joined. When it was over, a French staff officer told Marshal Pétain, that Germany's new model army had beaten a French foil designed for the last war.[86]

348 Section III—Survival of the Fittest: The Nations Collide

The Battle of Britain

It was generally believed that the war was over. "The British have lost the war," Hitler boasted on June 22, "but they don't know it; one must give them time, and they will come around."[87] Britain had gotten many of her men, but none of her equipment, off the beaches at Dunkirk. With her military hardware gone, the only advantage she might claim was her naval strength. However, even this was now endangered. By terms of the Franco-German armistice, Hitler had demanded that the French navy be disarmed. The fleet could have been handed over to the British prior to the French capitulation, but its self-seeking commander, Admiral Jean Darlan, reversed his own decision to do so when Pétain named him Minister of Marine on June 17. (What after all is the use of being a naval minister if one has already given away one's navy?) Thus, at the discretion of a vain commander, the French fleet remained in France, provoking widespread fear in Britain that it would one day be incorporated into Hitler's *Kriegsmarine*.

Churchill was determined to avoid this eventuality. On July 3, he ordered the seizure of all French ships in British ports. On the same day, a British naval squadron destroyed a French one at Mers-el-Kebir off the coast of Algeria with great loss of life. (Despite protests from the French government, Churchill also sent British ships into French ports to evacuate 19,000 marooned Polish fighters who had made their way to France to continue the fight against Hitler.[88]) In response, the Vichy Government angrily cut off relations with Britain.

The attack at Mers-el-Kebir served notice to Germany that Britain intended to continue fighting, whatever the odds.[89] Accordingly, Hitler set to work on Operation Sea Lion—a blueprint for the invasion of the British Isles. Others had had this idea before, but it always foundered on the tricky business of wresting control of the English Channel from the British fleet. Times had changed, however, and the idea now seemed conceivable. During the Norwegian Campaign, the *Luftwaffe* had inflicted an unexpected degree of damage on British ships. If it could now defeat Britain's Royal Air Force and gain control of the skies, the British Navy might be blown out of the water from the air. Finding his "common sense" peace proposals to Britain rejected, Hitler confidently declared that there were "no more islands."[90] On July 19, in a speech at the Kroll Opera House in Berlin, he took credit for victory in a battle that was yet to be fought—distributing a dozen field marshal's batons among his officer corps for "assisting" him in the triumphs to date, which he clearly attributed to his own genius.[91]

A month earlier, almost to the day, Churchill had addressed the House of Commons saying, "The whole fury and might of the enemy must very soon be turned on us. Hitler knows that he will have to break us in this island or lose the war.... Let us therefore brace ourselves to our duties, and so bear ourselves that, if the British Empire and its Commonwealth last for a thousand years, men will say, 'This was their finest hour.'"[92]

After some preliminary strikes in early July 1940, the "Battle of Britain" started in earnest on August 13, when the Germans launched countless sorties against British radar installations and airfields. A similar effort was carried out on the 15th, but the RAF and its radar remained intact. By the end of the month, the air fighting had become intense, and though the British held their own, they lost so many pilots that the concern soon became not the availability of planes—for these were being replaced rapidly enough by British factories—but of the men to fly them.[93] Polish, Czech, Belgian and French pilots—refugees from the battles on the continent—eagerly volunteered to help fill the void. (The Poles, composing the largest contingent, particularly impressed RAF command with the tactical skill they had gained from earlier battles. They would down some 200 German planes for the RAF at a cost of just 25.[94])

On August 24, a squadron of German bombers lost their way during a night raid and accidentally bombed central London. The British responded by bombing Berlin three times in a single week. In a fury, Hitler vowed that he would blot England's cities from the map.[95] His attempt to fulfill this boast would change the course of the battle—though hardly in the direction he intended. Although he did not know it, the RAF was on the brink of collapse.[96] But now, by his command, all attacks on airfields and radar installations were abandoned in favor of a terror campaign against London itself.

On September 7, the Führer dispatched more than 1,000 planes to the British capital. Much damage was done during this and succeeding raids, but the city held out no matter what the *Luftwaffe* threw at it. The "Blitz" (as the attacks on London were collectively known) served only to stiffen the resolve of the British people and spur the reprieved RAF to greater efforts. Inspecting the bombed-out docks of London's East End, Churchill heard shouts of "Good old Winnie. We knew you'd come and see us. We can take it. Now give it back!"[97]

As the air battle dragged on, the Germans, who had gotten the upper hand in the weeks preceding the decision to make London their primary target, began to lose significantly more planes than the British. A massive daylight raid on September 15 proved particularly disastrous. By October, it was clear that the *Luftwaffe* would not achieve air superiority. Operation Sea Lion, already postponed indefinitely, was now effectively abandoned. Acknowledging the effort and sacrifice of the Royal Air Force, Churchill issued his oft-quoted tribute in the Commons: "Never in the field of human conflict was so much owed by so many to so few."[98] In the course of the battle, the RAF lost 915 planes and 1,345 airmen killed, the Germans 1,733 planes and nearly 2,700 killed.[99] Britain had obtained her first victory. In the opinion of the military historian Lynn Montross, it was as decisive as the Marne had been in World War I.[100]

Italian Military Incompetence Unveiled

Embarking on the Battle of Britain, says Max Hastings, was one of Hitler's "great blunders," for the direct attack on the British homeland—particularly the bombing of its cities—galvanized the nation behind Churchill and the war. A better alternative, in Hasting's view, would have been to chip away at British resolve with easy victories elsewhere—for example, by joining Italy in ousting British forces from Egypt—leaving the home populace to ruminate over continuing defeats on faraway battlefields and the unnerving *possibility* of assault from the air.[101]

Instead, while the air battle raged over the English Channel in September 1940, Benito Mussolini decided to invade British-controlled Egypt on his own. In theory, this was all part of his master plan to convert the Mediterranean into an Italian lake. But by declaring war on Britain, he forfeited access to the British-controlled Suez Canal, thereby marooning his "East African Empire" (which henceforth could be reached only by sailing around the Cape of Good Hope—which was something of an inconvenience—or by air). His forces in Ethiopia and Eritrea did manage (at some cost) to occupy British Somaliland, but this did not change matters. Hence, on September 13, Italian colonial troops struck eastwards from Libya into Egypt. The following month (perhaps due to jealousy over Hitler's European conquests), the *Duce* sent a second army into Greece from occupied Albania.[102]

Both campaigns ended in disaster. Following the arrival of reinforcements, the British counterattacked from Egypt in December. Relying on mobile tactics and tank superiority, they pierced the Italian line at Sidi Barrani, driving Mussolini's legions into chaotic retreat. Within two months, the British had taken 130,000 Italian prisoners at a cost of but 2,000 casualties.[103]

At nearly the same time (January 1941), British forces stationed in Kenya and Sudan invaded Italian East Africa. Though vastly outnumbered, their tactical deployment again proved superior, as they routed the Italians in Somaliland, Eritrea and Ethiopia reducing Mussolini's East African Empire to a shambles. In May 1941, they restored the deposed Ethiopian Emperor, Haile Selassie, to his throne in Addis Ababa. More than 230,000 Italian soldiers became prisoners of war in this campaign.[104]

By this time, however, Churchill had entered upon a gamble that was to throw away much of the African achievement. Had he completed the campaign against Libya by seizing Tripoli at the end of 1940, the victory over Mussolini's African forces would have been complete. But a new strategic possibility had attracted his attention. In September 1940, Nazi Germany had served as "arbiter" in a "boundary dispute" between Romania and Hungary. Romania had already been made to surrender Bessarabia and northern Bukovina to the Soviet Union (June 1940) and southern Dobruja to Bulgaria (August 1940). Hungary now demanded Transylvania. With his usual diplomatic panache, Hitler worked out a "compromise" whereby Romania handed over *most* of Transylvania to Hungary, while the rest of the Romanian nation became a German protectorate. (King Karol II abdicated on September 6.) This was no insignificant matter, for it gave Hitler access to Romania's oil fields. Rather than let his foe exploit this resource with impunity, Churchill sought to bring the Romanian oil fields within range of the RAF ... which brings us back to Mussolini's campaign in Greece.[105]

Mussolini had not apprised Hitler of his plan to invade Greece, which was only fair since Hitler, just weeks earlier, had neglected to apprise Mussolini of his design to occupy Romania.[106] When, on October 28, 1940, Mussolini's legions struck into Greece, they deployed modern armaments, including tanks, against a Greek army that relied upon pack mules for mobility. All things considered, the Greeks were better prepared. The terrain on the Greco-Albanian border is exceedingly mountainous. Attempting to negotiate narrow, twisting, iced-over trails amid freezing temperatures, the Italian tanks could make no headway.[107] Time and again, the Greeks (and their mules) got around them, employing guerrilla tactics conceived by the Greek premier, Ioannis Metaxas (who had formerly served as a general in the Greek army). Stumbling out of Greece in panicked flight, the Italians sustained tens of thousands of casualties and left an additional 10,000 of their comrades behind as prisoners of war. Although Metaxas succumbed during an operation for a throat abscess during this campaign, the Greeks continued their drive, harrying the Italians towards Valona, their principle Albanian port.

Thus, when Churchill halted his potentially decisive advance on Tripoli and diverted a large proportion of the British Army of Egypt to Greece, it was not primarily a matter of military necessity, but rather a bid to threaten Hitler's Romanian oil fields. Alas for Churchill, the theory of unintended consequences now supervened. Hitler espied the strategic implications of the British move with immediacy, and decided to nip the problem in the bud. In February 1941, he dispatched ground forces to North Africa to assist Mussolini's dispirited army. Led by Erwin Rommel, the German troops dislodged the British from their forward base at El Agheila. Apart from a lone garrison that managed to hold out at Tobruk, the British were harried all the way back to their start line in Egypt, whither the pugnacious Rommel pursued them, even though he had been ordered not to do so and lacked the strength for a decisive blow—something he attempted to conceal by employing Volkswagens surmounted with tank façades to magnify his apparent numbers.[108]

In the meantime, Hitler struck in the Balkans. Ignoring Russian protests that Bulgaria was in the Soviet sphere of influence, the Führer convinced Bulgaria to join the Axis. On March 1, 1941, an army of occupation entered the country. In neighboring Yugoslavia, diplomacy nearly accomplished the same thing. But two days after accepting the German terms, the regent, Prince Paul, was overthrown in favor of his 17-year-old ward, King Peter II, who promptly abrogated the pact in favor of a treaty of friendship with Russia (April 5, 1941). The chess turn was now Hitler's and he responded with his trademark maneuver: *Blitzkreig*. On April 6, Belgrade was subjected to a merciless bombing raid in which 17,000 civilians were killed. The city zoo was hit and the terrified animals took to the streets in a peculiar procession that included a bewildered bear, which swam the Danube in order to escape the flames.[109] Suffering casualties numbered in the hundreds, the *Wehrmacht* overwhelmed the Yugoslav Army, taking 330,000 prisoners.[110]

Greece was attacked on the same day as Yugoslavia. Sadly, she had divided her forces between her Western (Albanian) and Eastern (Bulgarian) fronts, thus leaving a large, unprotected interval along her northern (Yugoslav) frontier. The *Wehrmacht* drove into the chasm (the so-called Monastir Gap) to outflank the Greeks and trap them in their forward positions. On April 24—just one week after battered Yugoslavia surrendered—Greece was ready to do the same. Accordingly, her government advised the British, who were still in the process of landing troops, to evacuate while there was still time. Of 57,000 troops landed, 50,000 got back out.[111]

The British attempted to stand firm on the neighboring island of Crete, but the effort was thwarted by the arrival of German paratroopers, who managed to secure an airstrip with which to reinforce themselves despite suffering abysmal casualties as they floated to earth under fire from British ground forces. Although dead paratroopers were to be seen dangling from tree limbs and strewn liberally about the ground,[112] the British position rapidly became untenable, forcing them to quit the island within a fortnight.

Warned by Archibald Wavell, the commander of British military forces in Egypt, that the RAF could not protect his ships and that he ought not even attempt an evacuation by sea since the anticipated naval losses might take three years to make good, the commander of the Mediterranean fleet, Admiral Sir Andrew Cunningham, answered that if the Royal Navy did not try to get the men off Crete after bringing them there, it would destroy a tradition of naval dependability that could not be rebuilt in 300 years.[113] The fleet ultimately carried 16,000 men to safety—most embarking at night from the beaches near Sphakia. Another 15,000 were killed, wounded or taken prisoner—including the loss at sea of 2,000 sailors (and ten ships) as the flotilla ran a gauntlet of German air attacks all the way from Crete to Alexandria.[114]

Germany's Balkan Campaign was stunningly victorious—but it had not come without cost. Germany's sole airborne division was decimated in the Crete operation, and the carnage convinced Hitler (erroneously) that airborne attacks were no longer practicable. Had he repeated the tactic against Malta, he might have deprived Britain of a vital Mediterranean base, but he would not hear of it.[115] Still, it remained only to wrest control of Egypt from the British to bring the Mediterranean campaign to a successful conclusion. Hitler's generals counseled just such a course, for if England could not be directly invaded, she might still be brought to her knees by seizing the transit center of her colonial empire—Egypt and Suez.[116] But it was now Hitler's turn to halt a campaign one step shy of a thoroughgoing strategic victory. Rommel was left in the lurch at Tobruk, whose garrison held out with dogged determination, while men and materiel were diverted to a much bigger prize: Soviet Russia.

Operation Barbarossa

While Hitler's legions marched from victory to victory at the outset of the war, Russia carried out her own aggressions. In June 1940, she ceased her protectorate policy, and simply annexed the Baltic States. Shortly thereafter, she notified Romania that she must return Bessarabia—one of her spoils from the peace treaties of 1919—to the Soviet Union, and that she had but twenty-four hours to do it. Northern Bukovina, to which Russia had no legitimate claim whatsoever, was to be thrown in as an interest payment.[117]

These actions provoked great anxiety at Berchtesgaden. While Russia, more likely than not, was merely jockeying for position against the day when relations with Germany turned sour, Hitler suspected something more immediately sinister—perceiving at the very least a rival claim to Romania's oil fields, which he had not yet seized for himself. But the conjecture did not stop there. Hitler was increasingly confounded by Britain's refusal to capitulate in the face of overwhelming odds. The visit of her emissary, Sir Stafford Cripps, to Moscow in the fall of 1940 seemed to solve the riddle. Britain was conspiring to bring Russia into the war![118] For a madman rapidly losing touch with reality, it was an inspired guess, but the evidence suggests that Russia had no intention, in 1940 or 1941, of fighting Britain's battles.

In an effort to thwart Britain's imaginary design, Hitler met with the Russian foreign minister, V.M. Molotov, in Berlin (November 1940). But their discussions—aimed at converting the Nazi-Soviet Pact into a formal alliance—proceeded so badly that the exasperated Führer stopped attending the meetings. The final negotiations were left to the German foreign minister, Joachim von Ribbentrop. Sitting with Molotov in an air raid shelter while British bombers ranged overhead, Ribbentrop boasted that England was already defeated and had only to realize the fact. While Molotov could not deny the boldness of this assertion, made by a man cowering in an air raid bunker, he nonetheless expressed wonderment as to who might be bombing Berlin if such were true.[119]

Clearly, no formal alliance was forthcoming, and this confirmed Hitler in his delusion that Russia planned to intervene against him. The logical decision would be to strike first. In so doing, he would not only realize his dream of hurling the Communists into Asia, thus providing *Lebensraum* (living space) for the German people and a vast cache of natural resources for the Reich, but he would thrust upon the British one final demoralization by removing their last hope for a continental alliance.[120]

On June 22, 1941, Germany launched a massive blitzkrieg against the colossus of Eastern Europe. "Operation Barbarossa" was slated to begin five weeks before it actually got rolling, and it is frequently argued that Hitler's diversion into Greece was responsible for the delayed start of the campaign, and thus for its disastrous conclusion. Churchill himself championed this view, though he must be regarded as a biased observer, needing as he did to shed a favorable light on his decision to intervene in Greece.[121] More recently historians have noted that the rainy spring of 1941 left the ground too muddy for the passage of heavy equipment until late June, and that the interlude in Greece did not actually influence the starting date of the offensive.[122]

In any event, when the attack began at 3:00 a.m. on June 22, it showed every sign of being unstoppable. Despite detailed warnings from England and the United States of an impending German invasion, Russia was taken completely by surprise. When the German attaché in Moscow finally handed a (tardy) diplomatic note to Molotov declaring the state of war, the disgusted foreign minister spat on the document and tore it in pieces.[123] Three German armies, totaling over three million men, were already pouring across the Russian frontier: Army Group North driving toward Leningrad, Army Group Center toward Smolensk, and Army Group South toward Kiev. Much of Russia's air force and heavy equipment were destroyed before her soldiers had time to man them. On the first day alone, 1,200 aircraft were obliterated—most of them still neatly lined up wingtip-to-wingtip on the Russian airfields.[124] Told of the attack, a disbelieving Stalin had the messenger taken away and shot.[125] His first inclination was to lock himself in his study and fortify himself with vodka[126]—and this, for a time, seemed to do the trick. But by week's end, the "Man of Steel" had suffered a nervous breakdown at his seasonal home outside Moscow, where he wandered speechless, until a deputation of high-ranking officials arrived to insist that he return to the Kremlin and lead the nation. On seeing them approach, he assumed that he had been ousted from power and that they had come to arrest him. Instead, they offered him the leadership of a newly formed, all-powerful "State Committee of Defense" (Stavka). He accepted.[127]

Both inside and outside Germany, it was believed that Russia would capitulate in a matter of weeks.[128] Outgunned and outmaneuvered, the Russian soldiery had no alternative but to fight to the death since the Germans indiscriminately murdered many of those who surrendered, and the Soviet Secret Police (NKVD) machine-gunned anyone who tried to flee to the rear.[129] No concession was made to the natural drive for self-preservation. A directive from the Russian High Command instructed wounded soldiers to feign dead, and then to pounce upon the first German who came close in order "to drag one with you" to the grave.[130]

Despite such inducements, the Russians could do little to stem the German tide. By early August, Army Group Center had taken Smolensk. Its commanders begged Hitler to send them on to Moscow, less than 200 miles to the east, arguing that since Stalin would have to stake his regime on its defense, the war could be brought to a rapid decision.[131] Indeed, the capture of Moscow would be a double-blow, since it would not only entail the destruction of Russia's main armies, but also the capture of her national transport and communications hub, without which she could not hope to supply or reinforce other fronts.[132] But Hitler denied his field commanders their opportunity. Army Group Center was ordered to remain at Smolensk while attention and armor were diverted to the drives on Leningrad and Kiev. The decision was irrevocable. The Russians must be wrenched from the Baltic coast. The abundant produce of the Ukraine must be seized

German troops in Russia, 1941. National Archives at College Park, Maryland (Wikimedia Commons).

to supply the army and the Reich.[133] Only then, when the flanks were secure, was Hitler willing to consider a bid for the capital.

At first, the disgruntled generals dragged their feet, hoping the Führer would change his mind.[134] But this merely resulted in further delays—which, incidentally, the Russians put to impressive use, dismantling entire factories from the ground up in threatened areas and transporting them by rail for reassembly out of harm's way beyond the Urals and the Volga. (Ominously for Germany, more than 1,300 industrial complexes were thus reconstituted in the first six months of fighting—many resuming production before walls and ceilings had even been built.)[135] Desperate to achieve total victory before winter set in, the German field commanders ultimately deferred to their leader and sent the panzers into the Ukraine. To their surprise, they were greeted by cheering throngs of anti–Soviet Ukrainians. Literally millions of these people were ready to rally to the Nazi banner if that meant getting rid of the Communists.[136] The peoples of the Baltic States and Belorussia were likewise eager to cast off Stalin's dictatorship. They awaited only a liberator; but if they thought they had found one in Hitler, they were sadly mistaken. The Nazi plan was to seize Russia's industrial plants, oil fields and grain-producing zones for the benefit of the Reich, and to let the Russian "*Untermensch*" (i.e., "Sub-humans") starve by the millions,[137] while German soldiers stood by ready to kill anyone who looked the least bit unhappy about it.[138]

Most enthusiastic in carrying out these orders were the Special Task Forces (*Einsatzgruppen*) of Heinrich Himmler's SS. At their discretion, civilians suspected of being Stalinist "partisans"—men and women—were hung from hastily erected gallows, or lined up in front of pits and gunned down. Some were sadistically shot in the abdomen and cast alive into their graves.[139] Successful partisan attacks were routinely punished by the execution of all civilians in the nearest village.[140] A special "Barbarossa Decree" issued at the outset of the campaign forbade the prosecution of soldiers for the commission of such war crimes, provided that combat discipline was not adversely affected.[141]

Areas that submitted without resistance to German occupation fared no better. Himmler boasted that 30 million Slavs would be wiped out to make room for an equal number of German colonists.[142] Survivors would be used for forced labor. As Himmler told a group of SS men departing for the front: "Whether 10,000 Russian females fall down from exhaustion while digging an anti-tank ditch interests me only in so far as the anti-tank ditch for Germany is finished…. We Germans, who are the only people in the world to have a decent attitude towards animals, will also assume a decent attitude towards these human animals. But it is a crime against our own blood to worry about them…. When somebody comes to me and says, 'I cannot dig the anti-tank ditch with women and children, it is inhuman, for it would kill them,' then I have to say, 'You are a murderer of your own blood because if the anti-tank ditch is not dug, German soldiers will die…. Our concern, our duty is our people and our blood…. We can be indifferent to everything else.'"[143]

Subjected to rape, pillage and murder, the Ukrainians began to lose their enthusiasm for the Nazis. By the time the German Army reached and encircled Kiev in late August, the cheering throngs had melted away. At the time, it didn't seem to matter. When the Ukrainian capital capitulated in September, 665,000 Russian prisoners were taken, bringing the total for the campaign to well over a million.[144] (Most would starve to death, penned up in barbed wire enclosures, as their German captors made no effort to feed them.[145] Of 5 million Russian prisoners taken during the course of the war, more than 60 percent died in captivity.[146])

One hundred Russian divisions had already been cut off or destroyed during Operation Barbarossa. Still, Leningrad held out in the North, and it became questionable if the Germans could put the Russians out of the war before winter relying on the present strategy. In late September, Hitler finally gave in to the wishes of his generals, and sanctioned a renewal of the drive on Moscow. But after two months of delay, the latter were no longer confident. It was too late in the year. Winter was approaching. German commanders, looking haggard and worried, were seen carrying about personal copies of Armand Caulaincourt's memoirs of Napoleon's disastrous campaign of 1812.[147] The rank and file were likewise nervous—most especially, the *Wehrmacht*'s Romanian and Hungarian auxiliaries, who frightened one another with old wives' tales averring that a Russian wasn't dead until he had been killed twice, and that he who kills a Russian on his own soil never makes it home.[148]

But Hitler was insistent, so the German panzers were diverted back to Smolensk for a drive on Moscow to begin on October 2. Despite rumors about the new push, the Russians were ill prepared. By October 4, their defensive line was broken, and the bulk of their forward troops were encircled near Vyazma, a city located roughly halfway between Smolensk and Moscow. Although the surrounded forces fought on, more than 600,000 were eventually taken prisoner. Worse still, Moscow lost radio contact with the front-line commanders, and Stalin could not even get updates on the evolving situation. Reconnaissance planes reported large German columns approaching to within 100 miles of Moscow, and it wasn't clearly established what (if anything) might be standing in their way.[149]

At this critical juncture, Stalin placed Georgi Zhukov in charge of Moscow's defense. Zhukov had already stemmed the German tide twice during Operation

Barbarossa. In August, he defeated the Germans at the four-week battle of Yelnya, some 225 miles to the west of Moscow. He was then sent to Leningrad, where he stopped the onslaught of Army Group North by convincing the city's defenders that they had more to fear from *him* than the from the Germans. He typically barked his orders over the phone and then hung up without waiting for a reply. He didn't need one. His command was Gospel. Failure to comply meant death.[150]

Zhukov's formula worked like a charm. The Germans never breached the defensive perimeter at Leningrad—a lucky thing for the starving inhabitants, since Hitler was planning to raze their city and slaughter them.[151] To be sure, Zhukov's merciless counterattacks after the German drive ground down proved as costly to his own troops as to the enemy, but the unrelenting commander had no qualms about making the lives of his men the chief currency of his own success. Later in the war, he gave Dwight Eisenhower a tutorial on how to clear a minefield, saying the most efficient way was to march troops across it, since the number of men killed would be roughly equal to the number lost had the Germans defended the ground with men rather than mines.[152] Needless to say, a man with such facile command of logical analysis (to say nothing of mathematics) was not likely to escape the notice of Stalin. The general was summoned from Leningrad, and arrived in Moscow on October 7.

By this time the capital's defenses were in complete disarray. Although, in his memoirs, Zhukov presents himself as a reasonable man making reasonable demands in a reasonable way, he must have made a few of his patented phone calls, for in scarcely any time at all, an intact line of defense in depth had been established, centered on Mozhiask. Unfortunately, it failed to hold. In desperation, the army withdrew to a new line on October 19. Most members of the government fled the capital. Having regained his nerve, however, Stalin remained, providing a much-needed boost to the morale of the city's defenders.

At Tula, just south of Moscow, inadequately armed troops fought off Guderian's panzers with clusters of grenades. When the supply of these was exhausted, they resorted to Molotov cocktails.[153] In front of the capital, the city's women took up shovels and slogged through the mud to help construct hundreds of miles of anti-tank ditches. Rain and mud also did its part to slow the German advance, but by early November, the ground was frozen, and the Germans were again on the move. In the first week of December, they broke into the Moscow suburbs, and could see the famed cupolas of the Kremlin on the horizon.

This, however, was the furthest extent of their advance. Despite enormous casualties, the Russians clung to their positions. Civilians joined the fray, armed with factory tools and other rudimentary weapons.[154] And then the subzero temperatures struck. Without winter clothing, thousands of German troops succumbed to frostbite. The snowbound roads became impassible to tanks whose motors could not be started in any event unless fires were set below them to warm them up.[155] By December 5, forward movement had ceased. On the following day, Zhukov ordered a counteroffensive involving 100 Russian divisions. A quarter of these had just arrived from the Manchurian front, well supplied and warmly clad (for the Russians had learned the value of winter clothing and snow camouflage during the Finnish War).[156] Their unexpected onslaught threatened catastrophe for the war-weary, freezing Germans. The date was December 6, 1941. The following day, destiny would deliver another momentous blow.

The United States Enters the War

The history of the United States of America is peculiar among the nations of the West. She had come into being in 1776 with a declaration of independence from England—the peculiar part being that she established herself as a republic. By 1861, she already boasted the oldest surviving republic still existent on the face of the earth, and was locked in a bloody, four-year Civil War to preserve it—indeed, to prove that that form of government could be preserved, even when challenged from within by bitter political controversy. Lincoln's Gettysburg Address, though amazingly brief, is perhaps the most poignant statement in defense of this principle ever made.

Though isolationist by nature, the United States had entered World War I in 1917 because she felt that her rights as a neutral power were being infringed upon; because she had evidence that Germany was conspiring to embroil Mexico in a war against her; and—to take a more cynical view—because the Allies owed her a good deal of money and were about to be defeated (in which event, the money would not be repaid).[157] The experience of the war and its aftermath served to confirm many Americans in their isolationist tendencies. They had spent their treasure and spilt their blood to bail out the Allies, and in return, the wily Europeans had reneged on their war debts, thus contributing to the onset of the Depression. America would not fall for *that one* a second time.[158] Safe behind the vast Atlantic barrier, the United States Congress busied itself with the drafting of new Neutrality Acts—the latest being passed in 1937.

The rapid German victories over Poland and France in 1939–1940, however, created a dilemma for the United States. The Western European democracies had proven themselves weak, inefficient and, in the view of many people, untrustworthy; but could the United States sit by idly while nations whose principles were akin to her own fell victim to a tyrannical aggressor? Was she willing to let the world's major democracies be wiped out in the lame hope that she might yet preserve her own freedom? (As Churchill put the "dilemma" in the case of the neutral states of Europe—Switzerland, Sweden, Ireland, Spain and Portugal—"Each one hopes that if he feeds the crocodile enough, the crocodile will eat him last."[159])

For the United States, the answer to these questions was very nearly "yes." There was still widespread feeling that the country should remain aloof. There was even some sympathy for Hitler's anthropological views. While Poland succumbed to blitzkrieg, the American flying hero, Charles Lindbergh, wrote an article for *Reader's Digest* entitled "Aviation, Geography and Race" in which he said that Americans needed to be on their guard "against attack by foreign armies and dilution by foreign races…." (Further on, he characterized "aviation" as "one of the priceless possessions which permit the White race to live at all in a pressing sea of Yellow, Black and Brown.")[160]

It may be disputed whether Lindbergh was more to blame for uttering such a statement or *Reader's Digest* was more culpable for printing it. In either event, it was the pressing sea of *dictatorship* that concerned President Roosevelt. After the fall of Poland, he convinced Congress to amend the Neutrality Act of 1937, and allow the sale of military equipment to France and England. The agreed revision was called "Cash and Carry," because it stipulated that the Allies could not purchase on credit (and thereby accumulate debt as in the previous war), but had to *pay cash* for all supplies and *carry them on their own ships* (lest America be drawn in through the sinking of her merchant vessels by German U-boats).[161] Much of the American public did not want to go even this far, and in order to garner sufficient support, Roosevelt had to portray the selling of weapons to Britain and France as enabling the European democracies to do the fighting themselves so that the United States would not need to get involved.[162]

With the fall of France in 1940, Roosevelt's efforts took on greater urgency. The year's annual budget included liberal funding for munitions production and naval expansion, and the cabinet was reshuffled to include a pair of Republican hawks—Henry L. Stimson (who became secretary of war) and Colonel Frank Knox (who was named secretary of the navy).[163] In September, a draft lottery system—the so-called "Selective Service Act"—was instituted. More important, Roosevelt gained passage of a "Lend-Lease Act" that allowed him to "lend" equipment to Great Britain for the duration of the war in return for 99-year leases on several British naval and air bases in the Western Hemisphere (March 1941). The agreement was a veritable godsend to the island nation whose material needs had so increased, and whose cash and gold reserves had so diminished, that even loan-based financing no longer remained a feasible option.[164] To ensure safe delivery of the "leased" equipment, United States ships began participating in naval convoys bound for England. This put them in harm's way in the so-called "Battle of the Atlantic."

The German navy was already doing everything it could to interfere with British shipping. Lacking U-boats at the outset of the war (the Admiralty had asked for 300, but had only 43 ready for use),[165] the Germans carried out their raids with surface vessels. The pocket battleship, *Graf Spee*, had an impressive, if brief, career in this capacity—sinking ten merchant vessels before being chased down and crippled off the coast of Uruguay. Despairing of escape, her captain, Hans Langsdorff, scuttled her in Montevideo Harbor and shot himself (December 1939). In a rather more awe-inspiring episode, the battleship *Bismarck* blew the slightly larger HMS *Hood* (the pride of the Royal Navy) out of the water with the loss of all but three of her crew. Built prior to the Battle of Jutland in 1916, the *Hood* lacked deck armor, and as occurred with several ships in that engagement, a shell appears to have pierced her deck and set off a chain explosion in her magazines.[166] In the ensuing days, however, the *Bismarck* was sunk in her turn, and thereafter, convoy raiding became the task of the U-boats alone (May 1941).

To compensate for their lack of numbers, the U-boats resorted to "wolf-pack" tactics whereby they prowled their own sectors individually until one of them located a convoy. The others would then converge on the target and attack en masse. In response, the U.S. Navy began locating German U-boats and giving their positions to the British so that they could sink them. To say the least, such actions stretched the definition of "neutrality," and by the fall of 1941, the U.S. and Germany were perilously close to war. Indeed, it was at this juncture that Roosevelt and Churchill held their famed meeting at Placentia Bay off the coast of Newfoundland to confer on war aims. There, they issued the so-called "Atlantic Charter"—a lofty joint declaration on freedom from oppression—while privately conceding that for freedom to triumph over tyranny the United States would likely have to enter the war, and that Germany would be considered the primary enemy when she did.[167] Yet, it was not the Germans who finally forced the United States to fight. It was the Japanese.

Even as late as July 1941, Japan was not yet thinking about an attack on Pearl Harbor, for she was still deeply embroiled in war with China, against whom she had been fighting since the invasion of Manchuria a decade earlier. As decisive victory continued to elude her, however, she decided to attack China's supply lines by encroaching on regions hitherto controlled by the European colonial powers.[168] Vichy France, being in no position to defend her Pacific possessions, acceded to Japanese occupation of French Indochina on July 24. President Roosevelt lodged an immediate protest against this aggression, and when his words went unheeded, he froze Japanese assets in the United States and arranged (with the cooperation of England and Holland) an oil embargo against Japan.

Thus, the first brush with the colonial powers created for Japan a much bigger problem than it solved, for the Japanese lacked sufficient oil reserves to prosecute a successful war against China, and would have to make good on the lost imports. To do so, they decided to seize the oil-rich Dutch East Indies, a move that was certain to provoke a more general war.[169] This, of course, would bring even bigger problems, and to deal with *them*, Japan devised the biggest solution of all: the creation of a so-called "Greater East Asian Co-Prosperity Sphere." The fulfillment of this encouragingly named program would require the eviction of the colonial powers from the Southeast Asian mainland and neighboring island archipelagos so that Japan might seize them for herself. She would then fortify them to create a defensive perimeter that would shield her home islands from retaliatory attacks, while allowing her—and this is where the euphemism "co-prosperity" came in—to exploit their resources to pay for the ongoing war effort. In short, Japan meant to create her own "Greater East Asian Empire." Of course, the entire scheme hinged on securing control of the Pacific until her aims could be attained, and to do so, Japan would have to eliminate the only fleet capable of rivaling her in those waters—the United States Pacific Fleet lying at anchor in the Hawaiian port of Pearl Harbor.[170]

As late as October 15, these plans were wholly theoretical, and significant steps were being taken to render their implementation unnecessary. Japan's prime minister, Prince Fumimaro Konoe, sincerely desired peace. Believing that his country could not win a protracted war with the United States, he practically begged Roosevelt to meet with him personally to hash out the differences between their respective nations. He was willing to withdraw Japanese forces from Indochina—eventually even from China itself, with the exception of Manchukuo.[171] But he was never given the opportunity to place these proposals on the table. Japan's previous actions had engendered mistrust, and Roosevelt's advisors counseled against the summit meeting in the belief that Konoe was attempting to lure the President into another Munich.[172] Having promised the military a free hand if he did not achieve a negotiated settlement by mid–October, and having been rebuffed repeatedly in his diplomatic overtures, Konoe resigned in despair on October 16. His successor was Hideki Tojo.

Though a hawk by nature, Tojo doubted Japan's capacity to defeat the United States. Consequently, he gave negotiation another try. The attempt did not get very far—mainly because Tojo's notion of a "concession" was to promise a Japanese withdrawal from China by 1966.[173] Roosevelt and his secretary of state, Cordell Hull, rather hoped to see progress within their own lifetimes. As a result, although there was an exchange of diplomatic notes, nothing of consequence was achieved. Accordingly, on December 1, the Japanese military received the go ahead for "Operation Z"—its codename for the attack on Pearl Harbor.

When this attack came, at dawn on December 7, 1941, it was completely unexpected. Adhering to the plan of Admiral Isoroku Yamamoto, the Japanese Imperial fleet sailed clandestinely to a position just north of Hawaii. Well before dawn, hundreds of planes took off from his carriers to make their assault. The first incoming wave was picked up on radar, but the instrument's operators could not locate anyone higher up who had the slightest interest. None of the officers at Pearl Harbor expected an air raid. Thus, no general warning was issued. (The radar station actually shut down for Sunday church services a few minutes later.)

All eight U.S. battleships in port were hit. Two—the *Oklahoma*, which capsized, and the *Arizona*, which exploded and burned with over 1,000 men aboard—were destroyed completely. Hundreds of aircraft, parked wingtip-to-wingtip, were damaged or destroyed on the ground, and more than 3500 American casualties were sustained. By a stroke of luck, the three active aircraft carriers of the U.S. Pacific Fleet were out on maneuvers at the time of the attack.

Characterizing the day of the attack as "a date that will live in infamy," Franklin Roosevelt obtained a declaration of war against Japan from the United States Congress on December 8, 1941. A cadre of conspiracy theorists have maintained ever since that Roosevelt knew about the attack in advance, and allowed it to occur in order to sway American public opinion in favor of the war.[174] Most historians, however, discount this theory, noting that, beyond the fact that there is no evidence for it, the deliberate sacrifice of so much of the U.S. fleet was simply too large a price to pay.[175] Nonetheless, the attack did push America into the war. Indeed, it pushed her into two wars at once. For Hitler, believing that the Japanese would keep the Americans occupied and

The USS *Arizona* burning after the Japanese attack on Pearl Harbor, 7 December 1941. Photographer unknown (Wikimedia Commons).

out of Europe so that he might focus all his energy on the war with Russia,[176] immediately declared war on the "half Judaized ... half Negrified" United States.[177] Based on the decisions taken at Placentia Bay earlier in the year, the decision was fraught with peril for Germany, and there were many high-ranking Germans who already knew it. In the fall of 1941, Albert Speer (soon to be named Hitler's armaments minister) received a projection for aircraft production over the next several years. The numbers showed that Germany's output would be dwarfed by that of the United States owing to the latter's tremendous industrial capacity. As Speer tells it, the aircraft plant manager who submitted the forecast added (in tears) that he had sent the information to the party leadership and that rather than acknowledge facts they had refused to credit the report.[178]

Germany's 1942 Campaign in Russia

In fairness to the higher ups, they were rather distracted at the time by the course of events in Russia. As the Red Army counterattacked around Moscow in the aftermath of the *Wehrmacht's* failed drive on the capital in December 1941, the Führer cashiered his top-ranking generals, assumed supreme command of Germany's armed forces, and forbade any mention of retreat. Countless lives were lost in an effort to comply with his orders, and ground was lost in spite of them, but eventually the German hedgehog defenses, mounting snows (which sometimes necessitated the towing of Russian infantry into battle on sleds drawn by Cossack cavalry[179]), and spring mud (which rendered even the sleds impracticable) brought the Russians to a halt.

By the time the ground hardened again in May, the *Wehrmacht* had recovered from the winter setback, and Hitler was busily outlining an elaborate scheme for a new German offensive. Codenamed *Operation Blue*, it called for a southern drive to seize Stalingrad, the communications hub linking the oil reserves of the Caucasus Mountains to the Russian armies in the field. Hitler believed that a successful campaign here would leave the Red Army paralyzed for lack of fuel.[180] Moreover, Hitler's industrial advisors had assured him—incorrectly as it turned out—that Germany itself would run out of fuel if the Caucasian oil fields were not seized.[181] Accordingly, once Stalingrad was taken, the army was to press on into the Caucasus towards Baku.

Between May and July 1942, the southern flank of the intended drive was secured with German victories at Kerch and Sevastopol in the Crimea.[182] There followed a pair of lightning blows further north—"Army Group B" piercing the Russian defenses east of Kursk on July 1 (the day that Sevastopol fell), while "Army Group A" smashed a second hole in the Russian line near Kharkov the following day. Hundreds of thousands of hapless Russians were either slaughtered or taken prisoner in these operations, and those remaining between the Donetz and Don Rivers seemed destined for encirclement as the German pincers swept around them. Indeed, so dire was the threat to Russia, that Winston Churchill sanctioned an improvised (and, as it turned out, disastrous) British amphibious raid on the French port of Dieppe to help divert the *Wehrmacht's* attention and provide some relief.[183]

Only Hitler's meddling saved the Russians from catastrophe. Intent on seizing geographical objectives rather than on destroying enemy armies in the field, the Führer opted against closing his pincers.[184] Had he stuck to his own plan, he would likely have decimated the Russian forces opposing him, leaving his panzers free to roll into

Despite a valiant effort by the predominantly Canadian attack force, the Dieppe Raid of 9 August 1942 (also known as Operation Jubilee) proved an unmitigated disaster. In the aftermath, abandoned "Churchill" tanks and Allied dead are seen in the foreground while a crippled landing craft burns offshore (Wikimedia Commons).

Stalingrad while the city lay defenseless. He might then have pressed into the Caucasus with impunity. (Alternatively, he might have turned north to attack Moscow from behind.) Instead, he decided to leave Stalingrad to the infantry, while diverting the bulk of his armor—the First and Fourth Panzer Armies—southwards in an attempt to overrun the Caucasian oil fields in yet another lightning strike (July 13). Alas, without tanks, the all-important drive on Stalingrad sputtered to a halt. Hitler, therefore, changed his mind once more. The Fourth Panzer Army, which he had just sent toward the Caucasus, was now told to turn around and resume its drive on Stalingrad (July 29).[185]

Two weeks had been lost in these comings and goings, and with them, the chance of easy victory. For during the interlude, Comrade Stalin did something he had never done before—he listened to his generals and allowed his threatened forces to retreat out of their snare.[186] Joined by reserves from the Moscow front, these refugee units dug themselves in at Stalingrad.

Hitler's Empire of Barbarism

"If the international Jewish financiers within and without
Europe succeed in plunging the nations once more into a world war,
the result will not be the Bolshevization of the world and the victory
of Jewry, but the obliteration of the Jewish race in Europe."[187]
—Adolf Hitler, Reichstag Speech, January 30, 1939

Hitler speaking to the Reichstag during the speech of 30 January 1939, in which he threatened the destruction of European Jewry. Seated on the top chair behind him is Hermann Goering. Arquival Nacional Collection, Brazil. Photographer unknown (Wikimedia Commons).

Despite Hitler's blundering, the gains of the campaign, to this point, were impressive. The arrival of *Wehrmacht* troops on the outskirts of Stalingrad brought the Nazi empire to its territorial zenith. From Scandinavia to North Africa and from the Atlantic to the Volga, Nazism reigned supreme to the detriment of friend and foe alike. In order to boost the *Wehrmacht's* manpower reserves for *Operation Blue*, Hitler had requisitioned factory laborers from his allies, thereby freeing many of his own laborers for military service. Mussolini, for example, dispatched Italian workers to Germany at the Führer's bidding, only to receive harrowing reports about their subsequent treatment (which, according to Count Ciano's diary, included the use of vicious watchdogs to keep them at their jobs).[188]

The real brutality, however, was reserved for the Russian enemy and, even more so, for putative "undesirables" among the civil populace—gypsies, invalids and, of course, the Jews. Branded by Hitler as "racial" degenerates, the Jews were subjected to bullying from the Nazi regime's earliest days. In the 1930s, the goal had been to impoverish them in order to make them emigrate. For a time, cynical support was even given to Zionism to encourage Jewish emigration to Palestine.[189] But with the attack on Russia in June 1941 the decision was taken to render a "Final Solution" to the "Jewish question." At the Wannsee Conference—convened at the order of Hermann Goering in January 1942 and presided over by Reinhard Heydrich (the number-two man in Himmler's *SS*)—it was confirmed that the entire "race" was to be wiped out. The ensuing events spawned new terms in the human vocabulary: "Genocide" and "Holocaust."

The horrors of the gas chambers and concentration camps have been widely described. Perhaps less familiar to the modern reader are the methods employed in the embryonic stage of the Holocaust. Lacking a modus operandi for their grotesque policy, the Nazis improvised. In the Baltic States and the Ukraine, they capitalized on local anti–Semitism to incite a wave of violent pogroms, with the result that local Jews were murdered in the streets—in some cases as a form of public entertainment. In Kovno (Kaunas), Lithuania, on June 27, 1941, for example, a German soldier stumbled upon an enthralled crowd of men, women and children watching a muscular youth (known afterwards as the "Death-dealer of Kovno") dashing out the brains of innocent Jews with a wooden club. There were already a score of dead in the street when the eyewitness arrived. Another twenty or thirty were huddled together with no hope of escape, awaiting their own turn, one by one, while the jovial crowd shouted encouragement to the executioner.[190] The incident was part of a pogrom that went on for several days, claiming 3,800 Jewish lives.[191] Photos taken by *Wehrmacht* photographers show large numbers of German soldiers standing among the spectators. Pitiably few were troubled enough to mention the atrocities to their superiors. Those who did were told that the murders were purely an "internal matter" for the Lithuanians to handle. This was entirely false. The SS had put the Lithuanian fanatics up to it—actively recruiting armed partisans (who until then had been fighting the retreating Soviets) and unloosing them on the Jews.[192]

Though widespread, the campaign of pogroms was neither spontaneous nor independently sustainable. Consequently, while zealous civilian collaborators continued to play a role, a special force of 3,000 SS enlistees became the leading henchmen in carrying out the genocide.[193] Organized into four squads, known collectively as the *Einsatzgruppen* ("deployment groups"), they had been recruited by Reinhard Heydrich prior to the invasion of Poland and had been killing civilians ever since. Between June and November 1941, they murdered 130,000 Lithuanian Jews, prompting the local SS commander to boast that there wasn't a Jew left except those needed for forced labor.[194] (Because the *Wehrmacht* had insisted on preserving these workers, some historians have sought to exonerate the German regular army from guilt in the Holocaust, but this is fiction. In most instances, the army rendered full cooperation, with rank-and-file soldiers often vying for the opportunity to participate in the butchery.[195])

As the German armies advanced, the massacres multiplied—the victims being so numerous that they had to be recruited to dig their own burial trenches before they could be shot. We read of Nazi cutthroats shooting pregnant women in the abdomen, beating defenseless children to death or holding them by the hair and shooting them in the back of the head before casting them into the pits.[196] In December 1941, at the Latvian port of Liepaja, SS and Latvian gunmen murdered 2,700 Jews—most of them women who had been forced to strip naked in the freezing cold. An eyewitness watching from the city's harbor reported that marksmen shot the victims in the head with rifles and that an SS officer completed the work, when necessary, with his pistol.[197] In August, the Russian town of Zhitomir began advertising Jewish hangings on huge placards so that the public could attend. On September 29–30, 1941, more than 33,000 Jewish men, women and children were shot in the back of the head at point blank range in the Babi Yar ravine outside Kiev. As the bodies piled up, new victims were made to lie face down atop those who were already dead until the busy executioners could get to them.[198]

A few SS men opted out of the death squads, but others were readily found to take their place. Indeed, by the end of 1941, tens of thousands of auxiliaries (SS members,

A German police officer shoots Jewish women still alive after a mass execution of Jews from the Mizocz ghetto. October 14, 1942. Published in 1946. Gustav Hille (Wikimedia Commons).

German police and local collaborators) had been enlisted in their support.[199] In all, as many as two million Jews perished by their hands.[200] But following Heinrich Himmler's personal excursion to Minsk to witness a mass execution of this type in early 1942, the Holocaust underwent a fundamental change in character. According to an SS officer, Himmler became visibly ill on viewing the proceedings, and afterwards demanded that the bloody work be accomplished in some other way lest his cherished SS warriors be traumatized by the experience of their own criminal actions.[201] An experiment was duly undertaken in which a group of mental asylum patients were blown up with dynamite. The outcome was no less grisly, so the next victims were packed into vans and suffocated by the fumes of carbon monoxide.[202] The occupants struggled and screamed as they died. Witnessing one of the vehicles being emptied, Adolf Eichmann claimed that he had never seen a more appalling sight. (As with Himmler, it was the "unpleasantness" of the process that troubled him, not the immorality.)[203] The method was adopted but was ultimately deemed too inefficient due to the limited numbers who could be killed.

The "solution" to the dilemma, as it turns out, had already been produced by German industry. In the fall of 1941, a new formulation of lethal cyanide gas—Zyklon B—was employed successfully on Russian prisoners of war being held at Auschwitz.[204] Death was seen to be rapid and certain. Henceforth, the Jews were to be gassed. Six extermination camps were promptly established in Poland, transforming the gassing operations into a centralized industry that would claim more than three million additional Jewish lives.[205]

To this point in the war, the Nazis had herded most Eastern European Jews into starvation ghettos in major cities like Warsaw, Krakow and Lodz. At intervals, portions of the ghetto populaces—typically those lacking the skills to perform productive work for the Reich—were either brought to the killing trenches to be shot or gassed with carbon monoxide. But Zyklon B made it possible to carry out the killing on an industrial scale. Between July and September 1942, the population of the Warsaw ghetto plummeted from 350,000 to 45,000.[206] So intent were the Nazis on pressing ahead with the genocide, that trains carrying Jews to the death camps were given precedence over those bringing troops to the Russian front.[207] Many died en route in appalling circumstances. Crammed into freight cars without water, parents sought to save their children by breaking window gratings and throwing them from the moving trains. Guards stationed on the roof answered these efforts with gunfire.[208] When rail traffic was especially heavy, the trains might sit motionless for days while those inside the sealed cars expired from thirst or suffocation. On one occasion, an unmarked *Wehrmacht* hospital train accidentally got entangled with the rest. By the time the mistake was discovered, 200 wounded German soldiers were dead.[209]

At Auschwitz and Madjanek, the fittest inmates were used as slave labor until they starved or died of exhaustion. At Chelmno, Sobibór, Treblinka and Belzec, victims went directly from train to undressing station to gas chamber to oven, all on the day of arrival.[210] Where gas chambers and crematoriums were lacking, victims were still shot and dumped into pits, but now, rather than being covered with dirt, the bodies were doused with gasoline and burned so that there would be no evidence.

Auschwitz was the system's "state-of-the-art" facility. On entering, the victims were told that they were going to shower, and were even instructed to place their clothes in an assigned spot for later use. They were then corralled into a large chamber with pillars resembling shower fixtures. Instead of water, however, Zyklon B was disgorged. The hapless victims suffered for up to thirty minutes,[211] choking, screaming, banging on the doors, struggling against each other, even attempting to claw their way through the gas chamber walls. To hide the noise from living prisoners, trucks sometimes revved their engines in high gear outside the death chambers,[212] but this precaution was not universally taken. At Treblinka, the next in line were made to wait naked in the cold, listening to the screams of those sent into the chambers ahead of them.[213] An eyewitness at Belzec saw the dead so closely packed together that they died standing upright.[214] Alternatively, there might be mounds of people—the last to die having climbed atop those who had already succumbed to escape the rising gas.[215] If hair and gold fillings had not been harvested prior to this point, it was done now, whereupon the corpses were thrust into freight elevators from which they were unloaded with pitchforks for incineration in the ovens.[216] Under threat of death, fit Jewish inmates were organized into so-called *Sonderkommando* ("special unit") work groups to help the SS dispose of the bodies and clean out the crematoria—the entire process taking about 90 minutes for 2,000 victims.[217] After the war, the commandant of Auschwitz was asked how millions of people could have been exterminated in this fashion. Without any sign of emotion, he replied that if the ovens hadn't slowed down the process, they could have killed far more.[218]

Attempts to organize resistance to the Holocaust were hampered by the almost universal disbelief that the Nazis actually intended to murder the entire Jewish population of Europe. Even in the ghettos, Jews discounted the initial reports given them by death camp escapees and killing ground survivors.[219] Indeed, for an extended period, ghetto community leaders cooperated in designating people for "deportation" in the mistaken belief that this would ensure more humane treatment both for themselves and for the deportees. Even when it became undeniable that the victims were being sent to their deaths, the community leaders continued to cooperate, either out of despair—for they lacked the means to resist—or in the belief that resistance would provoke disastrous reprisals against other ghettos or against those left behind in their own.[220]

In January 1943, however, the last 45,000 inhabitants of the Warsaw ghetto decided to fight rather than cooperate in their own destruction. Using a small cache of smuggled handguns, grenades, Molotov cocktails and other rudimentary explosives, they fought off German incursions until May. Aghast at their own casualties—which included a hundred killed by the detonation of a single electrical mine—the SS forces finally set fire to the ghetto with flamethrowers and rounded up the survivors as they struggled to escape the flames. Many preferred death to capture, and leapt from upper story windows or died amidst the blaze.[221] According to an SS report, some of the former survived their falls, and "tried to crawl with broken bones across the street into buildings which were not afire."[222] On May 8, the organizers of the uprising committed suicide in their burning command bunker rather than yield.

In all, the Holocaust claimed six million Jewish lives, most of them by the end of 1943. When the camps were liberated two years later very few Jews had survived.[223] But Jews were not the only victims. In the absurd world of Nazi anthropology, gypsies were also deemed a threat to the pure blood of the Aryan race. Though less numerous than the Jews, they were dispensed with in parallel fashion—with the single heinous addition that there appears to have been a small collection of shrunken gypsy heads on a political department office shelf at Sachsenhausen.[224] Up to a half-million gypsies died in the extermination camps.[225] Invalids fared no better. Insane, demented and crippled adults, mentally and physically handicapped children—all were targeted in a grisly euthanasia campaign. On the basis of a questionnaire filled out by private physicians, and reviewed by a committee of government doctors, a patient's life could be deemed "not worth living"—not worth it, because the patient was of no value to the state. The hapless individuals were then taken to one of six centralized execution facilities to be gassed or killed by lethal injection under a doctor's supervision. Afterwards, ashes from the euthanasia crematoriums were forwarded to the family along with a sham explanation of the cause of death. But the centers were in Germany and the murders were an open secret. Irate family members began to complain, and owing to an increasing public outcry, Hitler declared the program terminated in late 1941. Nonetheless, the killings proceeded—only now in a decentralized way, at the discretion and prerogative of the family doctor. The total number "euthanized" has been estimated at 200,000 or more.[226]

Towards the end, with the fortunes of war turning inexorably against them, the Nazis attempted to erase all trace of their handiwork. The mass graves in Russia and the Baltic States were exhumed, and the decaying corpses were burnt in makeshift ovens.[227] Several of the extermination centers were razed, and the ground where they stood was camouflaged with woods or farmland.[228] But the work was done hurriedly, and the evidence was too ubiquitous to hide. The Russians liberated Auschwitz in January 1945, finding it nearly empty and partially demolished, while many slave labor camps inside the Reich were still operating when Allied troops arrived.[229]

Hitler's genocidal program met with varying degrees of cooperation in the conquered states of Europe. The zeal of the Baltic States and the Ukraine has already been described. Romania carried out deportations and sadistic pogroms, and also provided killing squad volunteers who distinguished themselves at Dalnik and Bogdanovca by packing Jews into buildings and immolating them.[230] Vichy France gutlessly handed over thousands of Jews. Many others fled to the Swiss border only to be denied entry. In despair, some killed themselves before the eyes of the Swiss border guards, but under strict orders from their government, the latter would not relent. (As Andrew Roberts notes, they were rather more helpful to Nazi fugitives at war's end.)[231] Pope Pius XII failed to speak out against the Holocaust and has been held in ill repute ever since.

On the other hand, despite passing anti–Semitic legislation, Bulgaria would not cooperate with the Reich's deportation policy. Nor would Italy or Hungary (until the Germans assumed direct control of their governments late in the war).[232] Singularly heroic were the Danes, who reacted to German efforts to seize their Jewish populace first by providing the latter with hiding places, and then by shuttling them to sanctuary in neutral Sweden. Likewise, the Finns gave full protection to their Jews.[233] The Czech government-in-exile, with assistance from the British Special Operations Executive, sent exiled Czech paratroopers to Prague to assassinate Himmler's lieutenant, Reinhard Heydrich. On May 27, 1942, they succeeded in their mission by hurling a bomb at his Mercedes. Believing (erroneously) that the town of Lidice had harbored the assailants, the Nazis leveled all its buildings, shot every man and sent the women and children to death camps. Afterwards, on receiving a tip, the Nazis cornered the assassins and a number of Czech resistance fighters at the Karl Borromaeus Church in Prague, killing them to a man after a short siege. Czech civilians suspected of collaborating in the plot were executed.[234]

13

World War II:
Allied Victory, 1942–1945

The Reich Overreaches Itself: Stalingrad

Such was the universe Nazism had conjured into being when, on August 23, 1942, the German Sixth Army appeared on the outskirts of Stalingrad. Ten days later, the German Fourth Panzer Army, back from the Caucasus, took up position alongside them. Hitler was now absolutely intent on taking Stalingrad—dreaming that his troops might then break out to the north and attack Moscow from the rear. Little did he realize that the city on the Volga was to be the final stop on the Sixth Army's itinerary, and that for the first time, on a massive scale, his own soldiery would be made to drink from the cup that hitherto they had served unto others.

The battle began propitiously enough. On the first day, German air raids reaped a deadly harvest, slaughtering 40,000 of the city's inhabitants.[1] With their homes reduced to rubble, hordes of civilians sought refuge across the Volga, only to be strafed by German aircraft as they fled. The onslaught threatened to provoke a panic among the city's stunned defenders. To spur them to duty, one Russian officer declared that cowardice would not be tolerated and then marched along the line shooting every tenth man in the head until his pistol was empty.[2]

With soldiers on both sides now irrevocably committed to the struggle, the battle for Stalingrad degenerated into a bloody house-to-house stalemate necessitating the commitment of an ever-increasing number of *Wehrmacht* troops. Opposing forces sometimes hunkered down on different floors of the same building or in different rooms in the same house.[3] The Red Army stopped at nothing to keep the attackers at bay—even creeping through the sewer system in an effort to infiltrate the German lines.[4] Faced with a German preponderance in tanks, Vasily Chuikov, the Russian commander, created a series of impassable strongpoints, forcing the panzers to detour into areas where pre-aimed heavy artillery lay in wait for them.[5] As the battle bogged down amid the ruins making mobile warfare unfeasible, the panzers ceased to afford the Germans any advantage whatsoever.[6] For an army accustomed to a war of movement, the atmosphere was stifling and claustrophobic. Anyone careless enough to raise his head immediately fell prey to sniper-fire. German morale began to plummet.

Nevertheless, over the next two months, the Russian perimeter at Stalingrad receded inexorably towards the Volga. Already, tens of thousands of the city's defenders had been killed, while reinforcements streaming across the river to replace them were informed that no one had the least interest in seeing them return if the city fell.[7] Many of these unfortunates never even made it to the opposite shore—having been blown to pieces by German aircraft while being ferried across.

Unbeknownst to the German High Command, however, the Russians actually were not sending the bulk of their reserves *into* Stalingrad. Rather, they were massing them secretly against the German flanks to the north and south of the city—where the *Wehrmacht* defenses had been denuded by the steady diversion of troops into the urban battleground.

Hitler's ill-founded strategy and tactics were now to catch up with him. In J.F.C. Fuller's view, the campaign had been a blunder from its very inception. In attacking a country the size of Russia, the goal ought to have been the immobilization of the Russian Army, so that the nation's vastness would work to the German benefit rather than to the Russian. The way to accomplish this feat was not to capture Stalingrad, but to capture Moscow—Russia's great railway hub. By moving on Stalingrad instead, Hitler had left Russia's mobility intact, while leaving his own army exposed at the apex of a narrow salient whose lengthy sides could never be made proof against Russian penetrations, and whose internal area was too small to allow for an effective defense in depth.[8] On November 19, the Russians, now under the overall command of Georgi Zhukov, surprised the Germans by staging massive counterattacks on both flanks of this salient. The forces defending these sectors—mostly untried conscript levies from Hungary, Italy and Romania—ran for their lives or were plowed over by a veritable Russian steamroller.

The only hope for the Sixth Army lay in immediate withdrawal, but Hitler absolutely forbade it. As a result, the Russian pincers slammed shut, transforming the besiegers of Stalingrad into the besieged. The only rational course of action now was for the Sixth Army to attempt a breakout. Against the advice of his generals, Hitler demanded the very opposite—insisting that the *Wehrmacht* launch a new attack from the Don River *to break back in* for the impossible purpose of reestablishing the indefensible Stalingrad salient.[9] On December 12, Erich von Manstein dutifully led a new army, hastily assembled on the Don, into the assault. Although he made some initial progress, the drive faltered well short of its goal.

The suggestion was now made that the Sixth Army attempt to break out and link up with Manstein's force so that together they could withdraw to safety. Hitler again refused. With his own forces threatened on both flanks, Manstein abandoned his attempt to reach Stalingrad on December 24. On the same day, Russian artillery shells began to rain down on the German airfield at Tatsinskaya, provoking a panicked attempt at evacuation. Before it was over, 56 transport planes out of a fleet of 180 had been destroyed on the ground—some colliding with one another (or with debris on the runway) as they sought to take off, others falling prey to Russian tanks, which overran the airfield when the shelling ceased. While the remaining planes did manage to get off the ground, they had lost their chief base of operations for airlifting supplies to the doomed men along the Volga.[10] On January 17, Russian forces overran the primary airstrip inside the Stalingrad pocket—Pitomnik—where crowds of wounded Germans had been vying with one another for days for the chance to be evacuated. Those seeking to get aboard planes out of turn were shot dead. A few desperate souls clung to the landing gear as the last planes took off, only to plunge to their deaths once the planes were airborne.[11]

Surrender was now the sole alternative for the marooned Sixth Army, but when permission was sought from Hitler, the latter replied that the army must hold out to the last man for the defense of Germany and Western Civilization.[12] On January 30, Hitler promoted the Sixth Army commander, Friedrich von Paulus, to the rank of Field Marshal. It wasn't intended as a compliment. No Field Marshal had ever capitulated in battle. The promotion was meant to tie Paulus' hands, but it failed to do so. He surrendered a few hours later. Scarcely a third of the 285,000 men that had set out under the Sixth Army's pennon the preceding spring were still alive. Starving and crippled with frostbite, most would not survive the looming march into Russian captivity.

The Course of the War on Other Fronts

Russia constituted but one theater of what was now a global war. In the Far East, Japan's attack on Pearl Harbor (December 7, 1941) had been carried out in synchrony with offensives against the myriad British, American and Dutch holdings that lay within her proposed Greater East Asian Co-Prosperity Sphere. Within six months, the Japanese had consolidated their hold on the whole of the western Pacific. At Singapore, a British garrison numbering 130,000 men surrendered to a Japanese force scarcely a third that size in February 1942. The heavy gun emplacements of the island fortress (which lies off the southern tip of the Malay Peninsula) faced permanently out to sea to guard against naval attack. The Japanese, therefore, had attacked from the landward side across the narrow Straits of Johore separating the island from the Malayan mainland.[13] A British blunder had made this approach possible, for the theater's supporting naval forces led by the battleship *Prince of Wales* and the battlecruiser *Repulse*—the only "capital" ships Britain possessed in the Far East—had been deployed without air support, making them sitting ducks for Japanese bombers, which promptly blew them out of the water on December 10, 1941 (eight days after their arrival and three days after Pearl Harbor).[14]

There is an adage, coined by William S. Lind, that "if the capital ships are beaten, the navy is beaten."[15] News of the disaster left Churchill tossing and turning in bed. "Over all this vast expanse of waters," he wrote in reference to the western Pacific, "Japan was supreme, and we everywhere were weak and naked."[16] Having likewise obtained superiority in the air, the Japanese drove southward through Malaya, outflanking one British position after another with bicycle reconnaissance teams leading the way.[17] Disposed to deride the invaders as "monkeys" and "little yellow men," the British defenders now learned, to their detriment, that their adversaries knew how to seize the initiative in jungle warfare.[18] Trained to remain awake for long periods, the Japanese were wont to deprive the British of sleep by attacking through the night (and, when they were not doing so, by playing recordings of the sounds of battle, replete with the screams of supposedly wounded men, over loudspeakers near the British lines).[19] In a matter of weeks, the Japanese had harried the British defenders all the way down the peninsula before storming across the straits to Singapore on steel barges. With victory in hand, the attackers perpetrated barbaric atrocities—shooting and bayoneting men who had ceased to resist or lay wounded in their hospital beds.[20] The garrison surrendered on February 15.

At the opposite extreme of the Malay Peninsula, the Japanese overran Thailand and eastern Burma, thereby closing the "Burma Road" over which Anglo-American supplies had been filtering into China. After a dogged resistance, the strategic Dutch East Indies were seized, delivering their all-important oil fields into Japanese hands (March

9, 1942). So, too, were the Philippines, where over half of General Douglas MacArthur's air force was destroyed on the ground just ten hours after the attack on Pearl Harbor. Faced thereafter with a two-pronged amphibious invasion, MacArthur withdrew his forces into Luzon Island's Bataan Peninsula, west of Manila (the Philippine capital), where he hoped to hold out until reinforcements arrived. Retreating down the peninsula through a series of fortified lines, the Americans and their Filipino allies inflicted enormous casualties on the advancing enemy.[21] Unfortunately, Bataan was inadequately provisioned. The men were already on reduced rations, and time told relentlessly against them. With the situation growing less tenable by the hour, MacArthur was ordered off the island. He refused initially, but ultimately gave in at President Roosevelt's insistence. His departure, though involuntary, led to recriminations of abandonment by those left behind. (Indeed, even while he was there, some troops had dubbed him "Dugout Doug," since he directed the defense of the Philippine archipelago from the bombproof tunnels of Corregidor—a fortified island located just off the Bataan coast—while they fought and starved in the jungle.[22]) MacArthur departed by PT boat and afterwards reached Australia on a B-17 to issue his famous pledge, "I shall return."

Bataan's defenders held out for another month before surrendering unconditionally (April 9, 1942). The Japanese led them into captivity on a brutal sixty-mile trek that came to be known as the "Bataan Death March." Men already sick and malnourished could not help but become stragglers on the dusty sun-scorched roads. In many cases, those who could not keep up were beaten, shot or bayoneted to death. Distraught Filipino civilians, seeking to provide the suffering marchers with food, were bludgeoned by Japanese rifle butts for their efforts.[23] Some units received orders to shoot all of their prisoners. But at least one recipient of this command—a certain Colonel Takeo Imai—set over a thousand prisoners free rather than do so. (He even advised the liberated men of the best route of escape.)[24] The number who died is not definitely known, but the toll may have been as high as 10,000.[25]

In the meantime, General Jonathan Wainwright, MacArthur's successor in the Philippines, was still holding out with a skeleton force on Corregidor. After an unrelenting bombardment lasting four weeks, the Japanese finally stormed the island with a force of 2,000 men. Half of these were killed or wounded in the assault,[26] but Wainwright was forced to capitulate—this time in the name of the entire Philippines (May 6, 1942).

All told, the Japanese onslaught on the islands of the Pacific had been a striking success. But when they attempted to threaten northern Australia, their attacks finally stalled. On the island of New Guinea, the terrain proved impenetrable. At sea, the Japanese navy received its first check in a duel with American aircraft carriers in the Coral Sea (May 4–8, 1942). It was the first sea engagement in history where carrier planes did all the attacking, since the fleets were too far apart to fire on each other directly.[27]

More troubling to the Japanese—although of less strategic import—was a daring raid pulled off by the United States the preceding month wherein American bombers attacked no less a target than Tokyo. Little damage was done, and the flyers had to ditch their planes on the Asian mainland due to a lack of fuel, but the Japanese were so appalled by what they viewed as an act of insolence against their sacred homeland that they convicted three of the eight American airmen captured during the raid on trumped-up charges of war crimes and executed them, in violation of international law. They could not fathom how the raid had even been possible in the absence of American air

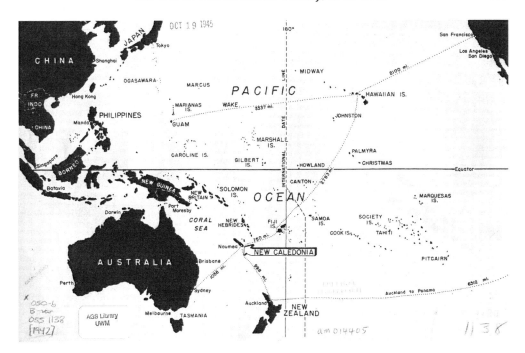

Pacific Theatre, 1942. Central Intelligence Agency from Washington, D.C. (Wikimedia Commons).

bases anywhere near their home islands. (President Roosevelt's helpful assurances that the bombers had taken off from "Shangri-La" did nothing to assuage their anxiety.[28])

At length, the Japanese concluded that the bombers had come from Midway Island, site of the nearest American airbase. This entirely erroneous guess was to change the course of the Pacific War. The bombers had actually taken off from the American aircraft carrier *Hornet*, which had approached to within 700 miles of the Japanese mainland. The Japanese had not considered this alternative since it was well known that U.S. army bombers were too heavy to take off from the short carrier runways. But the Americans had circumvented the problem by ripping out all unnecessary equipment (including radios and gun emplacements) from a squadron of B25s, thereby rendering them light enough to accomplish the task.[29]

Though it had not been meant to do so, the "Doolittle Raid" (named after its commander, Lieutenant Colonel James Doolittle) instilled in Japan a hysterical obsession over the origin of the bombers—and this is what transformed it from a minor morale-raising raid into an action of the utmost strategic significance. Intent on eradicating the Midway airfields, the Japanese sent a massive fleet eastward. Unbeknownst to them, however, the Americans had broken their cipher codes, and were aware they were coming. Awaiting them in ambush—behind Midway, and out of range of the Japanese carrier planes—were the remnants of the American Pacific Fleet, commanded by Admirals Fletcher and Spruance.

On the morning of June 4, 1942, Admiral Yamamoto, the Japanese commander, launched his opening air strike. American planes on Midway took off to counter it and were blown out of the sky. In the meantime, however, U.S. reconnaissance planes had located Yamamoto's armada and relayed its position to the American admirals. While the Japanese planes returned to their carriers to refuel, Fletcher and Spruance secreted their carriers into striking range and unleashed their unexpected counterblow against the Imperial fleet. The first wave of American planes—low-flying torpedo aircraft—were obliterated without inflicting any damage. They did, however, keep the Japanese fighters busy at low altitude while higher-flying American dive-bombers arrived in their wake to score devastating hits. In an attack lasting just minutes, enough damage was done to send three Japanese carriers to the bottom, their decks laden with aircraft being refueled and rearmed for further sorties against Midway. Unfortunately, a fourth Japanese carrier, the *Hiryu*, was still in action, and got its planes into the air in time to follow the American flyers back to their carrier, the *Yorktown*.[30] Two torpedo bombs drove into the *Yorktown*'s hull, crippling her. (Later, as she tried to hobble out of action, a Japanese submarine finished her off.) The *Hiryu*, however, was sunk in her turn by dive-bombers from the other American carrier, the *Enterprise*, thereby bringing the battle to an end.

For the Japanese, Midway was a decisive reverse. The battles of the Coral Sea and Midway had demonstrated beyond doubt that aircraft carriers were the key to modern naval success, and the Imperial fleet had been the clear loser from this standpoint. The months' long Japanese naval *blitzkrieg* in the Far East had been brought to a halt. There could be no further chance of rapid victory. Like Germany after Stalingrad, Japan was now committed to a war of attrition against an enemy with far greater resources.

The Americans, in contrast, were so emboldened by their victory at Midway that they embarked on their first Pacific offensive. In the ensuing months, U.S. Army forces under the command of Douglas MacArthur fought their way up New Guinea's Huon Peninsula, while the U.S. Navy carried out an amphibious attack on the island of Guadalcanal (one of the Solomon Islands). The Japanese had extended their perimeter into the Solomons in April 1942, in order to menace American communications with Australia. On August 7, 1942, U.S. Marines stormed ashore without opposition. Two days later, however, a Japanese squadron defeated their escort fleet near Savo Island, just north of Guadalcanal. The surprise night attack—an old-fashioned surface-ship affair without carrier involvement—claimed four American cruisers, and forced a temporary withdrawal of the rest, thus marooning the Marines on Guadalcanal. The Japanese got away without losing a single vessel.

There ensued an epic battle by land and sea. While the Marines slugged it out with the Japanese on Guadalcanal, the rival navies embarked on a months-long duel for hegemony of the surrounding waters. Nighttime convoys, dubbed the "Tokyo Express" by the Marines, ferried Japanese soldiers to the island and bombarded Henderson Field (a rudimentary airstrip built by the Japanese but captured by the Marines in their initial assault). Short on heavy weapons, the Japanese resorted to "*banzai*" or "human wave" attacks in an effort to retake the airstrip, but the Marines held them off and inflicted heavy casualties (September–October 1942). Afterwards, the naval battle reached a crescendo with a succession of bloody engagements wherein the Americans lost the carrier *Hornet* (the ship that had launched Doolittle's Tokyo raiders) and the *Juneau* (the death ship of the five Sullivan brothers).[31] But the Japanese suffered too. In the midst of one crushing defeat, four beached Japanese transports—their men still in the process of debarking—were bombed and strafed so horribly that their American assailants could not view the carnage without vomiting.[32] In mid–November, the Americans finally won the naval battle and cut off enemy supplies to the island.

In February 1943, the Japanese were forced to evacuate their last troops from

Guadalcanal. Two months later, they suffered another shattering loss when the Allies intercepted a message containing the flight itinerary of Admiral Isoroku Yamamoto (mastermind of the attacks on Pearl Harbor and Midway). On April 18, 1943, the bomber transporting Yamamoto was intercepted and shot down over the Solomon Islands. Thus, by the spring of 1943, Japan had lost not only a series of key battles, but also her supreme military strategist. She would not recover from the blow.

The Battle for North Africa

The other major theater of the global struggle was North Africa. There, Rommel had attacked the British again in January 1942, driving them once more from El Agheila back toward the Egyptian border. A second push secured the capture of Tobruk with its large garrison and copious supplies—a disaster of sufficient proportions to bring a vote of censure against Churchill in the House of Commons (June–July 1942).

Relieved of the threat to his supply line that Tobruk had represented, Rommel crossed into Egypt and pressed on to El Alamein, just sixty miles from Alexandria. In August, he staged an assault against the last defensible British line, which stretched from the Mediterranean Coast near El Alamein southwards across the desert to the impenetrable Qattara Depression, a region of salt marshes and quicksand impassable to tanks. Opposite him was the well-entrenched and (more importantly) well-supplied British Eighth Army commanded by Bernard Montgomery, who characterized Rommel's attack as "a gambler's last throw."[33]

"I had pondered deeply over Rommel's previous successes in the desert," Montgomery later wrote, "and had observed that his favorite tactic was to induce the British tanks to attack his armour which he protected with a screen of anti-tank guns; he thus knocked out most of the British armour—having done which he launched his own armour and won the *mêlée*. I decided to play this tactic with him ... his forces had a good hammering from my anti-tank guns ... and he gave up the contest and withdrew. So I won my first battle with Rommel, a defensive one."[34]

For Rommel, the defeat had decisive implications. With the British airbase on Malta wreaking havoc with Axis shipping in the Mediterranean, Rommel could not make good his losses.[35] With munitions running short, his position grew daily more precarious. Montgomery, in contrast, had an intact, line of supply (even if much of his materiel had to sail from Britain around the Cape of Good Hope).[36] Regarded as arrogant and self-promoting by his fellow officers (who were wont to say of him, "In defense, indomitable; in attack indefatigable; in victory, insufferable!"[37]), the Eighth Army commander had a knack for raising the morale of his men. He seemed to be ever present—driving about in a tank emblazoned with his nickname, "Monty,"[38] and sporting the black beret of the Royal Tank Corps. (The beret was a gift from a member of the corps who did not want him to hazard a tank's hatch wearing the wide-brimmed Australian "slouch hat" that he had shown up in.)[39] On October 23, 1942, while Rommel was in Austria on sick leave, Montgomery counterattacked. General Stumme, the interim commander of the Afrika Korps, was nearly captured at the outset of the fighting and, in attempting to elude his pursuers, suffered a heart attack and died.[40]

Montgomery possessed a three-to-one advantage in air power, more than twice the number of tanks and nearly twice the number of men as the Axis defenders. The first obstacle to his advance was the no man's land known as the "Devil's Garden," composed of one-half million Axis mines.[41] Infantry employing mine detectors and Scorpion flail tanks cleared a path forward, allowing Montgomery's Australian division to capture a key position overlooking the coastal road. Unfortunately, a diversionary attack at the south end of the line failed to lure German troops away from the main point of attack. Consequently, by October 26, the British advance had been stopped with the loss of 200 tanks.[42]

Having returned by this time, Rommel launched a ferocious, if unsuccessful, counterstrike, after which the battle degenerated into a stalemate that lasted the better part of a week. Churchill issued impatient inquiries during this interval,[43] but by the end of it, Montgomery had formulated two tactical improvisations that would allow him to deliver a decisive blow. The first was to assemble fresh reserves for a new thrust in the north by creatively thinning out his defenses in the south. The second—prudently instituted at the 11th-hour on the advice of his staff—was to alter his line of attack from a direct assault towards the coastal road, which was heavily guarded by German troops, to a point further south, which was defended by Mussolini's poorly supplied Italians.[44] Launched on November 2, 1942, "Operation Supercharge" achieved a breakthrough the following night.

Rommel saw no option now other than retreat. He made his intention known to Hitler, who predictably countermanded the decision and ordered him to hold his ground. The situation dictated otherwise. Montgomery's thrust sent Rommel reeling across the Libyan Desert for a distance of 1,200 miles. Short on petrol, the "Desert Fox" had to abandon large amounts of armor en route. Nor was this the worst of it. To coincide with Montgomery's push, American and British forces had debouched in Rommel's rear—having made successful amphibious landings at Casablanca, Oran and Algiers in French North Africa.

Initially, the United States chiefs-of-staff had opposed the idea of a North African landing. Stalin had long been insistent on the establishment of a second front in Europe, and the American chiefs were inclined to oblige him. But Churchill—the principal proponent of the North African operation—had won them over by degrees with the convincing argument that a cross-Channel attack against the European mainland was not within the Allies' means in 1942. Because this decision was sure to come as a great blow to Stalin, Churchill volunteered for the unenviable task of traveling to Moscow to inform him personally.[45]

For a time, the Americans thought of limiting the assault force to United States troops in the belief that North Africa's French defenders would be less likely to oppose an all-American invasion than one that included the British. Happy to make any accommodation, Churchill assured Roosevelt that his own soldiers would be proud to don American uniforms if such a ruse might be helpful.[46] Roosevelt, however, did not think it necessary. On November 8, 1942, Operation Torch commenced as a joint venture of British and American troops.

Marshal Pétain, head of the Vichy government, directed his colonial outposts to resist. Consequently, the Allies encountered stiff opposition at Casablanca and Oran on the first day. Hoping to arrange a speedy cease-fire, the Americans sought the support of General Henri Giraud, lately rescued by submarine from the south coast of France. But Giraud insisted that he be named Allied commander-in-chief as the price of his cooperation, and bitter negotiations ensued before the general reluctantly dropped this demand

and made the necessary radio address calling upon all Frenchmen to lay down their arms. Much to the dismay of the exhausted American negotiators, none of the French were disposed to obey. Giraud suggested that the Americans try their luck with Admiral Jean Darlan, who happened to be in Algiers visiting his hospitalized son. The Allies disliked and distrusted Darlan, but knew that *his* word, at least, carried weight. After some cajolery, the Admiral agreed to cooperate in return for being named high commissioner of the French State, and on November 10, French resistance in North Africa ceased.[47] Hitler riposted by occupying the Vichy-held portions of France, and advancing on Toulon where the remnants of the French fleet were stationed. Darlan ordered the fleet to slip away to North Africa, but the local commander at Toulon, Admiral de Laborde, answered this directive with a single word—"*merde.*"[48] (To his credit, de Laborde had the fleet scuttled rather than allow the Germans to seize it.) Several weeks later, a fanatical royalist assassinated Darlan for his prior collaboration with the Nazis (December 24, 1942).

With the western Mediterranean coastline now in Allied hands, Rommel's retreating Afrika Korps found itself racing away from one enemy force and towards another. After ignoring another inane order from his superiors to stand and fight in the vicinity of Tripoli, he outpaced his pursuers and arrived in Tunisia with some breathing space (January 1943). There he received the promising news that Axis forces already on the scene had halted the progress of Operation Torch, whose commander, Dwight Eisenhower, had hoped to capture Tunis from the west before Rommel arrived.

The temporary respite gave Hitler a belated opportunity to send reinforcements to North Africa. In all, some 250,000 German and Italian troops arrived. Had these same troops been sent to Rommel prior to the battle of El Alamein, they might have won a decisive victory.[49] Their arrival at this juncture promised only to magnify the catastrophe. Hitler could not hope to keep pace with the Allied build-up in North Africa, and his decision to dispatch reinforcements despite this reality meant certain doom for those sent into the maelstrom. Even worse, it denuded Sicily and Italy of troops they would soon need for their own defense.[50]

Seeking to delay the inevitable, Rommel mapped out an audacious plan to defeat the converging Allied forces in detail before they could combine for joint operation.[51] Employing state-of-the-art Tiger tanks he defeated the advancing Americans at the Kasserine Pass near the eastern Tunisian border (February 1943). However, his subsequent push towards Thala and Tebessa—success in which would have disrupted American communications and compelled retreat—was halted after a promising beginning.[52] The subsequent arrival of American reinforcements convinced Rommel to wheel about and try his luck with the other advancing pincer—Montgomery's Eighth Army, which was approaching the Axis defensive works known as the "Mareth Line" to the southeast. Here, he was sharply repulsed (March 6, 1943).

With no hope of victory, Rommel advised a total withdrawal from Africa. Hitler would not agree. In an unavailing attempt to make the Führer see reason, Rommel flew to Europe. He would not return. Pressed from two directions, the Axis perimeter in North Africa now shrank inexorably. By the end of April, Hitler's forces had been confined to a strip of coastal territory surrounding Tunis. On May 6, a new Allied push wrought a general collapse. Frantic German soldiers broke and fled to the beaches of Cape Porta Farina and the Cape Bon Peninsula only to find that no transport vessels were available to take them away.[53] On May 13, Rommel's successor, General Juergen von Arnim, surrendered, leaving the whole of North Africa in Allied hands.

The implications of the Russian victory at Stalingrad, Montgomery's victory at El Alamein and the success of Operation Torch were momentous. Henceforth, says Alan Bullock, the Allies would be the attackers, and the Germans the defenders.[54] On the Eastern Front, the remnants of Army Group South were reeling in retreat. By mid–February the Russians had retaken the communications center of Kharkov on the Donetz River. From there, they struck southwest in an attempt to trap Army Group South with their backs to the Sea of Azov.

If Hitler had had his way, the Russians would undoubtedly have succeeded. But the commander of Army Group South, Erich von Manstein—the same man who had masterminded the Ardennes offensive in 1940 and who had attempted to relieve Paulus at Stalingrad—convinced Hitler to allow a strategic withdrawal (a startling feat in itself!) so as to draw the Russians forward into an exposed position. When the Russians took the bait, Manstein caught them in a pincer movement—casting them out of Kharkov and back across the Donetz. In so doing he restored an intact line of defense in southern Russia just when disaster seemed imminent.[55]

Despite Manstein's success, the notion of retreat continued to rankle with Hitler. Consequently, when the Army Group South commander argued for a continued policy of strategic withdrawals and timely counterthrusts such as the one he had just pulled off, Hitler opted instead for another offensive.[56] Although the Führer was now sick with doubt—indeed, he admitted that the very thought of the new attack made his stomach turn[57]—he remained incapable of heeding sound advice.

Kursk

Stalin, too, was impatient for an offensive, but his generals convinced him to let the Germans make the next move. Hitler's attack, codenamed Operation Citadel, opened on July 4, and was directed at the Russian salient around Kursk. The Germans attempted their characteristic blitzkrieg and encirclement tactics, but the Russians had anticipated the assault and had constructed a labyrinthine defense. After running a gauntlet of minefields, anti-tank guns and artillery fire for over a week, the German southern pincer seemed on the verge of a breakthrough. Instead of finding open country, however, the Germans were pounced upon by the Soviet Fifth Guards Tank Army, which had been stationed in reserve. On July 12, some 1,800 tanks engaged one another on the southern approaches to Kursk, in what remains the "greatest tank battle in history." Much of the contest was fought at point-blank range after tanks on both sides infiltrated each other's ranks. At such close quarters, machines were blown to smithereens as explosions sent tank turrets lurching through the air.[58] Despite a herculean effort, the offensive ground to a halt on July 15. It was the last offensive thrust the Germans were able to mount on the Eastern Front. Losses were staggering on both sides, but whereas the Russians could readily replace their men and machines, the Germans could not hope to do so.

Still, doom was not inevitable, provided Hitler would agree to a strategy of elastic defense, whereby the German forces would withdraw to defensible positions on a shorter front against which the Russians might exhaust themselves with fruitless attacks. The Germans could then reserve their striking capacity for timely and calculated counterstrokes, staving off defeat indefinitely no matter how forcefully the Russians came on.

Red Army infantrymen keep pace with a tank during the advance through Ukraine 1943 (*Geschichte des Grossen Vaterländischen Krieges der Sowjetunion*, Bd.3, Berlin 1964, Wikimedia Commons).

The line of the Dnieper River was put forward as a suitable position. Hitler, however, did not give his grudging assent to this strategy until September, and by then the Wehrmacht was out of time. Russian troops pushed across the Dnieper before the Germans could entrench themselves on the opposite bank.[59] By late September, they had breached the Dnieper at five separate points and had retaken Smolensk. In November, they liberated Kiev and cut off the German garrisons in the Crimea.

With the front pierced at multiple points, Manstein's Army Group South sought to extricate itself from the great bend of the Dnieper. Surging forward in pursuit, Russian tanks overtook straggling horse-drawn carts filled with German wounded and purposely crushed them to pulp beneath their treads. Panicked German troops sought to swim across freezing streams only to have their clothes turn to ice the moment they emerged on the far bank.[60]

All along the front, the Germans were thrown into retreat. In January 1944, a Russian push in the north relieved Leningrad. The city had been under siege for two and a half years, sustaining a death toll from hunger and battle that may have been as high as forty percent.[61] According to Harrison E. Salisbury, if corpses were brought to the cemeteries at all, they had to be stacked up like cordwood until the ground thawed enough to dig trenches for their mass burial. Apart from ice trails across the frozen waters of Lake Ladoga, the city had been entirely cut off, leaving the inhabitants to vie with one another—sometimes to the death—for a scrap of bread. With every last pigeon, crow and rat already devoured, nourishment was sought in grass, leather, wallpaper paste and other inedible substances.[62] At the height of the crisis, resort was had to that appalling expedient, cannibalism, with innocents—children among them—being kidnapped as fodder. The beneficiaries of this trade pretended not to know the origin of what they were eating and made sure not to ask.[63] If apprehended, the punishment was death. Now, however, Leningrad was free, and it was the Reich's turn to suffer.

The Strategic Bombing Campaign and the Assault on the Soft Underbelly

On April 20, 1939, the renowned British military historian, tank warfare expert and unabashed fascist, General J.F.C. Fuller, was one of two Englishmen to attend Adolf Hitler's fiftieth birthday parade in Berlin. "For some three hours," he later wrote, "a mechanized and motorized army roared past.... Never before or since have I watched such a formidable mass of moving metal." Meeting face to face later in the day, Hitler shook Fuller's hand, remarking, "I hope you were pleased with your children?" Fuller answered, "Your Excellency, they have grown up so quickly that I no longer recognize them."[64]

Between 1918 and 1939, the theory of warfare had come to be dominated by two revolutionary tactical concepts. The first, formulated in large measure by Fuller himself, envisioned massive tank formations, covered by aircraft, piercing the enemy's front lines and pressing to the rear to disrupt the enemy's command structure and communications. Deprived of leadership and supply, the demoralized foe would lose all coordination of effort and must either capitulate or be annihilated. During the 1930s, Fuller's theory found its warmest adherents (Heinz Guderian chief among them) in Nazi Germany, where its tenets were encapsulated in a single word: *Blitzkrieg*.[65]

The second concept was known as "strategic" bombing. Its chief advocate was an Italian general named Giulio Douhet,[66] who argued that the key to victory in subsequent wars would be command of the air. Once this had been obtained, the enemy's civilian centers could be bombed to destruction. The actions of soldiers at the front would be rendered meaningless, because the nation's industrial centers would be ruined, and its terrified populace would lose the will to fight.[67] By the late 1930s, this theory had obtained its predominant foothold in Great Britain, prompting that nation to focus her belated rearmament program on air power. (As Prime Minister Stanley Baldwin famously lamented in 1932, "I think it is well also for the man in the street to realize that there is no power on earth that can protect him from being bombed. Whatever people may tell him, the bomber will always get through."[68])

Amongst Douhet's foremost disciples was Britain's Air Chief, Arthur "Bomber" Harris. Throughout the war, Harris positively insisted that he could defeat Germany using air power alone, without the need for ground troops. The United States Air Force was equally intrigued—although its leaders seem not to have mastered the part about gaining control of the skies first. The British had learned this lesson the hard way in 1941 as RAF flyers sustained higher casualties than did their targets on the ground.[69] Bomber Command promptly concluded that daylight bombing was insupportable without fighter escort. The Americans, however, remained convinced that their B-17 "Flying Fortresses" (which fairly bristled with machine-guns) could defend themselves, and it was not until hundreds of these mighty aircraft had been shot out of the sky—most notably in the raids on the Ploesti oil fields (August 1943) and the Schweinfurt ball-bearing factory (October 1943)—that they finally grasped what their allies were telling them.[70] In 1942 and 1943, an Allied crewman's chance of surviving a full tour of duty

(30 bombing missions) was less than 50 percent. By war's end, 44 percent of the 125,000 crewmen serving in RAF bombers and 26 percent of 100,000 crewmen serving in American bombers had been killed.[71] Body parts pitched out of exploding aircraft were often visible to the crews of other planes.[72]

Despite the toll, by mid–1942 the Allies had already carried out some impressive raids—most notably, the RAF bombings of Cologne, Essen and Bremen in May and June. Over 1,000 planes participated in the nocturnal Cologne raid, wreaking havoc as yet unseen. By the following year, the Allies had accumulated an immense arsenal of planes and bombs, and it was believed that the combined air forces could finally deliver on Harris' promises.

To prove their point, they carried out four massive raids against the city of Hamburg, beginning on July 24, 1943. During the second of these, twenty-four hundred tons of incendiary bombs were dropped on the city in less than one hour[73]—their individual fire-jets coalescing into one devastating man-made firestorm that consumed the surrounding air to produce overpowering suction winds. According to an official German report, living persons were propelled into the maelstrom by 150 mile-per-hour gusts, with large trees being torn up by the roots to follow after them.[74] Unable to survive above ground, panicked citizens crowded into air raid shelters only to be roasted alive or poisoned by carbon monoxide from the combustion overhead.[75] Most authorities place the

One of 100 U.S. B-17 bombers sent to bomb the Focke-Wulf plant at Marienburg on October 9, 1943. Unknown photographer (Wikimedia Commons).

death toll above 30,000. Goebbels claimed in his diary that 800,000 civilians were left homeless,[76] while Albert Speer estimated that if the Allies had staged like attacks on six more German industrial centers they might have terminated all armaments production in the Reich.[77]

The moral effect of the raid seemed to vindicate Bomber Harris' claims. Across Germany, people wondered whether their city would be next.[78] Nuremberg, Darmstadt, Magdeburg and other cities were soon targeted. But the ultimate effect of these raids remains controversial. Far from bringing a speedy end to the war, some critics argue that they merely intensified the enemy's determination to resist—much as the Blitz had done in London. Nor did the raids entirely cripple Germany's industry. German war production actually continued to rise until mid–1944—albeit it at a decisively slower pace that it would have done.[79]

While others pondered the pros and cons of strategic bombing, Winston Churchill argued successfully for an Allied attack on Sicily. On July 10, 1943 (in the midst of Hitler's failed attempt to pinch out the Kursk salient), a massive Allied amphibious assault was made on the island. Stormy weather with high winds helped the Allies to achieve surprise, but also made the attackers seasick,[80] while wreaking havoc with a simultaneous airborne assault. (Released too early, more than a third of the gliders employed "glided" directly into the Mediterranean, while 4,500 paratroopers landed wherever the winds took them.)[81] Nevertheless, within five weeks, the conquest of the island was complete, seemingly vindicating Churchill's portrayal of the Mediterranean as the "soft underbelly" of the Axis.

Alas, this notion would be belied by the subsequent Allied experience in Italy—not the least because of strategic and tactical blunders made in the Sicilian campaign. First, as Andrew Roberts has noted, the Allies had invaded Sicily before deciding whether they would follow it up with the invasion of Italy. Had this been determined in advance, a simultaneous assault could have been made on Reggio (where the toe of the Italian boot comes closest to Sicily), thereby cutting off the Axis route of escape from the island.[82] Similarly, the coordination of ground and air attacks in the Sicilian campaign was grossly mismanaged. With total command of the air, the Allied air forces should have been employed in *Blitzkrieg* fashion—flying in low and strafing the fleeing enemy troops as they were driven back. Instead, they adhered to Bomber Harris' strategic bombing dictums, annihilating various towns and villages from great height—killing rather more Sicilian noncombatants than was necessary while destroying the very roads upon which the Allies would soon need to advance. The retreating Germans, being more familiar with the lay of the land, were able to rely on alternate routes—easily outpacing their British and American pursuers in the race to Messina, opposite Reggio, whence more than 50,000 of them escaped to Italy, bringing their equipment with them.[83] Still, the island's defenders lost 164,000 men in killed, wounded and captured—32,000 of them Germans, the rest Italians who are reported to have surrendered in droves. (The Allies lost scarcely a tenth of this number.)[84]

The war's sudden arrival on Italy's shores provoked a palace revolution. On July 25, 1943, King Victor Emmanuel III informed Mussolini that the Italian people no longer wished to fight, and placed the Fascist ruler under arrest.[85] Fearing that Italy would now defect to the Allies, Hitler prohibited Italian forces fighting on other fronts from returning to their homeland. Utilizing (among others) the German troops that had escaped from Sicily, he placed the country under military occupation.[86] Erwin Rommel advised against defending the southern end of the peninsula, but Albert Kesselring (the German commander on the scene) insisted that such a defense could and should be made.[87] The Führer, of course, decided in favor of the latter—something the Allies had not counted upon, since intercepts of coded German messages had indicated that the Germans would withdraw to the Maritime Alps, leaving an open path up the peninsula.[88] The reality was to be devastatingly different.

On September 3, 1943, Italy's new government secretly agreed to an armistice with the Allies, who, on the same day, made successful landings at Calabria and Salerno on the Italian mainland. Hitler countered with a glider raid against Gran Sasso where Mussolini was incarcerated. The Duce was liberated and ushered into an overloaded spotter plane that nearly crashed into a ravine before sputtering to safety.[89]

The Duce's rescue, however, did little to support Hitler's Italian policy. Although the deposed Italian dictator was placed in charge of a new Italian puppet state—the so-called "Salò Republic"—he was now a broken reed, possessing neither the means nor the desire to provide the Germans with constructive help. Pressed on one occasion to render judgment on a critical issue, he refused on the grounds that he was only the "Mayor of Gargnano" (the small town north of Salò where he was then residing), and therefore not of sufficient rank to deal with important matters.[90] In fact, his plight was worse than that. When Hitler insisted that he take retribution against those who had been involved in the coup of July 25, the Duce could only feign indifference while his own son-in-law, Count Ciano, was brought before a firing squad. (Told afterwards by the attending priest that Ciano had forgiven him just moments before death, Mussolini is said to have wept.[91])

Meanwhile, in October 1943, the Americans and British had advanced from Salerno to take Naples. Here, however, their drive was brought to a halt by Kesselring's Germans, who had established a series of defensive lines between the sea in the west and the impassable Apennine Mountain range in the east. It was at this juncture, that Stalin, Roosevelt and Churchill held their first summit meeting—the Tehran Conference, which convened on November 28, 1943. In supposed deference to Stalin's greater experience in fighting the Germans, Roosevelt opened the meeting by asking the Russian dictator to suggest a reasonable strategy for defeating Hitler. Stalin gave a predictable response: the Western Allies must invade France. Roosevelt immediately agreed.[92] Churchill, in contrast, favored an exploitation of the Mediterranean gains already won. In his memoirs, he insists that he merely desired a continuation of the Italian campaign coincident to the landing in France, with the ultimate goal of seizing the Ljubljana gap and making a thrust toward Vienna.[93] His detractors have maintained ever since that his true desire was to invade the Balkans to forestall the Communist uprisings then occurring in Greece and Yugoslavia, and, afterwards, to dash into Eastern Europe ahead of the Russians.[94] Considering what ultimately happened, it doesn't seem such a bad idea (apart, perhaps, from its impracticality). But the point was already moot since Churchill was outvoted by two-to-one before being given a chance to speak. Knowing that Stalin and Roosevelt had fixed their opinions in advance, he saw little alternative but to nod his assent.[95]

Orchestrating a successful landing in France, however, was no easy thing, and in the interim, the battle for Italy continued. In January 1944, an Anglo-American force achieved a surprise landing at Anzio to the rear of the main German defenses. Unfortunately, the expedition's commanders failed to move inland in timely fashion.

From left to right: Joseph Stalin, Franklin D. Roosevelt and Winston Churchill on the portico of the Soviet Embassy during the Tehran Conference (28 November–1 December 1943). U.S. Signal Corps photo (Wikimedia Commons).

Consequently, a golden opportunity to cut Kesselring's communications was squandered, allowing the German commander to rush reinforcements to the scene and pin the Allies to their beachheads with punishing counterattacks (which, however, fell short of driving them into the sea).[96]

With "Operation Shingle" hopelessly bogged down, the Allies tried the direct approach again, assaulting the German "Gustav Line" from the south at Cassino. In their failed and costly attempt to take this town, they committed a mortifying offense. Monte Cassino—the great monastery founded by St. Benedict in the 6th century—was mistakenly suspected of being a German observation post, and was needlessly destroyed by Allied bombers (February 1944). After leaflets were dropped to give the monks a chance to run for their lives, the venerable structure was pulverized at a blow, leaving behind ruins that, in Churchill's estimation, were more defensible than the monastery had been.[97] In the view of J.F.C. Fuller, it was another example of misdirected air power. Treasures of antiquity aside, our bombs ought to have been directed not against targets like Monte Cassino, but against the tenuous roads and railways that stretched the length of the Italian boot; for without supply lines the Germans could not possibly hold their positions.[98]

After collecting massive reinforcements at Cassino and Anzio, the Allies launched another push in May 1944. This time, the Gustav Line caved in under the impetus of the southern drive while a simultaneous breakout was achieved from the Anzio beachheads. The entire German Army in Italy ought to have been trapped between the closing pincers, but just as the American Fifth Army was about to block the routes of egress, General Mark Clark defied orders and diverted most of its strength to Rome lest the British have the honor of getting there first.[99] (The vainglorious, publicity-minded Clark was so certain that the British meant to deprive him of the laurels he coveted that he actually threatened to open fire on them if they attempted to reach the city before his own troops.[100]) Consequently, on June 4, 1944, the first Axis capital fell to the advancing Allies—a political milestone, perhaps, but militarily, an error of the first magnitude, for it allowed the Germans to escape encirclement and withdraw to a new defensive line— the "Gothic"—against which Allied soldiers would have to toil and die.[101]

Operation Overlord

When Mark Clark made his entry into Rome on June 4, conditions over the English Channel were unseasonably stormy. Two days later, the weather broke, and though there was no guarantee that the sea would remain calm, General Dwight David Eisenhower gave the go ahead for the long-awaited Allied invasion of France. Once ashore, the first obstacle to be overcome would be Hitler's so-called "Atlantic Wall"—a series of minefields and pillboxes backed up by sixty German infantry and panzer divisions. The Allies possessed air superiority and could thus hamper the enemy's mobility, but the key to success was surprise. Accordingly, great efforts were taken to conceal the true point of attack—i.e., the beaches of Normandy—and to make the Germans believe that it would occur at Calais, further to the northeast, where the Channel is at its narrowest. Multiple ruses were employed towards this end. In the weeks leading up to the invasion, the Calais sector was targeted for twice as many bombing sorties as was Normandy.[102] Then, on the night of the Channel crossing, RAF bombers scattered aluminum strips over the route to Calais to create the appearance (on German radar) of a massive air attack, while beneath them, motorboats towed reflector balloons to produce the image of an invading fleet.[103]

Simultaneous with these feints, the Allies jammed the German radar stations at Normandy with radio waves or knocked them out all together in bombing runs. They also dropped dummy paratroopers all over the region, so that when reports of real paratroopers filtered in later, they would not be believed.[104] Once these preparations were complete, Allied airborne and glider forces made a nocturnal descent upon the flanks of the attack zone in order to secure key bridges and exit routes from the Normandy beaches, and to destroy bridges and communications that the enemy would need in order to stage counterattacks.

The Calais ruse paid off in spades. When the vast Allied armada—consisting of 5,300 ships carrying 150,000 troops and 1,500 tanks[105]—appeared off Normandy's coast at dawn on June 6, the German defenders were taken utterly by surprise. Hitler's chief of operations, Alfred Jodl, who received the disquieting news just as he was waking up, insisted that the action was only a feint, and refused to dispatch desperately needed reinforcements until a critical delay had occurred.[106] In the interim, five Allied beachheads were established. Furthest east, the British landed at "Sword." Next to them came the Canadians at "Juno," and then another British force at "Gold." Finally came two

American beaches. "Utah," located furthest west, was captured with relative ease—in part because the first wave of troops stormed ashore over a mile from their intended landing site in a region that was only sparsely defended.[107] Accompanying this wave was General Theodore Roosevelt Jr. (the son of former president Teddy Roosevelt). The German defenders were quickly overwhelmed, and a road was secured on which to advance inland.

At "Omaha Beach," however, the Americans came up against fierce resistance. The troubles began with the men being placed in their landing craft too many miles from shore. Some of these cumbersome vessels sank outright in the choppy waters, while others were tossed about so violently that their occupants became seasick. On reaching shore, the soldiers were greeted by the sound of German bullets rattling off their landing ramps, even as these were being lowered to allow them to debark.[108] Many were cut down before they could get out of the boats. Others drowned after jumping into water over their heads, laden with too much equipment to swim. Pinned down by machine-gun fire, those who made it onto the beach sought refuge behind the twisted metal beach obstacles that had been scattered along the waterline to allay an Allied landing—and it took no small amount of cajoling to convince them to leave these sanctuaries and move inland.[109]

At all the other landing sites, propeller-driven amphibious tanks successfully got ashore to support the assaulting infantry. At Omaha, where they were most needed,

General Dwight D. Eisenhower gives the Order of the Day ("Full victory—nothing less") to US Co. E, 502nd Parachute Infantry Regiment of the 101st Airborne Division at 8:30 PM on June 5, 1944, at Greenham Common Airfield in England (Library of Congress).

"Into the Jaws of Death." American GIs come ashore under fire at Omaha Beach during Operation Overlord. Photograph by Robert F. Sargent. National Archives and Records Administration (Wikimedia Commons).

fully half the tanks were released too far from the beach. Although they were equipped with collapsible canvas flotation screens, most sank in the rough seas, carrying their crews to the bottom with them.[110] Without their firepower, it took all day and a ghastly toll—3,000 in killed, wounded and missing—before Omaha was finally secured.

The Germans, meanwhile, were experiencing difficulties of their own. Prior to the invasion, Hitler's commanders in the West, Erwin Rommel and Gerd von Rundstedt had disagreed on tactical deployment. Rommel rightly believed that Allied air superiority would hinder the movement of reserves,[111] and insisted on forward deployment all along the coastline to prevent the Allies from getting ashore wherever they might attack. Von Rundstedt wanted a large force kept in reserve to be rushed to the scene of invasion. Hitler favored Rommel's plan but agreed to a compromise, whereby the bulk of the infantry was stationed on the beaches and the armor was kept in reserve.[112] On the morning of the invasion, Rommel was away from the front attending his wife's birthday party. Hitler, who would not let his generals act on their own initiative, was fast asleep, and since Jodl refused to wake him, valuable time was lost in obtaining permission to dispatch panzers to the threatened areas. Even when counterattacks were sanctioned, however, Allied control of the skies, where 12,000 planes roamed with impunity, made daylight maneuvers suicidal. Consequently, by day's end, at a cost of 4,500 killed,[113] the Allies were ashore with nearly 150,000 men—a figure that would rise to 300,000 by the following night.[114]

There ensued a battle of attrition lasting weeks, as the Allies attempted a break-out, while the Germans under Rommel and von Rundstedt sought to contain them. In the midst of it, Churchill crossed the Channel to have lunch with Bernard Montgomery three miles behind the front lines (June 12). At the start of his return journey, Churchill prevailed on Admiral Vian, commanding his transport destroyer, *Kelvin*, to participate in an ongoing naval bombardment of an enemy position. Content after a volley or two that he had done his part for the war effort, the prime minister gave the admiral leave to sail home.[115]

On June 27, American forces backtracking into the Cotentin Peninsula secured the port of Cherbourg, but found it so damaged by its German defenders as to be use-less pending major repairs. Fortunately, the calamitous Dieppe raid of 1942 had taught the Allies that ports could be difficult, if not impossible, to capture intact, and they had planned in advance to circumvent the problem by constructing artificial har-bors—known as "Mulberries"—right on the D-Day beaches. The idea—which involved towing concrete caissons across the Channel and then submerging them just offshore—was one of Churchill's, held over from the First World War.[116] When the king's cousin, Vice-Admiral Lord Louis Mountbatten, first suggested the idea to Eisenhower in 1942, the service chiefs had snickered at it. But ultimately Overlord's planners adopted the proposal out of necessity and made it work.[117] They likewise constructed a Pipeline Under the Ocean—"Pluto" for short—to transport vast amounts of petrol from the Isle of Wight.[118]

The initial breakout battle was centered on the town of Caen at the easternmost extreme of the Allied position, where Montgomery was pitted against his old nemesis, Rommel. If Caen could be taken, Rommel would be deprived of the sole crossroads by which his front in Normandy could be reinforced. He would thus be forced to carry out a drastic retreat to reestablish intact communications—something that Hitler would never allow.[119] Accordingly, Rommel threw in everything he had to keep the town and its vital communications in Axis hands. Determining that a breakthrough at Caen was now exceedingly unlikely, Montgomery decided to continue the operation as a feint—forcing Rommel to commit his main strength to the town's defense while the Ameri-cans attempted a breakout further to the west.[120] Alas, the new strategy necessitated an advance through the "*bocage*"—a maze of naturally defensible hedges and sunken roads that led outwards from the American part of the line. Harassed at every step, the Allied progress proved painfully slow. Indeed, by day fifty after the D-Day landings, the Allies had only achieved the objectives set for day five.[121]

Now that the "Second Front" against Germany was finally established, Joseph Sta-lin was not about to sit back and let it bog down. On June 22, 1944, three years to the day after Germany embarked on Operation Barbarossa, the Red Army launched a massive offensive on the Eastern Front, thereby crippling Germany's ability to divert resources to Normandy.

The German line in the East was composed of three "Army Groups": "Army Group North" guarding the Leningrad Front, "Army Group Center" guarding the Moscow Front and "Army Group North Ukraine" guarding the Ukrainian Front. The German High Command believed that any Russian offensive in 1944 would be confined to the Ukrainian Front—a view that was reinforced by Russian deception operations, includ-ing the "massing" of sham forces in that sector.[122] In truth, however, the Red Army intended to launch a series of full-scale attacks along the entire line from the Baltic to the Ukraine, beginning with an attack on Army Group Center. Codenamed "Operation Bagration," this initial assault pitted 1,700,000 Russian soldiers, 4,000 armored vehicles and 5,300 aircraft against 800,000 Germans supported by only 550 armored vehicles and 839 aircraft.[123]

Because the Germans had not expected an attack in this sector, they had denuded it of much of its armor to reinforce the Ukrainian Front. Consequently, when the attack opened on June 22 with an artillery barrage from 140,000 guns along a 350-mile front (an average of 400 guns per mile),[124] the unsuspecting defenders were overwhelmed. Within five days, large German garrisons had been encircled and annihilated at Vitebsk and Orsha. As the front crumbled, Hitler insisted that the army stand and fight. German soldiers who attempted to retreat without orders were shot on sight by SS troops stationed on the roads leading westward.[125] Notwithstanding these draconian measures, the Germans were rapidly thrown back from the Dnieper and Dvina Rivers. They thought briefly of establishing themselves on the Berezina, but had to abandon the idea when Red Army troops got there ahead of them. On July 3, the Russians took Minsk, on the 13th, Vilnius, on the 27th, Bialystok and on the 28th, Brest-Litovsk.

In the meantime, a second full-scale offensive was launched in the south against Army Group North Ukraine. Having reinforced this part of the line prior to Operation Bagration, the German defenders were able to mount a stouter resistance. Nevertheless, they were driven back. On July 26, the Red Army forced them out of Lvov, and in the ensuing week, harried them all the way to the outskirts of Warsaw—a distance of nearly 250 miles. Six weeks later, the final blow of the campaign was launched against Army Group North (September 17, 1944). The preceding offensives had left this portion of the German line isolated with its southern flank exposed. The Red Army now cut it off entirely, taking Memel on the Baltic coast to complete its encirclement on October 5. By the time Stalin's various offensives came to an end, the Germans had been thrown back to the Vistula (well beyond the start line of Operation Barbarossa) with the loss of sixty divisions and casualties approaching a half-million men.[126] In the view of Andrew Roberts, it had been "one of the most decisive campaigns in history."[127]

Nor was this the final Allied accomplishment of 1944. On the other side of the globe, General MacArthur and Admiral Nimitz had adopted a policy known as "leapfrogging" in order to press their Pacific advance without risking catastrophic casualties. Thus, instead of attempting to land on Japanese strongholds like Rabaul, they simply sailed around them—isolating them by sea as they pushed ahead to the next assailable target.

In June of 1944 that target was Saipan in the Mariana Islands. On June 15—nine days after D-Day and seven days prior to Operation Bagration—U.S. Marines secured a beachhead on the island at a cost of two thousand casualties. For the next two nights, they held off badly organized *Banzai* attacks, before springing forward to pierce the island's defenses. The Marianas were an integral part of Japan's defensive perimeter in the Pacific. As their loss would create a fatal breach, the Japanese had little alternative but to risk a decisive battle at sea to retain them.[128] Hoping to keep their fleet out of harm's way, they conceived the idea of launching their carrier planes from the furthest conceivable distance. After an initial strike on the American fleet, the planes were to refuel on nearby Guam and Rota, strike the American fleet a second time, and then return to their carriers. Alas for them, the Americans (who were still intercepting and decoding Japanese military dispatches, just as they had done at Midway) detected their approach on radar and bombed the Guam and Rota airfields before they arrived.[129]

The ensuing encounter has come to be known as the "Great Marianas Turkey Shoot."[130] Besides being nearly out of fuel with no place to land, Japan's Zero fighters were all but obsolete. Pitted against America's brand-new supremely maneuverable "Hellcat fighters," they were shot down with impunity. More than seventy-five percent of the planes launched from Japan's carriers during the battle were lost.[131]

Having scarcely any planes left for defense, the Japanese fleet sought to withdraw. The Americans, under Vice-Admiral Marc Mitscher, pursued them relentlessly, and by dusk on the battle's second day drew close enough to attack with their own carrier planes. So far and so late into the night did the American flyers pursue the fleeing enemy that, on attempting to return to their carriers, no less than 80 American pilots either crashed in the murky darkness or ditched their planes as they ran out of fuel.[132] (The loss of pilots and aircraft would have been far higher if the American carriers had not risked destruction by turning on their lights to help guide them to safety.)[133] The United States emerged from the two-day sea engagement with decisive naval and air superiority in the Pacific. All told, the Japanese lost nearly 500 planes, the Americans only a quarter of that number. The American fleet, moreover, was essentially undamaged, while two Japanese carriers were sent to the bottom by American submarines, and a third was destroyed from the air as the Imperial fleet withdrew.

Despite these advantages, it took three weeks of hard combat to subdue Saipan. In the last days, Japanese soldiers threw their lives away in hopeless *Banzai* attacks, while civilians, preferring death to surrender, committed suicide in droves—many by jumping from cliffs, often with their children.[134] In securing the island with its mountainous terrain and abundant defensible caves, U.S. forces sustained an estimated 15,000 casualties.[135]

The July Plot and the Normandy Breakout

On July 17, 1944, Allied aircraft strafed a German staff car traveling outside the village of Sainte Foy de Montgommery in Normandy. The car promptly crashed, leaving one of its passengers with a fractured skull. While convalescing at his home three months later, the passenger—Field Marshal Erwin Rommel—received a visit from two fellow generals. While SS troops surrounded the house, the visitors curtly offered the Desert Fox a choice between committing suicide immediately with poison they were prepared to supply (in which case he was to be given a state funeral with military honors) or standing trial for treason.

The thread tying these two events together had occurred in the conference barracks at the Wolf's Lair in Rastenburg, East Prussia, on July 20, 1944—just three days after the attack on Rommel's staff car. There, at 12:42 p.m., in the midst of a crowded daily briefing, a great explosion had occurred, blowing some of the room's occupants to bits and jettisoning others out the windows.[136] Emerging practically unscathed, however, was the blast's intended victim—Adolf Hitler. Meeting Mussolini a few hours later, Hitler declared, "After my miraculous escape from death today I am more than ever convinced that it is my fate to bring our common enterprise to a successful conclusion."[137] Apprised of this and similar comments, Winston Churchill told the House of Commons that "When I hear that after Hitler escaped his bomb he described his survival as providential, I think from a purely military point of view we can agree with him. Certainly it would be most unfortunate if the Allies were to be deprived in the closing phases of the struggle of that form of warlike genius by which Corporal Schickelgruber has so notably contributed to our victory."[138]

The explanation for his survival was more mundane than Hitler believed it to be. The chief conspirator in what has come to be known as the "July Plot" had brought a bomb into the conference room in a briefcase and had placed it in a very good position before exiting the room. Unfortunately, just prior to its detonation, an uninvolved officer found the briefcase in his way, and moved it. It thus exploded on the far side of a thick oaken support beam beneath the table at which Hitler was standing, shielding him from the blast and saving his life. (The Führer tended to be lucky that way. A few weeks earlier, after boasting that his new V-1 "buzz" bombs would bring England to its knees, one of the unpiloted rockets took a wrong turn and crashed into his bunker in Margival, France, without injuring him.[139])

The intention of the July Plot conspirators had been to assassinate Hitler and carry out a reactionary military coup with the goal of seeking peace with the Allies before enemy troops set foot on German soil. It was not long before the case was solved, since the aforementioned conspirator, Lieutenant-Colonel Claus von Stauffenberg (until then a trusted and distinguished staff officer), was seen leaving the compound in a rush as soon as the explosion occurred—too soon, indeed, to realize that Hitler had survived. He was apprehended and executed by firing squad later that day. After a disgraceful sham trial, eight other conspirators were hanged—literally "like cattle," at Hitler's insistence—using piano wire suspended from meat hooks. Their agonized strangulation was preserved on film, to be shown to members of the army as a macabre means of deterring further conspiracies, but as Shirer notes, most of its intended audience refused to watch. Goebbels himself felt faint on viewing it and had to cover his eyes.[140]

In the ensuing weeks, an SS investigation revealed that several of Germany's most celebrated generals had had foreknowledge of the plot. One of these was Field Marshal Günther von Kluge, Hitler's new commander-in-chief on the Western Front, who poisoned himself on learning that he was a suspect. Another was Erwin Rommel, who did the same in the backseat of the car of the two generals who had come to visit him within minutes of receiving their ultimatum. (Because his family was home, they drove him a mile or so from his house before insisting that he get on with it.)[141]

Amid it all, the Allies finally achieved their breakout from Normandy. On July 25, 1944, perfect flying weather allowed Allied bombers to pulverize the German lines near St. Lô.[142] Smashing through the gap, the Americans advanced to seize the key coastal city of Avranches on August 1, thereby opening the route to Brittany. Over the ensuing days, they cleared Brittany of all meaningful resistance, and then wheeled eastwards in an effort to envelop those units still opposed to Montgomery in the vicinity of Caen. Spearheading the U.S. advance was the indomitable General George S. Patton, whose zeal for battle was frequently as alarming to his own men as it was to the enemy. Under his ceaseless prodding, the Americans reached Laval on August 6. By the following day, they were making progress towards Le Mans, placing all Axis forces in Normandy at risk of encirclement. For the Germans, retreat was the obvious course. Hitler, however, became intrigued by the idea of a counterattack aimed at piercing the Allied line and recapturing Avranches—success in which would have cut Patton adrift from his supply base in Normandy.[143] Against his better judgment, Field Marshal von Kluge (still in command as he was not yet a suspect in the July Plot) struck westwards from Falaise August 7.

The ensuing two weeks of combat composed the largest tank battle of the war on the Western Front.[144] Owing to Allied air superiority, the German thrust never really had a chance of breaking through. It did, however, manage to produce a rather impressive dent in the Allied line. Known as the "Falaise Pocket," this dent was now chock full of German soldiers and badly exposed on either flank. When the Allies took the logical step of counterattacking it from both sides, the retreat that the Germans might have carried out in orderly fashion prior to the offensive, became a panicked rout in which fully 70,000 German troops were killed or captured. (Only about half this number got out.)[145] In addition to the human loss, a great deal of irreplaceable equipment was destroyed or abandoned. Allied flyers, carrying out bombing and strafing runs in the final days of the battle, reported a veritable foot race below them, with panzers, infantry, mounted transport and bicyclists all jockeying for position in their bid to escape.[146] On surveying the battleground afterwards, Eisenhower encountered corpse-strewn roads where one could scarcely take a step without treading upon the German dead.[147]

The Warsaw Uprising

Overall, the Normandy campaign cost the Germans nearly a quarter of a million men. Unfortunately, an equal number were able to regroup behind the Seine.[148] The cost to the Allies likewise had been high. Between D-Day and the St. Lô breakout on July 25, the Allies sustained 122,000 casualties. The victory at Falaise claimed another 29,000.[149]

On August 15, 1944, the Allies successfully landed in southern France, seizing the Mediterranean port of Marseilles in Operation Dragoon. Strategically, however, the accomplishment must be counted a liability, for it deprived the Italian campaign of much needed men and materiel—including landing craft that could have been used for amphibious strikes behind Germany's Gothic Line. As a result, the Allied march up the Italian peninsula slowed to a crawl, shattering Churchill's hopes of reaching Vienna ahead of the Russians. (He had, in any event, been unable to win the Americans over to his conception, since the latter viewed the idea as a diversion into Eastern European politics that would detract from the prime objective of defeating Germany.)[150]

By this time, on the Eastern Front, Operation Bagration had brought the Russian Army almost to the banks of the Vistula—well within range of Warsaw, the Polish capital. Fearing that liberation by the Russians would mean the imposition of Soviet tyranny, the people of Warsaw attempted to liberate themselves in the name of their legitimate government (now in London exile) before the Russians arrived.[151] The result was one of the great tragedies of the war.

At the signal of their local commander, Tadeusz "Bor" Komorowski, the Poles inaugurated the insurrection with a synchronized attack on the city's German garrisons at five o'clock P.M. on August 1, 1944.[152] Their chief weapons were small arms, augmented (thanks to Polish enterprise) by a few hand grenades manufactured from recovered German shells that had failed to detonate in 1939.[153] In the ensuing struggle, the Poles fought hand-to-hand and kept their lines of communication open by sending messengers through the city's sewer system where they had to negotiate fast-moving currents of excrement that engulfed them to the waist.[154]

Initially, the uprising encountered some success, but the outcome hinged on the imminent arrival of the Russians, and the Russians—who no doubt understood the political motives of the insurrection—never budged.[155] Reprieved by their inertia, the Germans brought tanks, heavy artillery and Stuka dive-bombers to bear against the insurgents. An SS force composed of violent criminals and Russian defectors was unloosed upon the city with barbarous consequences. According to Alan Clark, captured Poles were doused with gasoline and set alight, while babies, transfixed on bayonets, were displayed from the windows of captured buildings.[156] German soldiers and tanks advanced through the streets using Polish civilians as protective screens. The Poles attempted to combat the tanks with Molotov cocktails. The SS countered by tethering Polish women to the vehicles so that they would be the first to burn.[157] During one attack, German troops stormed a Polish barricade by forcing a crowd of captured Polish women to run ahead of them. At the last moment, the Germans trampled the women underfoot to get at their quarry.[158]

Britain and the United States protested Russia's inaction during these ghastly days, but to no avail. The Soviets feigned innocence in the matter, claiming, with some justification, that the sheer magnitude of their advance had overextended their supply lines, forcing them to halt until their materiel could catch up.[159] This does not, however, explain their refusal to allow Britain and the United States to use Russian airfields as bases from which to succor the insurrection.[160] Nor does it explain Russia's simultaneous ability to press forward into the Balkans on their southern front—an advance possessing the self-evident political advantage of establishing Russia's post-war claim to the region.[161]

On August 20, 1944, Russian troops crossed the River Pruth into Romania. On the 23rd, Romania's King Michael, who had been carrying out secret correspondence with the Allies for some time, sacked his pro–Nazi dictator, General Ion Antonescu. Hitler retaliated by bombing Bucharest, but this merely precipitated Romania's defection to the Allies.[162] The German Sixth Army—reconstituted after the original perished at Stalingrad—was now guarding the frontier of a belligerent power with both flanks uncovered. It was an odd, if short-lived predicament, as the Russians were already in the process of encircling it for the second time in the war.[163]

Bulgaria followed Romania's lead by defecting to the Allies in September. By October, partisan uprisings had hurled the Germans out of Greece, and out of Belgrade, Yugoslavia where Marshal Tito's Communist minions had been waging a guerrilla war since 1941. In the same month, Hungary's dictator, Admiral Horthy, signed an armistice with the Russians, but this document was nullified when the Nazis seized Horthy's son as a hostage, and forced the dictator to resign before the agreement took effect.[164] German reinforcements were funneled into the country, and for the time being the road to Budapest was blocked.

Operation Market Garden

A day prior to the Russian attack on Romania, strikes and uprisings in Paris forced the city's German garrison to carry out a hasty evacuation (August 19, 1944). On August 25, "Free French" and American forces advancing from Normandy made their triumphant return to the French capital, and, on the following day, Charles de Gaulle led a victory march past cheering throngs on the Champs Élysées. Nine days later, Canadian forces liberated Brussels, the capital of Belgium. These accomplishments were of great symbolic value, but the burden of defeating the German army still remained—and the British and Americans were at loggerheads as to how it should be accomplished. Eisenhower, as commander-in-chief, wanted to advance on a broad front in order to stretch Germany's resources to the utmost until, inevitably, an opportunity presented itself for a breakthrough. The chief drawback to this approach was that it would delay ultimate victory, because the Allied supply lines in Europe still stretched all the way back to Normandy and were insufficient to sustain a rapid advance in all sectors at once.[165] Of necessity, the war must drag on well into 1945 with this strategy.

As a speedier alternative, Bernard Montgomery lobbied for the investment of all available materiel in a single bold thrust through Belgium with the goals of breaching the Rhine and winning the war before Christmas.[166] Eisenhower, who was facing simultaneous demands for resources from his own headstrong generals, Patton and Bradley, did not think Montgomery's plan logistically feasible. Although Antwerp was captured on September 4, the Belgian port could not be used since the 50-mile-long Scheldt estuary leading into it from the Channel coast was still in German hands. To clear it, Montgomery would have had to backtrack when he was bent on continuing his advance. If he had done so (or if Eisenhower had ordered him to), he would have opened a direct supply route across the Channel. But he did not. Consequently, like his fellow generals, he was dependent upon the elongated route from Normandy.[167]

While Eisenhower ultimately rejected Montgomery's notion of a "full-blooded thrust" with forty divisions in favor of his own "broad front" strategy, he was nonetheless willing to let Montgomery launch a smaller scale effort to establish a bridgehead on the far bank of the Rhine—in part because it held out the promise of overrunning the launch sites for Hitler's new pilotless "V-weapons" which were already falling on London.[168] These included the coughing, sputtering V-1 "buzz bomb," which, owing to its noise and slow speed, eventually became an easy target for the RAF, and the more worrisome V-2, which was a full-fledged, high-speed rocket that struck before it could be detected.[169]

The result, after much heated debate, was Operation Market Garden, which opened on September 17, 1944, with the largest airborne offensive in history, encompassing thirty-five thousand men—two-thirds of them paratroopers, the remainder transported by glider.[170] Their immediate objectives were a series of bridges behind German lines in Holland, including those at Zon (over the Wilhelmina Canal), Nijmegen (over the River Waal) and Arnhem (over the Lower Rhine). Once these had been secured, infantry and armor were to pour across them to establish Monty's bridgehead across the Rhine, thereby opening an invasion route into the Ruhr—Germany's largest and most vital industrial district. The plan held the supreme advantage of bypassing Hitler's heavily fortified Siegfried Line, whose northern extremity ended just south of the targeted bridges. Alas, it was bound to fail—something the Allied High Command ought to have known at the outset from reconnaissance photos revealing the unwelcome presence of two panzer divisions at Arnhem (rather more than light-armed paratroopers were equipped to deal with). The information was passed on to Frederick Browning, commanding the 1st Airborne Corps, and to Montgomery himself. Both chose to ignore the implications, and when Eisenhower was alerted, he, too, failed to cancel the operation.[171]

While ground troops broke through on a narrow front and advanced along a single open road to the relief of the paratroopers, the American 101st Airborne Division

Parachutes open overhead as waves of paratroops land in Holland during operations by the 1st Allied Airborne Army during Operation Market Garden. September 1944 (Wikimedia Commons).

found the bridge at Zon already destroyed—a situation that was remedied, at the cost of some delay, by the assembly of a British-manufactured "Bailey" bridge from prefabricated components. A more serious delay occurred at Nijmegen, where the American 82nd Airborne assault force, having all been dropped on the near bank, had to stage a small-boat river crossing in broad daylight under heavy fire to secure the opposite end of the bridge.[172] Although British armor made it across directly after it was taken, another long delay ensued in waiting for the infantry to catch up.

In the meantime, the British effort at Arnhem failed disastrously. Most of the 1st British Airborne Division was hemmed in at its landing site at some distance from the bridge. Although a lone battalion got through to gain the bridge's northern end, it was afterwards encircled. Allied reinforcements (including the Polish 1st Independent Parachute Brigade, which ran a gauntlet of deadly ground fire while descending to earth[173]) were unable to relieve them, and the offensive had to be aborted at substantial loss on the 9th day. Of those engaged at Arnhem, nearly 1,500 were killed. Two thousand more got back across the Rhine by boat or by swimming, while an estimated six thousand were taken prisoner[174]—among them a number of Poles who had to disguise themselves as Brits, since the Germans shot Polish prisoners on sight.[175]

The Battle of the Bulge

Despite the failure of Operation Market Garden, Bernard Montgomery had not lost faith in the idea of outflanking the Siegfried Line from the Netherlands. Eisenhower, however, had other ideas—having now decided upon a series of converging blows aimed at obliterating the Siegfried defenses themselves. Once this had been accomplished, the Allies were to press forward to the left bank of the Rhine. Shielded by the river all along the front, Eisenhower believed he would be able to free up the bulk of his forces for offensive thrusts.[176]

Straightforward in conception, the plan ground to a crawl upon implementation. In the extreme north, Montgomery's progress toward the Rhine proved maddeningly slow. Behind the lines, in a belated effort to liberate the Scheldt estuary, Monty's First Canadian Division was forced to advance in small units across flat, mud-soaked terrain in the face of German machine gun fire. According to Max Hastings, the Canadian casualty rate in this drive approximated that sustained at Passchendaele in 1917.[177] Although the operation was ultimately successful, it was not until November 28 that the first Allied supply ships put in at Antwerp.

The Americans, meanwhile, were encountering similar difficulties. Despite massive air superiority, Omar Bradley and Courtney Hodges were unable to gain control of Aachen (the first German city to be occupied) until October 21. It then took them until December 15 to reach the Roer River Dam (their first objective en route to the Rhine). Concerned that the Germans would attack his right flank in the course of this slow advance, Hodges diverted three divisions into the Hürtgen Forest, where they sustained 13,000 casualties in ten weeks of brutal combat without attaining victory.[178] Further to the south, the unrelenting George Patton overcame intense resistance at Metz and pushed ahead to the outskirts of Saarbrücken at a total cost of 29,000 casualties,[179] while in the extreme south, Jacob Devers (commanding "Dragoon Force"—the troops that had come ashore at Marseilles in Operation Dragoon) actually broke through the German line between Belfort and Mulhouse to reach the Rhine on November 22.

Such was the situation in mid–December 1944. But even as Eisenhower pushed towards the Rhine in hopes of using the natural obstacle as a defensive shield behind which he could contemplate subsequent operations, he received a lesson in how vulnerable such obstacles could be. On December 16, 1944, Adolf Hitler launched his last offensive of the war—through the Ardennes.

Inexplicably, the Allies had regained their confidence in the "impassability" of this forest, through which the Germans had launched their decisive blow against France in 1940. North of the Ardennes, Bradley was pressing ahead with the American First and Ninth armies. South of it, Patton was outside Saarbrücken with the Third Army. But the Ardennes itself was protected with nothing more than a thin shielding force. Lacking any sense of proportion, Hitler thought he saw the chance for a decisive blow. As in 1940, he hoped to drive straight through to the coast—this time to Antwerp, which, following the capture of the Scheldt estuary in November, was finally getting up to speed as a major Allied supply base. All Allied troops north of the breakthrough line would be entrapped just as they had been four years earlier. The chances of success seemed to be enhanced by Eisenhower's "broad front" policy, for in pursuing it, the Allied commander had arrayed his forces linearly in end-to-end fashion with scarcely anything held in reserve.[180]

By this point in the war, however, Nazi Germany did not possess the means to exploit a victory even if one was achieved. In vain, Gerd von Rundstedt (reappointed as commander-in-chief on the Western Front after von Kluge's suicide) sought to dissuade the Führer from committing his last reserves to the enterprise, but Hitler was adamant, delivering his final instructions to Rundstedt with the handwritten annotation, "Not to be altered."[181]

Accordingly, on December 16, 1944, the Germans made their nocturnal lunge through the Ardennes under "artificial moonlight" created by reflecting searchlight beams off low-lying clouds. (The British had used the same technique in North Africa.)[182] To the credit of its planners—Hitler and his chief of operations, Alfred Jodl—a cataclysmic surprise was achieved. On hearing the first reports, American general, Omar Bradley, assumed the attack was merely a diversion, but in truth the Ardennes front was crumbling. By the third day, many of the Allied defenders had been captured or thrown into headlong retreat along a forty-mile front, leaving startled civilians to remove American flags and other Allied insignias before the Germans arrived and began asking questions.[183] To compound the mayhem, SS troops disguised in American uniforms and speaking immaculate English appeared behind the Allied lines to cut phone lines, alter road signs and spread misinformation. Reports of their presence soon had American troops as far to the rear as Paris leveling rifles at one another and calling out questions designed to stump enemy imposters: "Who plays second base for Brooklyn?" they might ask, or "Who's (actress) Betty Grable's husband?"[184] Exposed imposters were shot on sight.

By December 20, the German panzers had raced westwards to encircle Bastogne—a major supply junction and communications hub controlling the route to Antwerp. But when the attackers summoned Bastogne to surrender, the city's American commander, General Anthony McAuliffe,replied with the single word, "Nuts!" (This afterwards became his nickname.) Defending the town's perimeter was the battle-hardened 101st Airborne Division—veterans of the Normandy invasion and Operation Market Garden. For ten days, they fought the Germans to a bloody stalemate, sapping their last strength. By December 25, Hitler's Ardennes Offensive had sputtered to a halt well short of Antwerp. Known afterwards as the "Battle of the Bulge," it had achieved a maximum of surprise, but under the strain of insufficient means, it ended in failure, just as the Führer's generals had tried to tell him it would. Even if the drive had possessed sufficient armor, it would have foundered for lack of petrol.[185] The drive to Antwerp depended on the commandeering of Allied fuel supplies along the route, an object that was never achieved (although it was only narrowly missed at the town of Spa).

As at Falaise, Hitler's attack force was now exposed in the salient (or "Bulge") it had created in the Allied line; and, as in the former situation, the Allies counterattacked on both flanks—converging on the "Bulge" from the north (Hodges) and from the south (Patton) simultaneously. On December 26, Patton's Third Army, advancing with characteristic rapidity, relieved Bastogne (although its 101st Airborne defenders protested ever after that they hadn't needed relieving). On January 1, Hitler countered with another surprise, catching a large proportion of the American air force on the ground in a 1000-plane Luftwaffe raid (but destroying only 150 Allied aircraft at a cost of 300),[186] while eight fresh Wehrmacht divisions plunged forward in the direction of Strasbourg (the very spot left vulnerable by Patton's mad rush northwards).[187]

Apart from the shock value, however, there was nothing to be gained by these blows, for Hitler had nothing left to throw into the scales. He had achieved his surprises by ignoring the rules of war, *not* (as he thought) because he was a military genius able to see his way around them, *but because he was a rank amateur who didn't even know them.*[188] By January 16, 1945, the Germans were back to their start line. Apart from inflicting significant casualties—some 80,000, compared to 98,000 of their own[189]—the chief result of the Battle of the Bulge was to waste Germany's last remaining reserves, further crippling her capacity to defend her frontiers. It had, moreover, served as the venue for another Nazi war atrocity—the Malmédy Massacre, in which the SS gunned down 86 American prisoners in cold blood, laughing as they did so.[190]

The Fall of the Third Reich

For as long as he could, Hitler turned a blind eye to the ruinous developments around him. When told of an immense Russian troop build-up from the Carpathians to the Baltic consisting of 225 divisions, he dismissed the reports, saying that such wild rumors had not been heard since the days of Genghis Khan.[191] With a tidal wave ready to break upon him, he wasted precious reserve units in an irrelevant effort to relieve Budapest, whose encirclement had been completed by the converging Soviet armies at the end of December.

On January 12, 1945, the Russians staged a colossal attack along the entire front. (It was initially planned for January 20, but Stalin launched it eight days early to assist his Western Allies in their struggle to eliminate the German "Bulge.")[192] Warsaw and Krakow were overrun as Russian armor and motorized infantry poured across the Polish plains, crushing all resistance. Attempting to form new lines to the rear, the reeling Germans found themselves tangled into a knot by fleeing civilian refugees. By mid–February 1945, the Russians had reached the Oder River, less than fifty miles from Berlin, before overstretched supply lines and German reinforcements dispatched hastily from the Western Front brought a halt to their advance.

The removal of troops from the West wrought havoc with Germany's Rhine defenses. In February, the Allies enveloped the "Colmar Pocket" on the river's west bank just north of Switzerland, eliminating its large contingent of German troops. During the same month, the British and U.S. Air Forces bombed Dresden. The attack, delivered in three waves, created a firestorm reminiscent of Hamburg, killing at least 25,000 people.[193] A ground attack followed along the entire Western Front. Although casualties were frightful (particularly in the Hürtgen Forest, where the fighting was now renewed), the American First Army had the astounding luck, on March 7, to capture an intact bridge over the Rhine at Remagen (just south of Bonn) as it was about to be demolished. Thus, two months earlier than expected, four American divisions pushed across the river to establish a permanent bridgehead in the German heartland. Shortly thereafter, the bridge sustained damage from German artillery fire, but American engineers quickly erected a 1000-foot floating bridge to take its place. They had been promised two cases of champagne if they finished the project in less than twelve hours. They were done in ten.[194]

To the south, Patton broke into the industrial Saar Basin on March 13. By the 25th, he had reduced the entire region, ending all organized resistance on the west bank of the Rhine. In the meantime, his forces achieved a new crossing of the river near Oppenheim, driving northeastwards from the opposite bank (March 22–23). One day later,

Montgomery crossed at Wesel far to the north, and drove southeastwards (March 23–24). Their combined objective was the encirclement of Germany's sole remaining industrial center—the Ruhr.

In after years, Eisenhower characterized this region as still being essential to the German war effort, but by this point in the war, the Allies had bombarded it to the point of incapacitation. Indeed, Germany's Armaments Minister, Albert Speer, did not even take the Ruhr into account when, in January 1945, following the loss of Silesia's mining district to the Russians, he addressed a blunt memorandum to Hitler saying that the war was over.[195] Although the Germans fought tenaciously in the canton's defense, the "Ruhr Pocket" was encircled by April 1. In the ensuing days, it was annihilated in a series of hammer blows with the capture of over 325,000 prisoners (including 30 generals).

Later in the same month, Vienna fell to the Russians.

The reader may be astounded to learn that in the midst of these events Hitler and Goebbels were congratulating one another. The occasion was the announcement over the airwaves of the most "positive" sort of news: On April 12, 1945, Franklin Delano Roosevelt had died suddenly of a massive stroke. It had long been Hitler's view that if Roosevelt could only be gotten out of the way, the Western Allies would come to their senses and abandon their unnatural alliance with Bolshevik Russia. From his vantage point (and, before rushing to judgment, one must take into consideration that this was deep beneath the ground in a bunker), it seemed obvious that the Grand Alliance was foredoomed.[196]

On the planet's surface, of course, things looked rather different. On April 16, 1945, the Russians began a new drive toward Berlin, raping, pillaging and murdering all along the route in retaliation for atrocities the Germans had perpetrated on Russian soil. Certain that Britain and the United States would treat them more leniently, the German High Command concentrated their remaining defenses against the marauding Reds, leaving their western frontier all but open to an Anglo-American advance on Berlin. Despite Churchill's enthusiasm for such a drive, the Western Allies did not respond to their cue—Eisenhower choosing instead to attack Bavaria, where the Nazis had purportedly established a "National Redoubt" with the intention of making a last stand. (In fact, the "Redoubt" did not exist.)

On April 25, while Russian troops were in the process of encircling Berlin, American and Russian forces came into contact at Torgau, seventy miles southwest of the capital, where they confounded Hitler's predictions by embracing and drinking toasts to each other's health. Three days later, on April 28, 1945, Italian partisans apprehended Benito Mussolini in attempted flight. He was executed along with his mistress, Clara Petacci, who stepped in front of the Duce to shield him just prior to the fatal shots. The lone gunman assigned to the execution had two pistols jam on him during the process, and had to prevail upon his victims to excuse him while he borrowed a third.[197] When the deed was finally complete, the bodies were transported to Milan, where an angry mob set upon them with great brutality. One woman, who had lost five sons during the Duce's reign, repaid him by firing five bullets into his corpse. Others kicked and battered the bodies, until they had become unrecognizable before those in authority decided to put the bodies out of reach by suspending them, heads down, from the rafters of a Milanese petrol station.

Hitler avoided a similar spectacle. On the afternoon of April 30, 1945, he put a pistol to his mouth while his newlywed bride, Eva Braun, took cyanide. He had stayed close to his maps to the bitter end, for one of Germany's sole remaining advantages in the war was the superior method by which her leader could encompass great geographical distances with one sweep of his arm, while confidently explaining where his armies would strike their next blow. On being told that Russian troops were only a few blocks distant on April 29, however, it seems finally to have dawned on him that his fantastical armies did not exist.[198] In his last hours, he dictated a last will and testament blaming others—most especially the Jews—for Germany's defeat.[199]

Immediately after the suicides, loyal guards doused the corpses with petrol and burned them beyond recognition. Soon afterwards, Joseph Goebbels, and his wife, Magda, who had just poisoned their six children, asked an obliging SS officer to shoot them in the back of the head. Their corpses too, were burned, but with less success. The propaganda minister's grotesque remains were still identifiable when Russian troops arrived.

Meanwhile, even in these final hours, SS troops scoured the streets above for supposed cowards and deserters, and hanged them from the sidewalk lampposts.[200] By now, the city was in ruins—its citizens having long since taken to their basements to avoid the ubiquitous Russian artillery fire. There they awaited the inevitable arrival of their Soviet conquerors, whose indecent exploits recognized no asylum—not even a maternity home administered by nuns.[201] All attempts to obtain a ceasefire on terms less than unconditional surrender were rebuffed. To escape the nightmare, many Berliners resorted to suicide.[202] Only on May 2, when the triumphant Russians unfurled a Red flag atop the Reichstag (the last building to fall) did the guns fall silent. German forces in Italy surrendered on the same day, leaving only a few pathetic pockets of resistance in the entire Reich. "The downfall of any powerful nation is a tragic spectacle," writes the military historian, Lynn Montross, "but few observers were moved to pity for Germany."[203] The Allied advance through occupied German territory in 1944 and 1945 had revealed undeniable evidence of Nazi atrocities—the most horrifying being the concentration camps where sparse numbers of survivors, kept alive as slave laborers, were little more than walking skeletons.

The Fall of Japan

Acting on the orders of Admiral Karl Dönitz (Hitler's nominal successor), Alfred Jodl signed articles of unconditional surrender at Reims on May 7, 1945. The war in Germany thus came to an end. But in the Pacific, there was another still to be won. By the autumn of 1944, General Douglas MacArthur was more anxious than ever to fulfill his promise to return victoriously to the Philippines. The island archipelago, located due west of the Marianas, was defended by 250,000 Japanese troops, most of them dug in on the two largest islands—Luzon in the extreme north (from which MacArthur's forces had been ejected in 1942) and Mindanao in the extreme south. Between these large islands were a number of smaller ones. In consultations with Admiral Nimitz and the fleet, MacArthur proposed to launch an amphibious assault on one of these smaller islands—Leyte—thereby severing communications between the two Japanese strong points, before defeating them in detail.[204]

The plan was a controversial one. Nimitz and his fellow admirals believed that a more practicable approach would be to ignore the Philippines altogether, while striking

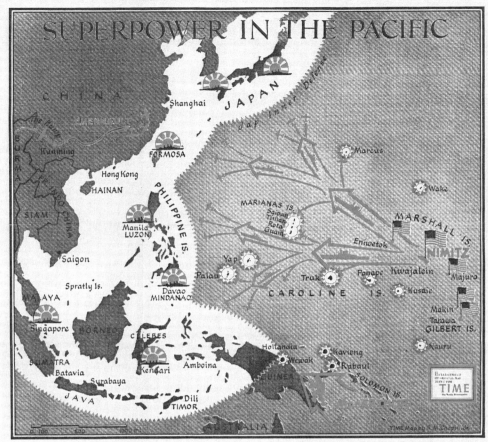

1944 Chapin map of American Progress in the Pacific during World War II for *Time Magazine.* **M. Chapin, Jr. (Wikimedia Commons).**

their next blows against Iwo Jima and Okinawa—a pair of islands located to the northwest of the Marianas in the direction of the Japanese mainland.[205] MacArthur, however, would not be deterred, and on October 20, he waded ashore on the heels of 130,000 marines at Leyte Gulf on the east coast of Leyte Island. Standing off the coast was the U.S. Seventh Fleet under Vice-Admiral Thomas Kinkaid, who was tasked with getting the troops ashore. A little further afield was the U.S. Third Fleet under Admiral William "Bull" Halsey. Possessing most of the carriers, Halsey's task was to shield the entire operation.

Unbeknownst to the Americans, a Japanese reconnaissance plane had spotted the approaching U.S. armada a day prior to the landings.[206] Japan's naval leaders decided to counterattack immediately. Organizing the fleet into three attack forces—Northern, Central and Southern—they mapped out a converging operation from three directions. The Northern Force, composed of four carriers and some support vessels, was to act as a decoy, since the carriers did not have enough planes to launch a meaningful attack.[207] Its task would be to lure Admiral Halsey's fleet away from Leyte Gulf while the other two forces sailed around the island from the far side to surprise Kinkaid's exposed fleet. The battle that ensued was the largest in naval history, lasting three days and pitting 216 U.S. ships against 64 Japanese.[208]

Though clever and shrouded in secrecy, the Japanese plan of attack required a degree of coordination that proved beyond its capability. Before the Northern Force had a chance to lure Admiral Halsey out of position, Halsey learned from his own reconnaissance that a Japanese squadron (Central Force) was sailing around Leyte Island's northern tip via the San Bernadino Strait (October 24). He promptly launched a carrier strike against it that sent it reeling in retreat. Learning only now of Northern Force's presence off Luzon far to the north, Halsey set off in pursuit. In so doing, however, he made the cardinal error of failing to alert Kinkaid, who, at about the same time, received word that the last Japanese squadron (Southern Force) was moving towards Leyte Gulf from the south via the Surigao Strait.

Believing that Halsey was still in position, Kinkaid sailed into the Surigao Strait, and that night inflicted a shattering defeat on Southern Force.[209] Alas, as dawn approached, he received a distress call telling him that Leyte Gulf (where he had left but a skeleton force of escort carriers) was under attack. The explanation, as it turns out, was that Central Force had not sustained a high degree of damage in its clash with Halsey's carrier planes the preceding afternoon. Afterwards, it had turned around and renewed its advance through the San Bernadino Strait, finding, to its utter surprise, that the route to Leyte Gulf was entirely clear.

Kinkaid's Seventh Fleet had expended its fuel and ammunition in the battle for the Surigao Strait and was in no position to make a timely return to Leyte Gulf. Nor was Halsey within range.[210] It seemed that the Gulf, where Kinkaid's skeleton force was now being mauled, must fall into hostile hands, leaving MacArthur's men on shore without an open supply line. Just as the situation reached its crisis point, however, Central Force suddenly and inexplicably withdrew. Its commander, Admiral Takeo Kurita, did not know that Halsey's fleet had actually fallen for the carrier decoy. Indeed, he was convinced that Halsey was still nearby and that Kinkaid must also arrive imminently. So with victory staring him in the face, he decided to break off his attack and turn back, squandering the opportunity that had been handed to him.[211]

In the aftermath, Northern Force was successfully pursued and all four of its carriers (decoys or not) were sent to the bottom. By October 27, the U.S. fleet had won a resounding victory. Irrevocably damaged, the Japanese fleet was finished as a viable force. It could no longer defend the home islands, much less what remained of Japan's Pacific empire.

Inevitably, Japan must face invasion—something that had not been threatened on a large scale since AD 1281, when a fleet carrying 140,000 irrepressible Mongols had been smashed to bits by a timely typhoon before making landfall. The storm was remembered ever after as the "Divine Wind" or "*Kamikaze*," and now, in her present hour of peril, Japan was determined to conjure a new one. On October 25, Leyte Gulf witnessed the first kamikaze raid of the war.[212] The Japanese suicide pilots sank one U.S. escort carrier and damaged several others. It was a pittance in comparison to the damage sustained by the Japanese fleet during the course of the battle, but it induced horror and revulsion in those who witnessed it. Thereafter, such attacks would become commonplace.

After Leyte, Japan was undeniably on the ropes, but her impending subjugation remained problematic. Her troops had resisted virtually to the last man on every island the Allies had captured in the Pacific. On Tarawa, Biak, Kwajalein Lagoon, Saipan and other islands, Japanese soldiers had staged suicidal *Banzai* attacks against entrenched Marines rather than surrender. The number of Japanese dead was consistently in the thousands or tens of thousands, the number taken prisoner in mere tens or hundreds. In the face of such fanaticism, it was estimated that an invasion of the Japanese home islands would cost the Allies in excess of one million casualties. Driving them out of China would exact an additional heavy cost.

As an alternative, the U.S. High Command decided to embark on a strategic bombing campaign, similar to that undertaken in Europe, with the object of breaking Japan's will to resist before an invasion of the homeland became necessary. Towards this end, it was necessary to seize airfields closer to the Japanese mainland so that short-range fighters could accompany the bombing raids and so that bombers that were damaged (or lacking fuel for the return journey to Marianas—1,500 miles distant) could land in an emergency. Iwo Jima and Okinawa were promptly targeted for this purpose.[213] In February 1945, American Marines forced a landing on the former. The island's defenders allowed them to crowd onto the beaches unopposed, and then opened up on them with a deadly barrage of mortar and artillery fire. The island's beaches were composed of volcanic ash. Armored personnel carriers could obtain no purchase on this powdery frictionless surface. Attempting to move forward on foot, soldiers sunk to the ankle, or even to the knee, with every step. Nor was it possible to dig in, since the surrounding sand and ash simply slid back into place as rapidly as it could be shoveled away.[214] Under intense fire, the Marines had no choice but to fight their way forward, capturing Mount Suribachi, where six of their number—among them a Native American named Ira Hayes—created an immortal image raising the American flag.[215] It took more than a month thereafter to subdue the island, for the Japanese had now abandoned the suicidal *Banzai* charges employed elsewhere. Instead, they held out to the last man in pillboxes and caves, exacting a devastating toll on the attacking Marines. Indeed, for the first time in the war, American forces sustained more casualties than they inflicted in taking a Japanese-held island.[216]

On Okinawa, which was seen as a jumping off point for the invasion of Japan itself,[217] the American invaders met even stiffer resistance. Here, it took three months to break through the enemy's three-tiered defensive line (April to June 1945). As the end approached, masses of civilians sought to "save face" by hurling themselves from the cliffs surrounding the Okinawan capital. Of 117,000 Japanese fighting casualties, only 7,000 were wounded. The rest were killed.[218] The Americans suffered 50,000 casualties, many of them at sea—for after the crippled remnant of the Japanese navy was blown out of the water attempting to sail to the island's defense (April 1945), Okinawa became the sight of a massive kamikaze campaign. To avoid radar detection in these attacks, the Japanese pilots approached at low altitude until the enemy was in sight. Then, after making a sudden and rapid ascent, they plummeted nose first into the targeted vessels. (Another technique was to approach at such high altitude that, even when warned by radar, U.S. planes simply could not climb fast enough to intercept them prior to their suicide dives.)[219] Over thirty American ships of varying sizes were sent to the bottom, while another 300 were damaged.[220] The success rate in striking an intended target has been reckoned at 20 percent for kamikaze pilots, compared to only 2 percent by dropping bombs or torpedoes.[221]

Having seized Iwo Jima and Okinawa, the Americans pressed ahead with their strategic bombing campaign, employing high altitude Boeing B-29 Superfortresses. Directed

One of the most iconic photographs from World War II: U.S. Marines raising the flag on Iwo Jima, 23 February 1945. From left to right, the four most visible Marines are Ira Hayes (native American), Harold Schultz, Franklin Sousely and Harlon Block. Only partly in view behind them are two more Marines (left to right): Michael Strank and Harold Keller. Photograph by Joe Rosenthal (Wikimedia Commons).

by General Curtis LeMay, the campaign relied heavily on incendiary bombs. On March 9, 1945, Tokyo was targeted, and a quarter of the city went up in flames. A fire tornado, so hot that it brought the city's canal water to a boil, destroyed over two hundred thousand buildings, and killed almost 90,000 of the city's inhabitants.[222] In the ensuing ten days, other major cities suffered similar devastation before the attacks were interrupted by a temporary shortage of incendiaries. (The raids resumed when more incendiaries became available.)[223] In all, 65 Japanese cities were destroyed in this fashion.[224]

Despite this relentless punishment, it appeared that Japan might hold out to force an invasion. The point remains controversial since the Imperial Cabinet contained a strong peace party supported by Emperor Hirohito. Even prior to the incendiary attacks, they had been anxious to cease hostilities, but two obstacles stood in their way. The first was the Allies' insistence that surrender be unconditional, which the Japanese could not abide because, at the very least, they required assurances that Emperor Hirohito (who was regarded as a divinity by his people) would be allowed to retain his throne. More problematic was the fact that, in addition to the peace party, the Japanese cabinet also had a strong war party, whose key figures believed that fierce resistance on the home islands might produce war weariness among the Allies and convince them to grant more valuable concessions—perhaps even permission to retain a portion of the Japanese empire.

To complicate matters, the peace party addressed their desire for surrender not to those with whom they were fighting, but to the Russians, who, being neutral, seemed a convenient intermediary. The first Japanese inquiries were made in February 1945. Alas, the Russians never told the United States about these overtures, since they were themselves intent on entering the Pacific War in order to claim a share of the spoils—namely, the right to pilfer the rich province of Manchuria of its natural resources. Thus, from the Russian standpoint, an early end to hostilities held little allure. Only in May, after Stalin had made clear his own expectations for a Far East peace settlement, did he utter so much as a hint about the Japanese initiatives.[225]

By this time, Emperor Hirohito was pressing for peace at any price. In July, he privately directed an envoy to say as much to Stalin, but the Japanese foreign minister, Shigenori Togo, sabotaged the effort in the erroneous belief that Stalin might be induced to broker a lenient peace in return for certain concessions in Asia.[226] The foreign minister was profoundly mistaken. On July 15, without even receiving the Japanese delegation, Stalin departed for Potsdam to confer with U.S. President Harry Truman. Two days later, he informed Truman that the Japanese had sent envoys to Moscow, but as they were seeking mediation rather than unconditional surrender, he would proceed with the invasion of Manchuria in early August.

This is exactly what the United States and Britain had desired of him at Yalta in February 1945, and they likely felt no different as late as July 15. On the 16th, however, the United States successfully tested its first atomic bomb in the New Mexico desert, and this gravely changed the situation. If the A-bomb could obviate the need for the million-plus-casualty invasion of Japan's home islands—as it seemed that it would—then Stalin's participation in the war was no longer desirable. A Russian attack now would only give Stalin unwarranted leverage in determining the peace terms to follow. When Truman informed Stalin of the weapon's existence on July 23, Stalin congratulated him and told him to use it, but made no change in his war preparations—save, perhaps, to speed them up.

After warning the Japanese that they had either to surrender or face weapons of unprecedented destructiveness, the first A-bomb was dropped on Hiroshima on August 6, by the U.S. B-29 Superfortress bomber, *Enola Gay*. According to the *Enola Gay*'s bombardier, the warhead tumbled out of the plane tail first and executed a backwards half-somersault before making its descent in the nose-down position.[227] The carnage that followed has oft been described—the brilliant flash that blinded many who witnessed it, the intense heat which instantaneously charred people to ash while leaving their silhouette imprinted on surrounding structures, and the concussive force that leveled or vaporized everything in its path. Survivors, whose last memory was of a bustling city, regained their wits to gaze upon a barren moonscape. On returning for a second look just two minutes after the explosion, the crew of the *Enola Gay* was shocked to see a colossal mushroom cloud already reaching their flying altitude of 33,000 feet, and speeding higher by the second.[228] Some 80,000 of the city's inhabitants died instantly— the overwhelming majority being civilians—while that number again succumbed to burns or radiation effects (the latter being augmented by condensed moisture in the mushroom cloud that rained down on the city a short time after the detonation).[229]

Two days later, on August 8, 1945, Russia declared war on Japan. On the following day, more than one million Russian troops stormed into Manchuria from two directions simultaneously. The emperor was now adamant regarding surrender. He met with the cabinet to express this view on August 9, but by then the Americans had decided to drop their second atomic weapon. Even as the emperor impressed upon his awed and tearful ministers the necessity of making peace, Nagasaki perished in a new atomic explosion.[230] Still, the cabinet would not render a decision. Culturally, surrender was viewed as a denigration of honor—something worse than death. It simply could not be approached pragmatically. Only on August 14, when Truman tacitly agreed to immunity for Hirohito, did the cabinet agree to sign a document of surrender, and even then a cadre of junior officers attempted an abortive coup in an effort to prevent it. On August 15, 1945, Emperor Hirohito personally broadcast news of the capitulation. Across Japan, men, women and children bowed in the streets and wept. They had never had the honor of hearing their emperor's voice before.[231]

The atomic attacks on Hiroshima and Nagasaki have long been the subject of bitter controversy. Even Churchill, who agreed to the attacks without reservation, recorded in his memoirs that Japan's defeat was inevitable even without the bomb.[232] Admiral William Leahy, Truman's chief-of-staff, went somewhat further, arguing that its use was immoral and unnecessary, and that by employing it, the United States "adopted an ethical standard common to the barbarians of the Dark Ages."[233]

Critics of the atomic attacks have frequently maintained (i) that a demonstration of the bomb's destructive power might have achieved the desired end without the attendant carnage; and (ii) that the only condition necessary for peace at this late date was to confirm Emperor Hirohito on his throne. But matters are not so clear-cut. As Andrew Roberts has noted, the United States had built only three atomic weapons, and one of these had already been detonated at Alamogordo in the initial test. Use of a second for demonstration purposes would have left only one with which to force Japan's surrender. In the end, we might have forfeited much of the weapon's shock value, employed the last one to no avail and then had to invade the home islands anyway.[234] Nor would a guarantee of Hirohito's status necessarily have altered the situation. The Japanese "war party" was composed largely of fanatics. We must bear in mind how few of the Japanese had been willing to surrender on the outlying islands, even when their plight had become hopeless; how not just soldiers, but civilians, had committed suicide rather than capitulate; and how even after the bombs were dropped and the emperor's position was guaranteed, the Japanese military attempted a coup d'état rather than countenance a "shameful" peace. When these facts are taken into consideration, there is room to doubt whether the Japanese would have surrendered on the basis of a minimalist concession rather than continue the struggle with their customary tenacity. Had they done the latter, and had the Allies relied on a conventional invasion to bring them to heel, the cost in casualties would very likely have been tremendous.[235] Douglas MacArthur predicted as many as one million American casualties,[236] while the lowest estimate—193,500 (put forward by the Joint War Plans Committee)—was hardly trivial. (Nor was it particularly realistic, since it underestimated the number of troops that Japan would have been able to concentrate on the home islands for their defense.)[237]

In considering the dilemma, Max Hastings wrote that "No sane person would suggest that the use of the atomic bombs represented an absolute good, or was even a righteous act."[238] Those who would declare it an absolute evil, however, might first consider the destiny consigned to those American soldiers who stood to die in an unnecessary invasion of Japan when those responsible for making the decision possessed an alternative—a terrible alternative to be sure, but one that was almost certain to end the war more quickly and with less total loss of life on both sides.

Atomic cloud rises over Nagasaki, Japan, 9 August 1945. Taken from one of the B-29 "Super-fortresses" used in the attack, by Charles Levy (Wikimedia Commons).

Retrospective: Was the Outcome Worth the Cost?

Japan's formal surrender was signed in Tokyo Bay aboard the battleship U.S.S. *Missouri* on September 2, 1945. As B.H. Liddell Hart notes, it had been six years and a day since the war began with Germany's attack on Poland.[239] During the course of the war, seventy million soldiers were mobilized. Of these, an estimated 17 million (or nearly 25 percent) were killed.[240] When civilian casualties are included, the overall death toll is thought to have exceeded fifty million,[241] meaning that for the first time since the Thirty Years' War (1618–1648), civilian deaths surpassed military deaths in a major conflict between nations.[242]

The war ended in the destruction of the Nazi Reich and Japanese empire—outcomes conjointly held to be desirable by the United States, Great Britain and Russia. Unfortunately, there was very little else on which the members of the "Grand Alliance" were destined to agree—least of all on the fate of Eastern Europe. Here, it may be argued, the war ended not in a victory for the alliance, but for Russia alone, which was not at all the same thing; it meant that the chief achievement of the great six-year struggle was not primarily the ousting of Hitler's totalitarian dictatorship from Eastern Europe—the battleground where the war began—but its replacement by the equally insipid rule of Stalin. As Winston Churchill famously phrased it in 1946, an "iron curtain" had descended upon the continent, behind which the ancient capitals of Eastern Europe were abandoned to Soviet tyranny.[243]

In volume three of his *A Military History of the Western World* (1956), the British military historian, Major General J.F.C. Fuller, blamed this undesirable outcome on putative blunders committed during the war by the Western Allies—the most fatal being: (i) the immediate support afforded to Russia in the wake of Operation Barbarossa, without first gaining nonaggression assurances regarding Eastern Europe; (ii) the insistence on "unconditional surrender," which allegedly frightened our Axis enemies into fighting to the bitter end at a staggering cost in lives to both sides; (iii) the decision to complement Operation Overlord with Operation Dragoon—the landing of troops in southern France in August 1944—rather than committing those same resources to the ongoing campaign in Italy with the goal of pressing through the Ljubljana Gap into Austria and Hungary. (While Operation Dragoon, in Fuller's view, had no strategic purpose, the Ljubljana operation might have allowed the Western Allies to beat the Russians to "the strategic center of Europe" and thus establish a post-war European settlement on their own terms); and (iv) the conversion of the meeting of the Big Three at Yalta in February 1945 into a veritable "super-Munich" by Roosevelt's alleged decision to "give Stalin a free hand in Europe as a *quid pro quo*" for the latter's participation in the war against Japan (which, at the time of the meeting was still expected to cost the United States as many as one million casualties).[244]

Fuller was an extraordinary military thinker, whose works may still be read with profit. In reviewing *A Military History of the Western World,* the *Spectator* referred to him as "the most eminent living writer on war," while *History Today* prophesied that his "work will stand the test of time and will be consulted and quoted when the very name of Creasy has been forgotten."[245] During World War I, Fuller had served as GSO of the nascent British Tank Corps, authoring a paper, entitled "Tank Raids," which served as a blueprint for the battle of Cambrai—the first successful tank assault in history.[246] Between the wars, he pushed for the mechanization of the British Army. The British higher-ups would not listen, but the Nazis, Czechs and others—including Charles de Gaulle in France—did, and his theories became the basis for what we now call *blitzkrieg.* A prolific writer (he wrote a book on yoga in addition to his military treatises), he was also an occultist who spoiled his own reputation by joining Oswald Mosley's British Fascist Union in the 1930s, expressing anti–Semitic, pro–Nazi sympathies, and, worst of all, attending Hitler's 50th birthday parade (where we last encountered him in this book). Having retired from the army in 1933, he was the only officer of his rank *not* called back to service when the war broke out. For a time, MI5 kept an eye on him, but unlike other leading members of the British Fascist Union he was not arrested. (There has been speculation that he was protected by Churchill, who knew him and respected his military theories.)[247] His postwar writings, which reflected a rectification of his more pernicious pre-war attitudes, went far to restore his reputation. Even then, however, his biographer, Anthony John Trythall, referred to him (metaphorically) as "a lapsed Catholic brought back to his religion by force of circumstance but still from time to time unable to prevent his past doubts and heresies from appearing through the chinks in his new orthodoxy...."[248]

It is necessary to recount the disreputable aspects of Fuller's history so that the reader should not feel hoodwinked or be denied the opportunity (if so disposed) to dismiss his arguments on an ad hominem basis. However, all four of his objections to Allied policy have also been trumpeted rather stridently by others, and, therefore, seem worth considering.

Churchill faced the first objection—i.e., of providing aid to Russia without preconditions—as soon as he announced his policy, which he did in a radio address on the very day that Hitler launched Operation Barbarossa: "We have but one aim and one single, irrevocable purpose. We are resolved to destroy Hitler and every vestige of the Nazi regime.... We will never parley, we will never negotiate with Hitler or any of his gang.... Any man or state who fights on against Nazidom will have our aid.... Any man or state who marches with Hitler is our foe.... That is our policy and that is our declaration."[249] Churchill's private secretary, Jock Colville, was among the first to express shock at this pronouncement, asking how the prime minister, as a longstanding enemy of Bolshevism, could possibly lend support to Russia (which had, after all, swallowed half of Poland at the outset of the war). Churchill's riposte stands prominently on the list of his famous utterings: "If Hitler invaded the realms of Hell, I would find some way to make a favorable reference to the devil in the House of Commons."[250]

Might Churchill instead have demanded assurances from Stalin about Eastern Europe before offering British assistance? The argument cannot be dismissed out of hand, but it assumes that Churchill could already apprehend dangers that lay in the distant future, and more immediately, that he had a strong enough hand to play—which he did not. Hitherto, Britain had been fighting alone and had not been winning. America was not yet in the war. France had been conquered and there was little indication that the Soviet Union would not be. Indeed, as we have seen, just days after Hitler's invasion, Stalin withdrew to his villa in the throes of a nervous breakdown. Of necessity, Churchill's chief concern must be in bolstering Russia's determination to continue the fight in the face of staggering defeats. To wager on preconditions at this juncture was also to wager that Russia would not simply capitulate or be overrun. Moreover, even if the requisite conditions had been obtained, one may doubt whether Stalin would have felt obliged to honor them in 1945 if all other variables remained the same—i.e., if the war ended with millions of Russian dead and Russian armies occupying the whole of Eastern Europe.

Fuller's second thesis—regarding "unconditional surrender"—has, in many quarters, taken on the character of accepted wisdom. On the final page of his *History of the Second World War* (1970), B.H. Liddell Hart seconded the opinion that the policy prolonged the war to no strategic benefit and at great cost in lives, saying, "If the Allied leaders had been wise enough to provide some assurance as to their peace terms, Hitler's grip on the German people would have been loosened long before 1945."[251] Roosevelt biographer Joseph Alsop went further, saying in *FDR, A Centenary Remembrance* (1982), "It is generally acknowledged now that insistence on an enemy's unconditional surrender is never justified."[252] Even Dwight D. Eisenhower concurred, saying in a 1964 *Washington Post* interview that Hitler "used something from the mouth of our own leader and persuaded the Germans to fight longer than they might have."[253]

The eminent British historian, A.J.P. Taylor, however, says that such charges are "without substance." Given the nature of Hitler's aggression, replete with its atrocities, there could be no satisfactory outcome to the war that did not begin with the eradication of Nazism and the withdrawal of German troops from all conquered territories. No one on the German side—not even the anti–Hitler "German Resistance" (such as it existed)—was willing to concede this much. Thus, "'Unconditional Surrender' was not so much a policy as a recognition of facts."[254]

The implication of the policy, moreover, was not necessarily as dire as its detractors suggest. Within weeks of announcing it, both Roosevelt and Churchill publicly spelled out its limitations. In a radio address given to the American public on February 12, 1943, Roosevelt said that "In our uncompromising policy we mean no harm to the common people of the Axis nations. But we do mean to impose punishment and retribution in full upon their guilty, barbaric leaders...."[255] Similarly, on February 22, 1943, Churchill told the House of Commons, "Unconditional surrender means that the victors have a free hand. It does not mean that they are entitled to behave in a barbarous manner, nor that they wish to blot out Germany from among the nations of Europe. If we are bound, we are bound by our own consciences to civilization. We are not to be bound to the Germans by a bargain struck. That is the meaning of 'unconditional surrender.'"[256]

There is a contextual aspect, too. When Roosevelt promulgated his unconditional surrender policy at Casablanca in late January 1943, Stalin was still fighting the battle of Stalingrad in which Russia sustained more casualties than the United States did in the entire war. For the whole of the preceding year, the Russian leader had been pressing the Western Allies to open a second front in Europe. After conferring at Casablanca, however, FDR and Churchill were forced to inform him via telegram that they would not have the means for a cross-Channel attack until 1944, and that in the interim their chief effort would be confined to driving the Axis forces out of North Africa, to be followed, if all went well, by an assault on Europe's "soft underbelly" via the Mediterranean. Part of Roosevelt's purpose in announcing the policy, then, must have been to reassure Stalin that Britain and the U.S. were truly committed to fight to the finish, and that they meant to adhere to their joint declaration of January 1, 1942, whereby the three powers had pledged themselves not to pursue a separate peace.[257] Roosevelt was also determined that Germany should be given no "escape clause" such as that claimed at Versailles, when the German delegation complained that they had surrendered on the basis of Wilson's Fourteen Points only to be handed a Carthaginian peace—a mentality that set the stage for Hitler's rise.[258]

The most intriguing of Fuller's indictments is, perhaps, the one regarding Operation Dragoon—not the least because Churchill and most of the British High Command also believed that the Allies ought to have pressed ahead in Italy and then through the Ljubljana Gap rather than launching Dragoon in the late summer of 1944. Eisenhower insisted on Dragoon, in part, because he needed more ports at which to land supplies. (Marseille and Toulon were captured in the operation.) Leaving aside the fact that from a strategic standpoint it made far more sense to clear the Scheldt estuary of German troops so that Antwerp could be used, Fuller argues that Eisenhower might still have landed troops in southern France to take the ports, but that he should then have sent the entire force southeastwards *into Italy* via the alpine passes rather than northwards to link with the Overlord forces. In conjunction with the British and American forces advancing from southern Italy, they would have crushed Kesselring's army between hammer and anvil. Thereafter, they could have concentrated in Venetia for the push through Ljubljana into central Europe.[259]

Had it all gone according to plan, the Allies might have reached the Ljubljana approaches by early winter 1944. Instead of facing Eisenhower's single "broad front" in the West, Hitler would have been caught between two pincers, either one of which might have broken through to capture the "strategic spine" of Europe—Berlin, Prague and Vienna—ahead of the Russians. The timing, moreover, might have forced Hitler to dispense with the Ardennes Offensive (in which the Americans suffered a punishing 77,000 casualties) out of a need to divert troops southwards.

There is, however, another side to the ledger. Given everything that had transpired in Italy prior to the summer of 1944, the Ljubljana effort, if made, might as easily have encountered disaster as success. The Germans had been extremely adept at blocking the Allied advance in southern Italy. It can hardly have been beyond them to mount a similarly resilient defense in the 30-mile-wide Ljubljana Gap. Moreover, even if the Allies broke through, they would still have had to fight and win costly battles with the Germans to attain the desired strategic goal. The United States leadership was disposed to let Stalin fight those battles for them, and therefore showed little regard for what they mischaracterized as Churchill's "Balkan adventures."[260] As Roosevelt told his son Elliott during the Tehran Conference in late 1943, "The only thing I'm sure of is this: if the way to save American lives, the way to win as short a war as possible is from the west, and from the west alone, without wasting landing craft and men and materials in the Balkan mountains, and our chiefs are convinced it is, then that's that."[261]

The origin of the Western Allies' contrasting outlooks may be traced to the circumstances under which they entered the war. Britain declared war on September 3, 1939, in response to Hitler's invasion of Poland. While Roosevelt was certainly opposed to Nazi aggression and in favor of the freedom of peoples—as the Atlantic Charter would later demonstrate—the American public remained staunchly isolationist in the face of Poland's tragedy. Indeed, Roosevelt won reelection to an unprecedented third presidential term the following year largely on his promise to American parents that "your boys are not going to be sent into any foreign wars."[262] As a result, when the United States was attacked by Japan and entered the war in December 1941, Roosevelt's and Churchill's priorities differed somewhat in regard to balancing casualties against geopolitical goals. The differing emphasis was evident at the Yalta Conference in February 1945. Possessing clearer insight into the threat Stalin posed to Eastern Europe, Churchill spent much of the conference seeking a guarantee of free and fair elections in countries occupied by the Russian armies—most especially, Poland. Roosevelt's chief objective, in contrast, was to obtain Stalin's active participation in the war against Japan—again with the idea of reducing American casualties. In the end, Roosevelt obtained his object. Stalin agreed to enter the war against Japan no later than three months after the war with Germany ended. In return, he was given leave to reclaim all territories lost to Japan in the disastrous Russo-Japanese War of 1904–1905.[263] As regards Europe, however, the settlement was less satisfactory. Zones of occupation, decided prior to the conference, were now finalized. The "strategic spine" of Eastern Europe—Berlin, Prague and Vienna—was confirmed as lying in the Russian sphere.[264] In return, Stalin offered nebulous promises for free and fair elections in Russian-occupied areas, but as no machinery was established to enforce these promises, he did not live up to them.[265] Consequently, when Churchill pressed the Russian leader to allow joint supervision of Poland's elections by English, American and Russian commissioners, Stalin answered (with high hypocrisy) that the Poles would be offended by such "flagrant interference" in their domestic affairs.[266]

Bernard Montgomery joined Fuller in likening Yalta unto a second "Munich." Just as Hitler was mistaken for a gentleman in 1938, so, too, was Stalin in 1945.[267] Such a charge would be difficult to level at Churchill, who was keenly aware of the threat posed by Stalin. But Roosevelt once said of the Russian leader, "I think if I give him everything that I possibly can and ask nothing from him in return, noblesse oblige, he won't try to annex anything and will work for a world of democracy and peace,"[268] and on the basis of such statements, he has been accused of "giving away" Eastern Europe out of sheer naiveté. FDR biographer Fiona Venn disagrees with this assessment, saying that Roosevelt "did no more than recognize realities; to argue that he 'gave away' Eastern Europe is to assume that it was his to give away. Cold logic—the logic of an occupying Red Army—dictated that Stalin would have a preeminent voice in the settlement of Eastern Europe. Short of outright war against the Soviets, the Western powers could do little more than acquiesce. And with the war in the Pacific still to be won, the alienation of Stalin was not to be lightly undertaken."[269]

When the Yalta Conference adjourned, Roosevelt had but two months to live. It was long enough for any remaining scales regarding Stalin to fall from his eyes. Recuperating from illness in Warm Springs, Georgia, on March 23, 1945, he exclaimed, "We can't do business with Stalin. He has broken every one of the promises he made at Yalta."[270] A temptation subsequently arose to return the favor. On April 13, 1945, one day after Roosevelt died, United States forces under General Omar Bradley and British forces under Bernard Montgomery took 325,000 German troops prisoner in the "Ruhr Pocket." The Russians took Vienna on the same day, but as Bradley later wrote, if the United States had been willing to take the requisite casualties, they could still have beaten the Russians to Berlin.[271] Montgomery certainly thought it should be done. (As Andrew Roberts notes, he counted the failure to try as one of the "five capital mistakes" made by America in the course of the war.[272]) So, too, did Churchill, who told Eisenhower in early April, "I deem it highly important that we should shake hands with the Russians as far to the east as possible" (i.e., in order to limit Soviet postwar influence).[273] Eisenhower expressed his understanding, but in the event decided that the "function of our forces must be to crush the German armies rather than dissipate our strength in the occupation of empty ruined cities."[274] He had already discussed the situation with army chief-of-staff, George C. Marshall, who concurred, saying, "Personally, and aside from any logistical, tactical, or strategical implications, I would be loath to hazard American lives for purely political purposes."[275] A chance to take Prague was similarly rejected during the first week of May.[276]

Given that the war broke out over Hitler's invasion of Poland and that it ended in the imposition of totalitarian puppet regimes throughout Eastern Europe, the question naturally arises as to whether the results achieved had been worth the cost in blood and treasure. In the course of the war, however, the Soviet Union suffered 27 million killed in comparison to 418,000 American and 449,000 British deaths in all theaters.[277] As Lee Baker comments, "The effort to destroy the Nazi threat, from the Soviet viewpoint, was a Soviet victory achieved by the blood of the Soviet people. And yet the western half of Europe was occupied by the United States and Britain as they evicted the *Wehrmacht* from those countries. The victory therefore had to be shared...."[278]

Was it then a victory at all? In the introduction to Hillsdale College's online course on World War II, College President Larry P. Arnn posits that the ultimate answer depends upon what was at stake in the war. And in answer to this, he poses a second question—one put forward by Winston Churchill: "Do[es] the government own the people or do the people own the government?"[279] The war's most obvious mixed result—the descent upon Eastern Europe of the "iron curtain" and the consequent birth of the Cold War—had its origin in the fact that the United States and Great Britain believed the latter proposition (i.e., that people ought to hold sway over their governments), while Stalinist Russia, as a totalitarian tyranny, believed the opposite.[280] While Stalin could claim his share of the victory on the grounds that he gained control of Eastern Europe and substantial territory in the Far East, irrespective of the human cost, the Western Allies might also claim victory—an imperfect one, perhaps, but one attained on loftier ground—for they had liberated Western Europe and much of Asia from fascist totalitarianism while remaining cognizant of the blood sacrifice their populations were called upon to endure in the process.

14

Societal Achievements, 1914–1945

The chief accomplishment of early 20th-century physics was to ruin everything for everyone. At the dawn of the century, as Wallbank and Taylor note, Victorian society believed in the certainty of its moral values, the inevitability of progress and the functioning of the Universe as something very like a "world machine,"[1] never deviating from the immutable laws of motion worked out by Isaac Newton (1642–1726) or from the immutable equations of electromagnetism worked out by James Clerk Maxwell (1831–1879).[2] Although the atom, which, hitherto, had been thought to be the smallest unit of matter ("atom" being Greek for "indivisible") had been found to contain an even smaller particle—the "electron"—in 1897, this was held to be of little account by most people in their day to day lives. The same could not be said, however, when Max Planck (1858–1947) proposed a new equation relating how the energy emitted by an object of a given temperature—we may take our sun as an example—corresponds to the frequency of the oscillating electromagnetic "waves" of which that energy is composed.

Planck's formula, $E = hf$, looks harmless enough, but it destroyed the entire edifice of the world. To understand this, we must break the equation down into its component parts. The E in the equation stands for "energy," and the f stands for "frequency." Neither of these is the problem. The h is the problem. It stands for "Planck's Constant." As the name implies, it is a *fixed* number—very small ($6.62607004 \times 10^{-34}\text{m}^2\text{kg/s}$)—but *fixed*. Hence, what Planck's formula says is that when the sun (or anything else) radiates its energy, if you divide the amount of energy emitted by the number of cycles the energy oscillates through per second[3] you will always get the *same number*. So, what, you say? Well, what it all means is that when the sun radiates its energy, it does not do so in continuous waves (as was previously known to be immutably "true"), but rather in discontinuous units, or "quanta"—all of which are exact multiples of $6.62607004 \times 10^{-34}\text{m}^2\text{kg/s}$. A brief analogy provided by Paul Looyen and based upon climbing a staircase may prove illuminating. While it is possible to climb a staircase one stair at a time, or even two or three or four stairs at a time, it is most definitely impossible to climb a staircase 1.7 stairs at a time. The physics of the staircase simply won't allow for it, and the person who attempts to defy this "first law of staircases" will make himself a tempting target for the serious-injury gods. In equivalent fashion, the physics of electromagnetic radiation won't allow for the radiation of energy in quantities that are not divisible by Planck's Constant. The energy is therefore emitted in particles or packets, not in waves.[4]

To make it all just a little less clear, in 1913, the Danish physicist, Niels Bohr, determined that, within the atom, an electron that absorbs or releases such a quantum of energy can move from one atomic orbit to another without crossing the space in between—the process being known as a "quantum leap."[5] (Slower out of the gate was Werner Heisenberg, who only informed the world in 1927 of his "uncertainty principle," proving that one could not know the precise position of a moving electron and its precise velocity at one and the same time.)

When Planck announced his new "quantum theory" at the Prussian Academy of Sciences in 1901, there was stunned silence until a member of the assembly shouted, "Gentlemen, this is *not* physics!" and stormed out of the room.[6] Four years later, Sir James Jeans put the finishing touches on an equation that was first conceived by Sir James Rayleigh in 1900, which was meant to express this same relationship (i.e., between energy emitted by a body at a given temperature and its electromagnetic frequency) by relying solely on the classical physics of Newton and Maxwell (which dictate that *mass*, and *mass* alone, is composed of particles, while *energy* is emitted in waves).[7] Their equation—known as the "Rayleigh-Jeans Equation"—which looks for all the world as if it was assembled using symbols chosen at random from the Rosetta Stone, proved highly accurate for low-frequency energy emission, as occurs, say, with a lightbulb, but was increasingly inaccurate when it came to objects emitting mostly high-frequency energy, such as the sun. Indeed, as the accompanying figure shows, on moving toward the very high-frequency end of the electromagnetic spectrum (i.e., into the range of ultraviolet, X-ray or gamma radiation) the equation predicts that the energy emitted should continue increasing to the point of infinity when in truth (as the experimentally derived, off-center bell-shaped curves show), it reaches a peak and then declines. So awry was the answer given by the Rayleigh-Jeans Equation at these high frequency wavelengths that it came to be known ever afterwards as the "ultraviolet catastrophe." Even so, it was a very important milestone in physics, for it showed that Planck had got it right, and the fellow who stormed out of the Prussian Academy had got it wrong.

In the same year that Rayleigh and Jeans produced their equation, Albert Einstein deduced his "special theory of relativity" from the fact that the speed of light is constant at 186,000 miles per second—even if viewed from the Earth as it rotates on its axis and hurtles through space. The speed of light, in other words, is an unvarying law of nature. This might, at first, seem reassuring, but because speed (also called "velocity") equals distance divided by time, and the speed of light is constant, Einstein's theory implied that observers moving at different velocities will have a different experience of time elapsed and distance traveled. Stated differently, time and distance are *not* the unvarying laws of nature that anyone with a modicum of sense formerly believed them to be. Rather, they vary with the velocity of the system in which they are measured. Hence, to take an example offered by Crane Brinton et al., if a traveler embarked from Earth on a 6-month round trip into space, flying along at 90 percent of the speed of light for the entire journey, his fellow Earthlings would have to tell him upon his return (gently, one would hope) that a whole year had elapsed since his departure, not 6 months. (The distance traveled would likewise differ when calculated by the traveler and by an observer on earth.)[8] Einstein's breakthrough transformed what Newtonian physicists had thought to be a three-dimensional world of height, length and depth, into a four-dimensional "space-time continuum" in which "time" constituted a fourth dimension.

Now, if we take everything physicists had been reassuring everyone about for more than two hundred years, tear it all asunder, and then pile on four years of carnage in the

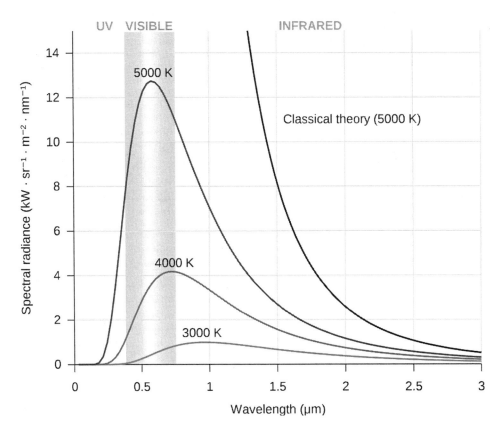

The "ultraviolet catastrophe" predicted by classical theory (Rayleigh-Jeans Equation) shows the curve of spectral radiance moving towards infinity as the wavelength shortens. Planck's Formula (exemplified by the three off-center bell-shaped curves) correctly predicts results found experimentally. Darth Kule (Wikimedia Commons).

trenches, the collapse of four European empires[9] and the partitioning of those empires into a hodgepodge of nations that had not been on the map only the day before (without, however, always including the right people in the right nations or giving everyone a nation who thought he should have one) and then mix in a worldwide pandemic—the Spanish Flu of 1918–1920 (which took more lives than the Great War itself)—we may begin to understand why there was a great deal less certainty in the world of 1920 than there had been in the world of 1900. We may understand, too, why, at the unveiling of a statue honoring his renowned grandfather, Thomas Huxley (the so-called "Bulldog of Darwinism," who in his day had been absolutely, positively certain about everything)— his six-year-old grandson, Aldous, might vomit into his hat, and then grow up to experiment with LSD and write *Brave New World*.[10]

The intolerable uncertainty came to be reflected in all sorts of things, most especially in art and literature. In the former, for example, it gave rise to "Cubism," which expanded upon Cézanne's dictum that "everything in nature adheres to the cone, cylinder or cube," not just to provide a new method of depicting a three dimensional scene on a two-dimensional canvas (as Cézanne had done), but also to depict a scene *from multiple vantage points* at one and the same time[11] (something that God never intended man to do, as a mere glance at the example provided will attest). This explains why a

Cubism: *Man in a Café* by Juan Gris, 1912. Philadelphia Museum of Art (Wikimedia Commons).

seemingly bright fellow like Picasso painted both of his subject's eyes on the same side of the nose so often (and to be a bit less irreverent, why "Cubism" remains an enduring testament to artistic forms of expression that cannot be produced merely by taking a photograph).

In literature, the implosion of all things gave rise to the experimental "stream of consciousness" novel—the chief exemplar of which was James Joyce's *Ulysses* (although one can get a general idea from his *Portrait of the Artist as a Young Man*, which has the merciful advantage of being shorter). Amid all the confusion and tumult, it is hardly surprising that Oswald Spengler, a nationalistic German historian, should produce a two-volume tome predicting the imminent collapse of Western civilization (*The Decline of the West*, 1922), or that people should be confused as to why anyone would have thought that 1919 was the proper year to pass Prohibition, or that T.S. Eliot should encapsulate the mindset of an entire generation in a poem, entitled *The Waste Land*, about the meaninglessness of human existence (1922), or that anyone who knew up from down spent the entire decade of the "Roaring Twenties" enormously drunk (Prohibition or no) until the Depression brought the merry-go-round to a screeching halt and forced everyone to sober up to the very uncertainty they had been seeking to escape.[12]

What takes hold of a society at such times, says the political philosopher Erich Fromm, is anxiety—anxiety that one has been left out or left behind by events and is therefore alone ("atomized" in the terminology of fellow philosopher, Hannah Arendt). Under such circumstances individual liberty becomes an affliction rather than a blessing, and the individual longs for escape into something that will provide meaning, or—what is more—a feeling of power. If a society is reasonably healthy, one might find such an escape in a fireside chat from Roosevelt and a new job from the WPA, or perhaps in an assurance from Churchill that we shall all "muddle through." If such empathetic gestures suffice in restoring a sense of dignity and belonging, individual liberty again becomes tolerable. If not, notes the Israeli historian J.L. Talmon, another type of escape presents itself—one in which the individual decides to surrender his or her personal liberty for a putative "collective" liberty provided by the state.

The above ideas (and a good many others) are outlined in a fascinating *Internet Encyclopedia of Philosophy* article entitled "Totalitarianism," by Eric B. Litwack, which summarizes what several leading philosophers—Arendt, Fromm, Talmon and Karl Popper among them—had to say about totalitarianism's nature and origins.[13] Before taking the conversation further, however, it will be useful to introduce two additional notions. The first is humankind's enduring desire for panaceas. The second is what Karl Popper termed "historicism." A quintessential example of the first can be found in the 18th-century Enlightenment, during which Europe's intelligentsia, spurred on by Newton's rational discovery of the laws of motion and universal gravitation, concluded that immutable laws might be found in all fields of human endeavor by the application "Reason." Reason was the panacea. Immutable laws were the common ideal. As it turns out, however, once you get beyond mathematics and certain scientific disciplines, there is very little else in the human experience that comes even close to being guided by immutable laws. Hence, when the Scottish adventurer, John Law, thought he had reasoned everything out in the field of economics, he produced the "Mississippi Bubble," which led to modern Europe's first stock market crash (1720).

As to the second notion—"historicism"—we have already mentioned an example in Oswald Spengler's *Decline of the West*. In it, Spengler looked back at history and determined that all previous cultures—take, for example, the Roman empire—had flourished, reached a peak, and then declined and fallen. He deduced from this that all cultures of the present and future must also do so—in effect pronouncing the decline and fall of cultures to be an immutable law of history. The idea that history is governed by immutable laws is called "historical determinism"—and the benefit it offers is that it allows one to predict with "certainty" what will happen in the future. By employing it to prophesize what was in store for the West in 1922, Spengler could say with confidence that the West had advanced so far along the highway of decline that the end must necessarily be nigh.

Having introduced these ideas, we can return to our anxious, atomized individual who imagines his or her individual liberty to be a burden and is seeking to trade it to the first person who can provide a suitable panacea for the putative anxiety-ridden, meaninglessness of his or her life. To such an individual, the idea that history is governed by laws that are leading towards some predetermined outcome might have some utility. But in bartering one's individual liberty for a panacea, he or she won't turn to Oswald Spengler's brand of historicism, because Spengler predicts only decline and death. Our individual will turn instead to someone like Jean-Jacques Rousseau, who promises in return a utopian society governed by "the general will," or to Karl Marx, who promises a "proletarian" utopia.

The proper medium to seek a Rousseau-style panacea was the Enlightenment—and with the attempt to implement his "solution" during the French Revolution the world obtained its first glimpse of modern totalitarianism. A totalitarian regime shall have no other gods before it, and therefore seeks to sever traditional bonds. Consequently, things like religious faith must be undermined. In revolutionary France, this was accomplished by such expedients as making the priesthood elective (with voting open to all, including people of differing denominations or even atheists) and re-dating the calendar so that 1792 (the year of the declaration of the French Republic) became the year "One." Further erasure of traditional bonds was accomplished by beheading the king and queen, renaming the months after seasonal themes and transforming the seven-day week into a ten-day "decade" (which fit much better with the new metric system). Any objections to such obliteration of tradition were dealt with then just as they were to be in later incarnations of totalitarianism—by terror.

The milieu of 20th-century totalitarianism was rather different from that of the French Revolution. As we have seen, at the dawn of the century, the immutable laws of Newtonian physics had been shown, at least in some instances, to be insufficient for the explanation of all physical phenomena—something that gave the Enlightenment approach something of a bad name. The 19th century, however, provided a new opportunity to misapply important scientific discoveries by producing its own Newtonian-scale breakthrough—namely, Darwin's theory of evolution (replete with its catchphrases "natural selection" and "survival of the fittest"). Just as Newton's revelations in physics during the 17th century were misapplied during the Enlightenment of the 18th, so, too, would Darwin's extraordinary achievement be perverted into the "Social Darwinist" panaceas of the 19th and 20th. Thus, Karl Marx's historicism, predicting the inevitable emergence of a proletarian utopia, was now seemingly buttressed by the misapplication of the catchphrase "survival of the fittest" to class conflict. Indeed, Marx was so enthralled with Darwin's theory that he offered to dedicate *Das Kapital* to him.[14] Nazism, in turn, misapplied the catchphrase to race.

Nineteenth century imperialism and the 20th-century clash of nations in the World Wars can likewise be viewed in Social Darwinist terms, but nationalism and imperialism feel most at home in the realm of conservatism (albeit of an authoritarian stripe), and here we are addressing the question of totalitarianism—an entity that may be seen as the very antithesis of conservatism. According to Hannah Arendt's works, *The Origins of Totalitarianism* (1951) and *Eichmann in Jerusalem: A Report on the Banality of Evil* (1963), what occurs under totalitarianism is the erasure of such things as traditional cultural bonds (including those between family and friends), ethical standards and critical thinking, and its replacement by ideology and propaganda as the sole binding glue for society's atomized citizens.[15] As noted earlier, terror is the necessary instrument used to bring about this "utopian" revolution. Consequently, says Litwack, the "twentieth century totalitarian state" became "what is undoubtedly the greatest intellectual justification for mass murder in history."[16] Even true believers are not safe in such societies, for as Arendt explains, "The ideal subject of totalitarian rule is not the convinced Nazi or the convinced Communist, but people for whom the distinction between fact and fiction (that is, the reality of experience) and the distinction between true and false (that is, the standards of thought) no longer exist."[17] Once society has been remade in this image, the individual is reduced to an automaton, and what was formerly regarded as "unthinkable" becomes "not just possible, but probable and even banal."[18]

Comparing totalitarianism to older forms of tyranny in 1941, George Orwell cited the example of the Medieval Church, saying that it may have "dictated what you should believe, but at least it allowed you to retain the same beliefs from birth to death. It did not tell you to believe one thing on Monday and another on Tuesday." Totalitarianism, in contrast, "sets up unquestionable dogmas, and alters them from day to day," and thereby "attacks the very concept of objective truth."[19] Taking contemporary Bolshevism as a case in point, Winston Churchill similarly observed in a 1925 address entitled "Mass Effects in Modern Life," that in such societies, the "individual becomes a function: the community is alone of interest ... thoughts dictated and propagated by the rulers are the only thoughts deemed respectable. No one is to think of himself as an immortal spirit, clothed in the flesh...." How, then, is the individual to view himself? Churchill answers: "In Soviet Russia we have a society which seeks to model itself upon the Ant. There is not one single social or economic principle or concept in the philosophy of the Russian Bolshevik which has not been realized, carried into action and enshrined in immutable laws a million years ago by the White Ant."

"But human nature," says Churchill, "is more intractable than ant-nature. The explosive nature of its phenomena disturb the smooth working out of the laws and forces which have subjugated the White Ant. It is at once the safeguard and the glory of mankind that they are easy to lead and hard to drive."[20] And on this more promising note, we will shift gears to examine some of the positive accomplishments that came to pass in the period under study despite the era's many uncertainties—not the least of them on the basis of the "individual," as opposed to the "collective," pursuit of excellence.

Exploration and Aviation

The quest for achievement may call upon the individual to show creativity or daring, but its most universal demand is for persistence in the face of adversity. It is, therefore, fitting to begin our discussion with Ernest Henry Shackleton's famous voyage on the *Endurance*—the last expedition of the "Heroic Age" of Polar exploration. Born in County Kildare, Ireland, Shackleton (1874–1922) was groomed by his physician-father to become a doctor, but at 16 he rebelled in favor of seafaring, ultimately earning his certificate as a "master mariner" in 1898. Three years later, he participated in Robert Falcon Scott's first attempt to reach the South Pole but became extremely ill along the way and had to bow out. He returned at the head of his own expedition in 1907 and came within 97 miles of being the first to attain the elusive polar goal before hostile conditions brought the trek to an end. Eventually beaten to the Pole by Roald Amundsen and the ill-fated Scott (1911), Shackleton conceived the new ambition of being the first to *cross* Antarctica—proposing to do so along the continent's narrow waistline between the Ross and Weddell Seas, visiting the South Pole en route.

The expedition was due to set sail in August 1914 when World War I broke out. Shackleton immediately offered to cancel his preparations and donate his two ships to the war effort, but the First Lord of the Admiralty, Winston Churchill, sent him a telegram with the single word, "Proceed."[21] The result was one of history's great, if unintended, survival adventures. Shackleton's team set out in two parties—one heading to the Ross Sea, where it was to make landfall and strike inland toward the Pole to establish supply depots for the second leg of the journey (i.e., from the South Pole to the Ross Sea), while Shackleton's own party, consisting of 28 men—one of whom was a stowaway[22]—was to land on the opposite side of the continent to begin the actual transcontinental trek from the coastline of the Weddell Sea. Unfortunately, before reaching the coast, Shackleton's ship, the *Endurance*, became trapped in the pack ice off Coat's Land (January 15, 1915), where it remained, drifting icebound in a northwesterly direction for ten months and three days, until the ice crushed it to pieces and swallowed it off Palmer Land near the opposite shore of the Weddell Sea (November 21, 1915).

To conserve food during the months adrift, the expedition party had to shoot the nearly seventy dogs (and one cat) they had brought. An attempt to walk across the pack ice toward land made little better than a mile a day and had to be abandoned. The group therefore camped alongside their three lifeboats and their sleds and waited for the ice to break up. On April 9, 1916, it did so within view of tiny Elephant Island, toward which they duly embarked—reaching it after a grueling seven-day journey at sea. It was their first foothold on actual land in nearly 500 days.[23]

There was, however, no chance that anyone would find them there, so Shackleton had the ship's carpenter, Chippy McNeish, fashion a wood and canvas deck for one of the three lifeboats—the *James Caird*. Thus fortified against sinking, Shackleton set off with five others for the Stromness Whaling Station on the island of South Georgia 800 miles away. For sixteen days, the little boat was tossed about like a cork in the gigantic waves. "Deep seemed the valleys when we lay between the reeling seas," wrote Shackleton afterwards. "High were the hills when we perched momentarily on the tops of giant combers."[24] Thanks to a magician-like job of navigation by Frank Arthur Worsley, skipper of the lost *Endurance*, the boat arrived safely at South Georgia with its crew of six. The whaling station was on the opposite side of the island, thereby necessitating an inland march across a mountain range never before traversed—a feat achieved in just 36 hours (May 20, 1916). After convincing the station manager that he was, indeed, Ernest Shackleton, the explorer asked his first question, "Tell me, when was the war over?" The manager said in reply, "The war is not over. Millions are being killed. Europe is mad. The world is mad."[25]

Shackleton and crew set off from Elephant Island for the island of South Georgia, April 1916. Underwood & Underwood (Wikimedia Commons).

Of course, there remained the tricky business of rescuing the 22 expedition members still subsisting on the occasional penguin or seal on Elephant Island 800 miles away (who, we may note, had no knowledge of Shackleton's success, and thus no knowledge of when, or if, they might be rescued). Two efforts to reach them proved unavailing due to frozen seas, but on August 30, 1916, all 22 were taken aboard the Chilean rescue ship *Yelcho* where they were greeted by Shackleton, and two other members of the group that had set off on the *James Caird* more than four months before. Not a man had been lost in the long ordeal. The leadership of Shackleton and Frank Wild (the expedition's second in command who was left in charge on Elephant Island) had been critical to this outcome.

When Shackleton died of a heart attack on his last expedition (1922), the "Heroic Age" of Polar exploration died with him. This did not, however, prevent the spinning of other exciting tales of adventure—nor of adventurous catastrophes. On May 9, 1926, navigator Richard E. Byrd and pilot, Floyd Bennett, set out from Spitsbergen, Norway, to fly over the North Pole in a three-engine Fokker monoplane. They returned in just under 16 hours reporting success. For their efforts, they each received the United States Medal of Honor. But they may not actually have achieved their objective. The flying time didn't match up. It ought to have put them more than 100 miles short (a calculation that was seemingly confirmed when Byrd's flight logbook, made public in 1996, was found to have suspicious erasures and corrections).[26] They had, in fact, made their hasty flight in a bid to reach the Pole ahead of the famed explorer, Roald Amundsen, who repeated the feat three days later in the dirigible, *Norge*, accompanied by the Italian aeronautical engineer and dirigible designer, Umberto Nobile. (Given the doubts about Robert Peary's 1909 overland trek to the Pole, Amundsen and Nobile may, in truth, have been first to get there.)

Richard Byrd, however, was hardly out of the adventure game. His North Pole pilot, Floyd Bennett, died of pneumonia in 1928 after rescuing three German flyers who had downed their plane in a bog on Greenly Island in Canada.[27] The following year, on November 28, 1929, Byrd, piloting a plane named the *Floyd Bennett* after his fallen colleague, with three others aboard, became the first to fly over the South Pole—this time with no questions. On his return, he was promoted to the rank of Rear Admiral and received the Navy Cross.[28]

Umberto Nobile, too, continued his adventures. On May 4, 1928, he returned to the North Pole in a new 350-foot-long dirigible, the *Italia*. After holding a ceremony high above the objective—during which the national flag of Italy and a large oaken cross (donated by Pope Pius XI) were dropped to the ice surface below[29]—Nobile and his crew began their return journey. Their progress, however, was hampered by fierce headwinds and heavy fog, until finally, without explanation, at 10:30 a.m. on May 25, the ship lurched into an uncontrollable tail-first dive, crashing onto the ice, where the cabin splintered free, leaving the dirigible superstructure to be swept skyward again by the winds, carrying six crew members to oblivion. On the ground, Nobile, whose leg was broken, and eight others (nine, if we include Nobile's pet fox terrier, Titina) were alive, but marooned. (One crew member had been killed on impact.) There ensued an ordeal, lasting two months. Five days into it, three of the men decided to set out on foot to seek help. (One, the expedition's Swedish meteorologist, Finn Malmgren, would perish. The other two were ultimately rescued—but not until July 12.) At the crash site, huddled beneath an expedition tent—painted red so that it could be seen more easily from the air—the remaining six men sent distress signals with a damaged radio and waited.[30] One of their plaintive signals was finally heard on June 3, by Nikolai Schmidt, an amateur shortwave radio hobbyist in remotest Russia, who alerted the government in Moscow by telegraph.[31] A number of rescue parties were promptly organized. Roald Amundsen, who considered Nobile an attention-seeker and did not like him, nonetheless set out by plane with five others on June 18 on one of these attempts. Alas, the plane vanished over the Barents Sea, leaving only some scattered debris to announce its fate.[32]

A Swedish aviator, Einar-Paal Lundborg, finally spotted the red tent on June 24—landing his ski-plane close by. The flyer insisted on taking Nobile away first. Nobile protested, but allowed himself to be convinced on the assurance that Lundborg would return forthwith to fetch another member of the party.[33] Lundborg was good to his word, but he crashed on returning to the tent and was stranded with the others for nearly three weeks while hostile weather prevented a general rescue—something that was not accomplished until July 12 by the Russian icebreaker, *Krasin*, commanded by Rudolf Samoylovich.

Nobile was received with popular adulation on his return to Italy,[34] but was officially pilloried by a Fascist commission of inquiry on a charge of abandoning his crew on the ice. (The Fascist government felt itself scandalized by the outcome of the expedition and by the death of Amundsen.) Nobile's name would be cleared in a second inquiry only after Mussolini's fall. (The fate of Rudolf Samoylovich, commander of the *Krasin*, and poor Nikolai Schmidt was far worse. They were executed in Stalin's purges of the late 1930s.[35])

The *Italia* was hardly the most famous airship to crash during this era—a distinction that goes, hands down, to the *Hindenburg*, which burst into flames when its hydrogen ignited above the airfield at Lakehurst, New Jersey, on May 6, 1937. The disaster, which was captured on newsreel (replete with Herbert Morrison's horrified lament, "Oh, the humanity!") received international attention and is credited with putting an end to the dirigible era. On the ground below, naval personnel can be seen running into the flames to rescue survivors. Their initial impulse had been to run in the opposite direction, but their commander, "Bull" Tobin, had called them to their duty, which they performed heroically.[36]

Twelve years earlier, Tobin had survived another airship disaster—that of the USS *Shenandoah*. Commanded by Zachary Lansdowne, the 680-foot dirigible took off from the airfield at Lakehurst on September 2, 1925, to begin a multi-city publicity tour. The following day, it ran into a squall line over Noble County, Ohio, which flung the ship up and down by as much as 3,000 feet before shearing it apart. Fourteen crew members were killed—six in freefall and eight (Lansdowne among them) in the control cabin, which plummeted 6,000 feet to the ground. The front end of the dirigible descended lightly enough for 18 crewmen to survive, while the tail section still had its gas cylinders intact and was safely piloted to the ground in the fashion of an aeronautical balloon by another ten survivors.[37]

In a court-martial the following year, Lansdowne's wife testified that her husband had opposed the publicity tour because of the unpredictable seasonal weather along the intended route and that he had written a letter to that effect to his superiors. She stated further that the Navy had attempted to make her say otherwise during a post-crash inquiry.[38] It was not the Navy, however that was on trial at the court-martial. Rather, it was U.S. Army Brigadier General William "Billy" Mitchell—the "Father of the United States Air Force."

Mitchell began his military career as an enlistee during the Spanish American War (1898). Drawn to aviation at the outbreak of World War I, he was initially rejected as a pilot due to his "advanced" age—he was 38. Undeterred, he paid for his own lessons to obtain a pilot's license and got his chance to fly anyway. At the Battle of St. Mihiel in 1918, he commanded 1,481 American and French planes in a mass bombing raid against German ground positions.[39] A gifted visionary, he was already advocating for strategic bombing and airborne (paratrooper) operations by war's end.[40] His enhanced vision, however, got him into increasing trouble. After the war, he campaigned for the creation of an independent air force, telling Congress (and the press) that America's current equipment was obsolete, outclassed by that of every other major nation. He stated, in addition, that in the next war battleships would be vulnerable to attack from the air. The Navy vehemently disagreed with the latter claim, but Mitchell would not relent, and the Navy grudgingly permitted him to attempt a demonstration. A supposedly unsinkable German battleship, captured intact during the war, was provided for the occasion. In July 1921, Mitchell successfully bombed it and sent it to the bottom. The Navy protested, saying he had only succeeded "by exceeding the parameter" outlined for the demonstration.[41] Mitchell answered by repeating the feat in 1923. Afterwards, he toured the Pacific, returning with the prediction that the Japanese would one day attack Pearl Harbor from the air and that the attack would occur on a Sunday morning (1924).[42] His prophesy was "rewarded" with a demotion to colonel and transfer to Fort Sam Houston in San Antonio, Texas (where the soldiers, regarding him as a hero, continued to address him as "General" Mitchell).[43] Five months later, the *Shenandoah* went down, and Mitchell went public with his criticisms, telling the press that "Brave airmen are being sent to their deaths by armchair admirals who don't care about air safety,"[44] and accusing the top brass of "incompetency, criminal negligence, and almost treasonable administration of the national defense."[45] The result was the convening of the aforementioned court-martial, which ended on December 17, 1925, with Mitchell being found guilty of insubordination. (Only one judge dissented: Douglas MacArthur, the youngest member of the panel.[46])

The trial created a public sensation, thrusting Mitchell's ideas into the limelight. Forced to resign his commission, he continued his advocacy as a civilian. He died in 1936, but his predictions were borne out in the Second World War during which his theories found practical application. Although his guilty verdict was never overturned, Mitchell did receive much posthumous recognition. The B25 "Mitchell" bombers used in the 1942 Doolittle Raid over Tokyo were named in tribute to him, and after the war he received a Congressional gold medal and a posthumous promotion to major general from Harry Truman. His dream of an independent United States Air Force was realized in 1947.

While Mitchell became the object of increasing reverence with the passage of time, another famed aviator of the era managed to achieve the opposite. A year and a half after Mitchell's court-martial, Charles Lindbergh became the first man to cross the Atlantic nonstop by air, flying 3,600 miles in the single engine *Spirit of St. Louis*, thereby winning a $25,000 competition for which Richard Byrd had also been a contestant. The plane's gas tank impeded the view from the cockpit, necessitating the installation of a periscope so that Lindbergh could see what was ahead of him during the flight.[47] Four aviators had died and two more had disappeared in prior attempts to achieve the crossing, but at 10:22 p.m. on May 21, 1927, after 33 and ½ hours flying time, Lindbergh landed success-fully in the darkness at Le Bourget Airport in Paris, where his plane was thronged by more than 100,000 delirious enthusiasts who proceeded to bear him about the airfield on their shoulders.[48]

According to the historian Felix Gilbert, "Lindbergh's feat touched the heart of the twentieth century in two ways: human pride in the continued existence of individual heroism and in advances in science and technology."[49] For a time, he was the most famous man in the world, but a little more than a decade later, he ruined it all by accepting a medal from (and praising the accomplishments of) the Nazi Regime after touring its military aircraft facilities in 1938 (the year of Munich and *kristallnacht*), writing a frankly racist article on aviation for *Reader's Digest* (1939) and preaching defeatism as a member of the isolationist America First Committee. On September 11, 1941, Lindbergh dealt the death blow to his once admirable persona by delivering a speech in Des Moines, Iowa, in which he blamed British and Jewish influence (along with the Roosevelt administration) for "pressing this country toward war."[50]

A decade or so earlier, while still at the height of his fame, Lindbergh convinced the philanthropic Guggenheim family to provide funding for the research of one Robert Hutchins Goddard of Worcester, Massachusetts. It may be counted as one of his more laudable actions, for Goddard is known today as the "Father of American Rocketry."

Drawn to the idea of space flight from the age of 15, when he read a serialized version of H.G. Wells' *War of the Worlds* in the Boston Post (a book, incidentally, that he reread annually throughout his adult life),[51] Goddard attempted his first powder-propelled rocket launch from the basement of the physics building at Worcester Polytechnic Institute while still an undergraduate. It seems to have achieved little other than to fill the basement with smoke.[52] Over the ensuing years, he filled notebooks with his calculations, envisioning a rocket propelled by gunpowder with a machine gun-type mechanism that would fire cartridges at intervals to provide periodic propulsion.[53] Although he took time out to invent a prototype bazooka for the army during World War I—the war ended before it could be employed—his mind remained fixed on reaching space. Helped by funding from the Smithsonian Institution, he produced a paper in 1919, entitled "A Method of Reaching Extreme Altitudes." It consisted mostly of academic minutia, but also summarized his experimental data showing that rocket propulsion was possible in a vacuum—and thus in space. As an intriguing afterthought, he added that a rocket thus propelled might reach the moon. The Smithsonian's subsequent press release created the false impression that his "moon rocket" would soon be completed, provoking a media craze that greatly embarrassed him. There followed a contemptuous *New York Times* editorial pronouncing propulsion in space an impossibility owing to Newton's Third Law (i.e., on actions producing equal and opposite reactions—which wasn't thought to apply in a vacuum where there is nothing to react *against*) and declaring Goddard ignorant of basic high school physics. (The *Times* did apologize; not until 50 years later, it is true, but the *Times* can't be blamed for that since Goddard's "moon rocket" wasn't ready until then—Apollo 11 being en route to the moon when the apology appeared in 1969.[54])

Despite the ill attention, Goddard pressed on with his work, carrying out the first successful liquid-fueled rocket launch in 1926. His wife stood by with a movie camera to immortalize the moment, which is now ranked alongside the Wright Brothers' flight at Kitty Hawk in significance.[55] The rocket soared to an altitude of 41 feet, achieved a peak velocity of 60 miles per hour and crashed to earth some 180 feet away, but the same principle would take us into space.

In subsequent years, Goddard continued his research, working on (among other things) gyroscopic guidance mechanisms. Germany's V-2 rocket and our modern space rockets have all employed his principles and patented inventions.[56] He died in 1945. Fourteen years later, Maryland's Goddard Space Flight Center was named in his honor.

Architecture and the Arts

Amid these achievements in aviation and rocketry, a different sort of "race to the sky"[57] occurred in New York City. It was an architectural contest, but it also encompassed a new art form. During the 1920s, a handful of perceptive French artists had finally figured out how the disconcerting puzzle pieces of "cubism" were meant to fit together. Their efforts culminated in an alluring art style that would be employed in art and architecture throughout the 1920s and 1930s. No one knew at first what to call it, and it was not until the 1960s that it finally obtained the name by which we know it today—"Art Deco." Sometimes referred to as "cubism tamed,"[58] Art Deco is characterized by richly accentuated geometric shapes, and at the time of its origination it seemed perfect for everything, from the stylized paintings of Tamara de Lempicka to the skyscraper. In the latter capacity, it added a number of famous geometric silhouettes to the New York City skyline, including those of the American Radiator Building (1924), the Bank of Manhattan Trust Building (1930), the Chrysler Building (1930) and the Empire State Building (1931).

The advent of steel-framing—the impact of which was first demonstrated in 1885 with the completion of Chicago's ten-story Home Insurance Building—made it possible to exceed the height limitations imposed by traditional masonry. Masonry construction requires increasing thickness of the walls at the base of a building in order to support advancing height—and before you get very high up, the required thickness at the bottom becomes impractical. Hence, it was not until steel-framing came into use that the "skyscraper" became feasible.

Thereafter, the world marveled at the construction of ever taller buildings. By the outbreak of World War I, the tallest building in the world was the 55-story, steel-framed, gothic-style Woolworth Building, which opened in Manhattan in 1913. At the end of the next decade, however, just before the Roaring Twenties roared to a halt, the architects of the proposed Bank of Manhattan Trust and Chrysler buildings (who were bitter personal rivals) decided to exceed the height of the world's then-tallest building—and to compete with each other to set a new record.

Even as the structures rose, the competitors redesigned them in a bid to outdo one another, ultimately coming up against the maximum height achievable based on their respective foundation sizes.[59] In April 1930, H. Craig Severance completed the 925-foot Bank of the Manhattan Trust Building, certain that he had won the contest. But his rival, William van Alen, whose design was thought to be complete when the Manhattan Trust opened its doors, had been erecting something secretly inside his building—a 125-foot spire, which was now raised to the top from the inside, bringing the Chrysler Building to 1,046 feet.[60] Hence, less than two months after its completion as the "world's tallest building," Severance's Manhattan Trust had been eclipsed. The triumphant Chrysler Building, however, would enjoy its championship standing for a mere eleven months before being outdone in its turn by what is perhaps still the world's most *iconic* building (if no longer its tallest). The 1,250-foot Empire State Building opened its doors on May 1, 1931, having risen at an average pace of 4.5 stories per week, with a total construction time of 410 days.[61] As part of the opening ceremony, the building's lights were turned on from Washington, D.C. by President Herbert Hoover. The Empire State Building's chief Art Deco features—shared with the Chrysler Building and to a lesser extent with the neo–Gothic Bank of Manhattan Building—are its spired crown (Chrysler's being perhaps the more striking) and stepwise tapering profile.[62] As it turns out, the latter feature—which harkens back to the ancient ziggurats and pyramids—was mandated by New York City's building code which prohibits the excessive blocking of sunlight.[63] (Of incidental note, the subsequent history of the Empire State Building possesses two elements that fit in well with our previous discussion of aviation, for the spire was designed to be a dirigible mooring station—a purpose that proved untenable owing to upward winds that massive skyscrapers create—and, in 1945, a U.S. B-25 "Mitchell" bomber crashed into the 79th floor in a dense fog, killing fourteen.)[64]

Despite the city's famed competition, the chief function of skyscrapers was not to serve as status symbols. As urban congestion increased at the dawn of the 20th century, particularly in financial centers such as New York and Chicago, the skyscraper was meant to solve the growing demand for office space—allowing vertical potential to compensate for an ever-decreasing supply of real estate at ground level.[65] As it happens, the most iconic architect of the period, Frank Lloyd Wright, envisioned the skyscraper as the means of doing away with urban congestion all together. The originator of "organic architecture" (which seeks to make a building's architectural design primarily a function of the landscape upon which it is built, tempered only by its internal requirements), Wright proposed to place an entire city inside a mile-high skyscraper so that the surrounding countryside could remain open and uncongested.[66] Alas, the project never got off the ground, leaving us to be content with Wright's existing masterpieces, such as his

An example of Art Deco art and architecture in one. Art Deco cartoon depicting the Empire State Building, RCA Building in Rockefeller Center and the Chrysler Building, 1936. Unknown artist (Wikimedia Commons).

1910 Prairie-style "Robie House" in Chicago, replete with its "geometric windows" (which let sunlight in while maintaining privacy), and his quintessentially organic "Fallingwater," which is built atop an actual waterfall in Mill Run, Pennsylvania (1938).

A last anecdote may be mentioned in our discussion of architecture—and it has to do with physics. In 1938, construction was completed on the Tacoma Narrows Bridge (Tacoma, Washington)—a new type of suspension bridge supported by solid steel girders instead of the commonly used open lattice-work trusses.[67] It was noted on completion that the bridge tended to undulate in the wind—a phenomenon that gained it the amusing nickname "Galloping Gertie." Things got significantly less funny, however, on November 7, 1940, when (amid traffic) the bridge went into something very like simple harmonic motion, with segments of the road rising for traffic in one direction and dropping for traffic in the other in repeating rhythmic oscillations until the whole structure broke apart and fell into Puget Sound. The disaster, which was provoked by 40 mph winds acting on the girders, was captured on film and long used in high school physics classes as an example of the danger of not taking "mechanical resonance" into account when embarking on building projects. It has since been determined, however, that the actual culprit was a more complex phenomenon called "aeroelastic flutter," which accelerates itself towards infinity in winds greater than 35 mph. Hence, it was more a matter of aerodynamics than resonance.[68]

The Assembly Line

Ground transportation, too, experienced revolutionary changes between the World Wars. On December 1, 1913, the Ford Motor Company unveiled a new innovation for the production of its signature Model T automobile: the moving assembly line. One hundred and fifty feet long and attended by 140 workers performing 84 distinct tasks,[69] it was initially powered by pulling vehicles along tracks with ropes as they were assembled.[70] (A power-driven conveyor belt was added in January 1914.) Manufacturing would never be the same. Henceforth, the worker would not need to hustle hither and yon, for the work would come to him.

The driving force behind it all was the company's founder, Henry Ford (1863–1947), whose mission was to build an inexpensive, reliable vehicle for the masses. The Model T (the ninth automobile designed by him) was introduced in 1908 at a retail price of $825[71]—far less expensive than the typical custom-built vehicles of the period, but still quite out of reach for most of the population. In order to reduce the cost, Ford set out to streamline the manufacturing process, using ideas gleaned by touring factories in Chicago, where he saw conveyor belts employed in granaries and overhead trolleys in the meat-packing industry.[72] Interchangeable parts, manufactured on his own machines by low-skilled workers (rather than handmade by craftsmen), were another cornerstone of the revolution.[73] Relying on his architect, Charles Sorenson (who designed the various components of the assembly line), his systems man, Clarence Avery (who organized the various production steps to allow for a continuous workflow) and ergonomics pioneer,[74] Frederick Taylor (who choreographed the exact timing and movements required of the workers manning the line),[75] Ford slashed vehicle production time from 12 hours to 93 minutes.[76] Production skyrocketed from some 13,840 vehicles per year in 1909 to 585,388 in 1916, in which year, the retail price dropped to $360.[77] By the time the Model T went out of production in 1927, Ford had produced 15 million in all, and the cost had come down to $260.[78]

To keep pace with rising demand, Ford *decreased* the workday from 9 hours to 8 and kept his factories running twenty-four hours a day in three successive shifts.[79] The work, however, was brutally monotonous, with each worker being assigned one task to be repeated ad nauseum under an exact and exacting time allotment. To keep workers from abandoning the company to find more interesting, less stressful work, Ford doubled their pay to $5 a day—a new industry standard. In so doing, he turned his workers into customers—for the salary increase allowed them to purchase their own Model Ts, the most affordable vehicle on the market.[80]

Alas, Ford had a malicious side. The first clue came with his generous pay increase; in order to qualify for it, his workers had to adhere to a strict code of conduct in their personal lives, enforced by a very nosy company "Sociological Department."[81] In the political sphere, Ford loudly opposed America's entry into World War I—during which Allied munitions factories (and to a lesser extent German) adopted his assembly line procedure, greatly enhancing the speed and volume of war material production.[82] In 1918, he ran for the U.S. Senate and was narrowly defeated, in part because of editorial attacks made on him in his hometown paper, the *Dearborn Independent*. Before the year was out, he had purchased the paper.[83] It was the beginning of a vile episode that would continue until the Model T went out of production in 1927.

On May 22, 1920, the first of a series of articles appeared in the *Independent* under the front-page headline, "The International Jew, the World's Foremost Problem." In ensuing editions, Jews were blamed for the world's myriads ills. Some accusations were merely denigrating. "Jazz," for example, was decried as "Yiddish moron music." But others amounted to blood libel—for example, the contention (purportedly "proven") that

Jewish financiers fomented World War I in order to profit from the killing of Christians.[84] Each edition contained an editorial under the title "Mr. Ford's Own Page," which reflected the boss's opinions, though authored by his editor, William Cameron. (A previous editor, Charles Pipp, had resigned rather than associate himself with Ford's anti–Semitism.)[85] In 1921, the paper serialized the infamous tsarist forgery, *The Protocols of the Elders of Zion*, "international Jewry's" putative blueprint for world domination. Suitably impressed, Adolf Hitler singled Ford out for praise in *Mein Kampf*.[86]

At its peak, the paper achieved a circulation of 900,000. Ford dealerships were told to purchase multiple copies and to hand them out to customers. Many dealerships refused, and the public fought back against Ford's propaganda with boycotts of his vehicles. The carnival came to an end in 1927 when a libel suit (ultimately settled out of court) resulted in a public apology from Ford and closure of the paper. Attempting to emerge from the sordid business with his reputation unsullied, Ford blamed the articles on his hired underlings and claimed that he had never read them.[87] (He would later disabuse anyone gullible enough to believe this far-fetched disclaimer by accepting a medal from Hitler [1938] and blaming the outbreak of World War II on "the Jews."[88]) He died in 1947. The assembly line and mass-ownership of motor vehicles survive him. So, too, does his tainted legacy.

Advances in Medicine

The period under study also witnessed revolutionary changes in the field of medicine. In 1910, after visiting all of America's 155 medical schools, Abraham Flexner of the Carnegie Foundation for the Advancement of Teaching issued a report exposing the pitiful quality of medical education in the United States. The so-called "Flexner Report" created a national scandal that led to the overhaul of American medical training along the lines pioneered at the Johns Hopkins Medical School by William Osler and William Halsted during the preceding two decades.[89]

At about the same time, a start was made on an entirely new form of medical treatment. Today, the term "chemotherapy" generally refers to the treatment of *cancer* with chemical medicines (as opposed to treating it with surgery or radiation); but when the term first came into usage, it was applied more broadly to denote the treatment of *any disease* with synthetic chemical compounds. The field of chemotherapy was founded by the German medical scientist, Paul Ehrlich (1854–1915). Two years after Ehrlich's birth, an English chemist named William Henry Perkin accidentally created a synthetic purple dye while attempting to manufacture the naturally occurring antimalarial drug quinine from lab chemicals.[90] The discovery inaugurated the synthetic aniline dye industry, which found myriad applications—most notably in the coloring of textiles. Among those who found use for such dyes was Ehrlich's mother's cousin, Carl Weigert, a pathologist who used them to stain animal tissues and cells for examination under the microscope. Ehrlich took a fascinated interest in this relative's work. In 1878, he obtained a medical degree from the University of Leipzig, writing his doctoral thesis on the use of synthetic dyes in tissue staining. In the process, he discerned that various dyes seemed to have special affinities for specific types of cells—a phenomenon that he attributed to the dye getting caught up in chemical processes at the cellular level.[91] It subsequently occurred to him that if chemical dyes had an affinity for *staining* bacterial pathogens, they might also have an affinity for *killing them* without causing harm to their hosts, thereby acting in the fashion of a "magic bullet." This was the foundational idea of "chemotherapy"—a term coined by Ehrlich himself.[92]

In 1905, a pair of German researchers, Fritz Schaudinn and Eric Hoffmann, isolated the spiral-shaped bacterium (or "spirochete") *Treponema pallidum*, which causes syphilis. The discovery immediately drew Ehrlich's attention. His young Japanese assistant, Sahachiro Hata, soon found a means of producing syphilis in rabbits through inoculation,[93] whereupon Ehrlich identified a chemical formulation of arsenic—a component of many aniline dyes—that produced a cure in such rabbits without undue toxicity. Initially called compound "606" because it was the 606th arsenic compound developed in his lab, Ehrlich renamed it "Salvarsan" ("salvation through arsenic"), proved its efficacy in humans, and published his results in April 1910.[94]

"Chemotherapy"—the treatment of disease with synthetic chemicals—thus found its first practical application.[95] But this was only one of Ehrlich's contributions to the field of medicine. A year after graduating medical school, he was appointed "Chief House Officer" at Berlin's famous Charité Hospital (the halls of which were roamed by such giants as Koch and Virchow). In this capacity, he discovered that the aniline dye carbol fuchsin could be used to stain the tubercle bacillus responsible for tuberculosis. (First isolated by Koch in 1882, the bacillus—known today as *Mycobacterium tuberculosis*—initially defied common staining techniques owing to the fatty composition of its cell wall.)[96] Ehrlich also established the fields of hematology and immunology. He founded the former by employing dyes to stain—and thereby distinguish—the various types of human blood cells. The latter resulted from his theory that the body's immune system combats disease by producing protein substances (now known as "antibodies") that bind receptors on invading microorganisms, tumor cells or allergens in the manner of a key being inserted into a lock. This hypothesis, known as the "side-chain theory of immunity," gained Ehrlich a Nobel Prize in 1908.[97] This was two years before his discovery of Salvarsan. It was also two years *after* the captain of the rifle team at St. Mary's Medical School in London changed the course of chemotherapeutic history forever by convincing a young graduate of that institution to abandon his dream of becoming a surgeon.

The graduate, a Scotsman named Alexander Fleming (1881–1955), happened to be a fine marksman, and the compelling argument made by his rifle team captain was that, if he forgot about becoming a surgeon and instead took a position as a researcher at St. Mary's, he could continue on as a member of the rifle team. That is precisely what Fleming did—taking a position in the school's inoculation department, which was headed by Almroth Wright, the inventor of the world's first typhoid vaccine (developed in 1896). During World War I, while British enlistees received Almroth's vaccine on their way to the Front, Fleming served as a captain in the British Army Medical Corps and made a study of infected battle wounds. His observations seemed to suggest that the application of antiseptics—the main treatment of the time—produced a rather worse outcome than doing nothing at all. After conducting a few experiments, he determined that the antiseptics, which were applied to the surface of the wounds, caused more damage to healthy tissue than they did to the causative bacteria. The reason, he discovered, was that the bacteria were anaerobic (which is to say they required no oxygen). They were thus able to flourish deep within the wound, out of reach of the antiseptic.[98] His subsequent work on the problem led to his discovery of lysozyme (1922), a natural enzyme found in saliva, tears and other secretions, that is modestly active against bacteria without being toxic to healthy tissue.

The discovery for which Fleming is famous, however, was one of medicine's most fortuitous accidents—resulting directly from his practice of keeping petri dishes strewn about his lab in the manner of an absent-minded professor until he got around to cleaning them up. On September 28, 1928, he returned to the lab from a vacation and decided that the time was ripe for just such a cleanup. Many of his petri dishes, upon which he had been culturing staphylococcal bacteria, were contaminated with mold—a finding that generally meant that they should be thrown away forthwith. He could not help but notice, however, that one of the moldy samples had a curious finding. Moisture from the mold had seeped onto the surrounding surface of the petri dish and wiped out every colony of staph within reach.[99] Determining that the mold was a member of the genus *Penicillium*, he gave its "mold juice" a name: "penicillin."[100]

Fleming published a paper on the matter in 1929 but was unable to isolate enough of the active ingredient to put it to practical use. He happily shared his samples with other researchers, however, in hopes that a process might be found.[101] Nearly a decade later, his paper was read by the biochemist Ernst Chain, a Jewish refugee from Nazism working in the laboratory of Australian researcher Howard Florey, at Oxford University. By 1940, Chain, Florey and another biochemist, Norman Heatley, had produced enough penicillin to perform an experiment on mice inoculated with deadly streptococci. Four mice were treated. Four were not. The next day, the former seemed unaffected, while the latter were stone dead.[102]

As Sutcliffe and Duin note, the new antibiotic was mass produced in the United States during World War II—finding its first mass application in the treatment of a gonorrhea outbreak among American troops in North Africa, who were thus rendered fit to return to duty in time for the 1943 invasion of Sicily.[103] Two years later, Fleming, Chain and Florey received a Nobel Prize for their momentous contribution.

Penicillin performs its work by killing bacteria. Before it went into widespread production, an antibiotic with a different mechanism of action was identified by the German medical researcher, Gerhard Domagk. "Prontosil" was a red dye invented in 1908 for use in the German textile industry. When metabolized, it cleaves into two parts, one of which, sulphanilamide, halts susceptible bacteria in its tracks—not by killing them, but by inhibiting their reproduction. Anticipating the 1940 experiment of Chain, Florey and Heatley by eight years, Domagk injected the compound into mice inoculated with hemolytic streptococci and found that it worked (1932).[104] He later employed it with success on his daughter after she developed a strep infection. In 1939, he received a Nobel Prize for his discovery, predicting thereafter that "chemotherapy" would find application in the treatment of cancer.[105]

While these advances were in train, the study of human hormones (termed "endocrinology") produced another Nobel Prize winning breakthrough. In 1869, a Dutch researcher named Paul Langerhans had noted that the human pancreas contains "islands" of tissue that are distinct from the rest of the gland. These areas came to be called "islets of Langerhans" in his honor, but their purpose was unknown until 1901 when Dr. Eugene Lindsay Opie of Johns Hopkins University discovered that the "islets" were diseased in individuals afflicted with diabetes—a scourge that produced deadly medical complications (all too often in children).[106] It was surmised afterwards that the islets produce a hormone in normal individuals that was deficient in diabetics. Even before it was isolated, the hormone was given a name: "insulin," derived from the Latin word "insula," meaning "island."[107]

Efforts to isolate insulin from pancreatic tissue were at first unavailing. But on October 30, 1920, Frederick Banting (1891–1941), an orthopedic surgeon from London, Ontario, learned an interesting fact while preparing a lecture on the pancreas—namely, that in experiments on dogs, removal of the pancreas resulted in diabetes, while merely tying off the ducts for the organ's digestive secretions did not. (We must note here that in addition to producing insulin, the pancreas also secretes several digestive enzymes.) Banting concluded that these digestive enzymes "digested" insulin as surely as they digested food, thereby foiling all prior attempts to isolate the elusive hormone. From this, he deduced that if the enzymatic ducts were tied off in live dogs, undigested insulin might be recovered from the remainder of the gland.[108] He took the idea to a leading researcher on diabetes, J.J.R. Macleod (1876–1935), at the University of Toronto, who supplied him with lab facilities, a group of highly unfortunate dogs, and an assistant, Charles Best (1899–1978), to further investigate the possibility.

In a mere 2½ months, Banting and Best achieved success, extracting the hormone using saline. Later, Macleod's protégé, James Bertram Collip (1892–1965), improved the extraction process by using alcohol.[109] In January 1922, the insulin extract was successfully administered to Leonard Thompson, a 13-year-old boy who was near death from diabetes, thereby saving his life. By this time (but too late to save Macleod's dogs), Banting and Best had realized that refrigeration inhibited the action of pancreatic enzymes, and that intact insulin could thus be obtained from refrigerated beef and pork pancreases without tormenting innocent canines.[110]

It was important to introduce all four individuals involved in this story, because by the time all was said and done, they had formed themselves into two rival pairings (Banting with Best, Macleod with Collip) whose quarrel over who deserved credit for their mutual accomplishment might, in the olden times, have ended in a duel. The Nobel committee's decision to award its 1923 prize in medicine only to Banting and Macleod, without recognizing Best or Collip, hardly settled the matter. In a bid to spite Macleod (whom he loathed), Banting announced that he would give half of his prize money to Best. Not to be outdone, Macleod split his with Collip. It was all rather petty, for all four had done good service to mankind—saving the lives of millions of diabetics.[111]

Before exiting our discussion of medical advances, we may mention an episode involving the cardiologist, Helen Taussig (1898–1986), who became interested in a pediatric illness known as "blue baby syndrome" and, more particularly, in its most frequent cause: the so-called "Tetralogy of Fallot"—a constellation of four congenital heart defects that work in lethal harmony to prevent venous blood from reaching the lungs in order to receive oxygen. Affected individuals are prone to develop a bluish discoloration of the skin due to oxygen deprivation (a condition known as "cyanosis"). As their bodies grow and their oxygen needs increase, the problem worsens, ultimately resulting in death.[112]

At the time that Taussig began her investigations at Johns Hopkins there was no treatment. But a minority of afflicted children inexplicably tended to have better outcomes—at least temporarily—and Taussig, who studied their hearts under a continuous X-ray monitor (known as a fluoroscope), found that such children had an additional congenital anomaly known as a "patent ductus arteriosus."[113] During pregnancy, the ductus arteriosus carries oxygenated maternal blood to the fetus (whose lungs, after all, have no exposure to air). The conduit typically closes at birth or within the first several weeks of life. What Taussig learned in studying tetralogy babies was that if the ductus arteriosus remained open (or "patent"), it shunted blood to the lungs, thereby bypassing the congenital narrowing that prevented it from getting there by the usual route. If this occurs in children with normal hearts, it can, over time, cause grave problems, but in Tetralogy of Fallot babies, it produced a solution.

Taussig approached Dr. Alfred Blalock (1899–1964), the chief of surgery at Johns Hopkins, about the possibility of surgically creating an "artificial" patent ductus arteriosus in affected children. Cardiac surgery had never before been undertaken, and the notion of doing it on the minuscule blood vessels of frail infants made the prospect all the more daunting. Nonetheless, on November 29, 1944, Blalock performed the operation successfully on one of Taussig's patients—11-month-old Eileen Saxon (whose death was felt to be imminent without intervention).

The feat would not have been possible, however, if it had not been for Blalock's assistant, Vivien Thomas (1910–1985), who now emerges as the most remarkable figure in the story. Thomas was a black man, the grandson of a slave, who had dreamed of becoming a doctor since childhood. Working as a carpenter, he had saved just enough for college when the bank in which he kept his deposits failed as a result of the Depression. If fate thus deprived him of his dream, however, it did not deprive him of his destiny, for it also arranged that he should become Blalock's laboratory assistant at Vanderbilt University at the tender age of nineteen (1930).

From the moment he embarked on this work, Thomas displayed a brilliant facility in performing surgery on dogs as part of Blalock's groundbreaking investigations on traumatic shock. Blalock's experimentation proved that the maintenance of adequate circulating blood volume by means of transfusion was the essential lifesaving intervention in shock cases—a discovery that saved countless lives during World War II. On being named chief of surgery at Johns Hopkins in 1941, Blalock convinced Thomas (upon whose technical expertise he had now come to rely) to come with him. When Taussig approached the two men with her request, it was Thomas who went into the trenches—learning the exact anatomy of the Fallot tetralogy from pathology specimens at the Hopkins pathological museum, recreating the anomalies in dogs, and then attempting to cure them by creating a shunt from the subclavian artery to the pulmonary artery (thus bypassing the blockage leading to the lungs through the creation of an artificial ductus arteriosis).[114]

By 1944, Thomas had performed the procedure successfully on 200 dogs—proving its safety and efficacy. When the time came to save Eileen Saxon, however, Alfred Blalock, his eminent chief, had not performed even one—at least not by himself. (He had assisted Thomas a handful of times.)[115] Consequently, during the entirety of the operation, Vivien Thomas stood on a stepstool, peering over Blalock's shoulder onto the operating field and offering the technical guidance that only he possessed, while Blalock and his surgical assistants, William Longmire Jr. and Denton Cooley (each famous in his own right), performed the delicate procedure. The operation was a success—revolutionizing the care of children with congenital heart defects and inaugurating the new field of cardiac surgery at one and the same time.

It is a comment on the times that Thomas, despite his many years as Blalock's lab assistant, still held the official position (and salary) of a "janitor" owing to the color of his skin. In 1946, Blalock finally got him reclassified as a lab technician with a commensurate salary.[116] Thomas would go on to become the director of surgical research laboratories at Johns Hopkins and a member of the medical school faculty with the title surgical instructor until his retirement in 1979. In 1976 he received an honorary doctorate from the school.[117]

Mathematics

In the field of mathematics, the most startling figure of the era was the self-taught Indian, Srinivasa Ramanujan. The son of a clerk in the cloth business, he was born near Madras, India, on December 22, 1887. From the first, he possessed an idiosyncratic intellect. Formal schooling left him unimpressed, and his parents had to hire a constable to ensure his attendance.[118] Although he excelled in all subjects, he was drawn especially to mathematics, mastering S.L. Loney's *Plane Trigonometry* without supervision, and setting to work on his own theorems by the age of 13. Two years later, he began tackling G.S. Carr's *A Synopsis of Elementary Results in Pure and Applied Mathematics*—an outdated Cambridge University entrance exam preparation book containing over 6,000 theorems intended for memorization with little in the way of proofs (proofs being unnecessary for the purpose at hand). Blessed with extraordinary intuition, Ramanujan worked out his own demonstrations, thereby becoming facile with the mathematical advances of the preceding two centuries while drawing conclusions that were well ahead of his time. In doing so, he showed a remarkable capacity for achieving results by induction (i.e., the process of deriving general conclusions from specific examples).[119] Because paper was an expensive commodity in the India of that time, Ramanujan did all of his calculations on slate, erasing them with his elbow before moving on to the next equation.[120] Of necessity, he reserved the precious space in his notebooks for summaries and conclusions without showing how he had arrived at them (Carr's little book having left him largely oblivious to the rigorous proofs required in formal mathematics).

Upon finishing high school, he obtained scholarships to two Indian universities, but lost both because he was too absorbed with his one passion to devote any effort to the other required subjects. He was, for a time, impoverished and unemployed, but in 1911, his 17-page treatise on Bernoulli numbers was published in the *Journal of the Indian Mathematical Society* and his genius earned a growing appreciation. Assisted by members of the society, he obtained a position as a shipping clerk, which allowed him to subsist while continuing his research. In 1913, he made inquiries by letter to three prominent British mathematicians, including with his correspondence 120 examples of his work. The first two recipients did not deign to respond. The third, G.H. Hardy, initially took it as an elaborate prank, but in reviewing it with his colleague, J.E. Littlewood, determined that Ramanujan's conclusions "must be true, because if they were not true, no one would have had the imagination to invent them."[121]

Hardy invited Ramanujan to continue his studies at Trinity College, Cambridge. As a devout Brahmin, he could not at first accept, but when his mother (who had been dead set against his going) confessed that the family goddess Namagiri had appeared to her in a dream forbidding her to stand between her son and his destiny, Ramanujan undertook the journey.[122] There followed a collaboration between Hardy and Ramanujan lasting five years and culminating in Ramanujan's acceptance as a Fellow of the Royal Society and a Fellow of Trinity College in 1918—accomplishments that were without precedent for an Indian scholar of that day owing to contemporary bigotries. Along the way, Ramanujan was converted into a mathematician of the formal type, capable of providing proofs for what he postulated. Hardy and Littlewood sought to guide him through this metamorphosis, and found it an exasperating process since, as Littlewood noted, "every time some matter, which it was thought that Ramanujan needed to know was mentioned, Ramanujan's response was an avalanche of original ideas" that caused the intended point to become quite lost.[123] Towards the end of his stay in England, Ramanujan became extremely sick. It was thought by his English doctors that he was suffering from tuberculosis, although this remains controversial and amebiasis has been put forward as an alternative diagnosis.[124] Once he felt well enough, he returned to India, but there he fell ill again, dying tragically at the age of thirty-two (April 1920).

His chief field of study had been "number theory" which involves the positive integers (i.e., whole numbers) and mathematical functions relating to them. While at Cambridge, his most celebrated breakthrough involved the derivation of a formula for determining the number of "partitions" into which an integer may be broken down. (The number 2 for example, can be broken down in two ways—or into two distinct "partitions"—using whole numbers. The first is "1 + 1," the second is "2." Similarly, the number 3 can be expressed by three partitions: "1 + 1 + 1," "1+ 2" and "3.") As the value of the integer rises (from 3 to 4 to 5 to 6, etc.), the number of partitions also rises but not in a predictable way. Using a new method of their own devising (known since as the "circle method," which continues to reap results to the present day), Ramanujan and Hardy derived a formula for calculating the number of partitions for any integer.[125]

To go into further detail on his myriad accomplishments is beyond the scope of this work (in large measure because it is beyond the comprehension of this author). Suffice to say that at his death, Ramanujan left behind three notebooks containing nearly 4,000 such theorems, giving generations of mathematicians proofs to work out and applications to identify—an output so prolific that Hardy could find no one with whom to compare his astonishing protégé other than Euler and Jacobi (the most prolific mathematicians of the 18th and 19th centuries, respectively).[126] To this day, Ramanujan is regarded as a national treasure in his home country—his birthday being celebrated annually as India's "National Mathematics Day."[127]

Epilogue: Brave New Atomic World

The world that emerged from the Second World War was profoundly different from that which had descended into it. Among the foremost changes was the diminished status of Europe on the world stage. Apart from the human cost of the war, much of the continent physically lay in ruins. Industrial plants were destroyed. Ports and railways were out of service. Millions of individuals, displaced from their homes, were either on the move with no definite destination or languishing in displaced persons camps with their futures in doubt. Amid such destruction, the once great states of Europe were in no condition to resume their standing at the head of world affairs, a mantle that was assumed instead by the emerging "superpowers"—the United States and the Soviet Union. With economic assistance (most especially that provided by the Marshall Plan at the outset of the Cold War), European *life* would be resuscitated but European *preeminence* would not.

The continent's prostration had worldwide implications. The performance of imperial powers like Britain, France and the Netherlands in the war with Japan had not proved a very good advertisement for European colonialism. The setbacks they sustained at the outset of the fighting (most especially the disastrous surrender of 130,000 British troops to the Japanese at Singapore) demonstrated that the European did not always come out on top—a fact that seems to have impressed itself not only on colonial natives in areas overrun by the Japanese, but also on Indian troops serving in the British Army and on native peoples further afield.[128] Imperialism was foredoomed—something that had been evident to many even prior to the war—and a process of global decolonization was now begun. In 1946, the United Nations consisted of 35 member states. Twenty-five years later, the number stood at 127, as myriad colonized territories in Asia and Africa obtained independent status. In some instances, the transition was peaceful. In others it was marred by horrific violence, whether between holdout colonial regimes and the native inhabitants or between the native inhabitants themselves.

For our purposes, two episodes are germane. The first is the Suez Crisis of 1956, in which Britain and France, aided by Israel, attempted to reestablish control over the Suez Canal after the Egyptian leader, Gamal Abdel Nasser, nationalized it. The result of this badly bungled military adventure (Israel was the only member of the triumvirate to carry out its mission competently) was to place the two European participants under the simultaneous censure of the United States and Soviet Union. The latter, indeed, threatened to intervene with ballistic missiles if the operation was not abandoned immediately. Thus reproached, Europe's two "preeminent" states were forced to climb down, and in doing so, they demonstrated unequivocally that the old powers of Europe could not compete with the new "superpowers" in the arena of international politics.

The second episode is the French-Algerian War, which began in 1954 (the year the French were beaten at Dien Bien Phu and forced out of Indochina, known henceforth as Vietnam)—and would not end would until 1962. In the interim, it would provoke the fall of the French "Fourth Republic" and give rise to a "Fifth" headed by Charles de Gaulle. The year was 1958, and though the French, by various brutalities, had gotten the upper hand in Algeria by that date it had not won over any Algerian hearts or minds. De Gaulle concluded from this and from the Suez Crisis that France could not maintain her global relevance by clinging to colonialism, and that she should instead pursue economic reform at home while relying on a nuclear weapons program to ensure her international standing.[129] The latter initiative achieved success in 1960, making France the world's fourth nuclear power after the United States, Great Britain and the Soviet Union.

The most interesting thing about the atom bomb—and this will be the last topic of our survey—is not the story of the Manhattan Project whereby it was brought into existence, but rather the nature of the energy we are talking about when we refer to atomic energy and atomic bombs. And that story begins with the composition of the atom. Although the idea of the atom as a fundamental indivisible particle was known to the Greeks, it did not enter into modern scientific thought until 1808, when John Dalton (1766–1844) published *A New System of Chemical Philosophy* proposing his "atomic theory"—namely, (i) that chemical elements (such as hydrogen, oxygen, nitrogen, etc.) are composed of small indivisible particles called atoms; (ii) that the atoms of a given element are all alike; (iii) that the atoms of different elements differ from each other in size and weight (with hydrogen atoms being the smallest); and (iv) that chemical reactions can combine different elements together to form chemical compounds (such as when two atoms of hydrogen combine with one atom of oxygen to form water).[130] Although some of the fine print was afterwards found to be wrong (for example, Dalton himself thought that water contained only one hydrogen atom for every oxygen atom rather than two),[131] the theory proved a very workable one and was not known to contain any fundamental flaws until 1897 when Joseph John Thomson (1856–1940) discovered the existence of something very much smaller than a hydrogen atom while studying the path of an electric current in a Crooks vacuum tube. In this experiment, he noted that if a positively charged "deflector" was placed along one side of the path taken by the electric current, and a negative deflector was placed along the opposite side, the path of the current would veer towards the positively charged deflector. Thomson knew, of course—since it is the one thing about electromagnetism which *everyone* knows—that "like" charges repel and "opposite" charges attract. He was thus able to conclude that the tiny particles that composed the electric current, which he at first called "corpuscles" and later renamed "electrons," must contain a *negative* charge since they were attracted to the positively charged deflector and repelled by the negative one.

His results, however, convinced him of something else—namely, that these electrons were "subatomic particles"—which is to say that they were not only smaller than atoms, but that they were component parts of atoms (meaning that atoms were not, after all, indivisible particles)—and that since atoms do not carry a net charge, there must be something within the milieu of the atom that carried a positive charge to neutralize the negative charge on the electron. What might this look like? Thomson gave the matter some thought and came up with what is known as the "plum pudding model," which depicted the atom as consisting of negatively charged electrons dispersed in a positively charged soup, just like pieces of plum are dispersed in plum pudding.[132]

And there matters stood until 1911, when a New Zealand physicist named Ernest Rutherford (1871–1937) set out to demonstrate the truth of this "plum pudding model" only to find that it was incorrect. In 1896, the husband-and-wife scientists, Pierre and Marie Curie, and the French physicist Antoine Becquerel, noted that some elements (particularly those whose atoms were very large, such as uranium and radium) were unstable and underwent a process of radioactive decay in which they emitted radiation of three types: alpha, beta and gamma. Alpha radiation, moreover, was found to consist of positively charged particles. (The beta particles were negatively charged and turned out to be electrons.)[133] Acting on this information, Rutherford devised an experiment in which he launched alpha particles at an extremely thin sheet of gold foil, just a few atoms thick, with the expectation that the alpha particles would be able to pierce the foil like bullets and pass straight through. This turned out to be true in most cases, but in a few cases the alpha particles changed direction somewhat on passing through the foil, and in rare cases—1 in every 8,000 or so—the alpha particle ricocheted back in the general direction of the start line.[134]

Rutherford concluded that the gold atoms of the foil must consist almost entirely of empty space surrounding a tiny central "nucleus" which contained most of the atom's mass. Further, much of this central mass or nucleus must be composed of positively charged particles—what we know today as protons. This explained why a minority of the positively charged alpha particles he had launched at the gold foil—those that came sufficiently close to the proton nucleus—were deflected off course: The positively charged alpha particle had come close enough to be repelled, and thus knocked off course, by the like-charged protons of the nucleus. However, if an alpha particle crashed directly into the nucleus, as occurred on average 1 in 8,000 times, it would not only be stopped in its tracks by the larger mass of the nucleus, but would ricochet back toward the start line, having been repelled in that direction by the nucleus' positive charge.[135] Rutherford's experiment led to a new conception of the atom as an infinitesimal solar system with the nucleus at the center—occupying roughly 1/4000th of the atom's diameter[136]—taking on the role of the sun and the electrons orbiting about it in the fashion of planets. In 1932, James Chadwick (1891–1974) identified uncharged particles that also exist within the nucleus, known today as "neutrons," thereby completing the "solar system" atomic model.

It might have occurred to the reader already that because like charges repel and opposite charges attract some serious difficulties should arise with this model. For example, why don't the negatively charged electrons simply hurtle into the nucleus under the power of opposite charges attracting one another? The Danish physicist, Neils Bohr (1885–1962), worked this one out, citing the action of a different force, known as "angular momentum," which, at fixed distances from the nucleus, allows for the establishment of stable orbits.[137] The second obvious question is why don't the protons of an atom's nucleus (given that they all possess a positive charge) repel one another and scatter in different directions? The answer to this one must lie in the existence of some "binding force" or "nuclear glue" strong enough to hold the protons together.[138] How strong is this force? The answer, as it turns out, was derived by Albert Einstein in his famous equation $E = mc^2$, which states that the potential energy of a thing equals its mass times the velocity of light (186,000 miles per second) squared—which is an awful lot of energy compared to mass. To get a general idea, we may cite an example provided by Wallbank and Taylor, which says that if one could harness the energy of *one pound* of coal by splitting its atoms to release 100 percent of its potential energy, the amount of energy obtained would be equivalent to the energy harvested by the (far less efficient) "combustion" of *1.3 million tons* of coal.[139]

This, then, is the sort of energy that we speak of when we discuss atomic energy and the atomic bomb. On a purely theoretical basis, such energy might be released from atoms either in controlled fashion (to provide a continuous energy source) or all at once (to produce a terrifying explosion). The latter notion occurred to H.G. Wells, who, in 1913, included an imaginary atomic bomb in his novel, *The World Set Free*. Nearly two decades later, the Hungarian physicist, Leo Szilard, read Wells' book and apprehended the possibility of making a real one.[140]

By Szilard's time, some efforts had already been made to split atoms one by one, including a 1919 experiment conducted by Ernest Rutherford. It was learned, however, that the energy required to split a single atom was far greater than the amount of energy released by splitting it. What was needed was a self-perpetuating "chain reaction," wherein the nucleus of one atom of a susceptible element is split apart in a crowd of other atoms. The nuclear particles jettisoned by the initial split atom, it was theorized, would careen outwards with great energy into the nuclei of nearby atoms, scattering their nuclear particles, which in turn would careen into even more atoms to scatter their nuclear particles in a self-perpetuating process releasing an ever increasing amount of energy along the way.[141] Further research revealed that such a chain reaction was theoretically possible, and that uranium, being unstable even when left alone, was likely the most suitable element for accomplishing the feat. This, in turn, led to the famous "Einstein letter," written to Franklin Delano Roosevelt by Albert Einstein in 1939, which served as the genesis of the Manhattan Project. And that—after a great deal of research and experiment—led to the first successful nuclear test explosion at Alamogordo, New Mexico on July 16, 1945, prompting Robert Oppenheimer (one of the lead scientists involved) to think, "Now I am become Death, the destroyer of worlds."[142]

The lament was not one of Oppenheimer's own devising. It is taken from the Bhagavad Gita, a Hindu scripture, and in calling it to mind, Oppenheimer was undoubtedly acknowledging the "'realization that science, has given men unprecedented power without a commensurate increase in wisdom."[143] The quoted phrase is taken from the third edition of Wallbank and Taylor's *Civilization Past and Present* (1955). The authors follow it with a Biblical quotation—Mark 8:36: "For what shall it profit a man, if he shall gain the whole world, and lose his soul?"—an apropos enough sentiment if civilization proposes to have a future.

As Hillsdale College president and Churchill scholar Larry P. Arnn has noted, from the time Winston Churchill was a young man at the dawn of the 20th century, he contemplated the "unprecedented power" that science has delivered into human hands and believed that it must be restrained—both in time of war (to prevent it from *destroying* everything), and in time of peace (to keep it from *controlling* everything).[144] The 20th-century philosopher, C.S. Lewis, as Arnn notes, voiced similar concerns, arguing in *The Abolition of Man* that humankind's putative scientific and technological victories "over nature can only be exercised as the power of some men over others," and that "Man's conquest over Nature, *if the dreams of some scientific planners are realized,* means the rule of a few hundreds of men over billions upon billions of men."[145]

Awful though it is to contemplate, this is not the only danger, for there is another at the opposite end of the spectrum—anarchy. In the introduction to *The History of Western Philosophy*, Bertrand Russell writes that "Every community is exposed to two opposite dangers: ossification through too much discipline and reverence for tradition, on the one hand; on the other hand, dissolution, or subjection to foreign conquest, through the growth of an individualism and personal independence that makes co-operation impossible." John Locke, as Russell notes, proposed as a solution to the conundrum "a half-way compromise philosophy, the doctrine of liberalism, which attempted to assign the respective spheres of government and the individual."[146]

When it comes to the essence of Western civilization, classical liberalism and its notion of "individual liberty constitutionally defined"[147] seems to hit the nail on the head. To see how this is so, we may reproduce a short passage from the first book of the current series (*The Ancient Near East, Greece and Rome*, McFarland, 2014) discussing the ultimate contribution of the ancient Greeks:

> Perhaps no modern writer has summed up the meaning of Ancient Greece more succinctly than Edith Hamilton. She credits the Greeks with developing the notion of individual freedom, and with founding Western civilization in order to foster it. While the wretched, unknowing, unrestrained Easterner required the external constraints inherent in slavish obedience to an omnipotent master, the Greek developed his own internal constraints with which to judge right from wrong and thereby guide his actions. The internal constraints, says Hamilton, released him from the need for external ones, thus making him free. He extended the idea to government, eagerly assisting in the generation of laws—a form of external constraint, to be sure, but one that was necessary to protect his freedoms from anarchy or tyranny.[148]
>
> It was this mindset that set the Greeks apart, and the miracle of it all, as Hamilton points out, is that whereas we had the Greeks to serve as our prototype, they had no one but

themselves. They are our cultural forebears, and the story of Europe and the West begins with them.[149]

In his 1925 speech, "Mass Effects in Modern Life," Churchill cautioned, "The magic of mass production has carried all before it. The public have a cheaper and even better article or a superior service; the workmen have better wages and greater security. The results upon the national character and psychology are more questionable. We are witnessing a great diminution in the number of independent people who had some standing of their own, albeit a small one, and who if they conducted their affairs with reasonable prudence could live by no man's leave underneath the law."[150] If we are to maintain any semblance of individual freedom—indeed, if we are to survive at all amid the twin specters of totalitarianism and anarchy—we would do well to keep the Greek example (and Churchill's admonition) always in mind.

Chapter Notes

Preface

1. Kohn, 9.
2. Wikipedia, "Demographics of Europe." https://en.wikipedia.org/wiki/Demographics_of_ Europe Accessed 7/28/21; F. Gilbert puts the figure closer to 450 million (3).
3. West, 485.
4. Phillips, 4.
5. Phillips, 6.

Chapter 1

1. Moscow, 116–17; Larousse, 287.
2. Du Coudray, 120–21, 142.
3. *Cambridge Modern History*, vol. 10, 10.
4. Kraehe, 3; May, *Metternich*, 3; Larousse, 283.
5. Kraehe, 2–3.
6. May, *Metternich*, 2.
7. Louis Madelin in Kraehe, 13–16.
8. Hazen, *ES1*, 22.
9. *Cambridge Modern History*, vol. 10, 10.
10. Kissinger, 155.
11. Phillips, 9–10.
12. Hazen, *ES1*, 20.
13. Hamilton-Williams, 159; see also Kissinger, 159 and Du Coudray, 140–41, for the offer of a duel.
14. Breunig, 122.
15. Kissinger, 161–62.
16. Kissinger, 174.
17. Phillips, 9 and 38.
18. May, *Metternich*, 8.
19. Larousse, 283; Artz, 116; May, *Metternich*, 13. As it happens, one of the first tasks deputed to this occupying army was the forcible suppression of a murderous "White Terror" perpetrated by French ultra-royalists against former revolutionaries in southern France (Phillips, 25).
20. Though it may have been expedient for Austria to have Prussia serve in this capacity in 1815, it allowed the latter to emerge as the natural protector of the lesser German principalities at Austrian expense, as would become evident a half-century later.
21. Phillips, 23.
22. Lowe, 19.
23. The severity of this judgment was lessened to some degree by the compensatory transfer of Holstein—a German principality—to the Danes. Ironically, the transfer of Holstein—amounting to little more than an afterthought at the time— would help trigger the cascade of events leading to the unification of Germany a half century later.
24. Hazen, *ES1*, 11.
25. Romilly was famed also for his anti-slavery sentiments and his prison reform efforts (Hazen, *ES1*, 10; Schapiro, *MCEH1*, 63).
26. *Cambridge Modern History*, vol. 10, 7.
27. *Cambridge Modern History*, vol. 10, 10. Hazen, *ES1*, 15–16.
28. From the "Treaty of Alliance and Friendship" (Quadruple Alliance), quoted in the *Cambridge Modern History*, vol. 10, 11.
29. Phillips, 19.
30. Hazen, *ES1*, 18.
31. *Cambridge Modern History*, vol. 10, 15.
32. Hazen, *ES1*, 71; see also Schapiro, *MCEH2*, 73.
33. Hazen, *ES1*, 69–70.
34. Hazen, *ES1*, 68.
35. Phillips, 29.
36. *Cambridge Modern History*, vol. 10, 15.
37. Phillips, 19.
38. Breunig, 179–80
39. *Encyclopedia Britannica*, vol. 15, 126.
40. Wallbank and Taylor, vol. 2, 192.
41. Artz, 140.
42. Hazen, *ES1*, 40.
43. Artz, 141.
44. Hazen, *ES1*, 40–41.
45. Phillips, 74.
46. May, *Metternich*, 43.
47. Hazen, *ES1*, 43–44.
48. Metternich, vol. 3, 250; see also Breunig, 119; Kraehe, 1.
49. Phillips, 75.
50. Jo. Burke, 231.
51. *Cambridge Modern History*, vol. 10, 575–76, 580.
52. Churchill, *HESP*, vol. 4, 12.
53. *Encyclopedia Britannica*, vol. 4, 41.
54. Hazen, *ES1*, 421.
55. The testimony of an eyewitness can be found in Carey, 299–301.
56. Press restriction was accomplished in part by a "stamp duty" imposed on all publications. In

1816, the radical, William Cobbett, began selling his *Weekly Political Register* at a price of just two pennies per issue—affordable even for the working masses. Now the added "stamp duty" raised the price beyond their means, driving Cobbett into debt (*Cambridge Modern History*, vol. 10, 577, 581).

57. Artz, 125 and 150; Jo. Burke, 233.
58. *Cambridge Modern History*, vol. 10, 22.
59. *Cambridge Modern History*, vol. 10, 16.
60. Hazen, *ES1*, 47.
61. Hazen, *ES1*, 50.
62. Wells, *OH1*, 906.
63. Phillips, 82–83.
64. Phillips, 84–85, 89.
65. Phillips, 103.
66. Hazen, *ES1*, 54.
67. Hazen, *ES1*, 53; Phillips, 92.
68. Hazen, *ES1*, 56–57.
69. *Cambridge Modern History*, vol. 10, 24.
70. Hazen, *ES1*, 58–59.
71. *Cambridge Modern History*, vol. 10, 25–27.
72. *Cambridge Modern History*, vol. 10, 28.
73. *Encyclopedia Britannica*, vol. 27, 307.
74. *Cambridge Modern History*, vol. 10, 28–29.
75. *Cambridge Modern History*, vol. 10, 29–30.
76. Hazen, *ES1*, 60.
77. *Encyclopedia Britannica*, vol. 16, 83; see also *Cambridge Modern History*, vol. 10, 30.
78. Phillips, 84–85, 117.
79. There was at this time a revolution in Piedmont that the tsar was likewise offering to help suppress. Austria ultimately quashed it without his help.
80. *Encyclopedia Britannica*, vol. 27, 1037; *Cambridge Modern History*, vol. 10, 35.
81. *Encyclopedia Britannica*, vol. 16, 972.
82. Phillips, 123.
83. Phillips, 125–26.
84. Hazen, *ES1*, 63.
85. Phillips, 127.
86. Phillips, 129.
87. *Cambridge Modern History*, vol. 10, 37–38; see also Phillips, 129.
88. Phillips, 125.
89. Hazen, *ES1*, 65.
90. *Cambridge Modern History*, vol. 10, 39.
91. Artz, 180–81; Schapiro, *MCEH1*, 504; Bergamini, 306; Breunig, 192; *Cambridge Modern History*, vol. 10, 441.
92. Schapiro, *MCEH1*, 504; Bergamini, 305.
93. *Cambridge Modern History*, vol. 10, 436–37, 440.
94. Crankshaw, *SWP*, 13–17.
95. *Cambridge Modern History*, vol. 10, 442–43.
96. Hayes, *ME*, 41; Hazen *ES1*, 652.
97. Schapiro, *MCEH1*, 505. Hayes, *ME*, 41.
98. Asimov, 345; Hamilton-Williams, 133.
99. *Cambridge Modern History*, vol. 10, 88; Hazen, *ES1*, 83–84.
100. *Cambridge Modern History*, vol. 10, 89; Hazen *ES1*, 86.
101. Lamartine, *HRMF*, vol. 4, 409–10.
102. Artz, 268.

103. Wolf, 72; see also, Agnew, 18–19; Guizot, *France*, vol. 8, 285; Blanc, vol. 1, 196.
104. Agnew, 28; see also Wolf, 72. (Lamartine claims that Odilon Barrot made this statement—*HRMF*, 489.)
105. Hazen, *ES1*, 100.
106. Artz, 273–74; Breunig, 140; Brinton et al., vol. 2, 550; Phillips, 188.
107. Larousse, 292; Cobban, vol. 2, 95; Wolf, 90.
108. Hazen, *ES1*, 105; Phillips, 189–90.
109. The Dutch actually invaded Belgium and scored a series of victories but withdrew again when France mobilized its forces in answer to a Belgian appeal. Even so, the Netherlands did not give final consent until 1839 (Phillips, 196–99).
110. Breunig, 194; Larousse, 293; Crankshaw, *SWP*, 104; Artz, 283.
111. Hazen *ES1*, 108–09.
112. *Cambridge Modern History*, vol. 10, 474.
113. Crankshaw, *SWP*, 106; Artz, 284; Phillips, 208.
114. Hazen, *ES1*, 112–13.
115. Hazen, *ES1*, 423; see also Schapiro, *MCEH1*, 65–66.
116. *Cambridge Modern History*, vol. 10, 585.
117. *Cambridge Modern History*, vol. 10, 591–92.
118. Schapiro, *MCEH1*, 79; Jo. Burke, 234; Artz, 223; Hazen, *ES1*, 428. Old Sarum and Dunwich were actually "pocket boroughs," wherein the power to nominate candidates was in the "pocket" of an individual patron (typically the local landlord). In rotten boroughs, the patron had to contend with a small constituency of voters but was virtually able to control the nomination process through bribery or various other inducements (*Cambridge Modern History*, vol. 10, 603–04).
119. Schapiro, *MCEH1*, 46; Breunig, 208; Brinton et al., vol. 2, 590.
120. Breunig, 207.
121. Hazen, *ES1*, 429; *Cambridge Modern History*, vol. 10, 611–12.
122. Hazen, *ES1*, 429–30.
123. Quoted in *Cambridge Modern History*, vol. 10, 603.
124. Hazen, *ES1*, 431–435.
125. *Cambridge Modern History*, vol. 10, 610–11.
126. Woodham-Smith, 36; see also Guizot, *England*, vol. 4, 441.
127. Hazen, *ES1*, 435–37.
128. Hayes, *ME*, 108.
129. *Cambridge Modern History*, vol. 10, 596, 600–02. The quoted words are *Cambridge's*, not Macaulay's.
130. Hayes, *ME*, 110; Hazen, *ES1*, 447.
131. *Cambridge Modern History*, vol. 10, 618.
132. Hayes, *ME*, 111–12; *Encyclopedia Britannica*, vol. 5, 954; Hazen, *ES1*, 449.
133. Hayes, *ME*, 114–15; see also Schapiro, *MCEH1*, 62–64.
134. Hazen, *ES1*, 440–42.
135. "Many aristocrats took up the cause of factory reform," notes J. Salwyn Schapiro, "partly because they were sincerely desirous of improving

the lot of the workers, and partly because the burden of the reforms would fall upon the manufacturers, whom they cordially disliked" (Schapiro, *MCEH1*, 65–66).

136. Derry, 122–23.

137. An early victim of the repression was the brilliant twenty-year-old mathematician Evariste Galois, who was imprisoned for proposing a toast to Louis Philippe while brandishing a dagger (1831). Upon his release, he was duped into a duel with a renowned marksman who was widely thought to be in the pay of the government. Knowing that death was assured, Galois spent his last hours furiously summarizing his mathematical theories. A century and a half later, they would play a crucial role in the long-sought proof to Fermat's Last Theorem (Singh, 221–26; Bell, 372–77).

138. Hazen, *ES1*, 116–18.

139. *Cambridge Modern History*, vol. 10, 479 and 487.

140. …"the fragments sticking against the opposite wall" (Blanc, vol. 2, 280).

141. Schapiro *MCEH2*, 81; *Encyclopedia Britannica*, vol. 7, 849.

142. Brinton et al., vol. 2, 553.

143. Breunig, 216*fn*; Gavin, 90.

144. Gavin, 77; J.S.C. Abbott, *Louis Philippe*, 352.

145. Gavin, 73; J.S.C. Abbott, *Napoleon III*, 153–54.

146. *Cambridge Modern History*, vol. 10, 484.

147. *Cambridge Modern History*, vol. 10, 496–507.

148. Brinton et al., vol. 2, 549.

149. French commandos actually stumbled upon him in his bedclothes during a dawn shore raid, but failed to recognize him. Apprehending their confusion, the wily generalissimo directed them to the room of a fellow general who was still fast asleep. The Frenchmen thus made off with the wrong quarry. As the party re-embarked, Santa Anna led a mock cavalry charge along the pier they were vacating to give the appearance that he was driving them into the sea. Although a shot from a French artillery piece spoiled the drama by killing his horse and tearing off his leg, Santa Anna managed to salvage something from the episode by embalming the severed limb in a bottle of preservative to be displayed from time to time as a trophy of his "victory" over the French.

150. *Annual Register* [1839], 494.

151. Breunig, 218; Schapiro, *MCEH2*, 81–82.

152. Hayes, *ME*, 118

153. May, *Metternich*, 97; Schapiro, *MCEH2*, 82; Asimov, 358.

154. Breunig, 214.

155. Robertson, 31.

156. Roberston, 40; Lamartine, *HFR*, vol. 1, 100.

157. J.S.C. Abbott, *Napoleon III*, 308; Langer, 13.

158. Namier, 8–9.

159. Hazen, *ES1*, 189, 192.

160. Robertson, 70–74.

161. Langer, 25; Robertson, 76.

162. Langer, 29–32.

163. Langer, 32.

164. Hazen, *ES1*, 197.

165. The young prince actually boasted a dual claim of succession, for his father, Louis, was a brother of the great Napoleon, while his mother, Hortense, was the daughter of Napoleon's wife, Josephine (by a prior marriage). He was thus a nephew of the great Napoleon on his father's side and an adoptive grandson on his mother's side (*Encyclopedia Britannica*, vol. 19, 211).

166. *Encyclopedia Britannica*, vol. 19, 212.

167. Guérard, 31; Duff, 28–29; Bierman, 27.

168. Smith, 2.

169. Hazen, *ES1*, 129.

170. Bierman, 43–44.

171. Guérard, 41–42.

172. Quoted in *Encyclopedia Britannica*, vol. 19, 213.

173. Hazen *ES1*, 449; Derry, 134. Wellington had met Louis Napoleon in London in the late 1830s following the Strasbourg affair, and had not shared his faith in his ultimate destiny, saying, "Would you believe it, this young man will not have it said that he is not going to be emperor of the French … his chief thoughts are of what he will do when he is on the throne" (*Encyclopedia Britannica*, vol. 19, 212).

174. Robertson, 99; Geer, 120–21; J.S.C. Abbott, *Napoleon III*, 355; Guérard, 60; Bierman, 68.

175. Vandam, 237. (See also, Guérard, 20).

176. Vandam, 236–37. (See also, Robertson, 101.)

177. Robertson, 84.

178. Smith, 7.

179. Hazen, *ES1*, 168.

180. *Cambridge Modern History*, vol. 11, 48–49.

181. Robertson, 118–23, 135.

182. Breunig, 243.

183. Hayes, *ME*, 126.

184. In the absence of a constitution, says the *Cambridge Modern History* (vol. 10, 356–58), the empire was ruled by a bureaucracy of "systematic ineptitude" erected as if by design "to give no service its full reward, no faculty its complete development, no man his right role." Long before the revolution, the emperor characterized his realm as "a worm-eaten house; if one part is removed, one cannot tell how much will fall," while Metternich lamented that he had spent his life "propping up the mouldering edifice."

185. West, 485.

186. Phillips, 277.

187. Hazen, *ES1*, 171.

188. Hayes, *ME*, 133.

189. Phillips, 277.

190. Phillips, 279–80.

191. Hayes, *ME*, 130.

192. Phillips, 280.

193. Phillips, 280.

194. Hazen, *ES1*, 166.

195. Larousse, 306; Langer, 57–59.

196. Hayes, *ME*, 135.

197. Namier, 23; Brinton et al., vol. 2, 560; Breunig, 251; Langer, 153; Robertson, 245; Hayes, *ME*, 134.

198. Hayes, *ME*, 138.

199. Langer, 156.

200. Robertson, 253

201. Langer, 167, 170–71; Robertson, 292–95.

202. Langer, 116–18; Robertson, 364–67.

203. The French Catholic Party would accept nothing less than an unconditional restitution of the Pope's temporal authority over the city. Hence, a surrender on terms, negotiated by Ferdinand de Lesseps (later of Suez Canal fame) just days prior to the siege, was disavowed and the bloodshed commenced (*Cambridge Modern History*, vol. 11, 125–26).

204. Robertson, 379; Hazen, *FYE*, 12.

205. Hayes, *ME*, 124.

206. Phillips, 287; Langer, 59–60; Robertson, 362.

207. Wolf, 225–6.

208. Langer, 165–70; Robertson, 253–58.

209. Hazen, *ES1*, 179.

210. Hazen, *ES1*, 180.

211. Szabó, 38–41; Langer, 170–74.

212. Robertson, 266, 305–06; Breunig, 251; Schapiro, *MCEH2*, 195–198.

213. Hazen, *ES1*, 185–86; Hayes, *ME*, 144.

214. Phillips, 329–31; Hayes, *ME*, 142.

Chapter 2

1. Hazen, *ES1*, 202.

2. Cobban, vol. 2, 153–54.

3. Wolf, 232–33.

4. Guérard, 67; *Cambridge Modern History*, vol. 11, 134.

5. *Encyclopedia Britannica*, vol. 19, 213.

6. *Cambridge Modern History*, vol. 11, 135.

7. Hayes, *ME*, 155–56.

8. Hazen, *ES1*, 203–05; Cobban, vol. 2, 155.

9. Guérard, 73–74.

10. *Cambridge Modern History*, vol. 11, 138.

11. Cobban, vol. 2, 156.

12. *Cambridge Modern History*, vol. 11, 138.

13. Guérard, 74.

14. Cobban, vol. 2, 156.

15. J.S.C. Abbott, *Napoleon III*, 470; (see also Smith, 12).

16. Hayes, *ME*, 157.

17. Phillips, 332.

18. See Guizot, *England*, vol. 5, 173.

19. *Cambridge Modern History*, vol. 10, 170.

20. Schapiro, *MCEH1*, 625; Hayes, *ME*, 493.

21. Schapiro, *MCEH1*, 625.

22. Larousse, 287; Swallow, 22–23.

23. Hazen, *ES1*, 605–06.

24. Phillips, 136.

25. Goodwin, 282; A. Palmer, *DFOE*, 85–86; Kinross, 444.

26. Hazen, *ES1*, 607.

27. Hazen, *ES1*, 608.

28. Swallow, 9; Palmer, *DFOE*, 91.

29. Swallow, 40.

30. Macfie, 21–22.

31. *Encyclopedia Britannica*, vol. 27, 458.

32. Smith, 41; Crankshaw, *SWP*, 132. (A diplomatic initiative brokered by Austria—known as the Vienna Note—calling for a Russian withdrawal from the principalities in return for a written assurance that Turkey would not change her Christian policy without prior approval from France and Russia was accepted by the tsar, but was refused by Turkey, which regarded the agreement as an infringement upon her sovereignty [Royle, ch. 4]).

33. Hayes, *ME*, 161.

34. Hazen, *ES1*, 613; Phillips, 339.

35. Hayes, *ME*, 162.

36. Woodham-Smith, 144.

37. Mosse, *LE*, 132; Farwell, 69.

38. Woodham-Smith, 170–72; Mosse, *LE*, 132; P. Warner, *CW*, 34; Royle, 113.

39. Mosse, *LE*, 132; Royle, 106.

40. Farwell, 68–70.

41. Woodham-Smith, 177; Royle, 178, 193.

42. P. Warner, *CW*, 23; Phillips, 353.

43. *Cambridge Modern History*, vol. 11, 317.

44. Royle, 218–19; Woodham-Smith, 196–98; P. Warner, *CW*, 29.

45. Woodham-Smith, 200.

46. P. Warner, *CW*, 30–31; Royle, 225–26; Woodham-Smith, 201.

47. P. Warner, *CW*, 30–34; Woodham-Smith, 200–06.

48. Crankshaw, *SWP*, 137; Woodham-Smith, 209.

49. Woodham-Smith, 209–16; Guizot, *England*, vol. 5, 196–8; P. Warner, *CW*, 46ff.

50. Phillips, 353; *Cambridge Modern History*, vol. 11, 318.

51. Woodham-Smith, 272. Estimates of the carnage vary: Warner puts the dead at 113, the *Annual Register* at about 230 including the captured. Whatever the actual number, those who survived owed much of their good fortune to a brave French cavalry charge which silenced the enemy guns on the northern ridge above the valley.

52. Woodham-Smith, 267–72.

53. *Annual Register of 1854*, 334.

54. P. Warner, *CW*, 29; Woodham-Smith, 198–99.

55. Woodham-Smith, 209–11, and 216–17.

56. *Annual Register of 1854*, 338–39.

57. Royle, 284–90; P. Warner, *CW*, 74–78; *Annual Register of 1854*, 340–46.

58. Falls, *HYW*, 34; Churchill, *HESP*, vol. 4, 76.

59. Royle, 394–95. P. Warner, *CW*, 152–53.

60. Woodham-Smith, 289; *Encyclopedia Britannica*, vol. 7, 453.

61. Hazen, *ES1*, 615.

62. *Encyclopedia Britannica*, vol. 7, 453.

63. Crankshaw, *SWP*, 150; Royle, 412–14.

64. Hazen, *ES1*, 615.

65. *Encyclopedia Britannica*, vol. 7, 453.

66. Hayes, *ME*, 163.

67. The new king's steadfastness in this matter gained him the epithet of "the Honest King" (Hazen *ES1*, 216).

68. Schapiro *MCEH1*, 208.

69. Hazen, *FYE*, 15.

70. *Encyclopedia Britannica*, vol. 5, 582; Hazen, *ES1*, 216.

71. Brinton et al., vol. 2, 606; May, *HOC*, vol. 2, 369.

72. *Cambridge Modern History*, vol. 11, 376.

73. Hazen, *ES1*, 218–19.

74. Smith, 43.

75. *Encyclopedia Britannica*, vol. 5, 584.

76. *Cambridge Modern History*, vol. 11, 305.

77. Phillips, 362.

78. *Cambridge Modern History*, vol. 11, 323.

79. Phillips, 359–60. In a move calculated to win French favor, Cavour alone among the assembled leaders gave enthusiastic support to this proposal (Phillips, 362).

80. Guérard, 100.

81. Bierman, 197; Hazen, 227.

82. Hazen, *FYE*, 9; Falls, *HYW*, 43; Duff, 140–41; Bierman, 197–98: The Geneva Convention and International Red Cross owe their origins to Solferino's butchery.

83. Hayes, *ME*, 171.

84. Schapiro, *MCEH1*, 213.

85. Hazen *ES1*, 228–29.

86. Hazen, *ES1*, 230.

87. According to Phillips, the affirmative vote in Nice was falsely obtained (379).

88. Hazen, *ES1*, 230–31; Larousse, 314.

89. Phillips, 382.

90. Hayes, *ME*, 173.

91. Hazen, *FYE*, 10, 15.

92. Schapiro, *MCEH1*, 162; see also Phillips, 449–50.

93. Breunig, 220.

94. Guérard, 138.

95. Cobban, vol. 2, 167.

96. Horne, *TY*, 4.

97. Christiansen, 65.

98. Schapiro, *MCEH1*, 145–46.

99. Rich, *ANR* (95) notes that an economic recession following the financial panic of 1857 dampened some benefits of the new free trade policy, and that businesses adversely affected by tariff reductions would not be mollified even government subsidies.

100. John, 41.

101. John, 22, 41–42.

102. Hayes, *ME*, 158–59.

103. Schapiro, *MCEH1*, 156.

104. Schapiro, *MCEH1*, 155–56; Hazen, *ES1*, 272.

105. In 1868, the state took measures to provide workman's death and disability insurance (Hayes *ME*, 159.

106. *Cambridge Modern History*, vol. 11, 471.

107. Hayes, *ME*, 176; *Cambridge Modern History*, vol. 11, 475.

108. Hayes, *ME*, 178; *Cambridge Modern History*, vol. 11, 476.

109. Hayes, *ME*, 177.

110. Hayes, *ME*, 177–78.

111. Hazen, *ES1*, 278.

112. Bierman, 228.

113. *Cambridge Modern History*, vol. 11, 485.

114. *Cambridge Modern History*, vol. 10, 354.

115. Wikipedia contributors. "Thaler." https://en.wikipedia.org/wiki/Thaler#Legacy Accessed 8/5/21.

116. The County of Mark, the Duchy of Cleves, the bishoprics of Magdeburg, Minden and Halberstadt, the Pomeranias, the Prussias, Silesia, portions of Westphalia, *inter alia*.

117. *Cambridge Modern History*, vol. 10, 354.

118. *Cambridge Modern History*, vol. 10, 354–55, 372.

119. *Cambridge Modern History*, vol. 10, 373, 378–79; Hazen, *ES1*, 148–49.

120. *Cambridge Modern History*, vol. 10, 355.

121. Hazen, *FYE*, 17; Hayes, *ME*, 183–84.

122. A.J.P. Taylor, *BMS*, 58; Headlam, 168–69.

123. Brinton et al., vol. 2, 619.

124. Larousse, 316.

125. Brinton et al., vol. 2, 620; Churchill, *HESP*, vol. 4, 268.

126. Holmes, 117, 119.

127. Fair, 292; Parker, 233–34; Falls, *HYW*, 72–73.

128. Headlam, 247.

129. Parker, 233–34; R. Holmes, 119; Asimov, 381–83.

130. Parker, 236.

131. Holmes, 133; Falls, *HYW*, 94–95.

132. John, 91.

133. Duff, 176–77; Bierman, 299–302.

134. John, 92.

135. Fuller, *MHWW*, vol. 3, 98; Larousse, 317.

136. Christiansen, 133; Bierman, 334.

137. Hazen, *ES1*, 283; Schapiro, *MCEH1*, 159–60; *Cambridge Modern History*, vol. 11, 492.

138. Smith, 35; Bierman, 321.

139. Hazen, *ES1*, 283; Schapiro, *MCEH1*, 160.

140. Robinson, vol. 2, 590.

141. Hazen, *FYE*, 27.

142. Falls, ed., *GMB*, 192, 196; Fair, 292.

143. Wolf, 347; Fair, 292.

144. Fair, 293.

145. Fair, 293; Fuller, *MHWW*, vol. 3, 106.

146. Fair, 293.

147. Falls, *HYW*, 104–05; Fuller, *MHWW*, vol. 3, 114.

148. Falls, ed., *GMB*, 197, 200.

149. Parker, 239–40.

150. Guérard, 193; Hayes, *ME*, 200.

151. C. Morris, 221 (Moltke's quote); Holmes, 147; Christiansen, 152; Bierman, 356 (Ducrot's quote).

152. Fair, 300; Guérard, 193–94; Fuller, *MHWW*, vol. 3, 122–24.

153. Fair, 300–01.

154. Fair, 303; Fuller, *MHWW*, vol. 3, 126.

155. *Encyclopedia Britannica*, vol. 24, 576; Fair, 302–03.

156. Hooper, 278.

157. Hazen, *FYE*, 29; see also Bierman, 365.

158. Alistair Horne employs this term, *TY*, 33*ff*.

159. Horne, *TY*, 41.

160. Hazen, *FYE*, 31; Christiansen, 210; Horne, *TY*, 39, 46–47.

161. *Cambridge Modern History*, vol. 12, 136.

162. Christiansen, 282–85; Edwards, *PC*, 135–41.

163. Christiansen, 320; Smith, 67.

164. *Annual Register of 1871*, 197–98. (The Communard defenders had been chased off by artillery fire.)

165. Washburne, vol. 2, 212.

166. Cobban, vol. 2, 210. (Jim Morrison is buried in Père Lachaise—Christiansen, 368).

167. Hazen, *ES1*, 335–36.

168. Quoted in the introduction (by Freidrich Engels) to K. Marx, 22.

169. *Encyclopedia Britannica*, vol. 28, 665.

170. Oman, vol. 3, 647; *Gentlemen's Magazine*, February, 1868, 252; Derry, 108.

171. Strachey, 73.

172. Jo. Burke, 241; Strachey, 74.

173. *Cambridge Modern History*, vol. 10, 676.

174. *Encyclopedia Britannica*, vol. 21, 40.

175. Jenkins, 8.

176. Evans, 8; Jenkins, 16.

177. Evans, 36, 56.

178. Evans, 24.

179. Quoted in Evans, 34.

180. Oman, vol. 3, 662.

181. Evans, 51; Derry, 150.

182. Evans, 66.

183. The name, according to Guizot, had been decided at an early gathering of like-minded souls, where "Mr. Cobden had been describing the Hanseatic League, and other similar associations formed in the Middle Ages for the purpose of resisting aristocratic oppression and protecting the working classes. 'Why do we not have a League?' cried someone in the audience. 'Yes,' rejoined Cobden, 'an Anti-Corn'-Law League'" (Guizot, *England*, vol. 5, 71).

184. Derry, 159–162.

185. Schapiro, *MCEH1*, 70; Hazen, *ES1*, 452–53.

186. Evans, 29.

187. *Cambridge Modern History*, vol. 11, 3.

188. Evans, 64–65.

189. Woodham-Smith, 114–17; Schapiro, *MCEH2*, 309–10; Churchill, *HESP*, vol. 4, 343.

190. Hazen, *FYE*, 130.

191. Woodham-Smith, 122; May, *HOC*, vol. 2, 295.

192. Guizot, *England*, vol. 5, 94–95.

193. *Encyclopedia Britannica*, vol. 9, 561.

194. Evans, 69.

195. Churchill, *HESP*, vol. 4, 59–61.

196. Derry, 164; Oman, vol. 3, 667.

197. Trollope, 19; Chamberlain, *LP*, 21; Barton, 37.

198. Chamberlain, *LP*, 21; Barton, 38.

199. Trollope, 41–42; see also Barton, 41–42.

200. Chamberlain, *LP*, 31.

201. Chamberlain, *LP*, 27; Trollope, 32.

202. Trollope, 33.

203. Trollope, 60–61.

204. *Encyclopedia Britannica*, vol. 20, 647.

205. Barton, 75–76.

206. Barton, 67–69, 80–81.

207. Trollope, 110.

208. Chamberlain, *LP*, 59; *Encyclopedia Britannica*, vol. 20, 647. Aberdeen's more celebrated "Oregon Treaty" of 1846 established the 49th Parallel as the boundary between what is now the state of Washington and the Canadian province of British Columbia.

209. Chamberlain, *LP*, 60–61.

210. Trollope, 142–143.

211. Chamberlain, *LP*, 68.

212. *Encyclopedia Britannica*, vol. 20, 648.

213. Quoted in Guizot, *England*, vol. 5, 132; Chamberlain, *LP*, 74; Derry, 173, Barton, 80; see also reference in *Encyclopedia Britannica*, vol. 20, 648.

214. Trollope, 9–10.

215. Trollope, 190.

216. Chamberlain, *LP*, 80–82.

217. Chamberlain, *LP*, 64, 88.

218. Chamberlain, *LP*, 98.

219. *Encyclopedia Britannica*, vol. 20, 648.

220. Farwell, 101.

221. *Annual Register of 1857*, 292.

222. The troops had been dispatched by Palmerston to settle the concurrent *Arrow* Affair.

223. Churchill, *HESP*, vol. 4, 87.

224. Hazen, *ES1*, 522. (See also Churchill, *HESP*, vol. 4, 87.)

225. *Encyclopedia Britannica*, vol. 9, 572; Chamberlain, *LP*, 114–15; Trollope, 256.

226. *Encyclopedia Britannica*, vol. 9, 572.

227. *Encyclopedia Britannica*, vol. 9, 571; see also, Chamberlain, *LP*, 117; Guizot, *England*, vol. 5, 345–46.

228. *Encyclopedia Britannica*, vol. 9, 571.

229. Trevelyan, 489.

Chapter 3

1. *Cambridge Modern History*, vol. 12, 767–68.

2. *Cambridge Modern History*, vol. 12, 770.

3. Boak et al., 696, 701.

4. *Encyclopedia Britannica*, vol. 25, 888; Schapiro, *MCEH1*, 33; Wallbank and Taylor, vol. 2, 154. The *Rocket's* average speed on the Manchester-Liverpool line was 13 miles per hour. Prior to his work on steam locomotion, Stephenson invented a safe mining lamp very similar to that engineered by Humphrey Davey. In the 1850s, he built a railway between Alexandria and Cairo in Egypt, which facilitated overland communications between the Mediterranean and Red Sea coasts. Impractical for heavy commerce, it nonetheless

provided a critical shortcut for postal contacts with India during the Indian Mutiny of 1857 (Chamberlain, *SFA*, 35).

5. Mosse, *LE*, 23.

6. Wells, *OH1*, 925.

7. Schapiro, *MCEH1*, 32–33.

8. Hayes, *ME*, 74.

9. The ends were to be spliced together at sea once the first spool was exhausted.

10. Rich, *ANR*, 9–10.

11. The story of the transatlantic cable is stirringly told in J.S. Gordon's *A Thread Across the Ocean*.

12. Wells, *OH2*, 960, gives a fuller discussion.

13. Wells, *OH2*, 966.

14. Mosse, *LE*, 34.

15. *Encyclopedia Britannica*, vol. 26, 23–24. Harun al-Rashid had considered the construction of a canal as early as the 8th century, but had dropped the idea out of fear that it would invite a Byzantine naval assault on the Arabian peninsula. We shall never know if manual labor could have been used successfully at that distant date (*Encyclopedia Britannica*, vol. 26, 22).

16. Wallbank and Taylor, vol. 2, 153, 294.

17. *Encyclopedia Britannica*, vol. 26, 547–58.

18. *Encyclopedia Britannica*, vol. 11, 496.

19. Rich, *ANR*, 1–2.

20. Rich, *ANR*, 3. Liebig began his professional career in a pharmacy at age 15, but was sacked within the year, after his compulsive extra-curricular experimentation led to a number of mishaps—explosions included (*Encyclopedia Britannica*, vol. 16. 591).

21. *Encyclopedia Britannica*, vol. 20, 893.

22. He also solved the riddle of a silkworm plague in France and prevented its recurrence (*Encyclopedia Britannica*, vol. 20, 893–94).

23. Wallbank and Taylor, vol. 2, 295, 298.

24. Haggard, 345.

25. Haggard, 348–49.

26. Wallbank and Taylor, vol. 2, 295.

27. Haggard, 352.

28. Sutcliffe and Duin, 62–63; Haggard, 352–53.

29. Ashton, 9–10.

30. Previously, if a corporation was sued, its stockholders were liable and could lose their life savings. The limited-liability laws reduced their risk to the worth of their shares.

31. Schapiro, *MCEH1*, 37–41.

32. Hayes, *ME*, 65.

33. Ashton, 19–20; Breunig, 199.

34. Wallbank and Taylor, vol. 2, 163–64; Rich, *ANR*, 23–24.

35. Wallbank and Taylor, vol. 2, 163.

36. Brinton et al., vol. 2, 571; Rich, *ANR*, 23; Hazen, *ES1*, 455–56.

37. Hayes, *ME*, 85; Wallbank and Taylor, vol. 2, 164.

38. Indeed, with the repeal of the Corn Laws in 1846, England's capitalists won a signal victory over the rival landed aristocracy, who championed protectionist tariffs in order to inflate the price of their agricultural products and thereby retain their wealth and influence at a time when the expansion of rail travel made large-scale, long-distance shipping of fresh produce feasible (which ought to have increased competition and lowered prices). Hayes, *ME*, 89–93.

39. Brinton et al., vol. 2, 572–73.

40. Wallbank and Taylor, vol. 2, 168; Brinton et al., vol. 2, 572. (The contemporary philosopher, Jeremy Bentham [1748–1832], generally agreed with the "hands off" [or *laissez faire*] approach of the "liberals" Malthus and Ricardo with regard to governmental economic regulation; yet his philosophy of utilitarianism—which taught that government institutions should be judged on the degree of happiness they provided to the greatest number— led him to concede that if the actions of a minority were creating widespread distress that government should indeed intervene. Only at mid-century did "liberalism" take on a more modern aspect with the writings of John Stuart Mill [1806–1873], a staunch believer in individual liberty, universal suffrage and women's rights, who generally subscribed to *laissez faire* economics, but favored government regulation to abolish abusive working conditions) (Brinton et al., vol. 2, 574–576).

41. Breunig, 220.

42. Schapiro, *MCEH2*, 565–66.

43. Breunig, 256–77.

44. *Encyclopedia Britannica*, vol. 21, 485.

45. Brinton et al., vol. 2, 660.

46. Brinton et al., vol. 2, 660. *Encyclopedia Britannica* (vol. 14, 344) agrees, saying the movement arose in response to "scientific research into the principles of light and colour, just as earlier movements in painting coincided with the scientific study of perspective and anatomy." Norman Rich (*ANR*, 60), however, argues that the involved artists were actually mistaken in their notion of the science behind light.

47. *Encyclopedia Britannica*, vol. 14, 343.

48. Rich, *ANR*, 54.

49. Rich, *ANR*, 55–57; Brinton et al., vol. 2, 657; Wallbank and Taylor, vol. 2, 286–92.

50. Rich, *ANR*, 63–65.

51. Talmon, 192–93; Breunig, 256–7; Brinton et al., vol. 2, 561. (Quote is from Hazen, *FYE*, 17; see also Headlam, 165.)

52. May, *HOC*, vol. 2, 393.

53. Sutcliffe and Duin, 67.

54. Brinton et al., vol. 2, 653.

55. Wallbank and Taylor, vol. 2, 300.

Chapter 4

1. In imposing this large indemnity on France, Germany had hoped to saddle that nation with financial burdens that would cripple its ability to embark on a war of revenge for fifty years (Schecter, 5). Instead, French finances enjoyed a remarkable recovery, while the sudden influx of indemnity payments into the German economy triggered

a short-lived speculative boom followed (when the payments ceased) by a financial panic—Germany's contribution to the Panic of 1873 (Wolf, 363).

2. There was in fact a third faction composed of Bonapartists, but defeat has so tarnished the reputation of Bonapartism that it commanded only a handful of supporters.

3. *Encyclopedia Britannica*, vol. 10, 874.

4. Hayes, *ME*, 339; *Encyclopedia Britannica*, vol. 10, 875.

5. Shirer, *Republic*, 37.

6. *Encyclopedia Britannica*, vol. 10, 875.

7. Wolf, 372–3.

8. Hazen, *FYE*, 78; Wolf, 374–6.

9. Wolf, 395; Cobban, vol. 2, 221.

10. Shirer, *Republic*, 42; *Encyclopedia Britannica*, vol. 10, 878.

11. As he nearly did after a minor incident on the German frontier.

12. Wolf, 401–02.

13. *Encyclopedia Britannica*, vol. 10, 879.

14. Rich, *ANR*, 197; Wolf, 402.

15. Defined by Cobban (vol. 2, 224) as "bonapartism without a Bonaparte."

16. *Encyclopedia Britannica*, vol. 4, 319.

17. Pope Leo XIII, it is true, issued a papal encyclical in 1892 entreating French Catholics to accept their form of government, which had now demonstrated its resilience; but his object seems to have been the creation of a Catholic republican party (which actually came into being under the name *Ralliés)* that could pursue legislation favorable to the church—and in any event, the majority of Catholic leaders would have no truck with France's "Atheistic Republic" even at the bidding of the pope (Wolf, 403–04)

18. Wolf, 406–07.

19. Shirer, *Republic*, 48*fn*; *Encyclopedia Britannica*, vol. 2, 143.

20. Bein, 80.

21. *Cambridge Modern History*, vol. 12, 120.

22. *Encyclopedia Britannica,* vol. 2, 134.

23. Bein, 80–81.

24. Quoted in Burns, 10–11.

25. Hayes, *ME*, 355.

26. *Encyclopedia Britannica*, vol. 2, 143; see also, Shirer, *Republic*, 48*fn*.

27. Bein, 115.

28. Shirer, *Republic*, 54.

29. Schechter, 19; Halasz, 31.

30. *Encyclopedia Britannica*, vol. 2, 119 and vol. 3, 812–813.

31. Schecter, 19; Halasz, 32.

32. Bredin, 74*fn*.

33. Bredin, 73.

34. Shirer, *Republic*, 59; Cobban, vol. 2, 239.

35. Originally entitled, *Letter to the President of the Republic*, the catchier title of *I Accuse* was suggested by Georges Clemenceau (Schechter, 125–26).

36. Tuchman, *Tower*, 227–31, Schechter, 131–35.

37. Schechter, 114; Burns, 45; Shirer, *Republic*, 48.

38. Schechter 159–61; Bredin, 309–10, 316.

39. Schechter, 162–63; Bredin, 324–25.

40. Shirer, *Republic*, 54; Schechter, 180–82.

41. Schapiro, *MCEH1*, 256.

42. Shirer, *Republic*, 71–72.

43. Schapiro, *MCEH1*, 263; Wolf, 418.

44. Hayes, *ME*, 361–63; Wolf, 380–83; Schapiro *MCEH1*, 235–36; F. Gilbert, 57–58.

45. Schapiro, *MCEH1*, 254–55.

46. Schechter, 253–55.

47. *Cambridge Modern History*, 12, 137.

48. Hayes [1920], 397.

49. Brinton et al., vol. 2, 624.

50. Schapiro, *MCEH1*, 278–79; Rich, *ANR*, 218.

51. Schapiro, *MCEH1*, 280.

52. Hazen, *FYE*, 59.

53. Hazen, *FYE*, 57.

54. Schapiro, *MCEH1*, 279.

55. Hazen, *FYE*, 55–6.

56. D. Stevenson, quoted in Abrams, 13.

57. *Cambridge Modern History*, vol. 12, 137.

58. *Encyclopedia Britannica*, vol. 4, 8.

59. *Encyclopedia Britannica*, vol. 11, 875–77.

60. Hayes, *ME*, 401.

61. Hayes, *ME*, 404–05.

62. Hayes, *ME*, 404; *Encyclopedia Britannica*, vol. 11, 877–78.

63. *Encyclopedia Britannica*, vol. 11, 874, 879.

64. Hayes, *ME*, 405–06.

65. These included Bavaria, Baden, Württemberg and Hesse-Darmstadt.

66. A.J.P. Taylor, *BMS*, 149; *Cambridge Modern History*, 137; Porter and Armour, 5; *Encyclopedia Britannica*, vol. 12, 876–77. Bismarck referred to these groups, together with Jews and socialists, as *Reichsfeinde* or "enemies of the Reich" (Abrams, 28*ff*).

67. Schapiro, *MCEH1*, 290; *Cambridge Modern History*, vol. 12, 148.

68. Williamson, *BG*, 54.

69. Schapiro, *MCEH1*, 290–91; Hayes, *ME*, 408; Hazen, *ES1*, 308.

70. Brinton et al., vol. 2, 623; Schapiro, *MCEH1*, 291. In this controversy the pope and emperor had locked horns over which of them should have the authority to invest bishops.

71. Hayes, *ME*, 409; see also *Encyclopedia Britannica*, vol. 11, 881.

72. *Cambridge Modern History*, vol. 12, 149.

73. Hazen, *ES1*, 309.

74. *Encyclopedia Britannica*, vol. 11, 881.

75. Hayes, *ME*, 409.

76. Williamson, *BG*, 53.

77. *Encyclopedia Britannica*, vol. 11, 881; *Cambridge Modern History*, vol. 12, 149.

78. A growing chorus of anti-Semitic conspiracy theorists, of course, blamed this crisis entirely on the Jews (Williamson, *BG*, 51–52).

79. Rich, *ANR*, 223; Brinton et al., vol. 2, 624.

80. Schapiro, *MCEH1*, 292.

81. Hazen, *ES1*, 314.

82. Schapiro, *MCEH1*, 288.

83. Shapiro, *MCEH1*, 296 [emphasis added].

84. Hazen, *ES1*, 316.

85. A.J.P. Taylor, *BMS*, 203; Abrams, 40–41.

86. Röhl, 34; Hazen, *FYE*, 52.

87. Although the Catholic Center Party had supported Bismarck in his pivot to protectionism at the end of the *Kulturkampf*, the party proved an inconsistent political ally, employing its significant voting clout to place a brake on many of the chancellor's favored initiatives. Indeed, for most of the ensuing decade, Bismarck lost control of the *Reichstag*. Only after the elections of 1887 was he able to forge a dependable *Kartell*, or coalition of parties, in that body (Williamson, *BG*, 60–61).

88. Hazen, *ES1*, 415.

89. Schapiro, *MCEH1*, 309.

90. Hazen, *FYE*, 302; Wallbank and Taylor, vol. 2, 253.

91. Wallbank and Taylor, vol. 2, 253; May, *HOC*, vol. 2, 431–32.

92. May, *HOC*, vol. 2 430.

93. May, *HOC*, vol. 2, 433.

94. Brinton et al., vol. 2, 625; Hayes, *ME*, 416.

95. Wallbank and Taylor, vol. 2, 254.

96. Wallbank and Taylor, vol. 2, 254; Brinton et al., vol. 2, 625; May, *HOC*, vol. 2, 435.

97. Wallbank and Taylor, vol. 2, 255.

98. Brinton et al., vol. 2, 625; Schapiro, *MCEH1*, 310; Hayes, *ME*, 420.

99. Wallbank and Taylor, vol. 2, 254; Schapiro, *MCEH1*, 310.

100. Schapiro, *MCEH1*, 313, 319.

101. Schapiro, *MCEH1*, 308–09; see also, Hayes, *ME*, 415–16.

102. Brinton et al., vol. 2, 625; Schapiro, *MCEH1*, 308.

103. *Encyclopedia Britannica*, vol. 28, 668.

104. Abrams, 52.

105. Röhl, 3–9.

106. Schapiro, *MCEH1*, 308.

107. Hayes, *ME*, 416; *Encyclopedia Britannica*, vol. 28, 667.

108. Wells, *OH1*, 1005.

109. Their bourgeois and aristocratic betters attended different schools preparing them for the university and for serving as leaders (Wallbank and Taylor, vol. 2, 254).

110. Schapiro, *MCEH1*, 322–23.

111. See Wolfgang Mommsen's quote in Abrams, 50; see also Porter and Armour, 20.

112. Abrams, 66.

113. Schapiro, *MCEH1*, 323.

114. Porter and Armour, 16, 19.

115. Brinton et al., vol. 2, 625–26; Schapiro, *MCEH1*, 317.

116. Abrams, 54, 66–67.

117. Porter and Armour, 19–20.

118. Abrams, 68–69.

Chapter 5

1. Barton, 121.

2. Trevelyan, 483.

3. Trevelyan, 483.

4. Quoted in Chamberlain, *LP*, 123.

5. Chamberlain, *LP*, 109; *Cambridge Modern History*, vol. 11, 339.

6. Derry, 188.

7. Chamberlain, *LP*, 109.

8. Hazen, *ES1*, 462.

9. Roth, 27.

10. *Encyclopedia Britannica*, vol. 3, 564.

11. Aldous, 16; Parry, 5.

12. Roth, 28–29; *Encyclopedia Britannica*, vol. 3, 564.

13. *Encyclopedia Britannica*, vol. 3, 564.

14. Parry, 5; Aldous, 16–17.

15. Roth, 36.

16. Roth, 41–42.

17. Roth supplies the term, 47.

18. Disraeli's speech in the Debate on Opening Letters at the Post Office, February 28, 1845; Hansard's Parliamentary Debates, vol. 78 cc138–208, reproduced at https://api.parliament.uk/historic-hansard/commons/1845/feb/28/opening-letters-at-the-post-office accessed 8/7/21.

19. Disraeli's speech on the third reading of the Bill on the Repeal of the Corn Laws: 15 May 1846; *Hansard's Parliamentary Debates*, 3/LXXVI, cols. 665–679, http://www.historyhome.co.uk/polspeech/dizcorn.html accessed 8/7/21.

20. Roth, 97; Aldous, 63–64.

21. Roth, 98; Aldous, 61.

22. Roth, 99; Parry, 51.

23. MP Sydney Herbert quoted in Weintraub, Stanley. *Disraeli: A Biography*. New York: Turman Talley Books and reproduced at https://en.wikipedia.org/wiki/Benjamin_Disraeli accessed 8/7/21; see also Aldous, 67.

24. Parry, 62.

25. *Cambridge Modern History*, vol. 11, 340.

26. Derry, 196.

27. Roth, 106.

28. Parry, 75; Derry, 197; Aldous, 175–76, 179.

29. Roth, 107; Hazen, *ES1*, 464.

30. Schapiro, *MCEH1*, 76.

31. *Cambridge Modern History*, vol. 11, 342; Hazen, *ES1*, 464; Schapiro, *MCEH1*, 76.

32. Walton, *SRA*, 28; see Derry, 193–94 for a fuller illustration of Lowe's views.

33. Hazen, *ES1*, 464.

34. Hazen, *ES1*, 463.

35. Hayes, *ME*, 284.

36. Roth, 100.

37. Disraeli, 282. The Albert Memorial came to fruition in 1876 and stands in Kensington Gardens, London.

38. Woodham-Smith, 119–20.

39. *Cambridge Modern History*, vol. 11, 343.

40. Oman, 704; *Cambridge Modern History*, vol. 11, 343; *Encyclopedia Britannica*, vol. 10, 255.

41. *Encyclopedia Britannica*, vol. 10, 255.

42. *Cambridge Modern History*, vol. 11, 344.

43. Hazen, *ES1*, 467.

44. *Cambridge Modern History*, vol. 11, 344.

45. Aldous, 192–93.

46. Parry, 79; Apjohn,169.
47. *Cambridge Modern History*, vol. 11, 345.
48. Apjohn, 172.
49. Roth, 112.
50. Oman, 702.
51. *Encyclopedia Britannica*, vol. 12, 67.
52. *Encyclopedia Britannica*, vol. 12, 68.
53. *Encyclopedia Britannica*, vol. 12, 69.
54. Aldous, 53–54, 84–86.
55. Apjohn, 118.
56. Winstanley, *GLP*, 38–39.
57. Winstanley, *GLP*, 10.
58. Winstanley, *GLP*, 9.
59. Apjohn, 144.
60. Winstanley, *GLP*, 12–13.
61. Asimov, 396.
62. Hazen, *FYE*, 131, 138; Jo. Burke, 263.
63. Hazen, *ES1*, 467; see Aldous, 202, for a description of the circumstances.
64. Oman, 706; *Cambridge Modern History*, vol. 12, 24.
65. Hazen, *ES1*, 478; Rich, *ANR*, 156; *Cambridge Modern History*, vol. 12, 24–25.
66. Rich, *ANR*, 157; *Cambridge Modern History*, vol. 12, 25.
67. Jarman, 21.
68. Oman, 708.
69. Hazen, *ES1*, 482.
70. Hazen, *ES1*, 485–86; Rich, *ANR*, 158–59.
71. Rich, *ANR*, 158; Winstanley, *GLP*, 48.
72. Disraeli, 187 (from a speech delivered in the Free Trade Hall at Manchester, April 3, 1872); see also Trevelyan, 513; Rich, *ANR*, 158.
73. Disraeli, 185.
74. Hazen, *ES1*, 485.
75. Roth, 134–35.
76. He thereupon entered the House of Lords but remained prime minister.
77. *Cambridge Modern History*, vol. 12, 33; *Encyclopedia Britannica*, vol. 9, 576.
78. D. Morris, 47, 50; Barthorp, 18.
79. Barthorp, 18*ff*.
80. Barthorp, 55–56; D. Morris, 362; Farwell, 226.
81. Barthorp, 139–45; Morris, 517–34.
82. Oman, 712.
83. Rich, *ANR*, 161; *Cambridge Modern History*, vol. 12, 36.
84. Aldous, 271–72.
85. Rich, *ANR*, 162.
86. See Aldous, 297–98 for the numbers, recorded by Gladstone himself in his diary.
87. Aldous, 317–19. (Aldous notes that the £10,000 advance Disraeli received for *Endymion* broke a previous record of £9,000 obtained by Charles Dickens [Aldous, 311]).
88. *Encyclopedia Britannica*, vol. 14, 782–84; Rich, *ANR*, 164.
89. Oman, 715–16; *Encyclopedia Britannica*, vol. 14, 783.
90. Oman, 716; *Encyclopedia Britannica*, vol. 14, 782–83; Rich, *ANR*, 164.
91. *Encyclopedia Britannica*, vol. 17, 447–48.

92. *Cambridge Modern History*, vol. 12, 39.
93. *Encyclopedia Britannica*, vol. 9, 577.
94. *Cambridge Modern History*, vol. 12, 39.
95. Hazen, *ES1*, 540.
96. *Encyclopedia Britannica*, vol. 9, 114.
97. Oman, 713.
98. *Encyclopedia Britannica*, vol. 9, 114; Oman, 714; *Cambridge Modern History*, vol. 12, 439.
99. Farwell, 275.
100. Moorehead, *WN*, 238–39.
101. Jo. Burke, 266–67.
102. Oman, 716; Hazen, *ES1*, 493–95.
103. *Encyclopedia Britannica*, vol. 9, 578.
104. Hazen, *ES1*, 497.
105. Jarman, 39.
106. Hazen, *FYE*, 141–6.
107. Hazen, *ES1*, 503.
108. Hazen, *ES1*, 505–06.
109. Schapiro, *MCEH1*, 391.
110. Hazen, *ES1*, 506–07.
111. Jarman, 55.
112. Hazen, *FYE*, 149.
113. Hazen, *FYE*, 150; Tuchman, *Tower*, 41–42.
114. Aldous, 320.
115. Powell, 94.
116. Hazen, *ES1*, 506.
117. May, vol. 2, 507; Kiernan, 85–6; Asimov, 459.
118. *Encyclopedia Britannica*, vol. 9, 127–28.
119. *Encyclopedia Britannica*, vol. 9, 128–29.
120. Farwell, 336–37.
121. *Encyclopedia Britannica*, vol. 9, 129.
122. Moorhead, *WN*, 337.
123. *Encyclopedia Britannica*, vol. 9, 129; Churchill, *RW*, 181.
124. F. Gilbert, 41; Rice, *GPD*, 275.
125. Hazen, *FYE*, 184–85; Schapiro, *MCEH1*, 415.
126. Jarman, 56; Schapiro, *MCEH1*, 415; Ward, 49.
127. *Encyclopedia Britannica*, vol. 15, 147.
128. Jo. Burke, 279; *Encyclopedia Britannica*, vol. 23, 256.
129. See the conflicting descriptions of Hazen, *FYE*, 185, and Jo. Burke, 279.
130. *Encyclopedia Britannica*, vol. 23, 256.
131. Powell, 106–08.
132. *Encyclopedia Britannica*, vol. 27, 201.
133. Hazen, *ES1*, 542.
134. *Encyclopedia Britannica*, vol. 27, 202.
135. Jo. Burke, 280; F. Gilbert, 45; *Encyclopedia Britannica*, vol. 27, 203.
136. Tuchman, *Tower*, 67.
137. Churchill, *HESP*; vol. 4, 383. (Jo. Burke, 281, says one in five.)
138. F. Gilbert, 46.
139. Jarman, 64.
140. Hazen, *ES1*, 514; see also, Schapiro, *MCEH1*, 342.
141. Ward, 20–22.
142. *Encyclopedia Britannica*, vol. 5, 814.
143. *Encyclopedia Britannica*, vol. 5, 814; Ward, 37.

144. *Encyclopedia Britannica*, vol. 5, 814.

145. Ward, 51; Tuchman, *Tower*, 64.

146. Jarman, 99–100.

147. *Encyclopedia Britannica*, vol. 5, 815; Jarman, 60–61.

148. Jarman, 61; *Encyclopedia Britannica*, vol. 5, 815; Ward, 47.

149. Jarman, 61; Powell, 112–13.

150. *Encyclopedia Britannica*, vol. 5, 816.

151. Hayes, *ME*, 302.

152. Powell, 136.

153. *Encyclopedia Britannica*, vol. 5, 818.

154. Hazen, *FYE*, 156–59; Tuchman, *Tower*, 452–55.

155. Hazen, *FYE*, 159.

Chapter 6

1. Quoted in Wallbank and Taylor, vol. 2, 218.

2. *Encyclopedia Britannica*, vol. 3, 17.

3. Brinton et al., vol. 2, 626; Palmer, *TOTH*, 82–83, 102.

4. Wallbank and Taylor, vol. 2, 236.

5. Hazen, *ES1*, 389; Rich, *ANR*, 202.

6. *Cambridge Modern History*, vol. 12, 176; Wallbank and Taylor, vol. 2, 236; Austrian and Czech troops that might have turned the tide in Italy had to be left behind to guard against rebellion in Hungary. (Palmer, *TOTH*, 110–11).

7. Crankshaw, *FHH*, 185–88.

8. Schapiro, *MCEH1*, 425.

9. Wallbank and Taylor, vol. 2, 237.

10. Hazen, *ES1*, 390, 393.

11. *Cambridge Modern History*, vol. 12, 183; Schapiro, *MCEH1*, 426; see also, Wallbank and Taylor, vol. 2, 237.

12. Mason, 7.

13. Phillips, 447.

14. *Encyclopedia Britannica*, vol. 3, 18; Schapiro, *MCEH1*, 426.

15. Hayes, *ME*, 430.

16. The various Slavic peoples of the empire held the plurality with 24 million.

17. Hayes, *ME*, 427.

18. Brinton et al., vol. 2, 627–28.

19. Hayes, *ME*, 433.

20. Brinton et al., vol. 2, 633–35; Schapiro, *MCEH1*, 440.

21. Crankshaw, *FHH*, 260; see also Wallbank and Taylor, vol. 2, 368; Davis, 48; Wawro, 4.

22. Schapiro, *MCEH1*, 432–33; Hazen, *ES1*, 399; Rich, *ANR*, 207. While the towns sent one deputy to the *Reichsrath* for every 2900 voters, the rural districts had but one deputy for every 11,600 voters.

23. Hazen, *ES1*, 397.

24. Schapiro, *MCEH1*, 432; Crankshaw, *FHH*, 252.

25. *Cambridge Modern History*, vol. 12, 189, 193. Excluded from most career pathways, many Jews excelled at business. The very anti-Semites who excluded them from other pursuits, now singled them out as convenient scapegoats for the lower middle class, many of whom were losing out to Jewish competitors in small business pursuits (Brinton et al., vol. 2, 632–33).

26. *Cambridge Modern History*, vol. 12, 194; Crankshaw, *FHH*, 280.

27. The term was his and only later adopted by the British (Rich, *ANR*, 208; Crankshaw, *FHH*, 280.

28. Quoted in Rich, *ANR*, 208; see also, Wawro, 26; Palmer, *TOTH*, 218.

29. *Cambridge Modern History*, vol. 12, 194.

30. *Encyclopedia Britannica*, vol. 3, 31.

31. Mason, 35.

32. Hazen, *ES1*, 400; *Cambridge Modern History*, vol. 12, 194–95.

33. Hazen, *ES1*, 401.

34. *Encyclopedia Britannica*, vol. 3, 34.

35. Mason, 40.

36. *Encyclopedia Britannica*, vol. 3, 36; Schapiro, *MCEH1*, 434.

37. Crankshaw, *FHH*, 313; Schaprio, *MCEH1*, 434.

38. *Cambridge Modern History*, vol. 12, 208–09.

39. Mason, 41–42.

40. Mason, 9; Crankshaw, *FHH*, 314–15, 317–18.

41. Hayes, *ME*, 434–35.

42. Crankshaw, *FHH*, 289.

43. Bergamini, 332–34.

44. Bergamini, 316; May, *HOC*, vol. 2, 455–56.

45. May, *HOC*, vol. 2, 455; Mosse, *AMR*, 12–17.

46. May, *HOC*, vol. 2, 456; Walbank and Taylor, vol. 2, 256–57. Rendered apathetic by generations of servitude and lacking even the rudiments of education, the serfs had made very poor students of the modern military art while composing the rank and file of the army during the Crimean War (Rich, *ANR*, 170).

47. Bergamini, 316.

48. Quoted in Grahame, 101.

49. Schapiro, *MCEH1*, 511.

50. May, *HOC*, vol. 2, 456; Asimov, 392; Rich, *ANR*, 171.

51. Families included (Crankshaw, *SWP*, 168).

52. Rich, *ANR*, 171; Crankshaw, *SWP*, 168–69, and 175; Mosse, *AMR*, 67.

53. Rich, *ANR*, 171–72; Schapiro, *MCEH1*, 514–15; Hayes, *ME*, 455; *Cambridge Modern History*, vol. 11, 615–17.

54. Bergamini, 336.

55. Hayes, *ME*, 455; Schapiro, *MCEH1*, 512.

56. Mosse, *AMR*, 9.

57. Brinton et al., vol. 2, 639; Shapiro, *MCEH1*, 514; Walbank and Taylor, 258; *Cambridge Modern History*, vol. 11, 620.

58. *Cambridge Modern History*, vol. 11, 619.

59. Mosse, *AMR*, 9; *Cambridge Modern History*, vol. 11, 619.

60. Van Der Kiste, 59; Brinton et al., vol. 2, 639; Hazen, *ES1*, 665–66.

61. Phillips, 401.

62. Arnold and Zychowski, 132. Potebnia had formerly been a tsarist officer.

63. Phillips, 406.

64. Arnold and Zychowski, 132.

65. Indeed, by allowing Russian troops to pursue Polish fugitives into Prussian territory, Bismarck strengthened Russia's hand, while forging an entente that helped ensure Austria's isolation in the Seven Weeks' War.

66. Phillips, 406; Arnold and Zychowski, 132–33; Kuczynski et al., 97.

67. Van Der Kiste, 60; Bergamini, 342.

68. Bergamini, 343.

69. Hayes, *ME*, 457; Schapiro, *MCEH1*, 515.

70. Brinton et al., vol. 2, 642; Hazen, *ES1*, 666.

71. Many Nihilists were students of the sciences. At the outset of the reign, the government had promoted education in the sciences in hopes training future bureaucrats. But, says *Encyclopedia Britannica*, "it discovered to its astonishment that there was some mysterious connexion between natural science and revolutionary tendencies. Many of the young men and women, who were supposed to be qualifying as specialists in the various spheres of industrial and commercial enterprise, were in reality devoting their time to considering how human society … could be reconstructed in accordance with the latest physiological, biological and sociological principles. Some of these young people wished to put their crude notions immediately into practice, and … their desire to make gigantic socialist experiments naturally alarmed the government…." Accordingly, scientific teaching was restricted, and emphasis was placed on learning foreign languages. *Encyclopedia Britannica*, vol. 1, 561.

72. Hazen, *FYE*, 257; Asimov, 421; Crankshaw, *SWP*, 270.

73. *Cambridge Modern History*, vol. 12, 310.

74. Crankshaw, *SWP*, 270; Duffy and Ricci, 320–21; Bergamini, 355.

75. Schapiro, *MCEH1*, 528; Hazen, *ES1*, 673.

76. Bergamini, 379.

77. Hazen, *ES1*, 674; Schapiro, *MCEH1*, 543.

78. Mosse, *AMR*, 11, 88.

79. Schapiro, *MCEH1*, 543.

80. Schapiro, *MCEH1*, 524; see also Hayes, *ME*, 461.

81. Hazen, *ES1*, 670–71; Schapiro, *MCEH1*, 525; Hayes, *ME*, 461.

82. Schapiro, *MCEH1*, 527.

83. Schapiro, *MCEH1*, 532; Van Der Kiste, 125; Bergamini, 364.

84. Hayes, *ME*, 472.

85. Hayes, *ME*, 462.

86. Bergamini, 365.

87. Wallbank and Taylor, vol. 2, 260.

88. Duffy and Ricci, 327.

89. Bergamini, 386; Crankshaw, *SWP*, 305.

90. Van Der Kiste, 187.

91. Duffy and Ricci, 329; Bergamini, 391.

92. Duffy and Ricci, 329–30.

93. Duffy and Ricci, 330–31; Van Der Kiste, 194.

94. Schapiro, *MCEH1*, 546.

95. Crankshaw, *SWP*, 310–311.

96. Schapiro, *MCEH!*, 546.

97. Hazen, *ES1*, 677–78.

98. Hayes, *ME*, 473; Schapiro, *MCEH1*, 543; *Cambridge Modern History*, vol. 12, 320.

99. Hazen, *ES1*, 675.

100. *Cambridge Modern History*, vol. 12, 320.

101. Crankshaw, *SWP*, 290; Hayes, *ME*, 473–74; *Cambridge Modern History*, vol. 12, 321.

102. *Cambridge Modern History*, vol. 12, 320.

103. Hazen, *ES1*, 677.

104. Crankshaw, *SWP*, 287.

105. Hazen, *ES1*, 677.

106. Shapiro, *MCEH1*, 540–41.

107. Schapiro, *MCEH1*, 541.

108. Hayes, *ME*, 476–78.

109. Crankshaw, *SWP*, 291–93.

110. Hayes, *ME*, 477.

111. Crankshaw, *SWP*, 298.

112. *Encyclopedia Britannica*, vol. 21, 835.

113. Tuchman, *Tower*, 130; Schapiro, *MCEH2*, 457.

114. More insidious was the publication of a phony document entitled *The Protocols of the Learned Elders of Zion*, which was purported to be proof of a Jewish conspiracy to conquer the world by financial means. *Okhrana*, the Russian secret police, had plagiarized most of it from a polemical satire written in France against Napoleon III, and even the dull-witted Nicholas II knew it to be a forgery. Nevertheless, it was popularly accepted, and remains a staple of anti–Semitism down to our own day (M. Gilbert, *AJC*, 152).

115. Schapiro, *MCEH1*, 549.

116. See Nigel Fowler Sutton's brief photo-documentary at https://www.youtube.com/watch?v=-gtmfmi6D6I Accessed 11/13/18. Sipyagin's assassination was also Azev's doing. It was not until 1908 that he was exposed as a double agent (Schapiro, *MCEH1*, 548–49; Crankshaw, *SWP*, 298).

117. Farwell, 15–16.

118. Farwell, 19–20.

119. Schapiro, *MCEH1*, 661; Hayes, *ME*, 566.

120. Hazen, *ES1*, 683; Schapiro, *MCEH1*, 662.

121. Hazen, *ES1*, 698.

122. Hazen, *FYE*, 275–76; Schapiro, *MCEH1*, 668.

123. Duffy and Ricci, 334; Bergamini, 401.

124. Reischauer et al., vol. 2, 469–70, 480; Schapiro, *MCEH2*, 629. (French loans had also been involved.)

125. Hazen, *FYE*, 277–78; Falls, *HYW*, 178–79.

126. Crankshaw, *SWP*, 329.

127. Duffy and Ricci, 334–35.

128. Crankshaw, *SWP*, 331.

129. Bergamini, 403.

130. Hazen, *ES1*, 709; Schapiro, *MCEH1*, 551.

131. *Cambridge Modern History*, vol. 12, 349.

132. Crankshaw, *SWP*, 345.

133. Hazen, *ES1*, 711–12; Schapiro, *MCEH1*, 555–56; *Cambridge Modern History*, vol. 12, 358.

134. It was at this point that Pobiedonostsev was finally dismissed from public office.

135. Schapiro, *MCEH1*, 559–60.

136. Brinton et al., vol. 2, 646.

137. Hazen [1910], 713; *Cambridge Modern History*, vol. 12, 364.

138. Schapiro, *MCEH1*, 560–61; Hazen, *ES1*, 714–15; Crankshaw, *SWP*, 364–65; *Cambridge Modern History*, vol. 12, 368.

139. "… a vital assault," as Hazen notes, "on the integrity of the assembly." (Hazen, *ES1*, 715.)

140. *Encyclopedia Britannica*, vol. 23, 910–11. Under article 87 of Goremykin's "organic laws" the government had the right to rule by decree when the Duma was not in session. But any decrees thus passed were to be subject to review by the Duma within 60 days of its reconvening. Here, the government altered the electoral law by decree in order to ensure that the Duma would be *an entirely different body* when it returned to session, in effect making a mockery of its power of review—scarcely a sign of respect for the rule of law (Crankshaw, *SWP*, 369–370). The effect of the electoral decree, as Bergamini, has noted was to render "the vote of 1 landowner … worth that of about 26 peasants or of 540 city workers." (Bergamini, 409).

141. Schapiro, *MCEH1*, 563.

142. Brinton et al., vol. 2, 646.

143. Hayes, *ME*, 485; *Encyclopedia Britannica*, vol. 23, 911; Schapiro, *MCEH1*, 567–68; Duffy and Ricci, 339.

144. Hayes, *ME*, 484; *Cambridge Modern History*, vol. 12, 374; Duffy and Ricci, 338.

145. Duffy and Ricci, 338–39; Bergamini, 408.

146. Hayes, *ME*, 484.

147. Schapiro, *MCEH1*, 563; Bergamini, 408.

148. *Encyclopedia Britannica*, vol. 23, 911.

149. Stolypin, himself, had predicted that the police would kill him. (Crankshaw, *SWP*, 373; Bergamini, 410).

150. Victor Emmanuel did not enter the capital until December when a fortuitous flood of the Tiber gave him occasion to show his concern for the people of Rome. (*Encyclopedia Britannica*, vol. 15, 62).

151. Hazen, *FYE*, pp. 96–7; Schapiro, *MCEH1*, 446–47.

152. *Cambridge Modern History*, vol. 12, 216.

153. Schapiro, *MCEH1*, 450; *Encyclopedia Britannica*, vol. 15, 63.

154. Hazen, *FYE*, 98; *Cambridge Modern History*, vol. 12, 214.

155. Schapiro [1918], 443.

156. Rich, *ANR*, 199.

157. *Cambridge Modern History*, vol. 12, 214–15; *Encyclopedia Britannica*, vol. 15, 62.

158. Schapiro, *MCEH1*, 443; Hayes, *FYE*, 100.

159. *Cambridge Modern History*, vol. 12, 215.

160. Rich, *ANR*, 201.

161. Rich, *ANR*, 200–01. "With all their faults," says the *Cambridge Modern History* (vol. 12, 215–16), "the Right had been a political party: the Left initiated a system of government by factions and sectional interests … a system negative of all political rectitude and destructive of healthy party distinctions."

162. Hayes [1920], 373.

163. Schapiro [1918], 451.

164. *Cambridge Modern History*, vol. 12, 219.

165. Hayes, *ME*, 375; *Cambridge Modern History*, vol. 12, 224.

166. Schapiro, *MCEH1*, 452.

167. *Cambridge Modern History*, vol. 12, 219–20; Schapiro, *MCEH1*, 452.

168. *Cambridge Modern History*, vol. 12, 221–22.

169. *Cambridge Modern History*, vol. 12, 223–24.

170. *Cambridge Modern History*, vol. 12, 225–26; Schapiro, *MCEH1*, 453.

171. After Italy's railroads were redeemed from foreign investors (1875–1876), there was an initial period of government ownership during which large operating deficits were accrued (1876–1885). The railroads were then privatized among three Italian companies that continued to mismanage them (1885–1905), leading ultimately to a reinstatement of government control in that year (*Encyclopedia Britannica*, vol. 15, 71).

172. Hayes, *ME*, 374.

173. Schapiro, *MCEH1*, 443; Hazen, *FYE*, 100.

174. Schapiro, *MCEH1*, 445; Hazen, *FYE*, 99. (Hazen puts the illiteracy rate at 40% among army recruits in 1914.)

175. Hayes, *ME*, 377.

176. Hayes, *ME*, 373*fn*.

177. Hayes, *ME*, 377–78.

Chapter 7

1. Rich, *GPD*, 218–19.

2. Schechter, 5.

3. *Cambridge Modern History*, vol. 12, 136.

4. Menning, 177.

5. Crankshaw, *SWP*, 163–64.

6. Rich, *GPD*, 215.

7. Menning, 173.

8. Martel notes that Bismarck meant to make French republicanism seem a greater threat to stability than Germany's sudden increase in power (18).

9. Hayes, *ME*, 693.

10. Williamson, *BG*, 83–85; Abrams, 41–43.

11. Rich, *GPD*, 221.

12. Menning, 178–79.

13. Menning, 178.

14. Seymour, 201; Davis, 76. (See also, Taylor, *BMS*, 167.)

15. Kinross, 509; *Cambridge Modern History*, vol. 12, 384; Crampton, 82.

16. Furneaux, 13; Snyder and Morris, 212. (From the reports of the London *Daily News* correspondent, J. A, MacGahan, who went to Bulgaria to investigate).

17. *Encyclopedia Britannica*, vol. 9, 575; Roth, 141.

18. Davis, 77; Palmer, *DFOE*, 140.

19. Phillips, 496.

20. Palmer, *DFOE*, 142.
21. Annual Register [1876], 276; Hazen, *ES1*, 622.
22. Gladstone, 31.
23. Menning, 181.
24. Phillips, 497.
25. Hazen, *ES1*, 623; see also Phillips, 500; Schapiro, *MCEH1*, 633.
26. Taylor, *SME*, 239; Phillips, 501.
27. Rice, *GPD*, 223.
28. Taylor, *SME*, 241; Menning, 181.
29. Phillips, 505.
30. Rich, *GPD*, 223.
31. Hayes, *ME*, 518–19.
32. Haze, *ES1*, 619.
33. Phillips, 505; Davis, 85.
34. Furneaux (forward), 7.
35. Phillips, 506.
36. Crankshaw, *SWP*, 242; Kinross, 521; Furneaux, 46.
37. Furneaux, 55–77, 117–39, 146–47.
38. Furneaux, 150–216
39. Hazen, *FYE*, 239; Hayes, *ME*, 518.
40. Schapiro, *MCEH1*, 685.
41. Rich, *GPD*, 223; see Menning, 184, for the text of the agreement; see also, Hayes, *ME*, 507.
42. Davis, 90; see also, Rich, *GPD*, 224.
43. Oman, 711.
44. Davis, 89.
45. Hayes, *ME*, 505; see also Roth, 148.
46. Rich, *GPD*, 226.
47. Roth, 149.
48. Phillips, 517.
49. Taylor, *SME*, 246.
50. Davis, 83; Swallow, 76.
51. Taylor, *SME*, 246.
52. Parry, 105.
53. Roth, 150.
54. Roth, 150.
55. Schapiro, *MCEH1*, 635; see also, *Cambridge Modern History*, vol. 12, 394.
56. Schapiro, *MCEH2*, 471–72; Remak, 12–13.
57. Macfie, 44.
58. Davis, 95.
59. *Cambridge Modern History*, vol. 12, 392, 396.
60. Davis, 90.
61. *Encyclopedia Britannica*, vol. 9, 945.
62. Hazen, *FYE*, 50–51; Schapiro, *MCEH1*, 686; Remak, 12–16.
63. Williamson, *BG*, 76; Martel, 31.
64. Remak, 25.
65. Davis, 320; Schapiro, *MCEH1*, 687; Hayes, *ME*, 698.
66. Tuchman, *Tower*, 67.
67. Kinross, 566–67.
68. Hazen, *FYE*, 149.
69. Henig, *OFWW*, 9; Martel, 47.
70. Fuller, *MHWW*, vol. 3, 171–177 says Britain already feared this commercial threat; Henig, 9–11, describes it more in terms of a fear Germany wished to instill in Britain to bring her to the table.
71. Martel, 37.
72. Martel, 42.
73. Hayes, *ME*, 701.
74. Tuchman, *Guns*, 18–19; Jo. Burke, 288; Jarman, 121.
75. *Encyclopedia Britannica*, vol. 8, 999.
76. Tuchman, *Guns*, 63; Marshall, 47–48; Hayes, *ME*, 702.
77. Tuchman, *Guns*, 24.
78. Martel, 11.
79. Tuchman, *Guns*, 21; Jarman, 121.
80. Hazen, *FYE*, 235.
81. Hayes, *ME*, 518; Schapiro, *MCEH1*, 637.
82. Hazen, *FYE*, 240; Schapiro, *MCEH1*, 637–38.
83. Hayes, *ME*, 519.
84. Hazen, *FYE*, 242.
85. Hazen, *FYE*, 242.
86. Davis, 266.
87. Hayes, *ME*, 516.
88. Crampton, 95.
89. Davis, 252; see also *Cambridge Modern History*, vol. 12, 395–96.
90. *Cambridge Modern History*, vol. 12, 395.
91. Crampton, 101.
92. Davis, 249.
93. Crampton, 102.
94. *Cambridge Modern History*, vol. 12, 408.
95. Davis, 254.
96. *Cambridge Modern History*, vol. 12, 408; Hazen, *FYE*, 236–7; Kinross, 541; Hayes, *ME*, 522.
97. Davis, 255–56.
98. Davis, 256.
99. *Cambridge Modern History*, vol. 12, 410.
100. *Encyclopedia Britannica*, vol. 25, 768.
101. Hazen, *ES1*, 631.
102. *Encyclopedia Britannica*, vol. 25, 768–69; Crampton, 112.
103. *New York Times*, July 19, 1895.
104. Hazen, *FYE*, 240.
105. *Encyclopedia Britannica*, vol. 24, 694.
106. *Encyclopedia Britannica*, vol. 24, 694.
107. Davis, 261*fn*.
108. *Cambridge Modern History*, vol. 12, 413.
109. *Cambridge Modern History*, vol. 12, 413.
110. Hayes, *ME*, 521; *Encyclopedia Britannica*, vol. 24, 695.
111. *Encyclopedia Britannica*, vol. 24, 695.
112. Shapiro, *MCEH1*, 640.
113. Swallow, 89; Kinross, 573.
114. Davis, 270 (quote), 277 (moniker). Davis (277) cites a British estimate of 50,000 massacred versus an American estimate of 75,000. Hayes, *ME*, 524) puts the figure at 100,000 to 200,000.
115. Kinross, 574–75.
116. Hazen, *FYE*, 244; see also Kinross, 574.
117. Hayes, *ME*, 525.
118. Davis, 285.
119. *Encyclopedia Britannica*, vol. 27, 464; see also, Mason, 64–65; Wawro, 59.
120. Davis, 424.
121. Davis, 286.
122. Davis, 287.
123. Schapiro, *MCEH1*, 645.
124. Quoted in Kinross, 584.
125. Macfie, 51.

126. Hazen, *FYE*, 307.

127. Rich, *GPD*, 426.

128. Hazen, *FYE*, 304, 307; Hayes, *ME*, 528; Davis, 432.

129. Hayes, *ME*, 529. The starting date of October 8 is taken from Rich, *GPD*, 427.

130. Schapiro, *MCEH1*, 646–47.

131. Hazen, *FYE*, 309; Davis, 437.

132. Davis, 437–38.

133. Palmer, *DFOE*, 217; Kinross, 591.

134. Hazen, *FYE*, 309–10; Kinross, 590–91.

135. The demographics are taken from Henig, *OFWW*, 19.

136. Hazen, *FYE*, 310–11; Liddell-Hart, *RW*, 20.

137. Palmer, *DFOE*, 218. Enver posed as a conqueror, but there had been no resistance as the Serbs and Bulgarians had already departed.

138. Davis, 448. Taken out of context, the reference to Armageddon may strike the reader as amusing, but Davis does not refer here to the Biblical Armageddon. Rather, throughout his book he employs the term as a synonym for World War I—the closest thing to Armageddon the world had seen (apart perhaps from the Black Death) since the dawn of history.

139. Quoted in Henig, *OFWW*, 5.

140. Davis, 483.

141. Henig, *OFWW*, 22; Mason, 73–74; M. Gilbert, *FWW*, 6.

142. Davis, 484.

143. Henig, *OFWW*, 15–17.

Chapter 8

1. *Encyclopedia Britannica*, vol. 25, 633; see also Moorehead, *WN*, 83–85.

2. *Encyclopedia Britannica*, vol. 2, 726.

3. Chamberlain, *SFA*, 44–46.

4. *Encyclopedia Britannica*, vol. 2, 727–28.

5. H. A.C. Cairns employed the phrase "cultural arrogance" in a 1965 work (Chamberlain, *SFA*, 24).

6. *Encyclopedia Britannica*, vol. 16, 813–14.

7. Chamberlain, *SFA*, 25.

8. *Encyclopedia Britannica*, vol. 4, 864–65.

9. *Encyclopedia Britannica*, vol. 25, 633.

10. Traveling north along the river for some distance, they encountered Samuel Baker who was exploring from the opposite direction and informed him of their findings. Baker then proceeded on his way and following a separate branch of the Nile discovered Lake Albert, which fed into the Nile from the west (1864).

11. Moorehead, *WN*, 81–83.

12. Pakenham, 20; *Encyclopedia Britannica*, vol. 16, 814.

13. *Encyclopedia Britannica*, vol. 16, 815.

14. *Encyclopedia Britannica*, vol. 16, 815; Moorehead, *WN*, 125–26; Pakenham, 5–7.

15. *Encyclopedia Britannica*, vol. 16, 815.

16. Pakenham, 7.

17. *Encyclopedia Britannica*, vol. 25, 780.

18. Quoted in Moorehead, *WN*, 127.

19. Pakenham, xxii.

20. Chamberlain, *SFA*, 50.

21. Pakenham, 19–20; Chamberlain, *SFA*, 50.

22. Chamberlain, *SFA*, 50; *Encyclopedia Britannica*, vol. 25, 780; Pakenham, 20.

23. *Encyclopedia Britannica*, vol. 25, 780.

24. *Encyclopedia Britannica*, vol. 25, 780.

25. See Chamberlain, *SFA*, 28, 101–02 for Stanley's motives and outlook.

26. Chamberlain, *SFA*, 3.

27. In his short Lancaster pamphlet, *The Partition of Africa*, J.M. MacKenzie explores these factors in detail, neatly dividing them into causes arising in Europe (termed "metropolitan") and causes arising in Africa (termed "peripheral")—but the take home point is most pithily captured by M.E. Chamberlain in her statement that "overarching theories," which formerly dominated the debate, "are…in retreat before multi-causal explanations" (Chamberlain, *SFA*, 94).

28. Gollwitzer, 23.

29. Chamberlain, *SFA*, 95.

30. J.M. MacKenzie, 18; Chamberlain, *SFA*, 53–54.

31. Hayes, *ME*, 619.

32. *Encyclopedia Britannica*, vol. 6, 920; Pakenham, 411.

33. It's size was 112,000 square miles (*Encyclopedia Britannica*, vol. 6, 920), which Hayes notes as ten times the size of Belgium (Hayes, *ME*, 620).

34. Schapiro, *MCEH1*, 678.

35. Pakenham, 588 (using the conversion factor of $5 to the pound). The value was up from $30,000 annually in 1886, indicating the value of the monopoly.

36. Pakenham, 591.

37. Hazen, *ES1*, 557.

38. *Encyclopedia Britannica*, vol. 6, 922.

39. Totten et al., 13–15, 32–36.

40. Totten et al., 14, 19.

41. Totten et al., 14.

42. Totten et al., 3; Pakenham, 609–12.

43. Sources for the Herero genocide: Totten, et. al., 3–40; Pakenham, 602–615.

44. J. M. MacKenzie, 45.

45. Riffenburgh, 18–19.

46. *Encyclopedia Britannica*, vol. 21, 951.

47. *Encyclopedia Britannica*, vol. 19, 163.

48. Riffenburgh, 20–23; *Encyclopedia Britannica*, vol. 19, 163.

49. Riffenburgh, 24–25.

50. *Encyclopedia Britannica*, vol. 21, 30; Riffenburgh, 44.

51. Riffenburgh, 44–45.

52. Riffenburgh, 42–43.

53. *Encyclopedia Britannica*, vol. 21, 968.

54. Quoted in the *Oxford Dictionary of National Biography* under H.G.R. King's entry, *Scott, Robert Falcon [known as Scott of the Antarctic]*. Accessed 5/17/20. https://www.oxforddnb.com/view/10.1093/ref:odnb/9780198614128.001.0001/odnb-9780198614128-e-35994; for Scott's expedition, see also Riffenburgh, 46–49.

55. Chamberlain, *SFA*, 35–36; J.M. MacKenzie, 37.

56. Wikipedia contributors, "Turbinia." *Wikipedia.org* https://en.wikipedia.org/wiki/Turbinia Accessed 8/9/21.

57. Wells. *OH1*, 925; Schapiro, *MCEH1*, 651.

58. See Wikipedia contributors, "SS Aberdeen (1881)" and "*Titanic.*" *Wikipedia.org* https://en.wikipedia.org/wiki/SS_Aberdeen_(1881) ; https://en.wikipedia.org/wiki/Titanic Accessed 8/9/21.

59. Weightman, 279–82.

60. *Encyclopedia Britannica*, vol. 26, 867.

61. Schapiro, *MCEH1*, 652.

62. Wells, *OH1*, 926–27.

63. *Encyclopedia Britannica*, vol. 11, 496; Weightman, 312–13.

64. *Encyclopedia Britannica*, vol. 18, 915–16.

65. Dunlop was Scottish, but was practicing in Belfast, Ireland, when he invented his tire. During the patent search it was discovered that a fellow Scotsman, Robert W. Thomson, had already developed a pneumatic tire in 1846, although it had not caught on. Consequently, Thomson is still credited with the invention, and Dunlop could only patent those aspects of his tire that were different (Weightman, 304–07).

66. *Encyclopedia Britannica*, vol. 18, 919–20.

67. Weightman, 322.

68. *Encyclopedia Britannica*, vol. 10, 518.

69. *Encyclopedia Britannica*, vol. 26, 547–48.

70. *Encyclopedia Britannica*, vol. 26, 548–49 gives a confusing explanation; better is that given in Wikipedia contributors, "Invention of the Telephone." *Wikipedia.org* https://en.wikipedia.org/wiki/Invention_of_the_telephone Accessed 8.9.21

71. Weightman, 338; *Encyclopedia Britannica*, vol. 16, 667. Of historical note, prior to incandescence, Humphry Davy had produced battery-powered electric lighting as early as 1801 employing an "arc" method, wherein two electrodes were brought into contact and then separated, generating an electric arc between them accompanied by a painfully bright and maddeningly inconsistent light beam (*Encyclopedia Britannica*, vol. 16, 659). In 1878, the Russian inventor, Paul Jabochkov, created a commercially viable arc lighting system suitable for large areas such as streetlights and buildings using alternating current electricity (*Encyclopedia Britannica*, vol. 9, 188). It was incandescence, however, that made electric lighting viable for routine use.

72. The quoted analogy is from Wells, *OH1*, 927. See also, Henderson, 57; Van Doren, 270.

73. Wikipedia contributors, "Werner von Siemens." *Wikipedia.org.* https://en.wikipedia.org/wiki/Werner_von_Siemens Accessed 8/9/21.

74. The Russian, Fyodor Pirotsky, was the first to build a working electric tram. See Wikipedia contributors, https://en.wikipedia.org/wiki/History_of_trams Accessed 8/9/21.

75. *Encyclopedia Britannica*, vol. 9, 189.

76. Davis, 271.

77. *Encyclopedia Britannica*, vol. 9, 191.

78. *Encyclopedia Britannica*, vol. 9, 191; Henderson, 57.

79. Montross, 712.

80. Fuller, *MHWW*, vol. 3, 177.

81. *Encyclopedia Britannica*, vol. 17, 242.

82. *Encyclopedia Britannica*, vol. 17, 242–43; 918.

83. *Encyclopedia Britannica*, vol. 2, 689; vol. 20, 220–21.

84. *Encyclopedia Britannica*, vol. 1, 869; vol. 2, 689.

85. Wells, *OH1*, 1000–02.

86. Davis, 336–37.

87. Davis, 338–40.

88. Schapiro, *MCEH1*, 699.

89. Hayes, *ME*, 687.

90. Henig, *OFWW*, 14–15. The statistics provided are likewise from Henig.

91. Quoted in Wallbank and Taylor, vol. 2, 297.

92. Wallbank and Taylor, vol. 2, 300.

93. Quoted in Wallbank and Taylor, vol. 2, 300.

94. Freud's quoted phrases are from: Marcaggi, Geoffrey, and Guénolé, Fabian. "Freudarwin: Evolutionary Thinking as a Root of Psychoanalysis." *Frontiers in Psychology*, June 19, 2018. https://www.frontiersin.org/articles/10.3389/fpsyg.2018.00892/full#B33 Accessed 5/13/20; see also, Brinton, et al, vol. 2, 666 and 904–06.

95. May, *HOC*, vol. 2, 568; Wallbank and Taylor, vol. 2, 301; Brinton et al., vol. 2, 667.

96. Quoted in Brinton et al., vol. 2, 667.

97. Smithfield, Brad. "Friedrich Nietzsche went mad after allegedly seeing a horse being whipped in the Italian city of Turin." *The Vintage News*, February 5, 2017. https://www.thevintagenews.com/2017/02/05/friedrich-nietzsche-went-mad-after-allegedly-seeing-a-horse-being-whipped-in-the-italian-city-of-turin/ Accessed 5/14/20.

98. Brinton et al., vol. 2, 658.

99. Zola, front matter "about the author."

100. *Encyclopedia Britannica*, vol. 19, 275.

101. *Encyclopedia Britannica*, vol. 14, 225.

102. May, *HOC*, vol. 2, 559.

103. Wallbank and Taylor, vol. 2, 291.

104. *Encyclopedia Britannica*, vol. 7, 906; Wallbank and Taylor, vol. 2, 290.

105. *Encyclopedia Britannica*, vol. 23, 447 and vol. 7, 906.

106. The defense that the impressionistic artist "determines which of the shapes and tones are of chief importance to the *interested* eye, enforces these and sacrifices the rest," and that in so doing, "uses the same freedom of sacrifice as the man who at the other end of the scale expresses his interest in things by a few scratches of outline," could not hold back the critics indefinitely. (Quoted phrases are from *Encyclopedia Britannica*, vol. 14, 345–46.)

107. Wallbank and Taylor, vol. 2, 588.

108. Brinton et al., vol. 2, 661; Wallbank and Taylor, 587.

109. See Kelly Richman Abdou, "Why Post-Impressionist Painter Paul Cézanne is known as

"The Father of Modern Art." *My Modern Met*, May 11, 2018. https://mymodernmet.com/paul-cezanne-paintings/ Accessed 5/6/20; and Claudia Rousseau, Ph.D., "Cézanne Portraits in the National Gallery of Art." *East City Art*, June 6, 2018. https://www.eastcityart.com/reviews/cezanne-portraits-national-gallery-art/ Accessed 5/12/20.

110. May, *HOC*, vol. 2, 576.

111. Van Doren, 273.

112. Haggard, 377; Sutcliffe and Duin, 57; Osler, 211.

113. Wallbank and Taylor, vol. 2, 296.

114. Osler, 211–14; see also, Sutcliffe and Duin, 57.

115. Sutcliffe and Duin, 57–59.

116. Osler, 222.

117. Wallbank and Taylor, vol. 2, 295.

118. Osler, 222.

119. Firkin and Whitworth, 550.

120. *Encyclopedia Britannica*, vol. 28, 110.

121. Sutcliffe and Duin, 194.

122. Firkin and Whitworth, 550.

123. *Encyclopedia Britannica*, vol. 28, 110.

124. Sutcliffe and Duin, 65; *Encyclopedia Britannica*, vol. 28, 110.

125. *Encyclopedia Britannica*, vol. 28, 110.

126. Sutcliffe and Duin, 65; Firkin and Whitworth, 551.

127. *Encyclopedia Britannica*, vol. 28, 110; Sutcliffe and Duin, 65.

128. Osler, 228.

129. Osler, 224; Haggard, 389; Sutcliffe and Duin, 95. Alternatively, the surface of the stagnant water can be coated with oil.

130. Haggard, 385.

131. *Encyclopedia Britannica*, vol. 28, 911.

132. Osler, 227.

133. *Encyclopedia Britannica*, vol. 28, 911.

134. Osler, 229.

135. *Encyclopedia Britannica*, vol. 28, 911.

136. Wikipedia contributors, "Health Measures during the construction of the Panama Canal." *Wikipedia.org*. https://en.wikipedia.org/wiki/Health_measures_during_the_construction_of_the_Panama_Canal Accessed 5/15/20.

137. Sutcliffe and Duin, 88–89.

138. Sutcliffe and Duin, 90–91; Bishop, 173.

139. Sutcliffe and Duin, 126–27; Haggard, 335–37; Margotta, 170–71.

140. Wallbank and Taylor, vol. 2, 295.

141. For descriptions of the event, see The Jockey Club contributors, "The Suffragette Derby and Thereafter." Jockeyclub.com https://www.thejockeyclub.co.uk/epsom/events-tickets/epsom-derby/about-the-event/the-derby/suffragette-derby-and-thereafter/ Accessed 5/23/20; Ben Johnson, "Emily Davison, Death at the Derby." *Historic-UK.com* https://www.historic-uk.com/HistoryUK/HistoryofEngland/Emily-Davison-Death-at-the-Derby/ Accessed 5/21/20.

142. Hayes, *ME*, 212.

143. Hayes, *ME*, 214.

144. Hayes, *ME*, 214–17.

145. Schapiro, *MCEH1*, 585; May, *HOC*, vol. 2, 398.

146. Tuchman, *Tower*, 489.

147. Schapiro, *MCEH1*, 606.

148. Sutcliffe and Duin, 79; Haggard, 364–68; *Encyclopedia Britannica*, vol. 28, 787.

149. *Encyclopedia Britannica*, vol. 28, 787.

150. Ben Johnson, *op cit.*

151. Tuchman, *Tower*, 446–48; Schapiro 608.

152. The Jockey Club, *op cit.*; Ben Johnson, *op cit.*

153. Biography, "Emily Davison." *Biography.com* https://www.biography.com/activist/emily-davison; Accessed 5/20/20.

154. The Jockey Club, *op cit*; Ben Johnson, *op cit.*; Schapiro, *MCEH1*, 609.

155. Hayes, *ME*, 260.

156. Quoted in May, *HOC*, vol. 2, 402.

157. This is the opening line of Marx and Engel's *Communist Manifesto*.

158. Hayes, *ME*, 260.

159. Schapiro, *MCEH1*, 573.

160. Hayes, *ME*, 261; May *HOC*, vol. 2, 403.

161. Schapiro, *MCEH1*, 589.

162. May, *HOC*, vol. 2, 405.

163. Schapiro, *MCEH1*, 581; see also, May, *HOC*, vol. 2, 402.

164. Tuchman, *Tower*, 502.

165. Orthodox Marxism was predicated on the idea that proletarian misery must inexorably increase until the socialist revolution occurred in consequence. Hence, to participate in bourgeois government for the purpose of piecemeal reform would betray the very soul of the movement by postponing (or even obviating the need for) revolution. The very idea, therefore, was anathema. Ironically, the Revisionists were more in tune than the Orthodox with most flesh and blood workers, who desired above all not collective ownership of the means of production, but the amelioration of their plight (Tuchman, *Tower*, 480).

166. Hayes, *ME*, 266–67; *Encyclopedia Britannica*, vol. 22, 489–90.

167. Hayes, *ME*, 267.

168. From Sergei Nechayev's *Revolutionary Catechism*, quoted in Hayes, *ME*, 269–70.

169. May, *HOC*, vol. 2, 403.

170. *Encyclopedia Britannica*, vol. 15, 928.

171. *Encyclopedia Britannica*, vol. 1, 918. (Kropotkin authored this *E.B.* article).

172. *Encyclopedia Britannica*, vol. 1, 917.

173. Brinton et al., vol. 2, 584.

174. Tuchman, *Tower*, 88–92.

175. Tuchman, *Tower*, 105–08; quoted also in *Encyclopedia Britannica*, vol. 1, 917fn.

176. *Encyclopedia Britannica*, vol. 1, 916.

177. Tuchman, *Tower*, 102.

178. Crankshaw, *FHH*, 352–3; Tuchman, *Tower*, 118.

179. Tuchman, *Tower*, 121; Hazen, *FYE*, 102.

180. Wallbank and Taylor, vol. 2, 172.

181. Hayes, *ME*, 270–71.

182. Tuchman, *Tower*, 531–32; Schapiro, 269–70; Brinton et al., vol. 2, 605–06; Wolf, 420.

183. Schapiro, *MCEH1*, 269. Not all such strikes were failures: As we have seen, in 1905, a general strike in Moscow and Saint Petersburg led to the establishment of the Duma, while a similar event in Vienna, headed by the socialist Viktor Adler, played a pivotal part in the Austrian government's decision to grant universal male suffrage.

Chapter 9

1. A.J.P. Taylor, *WWI*, 22.

2. Remak, 103–04; Marshall, 11–12; Crankshaw, *FHH*, 400.

3. O'Shea, 21–22; Shermer, 15; Marshall, 8.

4. Palmer, *TOTH*, 323–24.

5. Eurnews, "WWI in historic newspapers: The assassination of Franz Ferdinand." *Europeana Newspapers*. http://www.europeana-newspapers.eu/wwi-in-historic-newspapers-the-assassination-of-franz-ferdinand/ Accessed 8/10/21.

6. Larousse, 347.

7. Remak, 105; Martel, 79.

8. Menning, 401; Martel, 100.

9. Rich, *GPD*, 440; Remak, 105.

10. Liddell Hart, *RW*, 23; see also, Remak, 110.

11. Dimitrijević had played a major role in ousting the Obrenovic Dynasty in favor of the ultra-nationalist Karageorgevics in 1903 (Menning, 399*fn*; Rich, *GPD*, 397).

12. Wawro, 52; Mason, 74; Menning, 397.

13. Remak, 98; Asimov, 491; Shermer, 16; Liddell Hart, *RW*, 22; Marshall, 9; Rich, *GPD*, 438. Franz Ferdinand's goal, it should be noted, was not altogether altruistic, for he was looking for an ally against Hungarian obstructionism in matters of state. His plan would likely have expanded the Dual Monarchy into a Triple monarchy, giving the Slavs their own capital at Zagreb and an equal standing with Hungary in imperial affairs (Mason, 77; Wawro, 54–55).

14. Remak, 97–100; Marshall, 26.

15. Menning, 402–03; 447; Rich, *GPD*, 444.

16. Hazen, *FYE*, 319–21; O'Shea, 24; Schapiro, *MCEH1*, 711–12.

17. Quoted in Remak, 115; see also, Menning, 420.

18. Hazen, *FYE*, 321–22.

19. Remak, 116.

20. Palmer, *TOTH*, 332.

21. Remak, 121–24; Rich, *GDP*, 454; see also, Menning, 430–31.

22. Remak, 127; Rich, *GDP*, 461. M. Gilbert (*FWW*, 30–31) notes that the Russian foreign minister was kind enough to assist the weeping ambassador to the door.

23. Larousse, 346.

24. Rich, *GPD*, 460. On the off chance that France had pledged her neutrality, Germany intended to demand Verdun and Toul as an earnest of her pledge. Röhl relates the further anecdote that on the day the German ultimatum was issued, the German Ambassador in London mistakenly informed Berlin that Britain and France would pledge their neutrality if Germany did not mobilize against France. In jubilation, the kaiser ordered German chief-of-staff Helmuth von Moltke to halt all troop movement in the West and redirect everything to the Russian front—a demand that caused the mortified chief-of-staff's face to change hue several times. The kaiser then telegraphed his effusive thanks to King George V of Britain, who telegraphed back (after consultation with British Foreign Secretary Sir Edward Grey) that the kaiser's information was mistaken. Much to Moltke's relief, the kaiser rescinded his order before mayhem set in (Röhl, 160–62; M. Gilbert, *FWW*, 30).

25. Terraine, 11.

26. Remak, 127. This Moltke was the nephew of the like-named victor of 1870–1871.

27. Hazen, *FYE*, 329; see also Schapiro, *MCEH1*, 716.

28. Fuller, *MHWW*, vol. 3, 189–90; Tuchman, *Guns*, 52–54.

29. Brinton et al., vol. 2, 704; Fuller, *MHWW*, vol. 3, 195.

30. Keegan, *FWW*, 36–39.

31. Fuller, *MHWW*, vol. 3, 196–98.

32. Tuchman, *Guns*, 199–207; Liddell Hart, *RW*, 54–55.

33. Snyder and Morris, 313.

34. M. Gilbert, *FWW*, 42.

35. Tuchman, *Guns*, 255–56; M. Gilbert, *FWW*, 42; Terraine, 40.

36. Keegan, *FWW*, 92–93; Tuchman, *Guns*, 356–60; Terraine, 39–40.

37. Tuchman, *Guns*, 354.

38. Tuchman, *Guns*, 55; A.J.P. Taylor, *WWI*, 32.

39. Robson, 9; Horne, *PG*, 25–26; Marshall, 72.

40. Keegan, *FWW*, 108–09.

41. Bernard John Denore, a soldier involved in the British portion of the retreat, reports that the harried troops fell back 251 miles in 12 days. Bereft of provisions, soldiers in tattered uniforms fell asleep from exhaustion, toppling to the ground in mid-step. Pursued relentlessly by the enemy—often by cavalrymen who dismounted to open fire from a distance—Denore's company sustained daily casualties, serving up a new blow to morale at each roll call (J. Lewis, *TWWS*, 1–9).

42. Liddell Hart, *RW*, 104–05; Tuchman, *Guns*, 302; Clark, *EF*, 24.

43. Fuller, *MHWW*, vol. 3, 205; Clark, *EF*, 30; Liddell Hart, *RW*, 107; Marshall, 98; Tuchman, *Guns*, 313; Strachan, 135.

44. Keegan, *FWW*, 159; Tuchman, *Guns*, 319.

45. Clark, *EF*, 39.

46. Tuchman, *Guns*, 344–45.

47. A.J.P. Taylor, *WWI*, 49; Robson, 16. Taylor puts the casualties at 100,000.

48. Fuller, *MHWW*, vol. 3, 211.

49. Terraine, 62; Liddell Hart, *RW*, 86.

50. Tuchman, *Guns*, 440–45; Churchill, *WC*, 164–65.

51. Namely, the newly formed, and already retreating, 6th Army and a few colonial troops.

52. Churchill, *WC*, 165.

53. Tuchman, *Guns*, 459.

54. Tuchman, *Guns*, 487; Robson, 13; Liddell Hart, *RW*, 93.

55. Tuchman, *Guns*, 483; Hazen, *FYE*, 334.

56. Liddell Hart, *RW*, 98–101; Marshall, 86–92.

57. Churchill, *WC*, 169.

58. Churchill, *WC*, 209–16.

59. Marshall, 138.

60. Terraine, 91.

61. Wolff, 122.

62. M. Gilbert, *FWW*, 41, 50; Wawro, 160–64.

63. M. Gilbert, *FWW*, 50; Wawro, 168.

64. Taylor, *WWI*, 49.

65. Marshall, 119–20; Liddell Hart, *RW*, 145; Tuchman, *Guns*, 185.

66. Tuchman, 186; Liddell Hart, *RW*, 146.

67. Taylor, *WWI*, 54; Keegan, *FWW*, 242; Marshall, 125.

68. Taylor, *WWI*, 54; Marshall, 121.

69. Keegan, *FWW*, 238–39.

70. Kinross, 558.

71. Totten et al., 45.

72. Totten et al., 45.

73. Keegan, *FWW*, 243.

74. M. Gilbert, *FWW*, 117–19; Terraine, 119–20.

75. Clark, *Donkeys*, 51–52; Liddell Hart, *RW*, 126; Keegan, *FWW*, 209.

76. Strachan, 176; M. Gilbert, *FWW*, 136.

77. Clark, *Donkeys*, 54–64; Keegan, *FWW*, 210–11.

78. Terraine, 146.

79. Churchill, *WC*, 392.

80. Liddell Hart, *RW*, 165; Fair, 329.

81. Fair, 329.

82. Swallow, 108; Keegan, *FWW*, 263–66; Marshall, 181; Churchill, *WC*, 429–31.

83. The canal cuts across German Schleswig-Holstein at the base of the Danish peninsula, to connect the North and Baltic Seas.

84. Robson, 22; Liddell Hart, *RW*, 178–79; Keegan, 213.

85. Marshall, 167–68; Liddell Hart, 175–76.

86. Snyder and Morris, 324; Robson, 103.

87. Liddell Hart, *RW*, 178–80.

88. Clark, *Donkeys*, 92–98.

89. M. Gilbert, *FWW*, 142, 151.

90. M. Gilbert, *FWW*, 160.

91. Clark, *Donkeys*, 150; M. Gilbert, FWW, 197; O'Shea, 64.

92. Clark, *Donkeys*, 157–62.

93. Clark, *Donkeys*, 163–64. (Marshall hotly contests this point, 230.)

94. Wolff, 52.

95. Fair, 320; Clark, *Donkeys*, 171–73; O'Shea, 63; M. Gilbert, *FWW*, 199.

96. Clark, *Donkeys*, 173; Keegan, *FWW*, 218; O'Shea, 63.

97. M. Gilbert, *FWW*, 181–83.

98. Churchill, *WC*, 502; Fuller, *MHWW*, vol. 3, 260.

99. Fuller, *MHWW*, vol. 3, 260; Churchill, *WC*, 514.

100. Churchill, *WC*, 514–15 (quote, 515); Terraine, 164–65 (Terraine cites the same quote).

101. Clark, *EF*, 66; Marshall, 223; Keegan, *FWW*, 249; Strachan, 146.

102. Robson, 23; Hazen, *FYE*, 346.

103. Strachan, 147.

104. A.J.P. Taylor, *WWI*, 117–19. The fortress had been the last to fall in the Franco-Prussian War.

105. Marshall, 235–37; Horne, *PG*, 48–49. Strachan (188) contests this view, saying that Falkenhayn only claimed that this had been his goal after failing to take the citadel.

106. Hayes, *GW*, 150.

107. "A futile innovation…" in the view of H.G. Wells, "the user of which was in constant danger of being burnt alive" (Wells, *OH1*, 1038).

108. Horne, *PG*, 117, 122–23; O'Shea, 165–66.

109. Churchill, *WC*, 567–68.

110. Strachan, 186.

111. Churchill, *WC*, 576.

112. Strachan, 189.

113. A.J.P. Taylor, *WWI*, 121; Horne, *PG*, 188–89.

114. A.J.P. Taylor, *WWI*, 121; Horne, *PG*, 199.

115. Some historians consign this story to legend (see O'Shea, 164; Horne, *PG*, 264–65).

116. M. Gilbert, *FWW*, 254.

117. Robson, 48–49.

118. Liddell Hart, *RW*, 225.

119. Clark, *EF*, 75–84.

120. Terraine, 226.

121. Robson, 40; Churchill, *WC*, 635–37 (text and diagram); Liddell Hart, *RW*, 293.

122. Hayes, *GW*, 166.

123. Robson, 51.

124. Churchill, *WC*, 641.

125. Churchill, *WC*, 641.

126. Keegan, *FOB*, 215.

127. Hayes, *GW*, 178.

128. Keegan, *FOB*, 230–31; A.J.P. Taylor, *WWI*, 122.

129. Churchill, *WC*, 645; Keegan, *FOB*, 234.

130. Keegan, *FOB*, 226, and *FWW*, 316; A.J.P. Taylor, *WWI*, 122–23; Robson, 53.

131. Keegan, *FOB*, 246, and *FWW*, 314–17; A.J.P. Taylor, *WWI*, 122–23.

132. M. Gilbert, *FWW*, 261.

133. Keegan, *FOB*, 248–52.

134. Churchill, *WC*, 647; see also, Robson, 53; Keegan, *FWW*, 317–18.

135. Liddell Hart, *RW*, 239–42; O'Shea, 96–97; Keegan, *FWW*, 319.

136. Hazen, *FYE*, 357; Keegan, *FWW*, 321.

137. Hazen, *FYE*, 359–61; Churchill, *WC*, 657–58; Liddell Hart, *RW*, 261–62.

138. Larousse, 355; Strachan, 278–81; Marshall, 264. (Even Germany's Bethmann-Hollweg proposed negotiations to the Allies at this time but was turned down as being insincere.)

139. Purcell, 56–58.

140. Strachan, 239.

141. Moorhead, *RR*, 107–10; Elson, 47; Marshall, 270; Brinton et al., vol. 2, 725.

142. Fuller, *MHWW*, vol. 3, 269; A.J.P. Taylor, *WWI*, 180; Elson, 48.

143. Horne, *PG*, 320.

144. Robson, 65–68.

145. Marshall, 288–89; Liddell Hart, *RW*, 299–300; Wolff, 81–85.

146. Keegan, *FWW*, 352–53.

147. Wolff, 81–3, 90; Churchill, *WC*, 696–700.

148. Wolff, 83; Churchill, *WC*, 698.

149. Quoted in Terraine, 293.

150. Horne, *PG*, 322.

151. Keegan, *FWW*, p. 354.

152. A.J.P. Taylor, *WWI*, 198.

153. Horne, *PG*, 322; Wolff, 97; Robson, 68–69; O'Shea, 127.

154. Liddell Hart, *RW*, 300–01; Wolff, 97.

155. Horne, *PG*, 324; Wolff, 100; O'Shea, 128.

156. Horne, *PG*, 324; Robson, 69; Wolff, 101.

157. Robson, 71; M. Gilbert, *FWW*, 338.

158. Robson, 70.

159. Strachan, 259.

160. Marshall, 300–01.

161. Wolff, 106–07.

162. Wolff, 130–39. (The depth was also needed to get below the water table.)

163. P. Warner, *PTV*, 113.

164. Liddell Hart, *RW*, 332.

165. Liddell Hart, *RW*, 339–40; Robson, 73; Churchill, *WC*, 714.

166. Prior and Wilson, 159–60; P. Warner, *PTV*, 139.

167. Taylor, *WWI*, 207.

168. Prior and Wilson, 93, 167, 177.

169. Keegan, *FWW*, 390–91; Prior and Wilson, 98; Wolff, 346–47.

170. P. Warner, *PTV*, 150; Keegan, *FWW*, 388.

171. Wolff, 212–14.

172. Liddell Hart, *RW*, 343; Wolff, 383; O'Shea, 42.

173. Robson, 75.

174. From Churchill, *The World* Crisis (quoted in Moorehead, *RR*, 173, and D. Bullock, 14).

175. A.J.P. Taylor, *WWI*, 186.

176. Snyder and Morris, 363. (The anecdote was related by John Reed in *Ten Days That Shook the World*.)

177. Fuller, *MHWW*, vol. 3, 273.

178. Churchill, *WC*, 309.

179. Churchill, *WC*, 312.

180. Churchill, *WC*, 317.

181. M. Gilbert, *FWW*, 373.

182. Tuchman, *Bible*, 339.

183. M. Gilbert, *FWW*, 374.

184. M. Gilbert, *FWW*, 384.

185. Marshall, 329–30.

186. Keegan, *FWW*, 411; Marshall, 333.

187. Moorehead, *RR*, 281; Schapiro, *MCEH2*, 766.

188. Liddell Hart, 368; Marshall, 343; Robson, 78.

189. Strachan, 295.

190. Strachan, 295.

191. Liddell Hart, *RW*, 391–92; Robson, 77–78; Strachan, 295.

192. Liddell Hart, *RW*, 369–70, 394–99.

193. Liddell Hart, *RW*, 400–02.

194. Marshall, 356; Churchill, *WC*, 759.

195. M. Gilbert, *FWW*, 407.

196. Marshall, 363–64; Taylor, *WWI*, 255.

197. Terraine, 340–42; Marshall, 369–70.

198. Marshall, 373; M. Gilbert, *FWW*, 428.

199. Churchill, *WC*, 782; Liddell Hart, *RW*, 419–22.

200. Hazen, *FYE*, 400; Marshall, 406; Fuller, *MHWW*, vol. 3, 274–75.

201. Churchill, *WC*, 792.

202. Keegan, *FWW*, 438.

203. Marshall, 413; Churchill, *WC*, 795.

204. Fuller, *MHWW*, vol. 3, 290, 297; A.J.P. Taylor, *WWI*, 258.

205. Foch wanted Haig to continue the push, but the latter, no longer profligate of human lives after the experiences of 1916 and 1917, refused to send his men forward against entrenched positions (Terraine, 354–55).

206. Marshall, 418; Fuller, *MHWW*, vol. 3, 298.

207. O'Shea, 148.

208. O'Shea, 153–54.

209. Hazen, *FYE*, 404.

210. Hazen, *FYE*, 409.

211. Strachan, 318.

212. Robson, 83; Liddell Hart, *RW*, 378; Marshall, 438–39.

213. Robson, 83–86; A.J.P. Taylor, *WWI*, 263.

214. Strachan, 326.

215. Larousse, 361; Liddell Hart, *RW*, 383–85; Keegan, 447–48.

216. Strachan, 326.

217. Terraine, 354–58.

218. Strachan, 326.

219. Marshall, 452; O'Shea, 185.

220. A.J.P. Taylor, *WWI*, 264; Elson, 19.

221. Elson, 19; Purcell, 72.

222. The so-called "Lansing Note" forwarded to Berlin on November 4 by Wilson in answer to a query on the matter seemed to indicate Anglo-French acquiescence in peace terms on the basis of the Fourteen Points with the reservation that Germany would make restitution for civilian damages including property loss in France and Belgium and the loss of British merchant ships (Lentin, 12–13).

223. Garraty, vol. 2, 673.

224. Langsam, 82.

225. May, *HOC*, vol. 2, 606; Lentin, 63.

226. Elson, 24–25.

227. Henig, *VA*, 4.

228. Neiberg, xiv.

229. Lentin, 109.

230. Langsam, 91; Henig, *VA*, 23–24; Neiberg, 26.

231. Langsam, 81.

232. P. Hastings, 10; Buell, 25–26. Goldston,

59–60; Elson, 25; Churchill, *Memoirs*, 6; Lentin, 24.

    233. Buell, 25–26; Jarman, 156.
    234. Purcell, 80–81.
    235. Langsam, 93–94.
    236. Langsam, 93; Neiberg, 48.
    237. All figures are from Langsam, 77.
    238. That is to say, ~10 billion dollars (Sontag, 26).
    239. Henig, *VA*, 21.
    240. Henig, *VA*, 20–21; Buell, 34–35; Lentin 12–13.
    241. This expectation was the result of notes exchanged with Woodrow Wilson prior to the armistice.
    242. Langsam, 98.
    243. Neiberg, 73; Lentin, 87.
    244. Buell, 28; Langsam, 98–99.
    245. Langsam, 100.
    246. Lentin, 67.
    247. The Rhineland was to be divided into three sectors, based respectively on the bridge-crossings at Cologne in the north, Coblenz in the center and Mainz in the south. The occupying troops were to evacuate the Cologne sector at five years, the Coblenz sector at ten and the Mainz sector at fifteen.
    248. Langsam, 91–93.
    249. Buell, 32–33.
    250. Lentin, 4.
    251. P. Hastings, 16–17; Buell, 36.
    252. Wiskemann, 17–18; Marshall, 477–78.
    253. Sontag, 61–62.
    254. B. Lewis, 236–37.
    255. Asimov, 551–52.
    256. B. Lewis, 348; Swallow, 111–20; Langsam, 633–34.
    257. The "mandate" idea was formulated by the former Boer general, Jan Smuts, to overcome Woodrow Wilson's aversion to colonialism as an infringement of self-determination (Neiberg, 56).
    258. Buell, 36.
    259. Boak et al., 765.
    260. Buell, 20.
    261. Neiberg, xi.
    262. Purcell, 76.
    263. See Sontag, 24–30, 111, and Marshall, 467–69 for a fuller discussion.
    264. Marshall, 470.
    265. Buell, 38.
    266. Lentin, 111.

Chapter 10

    1. Troy Lennon, "Blind female anarchist Fanya Kaplan executed for Lenin assassination plot," *The Daily Telegraph*, August 30, 2018 https://www.dailytelegraph.com.au/news/blind-female-anarchist-fanya-kaplan-executed-for-lenin-assassination-plot/news-story/90472a16e8fa49fec287aac7b71c3a7b Accessed 8/10/21; Elson, 53; P. Hastings, 26.

    2. Brinton et al., vol. 2, 726.
    3. Moorehead, *RR*, 48; Brinton et al., vol. 2, 643–44.
    4. Moorehead, *RR*, 42.
    5. Brinton et al., vol. 2, 727.
    6. Buell, 243.
    7. Elson, 50–51.
    8. Langsman, 548.
    9. Moorehead, *RR*, 261.
    10. Moorehead, *RR*, 264; Elson, 53.
    11. Moorehead, *RR*, 268.
    12. Moorehead, *RR*, 276–81.
    13. D. Bullock, 21.
    14. Quoted in Alan Wood, *SAS*, 21.
    15. Quoted in D. Bullock, 52.
    16. P. Hastings, 29.
    17. Elson, 40; Langsam, 552.
    18. Foley, 90; D. Bullock, 35.
    19. Schapiro, *MCEH2*, 767.
    20. Steinberg and Khrustalëv, 353, citing testimony of Yakov Yurovsky, one of the executioners.
    21. Steinberg and Khrustalëv, 353–54, 359–62; Van der Kiste, 244.
    22. Duffy and Ricci, 348; Elson, 54.
    23. Moorehead, *RR*, 284.
    24. D. Bullock, 36; Foley, 93.
    25. Elson, 34.
    26. Kravchenko, 27; Hastings (citing Kravchenko), 27–8.
    27. Moorehead, *RR*, 266, 270.
    28. Elson, 54; Buell, 246.
    29. Moorhead, *RR*, 56, 80*fn*.
    30. D. Bullock, 53, 83–84.
    31. Elson, 54.
    32. D. Bullock, 21, 137.
    33. P. Hastings, 28; D. Bullock, 124; ExecutedToday.com, *1920: The White Admiral Aleksandr Kolchak*. http://www.executedtoday.com/tag/ushakovka-river/ Accessed August 28, 2020.
    34. P. Hastings, 30.
    35. Davies, 63; Zamoyski, 285; Langsam, 518.
    36. Davies, 62–63; Lukowski and Zawadzki, 268, 279–86; Zamoyski, 285, 289–92.
    37. Zamoyski, 293.
    38. Lukowski and Zawadzki, 289–91; Davies, 30. Established in 1386, the Polish-Lithuanian Commonwealth encompassed a confederacy of ethnicities—Polish, Lithuanian, German, Latvian, Belorussian, Ukrainian and Tatar among others—all enjoying autonomy in their local cultural and political institutions and bound to each other only by allegiance to the same prince (Zamoyski, 78).
    39. Davies, 30.
    40. Alexander Ulyanov was hanged. Bronisław Piłsudski was exiled to Sakhalin Island where he ultimately became involved in important anthropological research.
    41. Davies, 50–51.
    42. Davies, 58.
    43. Davies, 120–23, 146–48.
    44. Davies, 131.
    45. Davies, 207.
    46. Davies, 49, 229; Lukowski and Zawadzki, 296.

47. Lukowski and Zawadzki, 296; Zamoyski, 296; Davies, 236–37.

48. Lukowski and Zawadzki, 296.

49. Buell, 259.

50. P. Hastings, 32–3.

51. Elson, 58.

52. Wells, *OH2*, 1134.

53. D. Bullock, 133; Elson (34) estimates as many as 15 million.

54. P. Hastings, 34; Elson, 55.

55. Hingley, 2–4; Caulkins, 15–16; Kerrigan, 32, 35–36, 42.

56. Kerrigan, 35–38.

57. Goldston, 168; Caulkins, 28–29; Hingley, 33*ff*; Kerrigan, 55, 74–75.

58. Kerrigan, 68–74.

59. Brinton et al., vol. 2, 736; Langsam, 573.

60. Hingley, 141–42; Kerrigan, 115–16; Archer, 71.

61. Hingley, 157–62, 168–69.

62. Caulkins, 73; Archer, 75–76.

63. Sontag, 152; Hastings, 33; Wiskemann, 75; May, *HOC*, vol. 2, 622; Langsam, 569–70.

64. Sontag, 153*ff*.

65. Wiskemann, 76; Archer, 87.

66. Brinton et al., vol. 2, 738–39; May *HOC*, vol. 2, 625–26; Alan Wood, *SAS*, 31–34; Archer, 88–89; Langsam, 580–82.

67. Sontag, 155.

68. Marrin, 110; Kravchenko, 119.

69. Sontag, 155–56; Marrin, 106; Alan Wood, *SAS*, 36.

70. Alsop, 249; Francine du Plessix Gray, "The Journalist and the Dictator." *New York Times*, June 24, 1990. https://www.nytimes.com/1990/06/24/books/the-journalist-and-the-dictator.html Accessed 8/11/21. (The article is a review of S.J. Taylor's 1990 biography of the tainted, Pulitzer Prize-winning Duranty, entitled, *Stalin's Apologist*.")

71. Hinglely, 206. Kerrigan believes this figure to be exaggerated (16).

72. Kerrigan, 139.

73. Alan Wood, *SAS*, 36.

74. Marrin, 83; see also, Langsam, 585–86.

75. Hingley, 243.

76. May, *HOC*, vol. 2, 623; Alan Wood, *SAS*, 36.

77. Hingley, 237–38; Alan Wood, *SAS*, 38; Marrin, 116–17; Archer, 97; Ziegler, *BTW*, 191.

78. Hingley, 244–45.

79. Caulkins, 100; Hingley, 245–46.

80. Marrin, 132.

81. Kerrigan, 16; Marrin, 136.

82. Wallbank and Taylor, vol. 2, 432.

83. Hingley, 257.

84. Sontag, 259; Marrin, 121. This was Nikolai Krestinsky.

85. Hingley, 179.

86. Langsam, 575.

87. Marrin, 75–85, 99, 128–34.

88. Davies, 32; Archer 49.

89. Goldston, 105–06; Fuller, *MHWW*, vol. 3, 334–35; Archer, 55.

90. Henig, *OSWW*, 13.

91. Langsam, 333.

92. Brinton et al., vol. 2, 755.

93. Langsam, 338.

94. Blinkhorn, *MFI*, 28.

95. Langsam, 338–39; Blinkhorn, *MFI*, 29–30.

96. Hibbert, 17.

97. Hibbert, 26. Besides being promiscuous, Mussolini was sexually violent towards women.

98. Hibbert, 32–33.

99. Hibbert 35–36; Blinkhorn, *MFI*, 22–23.

100. Hibbert, 40–41.

101. Blinkhorn, *MFI*, 24–25.

102. Blinkhorn, *MFI*, 32–33.

103. Langsam, 339.

104. Hibbert, 64.

105. Blinkhorn, *MFI*, 33–34.

106. Langsam, 340; Blinkhorn, *MFI*, 34; Elson, 91–92. Unruly members of his Grand Council were now threatening to oust him if he failed to do so (Blinkhorn, *MFI*, 34)

107. Langsam, 340–41; Wallbank and Taylor, vol. 2, 438.

108. One of intellectuals, and one each for capital and for labor in six different economic fields—industry, agriculture, commerce, banking and domestic and international transport (Brinton et al., vol. 2, 757.

109. Langsam, 344.

110. Langsam, 346–48.

111. May, *HOC*, vol. 2, 648.

112. Blinkhorn, *MFI*, 51.

113. Blinkhorn, *MFI*, 44–45, 48.

114. Langsam, 349.

115. May, *HOC*, vol. 2, 648.

116. Blinkhorn, *MFI*, 49.

117. Wallbank and Taylor, vol. 2, 439.

118. Langsam, 351.

119. Langsam, 351–52.

120. Freeman, 22.

121. Blinkhorn, *MFI*, 46; Wallbank and Taylor, vol. 2, 439.

122. Sontag, 49.

123. In fact, it had been Ludendorff who insisted that the war end when it did—i.e., before German territory had been invaded. By leaving the signing of the armistice to others, however, he conveniently evaded all responsibility—foisting it instead upon the unlucky politicians who appended their signatures (Strachan, 331).

124. Strachan, 331.

125. Henig, *WR*, 25.

126. Shirer, *Reich*, 43.

127. Henig, *WR*, 26.

128. Henig, *WR*, 27.

129. Sontag, 112; Wiskemann, 44–45.

130. Wiskemann, 42; Goldston, 109; Eubank, 30–31.

131. Wiskemann, 46.

132. Sontag, 113; P. Hastings, 43–46.

133. Larousse, 368.

134. Elson, 70.

135. P. Hastings, 46.

136. Brinton et al., vol. 2, 765.

137. Langsam, 412.

138. A. Bullock, 50–60.

139. Langsam, 414; Henig, *WR*, 37.

140. Goldston, 128–29; Sontag, p. 204.

141. Elson, 92; Brinton et al., vol. 2, 766.

142. Henig, *WR*, 41.

143. Stokesbury, 17–18.

144. Langsam, 183. Charles Dawes and Austen Chamberlain shared the prize in 1925.

145. Langsam, 156.

146. Henig, *WR*, 47, 59.

147. Gary Richardson, Alehandro Komai, Michael Gou and Daniel Park, "The Stock Market Crash of 1929." *federalreservehistory.org.* https://www.federalreservehistory.org/essays/stock_market_crash_of_1929. Accessed 10/5/20; Freeman, 4–5.

148. P. Hastings, 57–58.

149. Sontag, 137–38; Eubank, 22.

150. Hastings, 60–61; May, *HOC*, vol. 2, 649; Brinton et al., vol. 2, 785; Langsam, 163–64, 252.

151. Langsam, 161*fn*; Freeman, 25. It rose to 9 million the following year.

152. Turner, 6; P. Hastings, 70; Shirer, *Reich*, 152.

153. Churchill, *Memoirs*, 35. (Shirer and Bullock attribute Hindenburg's words to an earlier meeting.)

154. Turner, 59.

155. It may be mentioned, however, that an increase in the number of seats gained by the German Communist Party factored in the Nazis' favor by conjuring the specter of Bolshevism (Henig, *WR*, 73–74).

156. Shirer, *Reich*, 177–85; Brinton et al., vol. 2, 768; Turner, 112–18, 157–61.

157. Turner, 147; see also Henig, *WR*, 75.

158. Shirer, *Reich*, 6–7.

159. Shirer, *Reich*, 192–94; Elson, 93–94; P. Hastings, 74.

160. Langsam, 451*fn*.

161. Wallbank and Taylor, vol. 2, 445–46; Langsam, 448–51.

162. Shirer, *Reich*, 193–94; Elson, 93.

163. Gerould, 240–41.

164. Langsam, 455.

165. Langsam, 455–59; Wallbank and Taylor, vol. 2, 446.

166. Davidowicz, 69.

167. Davidowicz, 70.

168. Davidowicz, 260; Shirer, *Reich*, 233.

169. Shirer, *Reich*, 215, 219.

170. Asimov, 571.

171. Wells, *OH1*, 1103; P. Hastings, 55; Wallbank and Taylor, vol. 2, 459.

172. Jarman, 155.

173. Purcell, 87–88.

174. Churchill, *CS*, vol. 3, 3012.

175. Killeen, 5, 25; Cottrell, 29.

176. Cottrell, 86; see also Killeen, 52.

177. Cottrell, 29; Killeen, 21–22, 84–86.

178. Killeen, 59.

179. Cottrell, 32.

180. Killeen, 60.

181. De Valera was the son of a Spanish father and Irish mother, hence his surname. He was also an American citizen, which led to his death sentence for his role in the Easter Rising being commuted (Cottrell, 35).

182. Cottrell, 45–46, 52.

183. Killeen, 98; Cottrell, 56.

184. Killeen, 102.

185. Cottrell, 56–60.

186. Killeen, 103.

187. Killeen, 106.

188. Killeen, 109.

189. Killeen, 129.

190. Quoted in Cottrell, 7.

191. P. Hastings, 55; Brinton et al., vol. 2, 783.

192. Langsam, 238–39; Perkins, 39–40.

193. Langsam, 240; Wallbank and Taylor, vol. 2, 459.

194. Langsam, 240–41.

195. Langsam, 241; Morgan, 58–59; Jo. Burke, 318–19; Perkins, 46.

196. Langsam, 242.

197. Perkins, 52.

198. Jarman, 163–64.

199. Langsam, 243.

200. Quoted in Langsam, 244*fn*; see also Perkins, 51.

201. Perkins, 59.

202. May, *HOC*, vol. 2, 641; Langsam, 245.

203. Wallbank and Taylor, vol. 2, 459; Jarman, 165; Langsam, 247.

204. Jarman, 166.

205. Wallbank and Taylor, vol.2, 460; Langsam, 251.

206. Jarman, 165–66; Langsam, 252–53.

207. Jarman, 166, Wallbank and Taylor, vol. 2, 460.

208. Morgan, 80.

209. Perkins, 111–12.

210. Perkins, 114.

211. Perkins, 115–19.

212. Bouverie, 118*fn*.

213. Langsam, 303.

214. Shirer, *Republic*, 170–71.

215. F. Gilbert, 210; Shirer, *Republic*, 142; Wallbank and Taylor, vol. 2, 430.

216. Before doing so, Poincaré had proposed a compromise solution, granting a 2-year moratorium on reparations if Germany would issue bonds to pay off the Allied war loans, composed of about 80 billion marks (thus leaving only about 50 billion marks to paid directly by Germany to the Allies as reparations). Great Britain refused to support the plan. A week later, France occupied the Ruhr (Shirer, *Republic*, 148).

217. F. Gilbert, 211–12, 310.

218. Wallbank and Taylor, vol. 2, 450

219. Langsam, 306–07.

220. Shirer, *Republic*, 154–56.

221. Cobban, vol. 3, 134.

222. Shirer, *Republic*, 164.

223. Langsam, 306.
224. Sontag, 131; Shirer, *Republic*, 141.
225. Wallbank and Taylor, vol. 2, 451.
226. Shirer, *Republic*, 165–66, 188–89; F. Gilbert, 310; Brinton et al., vol. 2, 788.
227. Langsam, 302; Wallbank and Taylor, vol. 2, 451.
228. Wallbank and Taylor, vol. 2, 451; Langsam, 311.
229. F. Gilbert, 311; Brinton, vol. 2, 788; Cobban, vol. 3, 141–42; Shirer, *Republic*, 208, 225.
230. Langsam, 311; Wallbank and Taylor, 451.
231. Shirer, *Republic*, 209.
232. Brinton et al., vol. 2, 788.
233. Shirer, *Republic*, 213.
234. Shirer, *Republic*, 218–19.
235. May, *HOC*, vol. 2, 657–58.
236. Shirer, *Republic*, 216.
237. Shirer, *Republic*, 217–19.
238. Shirer, *Republic*, 220–22.
239. F. Gilbert, 312; Cobban, vol. 3, 145–46
240. Langsam, 313.
241. Wallbank and Taylor, vol. 2, 452; Langsam, 314.
242. Shirer, *Republic*, 285; Cobban, vol. 3, 148.
243. Langsam, 315.
244. F. Gilbert, 313.
245. Cobban, vol. 3, 154.
246. Cobban, vol. 3, 147–48, 152.
247. Wallbank and Taylor, vol. 2, 452.
248. Cobban, vol. 3, 153; F. Gilbert, 314.

Chapter 11

1. Henig, *OSWW*, 9–12.
2. Shirer, *Republic*, 240–41.
3. Shirer, *Republic*, 240–41.
4. Langsam, 622–24; Brinton et al., vol. 2, 777; Wiskemann, 64.
5. Churchill, *Memoirs*, 54; Langsam, 496.
6. Henig, *OSWW*, 24–25.
7. Henig, *OSWW*, 30; Shirer, *Reich*, 283–84.
8. Henig, *OSWW*, 31.
9. A.J.P. Taylor, *OSWW*, 85.
10. The French motivation in seeking this agreement was to have Stalin instruct France's unruly Communist Party to cease subverting attempts made by the French government to improve the nation's military preparedness (Churchill, *GS*, 135; A.J.P. Taylor, *OSWW*, 85).
11. Shirer, *Reich*, 288–89; Churchill, *GS*, 138.
12. Henig, *OSWW*, 33; Churchill, *GS*, 138.
13. Langsam, 651, 659.
14. Langsam, 651–52, 663.
15. Langsam, 654. (Woodrow Wilson strongly opposed the Japanese claims, but to no avail.)
16. Wallbank and Taylor, vol. 2, 494.
17. Sontag, 241–42.
18. Churchill, *GS*, 86; Langsam, 665; Wallbank and Taylor, vol. 2, 499; Henig, *OSWW*, 36.
19. Liddell Hart, *SWW*, 205; Fuller, *SWW*, 127; Asimov, 561.
20. Goldston, 191; Toland, *RS*, 8–10; Zich, 20.
21. Asimov, 561.
22. A.J.P. Taylor, *OSWW*, 62; P. Hastings, 96.
23. Churchill, *GS*, 87.
24. May, *HOC*, 707 and 719; P. Hastings, 96; Churchill, *GS*, 88.
25. Henig, *OSWW*, 32. Britain also regarded Japan as a safeguard against Soviet expansion in Asia (Sontag, 243).
26. Henig, *OSWW*, 32; Churchill, *GS*, 138.
27. Cobban, vol. 3, 165.
28. Churchill, *GS*, 133; Bouverie, 73.
29. It does not follow from pledging oneself to the peace of Europe that one is free to make *war* beyond its boundaries.
30. Langsam, 362.
31. P. Hastings, 100–04 (see particularly the pictures on 102); Goldston, 194–95; Elson, 151, 158–65.
32. Ziegler, *BTW*, 181; Elson, 151.
33. Ziegler, *BTW*, 182.
34. Langsam, 366–67.
35. Langsam, 367; Taylor, *OSWW*, 91; Elson, 151; Brinton et al., vol. 2, 807; Sontag, 288.
36. Elson, 151; Brinton et al., vol. 2, 807; Sontag, 289; Blinkhorn, *MFI*, 63.
37. Sontag, 290; A.J.P. Taylor, *OSWW*, 94; Bouverie, 80.
38. Henig, *OSWW*, 40; Langsam, 732.
39. Churchill, *GS*, 192.
40. Churchill, *GS*, 192–93; Eubank, 60.
41. Shirer, *Reich*, 294.
42. Larousse, vol. 2, 374.
43. Shirer, *Republic*, 267.
44. Shirer, *Reich*, p. 291-2.
45. Taylor, *OSWW*, 95; Langsam (367) mentions the tie to the Rhineland occupation.
46. Sontag, 294; Elson, 155.
47. Asimov, 566.
48. Wallbank and Taylor, vol. 2, 457.
49. Langsam, 373.
50. Langsam, 375.
51. Langsam, 375–77.
52. McKendrick, 195.
53. G. Jackson, 13.
54. Wallbank and Taylor, vol. 2, 266; Larousse, vol. 371.
55. McKendrick, 194.
56. Elson, 167.
57. Langsam, 383–83.
58. Langsam, 388.
59. R. Carr, 249.
60. G. Jackson, 24–25, 27; McKendrick, 199.
61. Blinkhorn, *CW*, 27.
62. McKendrick, 200; Blinkhorn, *CW*, 29.
63. G. Jackson, 36.
64. McKendrick, 200.
65. Langsam, 391.
66. Blinkhorn, *CW*, 28.
67. Langsam, 391–92.
68. Browne, 63; Blinkhorn, *CW*, 39–40; R. Carr, *SAH*, 257.
69. Eubank, 66.

70. P. Hastings, 105; Blinkhorn, *CW*, 37; Elson, 169.

71. P. Hastings, 106; Browne, 41; Elson, 169–70; G. Jackson, 58.

72. R. Carr, *MS*, 137; Browne, 56.

73. The Soviets insisted that their Communist minions in Spain avoid revolutionary activity lest they push the Western democracies into Franco's camp through fear of Bolshevism.

74. G. Jackson, 51, 107.

75. P. Hastings, 109; Ziegler, *BTW*, 200; Elson, 172.

76. Stokesbury, 37; Orwell, 10.

77. Salazar hated Bolshevism, but his main motivation seems to have been the profits to be made on the arms trade (G. Jackson, 50, 60, 146; Langsam, 396).

78. P. Hastings, 106.

79. Asimov, 569; P. Hastings, 109; G. Jackson, 124.

80. G. Jackson, 125.

81. Browne, 72.

82. Trapped in Vichy France a few years later, Picasso was accosted by a Nazi officer brandishing a reproduction of the painting and demanding to know, "You did that, didn't you?"—to which Picasso retorted, "No, you did!" (Ziegler, *BTW*, 206–07).

83. Eubank, 66; Goldston, 199.

84. Blinkhorn, *CW*, 49.

85. P. Hastings, 111.

86. P. Hastings, 97–98; Elson, 132–34.

87. Langsam, 675–76; Elson, 135; Toland, *RS*, 44–45; P. Hastings, 98; Asimov, 564.

88. Elson, 136; Zich, 23; Chang, 4, 6, 87–88.

89. Chang, 48.

90. Toland, *RS*, 56.

91. Chang, 4–6, 85–89.

92. Chang, 49–50, 52–3, 89–99.

93. Elson, 137.

94. Wallbank and Taylor, vol. 2, 454; Langsam, 469.

95. Langsam, 466–67.

96. Langsam, 470.

97. Langsam, 470–71.

98. Wallbank and Taylor, vol. 2, 454–55; Langsam, 472.

99. Langsam, 472–73; Wiskemann, 65–66.

100. Langsam, 475–76.

101. Langsam, 476–78; Elson, 185.

102. Langsam, 473–74; Blinkhorn, *MFI*, 62.

103. Elson, 186; Eubank, 34.

104. P. Hastings, 113.

105. Hibbert, 100.

106. Elson, 186; Langsam, 481–82.

107. Brinton et al., vol. 2, 776; Langsam, 482–83.

108. Shirer, *Reich*, 296; Eubank, 82–83.

109. Shirer, *Reich*, 323; Goldston, 203.

110. A. Bullock, 247–49.

111. Shirer, *Reich*, 351.

112. Anonymous. "How a Nazi Saved Sigmund Freud." *The Jewish Chronicle.* January 28, 2010. https://www.thejc.com/lifestyle/features/

how-a-nazi-saved-sigmund-freud-1.13679, Accessed 1/7/21.

113. Churchill, *GS*, 196–97.

114. Langsam, 511.

115. Langsam, 500–04.

116. Langsam, 504–07.

117. Langsam, 508–10; A. Bullock, 256–57.

118. Sontag, 336; Shirer, *Reich*, 359; A.J.P. Taylor, *OSWW*, 153; Elson, 194; Henig, *OSWW*, 51.

119. Langsam, 511.

120. Shirer, *Reich*, 363.

121. A. Bullock, 255.

122. Shirer, *Republic*, 342.

123. A. Bullock, 256; Henig, *OSWW*, 50; Shirer, *Reich*, 365; *Republic*, 342–43. As Shirer notes, the German troop movements cited by Czechoslovakia prior to the mobilization may have been routine maneuvers, and it is certain that Hitler was caught completely off guard by the Czech decision to mobilize.

124. Langsam, 511; Shirer, *Republic*, 340.

125. Shirer, *Republic*, 339–40.

126. Bouverie, 123.

127. Ward, 121.

128. Ward, 107.

129. Shirer, *Republic*, 340–41; A. Bullock, 255.

130. Ward, 122–23.

131. Shirer, *Republic*, 344–45.

132. Shirer, *Republic*, 345–46; A. Bullock, 256

133. Shirer, *Republic*, 351.

134. Ward, 152–53.

135. Shirer, *Republic*, 350–51; Langsam, 511.

136. Elson, 194; A. Bullock, 259; Shirer, *Reich*, 383; Bouverie, 235, 238.

137. Shirer, *Republic*, 358.

138. Shirer, *Republic*, 351–53.

139. A. Bullock, 261; Shirer, *Republic*, 359–60.

140. Ward, 153; Bouverie, 238.

141. A. Bullock, 261.

142. Churchill, *Memoirs*, 141; P. Hastings, 117–18; Goldston, 208.

143. From Keith Feiling's *Life of Neville Chamberlain*, quoted in Churchill, *GS*, 300; Shirer, *Republic*, 362.

144. Shirer, *Republic*, 363–64.

145. See Churchill, *GS*, 299.

146. Shirer, *Republic*, 364–65, 368–69.

147. A. Bullock, 264; Shirer, *Republic*, 369.

148. Ward, 155.

149. A. Bullock, 266.

150. Stokesbury, 61; Shirer, *Reich*, 379–80; A. Bullock, 268.

151. Churchill, *GS*, 315; P. Hastings, 117; Ward, 155.

152. Ward, 156; Shirer, *Republic*, 394; A.J.P. Taylor, *OSWW*, 183.

153. Ward, 153, 156; Bouverie, 277.

154. Shirer, *Republic*, 398; A.J.P. Taylor, *OSWW*, 184.

155. Churchill, *GS*, 318; Shirer, *Republic*, 402; Ward, 157; A.J.P. Taylor, *OSWW*, 186.

156. Shirer, *Republic*, 401; A.J.P. Taylor, *OSWW*, 185; Bouverie, 284.

157. P. Hastings, 120; Ward, 157; A.J.P. Taylor, *OSWW*, 186; Henig, *OSWW*, 54.

158. Shirer, *Republic*, 403. Elson, 196.

159. P. Hastings, 115.

160. Churchill, *GS*, 328.

161. Churchill, *GS*, 326; Shirer, *Republic*, 405.

162. Humes, 76.

163. P. Hastings, 118.

164. A. Bullock, 280.

165. A. Bullock, 282; A.J.P. Taylor, *OSWW*, 203; Hibbert, 125.

166. Shirer, *Republic*, 407; Bouverie, 294.

167. Henig, *OSWW*, 55.

168. Shirer, *Reich*, 454; Churchill, *GS*, 345–46.

169. A.J.P. Taylor, *OSWW*, 211; Bouverie, 326.

170. Zamoyski, 298.

171. Langsam, 528–29; 534–35.

172. Lukowski and Zawadski, 299; Langsam, 529–30; Zamoyski, 304.

173. Lukowski and Zawadski, 301; Zamoyski, 307.

174. Langsam, 530; Zamoyski, 305; Abramsky et al., 136.

175. Langsam, 530–31; Lukowski and Zawadski, 304.

176. James Carroll, "Pope Francis and the Problematic Sainthood Cause of Cardinal August Hlond." *The New Yorker*, July 11, 2018. https://www.newyorker.com/news/daily-comment/pope-francis-and-the-problematic-sainthood-cause-of-cardinal-august-hlond. Accessed 2/7/21.

177. Lukowski and Zawadski, 301–02; Abramsky et al., 136.

178. Zamoyski, 308.

179. Langsam, 525–26.

180. Lukowski and Zawadski, 298; Zamoyski, 308.

181. Langsam, 528.

182. Langsam, 522.

183. Lukowski and Zawadski, 308 (photo caption).

184. Zamoyski, 299–300.

185. Zamoyski, 300–02; Lukowski and Zawadski, 310–12.

186. Langsam, 524.

187. Langsam, 526–27.

188. Langsam, 527; Zamoyski, 308.

189. Zamoyski, 303–04.

190. Zamoyski, 309.

191. Lukowski and Zawadski, 321.

192. Lukowski and Zawadski, 304–05; Langsam, 535.

193. Lukowski and Zawadski, 316.

194. Zamoyski, 311.

195. Langsam, 535

196. Lukowski and Zawadski, 316.

197. Zamoyski, 311; see also, A. Bullock, 285–86.

198. Langsam, 532.

199. Langsam, 533.

200. Robert Hirsch, "Gdynia, Poland 1933 Historic Marine Station." *Docomomo U.S. Newsletter, October 14, 2024.* https://www.docomomo-us.org/news/gdynia-poland-1933-historic-marine-station, Accessed 2/10/21.

201. Langsam, 533–34. Langsam cites the figure of 7,200 ships docking at Gdynia in 1933. According to Zamoyski's more recent work, the figure rose to 12,900 in 1938.

202. Henig, *OSWW*, 57; Shirer, *Republic*, 431.

203. A.J.P. Taylor, *OSWW*, 195–96; A.J.P. Taylor, *SWW*, 32; Eubank, 125–27.

204. Lukowski and Zawadski, 323; A. Bullock, 285–86, 291.

205. Langsam, 733; A. Bullock, 294, 300.

206. Bouverie, 330–32.

207. Shirer, *Republic*, 409.

208. Shirer, *Reich*, 480, 543; Stokesbury, 65; A. Bullock, 293–94, 298.

209. Shirer, *Republic*, 425–26; A. Bullock, 298.

210. Henig, *OSWW*, 56–57; Shirer, *Republic*, 425.

211. P. Hastings, 123 (picture caption).

212. Lukowski and Zawadski, 325–26; Henig, *OSWW*, 58; A. Bullock, 304–05.

213. A. Bullock, 313; Shirer, *Reich*, 519–20; M. Hastings, 5.

214. Neville Chamberlain, "Chamberlain Declares War on Germany." https://www.history.com/speeches/chamberlain-declares-war-on-germany. Accessed 2/15/21.

215. In the view of A.J.P. Taylor, Hitler had not been spoiling for war with Britain and France, whom he viewed as spineless. Rather, he was continuing to pursue the goal he had mapped out in *Mein Kampf*—namely, the reversal of the Versailles judgment on the 1918 Treaty of Brest Litovsk. The reader will recall that prior to losing the First World War Germany had defeated Russia, and that she had annexed territories extending across Poland into the Ukraine. At Versailles, these acquisitions were rendered null and void. Had she been able to retain them, the resources at her disposal might well have established her as the self-sufficient "Thousand-Year Reich" envisioned by Hitler. At the very least, Germany would have been overwhelmingly dominant in Europe. If Britain and France wanted to go to war with him then, it was all to the good. But not now! (A.J.P. Taylor, *OSWW*, 68–70; see also Fuller, *MHWW*, vol. 3, 377).

216. From the account of Hitler's personal interpreter, Paul Schmidt (Shirer, *Reich*, 613; Stokesbury, *WWII*, 66; Bouverie, 377).

217. Speer, 227.

218. Churchill, *GS*, 408.

Chapter 12

1. Zaloga, 7–8; Koskodan, 19, 80–83; Williamson, *PB*, 69–73.

2. Fuller, *SWW*, 47; Liddell Hart, *SWW*, 27; Wernick, 26; Roberts, *SOW*, 17.

3. Wernick, 21 and 24.

4. Roberts, *SOW*, 24; M. Hastings, 7, 16; Hastings (12) notes that rumors of cardboard tanks were prevalent in Britain at the outset of the war.

5. Koskodan, 23–24; Zaloga, 8–9; Williamson, *PB*, 82–83.

6. Zaloga, 9–10; All About History Team, "Polish Cavalry did charge German tanks in World War II ... and they won!" *History of War*, December 2, 2015. https://www.historyanswers.co.uk/history-of-war/polish-cavalry-vs-german-tanks-the-lies-the-betrayal-and-the-unlikely-truth/ Accessed 2/23/21.

7. Langsam, 738.

8. Shirer, *Reich*, 635. More recent research by Andrew Roberts puts the number of French divisions at 85 as against 40 German, though the majority of the latter were poorly trained, badly equipped reserves (Roberts, *SOW*, 19, 22).

9. M. Hastings (4) relates that British and French assurances had not been made in earnest. They had been idle threats meant to deter Hitler from unleashing his war.

10. Shirer, *Reich*, 634.

11. Shirer, *Republic*, 520–24; Roberts, *SOW*, 23.

12. Stefan Starzynski (Langsam, 738).

13. Sulzberger, 58; A.J.P. Taylor, *SWW*, 41; Shirer, *Reich*, 628; M. Hastings, 17.

14. Lukowski and Zawadski, 326–27; see also Zamoyski, 316; S.P. MacKenzie, 13; Koskodan, 41.

15. Roberts, *SOW*, 25. Roberts puts German casualties at 35,000.

16. Koskodan, 41–46; Zaloga, 11–13; Roberts, *SOW*, 26; M. Hastings, 23–24.

17. Koskodan, 22.

18. Fair, 348*fn*; Koskodan, 29–30

19. Shirer, *Reich*, 639–41; A. Bullock, 317; Harman, 6.

20. Shirer, *Reich*, 674.

21. Shirer, *Reich*, 674; Stokesbury, 83.

22. Churchill, *GS*, 539; Liddell Hart, *SWW*, 43–44; Langsam, 745.

23. Stokesbury, 81.

24. Sulzberger, 72.

25. Roberts, *SOW*, 32.

26. Roberts, *SOW*, 31–32.

27. M. Hastings, 33.

28. Churchill, *GS*, 543–44; Liddell Hart, *SWW*, 44–45, 53–54; Roberts, *SOW*, 38–39.

29. M. Hastings, 38; Roberts, *SOW*, 34.

30. Shirer, *Reich*, 705.

31. Langsam, 759–60; Fuller, *SWW*, 60. Churchill says that the merchant ships contained supplies and ammunition, but does not mention the commandos (*GS*, 590–91). Of note, the British retook Narvik in May, but had to withdraw after 10 days owing to events in France.

32. Draper, 42.

33. Draper, 4–5, 36; S.P. MacKenzie, 14.

34. Colville, 122–23; see also interview with Colville in episode 2 of *World at War* series.

35. Later in life, after a long discussion with his own son—also named Randolph—Winston remarked that their conversation that day exceeded all the dialogue he had had with *his* father in a lifetime (Jenkisson, 23).

36. Jenkisson, 21–23; Johnson, 9; Humes, 17.

37. Jenkisson, 23.

38. Humes, 25–26, 30.

39. Jenkisson, 23–27; Johnson, 12–15; Humes, 30–31.

40. His captor, he was to find out years afterward, was none other than Louis Botha, who became the first prime minister of the Union of South Africa (Jenkisson, 28–29, 43).

41. Humes, 45–46; Johnson, 38, 42–43. He had been promoting tank development since his time at the Admiralty.

42. Jenkisson, 58, 70; Johnson, 58; Humes, 52.

43. Humes, 51.

44. Jenkisson, 73.

45. Although Churchill was a proponent of Zionism, Transjordan was forged wholly from territory originally assigned to the British Mandate for Palestine. The territory pledged to the establishment of a "National Home" for the Jewish people was thereby reduced by three-quarters. His object, according to James Humes, was to strengthen the hand of the moderate Hashemites (Faisal of Iraq and Abdullah of Transjordan), against the radically anti-Zionist Wahabists of Saudi Arabia (Humes, 54).

46. Jenkisson, 75; Humes, 54.

47. On the occasion of his investment, he proudly donned the chancellor's robe worn by his father.

48. Johnson, 47, 67.

49. Humes, 73. Harold MacMillan, then a young Conservative, coined the phrase.

50. Humes, 68.

51. Draper, 57.

52. Draper, 104–05; A.J.P. Taylor, *SWW*, 51; Liddell Hart, *SWW*, 68–69; Wernick, 116.

53. Liddell Hart, *SWW*, 68–69; Wernick, 118.

54. Fuller, *MHWW*, 387–88; Keegan, *SWW*, 55–58.

55. Liddell Hart, *GG*, 124–25.

56. Keegan, *SWW*, 70; Shirer, *Republic*, 676; Roberts, *SOW*, 57; M. Hastings, 56.

57. Churchill, *Memoirs*, 252.

58. Churchill, *Memoirs*, 257.

59. Draper, 139–41; A.J.P. Taylor, *SWW*, 54.

60. Liddell Hart, *SWW*, 74–75, 80–83; *GG*, 132–34. Churchill puts the blame on General Rundstedt, citing his diary (*Memoirs*, 265), while Fuller says Hitler was right about the ground in any event (*MHWW*, vol. 3, 404).

61. Roberts, *SOW*, 64.

62. Shirer, *Reich*, 729–30.

63. Churchill, *Memoirs*, 275; Harman, 93.

64. Harman, 92–93.

65. Churchill, *Memoirs*, 276; Montross, 814.

66. Harman, 133–4.

67. Sulzberger, 60.

68. Harman, 123, 145–46, 205.

69. Churchill, *FH*, 115–118.

70. See General Blumentritt's remarks in Liddell Hart, *SWW*, 83 and *GG*, 134–35; M. Hastings, 66. Roberts (*SOW*, 62–63) feels that this argument is utterly implausible.

71. Liddell Hart, *GG*, 133.
72. Draper, 233–43.
73. Shirer, *Republic*, 25–26.
74. Roberts, *SOW*, 70.
75. Draper, 4–5.
76. Draper, 258*fn*; Roberts, *SOW*, 73; Jenkisson, 96.
77. Churchill, *Memoirs*, 300.
78. The idea originated with de Gaulle, now Undersecretary of State for National Defense, who was in England attempting to coordinate Anglo-French strategy (Churchill, *FH*, 207).
79. Draper, 273–76, 305–06. (Laval was a principal of the infamous Hoare-Laval pact.)
80. Draper, 301.
81. Draper, 301–08.
82. See Harman, 31 (deserters) and 194–95 (brave defense of the perimeter to the last).
83. Harman, 5; Fuller, *SWW*, 36–37, 51–52.
84. Fuller, *MHWW*, 381–82; Fuller, *SWW*, 52, 82; Montross, 773; Harman, 5.
85. Fuller, *MHWW*, 390–91; Draper, 44, 113, 135–36; Shirer, *Reich*, 719.
86. Harman, 31.
87. A.J.P. Taylor, *SWW*, 65; Roberts, *SOW*, 91–92.
88. Koskodan, 56; Zaloga, 15.
89. Churchill, *Memoirs*, 329–34; Stokesbury, 104.
90. Langsam, 782–83.
91. Montross, 817; Roberts, *SOW*, 75.
92. Churchill, *Memoirs*, 326.
93. S. P. MacKenzie, 19–20; Keegan, *SWW*, 92; Stokesbury, 110–11; Liddell Hart, *SWW*, 93.
94. Koskodan, 90–96. The Polish 303 Squadron downed more German aircraft than any other RAF units during the campaign (Zaloga, 15).
95. Churchill, *Memoirs*, 368.
96. Shirer, *Reich*, 777; Asimov, 600; Jenkisson, 96; Stokesbury, 112.
97. Humes, 88.
98. Churchill, *Memoirs*, 366. (He actually said this in mid-campaign on August 20).
99. M. Hastings, 88; Roberts, *SOW*, 108; Jenkisson, 97.
100. Montross, 822.
101. M. Hastings, 78, 95–96; see also, Fuller, *SWW*, 84–85.
102. Langsam, 791–94.
103. Fuller, *SWW*, 98; Stokesbury, 140.
104. Liddell Hart, *SWW*, 127.
105. Stokesbury, 142; Shirer, *Reich*, 817, 823.
106. Roberts, *SOW*, 123; M. Hastings, 113.
107. Langsam, 795–96; Montross, 831–32.
108. Liddell Hart, *SWW*, 118–19.
109. Churchill, *Memoirs*, 428.
110. Stokesbury, 143.
111. Montross, 836.
112. Keegan, *SWW*, 171.
113. Roberts, *SOW*, 126–27; A.J.P. Taylor, *SWW*, 92; Churchill, *Memoirs*, 446.
114. Churchill, *Memoirs*, 445-7; Montross, 837.
115. Taylor, *SWW*, 93; Keegan, *SWW*, 171; Liddell Hart, *SWW*, 136–39; Roberts, *SOW*, 127.

116. Fuller, *MHWW*, vol. 3, 419; Shirer, *Reich*, 828–29.
117. Liddell Hart, *SWW*, 143; Shirer, *Reich*, 794–95.
118. Liddell Hart, *SWW*, 143–44; Shirer, *Reich*, 798; A.J.P. Taylor, *SWW*, 98.
119. Churchill, *FH*, 586; A. Bullock, 362; Shirer, *Reich*, 809; Sulzberger, 417–18.
120. Sulzberger, 101; Montross, 839–40; Roberts, *SOW*, 139, 147.
121. For Churchill's description, see *Memoirs*, 461, 464.
122. Fuller, *MHWW*, vol. 3, 420; Liddell Hart, *SWW*, 132; Keegan, *SWW*, 174; Roberts, *SOW*, 140–41.
123. Sulzberger, 250.
124. Marrin, 176; Roberts, *SOW*, 156–57; M. Hastings, 142.
125. Marrin, 176; Caulkins, 115.
126. Marrin, 176.
127. Roberts, *SOW*, 157; M. Hastings, 147.
128. A.J.P. Taylor, *SWW*, 98–99.
129. Keegan, *SWW*, 186–87, 190.
130. Clark, *Barbarossa*, 43.
131. Stokesbury, 156.
132. Shirer, *Reich*, 856; Marrin, 182; Roberts, *SOW*, 167.
133. Clark, *Barbarossa*, 102; A. Bullock, 382–83.
134. Clark, *Barbarossa*, 104–05.
135. A. Roberts, *SOW*, 182; M. Hastings, 150; Kerrigan, 165–67; Marrin, 193.
136. Fuller, *MHWW*, vol. 3, 435; Stokesbury, 156; Sulzberger, 258–59 (photos).
137. Shirer, *Reich*, 833–34; A. Bullock, 376; Stokesbury, 156–57.
138. Fuller, *MHWW*, vol. 3, 436.
139. Clark, *Barbarossa*, 153.
140. Bartov, 9.
141. Bartov, 6.
142. Roberts, *SOW*, 165; M. Hastings, 152.
143. Office of U.S. Chief Counsel... vol. 4, 559; see also S.P. MacKenzie, 109.
144. Fuller, *MHWW*, vol. 3, 434.
145. Marrin, 185; Bartov, 8.
146. Bartov, 3.
147. Liddell Hart, *GG*, 185. Eight years earlier, Caulaincourt's long-missing memoirs had been found in a metal chest in the ruins of the Caulaincourt estate. See George Libaire's introduction to Caulaincourt's *With Napoleon in Russia* for the full saga of these memoirs prior to publication.
148. Clark, *Barbarossa*, 146.
149. Zhukov (Salisbury's introduction), 24.
150. Zhukov (Salisbury's introduction), 12.
151. Shirer, *Reich*, 854.
152. Zhukov (Salisbury's introduction), 8; Eisenhower, 467–68.
153. Roberts, *SOW*, 182–83; Zhukov, 52.
154. Liddell Hart, *GG*, 187; Fuller, *MHWW*, vol. 3, 442.
155. Fuller, *MHWW*, vol. 3, 427; Shirer, *Reich*, 862.
156. M. Hastings, 39.

157. O'Shea, 124.

158. Asimov, 534.

159. Churchill, radio address, January 20, 1940 (quoted in Roberts, *SOW*, 113).

160. Lindbergh, Charles. *Aviation, Geography and Race*, Reader's Digest, vol. 35, n. 211, 1939.

161. Langsam, 817.

162. M. Hastings, 183.

163. Langsam, 817; Venn, 91.

164. Churchill, *Memoirs*, 384.

165. Battle attrition brought the number down to less than 30 by the end of 1940, but rapid production thereafter brought the number up to 150 by the end of 1941 (Roberts, *SOW*, 352–58; M. Hastings, 269; Liddell Hart, *SWW*, 377; S.P. MacKenzie, 63).

166. Roberts, *SOW*, 362; Liddell Hart, *SWW*, 377–78; Montross, 830.

167. Stokesbury, 120–21; Fuller, *MHWW*, vol. 3, 452: Keegan, *SWW*, 539, 542.

168. Fuller, *SWW*, 127–28; Liddell Hart, *SWW*, 199.

169. Liddell Hart, *SWW*, 206–07.

170. Sulzberger, 145, 150; Keegan, *SWW*, 246–47, 252; Fuller, *SWW*, 127–32.

171. Toland, *RS*, 80, 107–08, 115–17.

172. Toland, *RS*, 102.

173. Toland, *RS*, 144; see also, Keegan, *SWW*, 249.

174. See for example, J.F.C. Fuller (*MHWW*, vol. 3, 450–57), but bear in mind that Fuller was an enthusiastic contributor to Britain's *Fascist Quarterly*, and that he also believed that Roosevelt was the dupe of Russian spies within his own government (see 450).

175. Taylor, *SWW*, 121; Liddell Hart also finds the evidence flimsy (*SWW*, 219).

176. Shirer, *Reich*, 901.

177. Toland, *RS*, 278; Shirer, *Reich*, 895*fn*.

178. Speer, 250.

179. Montross, 850.

180. Stokesbury, 235; Keegan, *SWW*, 222–23; Craig, 18.

181. Liddell Hart, *GG*, 195, 204; Fuller, *MHWW*, vol. 3, 518.

182. Stokesbury, 236; Kerch was viewed as a potential base for amphibious assaults on the Caucusus (Liddell Hart, *SWW*, 248).

183. Fuller, *MHWW*, vol. 3, 527; Botting, 22; Churchill, *Memoirs*, 636–37.

184. Stokesbury, 235–37; see also, Montross, 893.

185. Shirer, *Reich*, 916; Fuller, *MHWW*, vol. 3, 526–28; Liddell Hart, *GG*, 204–05.

186. S. P. MacKenzie, 71; Keegan, *SWW*, 224; Clark, *Barbarossa*, 213.

187. Office of U.S. Chief Counsel... vol. 1, 984; see also Dawidowicz, 142.

188. Ciano, 383.

189. Dawidowicz, 110–15; Totten et al., 136.

190. Klee et al., 28.

191. Klee et al., 27; Hilberg, 121.

192. Klee et al., 26–33; Hilberg, 120–22.

193. Totten et al., 137; Hilberg, 121–22.

194. Klee et al., 54–55.

195. Hilberg, 111–14, 131; M. Hastings, 495.

196. Klee et al., 179, 197.

197. Klee et al., 133.

198. Klee et al., 63–65; see also, Roberts, *SOW*, 222–23.

199. Roberts, *SOW*, 222.

200. Dawidowicz, 171; Totten et al., 137.

201. Hilberg, 136–37; McManus, ed., 123; M. Hastings, 496.

202. McManus, ed., 123; Hilberg, 137.

203. Fleming, 74.

204. Fleming, 48–99.

205. Totten et al., 138.

206. Dawidowicz, 419. Most of Warsaw's victims were sent to the death camp at Treblinka, where the sadistic commandant had a dog with a talent for biting inmates in the groin (Klee et al., 248).

207. Dawidowicz, 188–91.

208. See testimony in Totten et al., 152–53.

209. Clark, *Barbarossa*, 194.

210. Hilberg, 221.

211. Dawidowicz, 199; Roberts, *SOW*, 229.

212. Fleming, 144.

213. Hilberg, 246.

214. Dawidowicz, 199.

215. Hilberg, 248–49; Shirer, *Reich*, 970.

216. Fleming, 143; Roberts, *SOW*, 230.

217. Roberts, *SOW*, 229–32.

218. S. P. MacKenzie, 118.

219. Dawidowicz, 385–86, 398–99, 474–75.

220. Hilberg, 200–01, 203, 294; Dawidowicz, 390–91.

221. Dawidowicz, 456–60; Shirer, *Reich*, 976–78.

222. Office of the U.S. Counsel... vol. 1, 143 (from an official SS report).

223. Keegan, *SWW*, 289.

224. Totten et al., 193.

225. Totten et al., 171.

226. Totten et al., 208, 211–16; Dawidowicz (176–81) gives a figure of 100,000.

227. Klee et al., 273–74.

228. Hilberg, 251–52.

229. Hilberg, pp. 254–7.

230. Hilberg, 118,142; Dawidowicz, 520.

231. Roberts, *SOW*, 113–14.

232. S. P. MacKenzie, 42; Dawidowicz, 490, 501, 515–17, 524–27; Totten, et al., 141.

233. Dawidowicz, 505–06; S.P. MacKenzie, 42.

234. Shirer, *Reich*, 991–94; Keegan, *SWW*, 488; Roberts, *SOW*, 242–43.

Chapter 13

1. Craig, 61; M. Hastings, 302.

2. Craig, 72.

3. Kerr, 182.

4. Falls, ed., *GMB*, 254.

5. Craig, 90.

6. Liddell Hart, *SWW*, 259–60. Montross, 891.

7. Stokesbury, 238–39.

8. Fuller, *SWW*, 178–87.

9. Fuller, *MHWW*, 534.

10. Craig, 280–81.

11. Clark, *Barbarossa*, 285–86; Roberts, *SOW*, 340.

12. Shirer, *Reich*, 930; A. Bullock, 404; Roberts, *SOW*, 342.

13. Toland, *RS*, 310; A.J.P. Taylor, *SWW*, 135.

14. For details, see Liddell Hart, *SWW*, 225–26.

15. William S. Lind, *America Can Win*, 90 (Quoted in Stitcher, "Sweep the Skies—Why Carriers aren't Capital Ships." *Imperium.news*. https://imperium.news/sweep-the-skies-why-carriers-arent-capital-ships/ Accessed 8/10/21.

16. Churchill, *Memoirs*, 510–11.

17. Zich, 122; Roberts, *SOW*, 206; M. Hastings, 205.

18. Montross, 857; Langsam, 829. Prior to Pearl Harbor, the Americans had not been less dismissive of the Japanese deeming the "slant-eyed Orientals" physiologically unfit to train as fighter pilots (Montross, 853; Roberts, *SOW*, 187).

19. Montross, 857–58.

20. M. Hastings, 208–12.

21. Montross, 860–61.

22. Zich, 95; Toland, *RS*, 328.

23. Toland, *RS*, 339–41; Zich, 100.

24. Toland, *RS*, 336–37.

25. Toland, *RS*, 343; Stokesbury, 211.

26. Liddell Hart, *SWW*, 223.

27. Churchill, *Memoirs*, 562; A.J.P. Taylor, *SWW*, 136; Sulzberger, 208; Montross, 864.

28. Toland, *RS*, 354; Sulzberger, 149; Stokesbury, 213.

29. R. Jackson, 69; Stokesbury, 213.

30. Zich, 182; Toland, *RS*, 385.

31. Toland, *RS*, 472–73.

32. Toland, *RS*, 475.

33. Montgomery, 513.

34. Montgomery, 513.

35. An intensive bombing campaign against Malta had previously starved the British of munitions, but the tide turned with Hitler's decision to call off an airborne assault on the island and the arrival of fresh munitions and planes (Shirer, *Reich*, 912–13; S.P. MacKenzie, 69; Asimov, 612; Goodenough, 49).

36. Roberts, *SOW*, 285.

37. Montross, 935.

38. Montross, 880.

39. John Welford, "Bernard Mongomery: An Insufferable Field Marshal." *Owlcation*, May 1, 2017. https://owlcation.com/humanities/Bernard-Montgomery-An-Insufferable-Field-Marshall. Accessed 4/5/21.

40. Shirer, *Reich*, 920*fn*.

41. Goodenough, 50–51.

42. Falls, ed., *GMB*, 266.

43. Goodenough, 52–53; Holmes, 205; Roberts, *SOW*, 295–96.

44. Holmes, 205–07; Montgomery, 514.

45. Churchill, *Memoirs*, 619.

46. Liddell Hart, *SWW*, 313–16.

47. Eisenhower, 99–107; Liddell Hart, *SWW*, 318–20, 327–31.

48. Shirer, *Reich*, 925*fn*.

49. Shirer, *Reich*, 925; M. Hastings, 365; Montross, 901.

50. Liddell Hart, *SWW*, 341–42, 432.

51. Liddell Hart, *SWW*, 401–02.

52. Liddell Hart, *SWW*, 405–10; Fuller, *SWW*, 244.

53. Liddell Hart, *SWW*, 430; Fuller, *MHWW*, vol. 3, 514.

54. A. Bullock, 402–03.

55. Livesey, 162–67; Liddell Hart, *GG*, 210–12; Keegan, *SWW*, 460–62.

56. S. P. MacKenzie, 74; Marrin, 198; Clark, *Barbarossa*, 312; Sulzberger, 253.

57. A.J.P. Taylor, *SWW*, 179; Clark, *Barbarossa*, 275; Roberts, *SOW*, 413.

58. Keegan, *SWW*, 469; Marrin, 202–03; Roberts, *SOW*, 423.

59. Keegan, *SWW*, 472–73; Clark, *Barbarossa*, 372–73.

60. Clark, *Barbarossa*, 377.

61. Reader's Digest, ed. (from Harrison Salisbury's *900 Days*), 43, 62.

62. M. Hastings, 167–68; Roberts, *SOW*, 172.

63. Reader's Digest (from Harrison Salisbury's *900 Days*), 51, 53, 57; Marrin, 190.

64. Trythall, 205.

65. Fuller, *SWW*, 37.

66. Liddell Hart contests Douhet's impact, saying that as late as 1935 few of Britain's Air Staff knew of Douhet's 1921 tome, *Command of the Air*, even though they subscribed to the same theories (Liddell Hart, *SWW*, 590*fn*).

67. Fuller, *SWW*, 39.

68. Perkins, 94.

69. Keegan, *SWW*, 420.

70. Keegan, *SWW*, 425–26; Stokesbury, 281; Montross, 919–20.

71. Roberts, *SOW*, 434–36; M. Hastings, 459.

72. M. Hastings, 464.

73. R. Jackson, 96.

74. R. Jackson, 96; see also Fuller, *SWW*, 228.

75. R. Jackson, 96.

76. Shirer, *Reich*, 1009.

77. Speer, 370.

78. R. Jackson, 99.

79. Fuller, *SWW*, 224–29; Speer, 501; Roberts, *SOW*, 442.

80. Montross, 903.

81. Liddell Hart, *SWW*, 441; M. Hastings, 430.

82. Roberts, *SOW*, 375.

83. Fuller, *SWW*, 265–66.

84. Roberts, *SOW*, 376.

85. Churchill, *Memoirs*, 711–12.

86. Stokesbury, 292.

87. Keegan, 350–51.

88. M. Hastings, 429.

89. Reader's Digest, ed. (from Richard Collier's *Duce!*), 395; Hibbert, 266.

90. Hibbert, 299.

91. Reader's Digest, ed. (from Richard Collier's *Duce!*), 396.

92. A.J.P. Taylor, *SWW*, 186.

93. Churchill, *Memoirs*, 740, 755–56, 771, 828–30; Fuller, *MHWW*, 576.

94. Sulzberger, 369; Stokesbury, 247; Churchill, *Memoirs*, 740, 755, 828–30.

95. In reference to another of his initiatives for saving Eastern Europe being rebuffed—namely, attempting to beat the Russians to Berlin in 1945—Churchill issued the gentle admonition that the United States oughtn't to have let its own lack of territorial ambitions blind it to the peril looming over Eastern Europe (Churchill, *Memoirs*, 937).

96. Roberts, *SOW*, 394–95.

97. Churchill, *Memoirs*, 799–800.

98. Fuller, *SWW*, 274.

99. Keegan, *SWW*, 361; Stokesbury, 306; A.J.P. Taylor, *SWW*, 191.

100. Roberts, *SOW*, 377, 401–02.

101. Stokesbury, 306; Keegan, *SWW*, 361.

102. Fuller, *MHWW*, vol. 3, 561.

103. Botting, 50 photo and caption, 94, 103.

104. Botting, 94.

105. Montgomery, 520; M. Hastings, 515.

106. Botting, 105; Liddell Hart, *GG*, 243; *SWW*, 549.

107. Botting, 129; Roberts, *SOW*, 473.

108. Botting, 137.

109. Sulzberger, 499–503; Botting, 137.

110. Botting, 134.

111. Roberts, *SOW*, 472; Liddell Hart, *SWW*, 549.

112. Montgomery, 520.

113. Roberts, *SOW*, 477. (M. Hastings puts the figure at 3,000, but Roberts provides a detailed breakdown according to nationality.)

114. M. Hastings, 518.

115. Churchill, *Memoirs*, 815; Neillands, *WC*, 174–75.

116. Churchill, *Memoirs*, 310–11.

117. Eisenhower, 234–35.

118. Roberts, *SOW*, 464; Montgomery, 520.

119. Eisenhower, 258.

120. Since "failure" was not in Montgomery's lexicon, he later claimed that his attack had been meant as a feint all along. In his world, *everything* went "according to plan."

121. Eisenhower, 267.

122. Baker, 89.

123. Baker, 88–89.

124. Roberts, *SOW*, 532; M. Hastings, 528.

125. S. P. MacKenzie, 116.

126. S. P. MacKenzie, 82; Hastings, 531.

127. Roberts, *SOW*, 532.

128. Churchill, *Memoirs*, 866; Fuller, *SWW*, 206; Liddell Hart, *SWW*, 617.

129. Montross, 929; M. Hastings, 547.

130. Liddell Hart, *SWW*, 619; Keegan, *SWW*, 307; A.J.P. Taylor, *SWW*, 310; M. Hastings, 548.

131. Toland, *RS*, 566–70.

132. M. Hastings, 548.

133. Sulzberger, 543; Toland, *RS*, 572; Stokesbury, 339.

134. Toland, *RS*, 588–90; M. Hastings, 550.

135. Fuller, *SWW*, 206; Toland, *RS*, 588–90.

136. Shirer, *Reich*, 1052.

137. A. Bullock, 441.

138. Quoted in Montross, 933.

139. Shirer, *Reich*, 1040–41; Botting, 193.

140. Shirer, *Reich*, 1071, 1071*fn*; Roberts, *SOW*, 482, says the piano wire part is a myth.

141. Shirer, *Reich*, 1078. The July Plot was not the first attempt on Hitler's life. In March 1943, a group of officers had cleverly disguised a bomb as a pair of brandy bottles and smuggled it aboard Hitler's plane at Smolensk. Unfortunately, the detonator malfunctioned, and Hitler made it back to the Wolf's Lair in safety. (To prevent the plot from being exposed, one of the conspirators hurriedly flew to Rastenburg, where he narrowly managed to replace the bomb with real brandy bottles before anyone became suspicious [Shirer, *Reich*, 1019–21; Clark, *Barbarossa*, 309–11; A. Bullock, 436]). Although the conspiracy was not uncovered, Hitler was already so certain that members of the army were out to kill him that he had his trademark peaked military cap reinforced with three and a half pounds of steel plating, thus converting it into a helmet of sorts (Shirer, *Reich*, 1020*fn*; Clark, *Barbarossa*, 309). After the July Plot, his paranoia intensified. He now trusted no one at all. With each passing day, his behavior became more spiteful and malignant so that his generals found it agonizing to deal with him (Shirer, *Reich*, 1081).

142. Montross, 933.

143. Churchill, *Memoirs*, 824; Eisenhower, 274–76; Fuller, *SWW*, 327.

144. Keegan, *SWW*, 396.

145. Montross, 935.

146. M. Hastings, 537–38.

147. Eisenhower, 279; Roberts, *SOW*, 487.

148. M. Hastings, 538.

149. Roberts, *SOW*, 486–87.

150. See Churchill, *Memoirs*, 827–34; Fuller, *SWW*, 322–25; *MHWW*, vol. 3, 575–77.

151. Keegan, *SWW*, 483; Stokesbury, 271–72; Zaloga, 24.

152. Reader's Digest, ed. (from Bor-Komorowski's *The Unconquerables*), 316.

153. Reader's Digest, ed. (from Bor-Komorowski's *The Unconquerables*), 327.

154. Reader's Digest, ed. (from Bor-Komorowski's *The Unconquerables*), 330; Churchill, *Memoirs*, 850–51.

155. Stokesbury, 271–2.

156. Clark, *Barbarossa*, 391.

157. Reader's Digest, ed. (from Bor-Komorowski's *The Unconquerables*), 318, 320.

158. Reader's Digest, ed. (from Bor-Komorowski's *The Unconquerables*), 335.

159. Stokesbury, 272; A.J.P. Taylor, *SWW*, 206–07; Clark, *Barbarossa*, 390*fn*; Roberts, *SOW*, 534.

160. Stokesbury, 272.

161. M. Hastings, 531–32; Fuller, *SWW*, 349.

162. Keegan, 504.
163. Clark, *Barbarossa*, 404.
164. Keegan, 506.
165. Montross, 946; Fuller, *MHWW*, vol. 3, 579.
166. Fuller, *MHWW*, vol. 3, 580; *SWW*, 339–40; Montross, 946; Montgomery, 526.
167. Keegan, *SWW*, 437; M. Hastings, 559; Roberts, *SOW*, 499.
168. Sulzberger, 520; Reader's Digest, ed. (from Cornelius Ryan's *A Bridge Too Far*), 342; Churchill, *Memoirs*, 877–78.
169. Eisenhower, 258.
170. Reader's Digest, ed. (from Cornelius Ryan's *A Bridge Too Far*), 343.
171. Reader's Digest, ed. (from Cornelius Ryan's *A Bridge Too Far*), 344.
172. M. Hastings, 560; Neillands, *BFR*, 112–118.
173. Zaloga, 21; Koskodan, 163.
174. M. Hastings, 561.
175. Koskodan, 174.
176. Eisenhower, 371.
177. M. Hastings, 564.
178. Montross, 948; M. Hastings, 563.
179. Montross, 948.
180. Fuller, *SWW*, 349.
181. A. Bullock, 455; Roberts, *SOW*, 508.
182. Liddell Hart, *GG*, 280.
183. Whiting, 140.
184. Stokesbury, 353–54, Liddell Hart, *SWW*, 645; Whiting, 151–53.
185. Liddell Hart, *GG*, p. 278.
186. M. Hastings, 573.
187. Whiting, 194–201.
188. Speer, 306.
189. Roberts, *SOW*, 509.
190. Whiting, 170; Roberts, *SOW*, 505.
191. Liddell Hart, *SWW*, 663; Shirer, *Reich*, 1091.
192. A.J.P. Taylor, *SWW*, 216.
193. According to A.J.P. Taylor, this is the city of Dresden's own estimate (*SWW*, 219).
194. Eisenhower, 381.
195. Shirer, *Reich*, 1097.
196. Speer, 586; Liddell Hart, *SWW*, 679–80.
197. Hibbert, 368; Reader's Digest, ed. (from Richard Collier's *Duce!*), 401.
198. Shirer, *Reich*, 1130; A.J.P. Taylor, *SWW*, 221.
199. A. Bullock, 478.
200. See Cornelius Ryan, *The Last Battle*, in Reader's Digest, ed., 418.
201. Reader's Digest, ed. (from Cornelius Ryan's *The Last Battle*), 423–24.
202. Reader's Digest, ed. (from Cornelius Ryan's *The Last Battle*), 423; Keegan, *SWW*, 532; M. Hastings, 608.
203. Montross, 956.
204. Fuller, *SWW*, 373–74.
205. M. Hastings, 551.
206. Fuller, *SWW*, 374.
207. Fuller, *SWW*, 374; Churchill, *Memoirs*, 869.
208. Roberts, *SOW*, 565.
209. Fuller, *MHWW*, vol. 3, 609–11.
210. Churchill, *Memoirs*, 872.
211. Liddell Hart, *SWW*, 626–27; Churchill, *Memoirs*, 872.
212. Sulzberger, 532.
213. Roberts, *SOW*, 568; Stokesbury, 366; Fuller, *SWW*, 380; M. Hastings, 614.
214. Keegan, *SWW*, 566.
215. Introverted and self-conscious, Hayes survived the carnage only to succumb to alcoholism after being forced to participate in a very public stateside bond tour (Toland, *RS*, 744*fn*).
216. Stokesbury, 368.
217. Roberts, *SOW*, 569; M. Hastings, 618.
218. Stokesbury, 372; Keegan, *SWW*, 568.
219. Inoguchi et al., 81–82.
220. Liddell Hart, *SWW*, 686; Sulzberger, 600.
221. M. Hastings, 622.
222. Keegan, *SWW*, 576.
223. Liddell Hart, *SWW*, 691.
224. M. Hastings, 617.
225. Liddell Hart, *SWW*, 693.
226. Robert James Maddox, "The Biggest Decision: Why We Had to Drop the Atomic Bomb." *American Heritage*. Volume 46, Issue 3. May/June 1995. https://www.americanheritage.com/biggest-decision-why-we-had-drop-atomic-bomb#2. Accessed May 7, 2021.
227. Toland, *RS*, 879.
228. J. Lewis, ed., 473.
229. Toland, *RS*, 886.
230. John Toland has uncovered the amazing anecdote of a survivor of the Hiroshima bomb, who made it home to Nagasaki just in time to be bombed again while describing the first strike to his wife. He lived to tell Toland about it personally. (See Toland, *RS*, 903–4.)
231. In actuality, the speech wasn't broadcast live. Hirohito had recorded it the previous day.
232. Churchill, *Memoirs*, 983.
233. Toland, *RS*, 898; Fuller, *MHWW*, vol. 3, 627.
234. Roberts, *SOW*, 576. Roberts quotes George Marshall regarding the forfeiture of shock value.
235. Maddox, *op cit*.
236. A.J.P. Taylor, *SWW*, 225.
237. Maddox, *op cit*.
238. M. Hastings, 627.
239. Liddell Hart, *SWW*, 698.
240. A.J.P. Taylor, *SWW*, 229; Stokesbury, 378.
241. Roberts, *SOW*, 579; Keegan, *SWW*, 590.
242. A.J.P. Taylor, *SWW*, 229.
243. Churchill, *Memoirs*, 997, from a speech delivered in Fulton, Missouri.
244. See Fuller, *MHWW*, vol. 3, 449–50, 508–09, 589; and *SWW*, 258–59, 281, 321–25.
245. Trythall, 245. Edward Creasy published an enormously successful work entitled *The Fifteen Decisive Battles of the World* in 1852.
246. Trythall, 56.
247. Trythall, 216–17.
248. Trythall, 245–46.
249. Churchill, *Memoirs*, 469–70.
250. Humes, 94; see also Neillands, *WC*, 159–60; Johnson, 122.

251. Liddell Hart, *SWW*, 713.

252. Alsop, 248.

253. "Eisenhower Regrets Policy of Total Surrender; Asserts Roosevelt Erred in his World War II Goal." Associated Press. *New York Times*, December 21, 1964. Accessed May 13, 2021. https://www.nytimes.com/1964/12/21/archives/eisenhower-regrets-policy-of-total-surrender-asserts-roosevelt.html Eisenhower said in the same interview that Chief-of-Staff George C. Marshall agreed with him.

254. A.J.P. Taylor, *SWW*, 170.

255. Franklin Roosevelt Administration: Address on the Casablanca Conference (February 12, 1943) https://www.jewishvirtuallibrary.org/president-roosevelt-address-on-the-casablanca-conference-february-1943 Accessed 5/13/21.

256. Churchill, *Memoirs*, 672–73.

257. Venn, 103.

258. Fuller, *MHWW*, vol. 3, 508; A.J.P. Taylor, *SWW*, 170; State Department, Office of the Historian, *The Casablanca Conference, 1943*. https://history.state.gov/milestones/1937-1945/casablanca Accessed 5/13/21.

259. Fuller, *SWW*, 325.

260. Neillands, *WC*, 176.

261. Quoted in Fuller, *MHWW*, vol. 3, 553, from Elliott Roosevelt's, *As He Saw It*."

262. Alsop, 204.

263. Sulzberger, 554; Fuller, *MHWW*, vol. 3, 585.

264. Roberts, *LIW*, 164; M. Hastings, 590.

265. Venn, 111–12; Churchill, *Memoirs*, 925.

266. Churchill, *Memoirs*, 927, 949.

267. Montgomery, 529; Fuller, *MHWW*, vol. 3, 584–85.

268. Arnold Beichman, "Roosevelt's Failure at Yalta," *Hoover Digest*, October 30, 2004. https://www.hoover.org/research/roosevelts-failure-yalta. Accessed 5/23/21.

269. Venn, 112.

270. Elie Abel, "We Can't Do Business With Stalin," *American Heritage*, August 1977, vol. 28, issue 5. https://www.americanheritage.com/we-cant-do-business-stalin#:~:text=%E2%80%9CWe%20can't%20do%20business,Stalin%2C%E2%80%9D%20the%20President%20exclaimed.&text=Stalin's%20bitter%20reproaches%20of%201942,witnessed%20such%20a%20grandiose%20operation. Accessed 5/23/21.

271. Fuller, *MHWW*, vol. 3, 586–87.

272. Roberts, *LIW*, 157 and 160.

273. Churchill, *Memoirs*, 937.

274. Fuller, *MHWW*, vol. 3, 587. Fuller finds Eisenhower's reasoning unfathomable, but Hitler would have done well to adopt the American commander's principle at Stalingrad.

275. Roberts, *LIW*, 163. In *SWW*, A.J.P. Taylor mistakenly attributes the quote to Truman.

276. A.J.P. Taylor, *SWW*, 223. Prague, it may be noted, was not a ruined city since it had not been bombed or fought over during the war. On May 5, 1945, Czech partisans rose up against their Nazi occupiers in a bid to liberate the city before the Russians arrived. The following morning General George S. Patton's U.S. Third Army reached Pilsen (sixty miles distant) and could have been the first to reach Prague. Eisenhower, however, insisted that Patton stand down. The Czechs came off the worse for this decision, suffering 8,000 casualties in the failed uprising before Russian troops arrived (on May 12) and then spending more than forty years in the stifling grip of Moscow.

277. Casualty figures: M. Hastings, 646, Baker, 104.

278. Baker, 105.

279. Winston Churchill. Address to the Estates-General of the Netherlands (1946), "Do the government own the people or do the people own the government?" https://winstonchurchill.org/publications/finest-hour/finest-hour-161/states-general-of-the-netherlands-1946-do-the-government-own-the-people-or-do-the-people-own-the-government/ Accessed May 7, 2021.

280. Larry Arnn, *The Second World Wars*, Hillsdale online course (based on the book of that title by Victor Davis Hanson). Lecture 1: *The Stakes of World War II*. https://online.hillsdale.edu/courses/the-second-world-wars , accessed 5/6/21.

Chapter 14

1. Wallbank and Taylor, vol. 2, 578.

2. 7.1: "The Wave Nature of Light." *Jove*. https://www.jove.com/science-education/11294/the-wave-nature-of-light Accessed 6/5/21.

3. If $E = h \times f$, then $E \div f = h$

4. Paul Looyen. "Understanding Max Planck and Black Body Radiation," *High School Physics Explained*, June 18, 2016. https://www.youtube.com/watch?v=7hxYGaegxAM accessed 6/5/21. A similar analogy is provided by the ancient Greek mathematician, Pythagoras (best remembered for the Pythagorean Theorem, proving that $a2 + b2 = c2$ for all right triangles, where c is the hypotenuse and a and b, the two sides that form a 90-degree angle). Hearing a blacksmith bang some metal with different hammers one day, Pythagoras noted that each hammer produced a sound that was harmonious with the others, except one, which produced a highly discordant sound. Thinking this curious, he made a study of the hammers and found that the masses of the harmonious hammers were in simple numerical ratio to one another, while the discordant one was not. Hence, the physics of harmony will not allow a hammer with a mass of 5, when struck against a piece of metal, to produce a sound harmonious with those produced by hammers with masses of 3, 6, 9 and 12 (all of which are divisible by 3, whereas 5 is not).

5. Stephen Ornes, "Scientists Capture a Quantum Jump as it Happens," *Discover* magazine, December 24, 2019 https://www.discovermagazine.com/the-sciences/scientists-

catch-a-quantum-jump-as-it-happens. December 24, 2019; Brinton et al., vol. 2, 911.

6. Wallbank and Taylor, 579.

7. To be fair, Newton did believe that light might be carried in particles that he called "corpuscles."

8. Brinton et al., vol. 2, 910. The correction factor for the lengthening of time and the shortening of distance is calculated by the formula $\gamma = $, where γ is the correction factor (also known as the "Lorentz factor"), v is the velocity of the traveler and c is the speed of light. Plugging in 0.92 for $v2/c2$ (90% of the speed of light squared), will calculate to a correction factor of 2.

9. i.e., the Hohenzollern, Hapsburg, Romanov and Ottoman.

10. Ian Samson, "Great Dynasties of the World: The Huxleys" *The Guardian*, November 12, 2010. https://www.theguardian.com/lifeandstyle/2010/nov/13/huxley-great-dynasties-aldous accessed 6/5/21.

11. Wallbank and Taylor, vol. 2, 587–88; Brinton et al., vol. 2, 661; Tate contributors, "Cubism," *Tate.org* https://www.tate.org.uk/art/art-terms/c/cubism Accessed 6/20/21.

12. The examples presented here to encapsulate the decade after the First World War are summarized from the discussion in Wallbank and Taylor, vol. 2, 591–92.

13. Eric B. Litwack, "Totalitarianism," *Internet Encyclopedia of Philosophy*. https://iep.utm.edu/totalita/ Accessed 5/26/21.

14. Rich, *ANR*, 39.

15. Litwack, *op cit.*

16. Litwack, *op cit.*

17. Quoted in Litwack (*op cit.*) from Hannah Arendt's *Origins of Totalitarianism*. San Diego: Harvest Books, Harcourt Brace Janovitch, 1968 (474).

18. Litwack, *op cit.* The reader may wish to keep that in mind the next time a "post-modernist," "moral relativist" or "critical theorist" hurls an absurdist whiffle ball his or her way (claiming, of course, that it is a regulation baseball); for such perversions of Heisenberg's "uncertainty principle" and Einstein's "theory of relativity" seem a very nice milieu for new incarnations of totalitarianism—and the "soft terror" of "cancel culture" seems a ready tool of implementation. (Dr. R. Albert Mohler, Jr., "Relativity, Moral Relativism, and the Modern Age," compares relativity and relativism. https://albertmohler.com/2015/12/07/relativity-moral-relativism-and-the-modern-age

19. George Orwell, "Literature and Totalitarianism," Orwell Project by O. Dag. 1999–2004, www. *Orwell.ru*. https://www.orwell.ru/library/articles/totalitarianism/english/e_lat Accessed 6/17/21.

20. Winston Churchill, "Mass Effects in Modern Life," 1925 (speech). https://www.nationalchurchillmuseum.org/mass-effects-in-modern-life.html Accessed 6/7/21.

21. Riffenburgh, 54.

22. Kieran Mulvaney, "The Stunning Survival Story of Ernest Shackleton and His Endurance Crew," History.com. https://www.history.com/news/shackleton-endurance-survival Accessed 6/9/21 ; Shackleton, preface.

23. Mulvaney, *op cit.* Shackleton, chapter 8.

24. Shackleton, chapter 12.

25. Shackleton, chapter 10.

26. Caryn E. Neumann, "Richard E. Byrd (1888–1957)," *Encyclopedia Virginia*. https://encyclopediavirginia.org/entries/byrd-richard-e-1888-1957/ Accessed 6/9/21; Riffenburgh, 56; History.com editors, "Explorer Richard Byrd flies over the South Pole. *History.com*. https://www.history.com/this-day-in-history/byrd-flies-over-south-pole Accessed 6/9/21.

27. Charles Lindbergh had flown nonstop from the U.S. to France in 1927. The three German pilots had just completed the first nonstop crossing in the opposite direction.

28. Neumann, *op cit*; History.com editors, "Explorer Richard Byrd flies over the South Pole. *History.com*. https://www.history.com/this-day-in-history/byrd-flies-over-south-pole Accessed 6/9/21. We may note, as an aside, that in 1933, Wiley Post became the first aviator to circumnavigate the globe, taking off from, and ultimately returning to, New York's Floyd Bennett Airfield. Post is best remembered today, however, for the fatal crash near Point Barrow, Alaska, in 1935, in which he and American humorist, Will Rogers, were killed.

29. Tass editors, "Polar Quest on the Italia. The Airship Crash Chronicle." *Tass*, 2018. https://italia.tass.com/ Accessed 6/10/21; Eva Holland, "Flying to the North Pole in an Airship Was Easy. Returning Wouldn't Be So Easy." *Smithsonianmag.com*. https://www.smithsonianmag.com/history/flying-north-pole-airship-was-easy-returning-wouldnt-be-so-easy-180964560/ Accessed 6/9/21.

30. Tass editors, *op cit.*

31. Tass editors, *op cit.*

32. John P. Rafferty, "What were the circumstances that surrounded Roald Amundsen's death?" *Britannica.com*. https://www.britannica.com/story/what-were-the-circumstances-that-surrounded-roald-amundsens-death Accessed 6/10/21.

33. Tass editors, *op cit.*

34. The Editor: Italy on This Day, "From Rome to the North Pole." *Italyonthisday.com*. https://www.italyonthisday.com/2016/04/from-rome-to-north-pole-Nobile-Ciampino-airship.html Accessed 6/10/21.

35. Tass editors, *op cit.*

36. Dan Grossman, "The Hindenburg Disaster," *Airships.net*. https://www.airships.net/hindenburg/disaster/#:~:text=Almost%2080%20years%20of%20research,spark)%20that%20ignited%20leaking%20hydrogen. Accessed 6/17/21.

37. Aviation, "From Sand Dunes to Sonic Booms, Shenandoah Crash Sites." *National Park Service* https://www.nps.gov/

articles/shenandoah-crash-sites.htm Accessed 6/17/21.

38. John T. Correll, "The Billy Mitchell Court-Martial." *Air Force Magazine*, August 1, 2012. https://www.airforcemag.com/article/0812mitchell/ Accessed 6/15/21.

39. Ms. Minnie L. Jones, "William 'Billy' Mitchell—the father of the United States Airforce." *United States Army*, October 17, 2019. https://www.army.mil/article/33680/william_billy_mitchell_the_father_of_the_united_states_air_force Accessed 6/15/21.

40. The Editors, Encyclopedia Britannica, "William Mitchell, United States Army general," *Britannica.com*, February 15, 2021. https://www.britannica.com/biography/William-Mitchell Accessed 6/15/21.

41. M. L. Jones, *op cit.*

42. National Museum of the United States Air Force, "Brigadier General William "Billy" Mitchell." *Nationalmuseum.af.* https://www.nationalmuseum.af.mil/Visit/Museum-Exhibits/Fact-Sheets/Display/Article/196418/brig-gen-william-billy-mitchell/ Accessed 6/18/21; see also Editors of Encyclopedia Britannica, *op cit*; M L. Jones, *op cit.*

43. J.T. Correll, *op cit.*

44. M.L. Jones, *op cit.*

45. Editors of Encyclopedia Britannica, *op cit.*

46. J.T. Correll, *op cit.*

47. History.com Editors, "Charles Lindbergh completes the first solo nonstop transatlantic flight," *History.com*, 2/9/10, updated 5/19/20. https://www.history.com/this-day-in-history/lindbergh-lands-in-paris Accessed 6/10/21.

48. Nola Taylor Redd, "Charles Lindbergh and the First Solo Transatlantic Flight. *Space.com*, 6/11/2019. https://www.space.com/16677-charles-lindbergh.html Accessed 6/10/21.

49. F. Gilbert, 249.

50. Quoted in "Fallen Hero," *American Experience* article. *WGBH Educational Foundation, PBS.org* https://www.pbs.org/wgbh/americanexperience/features/lindbergh-fallen-hero/ Accessed 6/17/21.

51. Richard Rhodes, "God Pity a One-Dream Man," *American Heritage Magazine*, June–July 1980. https://www.americanheritage.com/god-pity-one-dream-man Accessed 6/9/21.

52. Nola Taylor Redd, "Robert Goddard: American Father of Rocketry," *Space.com*, February 25, 2013. https://www.space.com/19944-robert-goddard.html Accessed 6/18/21. NASA, "Dr. Robert H. Goddard, American Rocketry Pioneer," *NASA.gov*. https://www.nasa.gov/centers/goddard/about/history/dr_goddard.html Accessed 6/1/9/21.

53. Richard Rhodes, *op cit.*

54. Frank H. Winter, "The Misunderstood Professor," *Air & Space Magazine*, May 2008. https://www.airspacemag.com/space/the-misunderstood-professor-26066829/ Accessed 6/9/21; Kiona N. Smith, "The Correction Heard 'Round the World: When the New York Times Apologized to Robert Goddard," *Forbes.com*. https://www.forbes.com/sites/kionasmith/2018/07/19/the-correction-heard-round-the-world-when-the-new-york-times-apologized-to-robert-goddard/?sh=ac5119145436 Accessed 6/9/21.

55. Richard Rhodes, *op cit.*

56. Towards the end of his life, he completed a treatise entitled, "The Last Migration," envisioning his life's work as the means for humankind to travel elsewhere in search of a new home "as the sun grows colder" in the distant future (Richard Rhodes, *op cit*).

57. The 1930–31 race to become the tallest building in the world is cataloged in Neal Bascomb's, *Higher: A Historic Race to the Sky and the Making of a City*. New York: Crown Publishing, 2004.

58. Artfinder, "What is Art Deco?" https://www.artfinder.com/blog/post/what-is-art-deco/#/ Accessed 6/20/21.

59. Warburg Realty, "The Battle to be the World's Tallest Building." *Warburgrealty.com*. January 29, 2020. https://www.warburgrealty.com/nabes/the-battle-to-be-the-worlds-tallest-building/ Accessed 6/19/21; Pucuda Corporation, "The Empire State Building: Race to the Sky," *Netting.com*. August 29, 2019. https://netting.com/the-empire-state-building-race-to-the-sky/ Accessed 6/19/21.

60. Warburg Realty, *op cit.*

61. *New World Encyclopedia*, "The Empire State Building," September 2017. https://www.newworldencyclopedia.org/entry/Empire_State_Building Accessed 6/19/21.

62. Leslie Postle, "The Empire State Building, An Art Deco Icon." *Decolish.com*. https://www.decolish.com/EmpireStateBuilding.html Accessed 6/19/21.

63. Postle, *op cit*; *New World Encyclopedia*, *op cit.*

64. Postle, *op cit*; *New World Encyclopedia*, *op cit.*

65. Wallbank and Taylor, vol. 2, 590.

66. Christopher James Botham, "Frank Lloyd Wright's Mile High Skyscraper," *Onverticality.com*. https://www.onverticality.com/blog/frank-lloyd-wright-mile-high-skyscraper Accessed 6/19/21; Mohamad Kashef, "The Race for the Sky: Unbuilt Skyscrapers," *Council on Tall Buildings and Urban Habitat*, 2008. https://global.ctbuh.org/resources/papers/download/305-the-race-for-the-sky-unbuilt-skyscrapers.pdf Accessed 6/19/21.

67. Wikipedia contributors, "Tacoma Narrows Bridge (1940)." *Wikipedia.org*. https://en.wikipedia.org/wiki/Tacoma_Narrows_Bridge_(1940)#Resonance_(due_to_Von_K%C3%A1rm%C3%A1n_vortex_street)_hypothesis (accessed 6/27/21).

68. Wikipedia contributors (Tacoma Bridge), *op cit.*

69. Jennifer L. Goss, "Henry Ford and the Auto

Assembly Line," *Thoughtco.com*, January 23, 2020. https://www.thoughtco.com/henry-ford-and-the-assembly-line-1779201 Accessed 6/11/21.

70. Ford Motor Company, "The Moving Assembly Line and the Five-Dollar Workday," *Corporate.Ford.com*. https://corporate.ford.com/articles/history/moving-assembly-line.html Accessed 6/11/21; History.com editors, "Ford's assembly line starts rolling," *History.com*. https://www.history.com/this-day-in-history/fords-assembly-line-starts-rolling Accessed 6/21/21.

71. Ford Motor Company, *op cit.*

72. Austin Weber, "The Moving Assembly Line Turns 100," *Assemblymag.com*, October 1, 2013. https://www.assemblymag.com/articles/91581-the-moving-assembly-line-turns-100 Accessed 6/11/21.

73. WGBH, "Ford installs first moving assembly line, 1913," *PBS.org*, 1998. https://www.pbs.org/wgbh/aso/databank/entries/dt13as.html Accessed 6/11/21.

74. A. Weber, *op cit.*

75. WGBH, *op cit.*

76. Goss, *op cit*; A. Weber, *op cit.*

77. A. Weber, *op cit.*

78. WGBH, *op cit.*; Ford Motor Company, *op cit.*; Goss, *op cit.*

79. Ford Motor Company, *op cit.*; Goss, *op cit.*

80. Ford Motor Company, *op cit.*; WGBH, *op cit.*

81. Kat Eschner, "In 1913, Henry Ford Introduced the Assembly Line: His Workers Hated It," *Smithsonian Magazine*, December 1, 2016. https://www.smithsonianmag.com/smart-news/one-hundred-and-three-years-ago-today-henry-ford-introduced-assembly-line-his-workers-hated-it-180961267/ Accessed 6/11/21.

82. Caitlan Reeg, "Mass Production," *Wall Street Journal Graphics*. https://graphics.wsj.com/100-legacies-from-world-war-1/mass-production Accessed 6/21/21.

83. History.com editors, "Henry Ford," *History.com*, November 9, 2009, updated March 26, 2020. https://www.history.com/topics/inventions/henry-ford Accessed 6/21/21.

84. Mitchell Bard, "Anti-Semitism in the United States: Henry Ford Invents a Jewish Conspiracy," *Jewishvirtuallibrary.org*. https://www.jewishvirtuallibrary.org/henry-ford-invents-a-jewish-conspiracy Accessed 6/11/21.

85. Bard, *op cit*. The Henry Ford Organization, "Henry Ford and Anti-Semitism: A Complex Story," *HenryFord.org*. https://www.thehenryford.org/collections-and-research/digital-resources/popular-topics/henry-ford-and-anti-semitism-a-complex-story Accessed 6/21/21.

86. Rabbi A. James Rudin, "The dark legacy of Henry Ford's anti-Semitism," *Washington Post*, October 10, 2014. https://www.washingtonpost.com/national/religion/the-dark-legacy-of-henry-fords-anti-semitism-commentary/2014/10/10/c95b7df2-509d-11e4-877c-335b53ffe736_story.html Accessed 6/11/21.

87. Bard, *op cit.*; Rudin, *op cit.*

88. Rudin, *op cit.*

89. Nuland, 425–26.

90. Science History Institute editors, "William Henry Perkin," *Sciencehistory.org*, 2021. https://www.sciencehistory.org/historical-profile/william-henry-perkin Accessed 6/27/21.

91. Heinrich Satter, "Paul Ehrlich, German Medical Scientist," *Encyclopedia Britannica online*, March 10, 2021. https://www.britannica.com/biography/Paul-Ehrlich, Accessed 6/26/21.

92. Margotta, 162–63; Satter, *op cit*. Robert Gaynes, "The Discovery of Penicillin—New Insights After More Than 75 Years of Clinical Use." *Emerging Infectious Diseases*, May 2017: 23 (5): 849–853. https://www.ncbi.nlm.nih.gov/pmc/articles/PMC5403050/ (accessed 6/26/21).

93. Paul Ehrlich—Biographical. *NobelPrize.org*. Nobel Prize Outreach AB 2021. Mon. 28 Jun 2021. https://www.nobelprize.org/prizes/medicine/1908/ehrlich/biographical/ (accessed 6/26/21). Edited and republished in *Nobel Lectures, Physiology or Medicine, 1901–1921*. Amsterdam: Elsevier Publishing Company, 1967.

94. "That which is saved by arsenic" is the rendering given for "Salvarsan" in WGBH contributors, "A Science Odyssey, People and Discoveries: Alexander Fleming, 1881–1955." *PBS.org*. https://www.pbs.org/wgbh/aso/databank/entries/bmflem.html Accessed 6/26/21.

95. Sutcliffe and Duin, 101; Wallbank and Taylor, 583.

96. Ehrlich would subsequently develop tuberculosis himself, but would recuperate after a convalescence in Egypt.

97. Sutcliffe and Duin, 101; Satter, *op cit.*; Nobel, "Ehrlich," *op cit.*

98. New World Encyclopedia contributors, "Alexander Fleming," *New World Encyclopedia*, , https://www.newworldencyclopedia.org/p/index.php?title=Alexander_Fleming&oldid=1024386 Accessed June 28, 2021; Siang Yong Tan, MD, JD and Yvonne Tatsumura, MA, MD. "Alexander Fleming (1881–1955): Discoverer of penicillin." *Singapore Medical Journal*, July 2015; 56(7): 366–67. http://www.smj.org.sg/article/alexander-fleming-1881-1955-discoverer-penicillin Accessed 6/26/21.

99. WGBH contributors, "A Science Odyssey, People and Discoveries: Alexander Fleming, 1881–1955." *PBS.org*. https://www.pbs.org/wgbh/aso/databank/entries/bmflem.html Accessed 6/26/21.

100. Tan and Tatsumura, *op cit.*

101. Gaynes, *op cit.*

102. Sutcliffe and Duin, 136–37; Gaynes, *op cit.*

103. Sutcliffe and Duin, 137.

104. Sutcliffe and Duin, 106.

105. Gerhard Domagk—Biographical. *NobelPrize.org*. Nobel Prize Outreach AB 2021. Mon. 28 Jun 2021. https://www.nobelprize.org/prizes/medicine/1939/domagk/biographical/ Accessed 6/27/21. Reproduced from Nobel Lectures, *Physiology or Medicine 1922–1941*, Amsterdam: Elsevier Publishing Company, , 1965.

106. Science History Institute contributors, "Frederick Banting, Charles Best, James Collip, and John Macleod." *Sciencehistory.org*. Updated December 1, 2017. https://www.sciencehistory.org/historical-profile/frederick-banting-charles-best-james-collip-and-john-macleod#:~:text=In%20the%20early%201920s%20Frederick,for%20their%20work%20in%201923. Accessed 6/26/21; Sutcliffe and Duin, 104.

107. Sutcliffe and Duin, 104; Bliss, Michael, "The Discovery of Insulin". *The Canadian Encyclopedia*. Historica Canada. Article published August 19, 2015; Last Edited November 8, 2018. https://www.thecanadianencyclopedia.ca/en/article/the-discovery-of-insulin Accessed 6/27/21; WGBH contributors, "A Science Odyssey, People and Discoveries: Banting and Best isolate insulin, 1922," https://www.pbs.org/wgbh/aso/databank/entries/dm22in.html Accessed 6/27/21.

108. Science History Institute contributors (Banting), *op cit.*; WGBH (Banting), *op cit.*; Bliss, *op cit.*

109. Science History Institute contributors (Banting), *op cit.*

110. Bliss, *op cit.*

111. Science History Institute contributors (Banting), *op cit.*; Bliss, *op cit.*

112. Nuland, 432.

113. Nuland, 437–38.

114. American College of Cardiology, "Just One More/Vivien Thomas: Remembering a Pioneering Legend," *Cardiology Magazine*. https://www.acc.org/latest-in-cardiology/articles/2021/02/01/01/42/just-one-more-vivien-thomas-remembering-a-pioneering-legend (accessed 6/28/21); Vanderbilt Medical Scientist Training Program contributors, "Vivien T. Thomas, LL.D." Vanderbilt School of Medicine https://medschool.vanderbilt.edu/mstp/person/vivien-t-thomas/ accessed 6/28/21; Nuland, 441.

115. Nuland, 441.

116. Vanderbilt, *op cit.*

117. Vanderbilt, *op cit.*; *Cardiology Magazine*, *op cit.*

118. India Today Web Desk, "Srinivasa Ramanujan: The mathematical genius who credited his 3900 formulae to visions from the Goddess Mahalakshmi." *India Today*. April 26, 2017. https://www.indiatoday.in/education-today/gk-current-affairs/story/srinivasa-ramanujan-life-story-973662-2017-04-26 Accessed 7/12/21.

119. M. Ram Murty and V. Kumar Murty, "The Legacy of Srinivasa Ramanujan," *The Hindu.com*. December 26, 2011, updated July 29, 2016. https://www.thehindu.com/news/national/the-legacy-of-srinivasa-ramanujan/article23683369.ece Accessed 6/22/21.

120. Murty and Murty, *op cit.*

121. Colm Mulcahy, "A Math Genius Like No Other Comes to the Big Screen." *Scientific American*. https://blogs.scientificamerican.com/guest-blog/a-math-genius-like-no-other-comes-to-the-big-screen/ Accessed 6/22/21; Murty and Murty, *op cit.*; Mike Hoffman, "Srinivasa Ramanujan." *USNA.edu*. https://www.usna.edu/Users/math/meh/ramanujan.html Accessed 7/12/21.

122. India Today Web Desk, *op cit.*

123. J. J. O'Connor and E.F. Robertson, "Srinivasa Aiynagar Ramanujan." *MacTutor*. https://mathshistory.st-andrews.ac.uk/Biographies/Ramanujan/ Accessed 7/12/21.

124. India Today Web Desk, *op cit.*

125. Biography.com Editors, "Srinivasa Ramanujan (1887–1920)." https://www.biography.com/scientist/srinivasa-ramanujan Accessed 6/22/21. The episode, explained by a like example, is stirringly told in the 2015 British movie, *The Man Who Knew Infinity*, based on a biography of that name by Robert Kanigel.

126. Hoffman, *op cit.*; Murty and Murty, *op cit.*

127. India Today Web Desk, *op cit.*

128. See Stokesbury, 384–85; M. Hastings, 210–11.

129. Encyclopedia Britannica online contributors, "Western Colonialism: Decolonization from 1945." *Britannica.com*. https://www.britannica.com/topic/Western-colonialism/Decolonization-from-1945 Accessed 6/25/21.

130. Christopher J. Wells, "Discovering the Atom—a Brief History." *TechnologyUK.net*, November 3, 2016, https://www.technologyuk.net/science/matter/discovering-the-atom.shtml Accessed 7/15/21.

131. Singer, 344.

132. C. J. Wells, *op cit.*

133. Gosling, 1.

134. No Brain Too Small Team, "History of Atoms." *Nobraintoosmall.co.nz*. Undated. https://www.nobraintoosmall.co.nz/students/physics/NCEA_Level2/L2_Atoms/pdfs/phys_90256_History_of_Atoms.pdf Accessed 7/15/21.

135. No Brain Too Small Team, *op cit.*

136. No Brain Too Small Team, *op cit.*

137. Wikipedia contributors, "Bohr Model." *Wikipedia.org*. https://en.wikipedia.org/wiki/Bohr_model Accessed 7/15/21. The distances providing stable orbits are all multiples of Planck's constant. It was also during this investigation that Bohr developed the notion of the "quantum leap" allowing them to skip from one orbit to another, without crossing the intervening space, upon releasing or gaining quantized amounts of energy.

138. Wallbank and Taylor, vol. 2, 580.

139. Wallbank and Taylor, vol. 2, 580; see also the similar statement in Boak et al., 844.

140. Cimino, 7–9; see also, Ferrell, 168–69; BBC contributors, "Was HG Wells the first to think of the atom bomb?" *BBC.com*, July 4, 2015. https://www.bbc.com/news/magazine-33365776 Accessed 7/13/21; Boak, 842*fn*.

141. Wallbank and Taylor, vol. 2, 580.

142. Cimino, 152; James Temperton, "'Now I am become Death, the destroyer of worlds,' the story of Oppenheimer's infamous quote." *Wired.co.uk*, August 9, 2017; https://www.wired.co.uk/

article/manhattan-project-robert-oppenheimer Accessed 7/14/21.

143. Wallbank and Taylor, 585.

144. Quoted in Larry P. Arnn, "Winston Churchill and Statesmanship." *Hillsdale College Online Courses* (DVD), volume 1, lecture 1, "Why Study Churchill."

145. The first quote is from Arnn, *op cit*. The second from Dr. Davey Naugle, "An introduction to and Themes from C.S. Lewis' *The Abolition of Man*." *Summer Institute in Christian Scholarship,* *Dallas Baptist University.* https://www3.dbu.edu/naugle/pdf/institute_handouts/lewis/abolition_summary.pdf

146. Russell, xxii–xxiii.

147. Phillips, 4.

148. Hamilton, *Echo*, 17–25.

149. Hamilton, *Greek Way*, 14.

150. Winston Churchill, "Mass Effects in Modern Life, 1925." *National Churchill Museum.org.* https://www.nationalchurchillmuseum.org/mass-effects-in-modern-life.html Accessed 8/20/21.

Bibliography

Short-form citations for frequently cited works
by authors who have multiple works in the bibliography
appear at the end of the entry, in *italics*.

Abbott, John S.C. *Austria: Its Rise and Present Power.* New York: P.F. Collier, 1898.
_____. *The History of Christianity.* Portland, ME: George Stinson & Co., 1885.
_____. *The History of Napoleon III.* Boston: B.B. Russell, 1873.
_____. *Louis Philippe.* New York and London: Harper & Brothers, 1899.
Abrams, Lynn. *Bismarck and the German Empire, 1871–1918.* 2nd edition. London: Routledge, 1995, 2006.
Abramsky, Chimen, Jachimczyk, Maciel, and Polonsky, Antony, eds. *The Jews in Poland.* New York: Basil Blackwell Ltd., 1986.
Adams, Arthur E., ed. *The Russian Revolution and Bolshevik Victory.* Lexington: D.C. Heath and Company, 1972.
Adams, Henry. *History of the United States of America.* 4 vol. New York: Charles Scribner's Sons, 1891.
Agnew, John Holmes, ed. *The Eclectic Magazine of Foreign Literature, Science, and Art.* New York & Philadelphia: Leavitt, Trow, & Co., January to April, 1844 (Specifically, the article *Reminiscences of Men and things, by one who has a good memory: Louis Philippe, King of the French.*)
Albright, William Foxwell, et al. *The Jewish People, Past and Present.* New York: Jewish Encyclopedic Handbooks, 1955.
Aldous, Richard. *The Lion and the Unicorn: Gladstone vs. Disraeli.* New York: W.W. Norton & Company, 2006.
Alsop, Joseph. *FDR: A Centenary Remembrance.* New York: Viking Press, 1982.
Annual Register. London: F. & J. Rivington (various years, as noted in chapter notes.)
Apjohn, Lewis. *William Ewart Gladstone, His Life and Times.* Glasgow: John McGready, 1881.
Archer, Jules. *Man of Steel: Joseph Stalin, Russia's Ruthless Leader.* New York: Sky Pony Press, 1965. (Foreword by Brianna Dumont, 2017.)
Arendt, Hannah. *The Portable Hannah Arendt.* Edited with an introduction by Peter Baehr. New York: Penguin Putnam, Inc., 2000.
Arnold, Stanislaw, and Zychowski, Marian. *Outline History of Poland.* Warsaw: Polonia Publishing House, undated.
Artz, Frederick B. *Reaction and Revolution, 1814–1832.* New York: Harper Torchbooks, 1963.
Ashley, Maurice. *A History of Europe, 1648–1815.* Englewood Cliffs, NJ: Prentice Hall, 1973.
Ashton, T.S. *The Industrial Revolution, 1760–1830.* London: Oxford University Press, 1980.
Asimov, Isaac. *Asimov's Chronology of the World.* New York: HarperCollins Publishers, 1991.
Asprey, Robert. *War in the Shadows.* Vol. 1. Garden City, NY: Doubleday & Company, Inc., 1975.
Baker, Lee. *The Second World War on the Eastern Front.* Harlow: Pearson/Longman, 2009.
Barthrop, Michael. *The Zulu War.* Poole: Blandford Press Ltd., 1980.
Barton, Gregory. *Lord Palmerston and the Empire of Trade.* Boston: Prentice Hall, 2012.
Bartov, Omer. *Germany's War and the Holocaust: Disputed Histories.* Ithaca, NY: Cornell University Press, 2003.
Beckmann, Petr. *A History of π.* New York: St. Martin's Press, 1971.
Bein, Alex. *Theodor Herzl.* Philadelphia: Jewish Publication Society of America, 1941.
Bell, E.T. *Men of Mathematics.* New York: Simon & Schuster, 1965.
Bergamini, John. *The Tragic Dynasty: A History of the Romanovs.* Old Saybrook, CT: Konecky & Konecky, 1969.
Berlinski, David. *A Tour of the Calculus.* New York: Vintage Books, 1995.
Bierman, John. *Napoleon III and his Carnival Empire.* New York: St. Martin's Press, 1988.
Bishop, W.J. *The Early History of Surgery.* New York: Barnes & Noble, 1995.

Blanc, Louis. *The History of Ten Years, 1830–1840.* 2 vol. Philadelphia: Lea & Blanchard, 1848.

Blinkhorn, Martin. *Democracy and Civil War in Spain, 1931–1939* London: Routledge, 1988. (*CW*)

_____. *Mussolini and Fascist Italy.* 3rd edition. London: Routledge, 2006 (*MFI*).

Boak, A.E.R., Hyma, Albert, and Slossen, Preston. *The Growth of Western Civilization.* New York: Appleton-Century-Crofts, 1951.

Botting, Douglas, et al. *The D-Day Invasion.* Richmond: Time-Life Books, 1978.

Bouverie, Tim. *Appeasement: Chamberlain, Hitler, Churchill and the Road to War.* New York: Tim Duggan Books, 2019.

Bray, R.S. *Armies of Pestilence, The Impact of Disease on History.* New York: Barnes and Noble, 1996.

Bredin, Jean-Denis. *The Affair: The Case of Albert Dreyfus.* New York: George Braziller, 1986.

Breunig, Charles. *The Age of Revolution and Reaction, 1789–1850.* New York: W.W. Norton and Company, Inc., 1970.

Brinton, C., Christopher, J.B. and Wolff, R.L. *A History of Civilization: 2 Volumes.* Englewood Cliffs, NJ: Prentice Hall, Inc., 5th Edition, 1976.

Browne, Harry. *Spain's Civil War.* London and New York: Longman, 1996.

Buell, Raymond Leslie. *Europe, A History of Ten Years.* New York: The Macmillan Company, 1928.

Bullock, Alan. *Hitler: A Study in Tyranny* (Abridged Edition). New York: HarperPerennial, 1991.

Bullock, David. *The Russian Civil War, 1918–22.* Oxford: Osprey, 2008.

Bulwer, Henry Lytton. *Sir Robert Peel, An Historical Sketch.* London: Richard Bentley and Son, 1874. [Forgotten Books Edition]

Burke, James. *Connections.* Boston: Little, Brown & Company, 1995. (*Connections*)

_____. *The Day the Universe Changed.* Boston: Little, Brown & Company, 1995. (*DUC*)

Burke, John. *An Illustrated History of England.* London: William Collins and Sons, 1985.

Burns, Michael. *France and the Dreyfus Affair.* Boston: Bedford/St. Martin's, 1999.

Burton, Richard Francis. *First Footsteps in East Africa.* Breinigsville, PA: Shepperd Publications, 2015.

Cambridge Modern History. Planned by Lord Acton. 14 volumes. New York: Macmillan, 1902–1912.

Carey, John, ed. *Eyewitness to History.* Cambridge: Harvard University Press, 1987.

Carr, Edward Hallett. *The Twenty Years' Crisis, 1919–1939.* New York: HarperCollins, 1946.

Carr, Raymond. *Modern Spain, 1875–1980.* Oxford: Oxford University Press, 1980. (*MS*)

_____, ed., *Spain: A History.* Oxford: Oxford University Press, 2000. (*SAH*)

Cartland, Barbara. *Metternich, The Passionate Diplomat.* New York: Pyramid Books, 1964.

Cartwright, Frederick F., and Biddiss, Michael D. *Disease and History.* New York: Barnes & Noble, 1972.

Caulkins, Janet. *Joseph Stalin.* New York: Franklin Watts, 1990.

Chamberlain, M.E. *The Scramble for Africa.* London: Pearson Education Ltd., 2010 (*SFA*).

Chamberlain, Muriel E. *Lord Palmerston.* Washington, D.C.: The Catholic University of America Press, 1987 (*LP*).

Chang, Iris. *The Rape of Nanking.* New York: Basic Books, 1997.

Charles River Editors. *The Birth of the Republic of Ireland.* Breinigsville, PA: Charles River Editors, 2018.

Christiansen, Rupert. *Paris Babylon.* New York: Penguin Books, 1994.

Churchill, Sir Winston. *The Gathering Storm.* Boston: Houghton Mifflin Company, 1948. (*GS*)

_____. *History of the English-Speaking Peoples.* 4 vol. New York: Dodd, Mead & Co., 1956. (*HESP*)

_____. *Memoirs of the Second World War.* New York: Bonanza Books, 1978. (*Memoirs*)

_____. *The River War.* N.p.: Seven Treasures Publications, 2008. (*RW*)

_____. *The Second World War.* Special Edition for Young Readers. New York: Golden Press, 1960. (*SWW*)

_____. *Their Finest Hour.* Boston: Houghton Mifflin Company, 1949. (*FH*)

_____. *Winston S. Churchill: His Complete Speeches 1897–1963.* Robert Rhodes James, ed. New York and London: Chelsea House/R. R. Bowker, 1974. (*CS*)

_____. *The World Crisis: 1911–1918.* Abridged and Revised Edition. London: Macmillan & Co., 1941. (*WC*)

Ciano, Count Galeazzo. *The Ciano Diaries, 1939–1943.* New York: Doubleday, Inc. 1946.

Cimino, Al. *The Manhattan Project, The Making of the Atomic Bomb.* London: Arcturus, 2016.

Clark, Alan. *Barbarossa.* New York: Quill (William Morrow & Co.), 1965. (*Barbarossa*)

_____. *The Donkeys.* New York: William Morrow and Company, 1962. (*Donkeys*)

_____. *The Eastern Front 1914–1918: Suicide of the Empires.* Gloucestershire: The Windrush Press Ltd, 1971. (*EF*)

Cobban, Alfred. *A History of Modern France.* 3 vol. Baltimore: Penguin Books, 1965.

Colville, John Rupert. *The Fringes of Power: 10 Downing Strette Diaries, 1939–1955.* New York: Norton, 1985.

Cottrell, Peter. *The Anglo-Irish War: The Troubles of 1913–1922.* Oxford: Osprey Publishing Ltd., 2006.

Craig, William. *Enemy at the Gates.* New York: Penguin Books, 1973.

Crampton, R.J. *A Concise History of Bulgaria,* Cambridge: Cambridge University Press, 1997.

Crankshaw, Edward. *The Fall of the House of Hapsburg.* London: Cardinal Books, 1974. (*FHH*)

_____. *The Shadow of the Winter Palace.* New York: The Viking Press, 1976. (*SWP*)

Creasy, Edward Shepherd. *Decisive Battles of the World.* New York: D. Appleton and Company, 1904.

Dahmus, Joseph. *Seven Medieval Kings.* New York: Barnes and Noble Books, 1994.

Davies, Norman. *White Eagle, Red Star: The Polish-Soviet War, 1919–20.* London: Orbis Books, Ltd., 1983.

Davis, William Stearns. *The Roots of the War, A Non-Technical History of Europe, 1870–1914 A.D.* New York: The Century Co., 1918.

Dawidowicz, Lucy S. *The War Agaisnt the Jews, 1933–1945.* New York: Bantam Books, 1975.

De Pree, Christopher Gordon. *Physics Made Simple.* New York: Broadway Books, 2004.

Derry, John W. *A Short History of 19th Century England: 1793–1868.* London: Mentor Books, 1963.

Disraeli, Benjamin. *Wit and Wisdom of Benjamin Disraeli, Earl of Beaconsfield. Collected from His Writings and Speeches.* London: Longman's, 1883 [Forgotten Books Edition].

Draper, Theodore. *The Six Weeks' War.* New York: Book Find Club, 1944.

Du Coudray, H. *Metternich.* New Haven: Yale University Press, 1936.

Duff, David. *Eugenie and Napoleon III.* New York: William Morrow and Company, Inc., 1978.

Duffy, James P., and Ricci, Vincent L. *Czars.* New York: Barnes & Noble Books, 2002.

Dunning, William Archibald. *A History of Political Theories from Rousseau to Spencer.* New York: The Macmillan Company, 1920.

Durant, Will. *The Story of Civilization.* 11 vol. New York: Simon & Schuster, 1954–75.

Edwards, Stuart. *The Paris Commune of 1871.* New York: Quadrangle Books, 1971.

_____, ed. *The Communards of Paris, 1871.* Ithaca: Cornell University Press, 1973.

Eisenhower, Dwight D. *Crusade in Europe.* Garden City, NJ: Doubleday & Company, Inc., 1948.

Elliot, Charles W. ed. *Scientific Papers.* New York: P.F. Collier & Son, 1910.

Elson, Robert T. *Prelude to War.* Alexandria, VA: Time-Life Books, 1977.

Encyclopedia Britannica. 11th ed. 29 vol. Cambridge: University Press, 1911.

Eubank, Keith. *The Origins of World War II.* Arlington Heights: Harlan Davidson, Inc., Second Edition, 1990.

Evans, Eric J. *Sir Robert Peel: Statesmanship, Power and Party.* London: Routledge, 1991.

Fair, Charles. *From the Jaws of Victory.* New York: Simon & Schuster, 1971.

Falls, Cyril. *A Hundred Years of War.* New York: Collier Books, 1962. (*HYW*)

_____, ed. *Great Military Battles.* London: Spring Books, 1964. (*GMB*)

Farwell, Byron. *Queen Victoria's Little Wars.* Ware, UK: Wordsworth Editions, 1999.

Ferrell, Keith. *H.G. Wells, First Citizen of the Future.* Lanham, MD: M. Evans, 1983.

Firkin, B. G., and Whitworth, J.A. *Dictionary of Medical Eponyms.* Casterton Hall, Carnforth, UK: The Parthenon Publishing Group, 1987.

Fisher, George Park. *Outlines of Universal History.* New York: Ivison, Blakeman, Taylor, and Company, 1885.

Fleming, Gerald. *Hitler and the Final Solution.* Berkeley: University of California Press, 1984.

Foley, Michael. *The Russian Civil War: Red Terror, White Terror, 1917–1922.* Barnsley, UK: Pen & Sword, 2018.

Freeman, Robert. *The InterWar Years (1919–1939), The Best One-Hour History.* Palo Alto: Kendall Lane Publishers, 2014.

Fuller, J.F.C. *A Military History of the Western World: 3 Vols.* New York: Minerva Press, 1956.

_____. *The Second World War.* New York: Da Capo Press, 1993.

Furneaux, Rupert. *The Breakfast War.* New York: Thomas Y. Crowell, Co., 1958.

Garraty, John A. *The American Nation: A History of the United States Since 1865.* 3rd ed. New York: Harper & Row, 1975.

Gavin, Catherine. *Louis Philippe, King of the French.* London: Methuen & Co., Ltd., 1933.

Geer, Walter. *Napoleon the Third: The Romance of an Emperor.* New York: Brentano's, 1920.

Gerould, Daniel. *Guillotine: Its Legend and Lore.* New York: Blast Books, 1992.

Gilbert, Felix. *The End of the European Era, 1890 to the Present,* 2nd ed. New York: W.W. Norton & Company, 1979.

Gilbert, Martin. *The First World War: A Complete History.* New York: Henry Holt and Company, 1994. (*FWW*)

_____, ed. *The Illustrated Atlas of Jewish Civilization.* New York: Macmillan Publishing Company, 1990. (*AJC*)

Gladstone, Willam Ewart. *Bulgarian Horrors and the Question of the East.* London: John Murray, 1876.

Goldston, Robert. *The Road Between the Wars: 1918–1941.* New York: Fawcett Crest, 1978.

Gollwitzer, Heinz. *Europe in the Age of Imperialism, 1880–1914.* New York: W.W. Norton and Co., 1969.

Goodenough, Simon. *Tactical Genius in Battle.* London: Phaidon Press, 1979.

Goodwin, Jason. *Lords of the Horizons.* New York: Henry Holt, 1998.

Gordon, John Steele. *A Thread Across the Ocean.* New York: Perennial, 2002.

Gosling, F.G. *The Manhattan Project, Making the Atomic Bomb.* Washington, D.C.: United States Department of Energy, National Security History Series, 2010.

Graetz, Heinrich Hirsch. *History of the Jews.* 6 volumes. Philadelphia: Jewish Publication Society of America, 1894.

Grahame, F.R. *Life of Alexander II, Emperor of all the Russias.* London: W.H. Allen & Co., 1883.

Grasso, Daniel. *Reading the Origins of Totalitarianism in 2020: A Short Guide to Mass Movements and Ideology.* Independently published through Amazon KDP, 2020.

Graves, Robert. *Good-bye to All That: An Autobiography*. Providence: Berghahn Books, 1995.

Guderian, Heinz. *Panzer Leader*. New York: E.P. Dutton & Co. Inc., 1952.

Guerard, Albert. *Napoleon III*. New York: Alfred A. Knopf, 1955.

Guizot, Francois. *The History of France*. 8 vol. English translation by Robert Black. New York: John B. Alden, Publisher, 1885. (*France*)

Guizot, Francois. *A Popular History of England*. 5 vol. Eng. Trans. by M.M. Ripley. Boston: Estes and Lauriat, 1874–81. (*England*)

Haggard, Howard W. *The Doctor in History*. New York: Barnes & Noble Books, 1996.

Halasz, Nicholas. *Captain Dreyfus, the Story of a Mass Hysteria*. New York: Simon & Schuster, 1955.

Hamilton, Edith. *The Echo of Greece*. New York: W.W. Norton & Company, 1957.

_____. *The Greek Way*. New York: W.W. Norton & Company, 1930.

Hamilton-Williams, David. *The Fall of Napoleon*. London: Arms and Armour Press, 1994.

Harman, Nicholas. *Dunkirk: The Patriotic Myth*. New York: Simon & Schuster, 1980.

Hastings, Max. *Inferno: The World at War, 1939–1945*. New York: Vintage Books, 2011.

Hastings, Paul. *Between the Wars*. London: Ernest Benn Limited, 1968.

Hayes, Carlton J.H. *A Brief History of the Great War*. New York: The Macmillan Company, 1922. (*GW*)

_____. *A Political and Social History of Modern Europe*, vol. 2 (1815–1915). New York: Macmillan, 1920. (*ME*)

Hazen, Charles Downer. *Europe Since 1815*. 2 vol. enlarged edition, New York: Henry Holt and Company, 1923. (*ES2*)

_____. *Europe Since 1815*. New York: Henry Holt and Company, 1910. (*ES1*)

_____. *Fifty Years of Europe 1870–1919*. New York: Henry Holt and Company, 1919. (*FYE*)

Headlam, James Wycliffe. *Bismarck and the Foundation of the German Empire*. New York: G.P. Putnam's Sons, 1899.

Henderson, W.O. *The Industrialization of Europe, 1780–1914*. London: Harcourt, Brace & World, Inc., 1969.

Henig, Ruth. *The Origins of the First World War*. 3rd edition. London: Routledge, 2002. (*OFWW*)

_____. *The Origins of the Second World War*. 2nd editon. London: Routledge, 2005. (*OSWW*)

_____. *Versailles and After, 1919–1933*. 2nd edition. London: Routledge, 1995. (*VA*)

_____. *The Weimar Republic*. London: Routledge, 1998. (*WR*)

Hibbert, Christopher. *Benito Mussolini: The Rise and Fall of il Duce*. London: Penguin Books, 1965.

Hilberg, Raul. *The Destruction of the European Jews*. Student edit. New York: Holmes & Meier, 1985.

Hingley, Ronald. *Joseph Stalin, Man and Legend*. New York: McGraw-Hill Book Company, 1974.

Holmes, Richard. *Epic Land Battles*. Secaucus: Chartwell Books, Inc., 1976.

Hooper, George. *The Campaign of Sedan*. London: Hodder and Stoughton, 1914.

Horne, Alistair. *The Price of Glory: Verdun, 1916*. Harmondsworth: Penguin Books, 1962. (*PG*)

_____. *The Terrible Year: The Paris Commune, 1871*. London: Phoenix, 2004. (*TY*)

Hourly History. *Irish Civil War: A History from Beginning to End*. Columbia: Hourly History, 2020. (*ICW*)

Hourly History. *The Spanish Flu: A History from Beginning to End*. Coppell, TX: Hourly History, 2021. (*SF*)

Howarth, T.E.B. *Citizen King: The Life of Louis Philippe, King of the French*. London: Eyre & Spottswoode, 1961.

Humes, James C. *Winston Churchill*. London: DK Publishing, 2003.

Hutchinson, John F. *Late Imperial Russia, 1890–1917*. New York: Addison Wesley Longman, 1999.

Inoguchi, Capt. Rikihei, Nakajima, Tadashi, and Pineau, Roger. *The Divine Wind*. New York: Bantam Books, 1958.

Irving, David. *The Destruction of Dresden*. New York: Ballantine Books, 1963.

Jackson, Gabriel. *A Concise History of the Spanish Civil War*. London: Thames and Hudson, 1974.

Jackson, Robert. *Bomber! Famous Bomber Missions of World War II*. New York: St. Martin's Press, 1980.

Jarman, T.L. *A Short History of 20th Century England, 1868–1962*. New York: Mentor Books, 1963.

Jenkins, T.A. *Sir Robert Peel*. St. Martin's Press, Inc., 1999.

Jenkisson, John, ed. *Winston Churchill: Giant of the Century*. New York: Time, Inc., 1965.

John, Katherine. *The Prince Imperial*. New York: G.P. Putnam's Sons, 1939.

Johnson, Paul. *Churchill*. New York: Viking, 2009.

Keegan, John. *The Face of Battle*. New York: Barnes & Noble Books, 1993. (*FOB*)

_____. *The First World War*. London: Hutchinson, 1998. (*FWW*)

_____. *The Mask of Command*. New York: Viking Press, 1987. (*MOC*)

_____. *The Second World War*. New York & London: Penguin Books, 1990. (*SWW*)

Kerr, Walter. *The Secret of Stalingrad*. Garden City, NY: Doubleday & Company, Inc., 1978.

Kerrigan, Michael. *Stalin: Man of Steel or Mass Murderer?* London: Amber Books, 2018.

Kiernan, V.G. *Colonial Empires and Armies 1815–1960*. Phoenix Mill: Sutton Publishing, 1998.

Killeen, Richard. *A Short History of the Irish Revolution 1912 to 1927*. Dublin: Gill Books, 2007.

King, C. Harold. *A History of Civilization*. 2nd Edition. Volume I. New York: Charles Scribner's Sons, 1964.

Kinross, Lord J., P.D.B. *The Ottoman Centuries*. New York: Morrow Quill Paberbacks, 1977.

Kissinger, Henry A. *A World Restored*. Boston: Houghton Mifflin Company, 1957.

Klee, E., Dressen, W., and Reiss, V. *The Good Old Days*. Eng. Trans. by Deborah Burnstone. Old Saybrook, CT: Konecky & Konecky, 1991.

Kohn, Hans. *Nationalism and Realism: 1852–1879*. Princeton: D. Van Nostrand Co., Inc, 1968.

Koskodan, Kenneth K. *No Greater Ally: The Untold Story of Poland's Forces in World War II*. Oxford: Osprey, 2009.

Kraehe, Enno E. *The Metternich Controversy*. New York: Holt, Rinehart and Winston, 1971.

Kranzberg, Melvin. *1848, A Turning Point?* Boston: D.C. Heath & Co., 1959.

Kravchenko, Victor A. *I Chose Freedom*. New Brunswick: Transaction Publishers, 1989.

Kuczynski, Stefan Krzysztof, et al. *A Panorama of Polish History*. Warsaw: Interpress Publishers, 1982.

Lamartine, Alphonse de. *History of the French Revolution of 1848*. 2 vol. Eng. Trans. by Francis A. Durivage and William S. Chase. Boston: Phillips, Sampson & Company, 1852. (*HFR*)

Lamartine, Alphonse de. *History of the Restoration of Monarchy in France*. 4 vol. Eng. Trans. by Captain Rafter. London: Bell and Daldy, 1865. (*HRMF*)

Langer, William E., *The Revolutions of 1848*. New York: Harper Torchbooks, 1969.

Langsam, Walter Consuelo. *The World Since 1914*. New York: Macmillan, 1943.

Larousse Encyclopedia of Modern History. Ed. Marcel Dunan. London: Paul Hamlyn, 1967.

Lentin, A. *Guilt at Versailles*. London: Methuen & Co., 1984.

Lewis, Bernard. *The Emergence of Modern Turkey*. London: Oxford University Press, 1961.

Lewis, Jon E. *True World War I Stories: Gripping Eyewitness Accounts from the Days of Conflict and Pain*. Guilford, CT: The Lyons Press, undated. Initially published under the title *Everyman at War* by C.B. Purdom in 1930. New Introduction by Jon E. Lewis. (*TWWS*)

_____, ed. *The Mammoth Book of Eye-Witness History*. New York: Carroll & Graf Publishers, 1998. (*EWH*)

Liddell Hart, B.H. *The German Generals Talk*. New York: William Morrow & Co., 1948. (*GG*)

_____. *History of the Second World War*. New York. G.P. Putnam's Sons, 1970. (*SWW*)

_____. *The Real War: 1914–1918*. Boston: Little, Brown and Company, 1964. (*RW*)

Littlefield, Henry Wilson. *New Outline-History of Europe, 1815–1940*. New York: Barnes & Noble, 1940.

Livesey, Anthony. *Great Commanders and their Battles*. Philadelphia: Courage Books, 1987.

Lowe, John. *Britain and Foreign Affairs, 1815–1885*. London: Routledge, 1998.

Lukowski, Jerzy, and Zawadzki, Hubert. *A Concise History of Poland, 3rd edtion*. Cambridge: Cambridge University Press, 2019.

Macaulay, Thomas Babington. *The Works of Lord Macaulay*. 8 vol. New York: D. Appleton & Co., 1866.

Macdonald, Lyn. *1915, the Death of Innocence*. New York: Henry Holt and Company, 1993.

Macfie, A.L. *The Eastern Question, 1774–1923*. London: Longman Group Ltd., 1989.

MacKenzie, J.M. *The Partition of Africa*. London: Methuen, 1983.

MacKenzie, S.P. *The Second World War in Europe*. London: Addison Wesley Longman Ltd., 1999.

Maddox, Robert James. "The Biggest Decision: Why We Had to Drop the Atomic Bomb." *American Heritage Magazine*, Vol. 46 (no. 3), 70–77. New York: American Heritage/Forbes, Inc., May/June 1995.

Magill, Frank. *Masterpieces of World Philosophy*. New York: HarperCollins, 1991.

Major, Ralph A. *Classic Descriptions of Disease*. Baltimore: Charles C. Thomas, 1932.

Manchester, William. *The Last Lion: Alone*. Boston: Little, Brown & Company, 1988.

_____. *The Last Lion: Visions of Glory*. New York: Dell Trade Paperback, 1984.

Margotta, Roberto. *The History of Medicine*. New York: Smithmark Publishers, 1996.

Markov, Walter, ed. *Battles of World History*. New York: Hippocrene Books, 1979.

Marrin, Albert. *Stalin, Russia's Man of Steel*. San Luis Obispo, CA: Beautiful Feet Books, 1988.

Marshall, S.L.A. *World War 1*. Boston: Houghton Mifflin Company, 1964.

Martel, Gordon. *The Origins of the First World War*. 2nd edition. London: Addison Wesley Longman Limited, 1996.

Marx, Karl, and Lenin, V.I. *Civil War in France: The Paris Commune*. New York: International Publishers, 1968.

Mason, John W. *The Dissolution of the Austro-Hungarian Empire, 1867–1918*. 2nd edition. London: Addison Wesley Longman Limited, 1985, 1997.

May, Arthur J. *The Age of Metternich, 1814–1848*. New York: Holt, Rinehart and Winston, 1963. (*Metternich*)

_____. *A History of Civilization*. 2nd Edition. Volume 2. New York: Charles Scribner's Sons, 1964. (*HOC*).

McKendrick, Melveena. *The Horizon Concise History of Spain*. New York: American Heritage Publishing, Co., Inc., 1972.

McManus, Jason. *The SS*. Alexandria, VA: Time-Life Books, Inc., 1989.

Mehring, Franz. *Absolutism and Revolution in Germany, 1525–1848*. London: New Park Publications, 1975.

Menning, Ralph R. *The Art of the Possible, Documents on Great Power Diplomacy, 1814–1914*. New York: McGraw-Hill, 1996.

Metternich, Clemen Wenzel von. *Memoirs of Prince Metternich*. 5 vol. Eng. Trans. by Mrs. Alexander Napier. New York: Charles Scribner's Sons, 1881.

Mommsen, Theodor. *A History of Rome*. Volume 2. Translated by William Purdie Dickson. London: J.M. Dent & Sons, n.d.

_____. *Mommsen's History of Rome.* Translated and abridged by C. Bryans and F.J.R. Hendy. New York: Charles Scribner's Sons, 1911 (abridged).

Monod, G. "Contemporary Life and Thought in France." *The Contemporary Review,* vol. 34. London: Strahan and Company Limited, 1879.

Montgomery of Alamein, Field Marshal Viscount Bernard. *A History of Warfare.* Cleveland: The World Publishing Company, 1968.

Montross, Lynn. *War Through the Ages.* New York: Harper & Brothers Publishers, 1960.

Moorehead, Alan. *The Russian Revolution.* New York: Harper & Brothers Publishers, 1958. (*RR*)

Moorehead, Alan. *The White Nile.* Middlesex: Penguin Books, 1960. (*WN*)

Morgan, Kevin. *Ramsay MacDonald.* London: Haus Publishing, 2006.

Morris, Charles. *The Marvelous Record of the Closing Century.* Philadelphia: American Book and Bible House, 1899.

Morris, Donald R. *The Washing of the Spears.* New York: Touchstone Books, 1965.

Moscow, Henry. *Russia Under the Czars.* New York: American Heritage Publishing Co., Inc., 1962.

Mosse, W.E. *Alexander II and the Modernization of Russia.* New York: Collier Books, 1962. (*AMR*).

_____. *Liberal Europe.* London: Harcourt, Brace, Jovanovich, 1974. (*LE*)

Namier, Lewis. *1848: The Revolution of the Intellectuals.* Garden City, NY: Anchor Books, 1964.

Neiberg, Michael S. *The Treaty of Versailles.* New York: Oxford University Press, 2017.

Neillands, Robin. *The Battle for the Rhine.* New York: The Overlook Press, 2005. (*BFR*)

_____. *Winston Churchill, Statesman of the Century.* Cold Spring Harbor, NY: Cold Spring Press, 2003. (*WC*)

Newark, Tim. *Turning the Tide of War.* London: Octopus Publishing Group, 2001.

Nuland, Sherwin. *Doctors: The Biography of Medicine.* New York: Vintage Books, 1988.

Office of the United States Chief Counsel for Prosecution of Axis Criminality. *Nazi Conspiracy and Aggression.* 8 vol plus 2 supplements. Washington, D.C.: United States Government Printing Office, 1946.

Oman, Charles. *A History of England. Division III: From A.D. 1688 to A.D. 1885.* London: Edward Arnold, undated.

Orwell, George. *Homage to Catalonia.* New York: Harcourt, Brace & World, 1952.

O'Shea, Stephen. *Back to the Front.* New York: Avon Books, 1996.

Osler, William. *The Evolution of Modern Medicine.* New Haven, CT: Yale University Press, 1913.

Pakenham, Thomas. *The Scramble for Africa.* New York: Perennial, 1991.

Palmer, Alan. *The Decline and Fall of the Ottoman Empire.* New York: Barnes and Noble Books, 1992. (*DFOE*)

_____. *Twilight of the Hapsburgs: The Life and Times of Emperor Francis Joseph.* New York: Atlantic Monthly Press, 1994. (*TOTH*)

Parker, Geoffrey, ed. *The Cambridge Illustrated History of Warfare.* Cambridge: Cambridge University Press, 1995.

Parry, Jonathan. *Benjamin Disraeli.* Oxford: Oxford University Press, 2007.

Perkins, Anne. *Baldwin.* London: Haus Publishing, 2006

Perlmutter, Amos. *The Life and Times of Menachem Begin.* Garden City, NY: Doubleday & Company, 1987.

Phillips, Alison. *Modern Europe, 1815–1899,* 4th ed. London: Rivingtons, 1905.

Porter, Ian, and Armour, Ian D. *Imperial Germany, 1890–1918.* London: Longman, 1991.

Powell, Enoch. *Joseph Chamberlain.* London: Thames and Hudson, 1977.

Pretorius, Fransjohan. *The Anglo-Boer War, 1899–1902.* Cape Town: Struik, 1998.

Prior, Robin, and Wilson, Trevor. *Passchendaele: The Untold Story.* New Haven, CT: Yale University Press, 1996.

Purcell, Hugh. *Lloyd George.* London: Haus Publishing, 2006.

Reader's Digest, ed. *True Stories of World War II.* Pleasantville, NY: Reader's Digest Association, Inc., 1980.

Reischauer, Edwin O., Fairbank, John K., and Craig, Albert M. *East Asia, The Great Tradition.* 2 Vol. Boston: Houghton Mifflin, 1958–65.

Reither, Joseph, ed. *Masterworks of History.* Garden City, NY: Doubleday and Company, Inc., 1948.

Remak, Joachim. *The Origins of World War I.* New York: Holt, Rinehart and Winston, 1967.

Rich, Norman. *The Age of Nationalism and Reform, 1850–1890.* 2nd ed. New York: Norton, 1977. (*ANR*)

Rich, Norman. *Great Power Diplomacy, 1814–1914.* Boston: McGraw-Hill, 1992. (*GPD*)

Riffenburgh, Beau. *Polar Exploration.* London: Royal Geographical Society in Association with Carlton Books Ltd., and Wildebeest Publishing, Ltd., 2009.

Roberts, Andrew. *Leadership in War: Essential Lessons from Those Who Made History.* New York: Viking, 2019. (*LIW*)

_____. *The Storm of War: A New History of the Second World War.* New York: Harper Perennial, 2012. (*SOW*)

Robertson, Priscilla. *Revolutions of 1848: A Social History.* New York: Harper Torchbooks, 1952.

Robinson, James Harvey. *Readings in European History, 2 volumes.* Boston: Atheneum Press, 1906.

Robson, Stuart. *The First World War.* London: Longman, 1998.

Röhl, John C.G. *Kaiser Wilhelm II.* Cambridge: Cambridge University Press, 2014.

Roth, Cecil. *Benjamin Disraeli, Earl of Beaconsfield.* New York: Philosophical Library, 1952.

Royle, Trevor. *Crimea.* London: Abacus, 1999.

Russell, Bertrand. *The History of Western Philosophy.* New York: Simon & Schuster, 1945.

Schapiro, J. Salwyn. *Modern and Contemporary European History (1815-1928).* Revised and Enlarged edition. Boston: Houghton Mifflin Company, 1929. (*MCEH2*)

_____. *Modern and Contemporary European History.* Boston: Houghton Mifflin Company, 1918. (*MCEH1*)

Schechter, Betty. *The Dreyfus Affair, A National Scandal.* Boston: Houghton Mifflin Company, 1965.

Seymour, Charles. *The Diplomatic Background of the War, 1870-1914.* New Haven, CT: Yale University Press, 1916.

Shackleton, Sir Ernest. *South: The Story of Shackleton's 1914-1917 Expedition.* A Project Gutenberg Ebook. Accessed 6/9/21. https://www.coolantarctica.com/Antarctica%20fact%20file/History/south/south_shackleton_preface.php

Shermer, David. *World War I.* Secaucus, NJ: Derbibooks, 1973.

Shirer, William. *The Collapse of the Third Republic.* New York: Simon & Schuster, 1969. (*Republic*)

_____. *The Rise and Fall of the Third Reich.* New York: Simon & Schuster, 1960. (*Reich*)

Singer, Charles. *A Short History of Scientific Ideas to 1900.* Oxford: Oxford University Press, 1959.

Singh, Simon. *Fermat's Enigma.* New York: Anchor Books (Doubleday), 1997.

Smith, William H.C. *Second Empire and Commune: France 1848-1871.* 2nd Edition. London: Longman, 1966.

Snyder, Louis L., and Morris, Richard B. *A Treasury of Great Reporting.* New York: Simon & Schuster, 1949.

Sontag, Raymond. *A Broken World, 1919-1939.* New York: Harper & Row, 1971.

Speer, Albert. *Inside the Third Reich.* New York: Avon Books, 1970.

Stanley, Henry M. *How I Found Livingstone.* Breinigsville, PA: Okitoks Press, 2017.

Stein, George H. *Great Lives Observed: Hitler.* Englewood Cliffs, NJ: Prentice Hall, 1968.

Steinberg, Mark D., and Khrustalëv, Vladimir M. *The Fall of the Romanovs.* London: Yale University Press, 1995.

Stokesbury, James L. *A Short History of World War II.* New York: William Morrow & Co., 1980.

Strachan, Hew. *The First World War.* New York: Penguin Books, 2003, 2013.

Strachey, Lytton. *Queen Victoria.* London: Chatto and Windus, 1955.

Sulzberger, C.L. *The American Heritage Picture History of World War II.* New York: American Heritage/Bonanza Books, 1966.

Sutcliffe, Dr. Jenny, and Duin, Nancy. *A History of Medicine.* New York: Barnes & Noble Books, 1992.

Swallow, Charles. *The Sick Man of Europe: Ottoman Empire to Turkish Republic, 1789-1923.* London: Ernest Benn, 1973.

Szabo, János B. "Hungary's Ill-fated War of Independence." *Military History*, August 1999, pp. 34-41.

Talmon, J.L. *Romanticism and Revolt, Europe 1815-1848.* England: Harcourt, Brace & World, 1967.

Taylor, A.J.P. *Bismarck: The Man and the Statesman.* New York: Vintage Books, 1955. (*BMS*)

_____. *The Habsburg Monarchy.* Harmondsworth, Middlesex: Peregrine Books, 1964. (*HM*)

_____, ed. *History of World War I.* London: Octopus Books, 1974. (*WWI*)

_____. *The Origins of the Second World War.* New York: Atheneum, 1961. (*OSWW*)

_____. *The Second World War.* New York: Berkley Windhover, 1975. (*SWW*)

_____. *The Struggle for Mastery in Europe, 1848-1918.* Oxford: Oxford University Press, 1954. (*SME*)

Taylor, Robert. *Lord Salisbury.* Edinburgh: Allen Lane, 1975.

Taylor, Robert Lewis. *Winston Churchill: An Informal Study of Greatness.* Garden City, NY: Doubleday and Company, 1952.

Terraine, John. *The Great War.* London: Wordsworth Editions, 1965.

Thompson, J.M. *Revolutionary Russia, 1917.* New York: Macmillan Publishing, 1989.

Toland, John. *Adolf Hitler.* Abridged ed. New York: Ballantine Books, 1976. (*AH*)

_____. *Hitler, the Pictorial Documentary of His Life.* Garden City, NY: Doubleday & Co., 1978. (*HPD*)

_____. *The Rising Sun.* New York: Bantam Books, 1970. (*RS*)

Totten, S., Parsons, W.S., and Charney, I., eds. *Century of Genocide.* New York: Garland Publishing, 1997.

Trevelyan, G.M. *A Shortened History of England.* Middlesex: Penguin Books, 1982.

Trew, Peter. *The Boer War Generals.* Gloucestershire: Wren's Park, 1999.

Trollope, Anthony. *Lord Palmerston.* London: Wm. Isbister, Ltd., 1882 [reprint 2018].

Trythall, Anthony John. *"Boney" Fuller.* New Brunswick: Rutgers University Press, 1977.

Tuchman, Barbara. *Bible and Sword.* New York: Ballantine Books, 1984. (*Bible*)

_____. *The Guns of August.* New York: Dell Contemporary Classics, 1962. (*Guns*)

_____. *The March of Folly.* New York: Alfred A. Knopf, 1984. (*Folly*)

_____. *The Proud Tower.* Toronto: Bantam Books, 1967. (*Tower*)

Turner, Henry Ashby. *Hitler's Thirty Days to Power: January 1933.* London: Bloomsbury, 1996.

Twiss, Miranda *The Most Evil Men and Women in History.* New York: Barnes and Noble Books, 2002.

Vandam, Albert Dresden. *An Englishman in Paris (Notes and Recollections)*. New York: D. Appleton and Company, 1892.

Van Der Kiste, John. *The Romanovs, 1818–1959*. Gloucestershire: The History Press, 2013.

Van Doren, Charles. *A History of Knowledge*. New York: Ballantine Books, 1991.

Venn, Fiona. *Franklin D. Roosevelt*. London: Cardinal Books, 1990.

Viorst, Milton. *The Great Documents of Western Civilization*. New York: Barnes and Noble Books, 1994.

Wallbank, T.W., and Taylor, A.M. *Civilization Past and Present*. 3rd Ed. Chicago: Scott Foresman and Company, 1954.

Walton, John K. *Disraeli*. London: Routledge, 1990.

_____. *The Second Reform Act*. London: Routledge, 1983. (*SRA*)

Ward, Roger. *The Chamberlains: Joseph, Austen and Neville, 1836–1940*. Croydon: Fonthill Media Ltd., 2015.

Warner, Oliver. *Great Sea Battles*. New York: The Macmillan Company, 1963.

Warner, Philip. *The Crimean War, A Reappraisal*. Ware: Wordsworth Editions, 2001. (*CW*)

_____. *Passchendaele: The Tragic Victory of 1917*. New York, Atheneum, 1988. (*PTV*)

Washburne, E.B. *Recollections of a Minister to France, 1869–1877*. 2 vol. New York: Charles Scribner's Sons, 1887.

Wawro, Geoffrey. *A Mad Catastrophe*. New York: Basic Books, 2014.

Weber, Eugen. *The Western Tradition. From the Ancient World to the Atomic Age*. Boston: D.C. Heath and Company, 1965.

Wedgwood, C.V. *The Spoils of Time*. Garden City, NY: Doubleday & Company, Inc., 1985.

Weightman, Gavin. *The Industrial Revolutionaries: The Making of the Modern World, 1776–1914*. New York: Grove Press, 2007.

Wells, H.G. *The Outline of History*. New York: Garden City Books, 1949. (*OH2*)

_____. *The Outline of History*. New York: The Macmillan Company, 1921. (*OH1*)

Wernick, Robert. *Blitzkrieg*. New York: Time-Life Books, 1976.

West, Willis Mason. *The Story of World Progress*. Boston: Allyn and Bacon, 1922.

Whiting, Charles. *Ardennes: The Secret War*. New York: Stein and Day, 1984.

Williams, Henry Smith. *The Historian's History of the World*. Vol. 10. New York: The Outlook Company, 1904.

Williamson, D.G. *Bismarck and Germany, 1862–1890*. 2nd edition. London: Addison Wesley Longman Limited, 1998. (*BG*)

Williamson, D.G. *Poland Betrayed: The Nazi-Soviet Invasions of 1939*. Barnsley: Pen & Sword, 2009. (*PB*)

Winstanley, Michael. *Gladstone and the Liberal Party*. London: Routledge, 1990. (*GLP*)

_____. *Ireland and The Land Question*. London: Methuen, 1984. (*ILQ*)

Wiskemann, Elizabeth. *Europe of the Dictators, 1919–1945*. New York: Harper Torchbooks, 1966.

Wolf, John B. *France, 1814–1919*. New York: Harper & Row, 1963.

Wolff, Leon. *In Flanders Fields*. New York: Time Incorporated, 1958.

Wood, Alan. *The Origins of the Russian Revolution*. 3rd edition. London: Routledge, 2003. (*ORR*).

_____. *Stalin and Stalinism*. 2nd edition. London: Routledge, 2005. (*SAS*)

Wood, Anthony. *The Russian Revolution*. 2nd edition. London: Longman Group UK Limited, 1976, 1986.

Woodham-Smith, Cecil. *The Reason Why*. New York: Time Incorporated, 1953.

World at War. Episode 2: "Distant War, 1939–40." London: Thames Video. Distributed in USA by HBO Home Video, 1973.

Yonge, Charlotte. *A Pictorial History of the World's Great Nations*. 3 volumes. New York: Selmar Hess, 1882.

Young, Peter ed. *World War II Encyclopedia*. vol 2. Westport: H.S. Stuttman Inc., 1978.

Zaloga, Steven J. *The Polish Army, 1939–1945*. Oxford: Osprey, 1982.

Zamoyski, Adam. *Poland: A History*. New York: Hippocrene Books, 2009.

Zeigler, Philip. *Between the Wars: 1919–19139*. New York: MacLehose Press, 2016. (*BTW*)

_____. *Omdurman*. New York: Dorset Press, 1973. (*OMD*)

Zhukov, Georgi K. *Marshal Zhukov's Greatest Battles*. New York: Harper & Row, 1969.

Zich, Arthur. *The Rising Sun*. Alexandria: Time-Life Books, 1977.

Zola, Émile. *The Debacle*. Translated with an introduction by Leonard Tancock. London: Penguin Classics, 1972.

Index

Numbers in *bold italics* indicate pages with illustrations

489